PUERTO RICO

SUZANNE VAN ATTEN

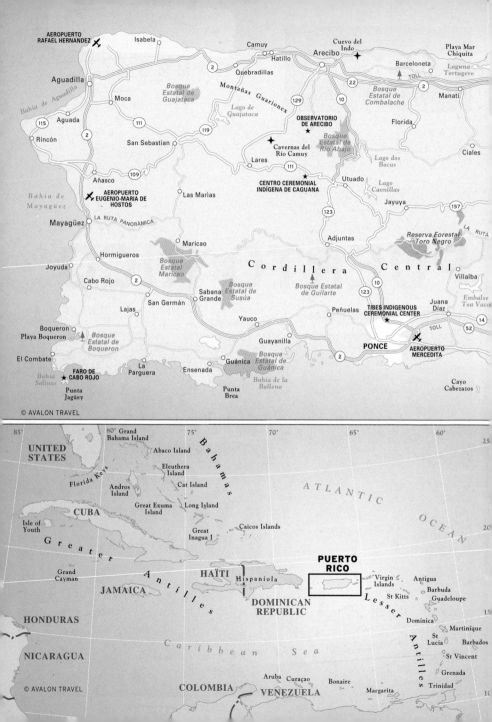

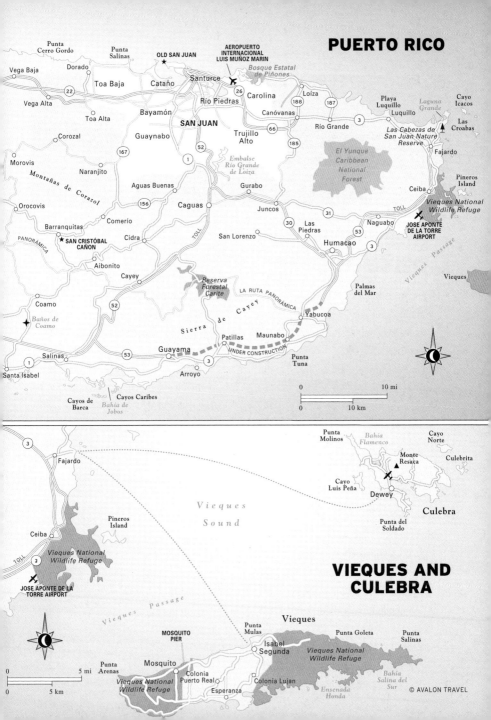

PUERTO RICO

Punta
Cerro Gordo
Vega Baja
Punta
Salinas
★ OLD SAN JUAN
✈ AEROPUERTO
INTERNACIONAL
LUIS MUÑOZ MARIN
Bosque Estatal
de Piñones
Cayo
Icacos
Dorado
Toa Baja
Cataño
Santurce
22
Vega Alta
Carolina
Loíza
188
187
Playa
Luquillo
Luquillo
Laguna
Grande
Las
Croabas
26
Bayamón
Río Piedras
Toa Alta
Canóvanas
66
185
Río Grande
3
Las Cabezas de
San Juan Nature
Reserve
Pineros
Island
Corozal
Guaynabo
SAN JUAN
Trujillo
Alto
52
Fajardo
Morovis
167
1
Embalse
Río Grande
de Loíza
El Yunque
Caribbean
National
Forest
Ceiba
Vieques National
Wildlife Refuge
Naranjito
Aguas Buenas
Gurabo
✈ JOSE APONTE
DE LA TORRE
AIRPORT
Montañas de Corozal
156
Caguas
Juncos
31
TOLL
Orocovis
Comerío
Juncos
30
Las
Piedras
Naguabo
53
Vieques
Passage
Barranquitas
Cidra
San Lorenzo
Humacao
3
Vieques
PANORÁMICA
★ SAN CRISTÓBAL
CAÑON
Aibonito
Cayey
Reserva
Forestal
Carite
Palmas
del Mar
Coamo
52
Sierra de Cayey
LA RUTA PANORÁMICA
Yabucoa
✦ Baños de
Coamo
Patillas
Maunabo
1
Salinas
53
Guayama
UNDER CONSTRUCTION
Punta
Tuna
Santa Isabel
3
Arroyo
Cayos de
Barca
Cayos Caribes
Bahía de
Jobos

0   10 mi
0   10 km

VIEQUES AND CULEBRA

3
Fajardo
Punta
Molinos
Bahía
Flamenco
Cayo
Norte
Culebrita
Monte
Resaca
Culebra
Cayo
Luis Peña
✈
Vieques
Sound
Dewey
Culebra
Pineros
Island
Ceiba
Vieques National
Wildlife Refuge
Punta del
Soldado
2
TOLL
✈ JOSE APONTE DE LA
TORRE AIRPORT
Vieques
Passage
Vieques
MOSQUITO
PIER
Punta
Mulas
Isabel
Segunda
Punta Goleta
Punta
Salinas
Mosquito
Punta
Arenas
Colonia
Puerto Real
Colonia Luján
Vieques National
Wildlife Refuge
Bahía
Salina del
Sur
Vieques National
Wildlife Refuge
Esperanza
Ensenada
Honda
© AVALON TRAVEL

0   5 mi
0   5 km

Contents

Discover Puerto Rico

Puerto Rico's nickname, Island of Enchantment, is a fitting sobriquet. Sandy beaches, palm trees, and tropical breezes make it a favorite getaway for the sun and surf crowd. Rugged mountains and a verdant rainforest attract adventure travelers, and lavish hotels with oceanside golf courses embrace vacationers who crave luxury.

But Puerto Rico is much more than a picture postcard. Four hundred years of Spanish heritage has left its mark on the island, giving it an Old World elegance. Its vibrant cultural life reflects not only the island's European history, but also its indigenous origins and African influences.

An added bonus is the hip, bustling metropolis of San Juan, which boasts world-class restaurants, nightclubs, and casinos that keep the party-hardy set up until dawn. Yet, a simple stroll through the cobblestone streets of Old San Juan steeps visitors in a concentrated dose of the island's history and cultural life.

Just 111 miles long and 36 miles wide, Puerto Rico has a population of 3.7 million people, making it one of the most densely populated places in the world. Despite the traffic jams and overdevelopment in some areas, natural beauty abounds in the many protected coves, mangrove lagoons, caves, and mountain streams. They provide the perfect backdrop for an immersion into the sensual pleasures of the tropics.

Less than an hour's drive from San Juan is one of the island's most popular sights, El Yunque Caribbean National Forest, which contains a semitropical rainforest. In the northwest karst country, there are limestone caves, easily explored at Las Cavernas del Río Camuy park, and several bioluminescent bays where kayakers can commune with the tiny luminescent organisms that turn the water a glittery green- or blue-specked sea on moonless nights.

Puerto Rico's central mountain region is one of the most dramatically beautiful areas of the island, where high mountain peaks, canyons, lush vegetation, orchids, streams, and cooler temperatures prevail. The indigenous Taíno culture was once a stronghold here, and their ancient ruins and petroglyphs can be found throughout the area.

All that is to say, there is a lot more to Puerto Rico than beaches. But if it is spectacular beaches one wants, there are plenty to be found, as is a bounty of water sports from surfing and diving to fishing and sailing.

Life is vivid in Puerto Rico. The sun shines brightly, rainbow-hued buildings pop with color, and tropical music fills the air. Prepare to have your senses awakened.

Planning Your Trip

▶ WHERE TO GO

San Juan

Situated on the northeast coast, sophisticated, fast-paced San Juan is Puerto Rico's capital and largest city. Its heart is Old San Juan, the original walled city founded by Spanish settlers in 1521, home to two fortresses: Castillo San Felipe del Morro and Castillo de San Cristóbal. Other significant neighborhoods include Isla Verde, with the city's best beaches and most exclusive hotels, and Condado, considered the tourist district, where you'll find high-rise hotels, high-end shops, and casinos. In nearby Santurce is a burgeoning arts district, home to galleries, studios, and Museo de Arte de Puerto Rico.

IF YOU HAVE . . .

Condado

- **THREE DAYS:** Visit Old San Juan, Luquillo, and El Yunque
- **FIVE DAYS:** Add Condado, Santurce, and Ponce
- **ONE WEEK:** Add Fajardo and Vieques or Culebra
- **TWO WEEKS:** Add Rincón and the Cordillera Central

Land-and-air vacation packages are available at resorts and hotels in Condado and Isla Verde. Because the island is only 111 miles by 36 miles, you can take a day trip to anywhere in Puerto Rico from San Juan; popular ones include El Yunque Caribbean National Forest in Río Grande, the beach and *kioskos* in Luquillo, and the colonial city of Ponce.

East Coast

The east coast contains Puerto Rico's most popular tourist sight, El Yunque Caribbean National Forest, a 28,000-acre nature preserve in the Sierra de Luquillo. The second most popular sight on the island is Balneario La Monserrate, a beautiful beach in Luquillo. Fajardo is the boating center of Puerto Rico, where you can go diving, snorkeling, fishing, sailing, and kayaking. It is also home to the small but ecologically diverse Reserva Natural Las Cabezas de San Juan, which contains a bioluminescent bay. The southern part of the east coast is the least touristy part of the island and features several nice beaches and good seafood restaurants. Land-and-air packages and all-inclusive meal plans are available at resorts in Río Grande. All-inclusive meal plans are offered by some hotels in the southeastern part of the island.

South Coast

Ponce, the island's second-largest city outside of metropolitan San Juan, was once a wealthy international port and a major player in the sugar and coffee industries. The city boasts gorgeous neoclassical and Spanish Revival architecture, a thriving plaza, and a strong cultural heritage preserved in its many museums. Just north of town is one of the island's

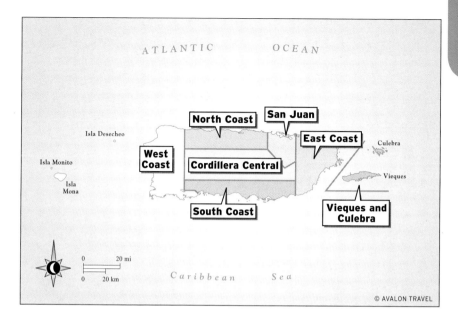

© AVALON TRAVEL

two major indigenous cultural sites. Centro Ceremonial Indígena de Tibes was once home to two indigenous tribes, the Igneri and the Pre-Taínos. Also north of town is Hacienda Buena Vista, a former 19th-century coffee plantation that has been restored.

El Faro Punta Mulas, Vieques

West Coast

Within the west coast region are the fun-loving surf towns of Isabela, Rincón, and Aguadilla; the colonial cities of Mayagüez and San Germán; the fishing village of Boquerón; the bioluminescent bay in La Parguera; and the salt flats of Cabo Rojo. In addition to being a major destination for surfing and diving, it has one of the island's loveliest public beaches, Balneario de Boquerón. And it is also home to two major forests, Bosque Estatal de Guajataca, a 2,357-acre subtropical wet forest in the north, and Bosque Estatal de Guánica, a 10,000-acre subtropical dry forest in the south.

North Coast

Much of the north coast is karst country, distinguished by limestone hills and caves, which makes for lots of rocky beaches and seaside cliffs. But there are two terrific sandy beaches—Balneario Cerro Gordo in Vega Alta and Playa Mar Chiquita in Manatí. Perhaps

Centro Ceremonial Indígena de Caguana

the biggest draw on this coast is Las Cavernas del Río Camuy, a gorgeous cave park featuring hikes through enormous caverns by a subterranean river. Another popular site is Observatorio de Arecibo, the world's largest radio telescope. And a bit off the beaten path is Cueva del Indio, huge petrified sand dunes where you can see natural arches, blow holes, and ancient Taíno petroglyphs.

Cordillera Central

The central mountain region is a wonderland of natural beauty and Taíno Indian culture. La Ruta Panorámica is a well-marked route that takes visitors on a scenic tour through the region. Bosque Estatal de Toro Negro, in the center of the region, contains the island's highest peak. Jayuya is the site of Museo del Cemi, an amulet-shaped museum containing indigenous artifacts, and La Piedra Escrita, a boulder covered with Taíno petroglyphs. But probably the most significant site is Centro Ceremonial Indígena de Caguana, a Taíno archaeological site dating to A.D. 1100 in Utuado. Also in Utuado is Bosque Estatal de Río Abajo, a 5,000-acre subtropical humid forest.

Vieques and Culebra

Vieques and Culebra are two small islands off the main island's east coast. Both offer some of the best wilderness beaches to be found in Puerto Rico—if not the entire Caribbean. Balneario Sun Bay in Vieques is a mile-long sandy crescent on crystal-blue waters. Playa Flamenco on Culebra is considered one of the best beaches in the United States. Both islands are renowned for their spectacular diving and snorkeling. Vieques is also the site of Mosquito Bay, Puerto Rico's most outstanding bioluminescent bay, where the water glows an electric blue at night. If you need a history fix, Vieques is home to El Fortín Conde de Mirasol, the last fort built by colonial Spain, which now holds the Vieques Museum of Art and History.

▶ WHEN TO GO

The climate in Puerto Rico is classified as tropical marine, which means it is sunny, hot, and humid year-round. The average year-round temperature ranges from 80°F on the coast to 68°F in the mountains.

Puerto Rico has two seasons. Dry season is January-April. This is when humidity is the lowest, and temperatures hit an average high of 84°F and an average low of 71°F. It should be noted that rain does occur during dry season, but at a much lower rate than in summer and fall. Airline tickets and hotel room rates tend to be higher during high season. From December through the end of dry season is high season for the tourist industry throughout much of the island, including San Juan, Vieques, Rincón, and resort areas, such as Dorado and Río Grande.

Rainy season is May-November, when an average of 4-6 inches of rain falls each month. The island's hottest months are June-September, when temperatures average 89°F, but it can spike as high as 97°F on the coast. The rainy season is also hurricane season. Airline ticket prices and hotel room rates are often reduced during rainy season.

In some parts of the island, particularly areas such as Cabo Rojo and La Parguera that cater primarily to Puerto Rican tourists, high season coincides with summer, when children are out of school.

Playa Zoni, Culebra

Explore Puerto Rico

▶ BEST OF PUERTO RICO

It would take at least a month to fully explore Puerto Rico, but this one-week tour gives visitors a little taste of everything Puerto Rico has to offer: beaches, nature preserves, colonial cities, surf and dive spots, and golf.

Day 1

Catch an early flight into San Juan and spend the day wandering Old San Juan's cobblestone streets. Shop for guayabera shirts at Panabrisa or *vejigante* masks at Puerto Rican Arts and Crafts. Enjoy a traditional Puerto Rican lunch of *mofongo* or *arroz con pollo* at Restaurante Raíces. That afternoon, tour the Spanish forts of Castillo San Felipe del Morro and Castillo de San Cristóbal. At night, do like the locals do and dine late on grilled lobster at Casa Lola Criolla Kitchen in Condado and return to Old San Juan to dance the night away to live salsa music at Nuyorican Café.

Day 2

In San Juan, rent a car and drive 35 miles east to El Yunque Caribbean National Forest. Enter at El Portal Tropical Forest Center and drive south, stopping at Las Cabezas Overlook, La Coca Falls, and Yokahu Tower along the way. If you packed a lunch, take a break at Caimitillo Picnic Area, and then spend the afternoon hiking the Mount Britton Trail. Or drive 11 miles to the Luquillo Kioskos and lunch on fritters and meat pies, then head next door to Balneario La Monserrate, one of the island's most celebrated beaches, and spend the afternoon swimming and sunning. Afterwards, shower and change at the public facilities and head back to San Juan, stopping at Kasalta Bakery on Avenida McLeary in Ocean Park for a casual dinner of *cubano* sandwiches and flan.

Old San Juan

¡MÚSICA! BOMBA, PLENA, Y MAS

Everywhere you go in Puerto Rico, you hear the melodic sounds of music, whether it's from the open door of a nightclub, a plaza bandstand, a concert hall, or a car stereo. There is a constant soundtrack to life on the island, and every note is meant to inspire you to get up and move your feet to the beat.

BOMBA AND PLENA

Bomba and plena are believed to have originated with Nigerian slaves who were shipped to Puerto Rico to work on sugar and coffee plantations. Bomba is a percussive, call-and-response form of music performed on a barril, similar to a conga drum, and accompanied by sticks, güiros (a washboard-style percussion instrument made from a gourd), and a maraca (one, never two). The call-and-response vocals are secondary to the dance, which is integral to bomba. The dancers match their movements to the rhythm of the drums, which go at a very fast clip, sending the dancers into a frenzy. Performances become a test of endurance between drummers and dancers as each group tries to best the other.

Plena is similar to bomba, but it adds horns and stringed instruments such as the cuatro (a double-stringed guitar-like instrument) to the mix, and the percussive emphasis is on the pandereta, a small handheld drum similar to a tambourine but without the cymbals. In plena, dance is secondary to the vocals, which consist of a kind of oral record that usually comments on topical subjects such as scandals, politics, or natural disasters.

Of the two musical forms, bomba is the one that has most endured. One of the best places to experience it is at the **Fiestas Tradicionales de Santiago Apóstol (St. James Carnival),** a six-day festival held in late July in Loíza. Bomba players and dancers gather in the town plaza every night and perform until the wee hours.

SALSA

The music most commonly heard throughout Puerto Rico is the festive sound of salsa. Salsa music earned its name in the late '60s, but the genre – a combination of Afro-Caribbean styles including Puerto Rican bomba and plena, Cuban mambo and rumba, Dominican merengue and

Spanish son – first emerged in the 1930s. It is typically a fast-paced, highly percussive musical style performed on a combination of instruments including conga drums, bongos, cowbells, timbales, maracas, bass, and horns. Most importantly, it is music meant to get you on the

cuatro

dance floor. If you want to learn a few moves, visit **The Latin Roots** in Old San Juan, where you can take a dance lesson during the day and demonstrate your mastery on the dance floor at night. Also in Old San Juan, **Nuyorican Café** is the hottest spot in town to hear live salsa music and get your move on. In July, San Juan hosts the annual **Salsa World Congress,** a weeklong convention featuring conferences, lessons, performances, exhibitions, and competitions.

REGGAETÓN

A combination of American hip-hop, bomba, plena, and Jamaican dancehall, reggaetón is a popular urban musical style typically heard in nightclubs and concerts around the island. Local pop stars Daddy Yankee, Don Omar, and Calle 13 have gained worldwide fame with the genre. **Club Lazer** and **The Noise** in Old San Juan are popular nightspots to hear reggaetón.

DANZA

A classical music style that originated in Ponce in the mid-1800s, danza combines Caribbean and European styles in a structured form often described as an Afro-Caribbean waltz. It is typically performed on piano and bombarino (similar to a trombone) to accompany ballroom dancers. Puerto Rico's national anthem, "La Borinqueña," was originally written as a danza. The best place to experience the musical style is at **Semana de la Danza,** a weeklong series of events held in Ponce in mid- to late-May. Events include conferences, concerts, parades, and dance competitions.

Day 3

In San Juan, eat a light breakfast at historic La Bombonera in Old San Juan and drive 62 miles to Las Cavernas del Río Camuy. Spend the morning exploring the subterranean world of the island's underground cave system. Have lunch at the snack bar. In the afternoon, drive 8 miles east to Observatorio de Arecibo and see the world's largest radio telescope. Drive 17 miles north to Hatillo and dine on *churrasco* at Mojitos Grill & Bar, then stay the night.

Day 4

In Hatillo, have breakfast at El Buen Café and drive 30 miles west to Aguadilla to play a round of golf at Punta Borinquen Golf and Country Club. Eat a light lunch at Panadería Borinqueña and drive 18 miles south to Rincón. Take a dip in the hotel pool and head to Black Eagle Restaurant for some conch fritters and cold Medalla beers and to watch the sunset. Next, head to Tapas Bar at Casa Isleña for a dinner of grilled octopus and then to Seaglass Bar for a nightcap.

Day 5

Wake up early and head to Black Eagle Marina for a snorkel or dive tour of Desecheo Island. Eat lunch on the boat. After you dock, drive 13 miles south to Mayagüez. Stroll around Plaza de Colón and tour Catedral Nuestra Señora de la Candelaria and Museo Casa Grande. Dine on traditional Puerto Rican cuisine at Siglo XX and stay the night at Hotel Colonial, a former convent.

Day 6

In Mayagüez, eat breakfast at Ricomini Panadería and drive 15 miles southeast to San Germán. Stop by the tourist office in Casa Alcaldía Antiqua on Plaza Francisco Mariano Quiñones and pick up a map for a self-guided walking tour of the town's lovely 17th-, 18th-, and 19th-century homes, plazas, and churches, including Porta Coéli Chapel and Museum of Religious Art. Drive 35 miles southeast to Ponce. Dine at one of the many seafood restaurants along La Guancha, the waterfront development overlooking the Caribbean Ocean. Stay the night at one of the hotels around Plaza de las Delicias.

Porta Coéli Chapel and Museum of Religious Art, Mayagüez

ON THE COFFEE TRAIL

drying tables at Hacienda Buena Vista

The gourmet coffee trade has exploded in Puerto Rico in recent years, recalling the island's heyday as a major exporter of the product during the 19th century. Today, historic coffee haciendas are reopening and new coffee farms are being established throughout the Cordillera Central as the world discovers the outstanding flavor of the beans produced from the island's nutrient-rich volcanic soil.

Along with the booming coffee industry has grown an interest in agritourism, resulting in more ways for visitors to get a closer look at the history, the process, and the culture of coffee production in Puerto Rico.

HACIENDA TOURS

The best time to visit haciendas is during harvest season, between September and December.

Established in 1833, **Hacienda Buena Vista**, a former coffee plantation north of Ponce has been restored by the Conservation Trust of Puerto Rico. Although it still produces a small crop of coffee and cocoa beans, its main purpose is historical preservation. Guided tours are available in Spanish and English by reservation.

Take a two-hour tour of **Hacienda Pomarrosa,** a working coffee farm located near Jayuya and enjoy a cup or two of the product, which is grown and processed on-site. Reservations are required. You can also stay overnight in one of two B&B-style accommodations located in the hacienda.

COFFEE FESTIVALS

Celebrate the end of harvest season in mid-February at **La Fiesta del Café**, a three-day celebration in Maricao, located in the west coast near San Germán. Festivities include musical performances, crafts, and food vendors.

Celebrated in Yauco in late February to coincide with the founding of the town, **Festival del Café** is a week-long celebration of the municipality's main crop. The event features parades, award ceremonies, musical and dance performances, arts, crafts, and food vendors.

HACIENDA HOTELS AND RESTAURANTS

Relive the glory days of Puerto Rico's 19th-century coffee trade by spending the night at **Hacienda Gripiñas**, a former coffee plantation, built in 1858 in Jayuya.

Make your reservations early for the exclusive, intimate dinners served once or twice a month at **Hacienda Luz de Luna,** a former 19th-century coffee plantation near Adjuntas, where chef-owner Ventura Vivoni serves an eight-course tasting menu to 36 guests at Restaurante Vida Ventura.

COFFEEHOUSES

The micro-roastery **Café Cuatro Sombras** in Old San Juan serves coffee grown at Hacienda Santa Clara in Yauco, which is then roasted on the premises and served in a variety of coffee drinks along with a light menu of pastries and sandwiches.

Located on the coffee farm in Jayuya, **Café Hacienda San Pedro Tienda y Museo** serves coffee drinks and sells bags of freshly ground and whole bean coffee. Next door, the museum displays coffee-processing equipment dating back to the plantation's origins in 1931.

pink frangipani in bloom

a shrine to the Virgin Mary

Day 7

In Ponce, have breakfast at Café Café Cocina Criolla Espresso Bar and tour the Museo de Arte de Ponce, the island's finest art museum. Drive 43 miles northeast to Cayey, stopping for a roast-pork lunch at one of the *lechoneras*. Drive 34 miles north to San Juan and catch a late flight home.

Options

If you have another week to spare, drive to Caguas and tour Jardín Botánico y Cultural de Caguas. Head west into the mountainous Cordillera Central to Jayuya, where you can tour Museo del Cemi, Casa Museo Canales, and La Piedra Escrita. Hop a flight or take a ferry to Vieques and go for a swim at Balneario Sun Bay during the day and tour the bioluminescent waters of Mosquito Bay at night. Then hop another flight or ferry to the smaller island of Culebra and sunbathe on Playa Flamenco, one of the most beautiful beaches in the Caribbean.

▶ BEST DAY TRIPS FROM SAN JUAN

Do yourself a favor. Rent a car, get out of San Juan, and explore some of the island. Puerto Rico is filled with so many surprising and delightful charms that are just a short drive away, it would be a shame to miss them.

Piñones

Spend the day exploring miles of primitive beach, riding bikes along Paseo Piñones Bike Path, kayaking in Laguna de Piñones or Laguna la Torrecilla, and dining on freshly made fritters at Boca de Cangrejos. Be sure to pack bug spray. Sand fleas are ferocious here in the afternoons. Piñones is 12 miles east of San Juan just past the international airport. Traffic can be excruciatingly slow

ROMANTIC ESCAPES

It's no wonder Puerto Rico is such a popular destination for honeymooners. The beautiful beaches, balmy breezes, and lush tropical foliage provide a perfect backdrop to a romantic getaway. But there's more to it than that. There is a palpable sensuality to life in Puerto Rico. The Spanish architecture, the salsa music, the Caribbean cuisine, the heat – all those elements and more come together to enliven the senses and set the stage for amorous pursuits. Couples can't help but fall sway to Puerto Rico's many aphrodisiacal charms.

OLD SAN JUAN

Book your stay at **Hotel El Convento,** a former Carmelite convent that dates back to 1651, and request the romantic getaway package including a bottle of champagne, rose petal turndown service, and chocolate-covered strawberries. Spend the day strolling through the historic town's cobblestone streets, playing hide and seek in **Castillo San Felipe del Morro,** and sipping café au lait at **Poetic Café.** That night, dine on expertly prepared French cuisine beneath a crystal chandelier at **Trois Cent Onze,** where the service is attentive and the ambiance quiet enough to hear a whisper. Spice things up with a passionfruit martini at **Tantra,** followed by a puff or two from the hookah.

LA PARGUERA

La Parguera is a romantic spot with an old-fashioned, rustic charm. Stay the night at **Parador Villa Parguera,** a quaint, weathered inn with pleasantly landscaped grounds right on the water. The next day go sailing to **Los Cayos,** where you can find your own private beach for swimming, sunning, and snorkeling. Dine at any number of excellent seafood restaurants in town, and take a private nighttime boat tour of glittery **Bahía Fosforescente.**

CULEBRA

Nothing says romance like privacy and seclusion, and nothing says privacy and seclusion like Culebra. Skip the ferry and hop a flight to this small island off the coast of Fajardo. Stay at **Club Seabourne**, a lovely, small property on Fulladoza Bay featuring private villas with luxurious beds and glass showers. Explore the primitive beaches in the **Culebra National Wildlife Refuge,** or go to famous **Playa Flamenco** and walk until you find a secluded spot. At night, dine at **Juanita Bananas,** specializing in fresh, seasonal seafood and produce. Stop by **Mamacita's** for a Bushwhacker, a sensuous and potent blend of Bailey's, Kahlua, Amaretto, coconut cream, rum, and ice cream.

Playa Flamenco, Culebra

and congested on weekends and holidays, so go early.

Río Grande

Give the sun and sand a break and spend the day exploring the rainforest at El Yunque Caribbean National Forest. First, grab picnic supplies from Kasalta Bakery in Ocean Park and then head to El Portal Tropical Forest Center for a briefing on the area. Drive into the forest, stopping at La Coca Falls and Yokahu Tower along the way. Put on your hiking shoes and hit one of the trails, like La Mina Trail, a moderate, 0.5-mile hike ending at La Mina waterfall, or El Yunque Trail, a strenuous 2.5-mile trail through the cloud forest ending at the top of El Yunque. Afterwards, stop at Coqui International in Palmer and shop for locally made arts and crafts. Río Grande is 27 miles east of San Juan along roadways that are often heavy with traffic.

Luquillo

Work on your tan and go for a dip in the tranquil waters of one of Puerto Rico's finest public beaches, Balneario La Monserrate, commonly called Playa Luquillo. If that's too tame, rent a surfboard and ride the waves at La Pared. When hunger pangs strike, hit a couple of vendors at Luquillo Kioskos and dine on a wide variety of fritters and traditional Puerto Rican dishes, or try one of the new upscale kiosks serving creative Caribbean cuisine. Luquillo is 33 miles east of San Juan along roadways typically thick with traffic, especially on weekends.

Fajardo

Prepare to spend the day at sea, sailing and snorkeling around the small islands that make up Reserva Natural La Cordillera. Dine on charcoal-grilled fish and shrimp at La Estación, and then take a nighttime kayak tour of Laguna Grande, the bioluminescent bay in Reserva Natural Las Cabezas de San Juan. Fajardo is 40 miles east of San Juan along congested roadways.

Caguas and Cayey

Spend the morning strolling through the lovely landscaped grounds of Jardín Botánico y Cultural de Caguas. Then head south into the

Museo del Cemi, Jayuya

coffee beans drying at Hacienda Buena Vista, north of Ponce

foothills of the Cordillera Central to the Guavate neighborhood of Cayey to chow down on moist, flavor-packed pork, cooked whole over open fire pits at any number of the *lechoneras* that line the streets. Afterwards, you can walk it off along the wooded trails at Reserva Forestal de Carite. Caguas is 20 miles south and Cayey is 33 miles south of San Juan, and it's highway all the way.

Jayuya

Drive along La Ruta Panorámica, a scenic route through the heart of the Cordillera Central to Jayuya. Visit Museo del Cemí to see the Taíno artifacts and Casa Museo Canales, a reconstruction of a traditional *criolla*-style house. Walk down to La Piedra Escrita to see the Taíno petroglyphs carved in stone and go for a dip in the natural river-fed pool beside it. Dine on traditional Puerto Rican cuisine and pit-cooked pork at El Lechón de la Piedra Escrita. Jayuya is 61 miles southwest of San Juan along winding mountain roads.

Orocovis

Mirador Orocovis-Villalba is one of the rare spots in the Puerto Rican landscape where

you can see both the north and south coasts at the same time, and it's easily accessible by car. For something more adventurous, strap yourself into a harness and fly through the trees on the canopy zipline tour at Toro Verde Nature Adventure Park. Afterwards, stop by Casa Bavaria, where it's Oktoberfest every day. Dine on schnitzel and bratwurst while admiring the mountain views from the patio. Orocovis is 54 miles southwest of San Juan along winding mountain roads.

Ponce

Tour the fabulous Castillo Serrallés, a four-story Spanish Moroccan mansion built in 1934 and filled with exquisite furnishings. Across the street is Cruceta del Vigía, a 100-foot-tall cross with observation deck. Enjoy a seafood lunch overlooking the ocean on the patio at Pito's Seafood Café and Restaurant. In the afternoon, tour the ceremonial grounds at Centro Ceremonial Indígena de Tibes or the 19th-century coffee plantation at Hacienda Buena Vista. Ponce is 72 miles southwest of San Juan, and it's highway all the way.

▶ EXPLORING THE CORDILLERA CENTRAL

As enticing as Puerto Rico's beaches are, there are plenty of reasons to spend time in the Cordillera Central, the island's interior mountain range. Gorgeous tropical jungle, hiking trails, natural pools, and indigenous culture are just some of the attractions to be explored.

One of the great things about the Cordillera Central is that it's possible to get a taste of its charms on a day trip from just about anywhere on the island. But travelers seeking a mountain getaway may want to escape there for two, three, or four days, to fully explore the mountainous region.

The only way to explore the Cordillera Central is by car, and be sure to allow plenty of time for travel. A good rule of thumb is to allow one hour for every 30 miles when traveling mountain roads. Try to stay on main roads whenever possible. Some mountain roads are so narrow, they seem more like one-way roads but they aren't. It is a common practice to blow the car horn when going around sharp turns to alert oncoming traffic to your approach.

Day 1

Fly into San Juan, rent a car, and drive 20 miles south to Caguas. Tour the lush grounds and historic ruins at Jardín Botánico y Cultural de Caguas. Head 14 miles south to Cayey and dine on juicy pit-roasted pork and other local delicacies at one of the *lechoneras*. If there's time, walk it off on the 0.5-mile hike in Reserva Forestal de Carite, a subtropical humid forest. Camp overnight at Área Recreativa Guavate or drive 31 miles south to Coamo for the night and relax in the hot springs.

Day 2

From Coamo, drive 13 miles north to Aibonito, stopping by Mirador Piedra Degetau to take in the amazing panoramic view before following the scenic route along La Ruta Panorámica

for 10 miles to Barranquitas. Visit the town square and tour Museo Luis Muñoz Rivera, the former home of the poet, journalist, and politician. If you want some adventure, take a hiking and rappelling tour of San Cristóbal Cañon. Dine at Vaca Brava, a kitschy restaurant specializing in abundant servings of grilled meats. Drive 30 miles west to Jayuya and stay the night in Hacienda Gripiñas, a former 19th-century coffee plantation.

Day 3

In Jayuya tour Museo del Cemí, a museum shaped like a Taíno amulet and featuring excavated artifacts from the island's indigenous culture. Stop by Casa Museo Canales next door to tour a traditional *criolla*-style house. Next visit La Piedra Escrita, a boulder covered with Taíno petroglyphs located in Río Saliente by a large natural pool where you can take a cool dip. Have lunch at nearby El Lechón de la Piedra Escrita. Take a two-mile hike to Torre Observación in Bosque Estatal de Toro Negro and admire the view from one of the highest points on the island. Camp overnight or return to Hacienda Gripiñas.

La Piedra Escrita, Jayuya

La Coca Falls in El Yunque Caribbean National Forest

BACKCOUNTRY HIKING

Discover the most remote part of **El Yunque Caribbean National Forest** by bypassing the paved trails in El Yunque Recreation Center and hiking **El Toro Trail,** a primitive trail starting at Carretera 186, kilometer 10.6, that passes through *tabonuco,* sierra palm, and cloud forests, offering spectacular views of the south coast. The arduous 2.2-mile trail connects with **Trade Winds Trail,** a 3.9-mile primitive trail that ends at the southern tip of El Yunque Recreation Center.

RAPPELLING

Hike, rappel, and body-surf your way through **San Cristóbal Cañon,** one of the biggest canyons in the Caribbean, located between Aibonito and Barranquitas in the Cordillera Central. Several adventure tour operators offer guided expeditions into the canyon and provide all the equipment and expertise you'll need. Thick with vegetation, the canyon is 4.5 miles long and 500-800 feet deep, providing a great place to test your mountaineering skills.

ZIPLINING

Toro Verde Nature Adventure Park in **Orocovis** boasts a variety of aerial challenges, including The Beast, a 4,745-foot double harness zipline that has you flying through the air in a prone position like a bird. There are also canopy tours, a hanging bridges tour, rappelling, and a mountain bike course.

SPELUNKING

Puerto Rico has the third largest underground river cave system in the world. The tamest way to witness this fascinating subterranean world is to visit **Las Cavernas del Río Camuy** on the north coast. Explore Cueva Clara, featuring a 170-foot-high room thick with stalagmites and stalactites and an underwater waterfall. For a more adventurous exploration of the cave system, contact one of several adventure tour operators and test your rappelling skills.

WILDERNESS CAMPING

Travel by boat at night over the choppy waters of Mona Passage and pitch a tent on uninhabited **Mona Island,** a semiarid subtropical island with 20 miles of coastline, most of which is vertical cliffs more than 200 feet high. Hike the island's trails, where you can spot feral pigs and goats as well as the prehistoric-looking Mona iguana, which grows up to four feet long. Snorkel or dive the crystal-clear waters that surround the island's perimeter. Several local outfitters provide transportation and equipment.

DIVING

Thanks to a modest fishing trade, Puerto Rico has some of the healthiest, most intact underwater reefs to be found in the Caribbean, which makes it ideal for diving and snorkeling. There are several world-class dive sites around the island, but one of the most spectacular is **La Pared** in **La Parguera.** The reef wall runs parallel to the coast from Guánica to Cabo Rojo, dropping from 55 feet to more than 1,500 feet in depth, with visibility ranging from 60 to 150 feet.

PADDLEBOARDING

The newest water sport to hit the island is stand-up paddleboarding, and it's quickly becoming one of the most popular pastimes for water sports enthusiasts. **Velauno Paddleboarding** in San Juan offers instruction in **Laguna del Condado** and tours in **La Parguera** and **Vieques,** as well as equipment rental and sales.

SURFING

Puerto Rico has many world-class surfing spots, especially on the northwest coast. For beginners who want a crash course in the sport, **Surf 787 Resort** in **Rincón** offers overnight accommodations and surf instruction for adults and a summer surf camp for kids.

Day 4

From Jayuya, drive 18 miles west to Utuado and explore Centro Ceremonial Indígena de Caguana, an archaeological site dating back to A.D. 1100 featuring *bateyes* (ball courts), monoliths, and petroglyphs left behind by the Taíno. Head 10 miles north toward Arecibo and stop for a 15-minute hike to Cueva Ventana for breathtaking views of the island's northern karst country. Take the highway 50 miles northeast to San Juan.

▶ SUNBATHING, SWIMMING, AND SURFING

No two beaches are alike in Puerto Rico. *Balnearios* are large, government-maintained beaches with bathroom and shower facilities, picnic tables, and snack bars. Some have lounge-chair rentals, lifeguards, and campsites. Expect to pay $3-5 per vehicle to get in, and be aware that they get crowded on weekends and holidays. There are also many wilderness beaches, which are typically remote and devoid of development and facilities. Some beaches have big waves best suited to surfing, and others are as calm as bathwater and ideal for swimming. One thing all the beaches have in common is their accessibility to the public. There is no such thing as a private beach in Puerto Rico.

Best *Balnearios*
BALNEARIO LA MONSERRATE

Balneario La Monserrate, commonly called Luquillo Beach, is considered one of the island's most beautiful beaches. It features a wide flat crescent of sand, a shady palm grove, and calm shallow waters. A couple of food vendors sell fritters and piña coladas, among other refreshments. There are several picnic shelters, as well as toilets and shower facilities. Camping is allowed with a permit.

BALNEARIO SUN BAY

Balneario Sun Bay is Vieques's crowning jewel of beaches. Pull your car to the edge of a sand dune and mark your spot on the smooth sand. Shade is spotty here, so bring a beach umbrella if you plan to stay for the day. Modest picnic shelters, bathrooms, and shower facilities are available. Camping is allowed with a permit.

PLAYA FLAMENCO

Culebra is the lucky site of Playa Flamenco, one of "America's Best Beaches," according to the Travel Channel. The wide, mile-long, horseshoe-shaped beach boasts fine white sand and calm, aquamarine water. Unlike Puerto Rico's other publicly maintained beaches, Playa Flamenco is home to two hotels—Villa Flamenco Beach and Culebra Beach Villas. An abandoned graffiti-covered tank on the sand is a reminder of the U.S. Navy's presence. Camping is allowed with a permit.

BALNEARIO DE BOQUERÓN

In addition to its long white beach and calm waters, this publicly maintained beach

Horses graze at Balneario Sun Bay.

The graffiti-covered tank on Playa Flamenco is a reminder of the U.S. Navy's presence.

is exceptional because of its excellent facilities, which are bigger, nicer, and more modern than those found at most *balnearios*. The property is quite shady, and in addition to the usual showers, toilets, and picnic tables, there is a huge events pavilion, a baseball field, and a cafeteria.

BALNEARIO CERRO GORDO

Balneario Cerro Gordo in Vega Alta on the north coast is a large protected cove with calm waters and a pristine sandy beach surrounded by hills covered in lush vegetation. It boasts the best campgrounds of any of the *balnearios* because of its spacious location atop a hilly peninsula overlooking the ocean. There's also great surfing to be had here.

Best Wilderness Beaches
BOSQUE ESTATAL DE PIÑONES

Bosque Estatal de Piñones offers several miles of gorgeous, undeveloped beach just minutes east of San Juan. Drive along Carretera 187 and look for sandy unmarked roads along the coast where you can pull your car right up to the beach and climb down the sand dunes into the water. For lunch, grab an *empanadilla* and *coco frio* from one of the food kiosks on the way. Plan on leaving by late afternoon because the sand fleas tend to attack when the sun starts to go down.

PLAYA MAR CHIQUITA

Playa Mar Chiquita in Manatí is a tiny protected cove located at the base of limestone cliffs on the north coast. A coral reef nearly encloses the calm, shallow basin of water, which is ideal for taking small children swimming. When you need some respite from the sun, explore the cliff-side caves.

CULEBRITA

It requires a boat ride to get there, but Culebrita, a *cayo* off the coast of Culebra, is the place to go if you really want to get away from it all. In addition to multiple beaches perfect for swimming or shore snorkeling, there are several tidal pools and a lovely, abandoned

walking along Playa Mar Chiquita in Manatí

lighthouse. To get there, either rent a boat or catch a water taxi at the docks in Dewey.

Best Beaches for Surfing

Although surf spots can be found all around Puerto Rico's coastline, the most popular area is the northwest coast in the municipalities of Isabela, Aguadilla, and Rincón.

PLAYA DE JOBOS

Playa de Jobos in Isabela is an island favorite. The break point off Puntas Jacinto is renowned for its right-breaking tube, and a shady parking lot right on the beach provides easy access. Within walking distance are a number of casual restaurants and bars. Happy Belly's Sports Bar and Grill offers beachside service.

DOMES

Rincón is the surfing capital of Puerto Rico, thanks to literally dozens of popular surf sites. By far the favorite is Domes, located in front of the green domes of an abandoned nuclear power plant known by the acronym BONUS. This easy-access spot features long hollow waves. Domes is often crowded, especially on weekends.

TRES PALMAS

This is a world-class site for experienced big wave surfers. Located in Rincón, the waves here are very long and fast. Waves reportedly reach heights of 40 feet.

WILDERNESS

Aguadilla also boasts several outstanding surf spots. One popular spot is Wilderness, located on the former Ramey Air Force Base. Just drive right through the golf course to get there. Waves break right and left, and swells reach up to 16 feet in height. Nearby El Rincón Surf Shop is a great source of information on current conditions and hot spots.

Best Beaches for Snorkeling and Diving

Puerto Rico's best snorkeling and diving is done offshore, but there are two beaches where underwater life can be explored.

BALNEARIO EL ESCAMBRÓN

The publicly maintained beach in the San Juan neighborhood of Puerta de Tierra features a small crescent beach on a protected cove. On the ocean floor is a collapsed bridge that provides an excellent site for underwater exploration.

PLAYA CARLOS ROSARIO

For easy access to a site rich in marine life, visit Playa Carlos Rosario, a narrow beach flanked by boulders and a protruding coral reef in Culebra. The underwater visibility is usually quite good here, and the coral reef, where you can see all kinds of colorful fish and coral formations, is teeming with marine life.

SAN JUAN

San Juan, Puerto Rico, is arguably the most cosmopolitan city in the Caribbean. The second-oldest European settlement in the Americas, it is a place where world-class restaurants and luxury hotels compete for space alongside glitzy nightclubs and casinos; where Spanish colonial and neoclassical buildings line cobblestone streets; where designer stores and import shops beckon spend-happy tourists; where art, music, and dance thrive in its theaters, museums, and festivals; and where you're never very far from wide strips of sand and surf, ideal for sailing, sunbathing, and swimming.

Situated on the northeastern coast of Puerto Rico, San Juan stretches along 25 miles of coastline and 10 miles inland. It spans 30,000 acres of coastal plain, encompassing rivers, bays, and lagoons, and is home to 1.1 million residents in the greater San Juan area. Established by Spain as the island's capital in 1521, the city's early role as a military stronghold is evident in its 16th- and 17th-century fortresses and a nearly 400-year-old city wall erected around the oldest part of the city to protect it from foreign attacks.

The heart of the city is historic Old San Juan, a 45-block grid of blue cobblestone streets lined with pastel 16th- to 18th-century buildings trimmed with ornamental ironwork and hanging balconies. By day its streets crawl with tourists shopping for souvenirs and designer duds. At night it throbs with locals and tourists

© GORAN MIHAJLOVSKI/123RF.COM

HIGHLIGHTS

LOOK FOR **◖** TO FIND RECOMMENDED SIGHTS, ACTIVITIES, DINING, AND LODGING.

◖ Castillo San Felipe del Morro: Established in 1539, this imposing Spanish colonial fortress was designed so sentries could spot enemies entering San Juan Bay. That's what makes it such an exceptional place to admire the views. The vast lawn is a great spot to fly a kite, too (page 34).

◖ Castillo de San Cristóbal: Built to protect San Juan from attack by land, San Cristóbal was begun in 1634 and eventually encompassed 27 acres, making it the largest fort on the island. It provides an excellent vantage point for checking out stunning views of the city (page 34).

◖ Catedral de San Juan Bautista: Established in 1521, the cathedral lays claim to being the oldest existing church in the western hemisphere. The current structure dates from the 1800s and contains the tomb of Juan Ponce de León (page 41).

◖ Museo de Arte de Puerto Rico: This impressive 130,000-square-foot museum showcases Puerto Rican art from the 17th century to the present, from classical portraiture to po-

litically charged conceptual art. As an added bonus, the wall text is in Spanish and English. Built in 2000, the museum was renovated in 2011 (page 46).

◖ Ocean Park Beach: Easy access and pristine sand make Ocean Park Beach an excellent place to spend the day in the sun. Due to its central location, it's a short cab ride from anywhere in the city. On weekends, lounge chairs are available for rent and street vendors patrol the area selling snacks and beverages (page 49).

◖ Nuyorican Café: The casual Old San Juan nightclub is the hot spot for live salsa music every night but Monday. This is where locals go to dance the night away on the tiny dance floor. Get there early if you want a seat (page 55).

◖ La Placita/Plaza del Mercado: By day Plaza del Mercado in Santurce is a popular farmers market selling fruits, veggies, and meats. By night, particularly Thursdays through Saturdays, it is the apex of a roving street party as revelers stroll from bar to bar, restaurant to restaurant, creating a festive atmosphere in their wake (page 58).

Old San Juan

alike, both partaking of some of the city's finest restaurants and nightclubs.

But Old San Juan is only the tip of the city. Travel eastward to Puerta de Tierra, a small, shady neighborhood with a lovely park, a small stadium, a classic hotel, and the closest public beach to Old San Juan. Continue eastward along the coast to Condado, considered the city's tourist district. High-rise hotels, condos, and apartment buildings overlook the Atlantic Ocean. High-end shops line the main thoroughfare, Avenida Ashford, and many fine restaurants and casinos serve night crawlers.

Farther eastward is Ocean Park, a fine stretch of beach with a stately residential community and a handful of guesthouses and restaurants. Beside it is Isla Verde, where the city's best beaches and most exclusive hotels are, along with fast-food restaurants and a cockfight arena.

Though it may seem so, San Juan isn't all beachfront property. Across the lagoon in Condado is Miramar, a high-rise residential

community and home of the Puerto Rico Convention Center, largest of its kind in the Caribbean. To the east is Santurce, a mix of working-class homes and small businesses that has transformed in recent years into an up-and-coming contemporary arts district.

Travel inland for a locals-only experience in Hato Rey, San Juan's commercial district; Río Piedras, home of the Universidad de Puerto Rico; and Bayamón, a bedroom community.

As in any large city, all is not paradise. San Juan is a densely populated metropolis thick with automobile traffic. A heavy cruise-ship trade dumps thousands of tourists in the city several days a week, and the number of trinket shops catering to day-trippers has proliferated. Burger Kings and Pizza Huts are not an uncommon sight. Neither are pockets of poor neighborhoods, some of whose residents contribute to a petty street-crime problem.

But despite its big-city ways, San Juan's natural beauty is apparent in its miles of sandy

SAN JUAN

beaches, its shady plazas, and its beloved coquí, a tiny tree frog whose "co-QUI" song fills the night air. As Puerto Rico is a commonwealth of the United States, American influence is clearly present, but San Juan proudly maintains its Spanish heritage in its language, its culture, and its customs. And although its future is firmly planted in the 21st century, San Juan's rich history endures in its carefully preserved architecture, its stately fortresses, and the hearts of its inhabitants.

PLANNING YOUR TIME

It's possible to hit San Juan's highlights in a single long weekend, but it's equally possible to spend a whole month here and not see all the city has to offer.

Six municipalities make up greater San Juan. They include San Juan, Cataño, Bayamón, Guaynabo, Trujillo Alto, and Carolina. The four sectors that visitors gravitate to are Old San Juan, Condado, Ocean Park, and Isla Verde in the municipalities of San Juan and Carolina. Not surprisingly, all four areas are along the coast, and luckily they are within about 20 minutes of one another by car, taxi or bus.

Old San Juan

Old San Juan is the cultural center of Puerto Rico. The 500-year-old walled city is filled with beautiful pastel-colored colonial buildings, Spanish forts, art and history museums, plazas, restaurants, bars, shops, and ship docks. Visitors could easily spend a couple of days wandering the cobblestone streets, exploring the city's history and culture. The downsides are that there is no beach in Old San Juan and hordes of tourists sometimes clog the sidewalks, especially when the cruise ships dock. But the town's copious charms are undeniable.

Many of the island's must-see sites are located in Old San Juan. They include two Spanish fortresses, **Castillo San Felipe del Morro** and **Castillo de San Cristóbal;** the historic churches

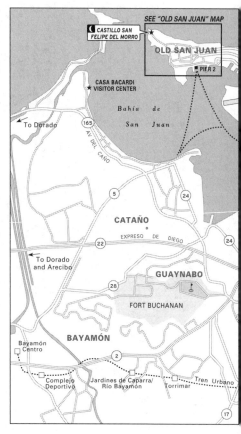

Catedral de San Juan Bautista and **Capilla del Cristo;** and a couple of terrific museums, including **Museo de las Americas.**

The best way to see Old San Juan is by foot. The roads are drivable, but they're narrow and one-way, and only residents' automobiles are permitted inside at night. Just be sure to wear flat, sturdy shoes; it's easy to turn an ankle on those cobblestones.

If walking gets to be too much, there is a free trolley service that runs throughout the town. Getting into and out of Old San Juan is easy. The main public bus terminal is near the cruise-ship piers on Calle de Marina, just south of Plaza de Colón, and there are taxi stands at

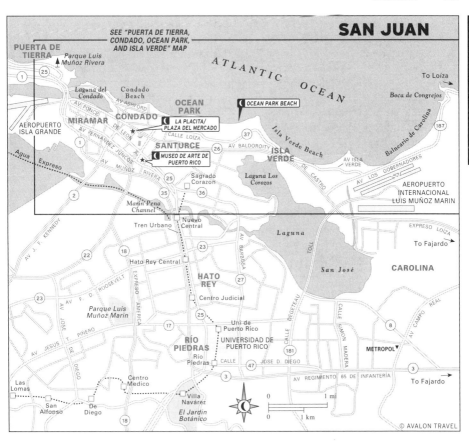

Plaza de las Armas and south of Plaza del Colón at Calle Tetuá and Calle Recinto Sur.

Puerta de Tierra

Geographically this small spit of land is part of Old San Juan, but it's located outside the walled city and lacks the cobblestone streets and pastel-colored colonial buildings that distinguish that part of town. Nevertheless, despite its size (little more than half a square mile), it packs in a diversity of sights.

Puerta de Tierra is the home of many government buildings, including **El Capitolio,** a neoclassical structure built in the 1920s. But it's also the site of two classic hotels, the Caribe

Hilton Hotel and the Normandie (closed at press time); **Fuerte San Jeronimo**, a diminutive fort; **Parque Luis Muñoz Rivera,** a lovely 27-acre park; **Balneario El Escambrón,** the closest beach to Old San Juan; and **Sixto Escobar Stadium.**

Condado

The strip of beachfront real estate that stretches between Isla Verde and Old San Juan has had undergone more facelifts than an aging Hollywood star. From its heady, glamorous days starting in the late 1950s to a period of decline in the 1980s to a new era of burgeoning prosperity in the 2000s, Condado has seen some ups and downs. The good news is its current renaissance seems to be on the ascent and gathering momentum.

Condado is home to some of San Juan's flashiest resorts, including the historic Caribe Hilton, Conrad Condado Plaza Hotel, and La Concha Resort, all of which appear to be flourishing. And where flashy resorts can be found, splashy restaurants can't be too far away. Some of San Juan's highest profile restaurants can be found in Condado, including *Iron Chef* competitor Roberto Treviño's Budatai and Casa Lola Criolla Kitchen, and *Top Chef Masters* competitor Wilo Benet's Pikayo. Naturally it follows that the area is home to shops selling the world's most exclusive designs, from Cartier and Louis Vuitton to Prada and Manolo Blahnik. Condado is not called the tourist district for nothing.

Granted, there are more vacant buildings in the area than one likes—both small high-rises

and large, traditional residences—which speak to the economic struggles of the times. But there are just as many buildings that are undergoing renovation. The most dramatic rehab project was the Condado Vanderbilt Hotel, a massive and stately hotel built in 1919 that is finished up its years-long renovation in 2012, and opened as a luxury condominium hotel with concierge and butler service.

There's more to Condado than commerce, of course, most notably that long, wide stretch of beach that attracted visitors in the first place. The waves can be big, especially in the winter, and the sand is coarse here, but that suits the tourists who flock here just fine. The neighborhood is pedestrian friendly with its wide, well-maintained sidewalks and strategically placed parks, such as Ventanas al Mar (Windows to the Sea), which features seaside picnic shelters, a promenade and several installations of contemporary public art. The area is also home to Laguna del Condado, a small, natural lagoon where fishing and kayaking are permitted and a wide boardwalk provides a place for runners and bicyclists to exercise.

Transportation in Condado is a breeze thanks to the reliable and comfortable bus system that serves the area and the constant flow of taxis, which can be flagged down from most any corner or outside area hotels. And there are a couple of car rental agencies in the vicinity if you want to explore outside San Juan.

Condado has more of a Miami vibe than a traditional Puerto Rican one, but visitors who stay here enjoy the creature comforts the area provides, not to mention the central location, which makes it a great home base for exploring other parts of the island.

Ocean Park

Ocean Park is a small community between Condado and Isla Verde comprising a cluster of modest shops, restaurants, and guest houses that have cropped up around an upscale

© SUZANNE VAN ATTEN

Laguna del Condado, Miramar

residential neighborhood of the same name. The neighborhood features wide, leafy streets and well-maintained homes built during the first half of the 1900s, and it includes some terrific examples of Caribbean-style midcentury modernist architecture. Enter the neighborhood via Calle Santa Ana, just off Calle McLeary. Visitors are free to come and go during the day, but after 6 P.M. a guard checks visitors' identification, and on weekends, car traffic is limited to residents and patrons of the neighborhood's restaurants and guesthouses.

For visitors, the best thing about Ocean Park is its long, wide strip of beach, which is free from the domination of high-rise buildings and resort hotels. Instead the sunny strip of sand and surf is lined with a wide, paved boardwalk, populated by an assortment of food vendors on weekends. The beach is called Ultimo Trolley by locals, because when the island's electric trolley system ceased to operate in 1946, the last trolley car was converted into a snack bar and placed in Parque Balboa, across the street from the beach. Speaking of **Parque Barbosa**, the park features several sports fields as well as a trail for biking, walking, and running. It also has a small parking lot, conveniently located across the street from the beach.

Ocean Park is also home to Kasalta Bakery, a large, popular spot for picking up freshly baked breads, cheesecakes, and pastries, as well as dining on outstanding *criolla* fare, from *cubano* sandwiches to empanadas to *carne guisada*. Traffic getting in out of the bakery's small parking lot is always congested. Parking in general is limited and challenging in Ocean Park. Walking or taking a taxi is recommended if you want to spend some time exploring the area.

Isla Verde

Technically part of a sector called Carolina, Isla Verde is renowned for its long, wide beaches, its luxury resorts, and some pretty spectacular nightclubs and casinos. When you're catching some rays on the beach or partying the night away in a glitzy hot spot, it can feel as glamorous as a mini-South Beach. Unfortunately, except for one entrance at the end of Calle Tatak, the only way to actually see Isla Verde's gorgeous coast is from one of the high-rise hotels and condominiums that line every inch of the way. And the traffic-choked main thoroughfare, Avenida Isla Verde, is a chaotic jumble of fast-food restaurants, pizzerias, and souvenir shops. The best way to enjoy Isla Verde is to ensconce oneself in one of the community's cushy seaside resorts and stay there. The community is also home to the Luis Muñoz Marín International Airport.

Santurce

Located between Isla Verde and Old San Juan, Santurce is one of the most densely populated districts on the island, and it has something of a split personality. On the one hand it is home to

Plaza del Mercado in Santurce

© SUZANNE VAN ATTEN

Miramar

Condado, the oceanfront tourist district, but that area is such an anomaly to the rest of Santurce, it is for all practical purposes its own separate district. The rest of Santurce—the real Santurce—had for many years a reputation as a somewhat gritty, occasionally dodgy, working-class neighborhood densely populated with mom-and-pop businesses and modest housing units. But in recent years Santurce has undergone a dramatic renaissance to become the epicenter of the island's exploding contemporary arts.

The transformation began with the opening in 2000 of the **Museo de Arte de Puerto Rico,** an institution built upon the permanent collection of works by Puerto Rican artists from the 17th century to the present. Santurce is also home to **Centro de Bellas Artes Luis A. Ferré,** a fine arts performance center and a number of contemporary galleries, art collectives, and design centers, many of which participate in Santurce es Ley, an annual arts festival held throughout the streets of Santurce

in mid-September. And naturally, where artists congregate, clubs and restaurants follow. Santurce is also the site of **La Placita/Plaza del Mercado,** a thriving farmers market, which provides the backdrop for nightly street parties on the weekends, when the surrounding restaurants and bars beckon revelers.

Miramar

Miramar is a neighborhood in transition. Located south of Condado, on the opposite side of **Laguna del Condado,** Miramar has long been home to the city's prosperous middle class, but it has suffered an economic decline over the years. The neighborhood's main one-way thoroughfares—Avenida Ponce de León and Avenida Fernández Juncos—run parallel from one tip of the community to the other, and a drive along either one of them reveals the spotty character of the neighborhood. Modern high-rise apartment buildings and classic colonial homes abut boarded-up storefronts and communities central to the lives of San Juan residents. Hato Rey is the city's business and financial district, chock-full of banks and restaurants that cater to businesspeople. It's connected by the 10-mile Tren Urbano metro system to Río Piedras, home of the Universidad de Puerto Rico, and the residential area of Bayamón, home of Parque de las Ciencias Luis A. Ferré science park.

Several spectacular day trips are less than an hour's drive east of San Juan, the most popular being **El Yunque Caribbean National Forest,** the rainforest, and **Balneario La Monserrate/ Luquillo Beach,** considered one of Puerto Rico's most beautiful beaches.

HISTORY

Christopher Columbus was on his second voyage in his quest to "discover" the New World when he arrived in Puerto Rico in 1493. He christened the island San Juan Bautista after John the Baptist, claimed it as a property of Spain, and went on his merry way. But among his crew was a lieutenant named Juan Ponce de León, who shared Columbus's passion for exploration and colonization. In 1508 Ponce de León returned to the island to establish a settlement in a nearly landlocked bit of marshland just west of San Juan, which he called Caparra. He couldn't have made a poorer choice for a new settlement. Virtually uninhabitable and strategically ineffective, the settlement was relocated around 1521 to what is now Old San Juan. Originally the new settlement was called Puerto Rico for its "rich port." It's not clear why—possibly a cartographer's mistake—but soon after it was founded, the name of the settlement was switched with the name of the island.

San Juan became a significant port to the Spanish empire, providing a stopping point for ships transporting goods from the New World to Europe. As a result, it became a target for foreign powers, which led Spain to begin constructing walls and fortresses to protect the harbor and the city.

© SUZANNE VAN ATTEN

La Fortaleza, home to the governor, in Old San Juan

abandoned buildings scrawled with graffiti. Most intersections contain at least one panhandler lurching from car to car seeking a handout.

The good news is that millions of dollars in public and corporate funds are being poured into the western tip of the community along San Juan Bay for the development of the Puerto Rico Convention Center District, at the center of which is the **Puerto Rico Convention Center,** a modern, 580,000-square-foot facility. Next door is the Sheraton Convention Center Hotel & Casino, and a second hotel is under construction. Future plans include office buildings and high-rise residential buildings. How much of this infusion of cash will trickle down to the rest of Miramar is hard to say, but it's a promising sign.

Miramar is also the site of Isla Grande Airport, which provides air service to the Caribbean.

Hato Rey, Río Piedras, and Bayamón

Outside San Juan's popular tourist areas are

Construction of the island's first Spanish fort, La Fortaleza, began in 1533 to protect gold from attack by Carib Indians. Today it serves as the governor's home. As the port grew in importance, Spain's enemies—England, Holland, and France—began to threaten it with attacks, making more elaborate defense systems necessary. Construction of El Morro began in 1539 to protect the harbor. To protect the land, San Cristóbal was begun in 1634. And in 1783, construction of the city wall, La Muralla, was begun. Construction continued on all three projects for hundreds of years.

For two centuries, from 1595 to 1797, San Juan endured multiple foreign attacks, primarily by the English and the Dutch. But by the early 1800s, peace finally reigned.

In 1868, the Puerto Rican independence movement began to gain steam and in 1897 Spain granted the island an autonomous constitution. But the following year, the Spanish-American War broke out, and when it ended eight months later, the Treaty of Paris ceded Puerto Rico to the United States.

Today Puerto Rico is a self-governing commonwealth. The seat of government is El Capitolio in the Puerta de Tierra sector of San Juan.

Sights

OLD SAN JUAN
Historic Sites
◖ CASTILLO SAN FELIPE DEL MORRO

It doesn't matter from which direction you approach El Morro (501 Calle Norzagaray, Old San Juan, 787/729-6777, daily 9 A.M.-6 P.M. Dec.-May, daily 9 A.M.-5 P.M. June-Nov., $3 adults, $5 for both forts, $2 seniors over 62, free for children under 16, orientation talks every hour on the hour in English and Spanish), it's an impressive sight to behold. From San Juan Bay, which it was constructed to protect from attack, it's an awesome feat of engineering and a daunting display of military defense featuring four levels of cannon-bearing batteries that rise 140 feet from the sea. From Old San Juan, the approach is more welcoming, thanks to an enormous expanse of grassy lawn and breathtaking views of the shore. It's easy to see why this is such a popular spot for kite-flyers.

Inside Castillo San Felipe del Morro is a maze of rooms, including gun rooms, soldiers' quarters, a chapel, turreted sentry posts, and a prison connected by tunnels, ramps, and a spiral stairway. The foundations for El Morro were laid in 1539, but it wasn't completed until 1787. It successfully endured many foreign attacks by the English in 1595, 1598, and 1797, and by the Dutch in 1625. During the Spanish-American War, the United States fired on El Morro and destroyed the lighthouse, which was later rebuilt.

On Saturdays and Sundays, guided tours are offered in Spanish and English.

◖ CASTILLO DE SAN CRISTÓBAL

Castillo de San Cristóbal (Calle Norzagaray at the entrance to Old San Juan, 787/729-6777, daily 9 A.M.-6 P.M. Dec.-May, daily 9 A.M.-5 P.M. June-Nov., $3 adults, $5 for both forts, $2 seniors over 62, free for children under 16, English tours at 10 A.M. and 2 P.M.) is the large fortress at the entrance to Old San Juan by Plaza de Colón. Before it was built, two significant attacks from land—first by the Earl of Cumberland in 1598, later by the Dutch in 1625—convinced the Spanish that protecting the walled city from attack by sea alone was not adequate.

The fort's construction began in 1634 and was completed in 1783. The fort eventually encompassed 27 acres of land, although some of it was destroyed to accommodate the expanding city. The fort's defense was tested

© BRYAN BUSOVICKI/123RF.COM

El Morro has protected San Juan since 1595.

in 1797 by another unsuccessful attack by the British. After the United States won the Spanish-American War, it took control of the fort and used it as a World War II observation post. Today, a section of the fort is open to the public, who can wander freely among its intriguing array of tunnels, ramps, stairways, batteries, magazines, soldiers' quarters, and turreted sentry posts.

CASA BLANCA

Casa Blanca (1 Calle San Sebastián, Old San Juan, 787/725-1454, Tues.-Sat. 9 A.M.-noon and 1-4 P.M., $2) was originally built as a home for the island's first governor, Juan Ponce de León, although he died on his quest for the Fountain of Youth before he could ever take up residence. Construction was begun in 1523, and for more than 200 years it served as the residence of Ponce de León's descendants. Today it's a museum of 17th- and 18th-century domestic life featuring lots of impressive Spanish

antiques. Don't miss the cool, lush gardens that surround the house and the views of both San Juan Bay and the Atlantic Ocean.

LA FORTALEZA

La Fortaleza (Calle Fortaleza, Old San Juan, 787/721-7000, ext. 2211, 2323, and 2358, Mon.-Fri. 9 A.M.-3:30 P.M., $3 donation) was the first fort built in Puerto Rico, completed in 1540 to provide refuge for the island's original Spanish settlers. Partially burned by the Dutch in 1625, it was rebuilt in the 1640s and received a new facade in 1846. It has been the official residence of the governor of Puerto Rico since the 16th century, which gives it the distinction of the longest continuous use of an executive mansion in the western hemisphere. Tours are limited mostly to the lovely gardens and first floor, with audio narration in Spanish and English.

LA MURALLA

La Muralla is the grand, dramatic, and impenetrable wall that once surrounded Old San Juan

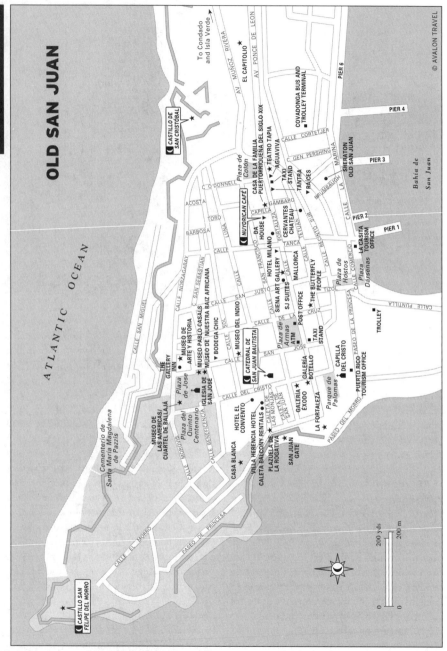

OLD SAN JUAN

© AVALON TRAVEL

ATLANTIC OCEAN

Bahía de San Juan

To Condado and Isla Verde

★ CASTILLO DE SAN CRISTÓBAL

EL CAPITOLIO

AV. MUÑOZ RIVERA

AV. PONCE DE LEON

PIER 6

PIER 4

PIER 3

PIER 2

PIER 1

COVADONGA BUS AND TROLLEY TERMINAL

CALLE CORTETJER

C. GEN PERSHING

SHERATON OLD SAN JUAN

MARINA

BRUMBAUGH

RAÍCES

TANTRA

AGUAVIVA

TAXI STAND

TEATRO TAPIA

CASA DE LA FAMILIA PUERTORRIQUEÑA DEL SIGLO XIX

Plaza de Colón

CERVANTES CHATEAU

GAMBARO

CAPILLA

DA HOUSE

CALLE RECINTO SUR

LA CASITA TOURISM OFFICE

Plaza de Hostos

Plaza Darsenas

CALLE COMERCIO

MALLORCA

THE BUTTERFLY PEOPLE

CALLE TIZOL

CALLE TETUÁN

CALLE FORTALEZA

HOTEL MILANO

CALLE SAN FRANCISCO

SIENA ART GALLERY

SJ SUITES

POST OFFICE

Plaza de Armas

ATM

TAXI STAND

CALLE CRUZ

CALLE SAN JOSE

CATEDRAL DE SAN JUAN BAUTISTA ★

GALERIA BOTELLO

CAPILLA DEL CRISTO

PUERTO RICO TOURISM OFFICE

PASEO DE LA PRINCESA

Parque de Palomas

TROLLEY

CALLE PUNTILLA

NUYORICAN CAFÉ

C. O'DONNELL

ACOSTA

TORO

BARBOSA

CALLE LUNA

CALLE SOL

CALLE SAN SEBASTIAN

CALLE NORZAGARAY

CALLE SAN MIGUEL

MUSEO DE ARTE Y HISTORIA ★

MUSEO PABLO CASALS ★

MUSEO DE NUESTRA RAÍZ AFRICANA

BODEGA CHIC

MUSEO DEL INDIO

THE GALLERY INN

CALLE NORZAGARAY

CALLE DEL CRISTO

CALLE SAN JUSTO

CALLE SAN JOSE

CALLE SAN JUAN

IGLESIA DE SAN JOSÉ ★

Plaza de José

Plaza del Quinto Centenario

Cementerio de Santa María Magdalena de Pazzis

MUSEO DE LAS AMÉRICAS/ CUARTEL DE BALLAJÁ

CASA BLANCA

CALLE MOROVIS

CALLE BENEFICENCIA

VILLA HERENCIA HOTEL

CALETA BALCONY RENTALS

HOTEL EL CONVENTO

PLAZUELA DE LA ROGATIVA

CALETA DE LAS MONJAS

GALERIA ÉXODO

LA FORTALEZA

SAN JUAN GATE

PASEO DEL MORRO

CALLE EL MORRO

PASEO DE PRINCESA

★ CASTILLO SAN FELIPE DEL MORRO

0   200 yds
0   200 m

LA MURALLA: AN ENDURING SYMBOL OF PUERTO RICO

SUZANNE VAN ATTEN

a section of La Muralla

The most enduring symbol of Puerto Rico is La Muralla. Nearly 400 years old, the city wall is composed of rock, rubble, and mortar that wraps around Old San Juan from the cruise-ship piers on San Juan Harbor to the capitol on the Atlantic Ocean. Its iconic sentry boxes serve as a symbol of the island's Spanish heritage and resilience in an ever-changing world.

Begun by Spanish colonists in the 1600s, the wall took 200 years to complete and has withstood multiple attacks by the English, the Dutch, and the Americans. But what proved nearly impenetrable to foreign attack has been rendered defenseless by modern life. Automo-bile traffic, pollution, and misguided attempts to preserve it have endangered the wall.

Forty-five feet wide and 40 feet high in some spots, La Muralla is crumbling in places. In 2004 a 70-foot section below the heavily traveled Calle Norzagaray fell, underscoring the urgency of stepping up preservation efforts. It wasn't the first time the wall's fragility was made apparent. A larger section fell into San Juan Bay in 1938, and in 1999, a Soviet oil tanker ran aground, damaging the wall's northwest corner.

When the U.S. Army seized Puerto Rico in 1898, it took over maintenance of the wall and attempted its first preservation efforts. Concrete was used to patch La Muralla, but that only served to add weight to the wall and trap moisture inside it, which weakened the structure through time.

Now a National Historic Site, La Muralla is maintained by the National Park Service, which has been overseeing efforts to repair the wall. Experts have spent years studying the 16th-century methods used to build the structure in an attempt to recreate the magic mixture of sand, water, and limestone used to stucco the wall. Not only is the repair method they've developed more effective than concrete, it serves to preserve the wall's historical integrity. The process is now being used to repair the wall's beloved sentry boxes. But it's a painstaking and costly process, requiring the services of specially trained masons, which the Park Service is hard-pressed to fund for large-scale repairs.

But La Muralla endures. Along with the fortresses of El Morro and San Cristóbal that adjoin it, the wall attracts 1.2 million visitors a year. Chances are, with the help of preservation efforts, it will continue to assert its soaring beauty and cultural significance as the proud protector of Old San Juan for years to come.

La Muralla City Gate

© SUZANNE VAN ATTEN

and still stands strong today along the coast and bay. Nearly 400 years old, the wall took 200 years to complete and stands 48 feet high in some places and 20 feet thick at its base. The wall once had five gates that permitted access into the city, but only one remains today.

LA PUERTA DE SAN JUAN

The commanding red La Puerta de San Juan was built in the late 1700s and is on the eastern end of Old San Juan beside La Fortaleza. Sixteen feet tall and 20 feet thick, the door is best seen from the wide bayside promenade, Paseo de Princesa.

PASEO DE PRINCESA

Named after La Princesa, a 19th-century prison that now houses the Puerto Rico Tourism Company, the promenade begins across from Plaza de Hostos at Calle Tizol near the cruise-ship piers in Old San Juan. Glorious royal palms, a view of the bay, the soaring city wall, the city gate, and an outlandish fountain comprising naked sea nymphs and goats are some of the sights along the way. The promenade continues along Castillo San Felipe del Morro, ending dramatically at the point containing the oldest part of the fort. Paseo de Princesa is the site of frequent festivals and events, and you can usually find a variety of vendors here selling *piraguas* (snow cones), popcorn, and *dulces* (sweets).

CUARTEL DE BALLAJÁ

Cuartel de Ballajá (Calle Norzagaray beside Plaza del Quinto Centenario near the entrance to Castillo San Felipe del Morro, Old San Juan) is a massive structure that once housed 1,000 Spanish soldiers. Built in 1854, the former barracks are three levels high with interior balconies and a dizzying series of arches that overlook an enormous courtyard. It was the last major building constructed by the Spanish in the New World. Today it houses the Museo de las Americas, featuring a fantastic folk art collection.

CEMENTERIO DE SANTA MARÍA MAGDALENA DE PAZZIS

Cementerio de Santa María Magdalena de Pazzis is the city's historic cemetery, outside the city wall just east of Castillo San Felipe del Morro and accessible from Calle Norzagaray in Old San Juan. In addition to a neoclassical chapel, there are many significant burial sites of some of the city's early colonists, as well as the tomb of Pedro Albizu Campos, the revered revolutionary who sought independence for the island of Puerto Rico. Avoid going alone or at night. Next door is **La Perla,** an impoverished community notorious for its drug trade; its illicit activities are known to spill over into the cemetery. If you don't want to venture in, you can get a great view of it from Plaza del Quinto Centenario on Calle Norzagaray.

TEATRO TAPIA

Teatro Tapia (Calle Fortaleza at Plaza de Colón, Old San Juan, 787/721-0180 or 787/721-0169, www.teatropr.com) is one of the oldest theaters in the western hemisphere. The lovely Romantic-style building was constructed in 1824 and renovated in 1987. Named after Puerto Rican playwright Alejandro Tapia y Rivera, the 642-seat theater still hosts a variety of performing arts events.

History Museums

MUSEO DE ARTE Y HISTORIA DE SAN JUAN

Museo de Arte y Historia de San Juan (150 Calle Norzagaray, Old San Juan, 787/724-1875, Wed.-Fri. 9 A.M.-noon and 1-4 P.M., Sat.-Sun. 10 A.M.-4 P.M., free) is in the city's former marketplace, built in 1857. In 1979 it was converted into a city museum. It contains two exhibition spaces, one housing temporary exhibits illuminating various aspects of the city's history, the other a permanent exhibition that gives a comprehensive look at the city's history from its geographical roots to the 21st century. Superbly produced wall graphics

and text include reproductions of old photographs, maps, prints, and paintings that tell the city's story. All the exhibits are in Spanish, but a photocopied handout in English encapsulates the exhibition highlights.

CASA DE LA FAMILIA PUERTORRIQUEÑA DEL SIGLO XIX AND MUSEO DE LA FARMACIA

One house holds two museums: Casa de la Familia Puertorriqueña del Siglo XIX and Museo de la Farmacia (319 Calle Fortaleza, Old San Juan, 787/977-2700 or 787/977-2701, Tues.-Sat. 8:30 A.M.-4:20 P.M., free). Upstairs is a re-creation of a typical (albeit wealthy) family's residence from the late 1800s filled with antiques, both locally made and imported from Germany, Belgium, and Italy. Downstairs is a re-created 19th-century pharmacy filled with authentic vessels, cabinets, and scales from a pharmacy in Cayey.

MUSEO DE NUESTRA RAÍZ AFRICANA

Museo de Nuestra Raíz Africana (Calle San Sebastián beside Plaza de San José, Old San Juan, 787/724-4294 or 787/724-4184, Tues.-Sat. 8:30 A.M.-4:20 P.M.) explores the African influence on Puerto Rican culture. Slavery and abolition figure prominently, including a display of handcuffs and collars and a simulated re-creation of what it was like to cross the ocean in a slave ship.

MUSEO DEL INDIO

San Juan's newest museum is Museo del Indio (119 San José, Old San Juan, 787/721-2864, Tues.-Sat. 9:30 A.M.-3:30 P.M., free). Devoted to the history of the island's Taíno Indian population, it contains many artifacts unearthed in excavations around the island, including pottery, stone tools, and *cemíes,* small carved stone talismans representative of various gods.

MUSEO PABLO CASALS

Museo Pablo Casals (101 Calle San Sebastián, Old San Juan, 787/723-9185, Tues.-Sat.

9:30 A.M.-4:30 P.M., $1 adults, $0.50 children age 12 and younger, seniors 60 and older) commemorates the career and accomplishments of Pablo Casals, the renowned cellist who performed for Queen Victoria and President Theodore Roosevelt, among other world movers and shakers. Born in Catalonia, Casals moved to Puerto Rico in 1956. A year later, the island established the annual Casals Festival of classical music, which continues today. Inside an 18th-century building, the museum contains Casals's music manuscripts, cello, and piano. You can hear recordings of Casals performing in the music room upstairs.

MUSEO DEL NIÑO

Museo del Niño (150 Calle Cristo near Hotel El Convento, Old San Juan, 787/722-3791, www.museodelninopr.org, Tues.-Thurs. 9 A.M.-3:30 P.M., Fri. 9 A.M.-5 P.M., Sat.-Sun. 12:30-5 P.M., $5 adults, $7 children) is a children's museum containing exhibits in geography, nutrition, weather, astronomy, biology, and more.

Art Museums and Galleries
MUSEO DE LAS AMERICAS

Museo de las Americas (Cuartel de Ballajá, 2nd floor, on Calle Norzagaray beside Plaza del Quinto Centenario, Old San Juan, 787/724-5052, fax 787/722-2848, www.museolasamericas.org, Tues.-Sat. 9 A.M.-noon and 1-4 P.M., Sun. 11 A.M.-4 P.M., $3 adults, $2 children age 12 and younger, students and seniors age 65 and older) is located inside an enormous structure that once housed 1,000 Spanish soldiers. The museum contains a fantastic collection of Latin American folk art, including masks, musical instruments, clothing, pottery, baskets, and tools. Highlights include altars representing Santería, voodoo, and Mexico's Day of the Dead celebration. Don't miss the collection of vintage santos, Puerto Rican wood carvings of saints. Wall text is in Spanish and English except in the second smaller exhibit dedicated

to Puerto Rico's African heritage. The **Tienda de Artesanías** on the first floor (Tues.-Fri. 10 A.M.-4 P.M., Sat.-Sun. 11 A.M.-5 P.M., 787/722-6057) has a small but quality selection of locally made crafts for sale.

GALERÍA BOTELLO

This gallery (208 Calle Cristo, Old San Juan, 787/723-9987 or 787/723-2879, fax 787/724-6776, www.botello.com, Mon.-Sat. 10 A.M.-6 P.M.) is a significant art museum dedicated to the work of Angel Botello. Although he was born in Spain, the renowned artist spent most of his life in the Caribbean, eventually settling in Puerto Rico, where he opened this gallery. Although he died in 1986, the artist lives on through his paintings and sculptures on view at the gallery, which also exhibits solo shows by contemporary artists.

SIENA ART GALLERY

Siena Art Gallery (253 Calle San Francisco, Old San Juan, 787/724-7223, www.sienagallery.com, Mon.-Sat. 11 A.M.-6 P.M.) is a fine art gallery featuring Puerto Rican and Caribbean artists including Mikicol and Rafael Colon Morales.

GALERÍA ÉXODO

Galería Éxodo (200-B Calle Cristo, Old San Juan, 787/725-4252 or 787/671-4159, www.galeriaexodo.com, daily 11 A.M.-7 P.M.)—formerly Fósil Arte—has a wide diversity of mostly high-quality works by contemporary artists, both Puerto Rican and international.

THE BUTTERFLY PEOPLE

The Butterfly People (257 Calle de la Cruz, Old San Juan, 787/723-2432 or 787/723-2201, www. butterflypeople.com, daily 11 A.M.-6 P.M.) is a unique gallery that sells fantastic colorful pieces composed of real butterflies mounted in Lucite.

© SUZANNE VAN ATTEN

Catedral de San Juan Bautista

Religious Sites

(CATEDRAL DE SAN JUAN BAUTISTA

Catedral de San Juan Bautista (151-153 Calle del Cristo, Old San Juan, 787/722-0861, www.catedralsanjuan.com, Mon.-Thurs. 9 A.M.-noon and 1:30-4 P.M., Fri. 9 A.M.-noon; Mass Sat. 9 A.M., 11 A.M., and 7 P.M., Sun.-Fri. 12:15 P.M.) holds the distinction of being the second-oldest church in the western hemisphere, the first being Catedral Basilica Menor de Santa in the Dominican Republic. The church was first built of wood and straw in 1521 but was destroyed by hurricanes and rebuilt multiple times. In 1917 the cathedral underwent major restoration and expansion. The large sanctuary features a marble altar and rows of arches with several side chapels appointed with elaborate statuary primarily depicting Mary and Jesus. In stark contrast is a chapel featuring an enormous contemporary oil painting of a man in a business suit. It was erected in honor of Carlos "Charlie" Rodríguez, a Puerto Rican layman who was beatified in 2001 by Pope John Paul II. Catedral de San Juan Bautista is the final resting place of Juan de Ponce de León, whose remains are encased in a marble tomb. It also holds a relic of San Pio, a Roman martyr.

CAPILLA DEL CRISTO

Built in 1753, the tiny picturesque Capilla del Cristo (south end of Calle de la Cristo, Old San Juan, 787/722-0861) is one of the most photographed sights in San Juan. Legend has it that horse races were held on Calle del Cristo, and one ill-fated rider was speeding down the hill so fast he couldn't stop in time and tumbled over the city wall to his death, and the chapel was built to prevent a similar occurrence. An alternative end to the legend is that the rider survived and the church was built to show thanks to God. Either way, the result was the construction of a beloved landmark.

Unfortunately, Capilla del Cristo is rarely open, but it's possible to peer through the windows and see the ornate gilded altarpiece. Beside it is **Parque de Palomas,** a gated park overlooking San Juan Harbor that is home to more pigeons than you might think imaginable. Bird seed is available for purchase if you want to get up close and personal with your fine feathered friends.

IGLESIA DE SAN JOSÉ

Iglesia de San José (Calle San Sebastián at Plaza de San José, Old San Juan, 787/725-7501) is one of the oldest structures in Old San Juan. Built in the 1530s, it was originally a chapel for the Dominican monastery, but it was taken over in 1865 by the Jesuits. The main chapel is an excellent example of 16th-century Spanish Gothic architecture. Originally Iglesia de San José was Juan Ponce de León's final resting place, but his body was later moved to Catedral de San Juan Bautista. Ponce de León himself is said to have donated the wooden 16th-century crucifix. Unfortunately, the church has

Capilla del Cristo

© SUZANNE VAN ATTEN

been closed for many years while it undergoes a seemingly endless renovation project.

Plazas and Parks

Most every town in Puerto Rico has a main plaza at its center that is flanked by a church and an *alcaldía* (town hall). Bigger towns like San Juan have several. There is no better way to spend the morning than strolling the perimeter of a plaza or spending time on a bench sipping coffee, fending off pigeons, and watching the parade of people pass by. The plazas are also popular sites for arts festivals and evening concerts. Not surprisingly, the largest concentration of historic plazas and parks is in Old San Juan.

PLAZA DE ARMAS

Plaza de Armas (Calle San Francisco, at Calle de la Cruz and Calle San José) is the main square in Old San Juan and a great place to people-watch. Once the site of military drills, it contains a large gazebo and a fountain surrounded by four 100-year-old statues that represent the four seasons. A couple of vendors sell coffee and snacks, and there's a bank of pay phones popular with cruise-ship visitors eager to check in with those back home. Across the street on Calle de la Cruz is a small grocery store. Across Calle Cordero is an ATM, and a taxi stand is just around the corner on Calle San José at Calle Fortaleza.

PLAZA DE COLÓN

Plaza de Colón (between Calle Fortaleza, Calle San Francisco, and Calle O'Donnell) is a large square at the entrance to Old San Juan by Castillo de San Cristóbal. In the center is a huge pedestal topped with a statue of Christopher Columbus, whom the plaza is named after. There's a small newsstand on one corner, and several restaurants and shops surround it on two sides. Unfortunately, there's little shade, so it's not that pleasant for lingering when the sun is high.

© SUZANNE VAN ATTEN

La Rogativa by sculptor Lindsay Daen, Plazuela de la Rogativa

by New Zealand artist Lindsay Daen in the 1950s. The piece depicts a procession of three women and a priest bearing crosses and torches. It commemorates one of San Juan's most beloved historic tales. In 1797 a British fleet led by Sir Ralph Abercrombie entered San Juan Bay and prepared to launch an attack in hopes of capturing the city. Because the city's men were away protecting the city's inland fronts, the only people remaining behind were women and clergy. In hopes of staving off an attack, the governor ordered a *rogativa,* a divine entreaty to ask the saints for help. As the story goes, the town's brave women formed a procession, carrying torches and ringing bells throughout the streets, which duped the British into thinking reinforcements had arrived, prompting them to sail away, leaving the city safe once again.

PLAZA DEL QUINTO CENTENARIO

Plaza del Quinto Centenario (between Calle Norzagaray and Calle Beneficencia near the entrance to Castillo San Felipe del Morro, Old San Juan) is Old San Juan's newest park. Built to commemorate the 500th anniversary of Christopher Columbus's "discovery" of the New World, the plaza features a striking 40-foot totem made from black granite and ceramic pieces created by local artist Jaime Suárez. The plaza provides a great view of the historic cemetery, El Morro, and all the kite flyers who gather on the fort's long green lawn.

PLAZUELA DE LA ROGATIVA

One of Puerto Rico's most beautiful pieces of public art is in Plazuela de la Rogativa, a tiny sliver of a park tucked between the city wall and Calle Clara Lair just west of El Convento in Old San Juan. At its center is a spectacular bronze sculpture called *La Rogativa,* designed

PLAZA DE JOSÉ

Plaza de José (Calle San Sebastián and Calle Cristo, Old San Juan) is in front of the Iglesia de San José and features a statue of its most celebrated parishioner, Juan Ponce de León. After successfully thwarting another attack by the British in 1797, citizens of San Juan melted the enemy's cannons to make the statue. This is a popular gathering place for young locals, especially at night when the string of nearby bars gets crowded.

PLAZA DE HOSTOS

Plaza de Hostos (between Calle San Justo and Calle Tizol, Old San Juan) is a bustling shady spot near the cruise-ship piers. On weekends it turns into a craft fair, and there are often food vendors selling fritters and snow cones. Just across the street, at **Plaza de la Dársena,** concerts are often held on the weekends on a covered stage overlooking the harbor.

PARQUE DE PALOMAS

Parque de Palomas (beside Capilla del Cristo on the south end of Calle de la Cristo) is home

PUERTA DE TIERRA, CONDADO, OCEAN PARK, AND ISLA VERDE

to a gazillion pigeons. A vendor sells small bags of feed for those who take pleasure in being swarmed by the feathered urban dwellers. Kids love it!

PUERTA DE TIERRA
PARQUE LUIS MUÑOZ RIVERA

Puerta de Tierra is a spot of land between Condado and Old San Juan that is home to Parque Luis Muñoz Rivera (between Ave. Ponce de León and Ave. Muñoz Rivera), a lovely, 27-acre green space established in 1929. Providing a welcome reprieve from the city's urban atmosphere, it features shady gardens, fountains, walking trails, a children's play area, and the Peace Pavilion.

FUERTE SAN JERÓNIMO

Fuerte San Jerónimo (behind the Caribe Hilton in Puerta de Tierra) is the only fort in San Juan that isn't part of the San Juan National Historic

Site. Instead, it's overseen by the Institute of Puerto Rican Culture and managed by the Caribe Hilton, on whose property it now sits. Various sources date its origins to the 17th and 18th centuries, but little is known about it. Unfortunately, it's rarely open to the public, but it can be seen from Puente Dos Hermanos bridge in Condado.

EL CAPITOLIO

El Capitolio (Ave. Ponce de Léon at Ave. Muñoz Rivera, 787/724-2030, ext. 2472 or 2518, www.nps.gov, Mon.-Fri. 9 A.M.-5 P.M.) is the seat of government for the island, and it is one of many government buildings located in Puerta de Tierra. The neoclassical revival-style building was completed in 1929, although the dome was added later in 1961. Inside are murals and mosaics that detail the island's history. Guided tours are available by appointment only.

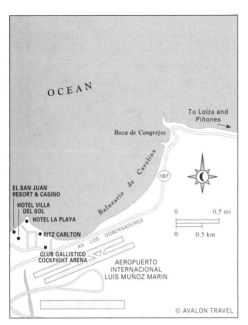

OCEAN

To Loíza and
Piñones

Boca de Congrejos

Balneario de Carolina

187

EL SAN JUAN
RESORT & CASINO

HOTEL VILLA
DEL SOL

HOTEL LA PLAYA

RITZ CARLTON

AV LOS GOBERNADORES

CLUB GALLISTICO
COCKFIGHT ARENA

AEROPUERTO
INTERNACIONAL
LUIS MUÑOZ MARIN

0   0.5 mi

0   0.5 km

© AVALON TRAVEL

bronze sculptures make this the perfect spot to relax or picnic. One of the highlights is a whimsical bronze sculpture called *Juan Bobo and the Basket*. Created in 1991 by New Zealand artist Lindsay Daen, who made the more famous *La Rogativa* statue in Old San Juan, it's inspired by a local fable.

MIRAMAR

PUERTO RICO CONVENTION CENTER

Puerto Rico Convention Center (100 Convention Blvd., Miramar, 800/214-0420, www.prconvention.com) is a shiny new facility that opened in 2009, and it lays claim to being the largest, most technologically advanced convention center in the Caribbean, with 580,000 square feet of meeting space that can accommodate up to 10,000 people. Events include art fairs, Puerto Rico Comic Con, bridal shows, volleyball championships, and shopping expos. Ficus Café is an open-air restaurant serving tapas and cocktails (Thurs.-Sat. 5 P.M.-midnight).

CONSERVATORIO DE MUSICA DE PUERTO RICO

Renowned cellist Pablo Casals established the Conservatorio de Musica de Puerto Rico (951 Ave. Ponce de León, Miramar, 787/751-0160, www.cmpr.edu) in 1959, and it underwent extensive renovation in 2011. The music conservatory provides undergraduate, graduate, and community education programs in areas of musical performance, composition, jazz, and education. The conservatory hosts a family concert series featuring performances by students, faculty, and guest artists; tickets are $10. In addition, free student concerts are held most Tuesdays at 5 P.M. in the Patio Luis Ferré, and free jazz concerts are held at 6 P.M. on Wednesdays in the Anfiteatro Rafael Hernández, in the Plaza de la Laguna.

GALERÍA PETRUS

Galería Petrus (726 Calle Hoare, Miramar, 787/289-0505, www.petrusgallery.com) is an

CONDADO

PARQUE NACIONAL LAGUNA DEL CONDADO JAIME BENÍTEZ

Parque Nacional Laguna del Condado Jaime Benítez (Avenida Baldorioty de Castro on the eastern side of the Condado Lagoon between Condado and Miramar, daily 24 hours) features a wide boardwalk along the lagoon's edge, park benches, and a public ramp for launching kayaks and canoes. Several natural restoration projects are underway at the site, including a seagrass restoration project in the lagoon and the cultivation of red mangrove trees, ceibas, and other native plants around its shore.

PARQUE LUCHETTI

A lovely oasis of quiet and lush green flora just two blocks away from the hubbub of Avenida Ashford, Parque Luchetti (between Calle Magdalena and Calle Luchetti at Calle Cervantes) is a hidden gem of a park. Shaded benches, flowering shrubs, palm trees, and

Puerto Rico Convention Center, Miramar

exhibit space that presents temporary shows featuring contemporary paintings, sculptures, and graphic arts from the 1960s to the present. The gallery's focus is on Puerto Rican artists, including painter Santiago Flores Charneco, painter and printmaker Luis Hernández Cruz, and sculptor Carlos Guzmán.

SANTURCE
Museums and Galleries
◖ MUSEO DE ARTE DE PUERTO RICO

Without a doubt, the crowning jewel of San Juan's cultural institutions is Museo de Arte de Puerto Rico (299 Ave. José de Diego, Santurce, 787/977-6277, fax 787/977-4446, www.mapr.org, Tues. and Thurs.-Sat. 10 A.M.-5 P.M., Wed. 10 A.M.-8 P.M., Sun. 11 A.M.-6 P.M., $6.50 adults, $3.50 children 5-12). Visitors with even a passing interest in art will be bowled over by the volume and quality of work produced by the many gifted artists who hail from this small island.

The 130,000-square-foot, neoclassical structure opened in 2000 and was renovated in 2011. It is devoted to Puerto Rican art from the 17th century to the present. And joy! The wall text is in Spanish and English. Exhibition highlights include works by the celebrated Francisco Manuel Oller, a European-trained 17th-century realist-impressionist, as well as a striking selection of *cartels,* a midcentury poster-art form distinguished by bold graphics and socially conscious themes.

Contemporary art is on the second floor, and it is not to be missed. One room is devoted to Rafael Trelles's 1957 installation *Visits to the Wake,* inspired by Oller's famous 19th-century painting of a family attending a child's wake, called *El Veloria.* The piece combines video, sculpture, found objects, and life-size cutouts of the painting's characters to astounding effect. Another remarkable work is Pepón Osorio's installation titled *No Crying Allowed in the Barbershop.* The simulated barbershop explores issues of male vanity, rites of passage, and early lessons in masculinity.

© SUZANNE VAN ATTEN

Conservatorio de Musica de Puerto Rico, Miramar

There are also temporary exhibition spaces for rotating shows, a children's gallery, a five-acre modern sculpture garden, and the Raul Julia Theater, featuring an intriguing curtain made of *mundillo,* a traditional hand-made lace. A museum shop is also on-site.

MUSEO DE ARTE CONTEMPORÁNEO DE PUERTO RICO

In a stricking red-brick Georgian structure completed in 1918, Museo de Arte Contemporáneo de Puerto Rico (Escuela Rafael M. de Labra, corner of Roberto H. Todd and Ponce de León, Santurce, 787/977-4030, 787/977-4031, or 787/977-4032, www.museo-contemporaneopr.org, Tues.-Fri. 10 A.M.-4 P.M., Sat. 11 A.M.-5 P.M., Sun. 1-5 P.M., $5 adults, $3 students with ID and seniors 60 and older) has two small exhibition spaces featuring rotating exhibitions from its permanent collection.

ESPACIO 1414

Espacio 1414 (1414 Ave. Fernandez Juncos, Santurce, 787/725-3899, www.espacio1414.org, open by appointment Mon.-Fri. 9 A.M.-1 P.M.) was established by art collectors Diana and Moises Berezdivin to house their collection of contemporary conceptual art with an emphasis on emerging artists. The nonprofit gallery is also the site of occasional visiting exhibitions, such as the group photography show "I Hate Karl Marx, Merry Christmas" in 2011.

C787 STUDIO

C787 Studio (734 Calle Cerra, Santurce, c787studios@gmail.com) is a slightly off-the-grid space that presents 10 group exhibitions a year featuring emerging contemporary, conceptual, and experimental artists. A gift shop sells T-shirts, hats, and other objects designed by local artists.

Performing Arts
CENTRO DE BELLAS ARTES LUIS A. FERRÉ

Centro de Bellas Artes Luis A. Ferré (Ave. Ponce de León, Santurce, 787/620-4444 or 787/725-7334, www.cba.gobierno.pr) is a fine arts performance space hosting classical, jazz, and folk concerts, as well as theater and dance productions. This is also the place to see *zarzuela,* a form of Spanish operetta, performed. Home to the Puerto Rico Symphony Orchestra and annual Festival Casals, it has four halls; the smallest can seat up to 200 and the largest can seat around 1,950. Ample parking is available on-site.

CATAÑO, HATO REY, AND RÍO PIEDRAS
CASA BACARDI VISITOR CENTER

Casa Bacardi Visitor Center (Carr. 165, km 2.6, Bay View Industrial Park, Cataño, 787/788-8400, www.casabacardi.org, Mon.-Sat. 8:30 A.M.-5:30 P.M., last tour at 4:15 P.M.; Sun. 10 A.M.-5 P.M., last tour at 3:45 P.M., free) is a tribute to the long, colorful role rum has played in the history and economic development of Puerto Rico. Established in 1862 by Don Facundo Bacardi Masó, Bacardi is the top-selling rum in the United States and is still owned and operated by its founder's descendants. But don't be misled into thinking you will take a tour of Bacardi's rum distillery operations. No rum is made on-site. Instead, expect to see a film about the company's origins in Cuba, historic objects used to make rum in its early days, and displays of advertisements through the years. The tour ends in The Lounge, where a bartender demonstrates how to make a variety of rum drinks and tour-goers get to imbibe two free rum cocktails. Most visitors to the visitor center arrive by ferry from Old San Juan. When you exit AcuaExpreso Cataño, you'll be instructed to turn right and walk about a quarter mile to a parking garage, from where vans will take visitors to Casa Bacardi. If you miss the vans, call a taxi. The walk is long and not pedestrian-friendly.

EL JARDÍN BOTÁNICO

Maintained by the Universidad de Puerto Rico, El Jardín Botánico (Río Piedras, Hwy. 1 at Carr. 847 in Río Piedras, 787/250-0000, ext. 6578, or 787/767-1701, daily 6 A.M.-6 P.M., free, guides available by special arrangement 10 A.M.-1 P.M.) is a 289-acre urban garden filled with tropical and subtropical vegetation, including orchids, heliconias, bromeliads, palms, and bamboo. There's also a native Taíno garden display of native plants.

PARQUE LUIS MUÑOZ MARÍN

Parque Luis Muñoz Marín (off Hwy. 18 between Ave. Jesús Piñero and Ave. F. D. Roosevelt, Wed.-Sun. and holidays) in Hato Rey is a modern 140-acre park with walking and bike trails, a children's play area, golf practice grounds, an amphitheater, pavilions, and more.

GREATER SAN JUAN
EL CAÑUELO

El Cañuelo (end of Carr. 870 on Isla de Cabras, Toa Alta, daily 8:30 A.M.-5:30 P.M., $2) is the ruins of a tiny fortress across the bay from Castillo San Felipe del Morro. Originally constructed of wood in the 1500s, it was destroyed in an attack by the Dutch in 1625. The current stone structure was built in the 1670s. Its purpose was to work in concert with El Morro to create cannon crossfire at the mouth of the bay. Unfortunately, the public is not allowed to enter the fort, but it provides a terrific view of El Morro. There's a small recreation area with picnic tables.

RUINAS DE CAPARRA

Ruinas de Caparra (Carr. 2, km 6.4, Guaynabo, 787/781-4795, Mon.-Fri. 8 A.M.-4:30 P.M.) is the site of Juan Ponce de León's first settlement on the island, established in 1508. All that's left is a few crumbling walls and foundations, but there is a small museum containing some historical documents and Taíno artifacts pertaining to the site.

Sports and Recreation

Puerto Rico's west coast is better known for diving and surfing, but there is plenty of opportunity to do both in San Juan. The most popular water sport these days seems to be stand-up paddleboarding. Riding personal watercraft like Jet Skis is also still popular. And good old-fashioned swimming, sailing, and fishing never go out of style.

BEACHES
Balneario El Escambrón

The closest beach to Old San Juan is Balneario El Escambrón (Ave. Muñoz Rivera, Puerta de Tierra, 8:30 A.M.-6 P.M. daily Apr.-Aug. and Wed.-Sun. Sept.-Mar., $4 per vehicle). The publicly maintained site offers basic amenities, such as public restrooms, showers, snack bar, lifeguards, and an outfitter renting scuba gear, snorkel gear, and kayaks. The small crescent beach is on a cove protected by a coral reef, so the water is quite calm, and there is excellent snorkeling and diving to be had along a collapsed bridge. Steer clear at night. It attracts unsavory types after dark.

Condado Beach

Condado Beach (along Ave. Ashford) is a perfectly fine beach for swimming and sunning,, although the terrain is hillier, the sand coarser, and the water less crystalline than San Juan's finest beaches in Isla Verde or Ocean Park. As in Isla Verde, the beach is lined with high-rise buildings, but it is easier for the public to access it thanks to several parks along the way, including **Ventanas al Mar, Plaza Ancla,** and **Parque del Indio.**

◖ Ocean Park Beach

Located along Park Boulevard, this gorgeous stretch of beach free from high-rise buildings is called Ultimo Trolley by locals, because when the island's electric trolley system ceased to operate in 1946, the last trolley car was converted into a snack bar and placed in Parque Balboa, a large recreation park located across the street with ample parking. The section of the beach directly across from the park is cleaned and raked daily, and a swimming area is protected with nets to keep out sea creatures. On weekends, lounge chairs are available for rent, and street vendors patrol the boardwalk selling snacks and beverages. Farther east the wind and surf are a little rougher, which makes it popular with sailboarders and kite-surfers.

Parque Barbosa (end of Calle McLeary) is right across the street from Ocean Park Beach and is the perfect place to park when visiting beach. It isn't the prettiest or best-maintained park in San Juan, but it does have hiking, jogging, and bike paths. Its proximity to a large public-housing project may deter some visitors.

El Alambique Beach

El Alambique Beach (Calle Tartak, Isla Verde) is a stunning strip of beach that makes Isla Verde a popular destination for sun-worshippers. Roughly two miles long, its wide stretches of sand and rolling surf make for great swimming, surfing, and windsurfing. Like all beaches in Puerto Rico, Isla Verde Beach is open to the public, but because it's lined cheek by jowl with high-rise hotels and apartment buildings, access is limited. Thank goodness for El Alambique, located at the dead-end of Calle Tartak by the San Juan Water Beach Club Hotel. Parking is limited, but there is a turnaround where you can unload your coolers and beach chairs. Once you find a spot to park the car, there is a pedestrian pathway from Avenida Isla Verde. On weekends you can find vendors along the beach renting beach chairs and selling *piraguas* (snow cones) on weekends.

Condado Beach

This is a popular spot to windsurf, parasail, ride Jet Skis, and take out small sailboats.

Balneario de Carolina

Balneario de Carolina (Carr. 187, Ave. Boca de Congrejas, 787/778-8811, $2) is huge a public beach maintained by the municipality of Carolina not far from Boca de Congrejas. Best suited for swimming and sunning, the facility features picnic shelters, bathroom facilities, and plenty of parking. Traffic can get very congested here on weekends.

DIVING AND SNORKELING

San Juan may be home to some beautiful beaches, but its snorkel and dive spots are virtually nil. Local outfitters typically head east toward Fajardo for underwater exploration tours.

Ocean Sports (77 Ave. Isla Verde, 787/268-2329, www.osdivers.com, Mon.-Fri. 9 A.M.-7 P.M., Sat. 9 A.M.-6 P.M., $115-175 pp) rents and sells snorkel and scuba equipment from its two stores and operates scuba and snorkel tours from Fajardo. Road transportation to and from San Juan is available.

Caribbean School of Aquatics (1 Calle Taft, 787/728-6606 or 787/383-5700, www.saildiveparty.com) offers full- and half-day sail, scuba, snorkel, and fishing trips from San Juan and Fajardo on a luxury catamaran with Captain Greg Korwek. Snorkel trips start at $69 per person; scuba trips start at $119 per person.

Scuba Dogs (Balneario El Escambrón, Ave. Muñoz Rivera, 787/783-6377 or 787/977-0000, www.scubadogs.net, Mon.-Thurs. 8 A.M.-4 P.M., Fri.-Sun. 8 A.M.-5 P.M.) offers guided snorkel, scuba, and kayak tours, as well as rents all the scuba, snorkel, and kayak gear you need to do it yourself. At Playa Escambrón, a Discover dive for first-timers is $95 and a single-tank dive for certified divers is $75. Kayak tours (2.5 hours) are $65 for adults and $55 for kids. Five-hour boat tours from Fajardo are $180 for first-time divers, $149 for certified

© SUZANNE VAN ATTEN

El Alambique Beach

divers, and $100 for snorkelers, including transportation from San Juan. Rental charges: full scuba gear for certified divers only, $55; regulator and tank, $40; full snorkel gear, $20; single kayak, $15 an hour; hybrid kayak or paddleboard, $20 an hour; double kayak, $25 an hour.

Caribe Aquatic Adventures (1062 Calle 19, 787/281-8858, www.scubadivingplanet.com) offers snorkel and reef dives four times daily, as well as light-tackle and deep-sea fishing trips. A day-long dive and picnic costs $140. A reef dive is $60.

SURFING
Wow Surfing School & Water Sports (on the beach at The Ritz Carlton San Juan and El San Juan Resort & Casino in Isla Verde, 787/955-6059, www.wowsurfingschool.com, daily 9 A.M.-5 P.M.) gives two-hour surf lessons for $85, including board. Group rates are available. Equipment rentals include surfboards ($25 an hour), paddleboards ($30), kayaks ($25), and snorkel equipment ($15 and up). Jet Ski

rentals and tours are available from Condado, Isla Verde, and San Juan Bay. Call for prices. **Caribbean Surf School** (787/637-8363, www.caribbeansurfpr.com) also offers lessons, tours, and equipment rental. Surfboard rentals are $30 per day and a one-hour surfing class is $65 (price includes day-long surfboard rental).

Tres Palmas Surf Shop (1911 Calle McLeary, Ocean Park, 787/728-3377, trespalmaspuertorico@yahoo.com, 9 A.M.-7 P.M. Mon.-Sat., 10 A.M.-6 P.M. Sun.) is the source for all your surfing needs, including boards, board shorts, flip-flops, sunglasses, T-shirts, bathing suits, and more. Rentals are $30 for surfboards, $35 for fun boards, $40 for long boards, and $25 for body boards.

Costazul (264 Calle San Francisco, Old San Juan, 787/722-0991 or 787/724-8085, fax 787/725-1097, Mon.-Fri. 9 A.M.-7 P.M., Sat. 11 A.M.-5 P.M.) sells surfboards and related equipment.

MASTER A WATER SPORT IN SAN JUAN

San Juan may be the most cosmopolitan city in the Caribbean, filled with sophisticated art museums, fine-dining restaurants, rooftop lounges, and designer shops, but it's the ocean that attracts most visitors, and there is no better way to enjoy it than mastering a new water sport. There are plenty of opportunities to take your first deep-sea dive, learn to ride the waves, or paddleboard, the hottest new water sport to hit the island.

- **Paddleboarding:** Having originated in Hawaii, the sport, which is sometimes called standup paddleboarding (SUP), involves standing on a board and using a long paddle to propel across the surface of the water. It can be done in the ocean, lagoons and rivers, and it is a fun way to explore the island's waterways. In San Juan, **Velauno Paddleboarding** offers private and group lessons at **Laguna de Condado,** as well as

eco-tours throughout the island.

- **Surfing:** Puerto Rico's primo surf spots are found on the west coast around Isabela, Aguadilla, and Rincón, but in San Juan, **Isla Verde**'s waves are just big enough to give novice surfers a challenge. Instructors with **Wow Surfing School & Water Sports** offer two-hour private lessons on land and in the water, as well as board rentals.

- **Diving:** Snorkeling can be fun, but if you really want to explore more exotic underwater sights, you need to strap on an air tank and take a deep sea plunge. **Scuba Dogs** at **Playa Escambrón** in **Puerta de Tierra** offers first-timers what's called a Discover Dive, which includes instruction and an underwater escort right there at the beach. If that's too tame, Discover Dives are also offered on a boat tour out of Fajardo.

PADDLEBOARDING

Velauno Paddleboarding (2430 Calle Loíza, Isla Verde, 787/982-0543, www.velaunopaddleboarding.com, Mon.-Fri. 10 A.M.-7 P.M., Sat. 11 A.M.-7 P.M.) is the go-to place for all things related to paddleboarding, including buying and renting equipment, instruction, and tours. Lessons are $100 for the first hour, $50 each subsequent hour. Tours are $75 for two hours, then $25 for each subsequent hour. Equipment rental is $50 for two hours or $60 for four hours.

BOATING

There are three marinas in San Juan. All three have fuel and water. The largest is **San Juan Bay Marina** (Calle Lindburgh, 787/721-8062), with a capacity of 191 boats, including 125 wet slips, 60 dry-stack spaces, and six spaces for yachts more than 100 feet long. There's also a restaurant on-site.

   Club Náutico de San Juan (482 Ave. Fernández Juncos, Miramar, bus stop 9.5, lat.

18°27'58" N, long. 66°05'32" W, 787/722-0177, www.nauticodesanjuan.com) is a secure port in San Juan Harbor featuring 117 wet slips that can accommodate vessels from 30 to 250 feet long. Amenities include a clubhouse, a fueling port, and 24-hour guard service. Club Náutico de San Juan also offers sailing lessons for children age 6 and up. For details, call 787/667-9936. It also hosts the annual International Regatta, which takes place every February, and the International Billfish Tournament, held every September.

   Cangrejos Yacht Club in Piñones (Carr. 187, km 3.8, Boca de Cangrejos, Piñones, 787/791-1015) has 180 wet slips, a boat ramp, and a restaurant.

FISHING

Mike Benitez Marina Services (Club Náutico de San Juan, 787/723-2292 or 787/724-6265, fax 787/725-4344, www.mikebenitezfishingpr.com) offers deep-sea fishing trips daily. Half-day charter trips last 8 A.M.-noon and 1-5 P.M. and cost

$650. Full-day excursions depart at 8 A.M. and return at 4 P.M. and cost $1,050. Reservations are required, and there's a six-passenger maximum.

Caribbean Outfitters (Cangrejos Yacht Club, 787/396-8346, www.fishinginpuertorico.com) offers fishing and fly-fishing charters throughout Puerto Rico, Vieques, Culebra, the Dominican Republic, and St. Thomas with Captain Omar.

Magic Tarpon (Cangrejos Yacht Club, 787/644-1444, www.puertoricomagictarpon. com) offers half-day fishing charters for $330-460 for 1-4 people.

CLIMBING, CAVING, AND ZIPLINES

Hacienda Campo Rico (Carr. 3, km 2, Carolina, 787/523-2001, www.hacienda-camporico.com) is a 2,300-acre estate featuring ziplines, kayaking, horseback riding, ATV riding, and a golf academy.

The go-to outfitter in San Juan for rappelling in the rainforest, cave tubing, zipline rides, and hiking is **EcoQuest** (New San Juan Building 6471, Ste. 5A, Isla Verde, 787/616-7543 or 787/529-2496, www.ecoquestpr.com). A hiking, kayaking, and zipline tour featuring five zipline courses is $119-169, including transportation.

TENNIS

There is no shortage of tennis courts in San Juan. Many of the large hotels have courts. In addition, there are several public courts, including: **Caribbean Mountain Villas Tennis Court** (Carr. 857, km 857, Canovanillas Sector, Carolina, 787/769-0860), **Central Park** (Calle Cerra off Carr. 2, Santurce, 787/722-1646), and **Isla Verde Tennis Club** (Villamar, Isla Verde, 787/727-6490). The general court rental rates are $4-10 per person, per hour.

GOLF

Río Bayamón Golf Course (Carr. 171 at Ave. Laurel, Bayamón, 787/740-1419, www.municipiodebayamon.com, Mon.-Sat. 7 A.M.-6 P.M.,

Sun. 6 A.M.-8 P.M., $30 greens fees) is the only golf course in the metropolitan San Juan area. The public course is 6,870 yards and par 72.

Caribbean Golf Academy (Hacienda Campo Rico, Carr. 3, km 2, Carolina, 787/523-2001, www.haciendacamporico. com) provides individualized instruction for beginning and advanced duffers. One-on-one instruction here is $100 per hour and a three-hour group session for a minimum of three people is $175 per person.

HORSEBACK RIDING

Tropical Trail Rides (Hacienda Campo Rico, Carr. 3, km 2, Carolina, 787/523-2001, www. haciendacamporico.com) provides horseback riding for $45 per person for two hours.

MOTORCYCLING

If land speed is more your style, **San Juan Motorcycle Rental** (6779 Ave. Isla Verde, 787/536-4731 or 787/317-1580, www.sanjuan-motorcyclerental.com) rents motorcycle for $20 for one hour to $60 for six hours.

BICYCLING

Rent the Bicycle (100 Calle del Muelle, Pier 6, Old San Juan, 787/602-9696 or 787/692-3200, www.rentthebicycle.net) will deliver bikes to your hotel. Rental rates are $17 for three hours, $25 a day. Bike tours of Old San Juan, Condado parks and beaches, and Piñones are $27 for three hours, with a two-person minimum.

YOGA

It's Yoga (1950 Calle McLeary, Ocean Park, 787/677-7585, www.itsyogapuertorico.com, $17 including mat and water, $2 towel rental) studio, on the second floor above a laundry, offers a variety of classes and workshops for beginners and beyond in the style of Ashtanga Vinyasa yoga. Pilates and fusion yoga classes are also offered.

SPAS

Eden Spa (331 Recinto Sur, Bldg. Acosta, Old San Juan, 787/721-6400, Mon.-Sat. 10 A.M.-7 P.M.) offers pure luxury pampering, including caviar facials, four-hands massage, honey-butter body wrap, chakra-balancing treatments, Reiki—you name it, Eden Spa has got it. Packages run $148-198.

Zen Spa (1054 Ave. Ashford, Condado, 787/722-8433, www.zen-spa.com, Mon.-Fri. 9 A.M.-7 P.M., Sat. 9 A.M.-6 P.M.) offers massage, body wraps, facials, manicures, and hair care. Day-spa packages run $145-450. There's also a health club on the premises.

Entertainment and Events

FESTIVALS

San Juan loves a festival. It seems as though there's one going on every weekend. Some have traditional origins, and others are products of the local tourism department, but they all promise insight into the island's culture and are loads of fun.

Noches de Galerías is held the first Tuesday of the month February-May and September-December. Roughly 20 museums and galleries throughout Old San Juan open 6-9 P.M. for this festive gallery crawl. Though its intentions may be high-minded, as the night progresses the event becomes more of a raucous pub crawl as young adults and teenagers fill the streets in revelry. Arts and crafts booths also line Plaza de San José.

Held in June, **Noche de San Juan Bautista** is the celebration of the island's patron saint. Festivities last several days and include religious processions, concerts, and dance performances. But the highlight of the event is on June 24, when celebrants from all over the island flock to the beach for the day for picnics and recreation. Then at midnight, everyone walks backward into the ocean three times to ward off evil spirits.

Street festivals don't get any more lively than **Festival de la Calle de San Sebastián** (787/724-0910), held in January on Calle San Sebastián in Old San Juan. For three days the street is filled with parades, folkloric dances, music, food, and crafts.

Founded in honor of the renowned cellist and composer Pablo Casals, the **Festival Casals** (787/725-7334) is held in June and July and features a slate of classical music concerts at the Centro de Bellas Artes Luis A. Ferré (Ave. de Diego at Ave. Ponce de León). Concerts are also held in Ponce and Mayagüez.

A new addition to the festival slate is **Santurce es Ley** (www.santurceesley.com), an annual independent artists street festival held in mid-September. More than a dozen galleries and design studios throughout Santurce stay open until midnight, hosting art exhibitions and musical performances featuring the work of more than 100 emerging local artists. Visit the website for a map of participating galleries and studios, as well as the musical lineup.

Each spring the **Heineken Jazz Festival** (Anfiteatro Tito Puente, Hato Rey, 866/994-0001) selects a single jazz master to celebrate with three nights of concerts, 8 P.M.-midnight.

The Puerto Rico Tourism Company presents an annual three-day arts festival in early June called **Feria de Artesanías** (787/723-0692, www.gotopuertorico.com). More than 200 artisans fill the walkways along Paseo La Princesa and Plaza de la Dársena, and the days are filled with music and dance performances as well as a folk-singer competition.

Less an actual festival and more a cultural series, **La Casita Festival** takes place every Saturday 5:30-7:30 P.M. year-round in Plaza de la Dársena by Pier 1 in Old San Juan.

Musicians and dance groups perform, and artisans sell their wares.

Similarly, **LeLoLai Festival** (787/723-3135, 787/791-1014, or 800/223-6530) presents traditional concerts and dance performances year-round at various sites throughout the island, including InterContinental San Juan Resort in Isla Verde and Castillo de San Cristóbal in Old San Juan.

NIGHTLIFE

If club- and bar-hopping is your thing, you've come to the right place. San Juan definitely knows how to party. Electronic music is prevalent, as is hip-hop and reggaetón, Puerto Rico's homegrown brand of hip-hop, combined with Jamaican dancehall and Caribbean musical styles. And there's always plenty of salsa to go around. The legal drinking age is 18, and there's no official bar-closing time, so many establishments stay open until 6 A.M. Things often don't get started until after midnight, so take a disco nap and put on your dancing shoes. It's sure to be a long, fun-filled night.

Old San Juan

There are two sides to Old San Juan's nightlife. On the southern end near the cruise ship docks are the more commercial and chain establishments like Señor Frog's. But the farther north you go toward Calle San Sebastián, the more authentic the offerings get.

◖ NUYORICAN CAFÉ

By far the best nightclub for live contemporary Latin music—from rock and jazz to salsa and merengue—is Nuyorican Café (312 Calle San Francisco, 787/977-1276, www.nuyoricancafepr.com, Tues.-Wed. 7 P.M.-3 A.M., Thurs.-Sun. 7 P.M.-5 A.M., free every night except $5 Fri., full bar). Don't bother looking for a sign; there isn't one. Just look for a gaggle of clubgoers clustered around a side door down Capilla alley, which connects Calle San Francisco and Calle Fortaleza. Locals and tourists alike pack

in, especially on weekends when the tiny dance floor gets jammed. The kitchen serves a limited menu of Puerto Rican cuisine until midnight. The music usually starts around 11 P.M. There's no direct link between this café and New York City's Nuyorican Poets Café, which was and still is the epicenter of the Nuyorican movement, although the name is a nod to the club in NYC.

OTHER CLUBS

San Juan's club scene revolves around techno and reggaetón, and there are any number of clubs devoted to the forms. Old San Juan's veteran nightclub is **Club Lazer** (251 Calle de la Cruz, 787/725-7581, www.clublazer.com, Fri.-Sun. 10 P.M.-3 or 4 A.M.). The three-level 1980s-era disco complete with a light show is popular with both gays and straights. The hottest DJs spin here, and Sunday is reggaetón night.

The Noise (203 Calle Tanca, 787/724-3739) is a white-hot club in a former house in Old San Juan, where reggaetón keeps the beat going until the wee hours. It's popular with the 18-21 crowd.

Blend (309 Calle Fortaleza, 787/977-7777, Tues.-Sat. 5 P.M.-3:30 A.M.) is a chic restaurant and lounge centered around an indoor patio and dramatic wall fountain. Local and touring DJs spin all forms of techno.

Club Le Cirque (357 Calle San Francisco, 787/725-3246, Wed.-Sat. 6 P.M.-4 A.M.) is a gay bar and lounge serving lunch and dinner. Smoking is allowed on the patio.

Another popular late-night bar for the casual bohemian crowd is **Galería Candela** (110 Calle San Sebastián, 787/594-5698 or 787/977-4305). The space is a hipster art gallery by day, but at night DJs spin into the wee hours.

BARS

If you need a place to rest your feet and just chill with a cool beverage, there is a wide variety of bars, both casual and upscale, where you can actually have a conversation, at least in the early part of the evening. The later it gets, though, the more crowded and louder it gets.

PIÑA COLADAS, *MOJITOS*, AND CUBA LIBRES: A COCKTAIL GUIDE

Nothing puts the exclamation point on a tropical island getaway like a fruity rum drink or two, and in Puerto Rico that usually means a piña colada. The sweet, frosty concoction of rum, coconut cream, and fresh pineapple juice is blended with ice and served in a tall glass garnished with a cherry and wedge of pineapple, and it takes the heat off the day in the most delightful way.

There are two establishments in San Juan that claim to have invented the drink, which may be served with or without rum. Located in Puerta de Tierra, **Caribe Hilton** has been an oasis of luxury and glamour in San Juan since it opened in 1949. It was here that bartender Ramon "Monchito" Marrero claimed to have created the first piña colada in 1954 after three months of experimentation. Rumor has it that Joan Crawford said the drink was "better than slapping Bette Davis in the face."

Rivaling Caribe Hilton as the birthplace of Puerto Rico's official drink is **Barrachina**, a restaurant in Old San Juan. Here Spanish-born bartender Ramon Portas Mingot claims to have created the first piña colada in 1963. The only difference between its recipe and Caribe Hilton's is that Barrachina mixes the rum, pineapple juice, and coconut cream with water (instead of ice) and freezes it before blending it.

No trip to San Juan is complete without trying a piña colada at both of these establishments and deciding for yourself which one is best.

Other popular rum drinks include the **Cuba libre,** made from rum, Coke, and a wedge of lime, and the *mojito,* featuring a fistful of fresh mint leaves muddled with sugar and topped with rum and a splash of club soda. Inventive interpretations of the *mojito* abound, featuring fresh fruit juice varieties made from watermelon, pineapple, and coconut.

If you have a strong constitution, order a *chichaito* (slang for little fornicator), a popular bar shot made from equal parts rum and anise-flavored liqueur.

Most of the world's supply of **rum** is produced in Puerto Rico and **Bacardi** is its most popular brand, but it's not the only game in town. Serralles distillery's **Don Q** brand is well regarded, but most locals recommend **Barrolito** as the island's most prized brand.

If rum isn't your thing, there are a few **local beer** options. The most popular brand is **Medalla Light pale ale,** produced by Cervecera de Puerto Rico in Mayaguez. In 2011, the company launched a premium lager called **Magna.** For a variety of microbrews, visit **Old Harbor Brewery** in Old San Juan.

At **El Farolito** (277 Calle Sol, Old San Juan, no phone, daily noon-midnight or later) artwork by local artists hangs on the walls and a chess set sits on the tiny bar of this narrow drinking spot favored by locals. Not the place for fruity, frozen drinks. Your best option is to stick with beer and shots, such as the *chichaito,* an anise- and coffee-flavored blast of booze.

If the painting outside of a monkey fallen into a martini glass doesn't get your attention, the bright red hue of this place will do the trick. **The Red Monkey** (252 Calle Cruz, Old San Juan, 787/565-3181, noon-midnight or later, $10-22, cash only) is a great spot for drinks, to watch Monday night football, or to hear live music. The food, including salmon burgers and wings, isn't bad either.

Although primarily an Indo-Latino fusion restaurant, **Tantra** (356 Calle Fortaleza, 787/977-8141, fax 787/977-4289, www.tantrapr.com, Sun.-Thurs. noon-11 P.M., Fri.-Sat. noon-midnight) turns into a late-night party spot with the after-dinner crowd who flock here for the sophisticated ambiance, the creative martinis, and a toke or two on one of the many hookahs that line the bar. The kitchen serves a limited late-night menu.

For something completely different, frozen tropical drinks and old kitschy decor create the perfect place for a shopping break at **María's**

(204 Calle de la Cristo, no telephone, daily 10:30 A.M.-3 A.M.). The tiny, pleasantly seedy bar primarily serves a variety of frozen drinks— piña colada, papaya frost, coconut blossom, and so on (with or without rum). Avoid the pedestrian tacos and nachos ($4-7) and check out the cheesy celebrity photos behind the bar, including Bill Clinton, Antonio Banderas, and Sly Stone. If the dark, narrow bar is full, look for a couple of tables in the back.

Looking for all the world like an old jail cell, **El Batey** (101 Calle Cristo, 787/725-1787, daily noon-4 A.M., cash only) is a barren dive bar covered top to bottom with scrawled graffiti and illuminated by bare bulbs suspended from the ceiling. There's one pool table and an interesting jukebox with lots of jazz mixed in with classic discs by the likes of Tom Waits, Jimi Hendrix, and Sly Stone. If you order a martini, they'll laugh at you. This is a beer and shots kind of place.

The barred windows and garish orange exterior don't offer much of a welcome at **Krugger** (52 Calle San José, 787/723-2474, Thurs.-Sat.), but the word is that this loud dive bar is the place to go for karaoke.

The Latin Roots (Galería Paseo Portuario, Calle Recinto Sur, 787/977-1877, www.thelatinroots.com, 11 A.M.-2 A.M. daily, $9-37) offers salsa dance lessons and exhibitions during the day, and a smokin' hot dance floor at night where you can strut your stuff. It also serves a full menu of Puerto Rican cuisine, including *mofongo* and roast pork.

Isla Verde

One of San Juan's most glamorous bars is **Mist**, atop the San Juan Water Beach Club Hotel (2 Calle Tartak, 787/728-3666 or 888/265-6699, fax 787/728-3610, www.waterbeachclubhotel.com). This posh rooftop bar features white leather sofas and beds arranged around tiny tables under a white awning. The minimal lighting is limited to elaborate Indonesian lanterns and candles, which complement the panoramic view of the city lights.

On the first floor of the San Juan Water Beach Club Hotel is **Zest** (2 Calle Tartak, 787/728-3666 or 888/265-6699, fax 787/728-3610, www.waterbeachclubhotel.com), a more intimate restaurant and bar. The attraction here is the interesting wall behind the bar— it's made from corrugated tin over which water pours all night long.

Another popular hotel hot spot is **Brava** (El San Juan Resort, 6063 Ave. Isla Verde, 787/791-2761 or 787/791-2781, www.bravapr.com). Formerly Club Babylon, this popular dance club still packs in the upscale trendy set, who dance to an eclectic mix of dance-club tunes, salsa, and '80s rock. Reservations are required for table service.

Iglu (5980 Ave. Isla Verde, 939/639-5616, 787/344-3699, 787/559-7322, or 787/632-4596, www.iglulife.com, opens 10 P.M., $10) is a late-night dance club under a domed roof featuring DJs, fashion shows, and ladies' nights.

More like a sports bar found in the continental U.S. than on a Caribbean island, **101 Sports Bar & Criolla Café** (101 Verde Mar, 787/791-3327, daily 11 A.M.-2 A.M., $6-13) is grungy little dive plastered with beer signs out front that beckon patrons with happy hour prices, flat-screen TVs, and a pub grub menu featuring wings, chicken fingers, quesadillas, and *mofongo*.

Condado

From the street level, **Di Zucchero Lavazza Restaurant & Lounge** (1210 Ave. Ashford, 787/946-0835, http://dizuccheropr.com, lounge Fri.-Sat. 11 P.M.-4 A.M.) is a hip Italian coffee bar and restaurant specializing in pasta, pizza, and panini in a dramatic red-and-black setting appointed with ornate white chandeliers. But venture upstairs and discover a massive two-level nightclub that continues the baroque theme from downstairs but sets it against an industrial-chic backdrop. Five extensively stocked bars serve up to 500 club-goers who come to dance to techno music, check out experimental film projections on the walls, and canoodle on overstuffed couches in dark corners.

Don't bother going to **Bed Lounge** (5390 Ave. Isla Verde, 787/728-0481 or 787/391-1576, Wed.-Sat. 9 P.M.-6 A.M., cover charge may apply) until midnight or later. That's when the action starts in the two-level club, where DJs play dance tunes and hip-hop.

The large open-air pavilion bar **La Terraza Condado** (intersection of Ave. Ashford and Calle McLeary, 787/723-2770, Sun.-Thurs. 5 P.M.-midnight, Fri.-Sat. 5 P.M.-2 A.M.) is popular with a young crowd that flocks here on the weekends for the cheap drinks, and it's an ideal perch for people-watching. There's a full bar, and it serves Puerto Rican cuisine ($9-18).

Santurce

At the nexus of all that is hip in Santurce, which is experiencing an arts renaissance, is **La Respuesta** (1600 Ave. Fernandez Juncos, Santurce, no phone, www.larespuestapr.com), a graffiti-covered industrial space that hosts DJs, live bands, and art exhibitions that celebrate both emerging young artists and oldsters with an edge. Musical acts run the gamut from hip-hop and R&B to metal and Latin jazz. Wednesday night is Noche de Cine, featuring film screenings. By day this place looks like an abandoned warehouse, but it smokes at night.

Santurce is home to several gay clubs. **Krash** (1257 Ave. Ponce de León, 787/722-1131, www.krashpr.com, Wed.-Sat. 10 P.M.-3 A.M., $6 after midnight), formerly Eros, is a major two-level party scene. Wednesday is urban pop night with three DJs spinning R&B, hip-hop, and reggaetón. Thursday and Friday nights feature DJs spinning house, tribal, and retro.

For a casual low-key gay bar, check out **Junior's Bar** (613 Calle Condado, 787/723-9477, daily, two-drink minimum). This is the place to have a beer, play some tunes on the jukebox, and check out the occasional drag queen or male stripper show.

Yet another popular gay bar and lounge in Santurce is **Starz** (365 Ave. de Diego, 787/721-8645).

The local lesbian crowd gathers in the laid-back ambiance of **Cups** (1708 Calle San Mateo, 787/268-3570, Wed.-Fri. 7 P.M.-3 A.M., Sat. 8 P.M.-3 A.M.). DJs spin dance music on Wednesday night, karaoke is Thursday night, and live music is Friday night. There are pool tables, too.

PARTY DISTRICTS

There's no doubt about it: Puerto Ricans love a good party, and it seems as if there's always one going on somewhere. San Juan has a couple of unofficial party districts where the concentration of bars and restaurants creates a street-party atmosphere that attracts young locals and tourists alike to bar-hop and people-watch. Although generally safe and contained, these areas can experience a certain level of rowdiness and petty crime, particularly the later it gets and the more alcohol is consumed. Visitors are encouraged to have a good time, but they should take care to keep their wits about them.

◀ La Placita/Plaza del Mercado

Santurce's historic marketplace, La Placita/Plaza del Mercado (Calle Roberts), is at the heart of this street party that spills into the narrow roads surrounding it. There is a high concentration of small bars and restaurants serving cheap drinks and local cuisine, and a bandstand hosts live music. The streets get especially crowded Thursday, Friday, and Saturday nights with locals, mostly middle aged, celebrating the weekend.

Boca de Cangrejos

Another popular party district is Boca de Cangrejos (end of Ave. Isla Verde, just past the airport), a sandy patch of beachfront bars, restaurants, clubs, and food kiosks. Since this is also a popular weekend beach spot, the party tends to start early here, but the fun still lasts late into the night. The best way to get to Boca de Cangrejos is to drive or take a taxi, although

© SUZANNE VAN ATTEN

Revelers gather on Saturday night at La Placita.

you'll have to call one to pick you up when you're ready to leave. If you drive, be sure not to leave anything of value visible in the car; break-ins are not uncommon.

Although most establishments are open-air concrete structures, there are a few more-upscale places, such as **Soleil Beach Club** (Carr. 187, km 4.8, Piñones, 787/253-1033, www. soleilbeachclub.com, Sun.-Thurs. 11:30 A.M.-10 P.M., Fri.-Sat. 11:30 A.M.-midnight, $10-25), near Boca de Cangrejos in Piñones. The beachside establishment with the palm-frond entrance serves Puerto Rican cuisine and offers live Latin music.

Calle San Sebastián

In Old San Juan, party central is along Calle San Sebastián. Restaurants, bars, clubs, and pool halls of every stripe line the street, making it a great place to bar-hop door-todoor. Standard stops include **Nono's** (109 Calle San Sebastián, 787/725-7819, daily noon-3 A.M.) and **Cafe San Sebastián** (153 Calle San Sebastián, 787/725-3998, Wed.-Sun. 8 P.M.-3 A.M.). This crowd skews young.

CASINOS

Puerto Rico's greatest concentration of casinos can be found in San Juan. Its gambling palaces are all in hotels. Although jacket and tie are not required, attire tends to be dressy. All the casinos have banks of slot machines, blackjack tables, and roulette wheels. Most have craps tables, Caribbean stud poker, and three-card poker. Some have mini-baccarat, let it ride, progressive blackjack, and Texas hold 'em.

Old San Juan

Old San Juan has only one casino, **Sheraton Old San Juan Hotel & Casino** (100 Calle Brumbaugh, Old San Juan, 787/721-5100, www.sheratonoldsanjuan.com, 8 A.M.-2 A.M.).

Condado

For a concentration of casino action, Condado

is the place to go. **Condado Plaza Hotel** (787/721-1000, daily 24 hours) boasts 402 slots, as well as 13 blackjack tables, six mini-baccarat games, and Texas hold 'em. Other 24-7 casinos in the area include **San Juan Marriott Resort & Stellaris Casino** (1309 Ave. Ashford, 787/722-7000, www.marriott.com, daily 24 hours) and the small **Diamond Palace Hotel and Casino** (55 Ave. Condado, 787/721-0810, daily 24 hours). Condado is also home to **Radisson Ambassador Plaza Hotel & Casino** (1369 Ave. Ashford, 787/721-7300, www.radisson.com, 10 A.M.-4 A.M.), with a whopping 489 slots.

Isla Verde

The largest casino is at the **Ritz-Carlton San Juan Hotel** (6961 Ave. of the Governors, Isla Verde, 787/253-1700, www.ritzcarlton.com, daily 24 hours, table games noon-6 A.M.). Within its 17,000 square feet are 335 slots, 11 blackjack tables, four mini-baccarat games, and Texas hold 'em.

Another 24-hour casino in Isla Verde is **Casino del Sol** in the Courtyard by Marriott Isla Verde Beach Resort (7012 Boca de Cangrejos Ave., Carolina, 787/791-0404, daily 24 hours). **El San Juan Resort & Casino** (6063 Ave. Isla Verde, Isla Verde, 787/791-1000, www.elsanjuanresort.com, 10 A.M.-4 A.M.) has the largest number of blackjack tables—14—and the added bonus of proximity to one of the most glamorous old-school hotel lobbies on the island, filled with gorgeous ornate woodwork and a massive antique chandelier. Other casinos in the area include **InterContinental San Juan** (787/791-6100, 10 A.M.-4 A.M.) and **Embassy Suites Hotel** (787/791-0505, 10 A.M.-4 A.M.).

Miramar

San Juan's newest casino is **Casino Metro** (Sheraton Convention Center Hotel & Casino, 200 Convention Blvd., Miramar, 787/993-3500, www.casinometro.com, daily 24 hours). It features more than 400 slot machines and 16 table games, including blackjack, roulette, baccarat, pai gow poker, and three-card poker. The Mezzanine Stage features live entertainment most nights of the week, and players receive complimentary snacks and beverages. Take a break from the action in the Metro Lounge, where you can enjoy a specialty cocktail and watch the game on one of 12 high-definition TVs.

MOVIE THEATERS

Puerto Rico gets all the major Hollywood releases, as well as a steady offering of Spanish-language films that don't make it to the States. Offering a modern megaplex experience is **Caribbean Cinemas Fine Arts Miramar** (654 Ave. Ponce de León, 787/721-4288, www.caribbeancinemas.com), showing a variety of English and Spanish films, most of which are subtitled. A second location is at Popular Center (Torre Norte, 208 Ave. Juan Ponce de León, Hato Rey, 787/765-2339).

HORSE RACING

Just 20 minutes east of San Juan, **Hipódromo Camarero** (Carr. 3, km 15.3, Canóvanas, 787/641-6060, www.comandantepr.com, free) is a modern upscale racetrack with a restaurant, sports bar, and clubhouse with a panoramic view of the track. Races are Wednesday-Sunday 3-6 P.M.

COCKFIGHTS

Granted, cockfighting isn't for everyone, but it is a part of Puerto Rican culture. Most cockfight arenas are in rural areas, but San Juan has a large, modern, tourist-friendly facility in **Club Gallistico de Puerto Rico** (Ave. Isla Verde at Ave. Los Gobernadores, 787/791-1557, Wed.-Thurs. 4:30-10 P.M., Sat. 2:30-10 P.M., $10 entry fee). Most of the betting action takes place in the seats closest to the ring. Odds are haggled over and then bets are placed on the honor system by shouting wagers until a taker is secured. Bets are made not only on which bird will win, but on how long the fight will last. Regulars tend to be high rollers who take their bets seriously, so novices may have difficulty placing bets. Food and beer are available for purchase. This is a highly charged, testosterone-rich environment. Women are welcome, but they are advised not to dress provocatively or go alone.

Shopping

In the current era of globalization, shopping is fast becoming similarly homogenized the world over, and Puerto Rico is no different. The island is rife with large shopping malls and outlet stores selling the same designer names you could buy at Anywhere, USA. But there is also a strong culture of artisanship in Puerto Rico, and many stores sell locally made traditional crafts and contemporary artwork in varying degrees of quality. Haitian, Indonesian, and Indian import shops are plentiful too, as are high-end fine-jewelry stores. And thanks to Condado, San Juan is the place to go for high-end fashion, including Louis Vuitton and Cartier.

OLD SAN JUAN

Visitors love to shop in Old San Juan because it offers the widest variety of unique shopping options in one pedestrian-friendly place. This is the place to go for fine jewelry, imported clothing and furnishings, cigars, folk art, tourist trinkets, and American chain stores, such as Marshalls, Walgreens, and Radio Shack.

Arts and Crafts

For visitors seeking high-quality crafts by local artisans, **Puerto Rican Arts and Crafts** (204 Calle Fortaleza, 787/725-5596, daily 9:30 A.M.-6 P.M.) is your one-stop shopping spot. This large two-level store has everything from original paintings and prints to ceramics, sculpture, jewelry, and more.

There is no end to cheap trinket shops in Old San Juan, so when you find a quality craft store selling unique, artisan-made items traditional to the island, it's a reason to stand up and take notice. **La Casa de las Casitas & Handcraft** (250 Calle del Cristo, 787/721-5195, and 208 Calle Fortaleza, 787/723-2276, www.handicraftpr.com, daily 10 A.M.-6 P.M.) is the place to go for original oil paintings, one-of-a-kind *vejigante* masks, and beautiful wood carvings of saints, a traditional form of handicraft called santos.

Natural Home (101 Calle Fortaleza, 787/721-5731, naturalhomeus@gmail.com, daily 10 A.M.-8 P.M.) is a gift shop selling hand-embroidered linens, unique crocheted jewelry, pottery, and unusual ceramic pieces.

For a small selection of authentic Caribbean crafts, stop by **Tienda de Artesanías** (Museo de las Americas in Ballajá Barracks, on Calle Norzagaray beside Quincentennial Plaza, 787/722-6057, Mon.-Sat. 9 A.M.-noon and 1-4 P.M., Sun. noon-5 P.M.). It has a nice but small mix of quality baskets, shawls, pottery, jewelry, santos, art posters, and CDs.

Máscaras de Puerto Rico (La Calle, 105 Calle Fortaleza, 787/725-1306, http://home. coqui.net/chilean, Mon.-Sat. 10 A.M.-6:30 P.M., Sun. 10:30 A.M.-5:30 P.M.) is a funky, narrow shop in a covered alleyway selling quality contemporary crafts, including masks and small reproductions of vintage *cartel* posters. In back is Café El Punto restaurant, serving traditional Puerto Rican cuisine.

There are two nearly identical shops on the same street called **Haitian Gallery** (367 Calle Fortaleza, 787/721-4362, and 206 Calle Fortaleza, 787/725-0986, www.haitiangallerypr. com, daily 10 A.M.-6 P.M.). They both sell a great selection of Haitian folk art, including brightly colored primitive-style paintings and tons of woodwork, from sublime bowls to ornately sculpted furniture. There's a small selection of Indonesian imports, such as leaf-covered picture frames and photo albums, and tourist trinkets.

Puerto Rico Homemade Crafts Gallery (403 Calle San Francisco, 787/724-3840, http://tallercocuyopr.com, Mon.-Sat. 10:30 A.M.-8 P.M., Sun. 10:30 A.M.-6 P.M.) is an excellent source for authentic local crafts and folk art—both traditional and contemporary. The shop carries a large selection of *vejigante* masks, plus native Taíno reproductions, *cartel* posters, coconut-shell tea sets, jewelry, and santos. Inside is a bar called Tres Cuernos (daily 10 A.M.-midnight).

The Poets Passage (203 Calle Cruz, 787/567-9275, daily 10 A.M.-6 P.M.) offers a funky collection of local arts, crafts, and books. The store is owned by local poet and publisher Lady Lee Andrews. Poetry nights are held every Tuesday at 7 P.M.

Tourist tchotchkes, shell jewelry, *vejigante* masks, gourds, beaded necklaces, and seed jewelry can be found at **Ezense** (353 Calle Fortaleza, 787/725-1782, ezense@yahoo.com, daily 10 A.M.-7 P.M.).

Clothing and Accessories

The guayabera is the classic linen shirt, detailed with symmetrical rows of tiny pleats that run down the front, traditionally worn by distinguished Puerto Rican gentlemen of a certain age, but they're making a comeback with younger men, too. **Panabrisa** (256 Calle San Francisco, 787/722-5151, panabrisapr@ yahoo.com, Mon.-Sat. 10 A.M.-5 P.M., Sun. 11 A.M.-5 P.M.) sells all varieties, from inexpensive cotton blend versions for around $25 to exquisitely crafted ones in linen for around $80. You'll also find trendy guayabera dresses and skirts for women and shirts for children.

For a large inventory of Panama hats, visit **Vaughn's Gifts & Crafts** (262 Calle Fortaleza,

787/721-8221, vaughns@operamail.com, Mon.-Sat. 10 A.M.-6 P.M., Sun. 11 A.M.-5 P.M.). Other hat styles, as well as handbags and souvenirs, also can be found.

Costazul (264 Calle San Francisco, 787/722-0991 or 787/724-8085, fax 787/725-1097, Mon.-Sat. 9 A.M.-7 P.M., Sun. 11 A.M.-5 P.M.) sells a great selection of surf and skate wear for men and women, including Oakley sunglasses and clothes by Billabong and Quiksilver. During surf season, it also stocks boards and related gear.

All along Calle del Cristo are a dozen or so designer outlets and stores including **Tommy Hilfiger, Couch, Guess, Crocs, Ralph Lauren, Dooney & Bourke, Polo Chopard, Harry Winston,** and **H. Stern.**

Cigars

Like Cuba, Puerto Rico has a long history of hand-rolled cigar-making, and you can often find street vendors rolling and selling their own in Plaza de Hostos's Mercado de Artesanías, a plaza near the cruise-ship piers at Calle Recinto Sur. There are also several good cigar shops selling anything you could want—except Cubans, of course. The biggest selection has to be at **The Cigar House** (255 Calle Fortaleza, 787/723-5223; 258 Calle Fortaleza, 787/725-9604; and 253 Calle San Justo, 787/725-0652; www.the-cigarhousepr.com, daily 10 A.M.-8:30 P.M.). Trinidad, Monte Cristo, Padron 1926 and 1964, Cohiba, Perdomo, Macanudo, Partagas, Romeo and Julieta, and Puerto Rican cigars aged in rum are among those sold. They also sell tons of tourist trinkets.

For a more intimate setting, visit **El Galpón** (154 Calle del Cristo, 787/725-3945 or 888/842-5766, Mon.-Sat. 10 A.M.-6 P.M., Sun. 10 A.M.-5 P.M.). This small, selective shop sells a variety of quality cigars, Panama hats, masks, art prints, and superb vintage and contemporary santos.

Imports

San Juan has several Indonesian import shops.

Eclectika (204 Calle O'Donnell, Plaza de Colón, and 205 Calle de la Cruz, 787/721-7236 or 787/725-3163, www.eclectikasanjuan.com, daily 10 A.M.-7 P.M.) has Indonesian imports specializing in home decor, purses, and jewelry.

Hecho a Mano (260 Calle San Francisco, 787/722-0203, and 250 Calle San José, 787/725-3992, fax 787/723-0880, www.hecho-amanopr.com) sells Indonesian decorative imports, locally designed women's wear, funky purses, and jewelry. There's another location at 1126 Avenida Ashford in Condado.

Kamel International Bazaar and Art Gallery (154-156 Calle de la Cristo, 787/722-1455 or 787/977-7659, kamelimports@yahoo.com, daily 10 A.M.-7 P.M.) sells inexpensive Indian clothing, jewelry, rugs, beaded handbags, and reproduction paintings on canvas.

Fine Jewelry

There are dozens of high-end fine-jewelry stores in Old San Juan, especially along Calle Fortaleza, including **N. Barquet Joyers** (201 Calle Fortaleza, 787/721-3366 or 787/721-4051, fax 787/721-4051, nbarquet@spiderlink.net, daily 10:30 A.M.-5 P.M.); **Casa Diamante** (252 Calle Fortaleza, 787/977-5555, daily 10 A.M.-6 P.M.); and **Emerald Isles** (105 Calle Fortaleza, 787/977-3769, Mon.-Sat. 11 A.M.-6 P.M.).

Vogue Bazaar (364 Calle San Francisco, 787/722-1100, Mon.-Wed. and Fri.-Sat. 10 A.M.-6:30 P.M.) specializes in pre-Columbian reproductions, gemstones from South America, and purses from Thailand.

Antiques and Collectibles

Thrift-store shoppers and collectors of vinyl will love **Frank's Thrift Store** (363 Calle San Francisco, 787/722-0691, daily 10 A.M.-6 P.M.). Come here to peruse the enormous used-record collection, from '80s kitsch to fresh electronica. There's even a turntable available, so you can listen to the stock before you buy. But this cluttered labyrinth of rooms is also packed with the widest assortment of junk and collectibles you could ever imagine. Decorative items, old photographs, dishes, toys, clothes—you name it.

Galería Don Pedro (254 Calle San Justo, 787/721-3126 or 787/429-7936, Mon.-Thurs. and Sat. 10:30 A.M.-7 P.M., Fri. 10:30 A.M.-5:30 P.M., closed Sun.) has three floors of antiques, vintage collectibles, and original artwork by local artists.

Kitchen Goods

Spicy Caribbee (154 Calle de la Cristo, 888/725-7529, www.spicycaribbee.com, Mon.-Sat. 10 A.M.-6 P.M., Sun. 11 A.M.-5 P.M.) sells Caribbean sauces, spice mixes, coffees, soaps, fragrances, candles, cookbooks, and more.

Groceries

Supermax (201 Calle Cruz, Old San Juan, 787/725-4839, www.supermaxpr.com, Mon.-Sat. 6 A.M.-midnight, Sun. 10 A.M.-8 P.M.) is a modern, full-service grocery store with a bakery, deli, fresh meat counter, and produce section. It carries a large selection of spirits and a wide variety of local coffees, but you'll have to get a clerk to unlock the case for you.

CONDADO

Condado has a couple of high-end stores like **Cartier** and **Louis Vuitton,** but in recent years more reasonably priced clothing stores have opened up. Don't be surprised if you try to enter a storefront along Condado and find the door locked during regular business hours. Many of the smaller shops are managed by a single person, and the doors are kept locked for their safety. Just ring the doorbell and the proprietor will buzz you in.

Clothing and Accessories

For one-of-a-kind designs, visit the eponymous store of one of the island's most renowned designers of casual wear and haute couture for both men and women, **Nono Maldonado** (1112 Ave. Ashford, 2nd floor, 787/721-0456, Mon.-Fri. 10 A.M.-6 P.M., Sat. 11 A.M.-6 P.M.). He was the former fashion editor of *Esquire* magazine.

Monsieur (1126 Ave. Ashford, 787/722-0918, Mon.-Sat. 10 A.M.-6:30 P.M., Sun. 2-7 P.M.) sells casual designer menswear for the young and clubby. Also for men is **Root** (1129 Ave. Ashford, 787/946-ROOT—787/946-7668, www.rootformen.com, Mon.-Thurs. 11 A.M.-7 P.M., Fri. 11 A.M.-10 P.M., Sat. 11 A.M.-10 P.M., Sun. noon-7 P.M.), a tiny black-and-white pocket store that sells two things: limited edition T-shirts designed by graphic artists ($25) and limited edition hand-made dress shirts ($49). Only 18 of each T-shirt is made, and only six of each dress shirt design is made, so it's a safe bet you'll be the only one on your block to have one when you go back home. The owners are Argentine, which explains the high style of the shop's unique designs.

Across the street from La Concha Resort, **Piña Colada Club** (1102 Ave. Magdalena, 787/998-1980, Mon.-Sat. 11 A.M.-7 P.M., Sun. noon-5 P.M.) specializes in stylish resort and beach wear. Labels include Trina Turk, Vitamin A Swim, Maaji, Echo, Bianca Coletti, Hale Bob, and the Piña Colada Club line of terry-cloth and jersey beachwear. Note: Don't confuse this clothing shop with the restaurant and bar of the same name located in the Caribe Hilton.

Charmé (1374 Ave. Ashford, 787/723-9065, Mon.-Sat. 10 A.M.-6:30 P.M.) is a tiny shop packed to the rafters with flowing resort wear for mature women, including the Flax Designs linen clothing line.

Nativa Boutique (55 Calle Cervantes, 787/724-1496, 350 Ave. Roosevelt, 787/783-0099, www.nativaboutique.net, Mon.-Sat. 10 A.M.-6 P.M.) is a clothing boutique selling micro mini club wear, crochet maxi dresses, and sky-high heels. It carries Maaji swimwear and designs by Maritza Camareno and Luis Antonio. Along the same vein, **Glam Boutique**

(1357 Ave. Ashford, 787/722-9197, daily 10 A.M.-7 P.M.) sells club wear and beachwear for the young and trendy, as does **Garbo** (1045 Ave. Ashford, inside the San Juan Beach Hotel, 787/724-5678 or 787/723-8000, ext. 1126, Mon.-Sat. 11 A.M.-7 P.M., Sun. noon-5 P.M.).

Imports

Indonesian imports and locally designed women's wear are available at **Hecho a Mano** (1126 Ave. Ashford, 787/722-5322, fax 787/723-0880, www.hechoamanopr.com, Mon.-Wed. 10 A.M.-7 P.M., Thurs.-Sat. 10:30 A.M.-8 P.M., Sun. 11 A.M.-6 P.M.). It also has two locations in Old San Juan (260 Calle San Francisco and 250 Calle San José).

Vintage Clothes

Fans of quality vintage clothing must beat a path to owner José Quióones's eclectic boutique, **Rockabilly** (53 Calle Barranquitas, 787/725-4665, Tues.-Sat. 10 A.M.-5 P.M.). We're talking about classic pieces by Chanel and Halston here, not to mention vintage prom dresses, stilettos, platforms, and purses. There are new vintage-inspired clothing styles too. In the back is a hair salon.

Surf Shop

It's not often you can buy a new surfboard and nosh on eggs Benedict at the same establishment, but **Lost Surf Shop** (1129 Ave. Ashford, 787/723-4750, daily 8 A.M.-10 P.M. or later on weekends) is a cut above the average. The shop stocks T-shirts, flip-flops, sunglasses, bathing suits, boards, and more. The restaurant serves breakfast, lunch, and dinner, and it has a full bar.

Groceries

Located in Miramar, **Supermax** (113 Ave. de Diego, 787/723-1611, www.supermaxpr.com, 24 hours) is a modern, full-service grocery store with a bakery, deli, fresh meat counter, and produce section. It carries a large selection of spirits and a wide variety of local coffees, but you'll have to get a clerk to unlock the case for you.

Eros Food Market (1357 Ave. Ashford, Condado, 787/722-3631, Mon.-Sat. 7:30 A.M.-10 P.M., Sun. 8 A.M.-9 P.M.) is a convenient place to stock up on provisions, including the essentials: coffee and rum. It includes a good supply of canned goods, health and beauty items, snacks, beverages, cigarettes, etc.

ISLA VERDE
Clothing

Owned by local designer Chrisnelia Guzman, **Dressed** (5980 Ave. Isla Verde, 787/726-3327, Mon.-Sat. 10:30 A.M.-7 P.M., Sun. noon.-4 P.M.) specializes in one-of-a-kind ball gowns, prom dresses, and club wear at surprisingly affordable prices. Most gowns are in the $100-200 range. **Creaciones Phylipa** (Ave. Isla Verde, 787/791-5051, daily 10 A.M.-7 P.M.) is a tiny shop packed full of inexpensive cotton gauze dresses for girls and women, jewelry made from beads and wood, purses, and tourist souvenirs.

Located at the end of La Plazoleta de Isla Verde shopping center, **Surf Face** (6150 Ave. Isla Verde, 787/640-9830 or 787/640-9638, Mon.-Sat. 9 A.M.-7 P.M., Sun. 9 A.M.-5 P.M.)

sells surfboards and skateboards, bathing suits, T-shirts, sunglasses, and flip-flops.

Groceries

Supermax (1 Calle Venus, Isla Verde, 787/268-3084 or 787/728-2050, www.supermaxpr.com, daily 24 hours) is a modern, full-service grocery store with a bakery, deli, fresh meat counter, and produce section. It carries a large selection of spirits and a wide variety of local coffees, but you'll have to get a clerk to unlock the case for you.

OCEAN PARK
Groceries

McLeary Mini Mart (1951 Calle McLeary at Calle Santa Ana, Ocean Park, 787/236-5057, Mon.-Tues. 8 A.M.-8 P.M., Wed.-Fri. 8 A.M.-9 P.M., Sat.-Sun. 9 A.M.-7:30 P.M.) is a convenient spot to pick up drinks and snacks for a day at the beach, or other last-minute essentials.

HATO REY

For all your American chain store needs, **Plaza Las Americas** (525 Ave. Franklin Delano Roosevelt, Hato Rey, www.plazalasamericas.com, Mon.-Sat. 9 A.M.-9 P.M., Sun. 11 A.M.-7 P.M.) is a two-level mall with more than 300 stores, including Macy's, JCPenney, Victoria's Secret, Ann Taylor, Foot Locker, Gap Kids, and Sears.

Accommodations

In addition to an enormous array of hotels, inns, and guesthouses offering every kind of accommodation imaginable, San Juan has a variety of daily, weekly, and monthly apartment rentals available to those seeking a homier or long-term place to stay. **El Viejo Adoquin** (6 Calle de la Cruz, Old San Juan, 787/977-3287, www.stay-inpr.com) offers several superbly located and decorated apartments in Old San Juan, as well as one in Rincón. **The Caleta Realty** (151 Calle Clara Lair, 787/725-3436, fax 787/977-5642,

www.thecaleta.com) also has many properties in Old San Juan and Condado.

OLD SAN JUAN

Aside from a Sheraton located near the cruise-ship docks, accommodations in Old San Juan are small boutique hotels and inns. In recent years a small hotel group has changed the landscape by developing several unique properties that are modestly priced but big on design, including Da House, Casablanca Hotel, and Villa

Herencia. No matter where you stay in Old San Juan, you're within easy walking distance to some of the city's finest restaurants, shops, and cultural sights.

$100-150

Catering to a young clientele, **Da House** (312 Calle San Francisco, 787/366-5074 or 787/977-1180, fax 787/725-3436, www.dahousehotelpr.com, $80-150 s/d) is owned and operated by the folks behind one of the city's hottest music clubs, Café Nuyorican. It's also located directly above the nightclub, making it a great spot for the late-night party crowd. Those inclined to go to bed early will no doubt be kept awake by the club downstairs, which doesn't close until 3 or 4 in the morning. But night owls looking to stay in elegant but casual surroundings on a student's budget would be hard-pressed to find a better hotel. The 27 units are small and sparsely furnished with just the basics—bed, lamp, mini-fridge, ceiling fan, and remote-control air-conditioning. There is no TV or phone, and fresh linens, irons, and hair dryers are available only upon request. And there's no elevator, so be prepared to walk up as many as four flights to your room—carrying your own luggage. Service is minimal—the pierced and tattooed employees that run the reception desk often do double duty in the bar downstairs. So what makes Da House so great? Besides the inexpensive rates and location in the heart of Old San Juan, it is a gorgeous building filled with fantastic contemporary art exhibitions that change every month.

A dramatic lobby and bar drenched in red velvet, crystal chandeliers, Moroccan lanterns and Pop Art paintings create a hip vibe at the 35-room **Casablanca Hotel** (316 Calle Fortaleza, Old San Juan, 787/725-3436, http://hotelcasablancapr.com, $114-234 plus tax), managed by the folks at Da House. Accommodations range from very small standard rooms to more spacious superior rooms

complete with sitting area and balcony. There's no elevator, so be prepared to carry your luggage up a flight or two of stairs. All rooms have air-conditioning, pillow-top mattresses, private baths, and iPod docks. Some rooms have satellite TV. Other amenities include a rooftop sun deck, complimentary high-speed Internet access, next-day laundry service, a business center, concierge service, and free shoe shine.

Also owned by the folks at Da House, **Pop Art Hotel** (103 Calle Cruz, Old San Juan, 787/722-3132, $125-150 s/d, $200 two-bedroom suite) is the newest addition to the group, and it's a funky property that offers self-serve accommodations in creatively designed digs featuring original contemporary art work and bright colors where you least expect them. More like a fancy hostel than a hotel, the rooms are furnished with bunk beds but come with private bathrooms, hair dryers, and air-conditioning. Some rooms have balconies. Continental breakfast is included.

For modern, generic accommodations, **Hotel Milano** (307 Calle Fortaleza, 787/729-9050 or 877/729-9050, fax 787/722-3379, www.hotelmilanopr.com, $95-185 s/d plus 9 percent tax) provides 30 clean, corporate-style rooms appointed with air-conditioning, satellite TV, hair dryers, and mini-refrigerators.

$150-250

A classic colonial home built in the 1700s has been converted into ◖ **Villa Herencia Hotel** (23 Caleta Las Monjas, Old San Juan, 787/722-0989, www.villaherencia.com, $150-180 s/d, $250 two-room suite, plus taxes), a stunning eight-room, limited service hotel featuring antique furnishings and huge, original Pop Art paintings by Puerto Rican artist Roberto Parrilla. A manager is on-site during the day only, and amenities are limited to an honor bar, a rooftop terrace, and some gorgeously appointed common areas. But it's hard to find such high style in Old San Juan at this price.

On the edge of Old San Juan overlooking the Atlantic Ocean is **The Gallery Inn** (204-206 Calle Norzagaray, 787/722-1808, fax 787/724-7360, www.thegalleryinn.com, $175-350 s/d, plus 18 percent tax and tariff, includes breakfast buffet), one of the unique hotels in San Juan. This 18th-century home is packed with 22 small rooms tucked into a multilevel labyrinth of patios, courtyards, balconies, archways, fountains, and interior gardens. As if that weren't enough, the hotel is chock-full of portrait sculptures and plaster reliefs by artist-owner Jan D'Esopo, as well as potted plants, hanging baskets, and an assortment of tropical birds, which have the run of the place. If the chockablock decor begins to feel a bit claustrophobic, there's an elegant, airy music room with a grand piano and a rooftop deck for a change of scenery. Small rooms are well appointed with quality antiques and reproductions. Each comes with air-conditioning and a telephone.

Nearby is the equally modern, corporate-style **SJ Suites** (253 Calle Fortaleza, 787/977-4873, 787/977-4873, or 787/725-1351, fax 787/977-7682, www.sjsuites.com, $125-250 s/d, plus 9 percent tax). Fifteen spanking-new, self-serve suites come with air-conditioning, satellite TV, and mini-refrigerators. There's no reception desk or on-site management. Check-in is inside Kury Jewelry Store next door.

Elegant simplicity defines **(Cervantes Chateau** (329 Recinto Sur, 787/724-7722, fax 787/289-8909, www.cervantespr.com, $224 s/d, $247 junior suite, $339 suites, $975 penthouse suite, plus tax and resort fees), a luxury boutique hotel near the piers in Old San Juan. Tastefully but playfully decorated by clothing designer Nono Maldonado, each room is different but features original artwork and a subdued modernist aesthetic in shades of gray, gold, and russet. The stunning penthouse suite takes up the whole top floor and features an outdoor terrace and a dining room table that seats up to

10. Each room has air-conditioning, flat panel TVs with cable access, free wireless Internet, and complimentary continental breakfast. Downstairs is a tiny lobby and Panza restaurant, serving international and local cuisine.

Over $250

To get a true sense of history, spend the night in a Carmelite convent completed in 1651 by order of King Phillip IV of Spain. **Hotel El Convento** (100 Calle Cristo, 787/723-9020, 787/721-2877, or 800/468-2779, www.elconvento.com, $325-445 s/d, $710-1,520 suite, plus taxes and resort fees). A recipient of many awards and accolades, the 58-room hotel encompasses a four-floor colonial structure with an enormous well-landscaped courtyard in the center. Common areas are filled with gorgeous Spanish antiques and reproductions. Rooms come with air-conditioning, cable TV, VCR, stereo, telephone, and refrigerator. Amenities include a fitness center, plunge pool, and whirlpool bath on the fourth floor, which overlooks Old San Juan and the bay. It has four restaurants.

If you want to know exactly what to expect, stay at the **Sheraton Old San Juan Hotel & Casino** (100 Calle Brumbaugh, Old San Juan, 787/721-5100, www.sheratonoldsanjuan.com, $399-429 s, $419 d, $449 suite, $499 one-room suite, plus tax and hotel service charges). The high-rise hotel by the cruise-ship docks features all the comforts one expects from the chain. Amenities include 42-inch LCD cable TVs, high-speed Internet, a rooftop pool, a health club, and a 7,000-square-foot casino. There are two restaurants, a seafood spot called Palio and Chicago Burger Company.

Apartment Rentals

If you want make like a local and live in a residential setting, **(Caleta Balcony Rentals** (11 Caleta de las Monjas, 787/725-3436, fax 787/977-5642, www.thecaleta.com/guesthouse.html, $80-150) offers six cozy, modest

Hotel El Convento

hiltoncaribbean.com, $319 s/d, $845 one-bedroom villa, $1,216 two-bedroom villa, includes 12 percent resort tax) is proof that all Hilton hotels are not all alike. This stunning display of modernist architecture and design is a beloved blast from the past, a reminder of a time when the Condado was an epicenter of glamour. Built in the late 1940s, the sprawling hotel features an enormous lobby awash in curved lines and modular shapes that merge elegantly with blond woods, polished steel, and thick glass. Be sure to gaze up at the ceiling, a stunning wooden structure that mimics the swooping shape of ocean waves. There are seemingly countless bars, including a swim-up bar at the pool. The Caribe Hilton is one of two places in Puerto Rico (the other being Barrachina in Old San Juan) that claims to have invented the piña colada, so tourists often stop by to have one, whether they're staying at the hotel or not. And don't miss the hard-to-find Tropical Garden. Tucked away in a quiet corner is an oasis of lushly landscaped grounds built around a pond and gazebo where peacocks, geese, and black swans roam freely. There are 814 units in the hotel and nine restaurants, including Morton's The Steakhouse. There is also a spa and boutiques for shopping.

CONDADO
$100-150

It's at the far eastern end of Condado, several blocks from the nearest restaurant or shop, but **At Wind Chimes Inn** (1750 Ave. McLeary, 787/727-4159, fax 787/728-0671, www.atwindchimesinn.com, $65-105 s, $99-150 d, $130-185 suite) is just a block from the beach. Two Spanish-style haciendas have been combined to create a quaint, artful, 22-room boutique hotel. Each room has air-conditioning, cable TV, telephone, and wireless Internet; some rooms have kitchenettes. Rooms are tastefully decorated with high-quality furnishings and bright cheery bedspreads. Amenities

units varying from studios to one-bedroom apartments in a three-story structure near the San Juan Gate. The property is a bit shabby, but it has a great location between Hotel El Convento and La Fortaleza, home of the governor. All apartments have balconies and a full kitchen or kitchenette; some have air-conditioning, TV, and telephones. Each room is different, and they all have character to spare, but the Sunshine Suite on the third floor is the best of the bunch. There's no reception desk or on-site management at this self-serve property.

PUERTA DE TIERRA
Over $250

Puerta de Tierra is a small bit of land between Condado and Old San Juan, just west of the bridge that connects those two communities. It includes a small beach, a large park, a stadium, several government buildings, and one classy hotel.

◖ **Caribe Hilton** (1 Calle San Geronimo, 787/721-0303, fax 787/725-8849, www.

include a small pool with jets and a waterfall, and a shady courtyard bar and grill.

Although it's about three blocks from the beach, **El Prado Inn** (1350 Calle Luchetti, 787/728-5925 or 800/468-4521, www.elpradoinn.net, $89-139 s/d, plus 9 percent tax and 6 percent service charge) has the benefit of being close to all the action on Avenida Ashford but with the quiet residential feel of Ocean Park. Each room is different, but they're all pleasant and comfortably decorated with a bohemian vibe. A modest continental breakfast is included, and there's a tiny pool in the courtyard. Another bonus is the lovely shaded Parque Luchetti across the street. Free parking is available.

The two **Canario** (800/533-2649, www.canariohotels.com) hotels in Condado offer small, clean, modern, no-frills accommodations at a budget rate. Rooms all come with air-conditioning, telephones, cable TV, and room safes. Service is minimal, continental breakfast is included, and both properties are within walking distance of the beach, restaurants, shops, and bars. The one with the most attractive entrance and lobby is **El Canario Boutique Hotel** (1317 Ave. Ashford, 787/722-3861, fax 787/722-0391, www.canaryboutiquehotel.com, $105 s, $119-134 d, $134 t, $149 q, plus 9 percent tax and $5 in surcharges). Dramatic black-and-white floors and lots of plants provide a cheery welcome to its 25 units. The largest property is **El Canario by the Lagoon** (4 Clemenceau, 787/722-5058, fax 787/723-8590, $114 s, $125-140 d, $140 t, $155 q, $155-185 penthouse suite, plus 9 percent tax and $5 surcharges), with 44 small basic rooms in a high-rise building beside Laguna del Condado. Rooms have balconies, and there's free parking on-site.

$150-250

Acacia Boutique Hotel (8 Calle Taft, 787/725-0668, 787/727-0626, or 877/725-0668, fax 787/268-2803, www.acaciaseasideinn.com, $105 s, $175-210 d) is a small, newish

beachfront property from the folks at nearby Wind Chimes. Modern, modest rooms have air-conditioning and basic cable TV; some have balconies. Wireless Internet is available in common areas. Guests can use the bar and pool of At Wind Chimes Inn.

✦ Conrad Condado Plaza Hotel (999 Ave. Ashford, 787/721-1000 or 866/316-8934, www.condadoplaza.com, $199-259 s/d, $329-459 suites, plus taxes and resort fees) is an interesting bookend to the 1940s-era modernism of the Caribe Hilton. The Conrad is a 21st-century modernist's dream with a minimalist aesthetic and a tastefully rendered nod to Pop Art sensibilities. The lobby is blindingly white with occasional touches of brilliant orange that draw the eye around the room, from the low-backed couches to the textured wooden wall treatments to the private nooks and crannies tucked behind beaded curtains. Modernist touches continue in the guest rooms, where billboard-size black-and-white photographs hang over the beds and the shower is a clear glass cube situated in the center of the spacious bathroom. The casino is open 24 hours a day, and there are multiple restaurants, including Tony Roma's and the dramatic Strip House, a steakhouse done up in red and black and appointed with black-and-white photographs of 1950s-era burlesque dancers. Other amenities include a fitness center, a business center, and two pools, one of which is filled with saltwater.

Over $250

La Concha Resort (1077 Ave. Ashford, 787/721-85000, fax 240/724-7929, www.laconcharesort.com, $309-369 s/d, $549 one-bedroom suite, plus tax and fees) was built in 1958 and is another huge, shimmering modernist hotel on the Condado. It closed and lay dormant for years, but a recent renovation has returned it to its former glory and beyond. Amenities include multilevel swimming pools with waterfalls and a sandy beach with food and beverage service, two lounges, and four restaurants, including Perla, an upscale restaurant serving contemporary American cuisine heavy on seafood in a stunning clamshell-shaped space right on the beach.

OCEAN PARK

Ocean Park boasts one of the better beaches in the metro area and some small, charming, gay-friendly guesthouses that pay a lot of attention to the kinds of details that can make an overnight stay memorable. Because this is primarily a residential neighborhood, there aren't a lot of restaurants, bars, or shops within walking distance. Also note that if you have a rental car, street parking can be scarce, especially on the weekends when locals flock to the beaches.

$100-150

Two side-by-side houses, connected by a courtyard, create **Tres Palmas Guest House** (2212 Park Blvd., Ocean Park, 787/727-4617, 888/290-2076, or 866/372-5627, fax 787/727-5434, www.trespalmasinn.com, $87-174 s/d plus tax), containing 18 modest guest rooms, offering possibly the most economical stay you can find this close to the beach in greater San Juan. Amenities include a tiny pool and two small hot tubs on the rooftop sundeck overlooking the ocean, which is about 15 steps away, right across the street. Rooms come with air-conditioning, cable TV, free wireless Internet, refrigerator, and complimentary continental breakfast. This is a great place to stay if you want to escape the city's congested tourist areas. Yet, all the action is just a short taxi ride away.

Located in the heart of Ocean Park's commercial district, just one block off the beach, **Oceana Hostal Playero** (1853 Calle McLeary, Ocean Park, 787/728-8119, fax 787/727-5748, www.oceanopuertorico.com, $90-130 s/d, $180 q, $230 suite, plus tax and service charge; two-night minimum required) is a modest, compact high-rise building with 27 rooms. Rooms come

with air-conditioning, cable television, wireless Internet, complimentary parking, and continental breakfast. Amenities include a tiny pool and Pura Vida Bistro, a vegetarian restaurant.

$150-250

Numero Uno Guest House (1 Santa Ana, 787/726-5010 or 866/726-5010, fax 787/727-5482, www.numero1guesthouse.com, $143-287 s/d, $277-287 suite, plus $25 for additional guests, plus 9 percent tax and 15 percent service charge; children under 12 stay with parents for free) is a small, well-maintained guesthouse with attentive service. There's no lobby to speak of, just a tiny reception office beside a petite black-bottomed pool. But the 11 rooms are newly furnished, tastefully decorated, and comfortable, if you don't mind the compactness. Amenities include air-conditioning, a minibar, and wireless Internet. The guesthouse also boasts the popular fine-dining restaurant Pamela's Caribbean Cuisine, serving internationally inspired cuisine.

You know you're in for something unique as soon as you pass the tall contemporary waterfall and koi pond at the entrance to **Hostería del Mar** (1 Calle Tapia, 787/727-3302, fax 787/727-0631 or 787/268-0772, www.hosteriadelmarpr.com, $89-199 s/d, $179-239 ocean view, $244-264 suites and one-bedroom apartment, plus 9 percent tax). This compact oceanfront hotel has a lot of pizzazz in its common areas. The small lobby features an artful mix of antiques and tropical-style decor that gives way to a tastefully designed Polynesian-style bar and restaurant filled with warm woods and rattan furnishings. The wooden top-hinged windows open out from the bottom, revealing the sand and sea just a few steps away. The restaurant, Uvva, specializes in what it calls Nuevo Mediterranean cuisine and serves three meals a day. The small, basic guest rooms have air-conditioning, cable TV, and telephones. A second-floor room is recommended for those sensitive to noise, which sometimes emanates from the bar at night.

ISLA VERDE

When it comes to accommodations, Isla Verde is mostly home to luxury chain hotels such as the Ritz-Carlton and the InterContinental. But it has a handful of small independent hotels and one swanky hotel for the glamour set.

$100-150

In a cheerful yellow faux hacienda-style building two blocks from the beach, **Hotel Villa del Sol** (4 Calle Rosa, 787/791-2600 or 787/791-1600, www.villadelsolpr.com, $100 s, $130 d, $180 minisuite) has 24 units with air-conditioning, cable TV, and mini-refrigerators. Some rooms are starkly furnished; others are a little nicer. Amenities include a tiny pool, restaurant, bar, free parking, and free wireless Internet in common areas. Vias Car Rental service is on-site.

$150-250

Under new management and renovated top to bottom in 2011, **San Juan Water Beach Club Hotel** (2 Calle Tartak, 787/728-3666 or 888/265-6699, fax 787/728-3610, www.waterclub.com, $195-220 s, $220-320 d, $390 suite) is a modern high-design boutique hotel offering super-luxurious accommodations for the young, trendy, and well-heeled crowd. The hotel's 75 rooms come with air-conditioning, satellite TV, CD players, two-line telephones, data ports, high-speed Internet, minibars, in-room safes, and superior beds topped with down comforters. Water is the theme of this stark white and aqua property: Bubbles float in Lucite countertops at the reception desk, and water features abound. Liquid, the lobby bar, has a corrugated tin wall with a constant flow of water trickling over it. Wet, the rooftop bar, features stunning views of the city and huge leather couches and beds—yes, beds—that spill out around the pool. The restaurant, Tangerine, serves American Asian cuisine.

Tucked away from the fray, **Hotel La Playa** (6 Calle Amapola, 787/791-1115 or 787/791-7298, www.hotellaplaya.com, $160-175 s/d, plus 9 percent tax and $5 energy surcharge) is a very casual, modest motel-style property right on the water. The quality and comfort of the rooms vary; some are windowless and stark while others have more stylish furnishings and feature terraces. The open-air lobby doubles as a bar and restaurant serving creative Caribbean cuisine. A tall vacant building next door mars the view. Beach access is across the street.

Catering to business travelers, **Verdanza Hotel** (820 Calle Tartak, Isla Verde, 855/222-5956, www.verdanzahotel.com, $168-188 s/d) is not located on the beach, but it's not a far walk. And the 220-room hotel offers all the amenities visitors could want, including a swimming pool with food and beverage service, a children's play area, a business center, a fitness center, and four restaurants serving Asian, Caribbean, Puerto Rican, and Spanish cuisine.

Over $250

The classic elegance of **El San Juan Resort & Casino** (6063 Ave. Isla Verde, 787/791-1000 or 888/579-2632, www.elsanjuanresort.com, $299-679 s, $359 d, $889 suite, $889-1,189 two-room suite, plus tax and resort fees) is apparent as soon as you step into the expansive lobby featuring a massive crystal chandelier, carved mahogany wood panels and columns, rose-colored marble floors, and antique French tapestries. Built in the late 1950s by Pan Am Airlines, the sprawling, 385-room resort is steeped in old-school luxury and consummate service. There are seven restaurants, including The Palm, and a spate of high-end shops, including David Yurman jewelry and Godiva chocolates. Other amenities include a nightclub, spa, beauty salon, fitness center, casino, three pools, tennis courts, and a gorgeous stretch of beach with food and beverage service. At press time, the rooftop restaurant was under renovation.

SAN JUAN

© SUZANNE VAN ATTEN

Hotel InterContinental San Juan Resort & Casino

Equally elegant is **Hotel InterContinental San Juan Resort & Casino** (5961 Ave. Isla Verde, 787/791-6100, www.ichotelsgroup.com, $285-342 s/d, $351-741 suites), a classic, oceanside hotel built in 1963. The lobby features long, low archways, burnished wood accents, marble tile floors, and subdued lighting that casts a flattering warm glow. There are 398 rooms, including junior and executive suites, and each one features a curved balcony that creates an undulating effect reminiscent of a waterfall on the building exterior. The grounds are lushly landscaped around a free-form, lagoon-style pool featuring waterfalls and a swim-up bar. Hotel amenities include a spa, fitness center, business center, and casino. The property has five restaurants, including Ruth's Chris Steak House and Alfredo's, where the namesake dish—fettuccine Alfredo—is the house specialty.

The Ritz-Carlton, San Juan (6961 Ave. of the Governors, Isla Verde, 787/253-7100.

www.ritzcarlton.com, $469-669 s/d, $679-4,000 suites) is the new kid on the block, relatively speaking. This luxury hotel was built in 1997 and features more than 400 luxury guest rooms on eight acres of beachfront property. It has a 24-hour casino and five restaurants, including BLT Steak and Il Mulino New York. Other amenities include a spa, fitness center, oceanfront pool, and concierge service.

MIRAMAR
$150-250

Hotel Miramar (606 Ave. Ponce de León, Miramar, 787/977-1000, www.miramarhotelpr.com, $149-154 s/d plus tax, including complimentary continental breakfast) is a modest high-rise hotel featuring cable television, air-conditioning, microwaves, mini-refrigerators, and free wireless Internet in the rooms. Other amenities include fitness center, laundry facilities, and a sundeck terrace. Bistro 606 serves breakfast and dinner daily and has a small bar. Check the board for dinner specials.

Over $250

The newest resort and casino in San Juan is **Sheraton Convention Center Hotel & Casino** (200 Convention Blvd., Miramar, 787/993-3500, www.starwoodhotels.com, $273-473 s/d, including tax and fees). Rooms run the gamut from standard guest rooms to a variety of multi-room suites, each one featuring a 40-inch flat screen TV with cable, high-speed Internet, and iPod docking station radio. Microwaves and mini refrigerators are available upon request. Amenities include a fitness center, full-service spa, two restaurants, a lounge, name-brand boutiques, a fourth-floor infinity pool with Jacuzzi, wading pool and sun deck, and Casino Metro. A business center provides copy shop services.

Food

San Juan's dining scene continues to evolve, becoming as sophisticated and unexpected as the city itself. Inventive reinterpretations of traditional *criolla* cuisine are in vogue these days, but traditional Puerto Rican dishes, as well as New American and global cuisines, are reaching new heights at the hands of trained chefs and home-style cooks throughout the metro area. Fast on the heels of homegrown celebrity chefs Roberto Treviño and Wilo Benet are young up-and-comers like Jose Enrique and Christophe Gourdain, who are transforming the culinary landscape.

OLD SAN JUAN
Puerto Rican

The hokey theme setting of ◖ **Restaurante Raíces** (315 Calle Recinto Sur, 787/289-2121, www.restauranteraices.com, Mon.-Sat. 11 A.M.-11 P.M., Sun. 11 A.M.-10 P.M., $12-39) threatens to undermine just how good its traditionally prepared *criolla* cuisine is. Based on a Disneyfied interpretation of the *jíbaro* (hillbilly) lifestyle, the enormous restaurant comprises multiple rooms tricked out like palm-thatched huts from the mountain region. Female servers wear long white dresses and turbans; male servers wear guayabera shirts and Panama hats. Drinks are served in tin cups. If you can look past the artifice, you can expect to dine on generous servings of expertly prepared rice and beans, *mofongo, churrasco, escabeche, alcapurrias* and *chuleta can can,* an enormous fried pork chop with ribs. Stop by the little shop in the center of the restaurant to pick up some traditional candies made from coconut and dried fruits. The original location is in Caguas (Urb. Villa Turabo, 787/258-1570).

For a more authentic experience, **La Fonda El Jibarito** (280 Calle Sol, 787/725-8375, www.eljibaritopr.com, daily 10 A.M.-9 P.M., $6-18) is one of the best bets for authentic Puerto Rican cuisine, including codfish stew, fried pork, fried snapper, great rice and beans, and *mofongo* (cooked and mashed plantain seasoned with garlic). It's a major staple. Sometimes it's stuffed with meat or seafood. Patrons share tables in this casual restaurant designed to look like a traditional country house. Between the blaring TV and many families with small children, the noise level can be overwhelming. Thank goodness there's a full bar.

Café Puerto Rico (208 Calle O'Donnell, 787/724-2281, www.cafepuertorico.com, Mon.-Sat. 11:30 A.M.-3:30 P.M. and 5:30-11 P.M., Sun. noon-9 P.M., $9-24) has a whole new lease on life. The plain little café beside Plaza Colón that was there forever and never changed a bit is no more: The place has been outfitted in rich dark wood paneling and a new tile bar with tastefully lit contemporary artwork hanging on the walls. It's quite a transformation, but the coffee is still outstanding, and the Puerto Rican cuisine is still good solid fare. You can get everything from *asopao* and *mofongo* to paella and steak.

Several historic restaurants in Old San Juan have been serving customers for more than 100 years. One of the most venerable is **La Mallorquina** (207 Calle San Justo, 787/722-3261, www.mallorquinapr.com, Mon.-Sat. noon-10 P.M., $9-36), which has been in operation since 1848. This Old World restaurant does so many things right—the linen table cloths, the proficient waiters in black and white, the enormous 19th-century vases in the corners, the massive carved mirror behind the bar, the outstanding *asopao,* a hearty traditional rice stew served with chicken or seafood. Now if they could just replace those cruddy laminated menus.

La Bombonera (259 Calle San Francisco, 787/722-0658, fax 787/795-2175, daily

La Mallorquina

© SUZANNE VAN ATTEN

6 A.M.-8 P.M., $7-14) was established in 1902. This huge dingy diner and bakery serves a large menu of fairly pedestrian Puerto Rican fare, including rice stews and sandwiches. But the best reason to go is for its famous *mallorca,* a light flaky piece of swirled pastry split lengthwise, stuffed with butter, smashed, heated on a grill press, and dusted with powdered sugar. The crispy breakfast sandwiches are also a good hearty way to start the day. But be prepared to wait: Service is excruciatingly slow, especially when you're waiting for the morning's first cup of coffee.

Cafeteria Mallorca (300 Calle San Francisco, 787/724-4607, daily 7 A.M.-6 P.M., $6-18) offers a very similar dining experience to that at La Bombonera, complete with its namesake pastry, but with friendlier, more attentive service.

Barrachina (104 Calle Fortaleza, 787/721-5852, 787/725-7912, www.barrachina.com, Sun.-Tues. and Thurs. 10 A.M.-10 P.M., Wed. 10 A.M.-5 P.M., Fri.-Sat. 10 A.M.-11 P.M., $14-49), located in the courtyard of a 17th-century building, is one of two places in Puerto Rico (the Caribe Hilton being the other) that claims to have invented the piña colada. They mix up a pretty good one. But the budget decor was looking pretty shabby on a recent visit, and the Puerto Rican cuisine was only adequate.

Café La Princesa (Paseo La Princesa, 787/724-2930 or 787/635-4173, www.cafelaprincesa.com, daily 11 A.M.-10 P.M., $10-25) is a shady sidewalk café located just outside the city wall that is particularly inviting at night, thanks to the dramatic lighting and sounds of live salsa music emanating from within. The menu features hearty fare, including paella, crab-stuffed *chillo* and *churrasco,* served three ways: in *chimichurri* sauce, in a red wine sauce, or stuffed with chorizo and mushrooms and topped with marinara and Swiss cheese.

Those in the know head to **Café El Punto** (105 Calle Fortaleza, 787/725-1306, http://home.coqui.net/chilean, Mon.-Thurs. 10 A.M.-8 P.M., Fri.-Sun. 10 A.M.-10 P.M., $8-15), tucked in the back of a gift shop, to dine on authentic *criolla* cuisine accompanied by fresh salads and tropical fruit shakes. *Tostones* stuffed with shrimp or chicken are popular, as is the avocado stuffed with shrimp salad. And if you've had your fill of fried foods, try the baked empanadas. The flan comes highly recommended, too.

Caribbean

Enter the dimly lit bar of ◧ **Bodega Chic** (5 Calle Cristo, 787/722-0124, Tues.-Sat. 6:30 P.M.-midnight or later, Sun. 11:30 A.M.-midnight or later, $15-26) and it feels as though you've time traveled back in time to the 1950s. Ceiling fans slowly turn over a few fourtop tables on a red cement floor surrounded by green walls hung with vintage black-and-white pages from old magazines. The ambiance is so authentic, you might think you walked onto a movie set. But the more contemporary dining room next door gives it away with its bright yellow walls and the restaurant's name emblazoned on the wall in huge letters. Atmosphere aside, the reason to come is the food. The chef-owner is Christophe Gourdain, who trained with the world-renowned French chef Jean-George Vongerichten, and the menu reflects his French-Algerian-meets-Puerto Rican roots. Dishes include roasted chicken breast with curry banana sauce, braised lamb shank, and a ceviche of mussels and calamari. For dessert, take a break from the ubiquitous offering of flan and indulge in the delicate profiteroles.

The locally owned OOF! Restaurants group was a pioneer in bringing San Juan into the 21st century of the culinary world. The first of its four restaurants is **The Parrot Club** (363 Calle Fortaleza, 787/725-7370, www.oofrestaurants. com, lunch Mon.-Fri. 11:30 A.M.-3 P.M. and Sat.-Sun. 11:30 A.M.-4 P.M., dinner Sun.-Thurs. 5-10 P.M. and Fri.-Sat. 5-10 P.M., bar Sun.-Wed. until midnight, Thurs.-Sat. until 1 A.M., $17-32), which opened in 1996. At first glance, this wildly popular restaurant might look like a prefab tourist attraction. It boasts an over-the-top tropical-island theme, complete with faux palm trees and wooden parrots, and the din around the crowded bar can make conversation a challenge. But the reality is the Parrot Club serves some of the island's finest interpretations of Nuevo Latino cuisine. If you prefer a nice, quiet, leisurely served meal, bypass the bar and ask to be seated in the calm, low-lit courtyard out back. The restaurant specializes in a smorgasbord of crisp, refreshing ceviches, featuring a wide selection of seafood marinated in fresh citrus juices and served chilled. The shrimp, *chillo* (snapper), and dorado (mahimahi) are the best of the bunch. If you want something a little heartier, try the thick slab of blackened tuna steak served in a dark, slightly sweet sauce of rum and orange essence. It's an addictive dish that will have you coming back for more.

Baru (150 Calle San Sebastián, 787/977-7107 or 787/977-5442, www.barupr.com, Tues.-Sun. 6 P.M.-midnight, $10-28) is a lovely, sensuous restaurant with a casually elegant atmosphere that melds classic architectural features with contemporary art and then bathes it all in warm low lighting that makes you want to linger long after your meal is over. The cuisine is a creative combination of Caribbean and Mediterranean dishes, carefully prepared and artfully presented. Serving sizes are slightly bigger than an appetizer and smaller than an entrée, so order several and share with your tablemates. For an excellent starter, go with the goat cheese and almond spread drizzled with mango sauce and served with long fried yuca chips. Its satisfying combination of creamy and crunchy textures pairs beautifully with the blend of sweet and savory flavors. The asparagus risotto is appropriately creamy and nubby on the tongue, and it's studded with just the right amount of freshly chopped stalks and tips. Plump, slightly charred scallops are served each in their own tiny shell-shaped dish, drizzled with a delicate coconut curry sauce, and flecked with fresh mint. But skip the pork ribs. Although falling-off-the-bone tender, they're slathered in a super-sweet guava sauce that overwhelms the flavor of the meat.

The atmospheric **El Asador Grill** (350 Calle San Francisco, 787/289-9966, www.elasadorpr. com, daily noon-4 A.M., $13-38), located in a contemporary faux hacienda-style setting, specializes in grilled meats prepared in a courtyard kitchen. Cream-colored stucco walls, dark wood beams, terra-cotta tile floors, and dramatic archways create an inviting environment. And the menu is a carnivore's delight. Beyond the usual grilled steak, chicken, pork, and fish, you can get sausages, sweetbreads, and kidney too.

Located in the space formerly occupied by Amadeus, **Aureola Café Restaurant** (106 Calle San Sebastián, 787/977/0100, Tues.-Sun. noon-midnight, $10-25) serves creative Caribbean cuisine specializing in seafood, including *chillo* fillet stuffed with shrimp, salmon pizza, mixed seafood ceviche, and *tostones* topped with caviar in a colorful atmosphere. In addition to the dining room, there is seating in an enclosed patio or outside on Plaza San Jose, located across the street.

Spanish

In the historic Hotel El Convento, the focal point of **El Picoteo** tapas and paella bar (100 Calle Cristo, 787/723-9020 or 800/468-2779, fax 787/721-2877, www.elconvento.com, daily noon-11 P.M., $7-29) is the original wood stove of the former convent, which was built in the mid-17th century. Visitors are greeted at the entrance by an enormous wax-covered altar packed willy-nilly with whimsical ceramic roosters and half-melted candles. The main dining room is in the hotel courtyard, but there's also dining at the long tile bar overlooking the open kitchen. The traditional Spanish tapas include stiff planks of Manchego cheese, thin slices of buttery serrano ham, fresh sardines, and a variety of olives. Bypass the mushy,

oily eggplant and roasted red-pepper salad, but definitely order the fiery bite-size chorizo sausages served in a pool of thin heady brandy sauce. Among the varieties of paellas is one prepared with nutty, earthy black rice and chock-full of shrimp, calamari, and chunks of dorado.

Mediterranean

Located in the lobby of Cervantes Chateau, **Panza** (329 Calle Recinto Sur, 787/724-7722, www.cervantespr.com, Wed.-Sun. noon-3 P.M. and 6-11 P.M., $21-32) is a fine dining restaurant offering a quiet, elegant respite from the crowds and chaos that sometimes reign on the streets of Old San Juan. Marble tile floors, white linen table cloths, and gold banquettes provide a serene atmosphere for a menu that combines Italian-influenced cuisine with flavors from the island. First-course offerings include dishes such as ceviche *taquitos* and sweet potato gnocchi; main courses include pan-seared cod loin and pan-roasted Peking duck breast. Four- and eight-course tasting menus are offered for $50 and $95 per person, respectively; the entire table is required to participate.

A whimsical atmosphere sets the scene for **Al Dente** (309 Calle Recinto Sur, 787/723-7303, www.aldentepr.com, Mon.-Thurs. 11:30 A.M.-10 P.M., Fri.-Sat. 11:30 A.M.-11 P.M., closed Sun., $17-32). Three intimate dining rooms are separated by huge red arches, and the ceiling is hung with stained-glass stars. A wooden, U-shaped bar is just inside the entrance, and large, colorful contemporary paintings brighten the walls. The menu features pastas, risottos, fresh catch of the day, and heavier traditional dishes such as *braciola* and *bistecca alla Fiorentina,* a one-pound steak served in a reduction of Barolo wine and fresh rosemary.

You'll think you've been transported to Turkey when you step into **Istanbul Turkish Restaurant** (325 Calle Recinto Sur, 787/722-5057, Sun.-Thurs. 11 A.M.-9:30 P.M., Fri.-Sat. 11 A.M.-10:30 P.M., $13-18). The high red and white walls are hung with a jumble of tapestries, flags, vintage pictures of Turkey, and large, severe portraits of Mustafa Ataturk, founder of the Turkish Republic. Waiters in fezzes wind their way around the tight-knit jumble of tables and chairs, carrying heaping platters of *dolma* (stuffed grape leaves), kebabs, lamb chops, and baklava. In addition to a full bar, beverage offerings include traditional Turkish coffee.

Steak and Seafood

For a hip, hot restaurant where the gorgeous wait staff is attitude-free, the seafood is amazing, and the decor is evocative of dining in an aquarium, get thee to ◖ **Aguaviva** (364 Calle Fortaleza, 787/722-0665, www.oofrestaurants. com, daily 11:30 A.M.-4 P.M., Mon.-Thurs. and Sun. 6-11 P.M., Fri.-Sat. 6 P.M.-midnight, $17-30), another of the OOF! Restaurants' purveyors of contemporary cuisine. The space is drenched in bright white, chrome, and aqua, with glass jellyfish lights hanging from the ceiling. In addition to an oyster and ceviche bar, dishes on a recent visit included grilled dorado with smoked shrimp salsa, grilled marlin with chorizo, and *nueva paella* with seared scallops. At the blue-lit bar, where seashells float in Lucite, sublime cocktails are prepared with fresh juices. Be sure to try the watermelon sangria.

Romance oozes from the patio of **Ostra Cosa** (154 Calle Cristo, 787/722-COSA—787/722-2672, Sun.-Wed. noon-10 P.M., Fri.-Sat. noon-11 P.M., $14-28). This lovely intimate restaurant in the back of Las Arcadas alley has just 11 tables on a redbrick patio under a white tent surrounded by scores of tropical plants and orchids. The cuisine is mostly seafood, including grilled prawns, Alaskan crab legs, and cheesy crepes stuffed with your choice of fillings. For something unusual, try the smoked calamari salad, a refreshing combination of thin slices of tender pink calamari with bits of seaweed in a spritz of light ginger sauce. Accompany that with the house cocktail, the

Spinoza, a bracing mixture of white rum and fresh-squeezed lime juice. There's live mood-setting music on weekends.

The long-standing, high-quality seafood restaurant **Marisquería Atlantica** (7 Calle Lugo Vinas, Puerta de Tierra, 787/722-0890 or 787/722-0894, www.marisqueriaatlantica.com, Tues.-Thurs. noon-10 P.M., Fri.-Sat. noon-11 P.M., Sun. noon-9 P.M., $18-49) serves everything imaginable from the sea, including *asopao*, grilled lobster, fresh fish including *chillo* and dorado, and a variety of ceviches and paellas. Valet parking is offered. A second location in Isla Verde also boasts a fresh seafood market (2475 Calle Loiza, Punta Las Marías).

Bringing a bit of a New England vibe to the island, **Old Harbor Brewery Steak & Lobster House** (202 Calle Tizol, daily 11:30 A.M.-1 A.M., 787/721-2100, www.old-harborbrewery.com, $10-44) is a microbrewery producing hand-crafted beers made on-site, including Coqui, a golden lager; Old Harbor Beer, a copper-colored pale ale; Kofresi, a dark stout; and Santo Viejo, a golden pilsner. As the name implies, the menu is heavy on local lobster and all varieties of beef, including Angus, Kobe, and dry aged. Lighter fare includes pizza and penne pasta served in a choice of sauce. Expect live entertainment on the weekends. Reservations are accepted.

Asian

Dragonfly (364 Calle Fortaleza, 787/977-3886, www.oofrestaurants.com, Mon.-Wed. 6-11 P.M., Thurs.-Sat. 6 P.M.-midnight, $12-26), another OOF! Restaurant establishment frequented by the young and beautiful party set, has recently been expanded from a tiny intimate space to encompass a lounge and second bar. Nevertheless, be prepared for the wait to get in, unless you go early in the night. The playful fusion menu offers delightfully creative cuisine combinations, such as Asian seared scallops and miso honey halibut. There's also a full-service sushi menu.

A fusion of Indian and Puerto Rican cuisine may seem an unusual combination, but ◖ Tantra (356 Calle Fortaleza, 787/977-8141, fax 787/977-4289, daily noon-midnight, late-night menu Mon.-Sat. midnight-2 A.M., $16-29) proves just how simpatico the dishes are. Sensual creations include crispy fried coconut sesame shrimp accompanied by a mango-peach salsa, and shredded tandoori chicken served over a platter of crispy fried plantain slices. The menu of eclectic small plates encourages sharing. If you can't decide, order one of the combo platters, which serve 2-4 diners ($55-75). The bar serves a variety of fruity martinis ($10) garnished with fresh flower petals. Forgo dessert and have a coconut martini rimmed in chocolate and freshly grated coconut instead. After dinner, fire up a bowl of fruit-flavored tobacco in one of the hookahs that line the bar ($20 a bowl). When the kitchen closes, Tantra turns into a late-night hot spot popular with service-industry workers who flock there when their restaurants close.

J-Taste (307 Calle Recinto Sur, 787/724-2003, www.j-taste.com, daily noon-11 P.M. or later, $17-25) serves Japanese cuisine, including sushi, teriyaki, tempura, rice, noodles, teppan-yaki, and more. It has a full bar.

French
For traditional French cuisine in a classic elegant setting featuring an enormous crystal chandelier and walls surrounded by long white flowing drapes, there's **Trois Cent Onze** (311 Calle Fortaleza, 787/725-7959, www.311restaurantpr.com, Wed.-Fri. noon-3 P.M., Tues.-Thurs. 6-10:30 P.M., Fri.-Sat. 6-11:30 P.M., $24-35). This is the place to go for snails and foie gras. Check out their highly lauded wine-pairing dinners.

Eclectic
Carli's Fine Bistro & Piano (Banco Popular building, corner of Recinto Sur and Calle San Justo, 787/725-4927, www.carlisworld. com, Mon.-Sat. 3:30-11:30 P.M., music starts at 8:30 P.M., $16-34) is a romantic, sophisticated lounge and restaurant serving a variety of dishes, including risottos, raviolis, quesadillas, and Caribbean-inspired tapas. The owner, a jazz pianist, performs nightly with a changing array of guest musicians. It's also a great place to just sit at the bar and enjoy one of a large selection of specialty cocktails. There's alfresco dining on the sidewalk too.

Some of the magic seems to have worn off **Marmalade** (317 Calle Fortaleza, 787/724-3969, fax 787/724-4001, www.marmaladepr. com, Mon.-Thurs. 6-11 P.M., Fri.-Sat. 6 P.M.-midnight, Sun. 6-10 P.M., bar daily 5 P.M. until late, $13-44). The silk organza appears a bit frayed around the edges and service on a recent visit was a confused muddle. But the menu, now featuring a medley of small plates, is still delightfully unexpected. Recent offerings on the seasonal menu included Kobe beef cheeks, poached snapper in Thai curry, and lamb tagine.

Sandwiches and Salads
Providing a welcome departure from more filling fare is **St. Germain Bistro & Café** (156 Calle Sol, 787/725-5830, Tues.-Sat. 11:30 A.M.-3 P.M. and 6-10 P.M., Sun. 10 A.M.-3 P.M. and 6-10 P.M., $5-12), serving a variety of soups, salads, sandwiches, quiches, pita pizzas, and cakes. A prix fixe brunch menu is served Sunday 10 A.M.-3 P.M., for $17 per person.

It's not necessarily worth a special trip, but if you take the ferry to Cataño to visit the Casa Bacardi Visitor Center, you might want to stop by **S.O.S. Burger** (36 Ave. Las Nereidas, Cataño, 787/788-3149, Wed.-Thurs. noon-7:30 P.M., Fri.-Sun. noon-11 P.M., $3-15), in a psychedelic-colored structure with a palm-frond roof, along the way. This is the quirky domain of Sammy Ortega Santiago (his initials inform the establishment's name), who sports waist-length dreadlocks and an infectious smile.

As the name implies, the brief menu serves a variety of burgers. But the real reason to go here is to kick back with some ice-cold Medallas and to nosh on the variety of tasty *pastelillos,* thin, crisp turnovers stuffed with meat, cheese, or seafood. Here they come stuffed with everything from crab, lobster, and *chapín* (boxfish) to cheese, beef, and pepperoni with tomato sauce. There's live music on weekends.

Breakfast

Although it serves three meals a day, breakfast is the best reason to visit **Caficultura** (401 Calle San Francisco, 787/723-7731, info@ caficulturapr.com, Mon.-Thurs. 8 A.M.-5 P.M., Fri. 8 A.M.-10 P.M., Sat.-Sun. 8 A.M.-8 P.M., breakfast $6-13, lunch $8-13, dinner $15-20). Pancakes banana flambé and coconut milk French toast are a few of the specialties that keep fans coming back.

Billing itself as a micro-roastery, **Cuatro Sombras** (259 Calle Recinto Sur, 787/724-9955, www.cuatrosombras.com, Mon.-Fri. 7:30 A.M.-6 P.M., Sat.-Sun. 10:30 A.M.-6 P.M., $2-8) is a coffeehouse that serves a brew made from beans grown in the Puerto Rican mountain town of Yauco, and then roasted right on the premises. In addition to all varieties of coffee drinks, panini, croissants, and muffins are available.

Catering to the literary minded, **Poetic Café** (203 Calle Cruz, 787/721-5020, daily 8 A.M.-9 P.M., $2-6) is a clever coffeehouse associated with the Poets Passage next door. Drink names sport literary references, such as the haiku espresso and couplet double espresso, and paper and pencil are provided on each table in case the writing muse strikes while you sip your metaphor café latte. A limited menu offers sandwiches and pastries, and there is a small bar.

Located beside Capilla del Cristo, **Waffle-era Tea Room** (Calle Tetuá, 787/721-1512, http:// waffle-era.com, Thurs.-Sun. 8 A.M.-8 P.M.,

© SUZANNE VAN ATTEN

S.O.S. Burger

$3-12) serves Belgian waffles, flambé dishes, coffees, and tea infusions.

CONDADO
Puerto Rican

Celebrated local chef Roberto Treviño's latest venture, **Ⓒ Casa Lola Criolla Kitchen** (1006 Ave. Ashford, 787/998-2918, www.casalolares-taurant.com, Sun.-Thurs. 11:30 A.M.-11 P.M., Fri.-Sat. 11:30 A.M.-midnight, $16-38), has moved into the space that once housed Ajili-Mójili. Not only has Treviño updated the space, giving it a playful pop of purple, but he's infused the *criolla* cuisine with his creative touch. Traditional corn sticks become *sorulli-tos* of blue cheese, empanadas are stuffed with a Cuban stew of *ropa vieja,* and the traditional mashed plantain dish of *mofongo* goes upscale with grilled lobster.

It's rare to find a true locals' place in Condado, and that's what makes **Ⓒ Cafe Condado** (Ashford Medical Center, Ave. Ashford, 787/722-5963, Mon.-Thurs. 5 A.M.-5 P.M., Fri. 5 A.M.-4 P.M., Sat. 5 A.M.-2 P.M., $3-9) so appealing. More diner than café, it features a long pink Formica bar with 16 aqua vinyl bar stools and a dozen or so four-top tables in an otherwise drab room. But the food is crazy cheap and very authentic. The *pollo empanada* (fried chicken breast), *cubano* sandwich, and red beans and rice are outstanding. They deliver, too.

The late-night party crowd likes **Latin Star Restaurant** (1128 Ave. Ashford, 787/724-8141, $11-40, daily 24 hours), less for the food and more for the fact that it's open 24-7. It serves a huge menu, including authentic local dishes such as goat or rabbit stew, tripe soup, and brandied guinea. There's indoor and sidewalk dining, and if you want to keep the party going, Dom Perignon is on the wine list. Breakfast and daily specials are also served.

Orozco's Restaurant (1126 Ave. Ashford, 787/721-7669, Wed.-Mon. 8 A.M.-11 P.M., Tues.

4-11 P.M., breakfast 8 A.M.-3 P.M. daily except Tues., live music Fri.-Sat., $11-25) serves tradi-tional Puerto Rican cuisine featuring *mofongo,* grilled steak, pork, and chicken, plus daily specials. There is a full bar; try the house-made sangria.

Steaks and Seafood

Previously located at Museo de Arte de Puerto Rico, the critically acclaimed **Ⓒ Pikayo** (999 Ave. Ashford, 787/721-6194, www.condadoplaza. com, www.wilobenet.com, daily 6:30-11 P.M., $34-39) is now located at Conrad Condado Plaza Hotel, where chef Wilo Benet continues to push culinary boundaries with dishes like duck *magret* in chocolate sherry sauce, Gouda cheese lollipops, and petit pork belly burgers.

A stunning example of midcentury mod-ern architecture at its best, **Perla** (La Concha Resort, 1077 Ave. Ashford, 787/977-3285, www.perlarestaurant.com, Sun.-Thurs. 6-10 P.M., Fri.-Sat. 6-11 P.M., $18-36) creates the sensation of dining inside a giant clam shell—albeit a devastatingly posh one—with views of an infinity pool and the Atlantic Ocean. Dinner selections include such deli-cacies as pan-roasted sea bass in lobster and truffle risotto and braised lamb shank with flaming raisin jam. Three- and five-course tasting menus are available for $40 and $55, respectively; wine pairings are extra.

Ⓒ Mar La Boquería (1108 Ave. Magdalena, 787/296-4943, daily noon-11 P.M., $21-24) is a petite, modernist eatery offering a menu that changes daily based on fresh products from local markets. The raw bar serves oysters, clam shooters, and a variety of ceviches. Main courses may include Marnier halibut or rabbit baked in wine. The wine list includes Veuve de Clicquot brut and Truchard Pino Noir.

Wedged between the traffic-clogged in-tersection of Avenida Condado and Avenida Magdalena on the eastern end of Condado, **Puerto Peru** (1105 Ave. Magdalena, 787/722-9583, Mon. 6 A.M.-10 P.M., Tues.-Thurs.

noon-3 P.M. and 6-10 P.M., Fri.-Sat. noon-11 P.M., Sun. noon-10 P.M., $18-29) is a cheerful spot offering refuge from the bustle of car and foot traffic just outside the door. The menu specializes in Peruvian seafood dishes, which are served in cool, fresh-tasting ceviches or grilled and topped with a choice of sauces that include *rocoto* hot pepper sauce, cheese and garlic sauce, tartar sauce, or traditional Puerto Rican *criolla* sauce, made of onions, tomatoes, cilantro, and lime.

Ikakos Restaurante Marisqueria (1108 Ave. Ashford, 787/723-5151, Tues. and Thurs. noon-10 P.M., Wed. and Fri. noon-10 P.M., Sat. 5-11 P.M., Sun. noon-10 P.M., $11-29) is a casual but elegantly appointed seafood restaurant specializing in fresh local lobster and whole fish. Oysters, mussels, and *empanadillas* make up the tapas menu, while entrées feature *mofongo* and *mamposteao,* a sautéed rice dish served with your choice of meat or seafood.

Waikiki Caribbean Food & Oyster Bar (1025 Ave. Ashford, 787/977-2267, daily 11 A.M.-late, $12-35), a casual oceanfront restaurant, features a long pinewood bar, sidewalk dining, a stone-grotto-style dining room inside, and a wood deck on the beach for alfresco dining. Dishes include mahimahi nuggets, crab-stuffed mushrooms, lobster tail, osso buco, and seafood *criolla.*

Cuban

A trendy take on Cuban cuisine can be found at **Ropa Vieja Grill** (1025 Ave. Ashford, 787/725-2665, Sun.-Wed. 11 A.M.-10:30 P.M., Thurs. 11:30 A.M.-11 P.M., Fri. 11:30 A.M.-midnight, Sat. 6 P.M.-midnight, $15-25). A modern space with a large cherrywood bar, tile floors, and a wall of windows that provides great people-watching, the restaurant serves risotto with pork rinds, filet medallions in Roquefort sauce, and grilled sea bass in pesto sauce.

Italian

In the heart of all the high-rises in Condado is a little seaside oasis called **Barlovento** (Plaza del Ancla on Ave. Ashford, 787/724-7286, Sun.-Wed. 5-11:30 P.M., Thurs.-Sat. 5 P.M.-midnight, $10-28). In a small park, the restaurant offers outdoor dining under a modernistic pavilion with purple awnings and chrome chairs. The menu features pizzas topped with shrimp, squid, prosciutto, capicola, or smoked salmon, and martinis made with mango and blackberries.

Via Appia's Deli (1350 Ave. Ashford, 787/725-8711 or 787/722-4325, daily 11:30 A.M.-11 P.M. or midnight, $11-20) serves standard red-sauce Italian dishes, including pasta, sandwiches, and pizzas. It has indoor and sidewalk dining.

Dine on prosciutto di Parma, fettuccine with basil tomato sauce, pizza, and panini at **Di Zucchero Lavazza Restaurant & Lounge** (1210 Ave. Ashford, 787/946-0835, http://dizuccheropr.com, Mon.-Thurs. 11 A.M.-11 P.M., Fri.-Sat. 11 A.M.-midnight, Sun. 11 A.M.-11 P.M., $14-17) while a DJ spins techno in this hip, black-and-red coffee bar and restaurant. After 11 P.M., the upstairs turns into a nightclub.

Mexican

If you're looking for nachos, slushy margaritas, and mariachi music, keep on looking. **Agave Cocina Mexicana Creativa** (1451 Ave. Ashford, 787/963-1793, daily noon-midnight, $10-30) is one of the first truly sophisticated Mexican restaurants on the island. The setting is sleek and understated, and the dishes are unexpected, ranging from beef ribs cooked in tequila and cola to Napoleon *chilaquiles* topped with a fried egg to fresh tuna seasoned with chilies, cinnamon, and achiote, served with clementines, plantains, and habanera foam. Valet parking is available.

Serving basic Tex-Mex cuisine, **Tijuana's Bar & Grill** (1350 Ave. Ashford, 787/723-3939, www.tijuanaspr.com, Mon.-Thurs. 11:30 A.M.-11 P.M., Fri.-Sat. 11:30 A.M.-midnight, Sun. 11:30 A.M.-11 P.M., $8-25) serves nachos, tacos, quesadillas, enchiladas, burritos, and fajitas indoors or on an outside terrace. Specialties include shrimp diablo and Mexican lasagna. It has a full bar. Another location is in Old San Juan (Pier No. 2, Fernández Juncos, 787/724-7070).

Asian

To step into ◖ **Budatai** (1056 Ave. Ashford, 787/725-6919, fax 787/725-2151, http://budatai.com, Mon.-Wed. 11:30 A.M.-11 P.M., Thurs.-Sat. 11:30 A.M.-midnight, Sun. 11:30 A.M.-10 P.M., $26-48) is to forget where you are. Nothing could seem farther away from the bustling tropical street outside than this luxurious, two-story restaurant and lounge. Deep red walls and drapes, iridescent stone tile columns, and massive gold light fixtures that resemble sea anemones create an exotic setting for premier chef Roberto Treviño, a competitor on the Food Network show *Iron Chef,* to serve his melding of Latin and Asian cuisines. Dishes include slow-roasted duck with Peking glaze, veal pot stickers, duck fried rice, and a variety of ceviches and sushi. The mixologist behind the bar surprises with creative twists on favorite cocktails, making margaritas with cilantro and *caipirinhas* with fresh watermelon juice.

Overlooking the Caribe Hilton's Tropical Garden, complete with pond, gazebo, and black swans, **Lemongrass Pan Asian Latino** (Caribe Hilton, 1 Calle San Germano, daily 5:30-10:30 P.M., $27-33) creates some lively dishes, including smoked eel over Chilean sea bass in a foie gras reduction and sea scallops and lamb cakes in mustard sesame sauce with fennel.

The elegant minimalist space at **Nori Sushi and Grill Bar** (1051 Ave. Ashford, 787/977-8263, Mon.-Thurs. 11 A.M.-3 P.M. and 6 P.M.-1:30 A.M., Fri.-Sun. 11:30 A.M.-1:30 A.M., $6-26) creates a fine dining atmosphere for sushi, tempura, teriyaki, and hibachi dishes. House special rolls include the Mango Dragon Roll, featuring eel, crab, avocado, and sliced mango, and sushi pizza made with choice of spicy salmon, tuna, eel, shrimp, or scallops. Chef specials include

pineapple seafood fried rice. Bento box lunch specials are served noon-3 P.M.

Pizza

Mike's Pizzeria (1024 Ave. Ashford, 787/723-0242, 787/723-0118, 787/722-2480, or 787/722-2484, www.mikespizzeriapr.com, Sun.-Thurs. 11 A.M.-midnight, Fri.-Sat. 11 A.M.-2 A.M., $6-18) serves New York-style pizza, salads, subs, calzones, pasta dishes, and burgers, plus a full bar. Delivery is free, but a $12 minimum purchase is required.

Breakfast

Picachos Café (1020 Ave. Ashford, 787/977-8681, www.picachoscafe.com, Tues.-Sun. 8 A.M.-6 P.M., $5-10) is a full-service coffeehouse that serves 100 percent Puerto Rican coffee in a variety of drinks, from espresso to iced coconut mocha. Noncaffeinated options include frozen lemonade and fruit smoothies. Menu options range from bagels and wraps to salads and sandwiches on baguettes.

Stop in **Lost Surf Shop** (1129 Ave. Ashford, 787/723-4750, daily 8 A.M.-10 P.M. or later on weekends, $4-25) for some sunglasses and a pair of board shorts and nosh on eggs Florentine or French toast for breakfast. The lunch and dinner menu includes Waldorf salad and grilled eggplant sandwich. The bar serves a variety of craft beers and spirits.

OCEAN PARK

There are few restaurants in Ocean Park, but the ones that are there are top-notch.

Puerto Rican

Despite its name, ◖ **Kasalta Bakery** (1966 Ave. McLeary, 787/727-7340 or 787/727-6593, fax 787/268-0864, www.kasalta.com, daily 6 A.M.-10 P.M.) is much more than a bakery. This large, professionally run operation sells piping hot *empanadillas, pastellillos,* and *alcapurrias* ($1.50), and super-thick toasted sandwiches

($5-8), including exceptional *cubanos, medias noches,* and a variety of breakfast sandwiches. There are also hot daily specials, including paella, seafood salads, and case after case of freshly made baked goods ($1.50), such as cheesecakes, jelly rolls, Danishes, cookies, and more. It also sells whole cakes and has an excellent wine and liquor selection. Order at the counter and grab a seat on a short bar stool at shared tables to feast. Be prepared to wait for a parking space and stand in line to order on the weekends.

Caribbean

In Numero Uno guesthouse, **Pamela's Caribbean Cuisine** (1 Calle Santa Ana, 787/726-5010, fax 787/727-5482, www.numero1guesthouse.com, lunch daily noon-3 P.M., tapas daily 3-6 P.M., dinner daily 6-10:30 P.M., $25-35) is the most popular restaurant in Ocean Park. This elegant fine-dining restaurant with excellent service features white linen tablecloths and mission-style furnishings inside, with casual seating outside right on the sandy beach. Specialties include grilled shrimp with tamarind sauce and rack of lamb with grilled pineapple and fresh mint chutney.

Uvva (Hostería del Mar, 1 Calle Tapia, 787/727-3302, fax 787/268-3302, www.hosteriadelmarpr.com, daily 8 A.M.-10 P.M., $20-45) is another popular fine-dining restaurant in Ocean Park. It features a tiny dining room decked out in warm woods and rattan furnishings. The cuisine is Mediterranean fusion, featuring several pasta dishes, fish, and lamb chops.

Pizza

For an unusual dining experience, **Pizza Cono** (1059 Calle McLeary, 787/317-3725, daily 11 A.M.-10 P.M., $2.50) is a closet-sized spot serving pizza cones to go. The sauce, cheese, and toppings are stuffed into a cone-shaped crust. Carryout only.

ISLA VERDE
Puerto Rican

Despite its location in an aging, nearly empty strip mall, ⬛ **Mi Casita** (La Plazoleta de Isla Verde, 6150 Ave. Isla Verde, 787/791-1777, daily 7 A.M.-10:45 P.M., $5-18) is a homey oasis of authentic Puerto Rican cuisine. The restaurant is designed to look like Mom's dining room, complete with china plates hanging on the green walls, and the menu features outstanding *criolla* cuisine, including a moist *mofongo, asopao, churrasco, chillo* and mahimahi.

At **Don Jose Restaurant and Bar** (6475 Ave. Isla Verde, km 6.3, 787/253-1281, Mon.-Wed. 7 A.M.-11 P.M., Thurs.-Sun. 24 hours, $7-22), a large, fully stocked bar dominates the center of this long, narrow dining room serving traditional Puerto Rican dishes, including shrimp *asopao, bifstec encebollado, chuleta can can, churrasco,* and *mofongo.* It also serves a traditional American breakfast (eggs, oatmeal, pancakes) as well as burgers, sandwiches, and salads. Daily specials and free delivery are offered.

Platos Restaurant (below Coral by the Sea hotel, 2 Calle Rosa, 787/791-7474 or 787/721-0396, Sun.-Thurs. 11:30 A.M.-11 P.M., Fri.-Sat. 11:30 A.M.-11:30, $17-23) is not named after the Greek philosopher but rather the Spanish word for "plates." This trendy, touristy restaurant is decorated in moss green and burnt orange with a large steel counter and big-screen TV in the bar. Tropical-drink specials are tall, but weak and pricey at $12 a pop. The formerly froufrou menu has been replaced with streamlined traditional dishes, including *mofongo,* steaks, pork chops, and fettuccine. Creativity reigns among the seafood dishes, which include mahimahi in coconut-passion fruit sauce.

Casa Dante (39 Ave. Isla Verde, 787/726-7310, Mon.-Thurs. 11:30 A.M.-1 A.M., Fri.-Sat. 11:30 A.M.-midnight, Sun. 11:30 A.M.-10:30 P.M., $8-30) is a casual, low-key locals' restaurant serving authentic Puerto Rican cuisine, specializing in a variety of *mofongos* with choice of fish, seafood, beef, chicken, or pork. There are also a few pasta dishes available.

Caribbean

If the restaurant didn't overlook the water, the

ambiance of this casual, open-air restaurant would be just plain sad, with its plastic deck chairs and tattered, dingy tent awning, not to mention the view of the abandoned building looming next door. But **La Playita** (Hotel La Playa, 787/791-1115, www.hotellaplaya.com, $16-26) serves a diverse and tasty menu heavy on seafood, including mahimahi in mango chipotle sauce and salmon filet in spicy guava sauce. There is also an extensive appetizer menu, including ceviche and mini *alcapurrias* and empanadas, making it a great spot for drinks and appetizers. Salads, wraps, and burgers round out the menu.

Part restaurant, part nightclub, **Spice** (6700 Ave. Isla Verde, 787/200-9967, daily 3:30 P.M.-midnight or later, $12-29) features a sidewalk bar, outdoor dining, and a stage big enough to accommodate a large band. The menu features a variety of grilled or fried meats and seafood served with your choice of sauce, including mango cilantro, mango pineapple, marsala, garlic and lemon, or marinara.

Seafood and Steak

Marisquería Atlántica (2475 Calle Loiza, Punta Las Marías, 787/728-5444 or 787/728-5662, www.marisqueriaatlantica.com, Mon.-Thurs. noon-10 P.M., Fri.-Sat. noon-11 P.M., $18-49) is a long-standing, high quality seafood restaurant, serving everything imaginable from the sea, including *asopao*, grilled lobster, fresh fish including *chillo* and dorado, and a variety of ceviches and paellas. There is also a market where you can pick up fresh seafood to prepare at home (Mon.-Sat. 9 A.M.-8 P.M., Sun. 10 A.M.-3 P.M.). A second location is in Puerta de Tierra (7 Calle Lugo Vinas).

Locals and tourists alike flock to 🄲 **Che's** (35 Calle Caoba at Calle Laurel, 787/726-7202 or 787/268-7507, www.chesrestaurant.com, Sun.-Thurs. 11:30 A.M.-10 P.M., Fri.-Sat. 11:30 A.M.-11 P.M., $13-48), a large casual restaurant serving excellent Argentine cuisine.

Grilled meats are the specialty—veal, lamb, *churrasco*, veal kidneys, and so on. There are also some unexpected offerings—a Greek-style spinach pie with a whole boiled egg buried inside and an apple and celery salad. Che's has good service and a full bar.

Two outposts of classic American steakhouses are located in two Isla Verde resorts. At El San Juan Resort & Casino is **The Palm Restaurant** (6063 Ave. Isla Verde, 787/791-1000 or 888/579-2632, www.elsanjuanresort.com, daily 5-11 P.M. or later, $17-54), which was established in New York in 1926. It brings its venerable menu of prime aged beef, double-cut lamb chops, and Novia Scotia lobster tail to the Caribbean. Meanwhile, over at The Ritz-Carlton is **BLT Steak** (6961 Ave. of the Governors, 787/253-1700, www.e2hospitality.com, daily 6-11 P.M., $28-50), offering a contemporary interpretation of the classic American steakhouse in a casual setting.

Cuban

Decor is secondary at the crowded casual Cuban restaurant 🄲 **Metropol** (Ave. Isla Verde, beside Club Gallistico cockfight arena, 787/791-4046, www.metropolpr.com, daily 11 A.M.-10:30 P.M., $9-40, most dishes $10-15). The house specialty is *gallinita rellena de congri*—succulent roasted Cornish hen stuffed with a perfectly seasoned combination of rice and black beans. The presentation is no-nonsense and the service expedient, designed to get you in and out so the folks lining up outside can have your table.

Italian

Despite its modest location on the busy thoroughfare, **Il Nonno** (41 Ave. Isla Verde, 787/728-8050, Sun.-Thurs. noon-10 P.M., Fri.-Sat. noon-11 P.M., $14-29) is a small fine-dining restaurant with a lovely setting. Pale green walls and walnut accents are complemented by an excellent selection of contemporary paintings.

The restaurant serves Italian cuisine from gnocchi gorgonzola to osso buco.

The casual modern Argentine-Italian restaurant **Ferrari Gourmet** (3046 Ave. Isla Verde, 787/982-3115, www.ferrarigourmet.com, Sun.-Thurs. noon-10 P.M., Fri.-Sat. noon-11 P.M., delivery after 6 P.M., $10-22) specializes in a wide variety of tasty creative pizzas. Selections include black olive and blue cheese; asparagus, parmesan cheese, and fresh tomato; and ham, roasted red peppers, and green olives. Entrées include *churrasco*, veal saltimbocca, and lasagna.

Il Mulino New York (The Ritz-Carlton, 6961 Ave. of the Governors, 787/791-8632, www.ilmulino.com, Mon.-Wed. 6-10:30 P.M., Thurs.-Sat. 6-11 P.M., Sun. 6-10 P.M., Sun. brunch 11 A.M.-3 P.M., $24-48) is the Caribbean arm of the celebrated Italian restaurant, specializing in meat and seafood dishes with a menu that includes rack of lamb, osso buco, and scampi *fra diavolo*.

Japanese

Catering to the late-night party crowd, **Kintaro** (5970 Ave. Isla Verde, 787/726-3096, Mon.-Thurs. and Sun. 5 P.M.-3 A.M., Fri.-Sat. 5 P.M.-4 A.M. $9-22) is a small, dark red eatery serving sushi, tempura, and teriyaki into the wee hours. It offers free delivery.

Pizza

Pizza City (5950 Ave. Isla Verde, 787/726-0356, daily 24 hours, $3-20) is an open-air restaurant best known for its tasty thin-crust pizza sold by the slice or pie, but it also serves breakfast, sandwiches, seafood salads, and *mofongo*. It has a full bar and offers free delivery.

Deli

Piu Bello (2 Calle Rosa, 787/791-0091, fax 787/791-0092, Mon.-Thurs. 7 A.M.-11 P.M., Fri.-Sun. 7 A.M.-midnight, $7-13) is a large, modern retro-style diner with indoor and outdoor dining. The enormous menu includes every sandwich imaginable, including wraps, Italian focaccia, flatbreads, panini, burgers, and clubs. It also serves breakfast, pasta dishes, and gelato. A second location is on Avenida Ashford in Condado. There's free wireless Internet.

Breakfast

Galluzzo Bistro Café (5757 Ave. Isla Verde, 787/903-1941 or 787/200-0465, galluzzobistro@gmail.com, Sun.-Thurs. 7 A.M.-8 P.M., Fri.-Sat. 7 A.M.-10 P.M., $7-9) is a small, modern spot that serves a variety of breakfast dishes, including Belgian waffles, crepes, and eggs Benedict, as well as soups, wraps, panini, salads, pastas, and coffee drinks. Be sure to check out the glass display case filled with housemade pastries and *macarons*. Free wireless Internet is available.

SANTURCE
Puerto Rican

During the day, ◖ **La Placita/Plaza del Mercado** (Calle Roberts) is a terrific open-air farmers market where shoppers can pick up a wide variety of fruits, vegetables, fresh meats, frozen fruit frappes, and herbal remedies. But at night the markets close up, sidewalk bars open for business, a live band strikes a tune, adjacent restaurants and bars fill up with patrons, and the surrounding neighborhood turns into a lively street party. This is a great place to drink, dine, dance, and people-watch. The action is especially hopping Thursdays through Saturdays.

It's easy to tell the chef-owned restaurant ◖ **Jose Enrique** (176 Calle Duffaut at La Placita, 787/725-3518, Tues.-Fri. 11:30 A.M.-10:30 P.M., Sat. 6:30-10 P.M., $10-26) is a foodie mecca by the size of the crowd congregated outside a modest-looking house that doesn't even bother with a sign indicating its name. When the 2011 Puerto Rico Wine and Food Festival ended, all the celebrity chefs made a beeline here to dine on the young chef's creative interpretations of *criolla* food. The menu changes every night, depending on what's fresh. A recent

SAN JUAN

night's offerings included house-smoked *longaniza* (pork sausage), *carne guisada* (beef stew), *churrasco* (Argentinean skirt steak), *dorado ajillo* (mahimahi in garlic sauce), and *tembleque* (a congealed coconut dessert). Reservations are not accepted, so be prepared to wait up to two hours, but not to worry. You can head someplace nearby for pre-dinner drinks and the hostess will call your cell phone when your table is ready. Ask to sit outside if there's space; the candlelit setting is more serene and atmospheric than the crowded, brightly lit dining room.

Boronia (Calle Capital at La Placita, 787/724-0636, daily noon-10 P.M., $9-20) is a modest, casual restaurant serving traditional *criolla* cuisine with a few surprises, such as mashed celery root with codfish for an appetizer and rabbit fricassee. There's live music on weekends.

Located on the first floor of a four-story apartment building, **Bebo's Café** (1600 Calle Loiza, 787/726-1008, http://beboscafepr.com, daily 7:30 A.M.-12:30 A.M., $6-21) is a casual restaurant serving an exhaustive menu of traditional *criolla* cuisine. Literally, just about anything you can think of is served here: Cuts of chicken, pork, and beef are prepared fried, breaded, grilled, stuffed, or stewed. Shrimp, crab, octopus, and conch are served in salads or stuffed in *mofongo*. All varieties of fritters, sandwiches, soups, fish, and flan are also represented, as are fruit shakes and frappes. Check the daily specials for delicacies such as stewed oxtail, goat fricassee, and *pastelón,* a dish similar to lasagna that uses plantain or breadfruit in place of pasta. This place is the real deal.

Considered by many to be the best place in town to dine on good, cheap Puerto Rican food, **La Casita Blanca** (351 Calle Tapia, 787/726-5501, Mon.-Thurs. 11:30 A.M.-4 P.M., Fri.-Sat. 11:30 A.M.-9 P.M., Sun. noon-4 P.M., $7-15) is an endearingly rustic restaurant serving rustic cuisine. The menu changes daily but typically includes classics such as *arroz con pollo, carne guisado, pastelón con carne,*

amarillos, tostones and *picadillo.* All meals end with a tasty complimentary shot of *chichaito,* made from rum and anisette. It's not far from Condado, but take a taxi. It can be a challenge to find and the neighborhood is a little rough around the edges.

Spanish

Set in a colonial mansion appointed with stained-glass windows, archways, patios, intricate tile work, and lush landscaping, **La Casona** (609 Calle San Jorge, corner of Ave. Fernández Juncos, 787/727-2717 or 787/727-3229, www.lacasonapr.net, Mon.-Fri. noon-3 P.M., Mon.-Sat. 6-11:30 P.M., $25-35) serves a menu of classic Spanish dishes. An extensive wine list complements the paella, rack of lamb, and pâté. It's a particularly popular spot for business lunches, banquets, receptions, and other private parties.

French

Located across from the Museo de Arte de Puerto Rico, **Bistro de Paris** (310 Ave. de Diego, 787/998-8929 or 787/721-8925, www.bistrodeparispr.com, Mon.-Wed. 11:30 A.M.-10 P.M., Thurs. 11:30 A.M.-11 P.M., Fri.-Sat. 11:30 A.M.-midnight, Sun. 11 A.M.-10 P.M., $25-37) specializes in authentic French nouvelle cuisine, including shrimp flambé and filet mignon topped with sautéed duck liver. Globe light fixtures and art posters create a cozy ambiance in the dining room, while more casual dining is available on the patio. Brunch is served Saturday and Sunday noon-4 P.M.

Breakfast

At **Abracadabra Counter Café** (1661 Ave. Ponce de León, 787/200-0447, Tues.-Thurs. 8:30 A.M.-7 P.M., Fri. 8:30 A.M.-9 P.M., Sat.-Sun. 10 A.M.-3 P.M., $5-15), bright yellow-and-white striped wallpaper and vintage photographs cover the walls of this whimsical bistro frequented by a hip, young clientele, as well as families attracted by the local coffee and the fresh, organic menu. Breakfast and brunch dishes are its specialties, including the Caprese omelet, Nutella-filled croissants, and bacon maple cupcakes. Live entertainment runs the gamut from magic shows to film nights to live musical performances. A full bar and free wireless Internet are available.

MIRAMAR
Puerto Rican

From the same folks who run the popular Casita Blanca in Santurce, equally popular **Casita Miramar** (605 Ave. Miramar, 787/200-8227, Mon.-Fri. 6-10 P.M., Sat. 11:30 A.M.-10 P.M., Sun. 11:30 A.M.-9 P.M., $18-32) serves traditional Puerto Rican cuisine in a two-story colonial building with a second-floor patio. The menu changes daily, based on what's fresh and in season. Be prepared to wait up to two hours if you go at prime time.

   Punta del Este (906 Ponce de León, 787/725-1235, Mon.-Wed. 11 A.M.-10 P.M., Thurs.-Fri. 11 A.M.-11 P.M., Sat. noon-midnight, Sun. noon-10 P.M., $7-13) is a narrow, casual restaurant specializing in Puerto Rican and Uruguayan cuisine. Daily specials are posted on its Facebook page and may include chicken fricassee with rice and beans, *mofongo* stuffed with *churrasco,* and chicken breast in champagne sauce. There is a full bar.

French

Although **Augusto's Cuisine** (801 Ave. Ponce de León, 787/725-7700, Tues.-Fri. noon-3 P.M., Tues.-Sat. 7-9:30 P.M., $26-40) is located in the Courtyard by Marriott, don't confuse it with generic chain hotel fare. The venerable French-influenced fine dining restaurant was located in this spot long before it was a Courtyard by

Marriott. It is the place to go to don your evening finery, make a selection from the extensive wine list, and enjoy a leisurely meal featuring chef Augusto Schreiner's lobster risotto, halibut in champagne sauce, or pine nut-encrusted scallops.

Breakfast and lunch

Neon green walls and bright orange chairs create a cheery place to start the day. **Al Gusto Deli** (950 Ave. Ponce de León, 787/723-4321, Mon.-Fri. 7:30 A.M.-3:30 P.M., $6-9) serves breakfast sandwiches and burritos, as well as deli sandwiches, wraps, salads, soups, and quesadillas.

RÍO PIEDRAS

Located in a densely developed commercial district on a frontage road that parallels busy Carretera 1, **C** **Sangria Global Cuisine** (1577 Calle Alda, Río Piedras, 787/758-8596, www. restaurantesangria.com, Mon.-Fri. 11:30 A.M.-10 P.M., Sat. 4-10 P.M., $18-28) is an oasis of sublime service, elegant ambiance, and outstanding creative *criolla* cuisine. The menu often changes, but a recent visit featured mini spring rolls stuffed with *ropa vieja,* rabbit empanadas with chipotle aioli, and *budin de pan* combining mango, pecans, and chocolate sauce. Features include a full bar, extensive wine list, and valet parking.

   Borges Café (1579 Calle Calda at Carr. 1 and Ave. de Diego, Río Piedras, 787/759-7642, Mon.-Fri. 5 A.M.-3 P.M., $3-11) serves cheap, tasty *criolla* cuisine cafeteria style in a no-frills atmosphere. In addition to menu regulars like *mofongo,* fried pork chops, and *biftec encebollado* (cube steak with caramelized onions) accompanied by choice of *tostones, amarillos,* etc., there are daily specials including *ropa vieja, chuletas can can, churrasco,* and whole fried *chillo.*

Information and Services

TOURIST INFORMATION

Puerto Rico Tourism Company (La Casita, Plaza de la Dársena, Old San Juan, 787/722-1709, fax 787/722-5208, www.seepuertorico.com, Mon.-Fri. 8 A.M.-4:30 P.M.) is in a small yellow colonial building near San Juan Bay, conveniently located near the cruise ship piers. It's a good place to pick up promotional brochures on various tourist sites, hotels, and tours, as well as a free rum cocktail.

Tourism Office of San Juan (250 Calle Teután at Calle San Justo, Old San Juan, 787/721-6363, Mon.-Sat. 8 A.M.-4 P.M.) offers self-guided audio tours of Old San Juan in English and Spanish for $10 per person. There's also a random selection of promotional materials for local tourist sites, hotels, and tours.

NEWSPAPERS AND MAGAZINES

El Nuevo Día (www.endi.com) is the islandwide Spanish-language daily newspaper. *La Perla del Sur* (www.periodicolaperla.com) is a daily paper serving Ponce.

The free bimonthly *Qué Pasa?* (www.qpsm.com) is an English language travel magazine published by Travel and Sports (www.travelandsports.com) for the Puerto Rico Tourism Company. The magazine's current issue is available online, and the publishing company's website is an exhaustive source of information about the entire island.

EMERGENCY SERVICES

The central hospital serving San Juan's tourist areas is **Ashford Medical Center** (1451 Ave. Ashford, Condado, 787/721-2160, clinic Mon.-Fri. 7 A.M.-7 P.M., Sat. 7 A.M.-noon). The emergency room is open 24 hours a day. Call 911 for ambulance service. There's a pharmacy on the first floor.

There are several **Walgreens** pharmacies

(201 Calle de la Cruz at Calle San Francisco, Old San Juan, 787/722-6290; 1130 Ave. Ashford, Condado, 787/725-1510; 5984 Ave. Isla Verde, Isla Verde, 787/982-0222). Another option is **Puerto Rico Pharmacy** (157 Calle San Francisco, Old San Juan, 787/725-2202).

Dial 911 to reach the fire or police department in case of emergency.

COMPUTER SERVICES

Cybernet Café (1128 Ave. Ashford, Condado, 787/724-4033, www.cybernetcafe.com, Mon.-Sat. 9 A.M.-9 P.M.) offers computer and Internet access, $3 for 20 minutes up to $9 for 65 minutes; discount memberships are available. Other business services are available, including fax and copies. A coffee bar is open on Saturday.

Rzone Computer & Phone (5980 Ave. Isla Verde, 787/294-6281, www.rzonecomputerphone.com, daily 9:30 A.M.-10:30 P.M.) is the place to go to update your Facebook status, print out your airline boarding pass, or Skype with friends back home. Internet services are $6 an hour, $3.50 for 30 minutes. Repair services also available for computers, phones, and game consoles.

OTHER SERVICES

There is no shortage of banks and ATMs in San Juan, the most popular being **Banco Popular** (206 Calle Teután, Old San Juan, 787/725-2636; 1060 Ave. Ashford, Condado, 787/725-4197; 4790 Ave. Isla Verde, Isla Verde, 787/726-5600).

Convenient **post office** facilities are at 153 Calle Fortaleza, Old San Juan, 787/723-1277, and 1108 Calle Magdalena, Condado, 787/723-8204.

Self-service laundries are available at **Coin Laundry** (1950 Calle Magdalena, Condado, 787/726-5955) and **Isla Verde Laundromat** (corner of Calle Emma and Calle Rodríguez, Isla Verde, 787/728-5990).

Getting There and Around

GETTING THERE
By Air

Luis Muñoz Marín International Airport (SJU, Isla Verde, 787/791-4670 or 787/791-3840, fax 787/253-3185 or 787/791-4834) is nine miles east of San Juan. It is a full-service airport with three terminals. It has a bank, restaurants, bars, and shops on the second floor alongside the departure gates. A tourist information office (787/791-1014) is in Terminal C, and a ground-service desk is on the first level by the baggage claim.

Isla Grande Airport (Aeropuerto de Isla Grande, SIG, end of Ave. Lindberg, Miramar near Old San Juan, 787/729-8790, fax 787/729-8751) is a regional airport that services flights throughout the island and the Caribbean.

For transportation into the city from the airport, there are several car-rental agencies on the first level, including **Wheelchair Getaway Rent A Car** (787/726-4023), which provides vehicles for drivers with disabilities. The first level is also where you can catch a taxi or bus into town. From the airport, take Baldorioty de Castro Avenue west toward Isla Verde, Ocean Park, and Condado and into Old San Juan.

The airport also is the site of the Luis Muñoz Marín International Airport Hotel (787/791-1700), which can be found in Terminal D on the second level.

Airline ticket prices fluctuate throughout the year, but the cheapest rates can usually be secured during the off-season, May-September, which is the rainy season. Note that late summer through early fall is also hurricane season.

These airlines service San Juan from the United States:

- **AirTran** (800/247-8726, www.airtran.com)
- **American Airlines** (800/433-7300, www.aa.com)
- **Continental Airlines** (800/231-0856 or 800/523-3273, www.continental.com)

- **Delta Air Lines** (800/221-1212 or 800/325-1999, www.delta.com)
- **JetBlue Airways** (800/538-2583, www.jetblue.com)
- **Northwest** (800/225-2525, www.nwa.com)
- **Spirit Airlines** (800/772-7117, www.spiritairlines.com)
- **United** (800/864-8331, www.united.com)
- **U.S. Airways** (800/428-4322, www.usairways.com)

By Cruise Ship

San Juan is the second-largest port in the western hemisphere, and it is a port of call or point of origin for nearly two dozen cruise-ship lines. The cruise-ship docks are at the piers along Calle La Marina in Old San Juan.

Some of the most popular cruise-ship lines serving San Juan include:

- **Carnival Cruise Lines** (866/299-5698 or 800/327-9501, www.carnival.com)
- **Celebrity Cruises** (800/647-2251, 800/722-5941, or 800/280-3423, www.celebritycruises.com)
- **Holland America Line** (877/724-5425, www.hollandamerica.com)
- **Norwegian Cruise Line** (800/327-7030, www.ncl.com)
- **Princess Cruises** (800/774-6237 or 800/421-0522, www.princess.com)
- **Radisson Seven Seas Cruises** (877/505-5370 or 800/285-1835, www.rssc.com)
- **Royal Caribbean International** (866/562-7625 or 800/327-6700, 305/539-6000, www.royalcaribbean.com)

GETTING AROUND
Taxi

Taxis are a terrific way to get around San Juan because you can catch them just about anywhere. In Old San Juan, there are taxi stands at Plaza de Colón, Plaza de Armas, and the

Sheraton near the cruise-ship piers. In Condado, you can flag them down on Avenida Ashford or at the Marriott hotel. In Isla Verde, flag one down on Avenida Isla Verde or find them congregating at the InterContinental San Juan Resort. In outlying areas such as Santurce, Bayamón, Hato Rey, or Río Piedras, you can sometimes flag one down on the major thoroughfares, but you might be better off calling one.

Licensed taxi services are well regulated. Operators include **Metro Taxi** (787/725-2870), **Rochdale Radio Taxi** (787/721-1900), and **Capetillo Taxi** (787/758-7000).

Fares between the airport and the piers in Old San Juan are fixed rates. From the airport, the rates are $10 to Isla Verde, $15 to Condado, $19 to Old San Juan, and $15 to Isla Grande Airport and the Puerto Rico Convention Center. From the piers, the rates are $12 to Condado and $19 to Isla Verde. There is a $1.50 gas surcharge, and each piece of luggage is $1. Metered fares are $3 minimum, $1.75 initial charge, and $0.10 every 19th of a mile. Customers pay all road tolls.

Bus
Autoridad Metropolitana de Autobuses (787/250-6064 or 787/294-0500, ext. 514, www.dtop.gov.pr/ama/mapaindex.htm) is an excellent public bus system that serves the entire metropolitan San Juan area. It's serviced by large air-conditioned vehicles with access for those with disabilities, and the cost is typically a low $0.75 per fare (exact change required). Bus stops are clearly marked along the routes with green signs that say "Parada," except in Old San Juan, where you have to catch the bus at **Covadonga Bus and Trolley Terminal,** the large terminal near the cruise-ship piers at the corner of Calle la Marina and Calle J. A. Corretjer. When waiting for a bus at a *parada,* it is necessary to wave to get the driver to stop. Operating hours are Monday-Friday

4:30 A.M.-10 P.M., Saturday-Sunday and holidays 5:30 A.M.-10 P.M.

The most commonly used routes for tourists are B-21 and A-5. Route B-21 starts at the terminal in Old San Juan and travels down Avenida Ashford in Condado and then south along Avenida Muñoz Rivera through Hato Rey to Plaza Las Americas, the island's largest shopping mall. B-21 runs every 20 minutes Monday-Saturday and every 30 minutes on Sunday and holidays.

Route A-5 connects Old San Juan and Isla Verde. The route travels along Avenida Isla Verde, Calle Loíza, Avenida de Diego, and Avenida Ponce de León into Old San Juan. A-5 does not go to Condado. It is possible to get to Condado from this route by transferring to B-21 at Parada 18 by Avenida De Diego, but keep in mind this stop is near a public-housing project in Santurce, which has been the site of violent crime. A-5 runs every seven minutes Monday-Friday, every 15 minutes Saturday, and every 30 minutes Sunday and holidays.

From the airport, visitors can take the C-45 bus to Isla Verde. To get to other parts of the city, it will be necessary to transfer to another route.

There are many other bus routes in San Juan. To obtain a free, detailed map of all routes, visit the bus terminal in Old San Juan. Riders should be aware, though, that buses serve tourist districts as well as housing projects, and some stops are in places where visitors who are unfamiliar with the lay of the land may not want to be. Make sure you know where you are before you disembark.

Trolley
Old San Juan Trolley (Mon.-Fri. 7 A.M.-7 P.M., Sat.-Sun. 9 A.M.-7 P.M., free) provides transportation from the cruise-ship piers throughout Old San Juan daily. You can catch the trolley at the Covadonga Bus and Trolley Terminal by Plaza de Colón, at La Puntilla parking lot on Calle Puntilla, or at marked stops throughout Old San Juan.

Ferry

The **AcuaExpreso San Juan** (Pier 2, Paseo Concepción de Gracia, Old San Juan, 787/729-8714 or 787/788-0940) ferry provides transportation across San Juan Bay from Old San Juan to the communities of Cataño ($0.50 one way) and Hato Rey ($0.75 one way). Even if you don't plan to get off and explore those neighborhoods, it's worth a ride to admire the view of Castillo San Felipe del Morro and Old San Juan on the return trip. The Cataño ferry takes about 10 minutes and operates daily 6 A.M.-9:40 P.M. The Hato Rey ferry, which takes about 15 minutes, operates weekdays only. Frequency is every 30 minutes except Monday-Friday, 6-10 A.M. and 3:45-7 P.M., when they run every 15 minutes except on holidays.

AcuaExpreso Cataño (Ave. Las Nereidas, 787/729-8714 or 787/788-0940) ferry service is provided to Old San Juan for $0.50 each way. The 10-minute ride operates daily 6 A.M.-9:40 P.M. Frequency is every 30 minutes except Monday-Friday 6-10 A.M. and 3:45-7 P.M., when they run every 15 minutes except on holidays.

Train

In 2005, San Juan launched **Tren Urbano** (866/900-1284, www.dtop.gov.pr), its first, long-awaited commuter train service. The system runs 10.7 miles, mostly aboveground, and has 16 stations, many of which house a terrific collection of specially commissioned public art. The train connects the communities of Bayamón, the Universidad de Puerto Rico in Río Piedras, Hato Rey, and Santurce at Universidad del Sagrado Corazón. The train runs daily 5:30 A.M.-11:30 P.M. Round-trip fares are $1.50; daily passes start at $5.

Público

Públicos are privately owned transport

© SUZANNE VAN ATTEN

ferry to Cataño

services that operate passenger vans along regular routes from San Juan to areas around the island. This is a very slow but inexpensive way to see the island. Providers include **Blue Line** (787/765-7733) to Río Piedras, Aguadilla, Aguada, Moca, Isabela, and other areas; **Choferes Unidos de Ponce** (787/764-0540) to Ponce and other areas; **Lina Boricua** (787/765-1908) to Lares, Ponce, Jayuya, Utuado, San Sebastián, and other areas; **Linea Caborrojeña** (787/723-9155) to Cabo Rojo, San Germán, and other areas; **Linea Sultana** (787/765-9377) to Mayagüez and other areas; and **Terminal de Transportación Pública** (787/250-0717) to Fajardo and other areas.

Car

Driving a car in San Juan can be a nerve-rattling experience for drivers not accustomed to inner-city traffic. The sheer volume of cars on the road at any given time can be daunting, and parking on sidewalks and driving up expressway shoulders are not atypical habits of Puerto Rican drivers. But renting a car is one of the best ways to explore the city and its outlying areas. In addition to most major car-rental agencies, several local companies provide comparable services.

Charlie Car Rental (6050 Ave. Isla Verde, 787/728-2418, and 890 Ave. Ashford, 787/721-6525, www.charliecars.com) is a cheap, reliable alternative to the national agencies. Drivers must be at least 21, and those younger than 25 must pay an additional $10 per day surcharge. Free pickup and drop-off at the airport, hotels, and cruise-ship port is available.

Vias Car Rental (Hotel Villa del Sol, 4 Calle Rosa, Isla Verde, 787/791-4120 or 787/791-2600; Carr. 693, km 8.2, Calle Marginal in Dorado, 787/796-6404 or 787/796-6882; and Carr. 3, km 88.8, Barrio Candelero in Humacao near Palmas del Mar, 787/852-1591 or 787/850-3070; www.viascar-rental.com, daily 8 A.M.-5 P.M.).

Scooter and Motorcycle

San Juan Motorcycle Rentals (102 Verde Mar, Ave. Isla Verde, 787/722-2111 or 787/791-5339) provides an alternative to renting a full-size car with its Vespa-style motor scooters available for rent by the hour. Free pickup and delivery service is provided.

Bicycle

Rent the Bicycle (100 Calle del Muelle, Pier 6, Old San Juan, 787/602-9696 or 787/692-3200, www.rentthebicycle.net) will deliver bikes to your hotel ($17 for three hours, $25 a day). Bike tours of Old San Juan, Condado parks and beaches, and Piñones are $27 for three hours, with a two-person minimum.

EAST COAST

Puerto Rico's east coast is rich in natural wonders, making it the most popular destination for day-trippers from San Juan. Less than an hour's drive from the island's capital are three quintessential Puerto Rican sights: El Yunque Caribbean National Forest, Balneario La Monserrate (Playa Luquillo), and Bosque Estatal de Piñones, all on the north end of the east coast. Farther east is Fajardo, the island's boating center renowned for its water sports, and Laguna Grande, a bioluminescent lagoon. Fajardo is also the point of departure for the ferry to the islands of Vieques and Culebra.

The southern side of the east coast is less developed and lacks the big-draw tourist sights found farther north, but its sleepy towns and beaches offer a quiet getaway for those wanting to escape the bustle and crowds.

The east coast is also home to several spectacular resorts, including El Conquistador in Fajardo and St. Regis Bahía Beach Resort in Río Grande. Río Grande also boasts several world-class golf courses, including the Robert Trent Jones Jr. course at the St. Regis and the Trump International Golf Club at the Gran Melia.

There are two officially designated scenic drives in the east coast. The Ruta Flamboyan (along Carretera 30 from Carretera 52 to Humacao) affords a lovely view of the spectacular *flamboyan* trees that bloom throughout the summer. These huge trees, also known as

© SUZANNE VAN ATTEN

HIGHLIGHTS

LOOK FOR **◖** TO FIND RECOMMENDED SIGHTS, ACTIVITIES, DINING, AND LODGING.

◖ Bosque Estatal de Piñones: Between the San Juan airport and the town of Loíza, this untouched parcel of natural beauty features several long stretches of wilderness beach, salt flats, mangroves, lagoons, and tropical forest, as well as six miles of bike path and a cluster of food kiosks serving some stellar Puerto Rican fast-food fare (page 97).

◖ El Yunque Caribbean National Forest: Puerto Rico's crowning jewel of natural treasures, the Caribbean National Forest is a 28,000-acre reserve that encompasses a rainforest, hiking trails, observation towers, waterfalls, and natural pools (page 101).

◖ Las Pailas: This natural water slide is formed by a mountain stream cascading over a smooth but rocky descent that bottoms out in a chest-deep pool of crystal-clear water (page 110).

◖ Balneario La Monserrate: Considered by many to be the main island's most beautiful beach, this publicly maintained facility, commonly called Playa Luquillo, features gentle waters, a wide crescent-shaped strip of sand, and a palm grove, which create the picture-perfect idyll of tropical paradise (page 110).

◖ Reserva Natural Las Cabezas de San Juan: Despite its small 300-acre size, the Fajardo nature reserve features seven different ecosystems, including coral reef, turtle grass, sandy beach, rocky beach, lagoon, dry forest, and mangrove forest. Its mangrove-enveloped Laguna Grande is bioluminescent – kayak here on a moonless night to see the water glow green, thanks to the harmless microscopic organisms that live here. It also boasts an 1880 lighthouse (page 117).

royal poinciana, have a broad, umbrella-shaped canopy that blooms a brilliant orange-red from June to early August. The Ruta Coqui doesn't necessarily get you any closer to its namesake, the coqui tree frog, than does a walk through any other forested part of the island. Instead the route (along Carretera 3 from San Juan to Humacao) passes by the east coast's most popular attractions—Playa Luquillo and El Yunque—and the town of Fajardo.

PLANNING YOUR TIME

It's actually possible to take a drive-by tour of the east coast's triumvirate of spectacular natural sights—Piñones, El Yunque, and Playa Luquillo—in a single day if you're pressed for time. But a better option is to spend a full day exploring each one. The attractions are less than an hour's drive from San Juan, and only minutes apart from one another.

When it comes to natural treasures, **El Yunque**

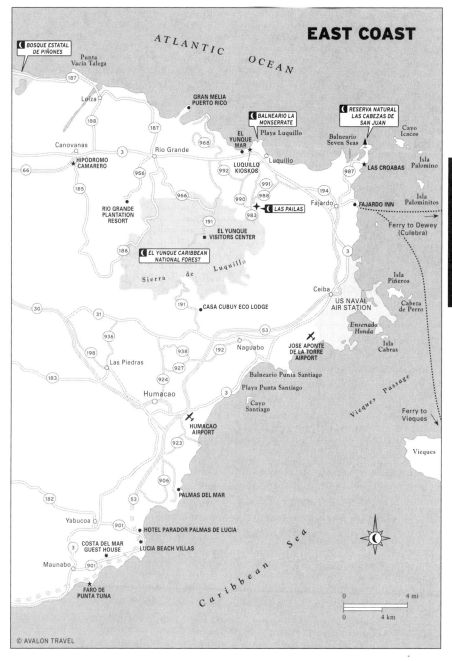

EAST COAST

EAST COAST

ATLANTIC OCEAN

BOSQUE ESTATAL DE PIÑONES

Punta Vacia Talega

Loíza

GRAN MELIA PUERTO RICO

BALNEARIO LA MONSERRATE

Playa Luquillo

RESERVA NATURAL LAS CABEZAS DE SAN JUAN

Cayo Icacos

Canovanas

Río Grande

EL YUNQUE MAR

Balneario Seven Seas

Isla Palomino

HIPÓDROMO CAMARERO

LUQUILLO KIOSKOS

Luquillo

LAS CROABAS

RIO GRANDE PLANTATION RESORT

Fajardo

FAJARDO INN

Isla Palominitos

LAS PAILAS

EL YUNQUE VISITORS CENTER

Ferry to Dewey (Culebra)

EL YUNQUE CARIBBEAN NATIONAL FOREST

Sierra de Luquillo

Ceiba

Isla Piñeros

US NAVAL AIR STATION

Cabeza de Perro

CASA CUBUY ECO LODGE

Ensenada Honda

Isla Cabras

Las Piedras

Naguabo

JOSE APONTE DE LA TORRE AIRPORT

Humacao

Balneario Punta Santiago

Playa Punta Santiago

Cayo Santiago

Vieques Passage

Ferry to Vieques

HUMACAO AIRPORT

Vieques

PALMAS DEL MAR

Yabucoa

HOTEL PARADOR PALMAS DE LUCIA

COSTA DEL MAR GUEST HOUSE

LUCIA BEACH VILLAS

Caribbean Sea

Maunabo

FARO DE PUNTA TUNA

0   4 mi

0   4 km

© AVALON TRAVEL

© SUZANNE VAN ATTEN

the pool and marina at El Conquistador Resort & Las Casitas Village in Fajardo

Caribbean National Forest is Puerto Rico's shining jewel. One of the world's most accessible rainforests, it offers hours of hiking, swimming, and bird-watching in a lush, tropical setting.

Coming in a close second as Puerto Rico's most popular attraction is Playa Luquillo, officially named **Balneario La Monserrate.** This is what picture postcards are made of: a long crescent of pristine sand gently lapped by the Atlantic Ocean and shaded by a thick palm grove.

Despite its proximity to San Juan, **Bosque Estatal de Piñones** is one of the most beautiful spots of coastal wilderness to be found on the island. It's easy to spend a day hiking or biking through the mangrove forest along the newly constructed bike path, kayaking through its lagoons, and swimming in the Atlantic surf beside palm-lined beaches.

Spending at least a long weekend in Fajardo is recommended for sports enthusiasts who want to enjoy all the boating, diving, fishing, and golfing to be had here. **Reserva Natural Las Cabezas de San Juan** is home to a diversity of ecosystems, as well as **Laguna Grande,** a bioluminescent lagoon that must be experienced at night.

Loíza and Piñones

Loíza holds a special place in Puerto Rican history because it was settled primarily by Yoruba slaves from Nigeria, who were brought over by the Spanish to work the island's sugar and coffee plantations. Emancipated slaves were relocated to Loíza, possibly because the east coast lacked much defense and it was hoped they could help repel foreign intruders. The town also served as a haven for escaped slaves who fled here in increasing numbers. Together they assimilated with the local Taíno Indians.

Loíza is a highly individual, tight-knit community rich in African-Caribbean culture, where traditional customs and art forms are preserved and cultivated. Unfortunately, Loíza is also severely economically depressed. There's virtually no industry, and many residents receive some form of public assistance. Not surprisingly, the crime rate is high, with the majority of offenses revolving around the thriving local drug trade.

Loíza's best option for economic viability may be in developing its tourism, because of its proximity to some of the island's most wonderfully unique cultural and natural gems. But that would undoubtedly change the nature of the municipality forever. For now, there's little American influence or tourist industry in Loíza, which makes it the kind of place you should experience sooner rather than later.

Loíza's big claim to fame is its annual weeklong festival, **Fiestas Tradicionales de Santiago Apóstol (St. James Carnival),** a not-to-be-missed celebration for young and old in late July. The festival's complex history, which dates to the Spanish Inquisition, is feted with parades, music, dance, food, and elaborately costumed street theater.

A big part of St. James Carnival is *bomba* and *plena* music, traditional drum-heavy styles of music and dance with African roots

that originated in Loíza and thrive there today. Some of the most celebrated artists of *bomba* and *plena* are from Loíza.

Among Loíza's greatest charms is its proximity to Piñones, the site of one of the most gorgeous pristine pieces of natural beauty on the island, **Bosque Estatal de Piñones.** This forest reserve features miles of wild coastline thick with palm groves, mangrove forests and canals, lagoons, sand dunes, and stretches of uninhabited beach as far as the eye can see.

Accommodations are limited to privately owned vacation rentals in Loíza, and dining options are best found in Piñones, which has a dizzying array of terrific roadside food kiosks and several decent restaurants specializing in seafood.

SIGHTS
Iglesia San Patricio
Iglesia San Patricio (Calle Espíritu Santo, Loíza, 787/876-2229, Mon.-Fri. 8 A.M.-4 P.M.) is claimed to be Puerto Rico's oldest church in continuous use, founded in 1670. It is also known as Espíritu Santo.

☀ Bosque Estatal de Piñones
There's no other place in Puerto Rico like the spectacular Bosque Estatal de Piñones (along Carr. 187 between San Juan and Loíza, 787/791-7750, office Mon.-Fri. 7 A.M.-3:30 P.M.). Stretching from the eastern tip of Isla Verde, San Juan, to the town of Loíza, this pristine reserve is a natural wonderland of deserted beaches; mangrove, pine, and palm forests; sand dunes, coral reefs; bays; salt flats; and lagoons. An important part of the island ecosystem, Piñones is home to 46 species of birds, including a variety of herons and pelicans.

Boca de Cangrejos (just east of the Luis Muñoz Marín International Airport in San Juan and the Cangrejos Yacht Club) is the

EAST COAST

gateway to Piñones from San Juan. At first glance, it looks like a shantytown of wooden shacks and concrete sheds barely clinging to a rocky point that juts into the sea. But you shouldn't bypass Boca de Cangrejos. It contains some of the best and cheapest local food you'll find, from stuffed fritters to all varieties of seafood. Walk from kiosk to kiosk and try a little bit of everything. Many items cost only $1. Expect crowds and a party atmosphere on weekends and holidays. Just east of Boca de Cangrejos along Carretera 187 are also several bars and nightclubs that keep the place hopping, day and night. Some people caution against venturing here at night, but it can be a fun, adventurous immersion into the local scene if you keep your wits about you. And definitely stop here during the day to stock up on provisions before entering the forest.

Carretera 187 is a narrow two-lane road that winds through Piñones to Loíza from San Juan. Tucked between the thick clusters of palms along the coastal side of the road are unmarked sandy turn-ins that lead to the beach, where you can park and walk down the dunes into the water to swim. You'll start to encounter the best swimming beaches around kilometer 9, where the reef recedes from the beach. Another option for a good swimming spot is **Vacia Talega,** a small unmarked crescent beach visible from the road on Carretera 187 just before you cross the river into Loíza. It has a small sandy parking lot but no facilities. This is also a good fishing spot. Piñones is also a popular place for surfing, especially at **Aviones,** just past Boca de Cangrejos.

In addition to swimming, surfing, and fishing, a major draw for Piñones is the **Paseo Piñones Bike Path,** a six-mile-long system of paved trails and boardwalks, which provides an excellent way to explore the forest. Bikes are available for rent at the restaurant **El**

pinchos cooking at Boca de Cangrejos in Bosque Estatal de Piñones

Pulpo Loco (Carr. 187, km 4.5, 787/791-8382, 10 A.M.-6 P.M.) for about $25 a day.

Venture away from the coast into the forest's interior and you encounter two lagoons, **Laguna de Piñones** and **Laguna la Torrecilla.** The best way to explore these rich mangrove ecosystems is by kayak. To reach the launch site, turn inland off Carretera 187 at kilometer 9 and follow the sign pointing to the Bosque Estatal de Piñones office. A couple of tour operators in the area offer kayak tours of the lagoons and hiking tours of the forest.

It is possible to take a bus (B-40 or B-45) from Isla Verde to Boca de Cangrejos or catch a taxi, but the best option for exploring Piñones is to drive there. Just be sure to lock your car, keep it in sight as much as possible, and don't leave anything of value visible inside.

SPORTS AND RECREATION

Piñones Ecotours (Carr. 187 at Boca de Cangrejos Bridge, 787/272-0005, fax 787/789-1730, www.ecotours.com) offers biking, hiking, and kayak tours in Bosque Estatal de Piñones. Gear rental is also available.

ENTERTAINMENT AND EVENTS

Fiestas Tradicionales de Santiago Apóstol (St. James Carnival) is one of Puerto Rico's liveliest and most colorful festivals, spanning about six days around July 25. Based in Plaza de Recreo de Loíza, the festival features lots of costumed parades, dances, street pageants, concerts, and traditional food vendors. Ostensibly it's a celebration of the town's patron saint, but religion takes a back seat to this raucous street party, which has origins in 13th-century Spain but is heavily influenced by African traditions. At the center of the celebration is a street pageant in which costumed caballeros (Spanish knights), masked *vejigantes* (Moors), and *locas* (trickster men dressed as old women) reenact Spain's defeat of the Moors. The colorful *vejigante* mask, made from coconut shell, wire, and papier-mâché and featuring protruding horns, has become a highly collectible, iconic symbol of the festival and Puerto Rico as a whole, and there are several local artisans in the area who produce them. St. James Carnival is also a prime place to revel in the African-influenced *bomba* music, which is performed late into the night.

SHOPPING

Estudio de Arte Samuel Lind (Carr. 187, km 6.6, Loíza, 787/876-1494, fax 787/876-1499, www.studioporto.com/guestsamuellind, Wed.-Sun. 10 A.M.-5 P.M.) is open to the public for the sale of paintings, prints, and sculptures by artist Samuel Lind.

Artesanías Castor Ayala (Carr. 187, km 6.6, 787/876-1130, rayala@libertypr.net, daily 10 A.M.-6 P.M.) sells highly collectible *vejigante* masks made by second-generation master mask-maker Raul Ayala.

ACCOMMODATIONS

The best option for accommodations in Loíza and Piñones is an **apartment rental** in one of the many new, modern, gated condominium developments that have cropped up. Several are on the beach. For information, visit www.vacationrentals411.com, www.rentalo.com, and www.vrbo.com.

FOOD

Venturing into Boca de Cangrejos for the first time can be a daunting experience, especially on the weekend. Located just east of San Juan International Airport on the western edge of Piñones, Boca de Cangrejos is a chaotic tangle of cars and pedestrians jockeying for position as people flock here to chow down at their favorite food kiosk, of which there are dozens and dozens. Like the Luquillo Kioskos, the food vendors specialize in fried street food like *alcapurrias* and *empanadas,* but Luquillo is as orderly as an English queue compared to the free-for-all at Boca de Cangrejos. The traffic moves at a snail's pace, parking is limited, lines for food can be long. But it's worth every bite.

EAST COAST

© SUZANNE VAN ATTEN

rolling *alcapurrias* in sea grape leaves at Donde Olga's

Choosing the best option from the scores of restaurants and fry shacks in Piñones isn't easy, but here's a tip: Skip establishments where the food is sitting under a heat lamp in a glass box and find a place where the cooks are making and frying the stuff while you wait.

◖ **Donde Olga's** (Carr. 187, km 5.0, 787/791-6900, fry shack and bar Sun.-Thurs. 11 A.M.-midnight, Fri.-Sat. 11 A.M.-3 A.M.; dining room Mon.-Wed. 11:30 A.M.-3 P.M. and 6:30-9:45 P.M., Thurs.-Sun. 11:30 A.M.-9:45 P.M., $2-26) is just such a place. If you're driving in from San Juan, pass the heart of Boca de Cangrejos and stay on Carretera 187 about a quarter-mile or so, and you'll find Donde Olga's? on the right. The large open-air dining area is located right beside the outdoor kitchen, where you can watch the cooks roll up *alcapurrias* in sea grape leaves and fry them in huge kettles over an open fire. Get in line and order your selection of fritters at the walkup bar, where you can also get super-cold cans of

Medalla beer. And don't forget to douse your piping hot goodies with a squirt or two from the spicy bottles of *pique* that dot the communal tables. If you want table service and a proper meal, go inside the dining room, where you can order grouper casserole, paella, and lamb chops.

The majority of eateries in Piñones are walk-up fry shacks, so one thing **Roger's Restaurant** (Carr. 187, km 0.05, 787/603-4296 or 787/791-2549, Sun.-Mon. and Wed.-Thurs. 11 A.M.-11 P.M., Fri.-Sat. 11 A.M.-2 A.M., $9-20) has going for it is that it's a full-service restaurant with indoor seating and ample parking. And if you like seafood you're in luck. The menu features all varieties, including conch, octopus, marlin, snapper, shrimp, lobster, and crabs, served in soups, salads, with rice, in *mofongo,* fried, and more. There's a full bar.

Soleil Beach Club (Carr. 187, km 4.8, Piñones, 787/253-1033, www.soleilbeach-club.com, Sun.-Thurs. 11 A.M.-10 P.M.,

Fri.-Sat. 11 A.M.-midnight, $10-25) is more upscale than the typical Piñones restaurant. Soleil Beach Club is an open-air waterfront eatery serving an ambitious menu of Caribbean dishes heavy on seafood, including shrimp in *mojito* sauce and salmon in curry tarragon butter.

INFORMATION AND SERVICES

For health and beauty needs, there is a **Walgreens** (1 Calle 3, Loíza, 787/256-2626). Banking services are available at **Banco Popular** (65 Calle San Patricio, Loíza, 787/876-3535, www.bancopopular.com). A **post office** is located at 64 Calle San Patricio, Suite 1.

GETTING THERE AND AROUND

Piñones is 19.2 kilometers or 12 miles east of San Juan. Take Highway 26 east to Carretera 187 east. Loíza is 39 kilometers or 24 miles east of San Juan. Take Highway 26 east to Carretera 66 east to Carretera 188 north.

Juan Carlos Transportation (787/876-3628 or 787/374-1056, Mon.-Fri. 8 A.M.-5 P.M.) offers taxi service and tours around Loíza. For 24-hour service, call 787/467-1222.

Río Grande

Río Grande has come into its own as a luxury resort destination in recent years. It's now home to three large properties, the newest one being a super-luxe St. Regis. And Marriott has another one under construction. The 371-room hotel with two beaches and a marina is scheduled to open in 2013. Several of the area's resorts offer discounted land-and-air packages on travel deal websites. In addition, several of the resorts offer all-inclusive packages so you can pay one price for accommodations and meals.

Where there are resorts, there are golf courses, and Río Grande boasts several world-class ones. The Trump International Golf Club at the Gran Melia hosts the annual PGA Tour Puerto Rico Open.

But even before the resorts and golf courses, Río Grande was a popular tourist destination because it lays claim to 45 percent of the Caribbean National Forest, including the popular El Yunque Recreation Area.

Meanwhile, the tiny community of **Palmer,** located at the base of El Yunque, is becoming something of an arts district. A number of shops, galleries, and eateries have opened up to serve the growing number of visitors who are coming to Río Grande to stay instead of just visiting El Yunque for the day and leaving.

◖ EL YUNQUE CARIBBEAN NATIONAL FOREST

It is commonly called El Yunque rainforest, but the official name of this spectacular natural preserve is the Caribbean National Forest. The name El Yunque technically refers to the forest's second-highest peak (3,469 feet), and it's also the name of the forest's recreational area. But regardless of its moniker, it is without a doubt Puerto Rico's crowning jewel of natural treasures.

The only tropical forest in the U.S. National Forest System—not to mention the smallest and most ecologically diverse—the Caribbean National Forest is a must-see for visitors to Puerto Rico. Nearly half of the 28,000-acre area contains some of the only virgin forest remaining on the island, which was completely covered in forest when Columbus arrived in 1493. It also contains one of the world's most accessible rainforests.

El Yunque is about 35 minutes east of San Juan off Carretera 3. Go south on Carretera 191 and it will take you into the forest and to El Portal Tropical Forest Center.

History

The name El Yunque is believed to be a Spanish

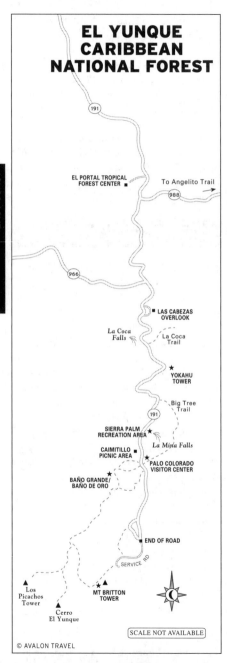

EL YUNQUE CARIBBEAN NATIONAL FOREST

191

EL PORTAL TROPICAL
FOREST CENTER ■ To Angelito Trail →
988

966

■ LAS CABEZAS
OVERLOOK

La Coca
Falls

La Coca
Trail

★ YOKAHU
TOWER

Big Tree
Trail

191

SIERRA PALM
RECREATION AREA ★

CAIMITILLO ■
PICNIC AREA

La Mina Falls

★ PALO COLORADO
VISITOR CENTER

BAÑO GRANDE/
BAÑO DE ORO ★

■ END OF ROAD

SERVICE RD

▲ Los
Picachos
Tower

▲▲ MT BRITTON
TOWER

▲ Cerro
El Yunque

SCALE NOT AVAILABLE

© AVALON TRAVEL

derivation of the Taíno Indian name for the area, Yuke, which means "white earth" because the mountaintops are often covered in clouds. The Taíno believed that El Yunque was a sacred place and home to their gods, the most powerful and revered being Yuquiyu, who protected mortals from evil. The Taíno visited the forest to cut trees, vines, and palm fronds to make canoes, baskets, and roofing thatch, and to gather its abundance of fruits, roots, and medicinal plants. It is also believed that religious ceremonies and rituals were held here. Many petroglyphs can be found carved into rocks and boulders throughout the forest.

Upon the arrival of Spanish settlers, attempts were made to exploit the forest's resources. The timber industry initiated forestation, and copper mining was pursued. But in 1876, King Alfonso XII of Spain decreed 12,300 acres of the forest a preserve, making it one of the oldest forest reserves in the western hemisphere. In 1903, after the United States gained control of Puerto Rico following the Spanish-American War, President Theodore Roosevelt designated the area the Luquillo Forest Reserve, and it was eventually expanded to its current size. Further securing its safekeeping, the United Nations designated it as part of the international network of biosphere reserves in 1976.

Flora

More than 240 inches of rain—100 billion gallons!—falls annually in the forest, making it a rich habitat for moisture-loving flora and fauna. It is home to more than 1,000 plant species, including 50 types of orchids, 150 ferns, and 240 species of trees, 23 of which are endemic only to El Yunque.

The Caribbean National Forest is in the Sierra de Luquillo, with mountains ranging in height from 600 feet to more than 3,500 feet above sea level, and it contains four distinct forests. Most of the area is covered in **tabonuco forest,** found in areas up to 2,000 feet above

© SUZANNE VAN ATTEN

ferns in El Yunque Caribbean National Forest

is the **cloud forest,** also known as the dwarf or elfin forest. This is a nearly mystical, otherworldly place where constant wind and moisture have stunted and twisted the dense vegetation. Roots snake across the windswept ground in thick tangles, and the trees, which don't exceed 12 feet in height, are covered with moss and algae. Here you also find many species of ferns and bromeliads, which bloom with brilliant red flowers. The air is cool, and visibility is often obscured by misty cloud covering.

Fauna

The majority of El Yunque's wildlife falls into three categories: birds, reptiles, and amphibians. There are more than 50 species of birds in the forest; the rarest and most beloved is the Puerto Rican parrot, which is classified as endangered. In 1987 an extensive program was initiated to try to bolster the population, though its success has been limited so far. Today there are about 35 Puerto Rican parrots living in the Caribbean National Forest. You're highly unlikely to spot one, but just in case, keep your eyes peeled for a foot-long, bright green Amazon parrot with blue wing tips, white eye rings, and a red band above its beak. When in flight, it emits a repetitive call that sounds like a bugle.

Other species of birds found in El Yunque include the sharp-skinned hawk, the broadwing hawk, the bananaquit, the Puerto Rican tody, the red-legged thrush, the Puerto Rican lizard-cuckoo, the green mango, the Puerto Rican emerald, the Puerto Rican woodpecker, the elfin woods warbler, the Puerto Rican bullfinch, and the stripe-headed tanager.

Even more beloved than the Puerto Rican parrot is the tiny coqui tree frog. There are 16 varieties of the species on the island, 13 of which live in El Yunque. You're only slightly more likely to see a coqui than a Puerto Rican parrot, but you're sure to hear its distinctive "co-QUI" call, particularly after a rain or at dusk. Even more elusive is the Puerto Rican

sea level. This is the most dramatic part of the forest and site of the true rainforest. The dominant tree species is the *tabonuco,* which grows up to 125 feet in height and is distinguished by its huge dark-green canopy and straight trunk, which has a smooth whitish bark.

The **sierra palm forest** is found along steep slopes and near rivers and creeks more than 1,500 feet above sea level. Its dominant tree, the sierra palm, is easily identified by the thick skirt of exposed roots around its base, which is an adaptation that allows it to thrive in the wet soil. The *palo colorado* **forest** is found in valleys and slopes at an altitude between 2,000 feet and 3,000 feet. The dominant tree is the *palo colorado,* also known as swamp cyrilla, which is characterized by its thick twisted trunk and red bark. Most of these trees have been around for ages—some reportedly more than 1,000 years.

On the uppermost peaks of El Yunque, between 2,500 and 3,500 feet above sea level, boa, a nonpoisonous snake that reaches lengths exceeding six feet.

Probably the most likely creature to be spotted in El Yunque is one of its many species of lizards. They are as common as ants at a picnic. The large Puerto Rican giant green lizard, which can grow as big as a cat, is commonly found along the limestone hills, and the smaller anoli, of which there are eight species, are ubiquitous.

The only mammals native to Puerto Rico are bats, of which there are 11 species in El Yunque. But rats and mongooses have been introduced to the island and now live in the forest. The rats were inadvertently brought over on trade ships and thrived on the island's sugar plantations. The mongooses were imported in a misguided attempt to control the rat population. They are vicious creatures and carriers of rabies, so give them a wide berth if you encounter them.

© SUZANNE VAN ATTEN

La Coca Falls

Recreation

The main thoroughfare through El Yunque is Carretera 191, which once completely bisected the forest from north to south, but recurrent landslides convinced engineers that the soil was too unstable to sustain a roadway at the forest's highest peaks. The forest is still accessible from the north and south on Carretera 191, but its midsection has been permanently closed. Most visitors to El Yunque drive in from the north end of Carretera 191 because it passes through the El Yunque Recreation Area. But there are efforts under way to close the north end of Carretera 191 and replace car traffic in the forest with a public transportation system to reduce the damaging effects of auto emissions.

The official entrance to the forest is **El Portal Tropical Forest Center** (Carr. 191, km 4, 787/888-1880, daily 9 A.M.-5 P.M., $3 adults, $1.50 children 4-12, free children under 4), a striking piece of architecture designed by the local firm Sierra Cardona Ferrer. Built in 1996, the bright white building is a modern interpretation of the traditional pavilion-style structure seen throughout the island. An elevated walkway leads visitors to its open-air interior filled with interactive educational displays. Features include an excellent gift shop heavy on educational materials, bathroom facilities, and a small screening room that continuously shows a film about the forest alternately in English and Spanish. This is also the place to obtain camping permits and arrange guided tours.

Travel farther south into the forest and you enter **El Yunque Recreation Area,** which encompasses El Yunque peak and the surrounding area, and which contains the forest's major tourist sights. The first stop you encounter is **La Coca Falls** (Carr. 191, km 8.1), the most accessible and photographed waterfall in the forest. It has an 85-foot drop and a constant flow of rushing water. There's plenty of parking space and a small snack bar nearby because this is also the trailhead for La Coca Trail.

The next stop on the route is **Yokahu Tower** (Carr. 191, km 8.8), a 69-foot-high observation tower built in 1963 from where you have terrific views of the forest and the Atlantic Ocean. Farther south is **Sierra Palm Recreation Area** (Carr. 191, km 11.3), offering more food concessions, restrooms, and a picnic area. Across the street is the Caimitillo Trailhead. The last stop is **Palo Colorado Visitors Center** (Carr. 191, km 11.8), an information center with still another snack bar and picnic area. Across the street is a short hike to **Baño Grande,** a picturesque stone pool built in the 1930s by the Civilian Conservation Corps. Slightly south of Palo Colorado is another pool, **Baño de Oro,** also built by the CCC. Although visitors are no longer allowed to swim in the pools, they're lovely spots that provide great photo opportunities. Palo Colorado is also the site of La Mina Trailhead and the Baño de Oro Trailhead.

Just before your reach the end of Carretera 191, the road intersects at kilometer 12.6 with a small loop road called Carretera 9938. This road takes you to the trailhead for Mount Britton Trail, which leads to **Mount Britton Tower,** built by the CCC. If visibility is good, you can see the south coast from here. From Mount Britton Trail, you can pick up the Mount Britton Spur Trail to the observation deck on the peak of El Yunque and **Los Picachos Tower,** another CCC tower.

Despite what many visitors might think, there is more to the Caribbean National Forest than El Yunque Recreation Center. In fact, the forest stretches way beyond Río Grande into the municipalities of Ceiba, Canóvanos, Fajardo, Naguabo, Luquillo, and Las Piedras. Many locals actually prefer the southern and western sides of the forest because they're less likely to attract busloads of tourists and they feature plenty of waterfalls and natural pools for swimming. To explore the western side, take Carretera 186 south from Carretera 3. To explore the southern side from Naguabo, proceed west on Carretera 31 and go north on Carretera 191.

Trails

Although it's possible to do a quick drive-by tour of El Yunque, the only way to fully appreciate its beauty and majesty is to park the car and hike into the jungle. It doesn't take more than a couple of dozen steps to become completely enveloped by the dense lush foliage. One of the greatest joys of hiking in El Yunque is the sound. Here the aural assault of the 21st century is replaced by a palpable hush and the comforting, sensual, eternal sounds of water-dripping, gurgling, rushing, raining. It's more restorative than a dozen trips to the spa.

There are 12 trails spanning about 14 miles in El Yunque. Many of the trails are paved or covered in gravel because the constant rain and erosive soil would require continuous maintenance to keep them passable. Nonetheless, hiking boots with good tread are a necessity. Even paved trails

© SUZANNE VAN ATTEN

a walking trail in El Yunque Caribbean National Forest

EAST COAST

can be slippery and muddy. The warm air and high humidity also require frequent hydration, so bring plenty of water. And naturally, it rains a lot, so light rain gear is recommended. Avoid streams during heavy rains as flash floods can occur. Primitive camping is permitted in some areas. Permits are required and can be obtained at El Portal Tropical Forest Center.

The following trails are found in El Yunque Recreation Area. All trail lengths and hiking times are approximate.

Angelito Trail (0.5 mile, 15 minutes, easy, clay and gravel) crosses a stream and leads to Las Damas, a natural pool in the Mameyes River. To get to the trailhead, proceed south on Carretera 191 just past El Portal and turn left on Carretera 988, 0.25 mile past Puente Roto Bridge.

La Coca Trail (2 miles, 1 hour, moderate to strenuous, gravel) starts at La Coca Falls and requires navigating over rocks to cross a couple of streams.

La Mina Trail (0.5 mile, 25 minutes, moderate, paved and steps) starts at Palo Colorado and follows the La Mina River, ending at La Mina waterfall, where it connects with Big Tree Trail.

Big Tree Trail (1 mile, 35 minutes, moderate, paved and steps) is an interpretive trail with signs in Spanish and English. It passes through *tabonuco* forest, over streams, and ends at La Mina waterfall, where it connects to La Mina Trail. The trailhead is by a small parking area at Carretera 191, kilometer 10.2.

Caimitillo Trail (0.5 mile, 25 minutes, easy, paved and steps) begins at Sierra Palm Recreation Area and crosses a stream. Along the way you'll pass a picnic area and structures used by the Puerto Rican parrot recovery program. It connects to the Palo Colorado Visitors Center and El Yunque Trail.

Baño de Oro Trail (0.25 mile, 20 minutes, moderate, paved and gravel) starts just south of the Palo Colorado Visitors Center and passes by Baño de Oro before connecting with El Yunque Trail.

El Yunque Trail (2.5 miles, 1 hour, strenuous, paved and gravel) is one of the forest's longest and most strenuous hikes. It starts a little north of the Palo Colorado Visitors Center and climbs to an altitude of 3,400 feet. Along the way it passes several rain shelters, through the cloud forest, and ends at the peak of El Yunque. The lower part of the trail is accessible from Caimitillo Trail and Baño de Oro Trail. The higher reaches of the trail connect with Mount Britton Trail and Los Picachos Tower Trail.

Mount Britton Trail (1 mile, 45 minutes, strenuous, paved) starts at Carretera 9938, a loop road at the end of Carretera 191. It is an uphill hike through *tabonuco,* sierra palm, and cloud forests. The trail crosses two streams and runs along a service road for a short distance—if you're not sure which way to go, just keep heading straight up. It ends at the Mount Britton Tower, built in the 1930s by the Civilian Conservation Corps.

Mount Britton Spur (1 mile, 30 minutes, moderate, paved) connects Mount Britton Trail to El Yunque Trail.

Los Picachos Trail (0.25 mile, 25 minutes, strenuous, unpaved and steps) is a steep ascent from El Yunque Trail to an observation deck built by the CCC.

The forest's remaining two trails are outside El Yunque Recreation Center on the western side of the forest. The trails are unpaved, muddy, not maintained, and often overgrown in parts. Long sleeves and pants are recommended for protection against brush, some of which can cause skin irritation on contact. These trails are for adventurous hikers who really want to get away from it all.

Trade Winds Trail (4 miles, 4 hours, strenuous, primitive) is the forest's longest trail. To reach the trailhead, drive all the way through El Yunque Recreation Area to the end of Carretera 191 where the road is closed. Be mindful not to block the gate. Walk past the gate 0.25 mile to the trailhead. The trail ascends to the peak of El Toro, the highest peak in the forest, where it connects with the El Toro Trail.

El Toro Trail (2 miles, 3 hours, difficult, primitive) starts at Carretera 186, kilometer 10.6, and traverses *tabonuco,* sierra palm, and cloud forests. It connects with the Trade Winds Trail.

SPORTS AND RECREATION
Golf

What made Río Grande a fertile, well-hydrated place for growing sugarcane and coffee has made it an excellent place for golf courses today.

Río Mar Beach Resort (Carr. 968, km 1.4, 787/888-8811, www.wyndhamriomar.com, 6:30 A.M.-6:30 P.M., greens fees $150-175 for resort guests, $185-200 nonguests, call 24 hours in advance, club rentals $50-60) has two courses. Ocean Course, built in 1975 by George and Tom Fazio, offers excellent views of the Atlantic Ocean and one of the best-rated holes (16) on the island. River Course, an 18-hole grass course with water in play, built in 1997 by Greg Norman, runs along the Río Mameyes. There's also a 35,000-square-foot clubhouse. Golf club rentals are available.

Trump International Golf Club (100 Club House Dr., Rio Grande, 787/657-2000, www.trumpgolfclubpuertorico.com, daily dawn-5 P.M.), formerly the Coco Beach Golf and Country Club, offers 36 holes of oceanside golf on courses designed by Tom Kite and Bruce Besse. Food and beverage service is provided on the course and in the clubhouse, which also has a pro shop. The club has a putting green and driving range as well. It has hosted the PGA Tour's Puerto Rico Open on multiple occasions, including 2012.

Robert Trent Jones Jr. Golf Course (St. Regis Bahía Beach Resort, Carr. 187, km 4.2, Río Grande, 787/957-1510, www.starwoodhotels.com, greens fees $225-275, club rentals $55) is a par 72, 6,979-yard course that meanders around saltwater lagoons and oceanfront views, with views of the rainforest rising overhead.

Tennis

Peter Burwash International Tennis (Río Mar Beach Resort, 6000 Río Mar Blvd., Río Grande, 787/888-6000, ext. 1140511, www.wyndhamriomar.com, court rental $25 single, $35 double, $3 an hour for lights, racquet rental $10) features 11 Har-Tru surface courts and two hard courts, four equipped with lights for nighttime play. Lessons, clinics, and packages are available. Appropriate tennis attire is required.

ENTERTAINMENT
Casinos

There are two casinos in Río Grande. **Gran Melia Puerto Rico** (1000 Coco Beach Blvd., Carr. 3 at Carr. 955, 787/809-1770, www.gran-melia-puerto-rico.com, daily 10 A.M.-2 A.M.) has a small casino with 130 slot machines, blackjack, progressive blackjack, roulette, craps, poker, and Texas hold 'em. **Río Mar Beach Resort** (Carr. 968, km 1.4, 787/888-6000, www.wyndhamriomar.com, daily 10 A.M.-2 A.M.) is even smaller space-wise, but it has 190 slots, blackjack, roulette, craps, Caribbean poker, Texas hold 'em, and three-card poker.

Horse Racing

Hipódromo Camarero (Carr. 3, km 15.3, Canóvanas, 787/641-6060, http://hipodromo-camarero.com, Wed., and Fri.-Sun., admission free) is technically in the municipality of Canóvanas, just east of Río Grande. The first race begins 2:45 P.M. except on Sunday, when it begins at 2:15 P.M.; the last race is at 6 P.M. Watch the races with food and beverage service from the grandstand, the clubhouse, or the Terrace Room restaurant. You can also watch the action on live monitors in the Winners Sports Bar.

SHOPPING

Coqui International (54 Calle Principal, Palmer, off Carr. 191 on the way to El Yunque, 787/887-0770, www.coquistores.com, Mon.-Sat. 10 A.M.-6 P.M., Sun. noon-6 P.M.) is a huge gallery selling a wide selection of crafts by local artisans as well as artisans from Haiti and the

Dominican Republic. It's a great place to buy contemporary and traditional *vejigante* masks, plus paintings, hammocks, food items, candles, and jewelry. Technically it is located in the community of Palmer, but it's on the way to the El Yunque rainforest. If you're traveling east on Carretera 3 from San Juan, turn right on Carretera 191 then left on Calle Principal; the store is on the left.

Caribbean Trading Company (4 Calle Principal, Palmer, 787/888-2762 or 800/576-1770, www.caribbeantrading.com, daily 10 A.M.-6 P.M.) is a great place to stock up on the flavors of the island. The shelves are stocked with local spices, hot sauces, coffees, and cigars, as well as CDs, books, and bath products.

Maji Lina Gallery & Art Center (57 Calle Principal, Palmer, 787/657-8962, www.majilinagallery.com, Mon.-Sat. 10 A.M.-5 P.M.) is a full-service art gallery representing several local painters, ceramicists, and sculptors. It also provides framing services and sells some crafts.

ACCOMMODATIONS

Gran Melia Puerto Rico (1000 Coco Beach Blvd., Carr. 3 at Carr. 955, 787/809-1770 or 866/436-3542, fax 787/807-1785, www.gran-melia-puerto-rico.com, $212-312 s/d, $337 suite, $1,300 oceanfront villa, plus taxes and resort fees, all-inclusive packages available) is a large 500-unit luxury resort, formerly known as Paradisus Puerto Rico. All accommodations are suites or villas and come with balconies or terraces, marble baths, air-conditioning, hair dryers, room safes, minibars, satellite TV, high-speed Internet, and room service. It has three restaurants serving Puerto Rican, Asian, and Italian fare, as well as two bars. Amenities include a lovely lagoon-style swimming pool, a spa and health club, three lighted tennis courts, and access to Trump International Golf Club. Guests can upgrade to what's called Royal Service to receive butler service and access to a private lounge and adults-only pool.

Río Mar Beach Resort (6000 Río Mar Blvd., Río Grande, 787/888-6000 or 877/999-3223, www.wyndhamriomar.com, $177-355 s/d, $455-1,055 suite, plus resort fees and taxes) is part of the Wyndham Grand Hotel chain. It is a massive property with nearly 700 rooms and suites appointed with lots of amenities, including 42-inch flat-screen HDTVs, high-speed Internet, cable TV, mini bar, air-conditioning, coffeemaker, and refrigerators upon request. Pets up to 20 pounds are permitted. Resort amenities include two oceanfront pools, a mile of secluded beach, seven restaurants, a casino, Mandara Spa, the Peter Burwash International Tennis Center, and two 18-hole golf courses.

◀ **St. Regis Bahía Beach Resort** (Carr. 187, km 4.2, Río Grande, 787/809-8000, www.starwoodhotels.com, $709-889 s/d, $1,470-1,500 suite, plus resort fees and tax) is a tropical oasis of moneyed luxury named one of *Forbes* magazine's Best New Hotels of 2011. The 483-acre seaside property boasts Fern, a restaurant from the celebrated French chef Jean-Georges Vongerichten; a golf course designed by Robert Trent Jones Jr.; nearly two miles of pristine sandy beach; and butler service. With only 139 units, there is plenty of space to get away from it all in style. Other amenities include a terraced, oceanfront swimming pool with cabanas, walking trails, kayaking, snorkeling, sailing, diving, windsurfing, fishing, a tennis center, a spa, and the Iguana Kids Club for children ages 5-12.

FOOD

The Grille Room (Río Mar Beach Resort, 6000 Río Mar Blvd., Río Grande, 787/888-6000, $36-55) is an Argentine-style grill located in the Club House at Río Mar Beach Resort. For $36, diners select three different meats. Choices include chorizo, lamb chops, sweetbreads, and rib-eye, among other meaty options. Sides such as grilled asparagus and sautéed spinach with blue cheese are served à la carte. Other entrée options include New York strip and asiago-crusted sea bass. All beef is USDA certified Angus, and the restaurant serves an extensive wine list, with an emphasis on Argentine wines.

Celebrated chef Jean-Georges Vongerichten, whose eponymous restaurant in New York City earned 3 Michelin stars, created **Fern** (St. Regis Bahía Beach Resort, Carr. 187, km 4.2, Río Grande, 787/809-8100 or 787/809-8000, www.fernrestaurant.com, breakfast daily 7-11:30 A.M., dinner Mon.-Thurs. 6-10 P.M., Fri.-Sat. 6-11 P.M., $18-46), the signature restaurant at the St. Regis Bahía Beach Resort. Hailed for his simple, well-sourced cuisine, his menu features roasted grouper, slow-cooked salmon, and veal Milanese among the entrées, all of which are served with select side dishes or à la carte for diners who like to mix things up. There is a five-course tasting menu for $78 or a three-course prix fixe meal for $48. Save room for dessert. Options include passion fruit soufflé with dark chocolate sorbet and crunchy milk chocolate mousse with banana-lime ice cream.

Most of the notable dining options in Río Grande are limited to the restaurants at the resorts, but there is one local nonhotel option worth checking out: **Antojitos Puertorriqueños** (#60, Carr. 968, Barrio Las Coles, 787/888-7378, daily 10 A.M.-9 P.M.) serves excellent local cuisine, including stuffed *mofongo* and *tostones,* rice and crab, *chillo* in garlic sauce, and salmon. Check out the changing exhibits of work by local artists.

And if you want to try some excellent Caribbean-style sangria, pay a visit to **Los Paraos Liquors** (54 Calle Pimentel, off Carr. 3, Río Grande, 787/888-3320, daily noon-2 A.M.), a modest-looking roadside liquor store with a popular outdoor stand-up bar. Those in the know flock here to buy the outstanding homemade sangria, a delicious pale-pink concoction packed with fresh fruit juices and sold in recycled liquor bottles for $7.50 apiece. Stock up! Once you try it, you'll want more. If traveling east on Carretera 3, turn left by the giant parrot sculptures onto Carretera 187R, and then take an immediate left on the one-way street. It's on the right-look for the large sign above the awning.

INFORMATION AND SERVICES

For pharmaceutical needs, there is a **Walgreens** (Carr. 3, km 29.1, 787/888-8755). Banking services are available at **Banco Popular** (Carr. 3, km 22.2, 787/887-3535, www.bancopopular.com). The **post office** is at 99 Calle Pimental, Suite 1.

GETTING THERE AND AROUND

Transportation is available through **Río Grande Taxi Service** (787/967-4119). Río Grande is 44 kilometers or 27 miles east of San Juan. Take Highway 26 east to Highway 66 east to Carretera 3 east.

EAST COAST

Luquillo

Luquillo attracts visitors from far and wide for two reasons. One is its beautiful public beach, commonly referred to as Playa Luquillo, although its proper name is Balneario La Monserrate. Many consider it one of the finest beaches on the main island. The other reason is for the Luquillo Kioskos, more than 50 food vendors serving some of the very best street food available in Puerto Rico.

Luquillo's town center has an uncommonly large plaza with very little charm, so there's little reason to tarry here. Instead, head over to the coastal side of town along La Pared, the seawall. On the street side is a cluster of restaurants and bars. On the sea side is a popular surfing spot.

◖ LAS PAILAS

Las Pailas (Carr. 983, Barrio Yuquiyu, Luquillo) is about as off the beaten path as you can get. This natural water slide is formed by a mountain stream cascading over a smooth but rocky descent that bottoms out in a chest-deep pool of crystal-clear water. Locals come here on weekends to mount the "horse," a saddle-shaped rock at the top of the descent, and slide down the rocks, landing in the natural pool below. If you're lucky, you'll see expert showboaters slide down on their bellies, face first, or even on foot. This is not an official tourist site. There are no signs, facilities, parking, or rules, although visitors should be mindful of respecting the property and not leave any trash behind. Although it's primarily a locals' spot, visitors are welcome, especially if they prove their mettle by taking a ride. To get here from San Juan, take Highway 3 east. Turn right on Carretera 992 and go toward Sabana, and then turn right on Carretera 983. Las Pailas is behind the homes that line the right side of the road. The best access is behind house number 6051, distinguished by a cyclone fence. Homeowners along this stretch

allow visitors to park for $5 and will point you toward a well-worn path that takes you to the nearby shoals. If you get lost, just ask.

BEACHES
◖ Balneario La Monserrate

Balneario La Monserrate, or Playa Luquillo (Carr. 3, east of San Juan, 787/889-5871, daily 8:30 A.M.-5:30 P.M.), is the kind of place people dream of when they envision an island paradise. A thick grove of tall, shady coconut palm trees sways in the breeze over a mile-long wide crescent of pristine sand gently lapped by the Atlantic Ocean. The only signs of civilization are a clean modern complex of bathrooms and showers, some covered picnic shelters, and a couple of snack bars serving fritters and piña coladas. Camping is permitted in a grassy area with picnic tables and grills on the western side. Rates are $10, $17 with electricity. Call 787/889-5871 for reservations.

The only drawback to this idyllic spot is that it gets packed with beachgoers on weekends, holidays, and during the summer, when beach chairs and umbrellas are available for rent and lifeguards keep an eye on things. If you want solitude, visit on a weekday during the low season, and you'll practically have the place to yourself.

On the far eastern side of the beach is **Mar Sin Barreras** (Sea Without Barriers), a staffed, **wheelchair-accessible beach** that caters to visitors with disabilities. In addition to a system of ramps that permits those in wheelchairs to roll right into the water, there are accessible bathrooms, showers, parking, and picnic shelters. The facility also rents special wheelchairs for entering the water.

Other Beaches

Although Balneario La Monserrate gets all the accolades and attention, it isn't the only beach

© SUZANNE VAN ATTEN

one of the many excellent Luquillo Kioskos

in Luquillo. A newly designated nature pre-serve, **La Selva Natural Reserve** (Carr. 193, just east of Luquillo) is a 3,240-acre tract of land comprising wetlands, mangroves, coastal forest, and pristine beaches ideal for swimming and surfing—just beware of the reefs. This is an important nesting site for leatherback turtles.

In the town of Luquillo along Carretera 193 is **Playa Azul,** a sandy crescent beach great for swimming and snorkeling. Parking is limited, and there are no facilities besides a few street vendors selling snacks. Farther eastward on Calle Herminio Diaz Navarro is **La Pared,** a great surfing spot adjacent to a picturesque sea-wall just one block from Luquillo's central plaza.

SPORTS AND RECREATION

Don't be confused by the sidewalk bar serv-ing up wings and beer. **Boardriders** (25 Calle Miguel Veve Calzada at La Pared, Luquillo, 787/355-5175, Mon., Tues, Thurs., Sun. noon-midnight; Fri.-Sat. noon-2 A.M.) is in fact a surf

shop, too. Surfboards, boogie boards, and pad-dleboards can be rented for $6-10 an hour or $20-40 a day. Schedule surf lessons or sign up for surf camp, too.

Hacienda Carabalí (Carr. 992, km 3, 787/889-5820 or 787/889-4954, www.haciendacarab-alipuertorico.com) is a 600-acre ranch offering guided horseback-riding tours on Paso Fino horses along mountainside and beachfront trails, along with ATV tours, mountain biking, and go-karts.

ACCOMMODATIONS

Despite Luquillo's popularity as a tourist desti-nation for locals and international travelers alike, it has a dearth of overnight accommodations.

Open since 2007, **Luquillo Sunrise Beach Inn** (A2 Ocean Blvd., Luquillo, 787/409-2929 or 787/889-1713, www.luquillosunrise.com, $145 s/d, $180 green room sleeps 5, $225 casita sleeps 6; all rates include breakfast) is a mod-est 17-room guest house conveniently located across the street from the surf beach La Pared

EAST COAST

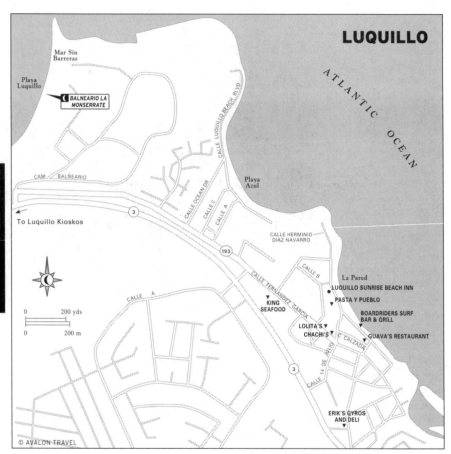

and two blocks away from the town center. The rooms are very basic but clean and come with air-conditioning and satellite TV. Some rooms have balconies, microwaves, and refrigerators. There is no swimming pool or bar, but a full breakfast is included with accommodations, and wireless Internet is available in common areas. Snorkeling equipment, surfboards, and boogie boards are available for rent.

El Yunque Mar (6 Calle 1, 787/889-5555, www.yunquemar.com, $119-139 s/d, suites $225-285, plus tax) is a small hotel in a residential area right on Playa Fortuna. This modest, faux Spanish-style hacienda offers 15 clean modern units with air-conditioning and cable TV. Suites come with mini-refrigerators and microwaves. There's no restaurant or bar, but there is a small pool.

FOOD
Food Kiosks
◖ **Luquillo Kioskos** (Carr. 193 at Carr. 3) is nearly as popular an attraction in Luquillo as Balneario La Monserrate. Along Carretera 3 just before you reach Luquillo from San Juan, this long stretch of 50-plus side-by-side kiosks

© SUZANNE VAN ATTEN

La Pared, a world-famous surfing spot in Luquillo

is one of the best places to experience Puerto Rico's array of traditional fritters. Shaped like discs, half moons, cigars, boats, and balls, these crispy deep-fried goodies come stuffed with a varied combination of meat, crab, cheese, plantain, coconut, and more. Most kiosks serve similar fare at stand-up bars where you can eat on your feet or seated at a table nearby. Pick one of each (they're only $1-3 apiece) and wash it all down with a cold beer, a cocktail, or *coco frio* (ice-cold coconut juice served from the shell). Be sure to buy a bag of *coco dulce*—sinfully rich patties of sugary coconut—for later. This place can get packed on the weekends and holidays, and the atmosphere can get rowdy at night. Despite the area's rustic nature, most kiosks accept credit and debit cards.

Puerto Rico's emergence as a culinary destination has not been lost on the kiosk proprietors in Luquillo. Many of the tried-and-true purveyors of Puerto Rican street food and home-style *criolla* dishes are still there of course, and thank goodness! But among them have cropped up some newer outlets that are serving some of the finest, most creative cuisine on the island, with an emphasis on fresh, seasonal ingredients. In addition to jazzing up the cuisine, these newcomers have created more aesthetically pleasing environments for their diners, painting their kiosks in tropical colors and creating alfresco dining areas out back, facing the ocean. The following are some of our favorites.

Ay Bonito Grill #21 (www.aybonitogrill. com, $10-22) is a sleek and modern space warmed up with colorful folk art paintings on the wall. Dine on a full menu of appetizers, salads, sandwiches, and entrées, including grilled mahimahi salad and pan-seared halibut topped with prosciutto and sage butter.

At **El Jefe Burger Shack #12** (787/615-0896, www.eljefeburger.com, daily noon-9:30 P.M., $9-12), burgers come in two sizes or stuffed with your choice of chorizo, beer-braised short ribs, or jalapeños and green chiles. Other gut-busters include bacon and cheese fries, beer-battered onion wedges and buckets of shrimp, and chicken or tilapia grilled or fried and served in your choice of sauce. The ginger *mojito* is outstanding.

Tapas 13 (787/615-0892, www.tapas13.com, Tues.-Sun. 5-10 P.M., tapas $4-14, entrées $15-21) is slightly more upscale but still casual. This kiosk serves Spanish dishes, including Manchego and serrano croquettes, chorizo in wine sauce, and paella. Owned by the same folks at El Jefe Burger Shack, located right next door, Tapas 13 is one of the few kiosks to take reservations.

La Parrilla #2 (787/889-0590, www.laparrillapr.com, $17-35) is a slightly upscale restaurant and bar serving an exhaustive menu of *criolla* and tropical dishes, including *chillo* stuffed with lobster or calamari rice and mahimahi in mango sauce.

Puerto Rican

Venture toward La Pared, the seawall, in the town of Luquillo for a concentration of more traditional restaurants. **Guava's Restaurant** (16 Calle Miguel Veve Calzada at La Pared, Luquillo, 787/889-2222, Mon. and Wed.-Thurs. 4 P.M.-midnight, Fri.-Sat. 4 P.M.-2 A.M., Sun. 11 A.M.-midnight, $15-30) does double duty as a casual restaurant serving an impressive menu of tropical dishes and a late-night hot spot for the party-hardy crowd. In addition to the usual *mofongo, churrasco,* and paella, the menu includes fried calamari with avocado and lime aioli, jerk pork *pinchos,* and chicken breast stuffed with chorizo and cilantro. Live music, a full bar specializing in fruity tropical drinks, and a rooftop terrace with an ocean view help create a lively scene.

Caribbean

What it lacks in ambiance, ◖ **Pasta y Pueblo** (Calle 14 de Julio Malecón, La Pared, Luquillo, 787/909-2015, Tues.-Sun. 5-10 P.M., $15-30)

makes up for in the quality of the food. Select your protein (chicken breast, skirt steak, mahi, scallops, etc.) and then your sauce (carbonara, Alfredo, garlic and oil, etc.), add a side (coconut rice or penne pasta), and voilà! You have dinner. Other options include coconut curry shrimp and a veggie plate.

Mexican

Lolita's Mexican Restaurant (Carr. 3, km 41.8, Luquillo, 787/889-5770 or 787/889-5770, 11 A.M.-10 P.M. daily, $3-17) is the place to go when you have a hankering for margaritas, tacos, burritos, and chiles rellenos.

Seafood

Boasting a menu as deep as the ocean, **King Seafood** (1 Calle Fernandez Garcia, Luquillo, 787/889-4300, www.kingseafoodpr.com, Tues.-Fri. 11 A.M.-10 P.M., Sat.-Sun. noon-10 P.M., $12-35) serves everything under the sea (lobster, shrimp, crab, octopus, fish, etc.) in a variety of preparations (fried, grilled, wrapped in bacon) and served in a variety of sauces (*criolla,* butter, garlic and oil, etc.). Specialties include paella and stuffed *chillo.*

American

As the name suggests, **Boardriders Surf Bar & Grill** (25 Calle Miguel Veve Calzada at La Pared, Luquillo, 787/355-5175, Mon., Tues., Thurs., Sun. noon-midnight, Fri.-Sat. noon-2 A.M., closed Wed., $6-21) is a haven for surfers, but even landlubbers are made to feel welcome at this casual bar/restaurant/surf shop located across the street from Luquillo's celebrated La Pared surf spot. Nosh on fish tacos, ribs, burgers, salads, and wraps and get the lowdown from the friendly, no-attitude staff on where the best surf breaks are. You can also rent boards and pick up any other surf supplies you might need.

Erik's Gyros and Deli (352 Calle Fernandez Garcia, at the intersection of Carr. 992 and Carr. 193 right by Carr. 3, 787/889-0615, Mon.-Sat.

KIOSK CUISINE

© SUZANNE VAN ATTEN

a typical kiosk lunch with *alcapurria,*
bacalaito, hot sauce, and Medalla beer

The roadways all over Puerto Rico are dotted with countless lean-tos, shacks, pavilions,
tents, and trucks where enterprising cooks sell
a variety of mostly fried local delicacies called
frituras. For the uninitiated, the assortment of
fried food can be daunting. But if you want a
truly traditional Puerto Rican experience, pop
an antacid and dive into an adventurous array
of some of the tastiest food on the island.

Most items sell for as little as a dollar apiece,
are served in napkins, and are eaten standing
up. Hot sauce is on hand to spice things up, and
nothing washes it all down better than an ice-
cold Medalla beer.

Luquillo and Piñones are famous for their
concentration of food kiosks, but kiosks can be
found all over, typically near beaches, parks,
and tourist sites, including Plaza de Hostos in
Old San Juan, Punta Sardinera beach in Isabela,
and Jardín de Atlantico park in Aguadilla.

Some of the most common items include:

- **alcapurria:** Mashed yuca (also called
cassava), yautia (taro root), and/or green
banana is stuffed with crab or beef and
deep-fried. They are elongated but fat in the
middle, like a thin sweet potato or fat cigar.

- **arepa:** South American in origin, it's
small, round patty of corn meal batter
fried, split open on one side, and stuffed
with meat or seafood. It looks like a small
fried hockey puck.

- **bacalaito:** A codfish fritter that looks like
a giant deep-fried pancake.

- **barcazas:** Whole plantains are sliced
lengthwise, stuffed with ground beef, and
topped with cheese. They look like banana
boats.

- **coco dulce:** This is an immensely sweet
confection of fresh, coarsely grated
coconut and caramelized sugar. It looks
like a brown craggy praline.

- **coco frio:** Chilled coconuts still in their
green husks have a hole cut in the top and a
straw stuck through it. Inside is a refreshing
thin coconut milk. After you drink all the
liquid, ask your server to chop it in half; you
can scoop the coconut out with a spoon if
it's unripe and soft, or you can chunk it out
with a knife if it's ripe and hard.

- **empanadilla:** A savory circle of pastry is
stuffed with meat, crab, lobster, shrimp,
or fish, folded into a half moon, thickly
crimped along the rounded side, and
deep-fried. It looks like an apple turnover.

- **papas rellenas:** A big lump of mashed
potatoes is stuffed with meat and
deep-fried. It looks like a fried baseball.

- **pastelillo:** Similar to an *empanadilla* but
typically smaller, a *pastelillo* has a thinner,
airier crust. Looks like an apple turnover.

- **pinchos:** Chunks of chicken, pork, or fish
are threaded on a skewer and grilled shish
kebab style. They're often served with a slice
of bread stuck on the point of the skewer.

- **pionono:** A ball of seasoned ground
beef is wrapped mummy style in slices
of plantain and deep-fried. Sometimes it
also contains egg. It looks like a craggy,
deep-fried softball.

- **taquitos:** Chicken, ground beef, crab,
or fish is rolled up in a tortilla and (you
guessed it) deep-fried. They look like fat
cigars or little fried envelopes, depending
on how the cook folds them up, and they
are sometimes called tacos, but they're
nothing like the Mexican version.

EAST COAST

EAST COAST

7 A.M.-6 P.M., Sun. 8:30 A.M.-2 P.M., $4-10) is an excellent place to get a cheap Greek-, American-, or Puerto Rican-style breakfast or lunch. This little corner deli serves gyros, burgers, lamb barbecue, Cuban sandwiches, *tortilla española* omelets, French toast, and more. It also sells chorizo and serrano ham by the pound.

Ice Cream

Located in front of the Plaza de Luquillo, **Chachi's** (119 Calle Fernandez Garcia, Luquillo, 787/536-9147, Sun.-Thurs. 3-9 P.M., Sat. 7-11 P.M., $2-8) serves ice creams and sorbets in a variety of tropical flavors, including coconut, pineapple, almond, tamarind, passion fruit and corn. You can order coffee drinks, fruit frappes, and milk shakes, too.

INFORMATION AND SERVICES

For health and beauty needs, visit **Walgreens** (889 Calle 2, 787/889-3107). **Banco Popular** (Carr. 193 and Calle B, 787/889-2610, www.bancopopular.com) provides banking services. The **post office** is at 160 Calle 14 de Julio.

GETTING THERE AND AROUND

For transportation call **Luquillo Taxi** (787/513-7685). Luquillo is 53 kilometers or 33 miles east of San Juan. Take Highway 26 east to Highway 66 east to Carretera 3 east.

Fajardo

Fajardo is a bustling little seaside town notable for its marinas and water sports enthusiasts. It's also an excellent seaborne transportation hub to Caribbean points east, where you can catch a ferry or sailboat to Vieques, Culebra, St. Thomas, and beyond.

Although it has a town proper with the requisite plaza and church, the heart of Fajardo is along the coast, where hundreds of vessels dock and dozens of seafood restaurants vie to serve the day-trippers who flock here for the superb diving, fishing, sailing, and golf.

Fajardo is also home to one of the island's bioluminescent lagoons, Laguna Grande, in Reserva Natural Las Cabezas de San Juan. Here you can kayak at night and marvel at the phosphorescent microorganisms that light up the water with a sparkling green glow.

SIGHTS
Balneario Seven Seas

Balneario Seven Seas (Carr. 987, beside Las Cabezas de San Juan, Las Croabas, 787/863-8180, Wed.-Sun. 8:30 A.M.-5 P.M., open daily during summer, $5 per vehicle) is a great beach for swimming and snorkeling. For underwater action, check out the reef on the far eastern end of the beach. Camping for RVs and tents is also available, although quarters are close so don't expect much privacy. Call 787/863-8180 for reservations.

Parque Las Croabas

Parque Las Croabas (Carr. 987) is a pleasant waterside park overlooking Bahía Las Croabas, dotted with moored fishing boats. From here you can see the island of Vieques. There are several concrete picnic shelters, poorly maintained bathroom facilities, and a small boat launch. Across the street are several bars and restaurants serving seafood. At dusk the park hums with activity because this is the launch site for all the kayak outfitters offering guided bio-bay tours in Laguna Grande.

Reserva Natural La Cordillera

Reserva Natural La Cordillera, comprising Icacos, Diablo, Palomino, and Palominitos, is a protected string of small sandy islands just north and east of Fajardo with lots of great

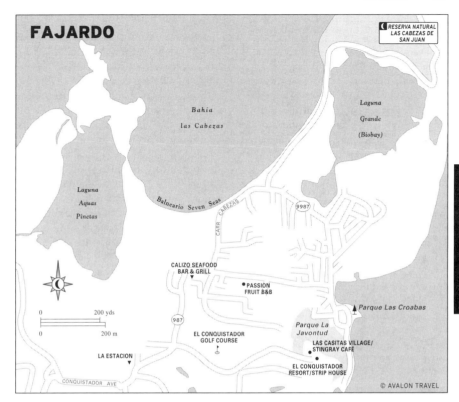

FAJARDO

RESERVA NATURAL
LAS CABEZAS DE
SAN JUAN

Bahía
las Cabezas

Laguna
Grande
(Biobay)

EAST COAST

Laguna
Aquas
Pinetas

Balneario Seven Seas

CARR. CABEZAS

9987

CALIZO SEAFOOD
BAR & GRILL

PASSION
FRUIT B&B

Parque Las Croabas

987

EL CONQUISTADOR
GOLF COURSE

Parque La
Javontud

LAS CASITAS VILLAGE/
STINGRAY CAFÉ

LA ESTACION

EL CONQUISTADOR
RESORT/STRIP HOUSE

CONQUISTADOR AVE

0   200 yds
0   200 m

© AVALON TRAVEL

snorkeling and diving spots around them. Bring plenty of water and sunscreen—there are no facilities or stores on the islands. To get there, go to the dock in Las Croabas and arrange a ride with one of the boat operators there. They'll drop you off and return later to pick you up. The cost is typically $10 each way. The islands can get crowded on weekends and holidays.

◖ Reserva Natural Las Cabezas de San Juan

Reserva Natural Las Cabezas de San Juan/ El Faro (Carr. 987, km 6, 787/860-2560 or 787/722-5882, guided tours Wed.-Sun. 9:30 A.M., 10 A.M., 10:30 A.M., 2 P.M., $7 adults, $5 seniors and children 11 and younger, free for children 4 and younger, reservations required)

is a unique and treasured piece of island property that has been protected from encroaching development. This 316-acre piece of land contains examples of all the island's natural habitats except for the rainforest: coral reefs, turtle grass, sandy and rocky beaches, lagoons, a dry forest, and a mangrove forest. It is home to many endangered wildlife species, including the osprey and the sea turtle, and artifacts of the Igneri Indians, precursors to the Taínos, have been excavated here.

Two main points of interest are found at Las Cabezas de San Juan. One is the neoclassical lighthouse *(el faro),* built by the Spanish in 1880, making it the island's second-oldest lighthouse. Today it houses facilities for scientific research in the areas of ecology, marine biology, geology, and archaeology.

The other highlight of Las Cabezas de San Juan is **Laguna Grande,** a mangrove lagoon filled with microscopic bioluminescent organisms that glow green at night when they sense motion. Several outfitters in the area offer canoe or kayak rides into the lagoon after dark on moonless nights so visitors can witness the biological phenomenon. Swimming in the lagoon is no longer permitted.

This rich nature reserve also features a nature center, hiking trails, a boardwalk, and an observation tower from which you can see El Yunque and nearby islands as far away as Tortola.

Entrance into Las Cabezas de San Juan is by guided tour only. Call for reservations. To get here, take Carretera 3 to the Conquistador Avenue exit and turn left on Carretera 987. The reserve is on the left after Balneario Seven Seas recreation area.

SPORTS AND RECREATION
Snorkeling, Diving, and Sailing
Most water-sports outfitters offer a variety of snorkeling, diving, and sailing opportunities to the northeast coast's natural attractions, as well as to Vieques and Culebra.

Sea Ventures Dive Center (Marina Puerto del Rey, Carr. 3, km 51.2, Fajardo, 787/863-3483 or 800/739-3483, www.divepuertorico.com) offers dive and snorkel trips to local reefs. A two-tank dive for certified divers is $120, including gear. A two-tank dive for beginners is $150, including gear and instruction. Snorkel tours are $60, including gear.

Salty Dog (787/717-6378 or 787/717-7259, www.saltydreams.com) offers catamaran snorkeling tours, including all-you-can-eat lunch buffet and unlimited rum drinks, $60 per person. A sunset cruise with cocktails and light snacks costs $59 per person.

Eco Adventures (787/206-0290, www.ecoadventurespr.com) offers bio-bay tours for $45 per person. Sailing snorkel tours cost $65 per person. Transportation from San Juan to Las Croabas is $20.

East Island Excursions (Puerto Del Rey Marina, Fajardo, 787/860-3434 or 877/937-4386, fax 787/860-1656, www.eastwindcats.com) offers sailing and snorkeling trips aboard a 62-foot sailing catamaran with a glass bottom and a slide, a 65-foot power catamaran, or a 45-foot catamaran. Excursions are available to Vieques, Culebra, Culebrita, and St. Thomas. Reservations are required.

Caribbean School of Aquatics (Villa Marina, Fajardo, 787/728-6606, www.saildiveparty.com) advertises itself with the slogan "Sail Dive Party" despite the scholarly name of its operation. It offers snorkeling, diving, and sailing trips to Vieques and Culebra aboard catamarans and sailing sloops. Reservations are required.

Traveler (Carr. 987, km 1.3, Villa Marina, Fajardo, 787/863-2821 or 787/412-9555, fax 787/655-4590, www.travelerpr.com) offers snorkeling and sailing on a 54-foot catamaran. Trips depart from Villa Marina at 10 A.M., and transportation can be arranged from San Juan. Group rates and charter packages are available.

Bio-Bay Tours
Capt. Suarez Electric Boat (Carr. 987, Las Croabas dock, Fajardo, 787/655-2739 or 787/472-3128, captainsuarezbiobaypr@gmail.com) offers electric boat rides into the bio-bay ($45 adults, $35 children).

Eco Adventures (787/206-0290, www.ecoadventurespr.com) offers bio-bay tours for $45 per person. Sailing snorkel tours cost $65 per person. Transportation from San Juan to Las Croabas is $20.

Yokahu Kayaks (Carr. 987, km 6.2, Las Croabas, Fajardo, 787/604-7375, yokahukayaks@hotmail.com) offers kayak tours to Laguna Grande in Las Cabezas de San Juan with licensed guides and equipment included ($45 per person). Reservations are required.

Kayaking Puerto Rico (787/435-1665 or 787/564-5629, www.kayakingpuertorico.com)

offers bio-bay tours in Laguna Grande ($45 per person). Combination kayak and snorkel expeditions are also available.

Las Tortugas Adventures (4 Calle La Puntilla, San Juan, 787/805-0253, www.kayak-pr.com) offers a variety of half- and full-day snorkeling and kayak tours on the east coast, launching from Bahía Las Croabas in Fajardo. Tours include Las Cabezas de San Juan in Fajardo, the bioluminescent lagoon, the mangrove forest in Piñones, and excursions to Cayo Icacos, Cayo Diablo, and Monkey Island. No experience is necessary, and all equipment is provided. Reservations are required.

Island Kayaking Adventures (787/444-0059 or 787/225-1808, www.ikapr.com) offers bio-bay kayak tours to Laguna Grande for $45 per person with a six-person minimum. Rainforest and bio-bay combo tours cost $100 per person.

Fishing

Light Tackle Paradise (Marina Puerto Chico, Carr. Road 987, km 2.4, 787/347-4464, $350-450 half-day for 4 or 6 people) offers fishing excursions on 22-foot and 26-foot catamarans or 17-foot skiffs.

Fish for dorado, wahoo, tuna, sailfish, and more with **Bill Wraps Fishing Charters PR** (787/364-4216, 787/347-9668, or 787/278-2729, www.billwrapsfishingpr.com. Half-day charters are $650, full-day charters are $950, including tackle, bait, and snacks. Lunch is included with full-day charter.

Golf and Tennis

El Conquistador Resort (1000 Conquistador Ave., 787/863-1000, www.elconresort.com) boasts the Arthur Hills Golf Course (daily 6:30 A.M.-6:30 P.M.), a par 72 hilly course overlooking the Atlantic Ocean and El Yunque rainforest. There are more than 50 bunkers and five water hazards, including a waterfall on the 18th hole. It also has a driving range and a putting green. It is home to the Ambassador's Cup

golf tournament in December. There are also seven tennis courts-four clay and three hard. Four are lit for 24-7 play.

Spa

Golden Door Spa (El Conquistador Resort, 1000 Conquistador Ave., 787/863-1000, www. elconresort.com) offers a wide variety of massages, hydrotherapy treatments, facials, reflexology, and energy-balancing treatments, including Reiki and craniosacral.

ENTERTAINMENT AND EVENTS

Carnaval de Fajardo (787/863-1400) is held in early August on Plaza de Recreo, featuring an artisans fair, a carnival, music, food, and arts and crafts.

The Casino at El Conquistador (El Conquistador Resort, 1000 Conquistador Ave., 787/863-1000, www.elconresort.com) features two Caribbean stud poker tables, five roulette wheels, three craps tables, 12 blackjack tables, and 224 slot machines.

ACCOMMODATIONS
$100-150

◖ **The Fajardo Inn** (52 Parcelas Beltrán, 787/860-6000, fax 787/860-5063, www.fajardoinn.com, $110-120 s, $140 d, $180 suite, $212 double suite, plus tax) is a large, bright white complex with 97 units high on a hill, affording gorgeous views of the ocean from one side and the mountains from the other. Formerly a property belonging to the U.S. military, this hotel has undergone a complete overhaul, making it a very pleasant family-friendly place to stay. The rooms are modern, well-maintained, and simply furnished. They all have air-conditioning, cable TV, and telephones, and some have kitchenettes, balconies, mini-refrigerators, and whirlpool baths. On the property are two pools, a playground, miniature golf, laundry facilities, and two restaurants.

Passion Fruit Bed & Breakfast (Carr. 987,

Las Croabas, 787/801-0106, www.passion-fruitbb.com, $119 s/d, $136 suite, $174 quad, plus taxes, includes full breakfast) offers comfortable, modern accommodations in a brightly colored, three-story structure that houses 11 units named after famous Puerto Ricans. Amenities include air-conditioning, satellite TV, and a pool. Wireless Internet is available in common areas.

Over $250

€ El Conquistador Resort & Las Casitas Village (1000 Conquistador Ave., 787/863-1000, www.elconresort.com, $309-499 s/d, $1,497 two-bedroom suite; Las Casitas Village $309 s/d, $509-609 one-bedroom, $809 two-bedroom, $1,009 three-bedroom, plus tax and resort fees) is one of Puerto Rico's best-known and most highly regarded luxury resorts. A behemoth property perched atop a dramatic cliff with a stunning panoramic view of the ocean, El Conquistador is more like a small town than a hotel. It boasts 750 rooms in five separate white stucco and terra-cotta complexes set amid beautifully landscaped cobblestone streets, plazas, and fountains. There are more than a dozen restaurants and bars, as well as a casino, fitness center, full-service spa, seven swimming pools, an oceanside water park, seven tennis courts, an 18-hole golf course, and a 35-slip marina. Every room has air-conditioning, satellite TV, telephone, minibar, marble bathroom, CD player, VCR, computer and fax connections, coffeemaker, and a sitting area. Snorkeling, scuba diving, and fishing tours and equipment are available on-site. There's also transportation available to the more secluded beaches on nearby Palomino Island. In addition to the hotel accommodations, Las Casitas Village offers luxury apartment stays with full kitchens in a separate complex with its own swimming pools, restaurants, and butler service. In 2007,

El Conquistador Resort & Las Casitas Village

© SUZANNE VAN ATTEN

Las Casitas was named the number one place for families to stay in the Caribbean by *Travel + Leisure Family* magazine.

FOOD
Caribbean

◖ **La Estación** (Carr. 987, km 3.5, next to Hotel Conquistador, Las Croabas, Fajardo, 787/863-4481, www.laestacionpr.com, Mon.-Wed. 5 P.M.-midnight, Fri.-Sun. 3 P.M.-midnight, $9-22), owned and operated by Kevin Roth from Brooklyn, New York, and Idalia Garcia from Puerto Rico, is a super-casual oasis of convivial fun and outstanding, freshly prepared cuisine. The kitchen is located in a converted gas station, but the sprawling dining areas are on open-air patios appointed with awnings, padded lawn furniture, butterfly chairs, and tabletops surrounded by tiki torches and festive strings of lights. There's also a partially enclosed bar with a juke box filled with contemporary Latino rock and reggaetón tunes and a pool table. The vibe is akin to hanging out in your coolest friend's basement. But it's the food that really puts this place on the map. Everything is charcoal grilled, right outside where you can watch the action—fresh fish of the day, shrimp, *churrasco*, strip steaks, chicken, and burgers. The green papaya salad makes for a refreshing starter. And many of the ingredients are locally sourced. Be sure to order the house cocktail, called the Low Tide. It features rum, Triple Sec, and fresh pineapple and tamarind juices.

Seafood and Steak

There is a small, intimate indoor dining room at ◖ **Callzu Seafood Bar & Grill** (Carr. 987, km 5.9, Las Croabas, 787/863-3664, Mon.-Fri. 5-10 P.M., Sat. 1-11 P.M., Sun. 1-10 P.M., $17-30), but why go there when you can dine alfresco on the large, romantic patio or at the lively outdoor bar? It's an ideal setting for the creative tropical cuisine coming out of this kitchen. The restaurant specializes in

interesting sauces—a ginger lime sauce for the frog legs in panko; a spicy red pepper sauce for the sautéed prawns—and those are just appetizers. For entrées, sautéed grouper is served in a cilantro Manchego sauce and baby back ribs are cooked in a guava sauce. Other selections include fried or steamed whole snapper, *mofongo* stuffed with Angus skirt steak and *chimichurri* sauce, and paella. The menu is conveniently printed in Spanish and English.

Stingray Café (1000 El Conquistador Ave., at La Marina Village of El Conquistador Resort, 787/863-6616, daily 6-11 P.M., $29-42) is something of a misnomer. Café implies a casual setting, but Stingray is an elegant fine dining establishment featuring a menu that melds tropical and Mediterranean flavors in a setting that overlooks the marina and Palomino Island. Dishes include warm lobster salad with shiitake mushrooms and a black truffle vinaigrette, grilled swordfish with green papaya salsa, and roasted lamb chops. A prix fixe three-course menu, including one glass of wine, is available for $45 per person.

Strip House (1000 El Conquistador Ave. at El Conquistador Resort, 787/863-6789, daily 5:30-11 P.M., $19-39) is an outpost of the celebrated New York restaurant, combining a vintage sexy vibe with sizzling slabs of beef for a decadent dining experience. The walls are drenched in bordello red and hung with black-and-white photographs of burlesque dancers from days gone by. And the menu is filled with rich favorites, such as gorgonzola fondue, lobster bisque, and a 24-ounce chateaubriand for two, with béarnaise sauce available upon request. Lighter options include seared diver scallops and broiled rock lobster tail. A $35 prix fixe menu is available.

Rosa's Sea Food (536 Calle Tablado, Marina Puerto Real, 787/863-0213, Mon., Thurs., and Fri. 11 A.M.-9:30 P.M., Sat.-Sun. 11 A.M.-9 P.M., $12-30) is a highly recommended spot for traditional Puerto Rican cuisine, especially the grilled fish and lobster.

Restaurante Ocean View (Carr. 987, km 6.8, 787/863-6104, Wed.-Mon. noon-11 P.M., $10-40) is right across the street from Parque Los Croabas and is a festive casual place to dine on fresh seafood under an open-air pavilion. It serves excellent combination seafood platters, *mofongo,* and paella, and it has a full bar.

Cuban

Metropol (Punta del Este Sur Court at the intersection of Carr. 3 and Carr. 194, 787/801-2877 or 787/801-2870, www.metropolpr.com, daily 11:30 A.M.-10:30 P.M., $10-36) is a modest casual restaurant serving excellent Cuban cuisine. The house special is *gallinita rellena de congri*—succulent roasted Cornish hen stuffed with a perfectly seasoned combination of rice and black beans. The presentation is no-nonsense and the service expedient.

Italian

Dining on northern Italian cuisine in a highly formal setting is not a culinary experience typically associated with Puerto Rico, but **La Piccola Fontana** (1000 El Conquistador Ave. on the mezzanine of El Conquistador Resort, 787/801-1008, daily 5:30-11 P.M., $26-38) has been offering just that for more than 20 years now. Entrées include lobster tail in honey truffle sauce, beef tenderloin risotto in Chianti sauce, veal lasagna, and shrimp Pinot Grigio. If you're not dining on an expense account, consider the three-course prix fixe menu special for $36 per person.

INFORMATION AND SERVICES

Bank service is available at **Banco Popular** (Centro Comercial Plaza, Fajardo Mall, Carr. 3, km 4.2, 787/860-5353, www.bancopopular.com). **HIMA-San Pablo Hospital** (404 Av. General Valero, 787/655-0505, www.himapr.com) offers emergency medical services. For pharmacy needs, there is a **Walgreens** (4203 Calle Marginal, 787/860-1600).

GETTING THERE AND AROUND

Fajardo is 65 kilometers or 40 miles east of San Juan. Take Highway 26 east to Highway 66 east to Carretera 3 east to Carretera 194 north. Getting to Fajardo requires flying from San Juan to the nearby airport in Ceiba, renting a car and driving, or taking a *público,* a privately operated van transport service.

Although its airport has closed and relocated about 4 miles south to Ceiba, Fajardo is still a gateway to the nearby islands of Vieques and Culebra, thanks to daily ferry service and boats operating out of its seven marinas. Nevertheless, all the transportation options in Fajardo point in one direction: eastward to Vieques, Culebra, or the Virgin Islands.

By Air

The Fajardo airport has closed, and all operations have relocated about 4 miles south to the **José Aponte de la Torre Airport** (787/863-4447) on the former Roosevelt Roads Naval Base in Ceiba. It is a small operation devoted to servicing transportation to the coast's neighboring islands. **Vieques Air Link** (888/901-9247, www.viequesairlink.com) flies to Vieques, Culebra, and St. Croix. Charter air service is available through **Air Flamenco** (787/901-8256).

By Ferry

The Puerto Rican Port Authority operates daily ferry service to Vieques and Culebra from the Fajardo ferry terminal at Puerto Real (Carr. 195, 787/863-0705 or 787/863-4560).

The **passenger ferry** is primarily a commuter operation during the week and can often be crowded—especially on the weekends and holidays. Reservations are not accepted, but you can buy tickets in advance. Arrive no later than one hour before departure. Sometimes the ferry cannot accommodate everyone who wants to ride. The trip typically takes about an hour to travel to Vieques ($4 round-trip) and 1.5 hours to Culebra ($4.50). There is no ferry service between Vieques and Culebra.

Note that ferry schedules are subject to change.

- **Fajardo to Vieques:** Daily 9:30 A.M., 1 P.M., 4:30 P.M., and 8 P.M.
- **Vieques to Fajardo:** Daily 6:30 A.M., 11 A.M., 3 P.M., and 6 P.M.
- **Fajardo to Culebra:** Daily 9 A.M., 3 P.M., and 7 P.M.
- **Culebra to Fajardo:** Daily 6:30 A.M., 1 P.M., and 5 P.M.

There is also a weekday **cargo/car ferry** from Fajardo that goes between Culebra and Fajardo, for which reservations are required. But be aware that most car-rental agencies in Puerto Rico do not permit their automobiles to leave the main island. The best option is to leave your car in Fajardo and rent another car on Culebra. The trip usually takes about 2.5 hours, and the cost is $15 for small vehicles and $19 for large vehicles. The schedule is as follows:

- **Fajardo to Vieques:** Monday-Friday 4 A.M., 9:30 A.M., and 4:30 P.M.
- **Vieques to Fajardo:** Monday-Friday 6 A.M., 1:30 P.M., and 6 P.M.
- **Fajardo to Culebra:** Monday, Tuesday, and Thursday 4 A.M. and 4:30 P.M.; Wednesday and Friday 4 A.M., 9:30 A.M., and 4:30 P.M.

- **Culebra to Fajardo:** Monday, Tuesday, and Thursday 7 A.M. and 6 P.M.; Wednesday and Friday 7 A.M., 1 P.M., and 6 P.M.

Marinas

Fajardo's main commercial marina is **Marina Puerto Real** (Carr. 195, 787/863-2188). This is where the Puerto Rican Port Authority operates daily ferry service to Vieques and Culebra.

Other marinas include the tony **Villa Marina Yacht Harbour** (Carr. 987, km 1.3, Fajardo, 787/863-5131, fax 787/863-2320, www.villamarinapr.com); **Puerto Del Rey** (Carr. 3, km 51.4, Fajardo, 809/860-1000 or 809/863-5792); and **Inversiones Isleta Marina** (787/643-2180, luisdiaz@coqui.net), offshore at Puerto Real Plaza, a startling high-rise development surrounded by ocean.

By *Público*

Travel with Padin (787/355-6746 after 6 P.M. for English, 787/644-3091 8 A.M.-6 P.M. for Spanish, http://enchanted-isle.com/padin/) operates 24-hour *público* service between Fajardo and the Luis Muñoz Marín International Airport in San Juan.

EAST COAST

Naguabo and Humacao

Check out the petite plaza with the umbrella-shaped trees in the town proper of Nagaubo, then go straight to its seaside community off Carretera 3. There's a slightly Mediterranean feel to this friendly little town, which overlooks a large bay and a hilly peninsula dotted with houses that cling to its sides. A long, wide *malécon,* a seawall with a balustrade, lines the ocean side of the road; shops, restaurants, and bars line the other side. Downtown Humacao is much more bustling with shops and restaurants clustered around a shady plaza flanked by a church and *alcaldía* (town hall). But the main reason to go is to catch some rays at Balneario Santiago or to pamper yourself in the luxury of Palmas del Mar resort.

SIGHTS

Balneario Santiago (Carr. 3, km 72.4, Humacao, 787/852-1660 or 787/852-3066, Mon.-Fri. 7:30 A.M.-3:30 P.M., Sat.-Sun. and Mon. holidays 7:30 A.M.-5 P.M., $3 cars, $2 motorcycles, $4 vans, $5 buses, camping $25-40) is a great stretch of publicly maintained beach and vacation center with a swimming pool featuring a big water slide, modest overnight accommodations, camping facilities, bathrooms, and picnic shelters. Adjacent to the *balneario,* along about kilometer 68.3, is a large shady **wilderness beach** that is unfortunately heavily littered and crawling with feral dogs. On the weekends you can find vendors there selling beverages, trinkets, oysters, and other food items. From here you can see **Cayo Santiago,** also known as Monkey Island because of the large population of rhesus monkeys placed there for safekeeping by animal researchers. Visitors are not allowed on the island, but they're welcome to dive and snorkel around its edges and watch the primates from a distance.

Reserva Natural de Humacao (Carr. 3, km 74.3, Humacao, 787/852-6058, Mon.-Fri. 7:30 A.M.-3:30 P.M., Sat.-Sun. and Mon. holidays 7:30 A.M.-6 P.M. May-Aug.; Sat.-Sun. and Mon. holidays 7:30 A.M.-5:30 P.M. Sept.-Apr., free) is a lovely natural reserve containing 3,186 acres of swamps, marshes, channels, and an interconnected lagoon system perfect for kayaking. It also has six miles of walking and bike trails. Sights along the way include an antique water-pumping station and bunkers constructed during World War II. Tour outfitter Water Sports & Ecotours operates out of the reserve, offering walking tours for $3.50 per person and kayak rentals for $10 per hour per person.

Iglesia Dulce Nombre de Jesus (3 Ave. Font Martelo, Humacao, 787/852-0868), located on the main plaza in downtown Humacao, is a Spanish colonial-style church built in 1793.

Museo Casa Roig (66 Calle Antonio Lopez, Humacao, 787/852-8380, fax 787/850-9144, Wed.-Fri. and Sun. 10 A.M.-4 P.M.) is a museum and cultural center operated by the Universidad de Puerto Rico in Humacao. It was originally a private home built in 1919 by Antonin Nechodoma, a student of the Frank Lloyd Wright style of architecture.

SPORTS AND RECREATION

Palmas del Mar Country Club (Palmas del Mar, Country Club Dr., Humacao, 787/285-2255, www.palmasdelmar.com) has two 18-hole, 72-par courses: Golf Club was built in 1974 by Gary Player, and Flamboyan, considered one of the island's most challenging, is a newer course designed by Rees Jones. There are

also tennis courts, an equestrian center, an enormous pool, a fitness center, and a modest spa.

Sea Ventures Palmas Dive Center (110 Harbour Dr., Palmas del Mar, Humacao, 787/781-8086 or 787/739-3483, www.divepalmasdelmar.com) offers daily two-tank dives in the morning and snorkeling trips in the afternoon. There are more than 35 dive sites in the area, including overhangs, caverns, reefs, and tunnels. It also goes to Cayo Santiago.

Rancho Buena Vista (Palmas Dr., Palmas Del Mar Resort, Humacao, 787/479-7479, www.ranchobuenavistapr.com) is an equestrian center offering horseback riding on the beach and pony rides for children.

Water Sports & Ecotours (Reserva Natural de Humacao, Carr. 3, km 74.3, Humacao, 787/852-6058, Mon.-Fri. 7:30 A.M.-3:30 P.M., Sat.-Sun. and Mon. holidays 7:30 A.M.-6 P.M. May-Aug.; Sat.-Sun. and Mon. holidays 7:30 A.M.-5:30 P.M. Sept.-Apr.) offers walking tours for $3.50 per person and kayak rental for $12 per hour per person in the 3,186-acre Reserva Natural de Humacao.

ENTERTAINMENT

Casino Real at Palmas de Mar (Four Points by Sheraton, 170 Candelero Dr., Palmas del Mar, 787/850-6000, daily 10 A.M.-2 A.M.) is a modest 7,000-square-foot casino with slot machines, blackjack, roulette, and Texas hold 'em.

ACCOMMODATIONS

Palmas del Mar (Carr. 3, km 86.4, Humacao, 787/852-8888, www.palmasdelmar.com) is a 2,700-acre planned community that includes residential and resort developments. For vacation rentals in Palmas del Mar, visit www.prwest.com. Police, fire, postal, banking, and medical services are all available at Palmas del Mar. **Wyndham Gardens at Palmas del Mar** (170 Candelero Dr., Humacao, 787/850-6000, fax 787/850-6001, www.wyndham.com, $145-314 s/d, plus tax, including breakfast) features

EAST COAST

107 guest rooms with air-conditioning and cable TV. Attractions include more than three miles of beach, a casino, an 8,000-square-foot pool, a 200-slip marina, two golf courses, tennis courts, a fitness center, a spa, an equestrian center, and 18 restaurants.

◖ Casa Cubuy Eco Lodge (Carr. 191, km 22, Naguabo, 787/874-6221, fax 787/874-4316, www.casacubuy.com, $100-110 s/d plus tax, includes breakfast, two-night minimum required) is a small, low-key lodge on the quiet, less visited southern side of El Yunque. Perched on a hill above a gurgling stream, this is definitely the place to go to get away from it all. Amenities are few (no TV!) beyond balconies and hammocks. But you're a short hike away from waterfalls and a natural pool where you can take an invigorating dip. A restaurant is onsite. In-room massages are available.

Centro Vacacional de Humacao Villas Punta Santiago (Carr. 3, km 72.4, Punta Santiago, Humacao, 787/622-5200, www.parquesnacionalespr.com, $65-71 cabanas, $109-115 villas, two-night minimum required) is a government-maintained and -operated vacation center patronized almost exclusively by Puerto Ricans but open to anyone looking for basic economical accommodations on the ocean. The gated property features a yellow-and-adobe-colored complex containing 99 cabanas and villas. Only the villas are air-conditioned, but both cabanas and villas have full kitchens. Linens, towels, and cooking utensils are not provided. Amenities include tennis courts, a playground, a pool with a water slide, and lovely shady grounds featuring almond trees, palms, and *flamboyans*.

FOOD

Chez Daniel (Palmas del Mar, Anchor's Village Marina, Humacao, 787/850-3838, fax 787/285-2330, www.chezdanielpalmasdelmar.com, Wed.-Mon. 6:30-10 P.M., $27-35; Sunday brunch noon-4 P.M., $45 per person; closed June) is an award-winning upscale fine-dining restaurant serving French cuisine with a Caribbean twist. Grilled duck breast, bouillabaisse, and Dover sole are among its specialties. It also has an extensive wine list. Dine inside or outside overlooking the marina. Check out the massive Sunday brunch buffet ($42 per person).

Los Makos Restaurant (Carr. 3, Nagaubo Playa, Naguabo, 787/874-2353, Tues.-Wed. 11:30 A.M.-8 P.M., Thurs. and Sun. 11 A.M.-10 P.M., Fri.-Sat. 11 A.M.-midnight, $10-40) is a large, modern restaurant with dining indoors and out, and a separate bar. It specializes in seafood, and its big seller by far is the local lobster, served in salads, soups, creole sauce, charbroiled, in garlic butter, or "Makos" style, accompanied by octopus, conch, and shrimp.

INFORMATION AND SERVICES

Emergency medical services are available at **Ryder Memorial Hospital** (355 Calle Font Martelo, Humacao, 787/852-0768). **Walgreens** (477 Carr. 3, Humacao, 787/852-1330) has a full pharmacy. Banking services are available at **Banco Popular** (Carr. 3, km 83.6, St. Triumph Plaza, Humacao, 787/852-8000). The **post office** is located at 122 Calle Font Martelo in Humacao.

GETTING THERE AND AROUND

For taxi services, call **Humacao Taxi** (787/852-6880). Humacao is 66 kilometers or 41 miles southeast of San Juan. Take Highway 52 south to Highway 30 south. Naguabo is 75 kilometers or 46 miles southeast of San Juan. Take Highway 52 south to Highway 30 south to Carretera 3 north.

Yabucoa and Maunabo

Often bypassed by visitors, Yabucoa and Maunabo are quiet, low-key, seaside municipalities in the southeastern corner of Puerto Rico that offer a tranquil getaway from the crowds, traffic, and American influence found elsewhere on the island. Nevertheless, the area is home to several small well-maintained hotels and restaurants that serve travelers who aren't looking for a lot of excitement or nightlife.

Unlike on the island's southwestern corner, the vegetation here is emerald-green thanks to the convergence of several rivers from the Cordillera Central. In Maunabo, the Cordillera Central descends into the Caribbean Ocean, creating lovely views where the mountains meet the sea. Maunabo was once the domain of Carib Indians and pirates, but it is primarily an agricultural community today, producing everything from cattle to grapes. Yabucoa was once integral to Puerto Rico's sugar production during the industry's heyday. At one time it had six sugar mills in operation. Today it is a manufacturing center, producing electronics, clothing, and cigarettes. Unfortunately, it's also home to an unsightly oil refinery that mars the view of its coast.

SIGHTS

The primary reason to visit the area is for its long stretches and private pockets of deserted beaches gently lapped by the Caribbean Sea. The most popular one is **Playa Punta Tuna** (Carr. 760, km 3, Maunabo), where the low-lying hills of the Cordillera Central kiss the sea. In addition to a nice wide mile-long beach and great surfing, this is where you'll find picturesque Faro de Punta Tuna, a lighthouse perched atop a hilly point that juts into the water.

Other beaches in Maunabo are **Los Bohíos** (Carr. 760, Bordaleza), which offers a wonderful view of the Punta Tuna lighthouse and great surfing, and **Los Pinos** (Carr. 901), northwest

of Playa Punta Tuna. **Playa Lucía** (Carr. 901, km 4) is a small beach in Yabucoa.

Faro de Punta Tuna (follow the signs from Carr. 760, Maunabo, 787/861-0301, Wed.-Sun. 9 A.M.-4 P.M., free) is a neoclassical-style lighthouse built in 1863. Stop by the office for information on the history of the lighthouse and the surrounding community, available in English and Spanish, then stroll the shady 0.25-mile path toward the octagonal tower high on a cliff offering 180-degree views of the ocean and mountains.

La Ruta Panorámica (Carr. 901) is the celebrated Panoramic Route that runs through the central mountain region of the island from east to west. The eastern leg of it along Carretera 901 in Maunabo offers stunning views of the east coast where the mountains meet the sea.

ENTERTAINMENT AND EVENTS

If you want something to do besides loll around on the beach all day, visit during festival time when things get lively. In Maunabo, the big draw is **Festival Jueyero,** a celebration that fêtes the land crab, held in September in the town plaza on Calle Santiago Iglesia. All sorts of crab dishes are on the menu, in addition to a parade, crab races, and more. Maunabo is also home to **Fiestas del Pueblo,** a town celebration held in late June in the plaza featuring music, dance, rides, games, and food kiosks. Yabucoa has a **Patron Saint Festival,** held in late September through early October in Parque Felix Millan, to commemorate Saint Angeles Custodios.

ACCOMMODATIONS

Hotel Parador Palmas de Lucía (Carr. 901 at Carr. 9911, Playa Lucía, Yabucoa, 787/893-4423, www.tropicalinnspr.com, $127 s/d, includes breakfast and snacks) is a modern motel-style property with a petite pool and a small sandy beach half a block away. It has 34 simple,

© SUZANNE VAN ATTEN

one of Maunabo's sandy beaches

comfortable rooms featuring air-conditioning, satellite TV, refrigerators, microwaves, coffee-makers, and balconies. There's a restaurant on-site serving breakfast, lunch, and dinner.

Lucia Beach Villas (Carr. 99011 at Carr. 901, Yabucoa, 787/266-1111 or 787/266-1716, $152 for 2 people, $185 for 4, $250 for 6) is a newly constructed, modern townhouse-style complex of 15 connected units located in a remote spot where you can see the mountains meet the sea. The two-story units with loft-style bedrooms feature air-conditioning, satellite TV, wireless Internet, full kitchens, 1.5 baths, and a pool with a dramatic backdrop that features a natural waterfall that trickles down the mountain behind it. Each unit sleeps up to six people. There's no restaurant on-site, but a secluded public beach is right across the street.

Costa del Mar Guest House (Carr. 901, km 5.6, Yabucoa, 787/893-4423, fax 787/893-6374, www.tropicalinnspr.com, two-night stay $379 for 2 people, $485 for 3, and $610 for 4, includes breakfast) is a new property with 16 units, 12 of which overlook the ocean (although there is no beach access). Amenities include air-conditioning, satellite TV, balconies, a pool, and a basketball court.

Located along the eastern leg of La Ruta Panorámica, **Parador MaunaCaribe** (Carr. 901, km 1.9, Barrio Emajagua, Maunabo, 787/861-3330, www.paradorinns.com, $102 s/d) is part of the Tropical Inns chain of economical, well-maintained and well-managed properties on the southeastern coast. The oceanfront property has 52 rooms, featuring air-conditioning, satellite TV, telephones, and wireless Internet. Amenities include a large infinity pool overlooking the Caribbean with bar service, a fitness room, a video game room, wireless Internet, and a restaurant serving breakfast, lunch, and dinner. All-inclusive packages are available.

FOOD

Gemelo y Su Rumba (Carr. 981, km 4.3, Yabucoa, 787/585-6284, Mon.-Thurs. 9 A.M.-9 P.M., Fri.-Sun. 9 A.M.-midnight, $1-18) is a casual open-air bar and restaurant serving exceptional empanadas during the week and fresh fish specials Thursday through Sunday.

The owner, Leftie, is a musician, and he turns the place into a lively music venue on Sundays when crowds flock there for the live salsa music and dancing that goes on throughout the day.

Restaurante El Nuevo Horizonte (Carr. 901, km 8.8, Yabucoa, 787/893-5492, fax 787/893-3768, Wed.-Thurs. 11 A.M.-8 P.M., Fri.-Sat. 11 A.M.-10 P.M., Sun. 11 A.M.-8 P.M., $13-29) offers inside dining on seafood and Puerto Rican cuisine while enjoying the ocean view from high up on a mountain peak. Outside is a kiosk serving empanadas and other Puerto Rican-style fritters and beers.

Palmas de Lucía (Hotel Parador Palmas de Lucía, Carr. 901 at Carr. 9911, Playa Lucía, Yabucoa, 787/893-4423, www.tropicalinnspr.com, Sun.-Thurs. 8 A.M.-9 P.M., Fri.-Sat. 8 A.M.-10 P.M., $11-17) serves three meals a day. Lunch consists of burgers, ribs, and chicken fingers, but dinner specializes in a variety of fresh seafood, including halibut, shrimp, and lobster, as well as Puerto Rican dishes such as *mofongo* and *asopao*.

Café Terraza Panadería y Repostería (11 Ave. Calimano, Maunabo, 787/861-3375, daily 7 A.M.-11 P.M., $2-5) serves everything you could want, from whole baked chickens and Puerto Rican cuisine to pastries and sandwiches. There is also a small market selling cold drinks and dry goods.

Los Bohios (Carr. 760, km 2.3, Maunabo, 787/861-2545, Fri.-Sun., $20-38) is a casual open-air restaurant overlooking the ocean that serves Puerto Rican cuisine, seafood, and steaks.

INFORMATION AND SERVICES

Walgreens (302 Ernesto Carrasquillo, Yabucoa, 787/893-4410) provides pharmaceutical services. Banking services are available at **Banco Popular** (561 Carr. Ernesto Carrasquillo, Yabucoa, 787/266-2600). The **post office** is located at 184 Ave Calimano in Maunabo.

GETTING THERE AND AROUND

For transportation services call **Yabucoa Taxi** (787/266-4047) or **Mauna Coqui Taxi** in Maunabo at 787/317-7258. Yabucoa is 64 kilometers or 40 miles southeast of San Juan. Take Highway 52 south to Highway 30 south to Carretera 921 south to Carretera 908 south. Maunabo is 80 kilometers or 50 miles southeast of San Juan. Take Highway 52 south to Highway 30 to Highway 53.

SOUTH COAST

The south coast stands in stark contrast to Puerto Rico's north coast. Instead of lush, rocky coastlines, rough Atlantic waters, mountainous karst country, and a dense population, the south coast features a flat, dry topography, and considerably less commercial development. It's a great place to go if you want to escape the traffic and American influence found elsewhere on the island. And there are many great historic and cultural sights to explore.

Historically, the south coast was a major player in the island's sugar industry. It was once dotted with enormous sugarcane plantations, as well as sugar refineries, rum distilleries, and shipping operations. As that industry died out, the south coast turned its economic development toward the manufacturing of goods, although it hasn't come close to restoring the area to the level of wealth it once enjoyed.

Ponce is the south coast's biggest city, and what a city it is. It has a large, lovely central plaza that bustles with activity night and day, and it rivals San Juan as the island's cultural, historical, and architectural center. Home to the founders of Don Q rum, Ponce was once a very wealthy city, which is apparent in its many beautiful buildings, museums, and elaborate festivals.

The south coast was home to a significant Taíno Indian community, established in the 1200s, that stretched from Guánica to Ponce. At the time of Columbus's arrival, its chief was

© SUZANNE VAN ATTEN

HIGHLIGHTS

© AVALON TRAVEL

LOOK FOR ◖ TO FIND RECOMMENDED SIGHTS, ACTIVITIES, DINING, AND LODGING.

◖ **Centro Ceremonial Indígena de Tibes:** Discovered in 1975, this site just a couple of miles north of the city of Ponce was once the ceremonial grounds to two indigenous groups, the Igneri and the Pre-Taínos. The site contains several ceremonial *bateyes* (ball fields), plazas, and petroglyphs (page 135).

◖ **Museo de Arte de Ponce:** Featuring arguably the finest art collection in Puerto Rico, the institution underwent a $30 million expansion in 2011 that included the addition of 600 new works of art. The collection features significant Italian baroque and British pre-Raphaelite work, as well as a solid body of work by Puerto Rican artists (page 135).

◖ **Castillo Serrallés:** An elaborate Spanish Revival mansion built in 1934 atop El Vigía Hill overlooking the city of Ponce and the Caribbean Sea, Castillo Serrallés was built for Eugenio Serrallés, a major player in the local sugarcane industry and founder of Serrallés Rum Distillery, maker of Don Q rum (page 135).

◖ **Hacienda Buena Vista:** The 19th-century coffee plantation has been painstakingly restored and turned into a working museum that still produces coffee and cocoa. Reservations are required to take the two-hour tour (page 136).

◖ **Paseo Tablado La Guancha:** This modern waterfront development in Ponce features a panoramic seaside boardwalk, lots of bars and restaurants, and a huge playground for children (page 137).

Cacique Agüeybaná, who is believed to have been the island's most powerful leader at that time. But the south coast's indigenous history predates the Taíno culture. Just north of Ponce, Centro Ceremonial Indígena de Tibes is one of Puerto Rico's most significant historical sites. Many ceremonial ball fields, plazas, and petroglyphs have been discovered on this site, which archaeologists have attributed to Pre-Taíno and Igneri cultures that date back as far as 300 B.C.

East of Ponce is Baños de Coamo, a natural hot springs near the center of the region. Believed to contain restorative powers, Baños de Coamo has been a tourist attraction since colonial times, and it remains one today.

The southeastern corner of Puerto Rico is the least populated part of the island. Official tourist sights are few in Patillas, but it has a couple of unique hotels, and its clear blue Caribbean waters beckon those eager to escape the hubbub of San Juan. And the fresh seafood is legend, especially among the restaurants the line the water's edge in the fishing village of Salinas.

PLANNING YOUR TIME

Most of the south coast is conveniently connected by multilane divided highways—Highway 2 west of Ponce, and toll roads Highway 52 and Highway 53 east of Ponce. Highway 52 also connects San Juan to the south coast near Salinas. Traffic along the south coast is generally pretty light, so all in all, getting around the area is fairly easy.

Ponce is 79 miles away from San Juan and takes about 1.5 hours to drive. You can get there and back in a day, but you'd be hard-pressed to see it all in that short span of time. Better to stay a weekend or longer, so you're sure to have time to visit the Indian grounds at **Centro Ceremonial Indígena de Tibes;** the city's impressive **Museo de Arte de Ponce;** the castle-like former home of the Don Q founder, the **Castillo Serrallés;** the former coffee plantation **Hacienda Buena Vista;** and the new waterfront development, **Paseo Tablado La Guancha.**

Salinas, on the other hand, is close enough to drive to from San Juan for dinner. Patillas is the kind of place where you want to kick back and chill out for a while. It's a great place to spend the weekend if you want to do nothing more than sunbathe, swim, and dine on fresh seafood.

© SUZANNE VAN A'TEN

Hacienda Buena Vista

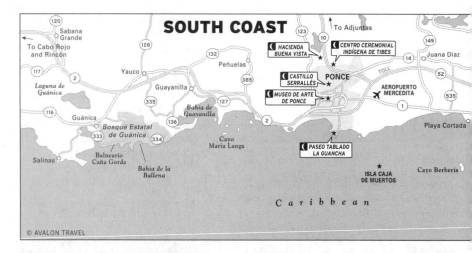

SOUTH COAST

Ponce and Vicinity

Ponce is like an elegant, cultured grande dame who started to deteriorate a bit over the years but has recently undergone a vigorous renewal program that has put a new sheen on all her best assets.

An economic and cultural rival to San Juan back in the day, Ponce experienced great growth and wealth during the 18th and 19th centuries thanks to its international shipping trade, which brought in an influx of European immigrants who established lucrative rum distilleries and plantations growing coffee and sugarcane. All that wealth translated into the construction of hundreds of gorgeous, ornate homes and buildings that combine rococo, neoclassical, and Spanish Revival architectural elements with traditional *criolla* building styles, distinguished by broad balconies, large doorways, and open-air patios. Unfortunately, many of them fell into disrepair over the course of the '80s and '90s due to economic hard times. But things are on an upswing, and many of the city's stunning buildings have been restored to their former glory.

At the city's core is Plaza de las Delicias, an enormous plaza anchored by a massive fountain, Fuentes de Leones, and the impressive Catedral de Nuestra Señora de Guadalupe.

HISTORY

Ponce's rich cultural life gave birth in the mid-1800s to a unique form of romantic classical music called *danza*. A melding of Caribbean and European styles, the formally structured musical style is often described as an Afro-Caribbean waltz and was typically performed on piano and *bombardino* (similar to a trombone) to accompany the dance. As with early rock and roll, conservatives disapproved of the new style because it encouraged couples to dance too closely. But it was eventually embraced by the whole island. In fact, Puerto Rico's national anthem, "La Borinqueña," was originally written as a *danza*. The form is still celebrated today with Ponce's annual Semana de la Danza festival.

The good times continued to roll for a while in Ponce. In 1882 the much ballyhooed Exposition-Fair was held in Plaza de las Delicias to celebrate and cultivate the city's standing as a cultural and agricultural center. Several pavilions were built, including a Moroccan-style structure, no longer

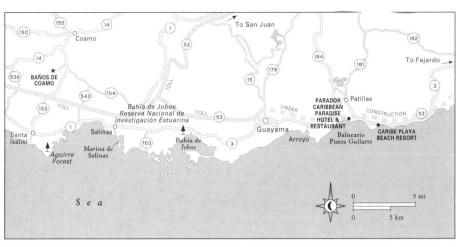

standing, that contained a bazaar and hosted children's dances. Another structure built for the fair was the startling black-and-red-striped structure known today as the Parque de Bombas, which later became the city's fire station and now houses the local tourism office. Many more tents and stalls filled the plaza displaying local produce, flora, and fauna. Horse races were held in the streets, and concerts, plays, and literary readings were held at Teatro La Perla.

But by the turn of the 20th century, the tides began to turn for Ponce. When the United States took control of the island in 1898, new trade restrictions choked the city's shipping industry. Sugar prices fell, sending that industry into decline, and hurricanes destroyed the coffee plantations. By the time the Depression rolled around, Ponce began to spiral into a severe economic decline.

Further demoralizing the social fabric of the city was an event in 1937 referred to as the Ponce Massacre, in which 19 people were gunned down during a demonstration by members of the island's Nationalist Party seeking independence from the United States. Two hundred people were injured in the melee, including many women and children. To learn more, visit the **Museo de la Historia de Ponce.**

Today Ponce is still struggling to find its economic foothold. In the early 1990s, millions of dollars were earmarked to revitalize the city, and much of the area around Plaza de las Delicias has been restored. The plaza is lined with many thriving businesses, including banks, hotels, bars, tourist shops, cafés, and fast-food restaurants. During the day, sidewalks are filled with shoppers, tourists, and street vendors selling everything from fresh flowers to hot dogs. At night there are often live concerts and lots of teenagers and lovers sitting on park benches, eating ice cream, and parading along the sidewalks. In addition, a recreational facility called La Guancha featuring restaurants, bars, and a playground was built near the harbor, and it has infused the tourist industry with some much-needed enthusiasm. And in 2005, JetBlue began flying direct from New York City's JFK airport into Ponce's Mercedita International Airport.

Ponce has a petty street crime problem, so stick close to Plaza de las Delicias at night, or take taxis to area restaurants and casinos. And if you're traveling by car, beware of Ponce drivers. They're arguably the worst on the island. Nevertheless, Ponce is full of many charms that are well worth taking a few extra precautions to enjoy.

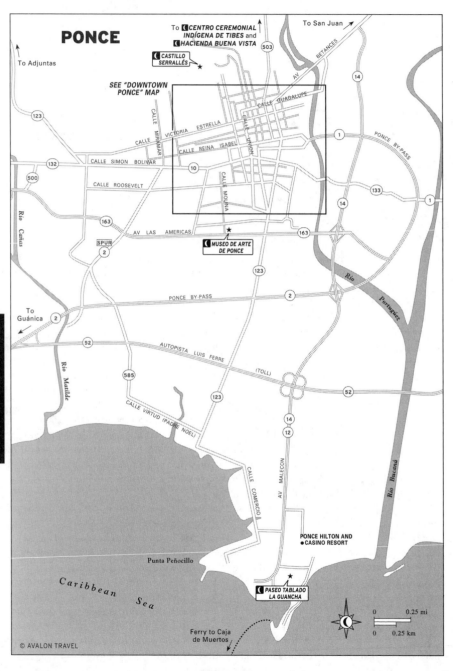

PONCE

To Adjuntas

To ☾ CENTRO CEREMONIAL INDÍGENA DE TIBES and ☾ HACIENDA BUENA VISTA

To San Juan

☾ CASTILLO SERRALLÉS ★

SEE "DOWNTOWN PONCE" MAP

503

BETANCES

AV

14

CALLE GUADALUPE

CALLE VICTORIA ESTRELLA

CALLE MIRAMAR

CALLE UNION

1

PONCE BY-PASS

CALLE REINA ISABEL

123

CALLE SIMON BOLIVAR

132

10

133

500

CALLE ROOSEVELT

CALLE MOLINA

Río Cañas

163

AV LAS AMERICAS

163

14

1

SPUR 2

☾ MUSEO DE ARTE DE PONCE ★

123

2

PONCE BY-PASS

To Guánica

2

52

AUTOPISTA LUIS FERRE

(TOLL)

52

585

123

14

CALLE VIRTUD (PADRE NOEL)

12

Río Matilde

CALLE COMERCIO

AV MALECON

Río Bucaná

Río Portugués

PONCE HILTON AND ● CASINO RESORT

Punta Peñocillo

★ ☾ PASEO TABLADO LA GUANCHA

Caribbean Sea

Ferry to Caja de Muertos

0   0.25 mi

0   0.25 km

© AVALON TRAVEL

SIGHTS
◖ Centro Ceremonial Indígena de Tibes

In 1975 the remains of two native civilizations were discovered a couple of miles north of Ponce on what is now called the Centro Ceremonial Indígena de Tibes (Carr. 503, km 2.5, 787/840-2255, www.nps.gov/nr/travel/prvi/pr15.htm, Tues.-Sun. 8 A.M.-3:30 P.M., except when holidays fall on Mon., then Wed.-Mon., $3 adults, $2 children, $1.50 seniors and visitors with disabilities). The Igneri reigned over the region from 300 B.C. to A.D. 600. On the same location, a Pre-Taíno culture thrived from A.D. 600 to 1200. Excavation of the site is still under way, but among the structures uncovered and restored are seven *bateyes,* or ball fields, and two rectangular stone-rimmed ceremonial plazas, around which you can spot faint petroglyphs carved into the rock.

The vegetation is rich with many of the same plants used by native cultures for medicinal and other purposes, including the *cohoba* tree (its red berries were used to induce hallucination and communication with the gods), the calabash tree (its gourd-like fruit was hollowed out and dried to make bowls), and the *mavi* tree (its bark was used to make a fermented drink). A small museum contains artifacts from both cultures found on the site, including *cemies,* amulets, vomit spatulas, *dujos* (stools), idols, necklaces, a mortar and pestle, flints, blades, and stone collars. In addition, there are the human remains of a woman, possibly sacrificed, found among 187 bodies discovered buried under one of the *bateyes.* There's also a gift shop selling literature about the native cultures and traditional crafts made by local artisans.

Don't be misled by the re-creation of a Taíno village on the site. That culture is not known to have inhabited this land, but it's interesting to see how the *bohio* (a conical wood and straw hut inhabited by commoners) and *caney* (a rectangular wood and straw structure where the cacique leaders lived) were constructed.

◖ Museo de Arte de Ponce

In 2010, Museo de Arte de Ponce (2325 Ave. Las Americas, 787/848-0505 or 787/840-1510, www.museoarteponce.org, Wed.-Mon. 10 A.M.-6 P.M., $6 adults, $3 children) underwent a $30 million renovation and expansion that includes a new glass pavilion entrance. The museum also added 600 new pieces to its permanent collection, including a 28-foot sculpture by Roy Lichtenstein. The crowning jewel of Puerto Rico's cultural institutions, the museum contains more than 3,000 pieces of European, North American, and Puerto Rican art from the 14th century to the present. In addition to its renowned collection of Italian baroque and British Pre-Raphaelite work, Puerto Rican artists are also represented with works by painters José Campeche (1759-1809) and Francisco Oller (1822-1917), as well as photographer Jack Delano (1914-1997), a member of a distinguished group of photographers who worked for the Farm Security Administration during the Depression and documented the island's people and places for more than 50 years.

The most celebrated piece in its collection is *Flaming June,* an 1895 classicist painting of a slumbering woman in a brilliant orange gown by Briton Lord Fredric Leighton. It may seem an unlikely symbol of Ponce's cultural heritage, but once you witness the power of the large gilt-framed painting in the Museo de Arte de Ponce, you can begin to understand why the image has not only been plastered on coffee cups, T-shirts, and mouse pads in the museum store but has been appropriated by local contemporary artists who've taken the liberty of altering her image in various ways, including wrapping her in the Puerto Rican flag.

◖ Castillo Serrallés

Set high on a hill overlooking Ponce is a startling reminder of the height of the city's flourishing sugar industry, when its port was the busiest on the island. Castillo Serrallés (17

Calle El Vigía, 787/259-1774, 787/259-1775, or 800/981-2275, fax 787/259-3463, www.castilloserralles.org, Thurs.-Sun. 9:30 A.M.-5 P.M., gardens $5.50 adults, $2.75 children; gardens, castle, and butterfly garden $12.80 adults, $6.40 seniors, $5.50 children) was built in 1934 for Eugenio Serrallés, a leader in the local sugarcane industry and founder of the still-operating Serrallés Rum Distillery, maker of the island's premier rum, Don Q.

Designed by architect Pedro Adolfo de Castro, the four-story Spanish Moroccan-style mansion was last inhabited in 1979 by Serrallés's daughter. It became a museum in 1991.

The house contains many of the Serrallés family's original furnishings, many of them made by Puerto Rican craftsman or imported from Europe, the oldest piece being a small 16th-century table in the foyer. No cost was spared in the construction of the house. The parquet wood floor in the parlor was imported from Brazil, and the dining room, which took 18 months to build, features a painted, hand-carved ceiling made of oak, mahogany, and ceiba woods, and the black-and-cream bathrooms are designed in an art deco style. The building was technologically advanced for the times: It even has an intercom system with 14 receivers as well as an elevator. In the kitchen is a 1929 GE side-by-side refrigerator that still works. One room in the house has been converted into an exhibition space that explains and illustrates sugarcane processing and rum-making.

Across the street from Castillo Serrallés is **Cruceta del Vigía** ($6 adults, $3 students and seniors, includes admittance to Castillo Serrallés and the gardens), an enormous concrete cross with an observation deck built in 1984. It marks the site of a Spanish lookout station established in 1801 to watch over the Ponce harbor. At that time, a crude wooden cross was erected on the site that remained there until it was destroyed in 1998 by Hurricane Georges. The cross was used as a flag-signaling system to alert troops to the arrival of merchant ships in the harbor. If a white flag was raised, it meant the harbor was under possible attack.

◖ Hacienda Buena Vista

Hacienda Buena Vista (Carr. 123, km 16.8, 787/722-5882, ext. 240 weekdays, 787/284-7020 weekends, www.fideicomiso.org, Wed.-Sun. by reservation only, English tours at 1:30 P.M., Spanish tours at 8:30 A.M., 10:30 A.M., 1:30 P.M., and 3:30 P.M., $8 adults, $5 children, reservations required, accessibility is limited) is a carefully restored 19th-century coffee plantation just north of Ponce and part of the network of historic sites operated under the auspices of the Conservation Trust of Puerto Rico.

Established in 1833, Hacienda Buena Vista was one of the most successful of the 50 plantations around Ponce. It was founded by a Venezuelan, Salvador de Vives, who started out as a small cash-crop farmer growing corn, plantains, yams, pineapples, and coffee. Eventually he added a corn mill, a rice husker, a cotton gin, and a coffee de-pulper to the operation. As Puerto Rico's coffee industry boomed, so did Hacienda Buena Vista, due in large part to the labor of as many as 57 slaves.

When the island's coffee industry went bust in 1897, the plantation was converted into orange groves and remained operational until the 1950s, when the land was expropriated by the Puerto Rican government and distributed in small lots to local farmers. Termites destroyed most of the original buildings, and the farm machinery was left to rust for many years, but in 1984 the Conservation Trust of Puerto Rico began an extensive restoration project using 19th-century construction techniques.

In addition to the restored structures, mill, and machinery, the plantation's lush natural setting is worth a visit. On the Canas River, the property features mature vegetation filled with a variety of birds, including the mangrove cuckoo and Puerto Rican screech owl, as well as plenty of coqui and lizards.

the kitchen at Hacienda Buena Vista

In October, coffee beans from the property are processed and sold by the bag. The Conservation Trust leads occasional guided hikes and bird-watching expeditions in Spanish. Check the website for details. Note that there is no sign at Hacienda Buena Vista. Look for the black metal gate with a guard shack, pull off the road onto the narrow shoulder, and wait for the gate to open at the appointed time.

C Paseo Tablado La Guancha

Commonly called La Guancha (end of Carr. 14 south), this brand-new waterfront facility compensates for the fact that although Ponce is on the coast, little of it is suitable for recreational use.

At first glance, the development isn't too welcoming. There are acres of asphalt parking and an enormous characterless park with tons of playground equipment and picnic tables yet not a lick of shade. Venture farther seaward, though, and you'll find a lovely wide boardwalk along the water that is lined with large pink-and-green matching pavilion-style buildings that house a variety of restaurants and bars. It also has an observation tower and clean, well-maintained bathroom facilities.

Things get particularly lively on the weekends. During the day you can catch a ferry to Caja de Muertos, five miles offshore, for swimming and snorkeling. And at night, families, teenagers, and couples flock here to parade up and down the boardwalk, feeding the fish and stopping in one of the many establishments for some refreshment.

Plaza de las Delicias

Plaza de las Delicias (bounded by Calles Isabel, Atocha, Unión, and Simon Bolívar) is a bustling Spanish colonial plaza surrounded by many lovely 19th-century buildings, many of them containing banks, but there is a bar and a couple of fast-food joints. Although it looks like one large plaza, Plaza de las Delicias is in fact composed of two smaller plazas: Plaza Degetau and

Plaza Luis Muñoz Rivera. Together they create what appears to be the central gathering spot for all of Ponce, especially on the weekends.

During the day the sidewalks along Calle Isabel and Calle Atocha are lined with dozens of brightly colored umbrellas, under which vendors sell hot dogs, silk flowers, lottery tickets, gift wrap by the yard, electronics, sneakers, jewelry, and more. At night, live bands give concerts, attracting multigenerational families, troops of preening teenagers, and love-struck couples who stake out cuddling corners on park benches. Street preachers also are known to get up on the soapboxes here, projecting their sermons through public address systems.

The plaza contains two enormous fountains, including the elaborate Fuentes de Leones (Fountain of Lions). This is also where you'll find the stunning **Catedral de Nuestra Señora de Guadalupe** (787/842-0134, office Mon.-Fri. 9 A.M.-1:30 P.M., services Mon.-Fri. 7 A.M.,

Catedral de Nuestra Señora de Guadalupe

9 A.M., and 12:05 P.M., Sat. 7 A.M., 4 P.M., and 7 P.M., Sun. 7 A.M., 9 A.M., 11 A.M., 4 P.M., and 7 P.M.), a gorgeous French neoclassical-style edifice reconstructed in the 1930s and featuring two bell towers, stone tile floors, and a sky-high arched ceiling painted a robin's-egg blue and hung with 20 crystal chandeliers. Check out the stunning religious statuary, including one of Mary dressed in a pale blue robe with a gold halo above her head, and the bloodied body of Christ in a glass coffin.

But by far the most exceptional structure in Plaza de las Delicias is **Parque de Bombas** (787/284-3338, daily 9 A.M.-5 P.M., free), a startlingly whimsical black-and-red-striped pavilion built in 1882 to provide exhibition space for the Exposition-Fair of Ponce. A year later it became home to the city's fire station. Today it is a museum honoring the history of the city's firefighters. It contains portraits of past fire chiefs, exhibits of fire helmets, hats, axes, and hose nozzles, and it also serves as the tourism office for the city. Lots of travel brochures on sights in the area and an interactive electronic display board provide directions and hours of operation for many of the city's sights.

Hanging around Plaza de las Delicias at night is probably not a good idea, if the armed police in bulletproof jackets who patrol it after dark are any indication.

Museums

Museo de la Música Puertorriqueña (Calle Isabel at Calle Salud, 787/848-7016, Wed.-Sun. 8 A.M.-4 P.M., free) is a tribute to the rich history of Puerto Rican music in a lovely neoclassical home built in 1912 for the Serrallés family, founders of the Serrallés Rum Distillery. Designed by architect Alfredo Wiechers Pieretti of Ponce, the home's stained-glass windows, stone tiles, and brass-embossed walls are reason enough to tour the museum.

Each room is dedicated to a different musical style and the vintage instruments used to

© SUZANNE VAN ATTEN

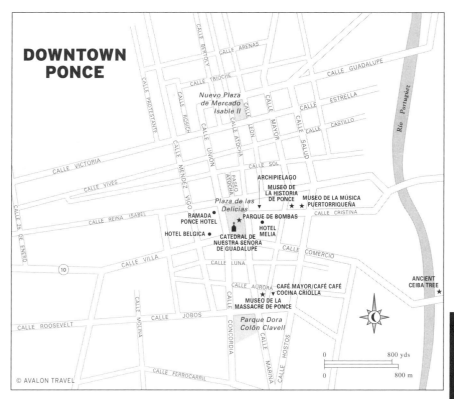

DOWNTOWN PONCE

CALLE BERTOLY

CALLE ARENAS

CALLE TRIOCHE

CALLE GUADALUPE

CALLE PROTESTANTE

CALLE ROSICH

Nuevo Plaza de Mercado Isabel II

CALLE MAYOR

CALLE ESTRELLA

CALLE ATOCHA

CALLE LEÓN

CALLE CASTILLO

CALLE SALUD

Río Portugués

CALLE VICTORIA

CALLE UNIÓN

CALLE MÉNDEZ VIGO

CALLE SOL

CALLE VIVES

PASEO ATOCHA

ARCHIPIELAGO

MUSEO DE LA HISTORIA DE PONCE ★

MUSEO DE LA MÚSICA PUERTORRIQUEÑA ★

CALLE 25 DE ENERO

CALLE REINA ISABEL

Plaza de las Delicias ▼

RAMADA PONCE HOTEL ●

★ PARQUE DE BOMBAS

CALLE CRISTINA

HOTEL BELGICA ●

HOTEL MELIA

CATEDRAL DE NUESTRA SEÑORA DE GUADALUPE

CALLE COMERCIO

10

CALLE VILLA

CALLE LUNA

CALLE AURORA

CAFÉ MAYOR/CAFÉ CAFÉ ▼ COCINA CRIOLLA

ANCIENT CEIBA TREE ★

CALLE ROOSEVELT

CALLE MOLINA

CALLE JOBOS

★ MUSEO DE LA MASSACRE DE PONCE

CALLE CONCORDIA

Parque Dora Colón Clavell

CALLE MARINA

CALLE HOSTOS

0   800 yds

0   800 m

© AVALON TRAVEL

CALLE FERROCARRIL

create it. In the *danza* room are cellos, violins, and French horns; in the salsa room are bongos, bells, maracas, trumpets, trombones, timbales, and *güiros* (gourds); in the *bomba y plena* room are tambourines, *güiros,* and accordions. There's also a room devoted to Taíno ceremonial instruments, including a drum made from a tree trunk, wooden maracas, conch shell horns, flutes made of royal palm and bamboo, and ocarinas (seeds made into flutes). Another room is devoted to the art of making bongos from wooden barrels. Free classes in bongo-making are held in June and July.

Museo de la Historia de Ponce (53 Calle Isabel, corner of Calle Mayor, 787/844-7071 or 787/842-7042, Tues.-Sun. 8 A.M.-4:15 P.M., free) is more than just a monument to the city's history. Its construction served to preserve and adapt two historic neoclassical homes, Casa Salazar and Casa Zapater, and thanks to the addition in 1998 of the Ernesto Ramos Antonini auditorium, it is a cultural center for the local arts community. Permanent exhibits focus on ecology, pre-Hispanic times, politics, economic development, and architecture. Wall text and information are in Spanish only.

A separate museum, **Museo de la Massacre de Ponce** (corner of Calle Marina and Calle Aurora, 787/844-9722, Tues.-Sun. 8 A.M.-4:30 P.M., free), has a very modest exhibit in Spanish dedicated to the memory of a bloody incident on Palm Sunday in 1937 when local police were ordered to fire on Puerto Rican nationalists demonstrating for Puerto Rico's independence

© SUZANNE VAN ATTEN

the black-and-red-striped pavilion Parque de Bombas

from the United States. Nineteen people were killed and more than 200 were injured.

Ancient Ceiba Tree

Puerto Rico's national tree, the ceiba, plays an important role in Puerto Rico's environment. Its massive ridged trunks were carved into canoes by the Taíno Indians, and its tall umbrella-shaped branches rise to 150 feet, high above the forest canopy, where the tree provides a habitat for birds, tree frogs, and insects. It is also host to many aerial plants, including bromeliads.

To see Ponce's 300-year-old ceiba tree, travel east from Plaza de las Delicias on Calle Comericio (Carr. 133) and turn left on Avenida La Ceiba just before you get to Highway 12. The massive gnarled trunk and thick canopy stand in majestic defiance of the surrounding urban blight that threatens to crowd it out.

Isla Caja de Muertos

Isla Caja de Muertos is a small uninhabited island five miles south of Ponce accessible by ferry (Sat.-Sun. and holidays 9 A.M.-5 P.M.) from La Guancha in Ponce. There are hiking trails through the island's interior, which is a semiarid forest containing a variety of cacti. Other features include a cave to explore, a lighthouse built in 1887, and a one-of-a-kind underwater snorkeling trail.

Parque Dora Colón Clavell

Built in 1995, the $11 million Parque Dora Clavell Colón (between Calle Marina and Calle Concordia) is a gorgeous city park with lacy wrought iron and glass pavilions and pergolas, landscaped walkways, and an amphitheater. Five kiosks sell breakfast, lunch, and dinner, as well as wine, beer, and coffee. It's four blocks south of Plaza de las Delicias.

SPORTS AND RECREATION

Caribbean Images Tours (787/244-6283 or 787/821-5312, info@caribbeanimagespr.com)

Parque Dora Colón Clavell amphitheater

offers half-day and full-day snorkeling tours to Caja de Muertos Island, Isla Ratones, and Gilligan's Island.

Island Venture Water Excursions (La Guancha, 787/842-8546, www.islandventurepr.com) offers transportation to Caja de Muertos for $20, $25 with lunch; two-tank diving excursions for $65 with lunch; and snorkeling excursions for $35 with lunch). On Friday and Saturday nights it offers sunset tours of the bay from La Guancha.

If you've got your own boat, **Ponce Yacht and Fishing Club** (787/842-9003 or 787/840-4388, fax 787/844-1300, www.ponceyachtandfishingclub.com) is a full-service marina with an enormous activities pavilion, including a bar and restaurant (seafood and Puerto Rican cuisine, daily noon-10 P.M.). Visiting boaters who pay a dockage fee can use the facilities (showers, cafeteria, restaurant, bar). Registration at the office (Mon.-Fri. 8 A.M.-5 P.M., Sat. 8 A.M.-3 P.M.) is required.

Acampa Adventure Tours (1211 Ave. Piñero, San Juan, 787/706-0695, www.acampapr.com) offers tours to Isla Caja de Muertos on a 37-foot sailing catamaran that include hikes and snorkeling. The tours depart from La Guancha pier in Ponce.

Costa Caribe Golf and Country Club (Ponce Hilton Golf and Casino Resort, 1150 Ave. Caribe, 787/259-7676, www.costacariberesort.com, www.ponce.hilton.com) is a 27-hole course designed by Bruce Besse on what was once sugarcane fields. It offers spectacular views of the Caribbean and Puerto Rico's central mountain region. The signature hole is number 12, featuring an island green.

ENTERTAINMENT AND EVENTS
Festivals

Río de Janeiro's celebration may be the world's most famous, but Ponce's **Carnaval** is no slouch. In February, during the five days preceding the first day of Lent, Plaza de las

Delicias is filled with festivities. Elaborate masquerade dances and parades are held each day, during which revelers show off their elaborate costumes and play out a symbolic battle between the Christians and the Moors. Traditional costumes include *caballeros,* who represent Spanish knights; *vejigantes* (horned entities), who represent the Moors; as well as the evil trickster spirits of the *viejos* (old men) and *locas* (crazy women).

In dramatic contrast to the frivolity of Carnaval is **Las Mañanitas** (787/841-8044). Every December 12 beginning at 5 A.M. a religious procession marches from Calle Lolita Tizol to Plaza de las Delicias. Leading the way are mariachis who sing songs honoring the city's patron saint, Our Lady of Guadalupe.

Semana de la Danza (787/841-8044) features a weeklong series of events celebrating *danza,* a turn-of-the-20th-century ballroom dance that originated in Ponce, and one of its most beloved composers, Juan Morel Campos. Held mid- to late May, the festival features conferences, concerts, parades, and dance competitions.

Feria de Turismo de Puerto Rico (787/287-0140) is an annual tourism fair held in late April at Paseo Tablado La Guancha from noon until midnight. Municipalities around the island represent themselves with their traditional foods, music, and crafts. There are also exhibits representing the island's hospitality industry.

In early April, Ponce hosts **Las Justas,** a massive athletic event that started as an intercollegiate track and field competition but now embraces all varieties of sporting events, including swimming, baseball, basketball, judo, table tennis, and cheerleading. Each year the event attracts more than 100,000 people, drawn as much by the athletic competition as by the nightly concerts featuring the island's biggest reggaetón stars. If this isn't your thing, stay far away from Ponce during Justas. Many businesses, including restaurants and hotels, not only close down but board up their windows; the heavy-drinking crowds are known to get rowdy.

Nightlife

The nightlife in Ponce appears to be pretty limited. There are two casinos in Ponce. **Ponce Hilton and Casino Resort** (1150 Ave. Caribe, 787/259-7676, fax 787/259-7674, www.ponce.hilton.com, daily 10 A.M.-4 A.M.) is a 7,000-square-foot casino with 230 slot machines plus blackjack, craps, roulette, Caribbean stud poker, Texas hold 'em, and three-card poker. **Holiday Inn and Tropical Casino** (3315 Ponce Bypass, 787/844-1200, open 24 hours) is a 9,800-square-foot casino with 346 slot machines plus blackjack, craps, roulette, let it ride, poker, three-card poker, and triple shot.

More bar than café, **Kenepa's Café Bar** (3 Calle Unión, Plaza de las Delicias, 787/363-6674, www.wix.com, bar Wed.-Sat. 4:30 P.M.-2:30 A.M., Sun. 4 P.M.-1 A.M.; restaurant Fri.-Sat. 4 P.M.-2:30 A.M., $8-17) is a popular nightspot for the young professional set. Serving Fridays and Saturdays only, the restaurant specializes in mini plantain baskets stuffed with a variety of fillings, including *churrasco,* chicken, chorizo, shrimp, and octopus. For bigger appetites, entrées include snapper fillet, *churrasco,* fried chicken, and fettuccine Alfredo.

SHOPPING

Paseo Atocha is a pedestrian part of Calle Atocha between Calle Isabel at Plaza de las Delicias and Calle Vives. The sidewalk is lined by a variety of shops selling shoes, clothing, jewelry, electronics, discount housewares, sewing notions, and tourist trinkets. On weekends, Friday-Sunday, the sidewalk fills with street vendors selling flowers, lottery tickets, gift wrap and cards, sewing notions, tourist trinkets, and more.

The newly renovated **Nueva Plaza de Mercado Isabel II** (corner of Paseo Atocha and Calle Victoria, Mon.-Fri. 6 A.M.-5 P.M., Sat. 6 A.M.-4 P.M., Sun. 6 A.M.-noon) is a thriving marketplace filled with vendors selling everything from fresh fruits, vegetables, meats, and seafood to souvenirs, lottery tickets, clothing,

© SUZANNE VAN ATTEN

Ponce's newly renovated Nueva Plaza de Mercado Isabel II was originally built in 1863.

and more. There are also several small eateries serving good, cheap *criolla* cuisine.

Pick up a bag of locally grown coffee roasted on the premises of **Café Mayor** (2638 Calle Mayor at Calle Aurora, 787/812-1941, Mon.-Fri. 8 A.M.-5 P.M.). Three roasts are available, but the French roast is the best.

Mi Coqui (9227 Calle Marina, facing Plaza de las Delicias, 787/841-0216, daily 9 A.M.-7 P.M.) is a two-level wonder. Downstairs is a large, densely packed trinket shop where you can find some low-end, locally made crafts, as well as bottles of rum and bags of coffee. But request access to go upstairs and you'll find a large gallery filled with original artwork, both traditional and contemporary, including oil paintings; *vejigante* masks; and the highly collectible santos, small hand-carved saints.

Utopia (14 Calle Isabel, 787/848-5441, fax 787/813-9899, daily 7:30 A.M.-6 P.M., $4-6) is a huge souvenir and import gift shop selling T-shirts, jewelry, and beachwear. A small lunch counter serves coffee and sandwiches.

ACCOMMODATIONS

Hotel Melia (75 Calle Cristina at Plaza de las Delicias, 787/842-0260 or 800/448-8355, fax 787/841-3602, www.hotelmeliapr.com, $95-130 s, $120-140 d, plus tax, includes a modest continental breakfast) was established in 1900 as a world-class European-style hotel. Thankfully, the outdated circa-1970s rehab of the lobby has been banished, replaced with tasteful dark wood paneling, attractive ceiling detail, and all-new furnishings. The renovated rooms have the budget-corporate look of a business traveler's motel. Rooms come with air-conditioning, phones, satellite TV, wireless Internet, and bathtubs (a rarity!). Amenities include a pool, a business center with two computers and free Internet access, laundry service, and room service.

Most recently renovated in 2011, **Hotel Bélgica** (122 Calle Villa, 1 block off Plaza de las Delicias, 787/844-3255, www.hotelbelgica.com, $77 s, $99 d) has been a continuously

the newly renovated Hotel Bélgica

operating hotel since its construction in 1872. The 20 very clean, simple rooms all have air-conditioning, satellite TV, and no telephones. Some rooms have shared balconies for no additional cost. Rooms have been recently furnished with pleasant Pier 1-style furnishings featuring brown basket weave and wrought-iron furniture. Rooms without windows have large mirrors tricked up with shutters and flower boxes to create a window effect, and all the bathrooms are modern. The hallways feature lovely patterned stone tile floors, while linoleum covers the floors in the rooms. There is no restaurant or bar on-site. If they're available, ask for room 9 or 10—they're the nicest of the bunch.

A welcome new addition to Plaza de las Delicias is **(Ramada Ponce Hotel** (Calle Reina at Calle Unión, Plaza de las Delicias, 787/813-5033, www.ramadaponce.com, $135 s, $140 d plus tax), a modern redo of a historic colonial building featuring 70 rooms, six in the 1882 building up front and the rest in a new modern building behind it that includes 12 junior suites with balconies. Rooms come with 32-inch LCD TVs, air-conditioning, and wireless Internet. Lola, the restaurant and bar in the lobby, is a popular hot spot at night.

FOOD

The waterfront development known as La Guancha is lined with a variety of dining spots, including **El Paladar Bar and Grill** (Paseo Tablado de la Guancha, 787/267-4491 or 787/842-1401, Mon. 11 A.M.-3 P.M., Tues.-Sun. 11 A.M.-11 P.M., $6-20). The casual eatery serves traditional Puerto Rican cuisine with an emphasis on fish, such as fried *chillo* (snapper) and dorado (mahimahi), and *asopao* (rice stew). The restaurant is in a large pavilion with enclosed dining downstairs and an open-air bar upstairs overlooking the boardwalk and marina.

The setting is everything at **Pito's Seafood Café and Restaurant** (Carr. 2, Sector Las Cucharas, 787/841-4977, fax 787/259-8328, www.pitosseafoodpr.com, Sun.-Thurs. 11 A.M.-11 P.M., Fri.-Sat. 11 A.M.-midnight, $16-35). Where else can you watch pelicans dive for their dinner while noshing on every type of seafood imaginable? For landlubbers, there are also plenty of beef, pork, and chicken dishes on the extensive menu. Trunkfish, a local delicacy, is served here when it's available. The three-level waterside restaurant has open-air dining, an enclosed fine-dining room, and private dining in the wine cellar. The wine list features 25 varieties by the glass from regions around the world. There is live music Fridays and Saturdays.

Located beside Pito's Seafood and similar in vibe, **La Monserrate Sea Port Restaurant** (Carr. 2, km 218, 787/841-2740, daily 11 A.M.-10 P.M., $12-35) offers oceanfront terrace dining and a menu featuring every type of seafood imaginable, including lobster, conch, octopus, red snapper, mahimahi, grouper, and shrimp.

Archipielago Restaurant (76 Calle Cristina, 6th floor, 787/812-8822, www.

archipielagopr.com, Wed.-Sat. noon-1 A.M., Sun. 10 A.M.-8 P.M., $10-40) is a chic, sexy rooftop restaurant that gets the cosmopolitan ambiance just right, and the menu is ambitious, with such tempting dishes as panko-crusted veal chop with onion jam and Spanish sausage risotto. Unfortunately the food is only OK. Nevertheless, it's a great place to admire the view while you have a drink and a couple of tapas at the bar.

At **Lola** (Ramada Ponce Hotel, Calle Reina at Calle Unión, Plaza de las Delicias, 787/813-5033, www.lolacuisine.com, Mon. 11:30 A.M.-9 P.M., Thurs.-Fri. 11:30 A.M.-11 P.M., Sat. noon-11 P.M., Sun. noon-9 P.M., $14-29), tile floors, colorful Pop Art paintings, and dim lighting create a glamorous setting for an eclectic menu, including risotto croquettes filled with prosciutto, lobster ravioli in vodka sauce, and lamb chops in tamarind sauce.

Serving breakfast and lunch only, **Café Café Cocina Criolla Espresso Bar** (2638 Calle Mayor, 787/841-7185, Mon.-Fri. 8 A.M.-3 P.M., $8-25) is an outstanding spot for expertly prepared Puerto Rican cuisine.

Kings Cream (9223 Calle Marina, 787/843-8520, daily 9 A.M.-midnight, cup $1.25-1.60, pint $2.75, gallon $11.50) is a no-frills operation serving soft ice cream in a variety of flavors for those on the go, as there's no seating on the premises. The fresh fruit flavors are the best.

INFORMATION AND SERVICES

Medical services are available at **Hospital San Lucas I** (184 Calle Guadalupe, 787/840-4545) and **Hospital San Lucas II** (917 Ave. Tito Castro, 787/844-2080). There's a 24-hour pharmacy at **Walgreens** (Ave. Fagot, 787/841-2135). The U.S. **post office** has branches at 93 Atocha (787/842-2997, 787/842-8303, or 787/284-2186) and Carretera 100, km 123.3 (787/812-0206, 787/812-0207, or 787/812-0208). **Late Night Cyber Café** (18 Calle Leon, Ponce, 407/401-9309 or 787/974-9345,

Mon.-Sat. 10 A.M.-1 A.M., Sun. 1 P.M.-1 A.M.) provides business services including copies, fax, and wireless Internet.

GETTING THERE AND AROUND

Ponce is 117 kilometers or 72 miles southwest of San Juan on Highway 52.

Plans are underway to expand and renovate **Mercedita International Airport** (PSE, 787/842-6292, fax 787/848-4715) to better accommodate bigger commercial jets. Currently there are two passenger terminals and one cargo terminal. JetBlue offers direct flights to Ponce from JFK airport in New York City and from Orlando, Florida. All other U.S. airline companies go through San Juan's Luis Muñoz Marín International Airport, where you can catch a plane to Ponce on one of several daily flights by Cape Air.

There is no public transportation service available from the airport, but you can catch a taxi waiting at the airport. There are several car-rental agencies at the airport, including Avis, Hertz, L&M, and Budget.

In central Ponce, it's fairly easy to wave down a taxi. You can also call **Abolition Taxi Cab** (787/843-0187), **Best Union Taxi Cab** (787/840-9126 or 787/840-9127), **Borinquen Taxi Cab** (787/843-6000 or 787/843-6100), and **Ponce Taxi Méndez** (787/842-3370 or 787/840-0088).

Ponce is a great place to spend a few days, but because this beautiful, culturally rich city is pocketed with economically depressed areas that can sometimes be unsafe, a car is recommended. Just be aware that Ponce drivers represent an old-school Caribbean style of driving that's less apparent in the rest of the island. Stop signs and traffic lights are more suggestion than law. Intersections can be a free-for-all, and horns are constantly blaring—often nanoseconds after a traffic light has turned from red to green.

YAUCO AND GUAYANILLA

The southwestern towns of Yauco and Guayanilla are primarily residential communities that don't often attract visitors, but there

SOUTH COAST

are three good reasons to go: a quirky museum, an annual festival, and one of the island's best restaurants. Together, they make an excellent reason for a day trip.

Sights

Purportedly one of the largest private collections of Volkswagens in the world, **Volkylandia** (Carr. 121, km 13.2, Yauco, 787/267-7774 or 787/267-7775, www.volkylandia.com, Thurs.-Sun. and holiday Mondays 9 A.M.-2 P.M., $10, children under 12 free) features 200 vehicles displayed in a former car dealership tricked out to look like an old-fashioned Puerto Rico town. The surprising variety of Bugs includes VW dragsters, taxis, and fire engines. It's 25 minutes west of Ponce.

Entertainment and Events

Festival del Café is an annual weeklong celebration of the coffee harvest held in late February in Yauco. Festivities take place in Plaza Fernando de Pacheco and include parades, award ceremonies, dance and musical performances, arts, crafts, and food vendors.

Food

In 1957, Don Juan Vera-Martinez fulfilled a special request for a patron at his cockfight arena by deep frying a pork chop specially cut so that it retained a thick rind of fat and part of the ribs. When cooked, the rind of fat curled in a way that recalled the petticoats of a can-can dancer, and *chuleta can can* was born. Now as much a tradition as *mofongo,* it's found on most every menu serving *criolla* cuisine. But the best is served by Don Juan's descendants at ◖ **La Guardarraya** (Carr. 127, km 6.0, Guayanilla, 787/856-4222, www.laguardarraya.com, Wed.-Sun. 11 A.M.-7:30 P.M., closed the last two weeks of Dec., $7-15), a destination restaurant halfway between Guánica and Ponce. Built in 1993, the restaurant is a large, lovely *criolla*-style wood structure with shuttered doors and windows tucked in the woods, and the service is highly professional. The house sangria made from fresh juices is outstanding and strong. This restaurant can be a challenge to find. If you're coming from Ponce, go west on Carretera 2, take exit 205 for Penuelas/Guayanilla, and turn left. Turn right at McDonald's, then take an immediate left onto Carretera 127 and cross the bridge. The restaurant is on the right. It's worth it.

Coamo and Salinas

COAMO

The town of Coamo is a modest little village in the hilly terrain just south of the island's majestic Cordillera Central mountain range. The compelling reason to venture here is not for the town but for its nearby claim to fame, the Coamo Baños, a natural hot springs reputed to have restorative powers.

Coamo is 103 kilometers or 64 miles south of San Juan. Take Highway 52 south to Carretera 153 north to Carretera 14 north.

Sights

Baños de Coamo (end of Carr. 546, daily 8 A.M.-6 P.M., free) may well be Puerto Rico's very first tourist attraction. The hot springs, which retain a constant 110°F temperature and which are rich in minerals, were first discovered by the Taíno Indians, who shared their find with the Spanish colonists. By the mid-16th century, visitors were making their way here in a steady stream, and in the 17th century a resort was built that operated until the 1950s. Wealthy visitors from all over the world visited

Coamo, including the most illustrious U.S. proponent of hot springs himself, President Franklin D. Roosevelt.

The springs look very different today than they did then. The water has actually been contained in two places. One, which looks like a small standard swimming pool, is on the private property of the Hotel Baños de Coamo and is reserved for its guests. The public bath is an easy half-mile hike down a dirt road behind the hotel. Unfortunately, despite the size of the hotel parking lot, visitors to the public bath are forbidden to use it, so it's necessary to park alongside the dead-end road, where local farmers sometimes sell produce from the backs of their trucks.

Until recently the bath was contained in a stone pool, but that structure has since been replaced by a square ceramic-tile enclosure that looks a lot like a giant bathtub set down in the great outdoors. Families with small children and many elderly folks gather here to relax for hours, bringing with them picnics (no alcohol allowed) and folding tables on which to play dominoes and cards. Whether the springs are truly healing can be debated, but that doesn't stop the clearly infirm who are drawn to the waters.

Dips are limited to 15 minutes at a time, and there is a small rustic changing room on-site.

Sports and Recreation

Coamo Springs Golf Club and Tennis Club (Carr. 546, km 1, 787/825-1370, www.coamosprings.com, daily 7 A.M.-7 P.M.) is an 18-hole course designed by Ferdinand Garbin in a residential community that will challenge your ability to golf in the wind.

Maratón de San Blas de Illesca (787/825-1370) is an internationally renowned half marathon held in early February.

Accommodations and Food

Parador Baños de Coamo (end of Carr. 546, 787/825-2186, fax 787/825-4739, hbcoamo@ coqui.net, $93 s/d, plus tax) has 46 very basic motel-style rooms on two levels, each with a private balcony. Rooms come with air-conditioning and cable TV and feature stone tile floors, worn furnishings, and institutional-looking bathrooms. But the thick, wild vegetation growing around the property creates a pleasant natural environment. At the center of the complex is a massive, reputedly 500-year-old *saman* tree covered in vines and cactus that shades the entire property. There are two pools, one for swimming adjoined by a bar, and the other containing water from the hot springs.

Aguas Termales (Hotel Baños de Coamo, end of Carr. 546, 787/825-2186 or 787/825-2239, daily 7-10 A.M., noon-3 P.M., and 5:30-9:30 P.M., $8-19) serves Puerto Rican cuisine, seafood, and steak.

At the Coamo Springs Golf Club & Resort is the **Coamo Springs Restaurant** (Carr. 153, km 1.5, 787/825-1370, www.coamosprings.com, Thurs. and Sun. noon-9 P.M., Fri.-Sat. 11:30 A.M.-10 P.M., $11-28), which is the nicest restaurant in town, serving Puerto Rican cuisine, paella, and *churrasco*.

Information and Services

Walgreens (106 Calle Piel Canela, Coamo, 787/803-6802) provides pharmaceutical services. **Banco Popular** (7 Calle Mario Braschi Bajos, Coamo, 787/825-1135) provides banking services. The **post office** is at 100 Calle A, Suite 1.

SALINAS

Salinas is an economically depressed and depressing fishing village with poorly maintained roads, a small marina, and a hotel that is best avoided. There's really only one reason to visit: to dine at one of the modest seafood restaurants that line the waterfront along Calle Principal.

Salinas is 103 kilometers or 64 miles south of San Juan on Highway 52.

Sights

Bahía de Jobos Reserva Nacional de

Museo Olímpico de Puerto Rico at Albergue Olímpico

© SUZANNE VAN ATTEN

Investigación Estuarina (Carr. 705, km 2.3, 787/853-4617 or 787/864-0105, Mon.-Fri. 8 A.M.-noon and 1-4 P.M., Sat. 9 A.M.-noon and 1-3 P.M., alternate Sun.) is a 2,800-acre reserve of mangrove forests and freshwater wetlands, pocketed with lagoons, salt flats, and mud beds. This is a great spot for kayaking, although rentals are not available on-site. Guided tours can be arranged in advance.

It has long been the dream of the Puerto Rico Olympic Committee to host the international games. San Juan hosted the 1966 and 1993 Central American Games and the 1979 Pan American Games, but Puerto Rico has yet to achieve its dream of bringing the Olympics to the island. Nevertheless, the competitive spirit lives on at **Albergue Olímpico** (Carr. 712, km 0.3, 787/824-2607 or 800/981-2210, museum daily 10 A.M.-5 P.M., water park daily 10 A.M.-5 P.M. June-July, museum $2, museum and water park $15). The 1,500-acre complex contains athletic training facilities for swimming, tennis, boxing,

fencing, track, and more; a school for 350 athletically gifted 7th-12th graders; an Olympic museum; and a water park with a miniature golf course and rock-climbing wall.

Sports and Recreation

Polita's Beach (Carr. 701, Marina de Salinas, $3 to park) is a small scrubby beach where you can rent personal watercraft for $5. It has a snack bar and portable toilets.

Marina de Salinas (end of Carr. 701, 787/752-8484 or 787/824-3185, fax 787/768-7676) accommodates 103 vessels and provides guests with water, electricity, ice, gas and diesel, private showers, laundry facilities, and a convenience store.

Accommodations

Marina de Salinas Waterfront Inn and Marina (end of Carr. 701, Playa Ward, 787/824-3185 or 787/824-5973, fax 787/768-7676, www.marinadesalinas.com, $95 s, $115-125 d, $135-175 suite, plus tax) is a poorly maintained two-level motel-style hotel with thin walls and thinner towels. But you get a modern bath with a shower, air-conditioning, TV, telephone, and coin-operated laundry facilities. Suites come with a microwave and a refrigerator. Amenities include a small pool, a snack bar, and a compact playground for toddlers.

Food

Restaurante Costa Marina (Marina de Salinas, end of Carr. 701, Playa Ward, 787/824-3185, Sun.-Thurs. noon-9 P.M., Fri.-Sat. noon-11 P.M., $10-32) is a tastefully decorated, nautical-themed restaurant with round porthole windows overlooking the marina. The extensive menu serves mostly seafood, including whole snapper and lobster. It also serves steaks and traditional Puerto Rican cuisine.

Ladi's (A-86 Calle Principal, Carr. 701, 787/824-2035, Tues.-Fri. 11 A.M.-9 P.M., Sat.-Sun. 11 A.M.-10 P.M., $8-29), an institution for 54 years, is a huge, elegantly casual open-air restaurant just feet from the water. The menu features traditional Puerto Rican cuisine specializing in seafood, including paella, whole snapper, and *mofongo.* The *tostones* are some of the best on the island. Ask for the accompanying sauce, a thin, spicy garlic tomato sauce. It's a much better and more traditional option than the Thousand Island dressing most restaurants serve nowadays. Ladi's offers excellent service and a full bar.

El Balcon del Capitan (A-54 Calle Principal, Carr. 701, 787/824-6210, daily 11 A.M.-10 P.M., $9-27) is a small casual waterfront restaurant. Seated on plastic patio furniture, dine on the large selection of *empanadillas,* stuffed with everything from lobster and beef to octopus and shrimp. Other specialties include lobster and paella. It's very popular among families with young children.

Guayama and Patillas

GUAYAMA

Guayama features a lovely central plaza, **Plaza de Recreo Cristóbal Colón,** distinguished by rows of unique umbrella-shaped trees and **Iglesia San Antonio de Padua,** a neo-Roman-style church with twin towers. Across the street is **Casa Cautino,** an architectural vision of white lacy iron work on a cream-colored *criolla*-style house with colonial details. Just east of town is the **Bellas Artes building,** another 19th-century architectural gem. The rest of the town is a gritty jumble of densely packed homes and businesses, many of which are in need of repair, and steady streams of traffic slowly navigating the narrow one-way streets lined with parked cars.

Guayama is 89 kilometers or 53 miles south of San Juan. Take Highway 52 south to Highway 53 west.

Sights

Centro de Bellas Artes de Guayama (Calle McArthur, 787/864-7765 or 787/864-0600, ext. 2306, Tues.-Sat. 9 A.M.-4 P.M., Sun. 10 A.M.-4:30 P.M., free) is a new art center in a restored 19th-century building. It contains 11 exhibition galleries devoted to art and history.

Museo Casa Cautiño (1 Calle Palmer, 787/864-9083, Tues.-Sat. 9 A.M.-4:30 P.M., Sun. 10 A.M.-4 P.M., free) is on the main plaza in Guayama in a lovely 19th-century neoclassic *criolla*-style home distinguished by an ornately decorated exterior and lacy ironwork. The one-story U-shaped house was built in 1887 and belonged to wealthy landowner General Cautiño Vázquez. During the Spanish-American War, the home served as headquarters for American forces. The home contains the family's original, locally made furnishings and artwork.

Bosque Estatal de Aguirre (Carr. 7710, south of Carr. 3, 787/864-0105, fax 787/853-4617, daily 7 A.M.-3:30 P.M.) is a pristine piece

© SUZANNE VAN ATTEN

Plaza de Recreo Cristóbal Colón, Guayama's central plaza

of undeveloped paradise containing mangrove forest, tidal flats, and large populations of birds and manatees. A wooden boardwalk provides easy access. Camping is not allowed.

Recreation and Entertainment

El Legado Golf Resort (Hwy. 52, 787/866-8894, www.ellegadogolfresort.com) is an 18-hole course designed by local legend Chi Chi Rodriguez in a residential condominium community. It includes several lakes, a waterfall, and a putting green shaped like the island.

Club Náutico de Guayama (end of Carr. 7701, 787/866-3162, fax 787/866-3162) is a private marina that accepts visitors.

Feria Dulces Sueños (787/864-7765, fax 787/864-5070) is a Paso Fino horse competition held at the fairgrounds in early March. Other festivities include food kiosks and music.

Fiesta de Reyes (787/864-7765, fax 787/864-5070) is held every year on January 6 to celebrate the traditional Puerto Rican

holiday Three Kings Day. The royal pilgrims visit each barrio in the municipality before proceeding to Plaza de Recreo Cristóbal Colón for music, games, and more.

The **tourism office** (787/864-7765, fax 787/864-5070) is on Plaza de Recreo Cristóbal Colón. It operates a free trolley tour from Casa Cautiño or Centro de Bellas Artes to points of interest in the area.

PATILLAS

Patillas is a charming small town located about four kilometers north of the Caribbean coast that boasts a shady plaza and a small but gorgeous Catholic parish. Ultimately, though, the main reason visitors go to Patillas is for a dip into the Caribbean and the quaint little inns and mom-and-pop restaurants that hug the narrow, rocky coast in a neighborhood called Barrio Guardarraya. This corner of the island is often overlooked by visitors because it doesn't have the wide, sandy beaches or the

© SUZANNE VAN ATTEN

Parroquia Inmaculado Corazón de María in Patillas

flashy restaurants, clubs, and shops found on the Atlantic side, but that is its draw for those who want to escape the more touristy parts of the island and enjoy a low-key getaway.

Patillas is 105 kilometers or 65 miles south of San Juan. Take Highway 52 south to Highway 53 west.

Sights

Located nearby in Arroyo, **Balneario Punta Guilarte** (Carr. 3, km 126, 787/839-3565, daily 8 A.M.-4:30 P.M., $2) is a publicly maintained beach with facilities on the west side of Puerto Patillas Bay. At the entrance is **Faro de Punta Figuras**, a recently renovated lighthouse built in 1893.

Parroquia Inmaculado Corazón de María (Patillas Plaza, 787/839-5333, daily mass) is a modest mission-style church containing a stunning turquoise nave with a gorgeous white, gilt-trimmed altarpiece. A spiral staircase leads to balcony seating and 10 round stained-glass windows look down on a painted tile floor.

Recreation

Wave Rebelz (8 Calle Cristo, east of Patillas Plaza, 787/236-4570, Mon.-Thurs. 10 A.M.-7 P.M., Fri.-Sat. 10 A.M.-8 P.M., Sun. 10 A.M.-5 P.M.) is the place to go to buy or rent all your surfing needs, from boards to board shorts. Brands include Element, Ripcurl, Creatures, VS, and Sol. Rental rates are $40 a day for surfboards, $50-60 for paddleboards, and $20-40 for boogie boards. Paddleboard lessons are available.

Accommodations

◖ **Caribe Playa Beach Resort** (Carr. 3, km 112, Patillas, 787/839-6339, fax 787/839-1817, www.caribeplaya.com, $130 s/d plus tax) is a bit of a misnomer. It's too small, modest, and low-key to qualify for what most people imagine when they think of a resort. Instead, it is old-fashioned, intimate, casual, and quiet. The pale yellow and white motel-style structure hugs the coastline so closely that you can practically hear the waves lapping the beach from the bed. The 27 units are very basic and come with air-conditioning, satellite TV, refrigerators, and coffeemakers. Wireless Internet is available in common areas. The grounds are landscaped with unusual tropical flowers and appointed with grills, shaded hammocks, umbrella tables, and lounge chairs. The seaside Ocean View Terrace serves three meals a day, breakfast being the best option. There is nothing fancy at all about this "resort," and that is a big part of its charm.

Parador Caribbean Paradise Hotel & Restaurant (Carr. 3, km 114.3, Barrio Guardarraya, Patillas, 787/839-5885 or 787/839-7388, www.caribbeanparadisepr.com, www.gotoparadores.com, $88-108 family rooms for two adults and two children under 12) is a sprawling, bright yellow inn catering to families traveling on a budget. There are 24 clean, motel-style rooms and a restaurant serving breakfast and dinner. Rooms are air-conditioned

© SUZANNE VAN ATTEN

Caribe Playa Beach Resort

and come with cable TV and coffeemakers. Amenities include a large swimming pool plus tennis and basketball courts. There is a children's day camp on-site during summer months.

Food

Newly opened in 2011, **◖Mustafá Restaurant** (Carr. 3, km 114, Barrio Guardarraya, 787/839-5428 or 787/644-5193, Mon.-Thurs. 11 A.M.-8 P.M., Fri.-Sun. till 10 P.M., $10-22) offers open-air dining so close to the water's edge that the sea practically laps at your feet. Sit at the outdoor bar or take a seat inside the enormous pavilion lined with coconut palms, where you can dine on an extensive *criolla* menu heavy on seafood dishes. Specialties include land crab stew; lobster stuffed with octopus, conch, and shrimp; and *chillo* fried whole or filleted and stuffed with shrimp. For landlubbers there is *chuleta can can* and *mofongo* stuffed with chicken. There's live entertainment on the weekends and karaoke on Thursday nights. Service

can be excruciatingly slow, so order a drink first and prepare to kick back and enjoy the view.

A neighborhood restaurant in the truest sense, **Lordemar Restaurant** (Carr. 3, km 112.5, Barrio Guardarraya, Patillas, 787/839-7692, Fri.-Sun. and holidays 11 A.M.-9 P.M., $7-27) is located on the covered patio in back of a small green house among a cluster of modest waterfront homes. The menu includes *asopao, churrasco, mofongo,* and crab stew. It has a full bar.

Nuevo Centro de Patillas (corner of Carr. 3 and Calle Soto, hours vary) is a long, low-slung metal building with green awnings that contains a dozen food and fruit vendors, as well as a bar or two and an ice cream shop.

INFORMATION AND SERVICES

Walgreens (1 Calle Marginal, Suite 2, Guayama, 787/864-5800) provides pharmaceutical services. **Banco Popular** (33 Calle Rivera, Patillas, 787/839-2130) provides banking services. The **post office** is at 101 Carr. 3 in Patillas.

WEST COAST

For many decades, the west coast of Puerto Rico has been a mecca for surfers and divers. The rocky coast—with its craggy points, protected lagoons, big swells, and underwater walls—is a nature-lover's wonderland. During surf season, from December to April, the population explodes, and a solid seasonal infrastructure of low-budget crash pads and burger bars has built up through the years to serve the seasonal visitors.

Recently nicknamed Porto del Sol by the tourism authority, the west coast is beginning to be promoted as a destination apart from San Juan. Thanks to the former Ramey Air Force Base, which once occupied much of Aguadilla, the infrastructure existed for the birth of Rafael Hernández International Airport, which now services flights from New York City, New Jersey, and Orlando, Florida. As a result, tourism has flourished, and more upscale resorts and restaurants are beginning to crop up in idyllic little spots along the coast to serve the leisure traveler.

The west coast has so much going on that it's worthy of an extended stay. It encompasses a huge range of environments within just a 50-mile range. Aside from the party-hardy surf towns of Isabela, Rincón, and Aguadilla, it includes the colonial city of Mayagüez, the fishing village of Boquerón, the phosphorescent bay in La Parguera, the salt flats of Cabo Rojo, and the 10,000-acre subtropical dry forest in Guánica.

© SUZANNE VAN ATTEN

HIGHLIGHTS

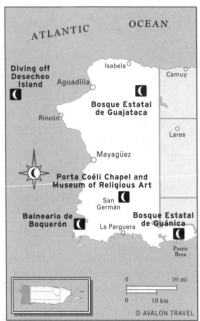

LOOK FOR **(** TO FIND RECOMMENDED SIGHTS, ACTIVITIES, DINING, AND LODGING.

(Bosque Estatal de Guajataca: This 2,357-acre forest reserve in the southern tip of Isabela is not only rich in flora and fauna, but the temperature hovers in the high 70s, making it a great escape from the summer heat (page 158).

(Diving off Desecheo Island: The west coast boasts an underwater wonderland, but the only way to see it is to don a mask and go deep. The waters around the uninhabited island of Desecheo provide spectacular spots to dive and snorkel. You can see all kinds of colorful marine life, including rays, parrot fish, grunts, porkpie fish, sharks, coral formations, and more (page 171).

(Balneario de Boquerón: One of the island's mostly lovely public beaches features a long, wide crescent beach and modern new facilities, including bathrooms, showers, picnic shelters, and snack bars (page 192).

(Porta Coéli Chapel and Museum of Religious Art: The tiny primitive chapel established in 1606 in San Germán is a rare example of Gothic architecture in the New World. It contains a collection of 18th- and 19th-century religious paintings and sculpture (page 202).

(Bosque Estatal de Guánica: The 10,000-acre subtropical dry forest and United Nations Biosphere Reserve features hiking trails, caves, beaches, the ruins of a Spanish fort, and great bird-watching opportunities (page 205).

Most important to some, the west coast is about as far away as you can get—both literally and figuratively—from San Juan. The fast-paced, high-stress urban environment in the island's capital is replaced by a slow-paced, nature-loving vibe that west coasters embrace.

PLANNING YOUR TIME

The entire west coast could be driven from tip to tail in less than two hours, but who would want to? There's so much to do and see, you could easily bypass San Juan and the eastern side altogether and spend an entire month on

the west coast. In a pinch, though, a long weekend will suffice.

There are two main reasons you want to plan on spending as much time as possible on the west coast. For one, most of the charms are to be found by taking up some form of water sport, and that takes time. Whether it is mastering the art of surfing on the beaches in Isabela, Rincón, or Aguadilla; taking a scuba-diving expedition to Desecheo Island or Mona Island; or paddling a kayak through the mangrove channels, taking a stand-up paddleboard tour, or kayaking through the Bahía

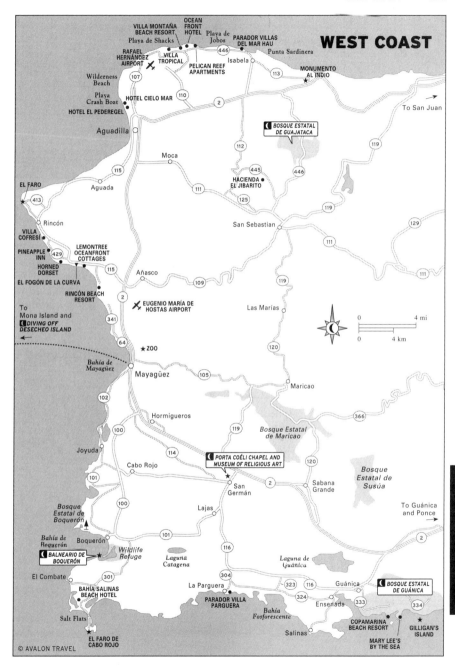

WEST COAST

VILLA MONTAÑA BEACH RESORT
OCEAN FRONT HOTEL
Playa de Shacks
Playa de Jobos
PARADOR VILLAS DEL MAR HAU
Punta Sardinera
RAFAEL HERNÁNDEZ AIRPORT
VILLA TROPICAL
PELICAN REEF APARTMENTS
Isabela
MONUMENTO AL INDIO
446
113
Wilderness Beach
107
Playa Crash Boat
HOTEL CIELO MAR
110
2
HOTEL EL PEDEREGEL
To San Juan
Aguadilla
BOSQUE ESTATAL DE GUAJATACA
Moca
112
119
445
446
115
HACIENDA EL JIBARITO
EL FARO
413
111
Aguada
125
VILLA COFRESÍ
Rincón
San Sebastian
119
129
PINEAPPLE INN
429
LEMONTREE OCEANFRONT COTTAGES
111
HORNED DORSET
115
111
EL FOGÓN DE LA CURVA
Añasco
119
RINCÓN BEACH RESORT
2
109
To Mona Island and
DIVING OFF DESECHEO ISLAND
341
EUGENIO MARÍA DE HOSTAS AIRPORT
Las Marías
64
ZOO
Bahía de Mayagüez
120
105
Mayagüez
Maricao
102
Hormigueros
366
100
119
Bosque Estatal de Maricao
Joyuda
114
PORTA COÉLI CHAPEL AND MUSEUM OF RELIGIOUS ART
120
Cabo Rojo
San Germán
2
Bosque Estatal de Susúa
101
100
Lajas
Sabana Grande
Bosque Estatal de Boquerón
Bahía de Boquerón
Boquerón
101
116
To Guánica and Ponce
2
BALNEARIO DE BOQUERÓN
Wildlife Refuge
Laguna Catagena
Laguna de Guánica
El Combate
301
304
323
116
Guánica
BOSQUE ESTATAL DE GUÁNICA
BAHÍA SALINAS BEACH HOTEL
La Parguera
324
333
334
Salt Flats
PARADOR VILLA PARGUERA
Ensenada
EL FARO DE CABO ROJO
Bahía Fosforescente
Salinas
COPAMARINA BEACH RESORT
GILLIGAN'S ISLAND
MARY LEE'S BY THE SEA

0   4 mi
0   4 km

WEST COAST

© AVALON TRAVEL

Fosforescente in La Parguera, you've got to get in the water to appreciate all the west coast has to offer.

The other reason you'll want to linger here is that there is a laid-back, easygoing rhythm to life on the west coast that compels you to slow down, take your time, have another beer, and watch the sunset. And if you don't let yourself be a part of that magic, you'll miss the whole reason for visiting.

To fully explore the west coast, a car is essential. If you're arriving via San Juan, it's about a 100-mile drive and takes about 2-4 hours, depending on time of day and road construction projects along the way. It's also possible to fly into Aguadilla and rent a car.

Isabela

The area known today as Isabela was once ruled by Cacique Mabodamaca, one of the island's most powerful Taíno chiefs. Legend has it that when faced with capture by the Spanish colonists, he leapt to his death off the cliffs of Isabela. When his body was recovered, the medallion that signified his lofty place in the hierarchy of Taíno culture was missing from around his neck and is still sought among the cliffs today. A striking monument to Mabodamaca exists at the intersection of Carretera 2 and Carretera 113. A large bust of the great Indian chief has been carved into the side of the mountain, his medallion respectfully replaced around his neck. The monument not only serves as a reminder of the Taíno culture that once prevailed in the area, but it marks the northern entrance to Puerto Rico's west coast.

WEST COAST

© MARY SIMPSON/123RF.COM

beach in Isabela

The first Spanish settlement in this area was called San Antonio de la Tuna. The date of its origin is unknown, but it was situated on the banks of the Río Guajataca, which separates Isabela from Quebradillas. In the early 1800s the residents of the town made a formal request to the island's governor asking that the town be relocated closer to the coast, and in 1819 a new town was established and called Isabela after Queen Isabel of Spain.

The town of Isabela features a charming little plaza anchored by a church, as are all town plazas. But most visitors head to the municipality's gorgeous beaches along coastal road Carretera 466. This is where you'll find lots of opportunities for swimming, surfing, diving, and horseback riding, as well as a variety of hotels, restaurants, and bars.

The westward drive along Carretera 466 is pretty remarkable. The long stretch of road passes through undeveloped land lined by palm groves and the sea on one side and flat grassy plains grazed upon by herds of cattle on the other. Beyond the plains is a huge ridge that runs parallel to the beach, creating a dramatic backdrop to the pastoral scene.

Those seeking an idyllic patch of wilderness beach must hurry if they hope to find it in Isabela, though: Condo construction has exploded, and it won't be long before everyone discovers this pristine parcel of paradise.

BEACHES

Surfing and diving are two great reasons to stay in Isabela. There are two excellent beaches perfect for doing both, just a couple of miles apart.

Playa de Jobos

Playa de Jobos (Carr. 466 just east of Carr. 4466) has no public facilities, but it has sufficient parking to support the serious surfers who flock to the break point off Punta Jacinto. It's renowned for its right-breaking tube just off the point. Carefully walk eastward on the point's rocky coral reef to find a big blowhole—where the ocean waves rush underneath and spray water into the air through a hole in the reef. It's a fantastic sight and a great place for photos.

Playa de Shacks

Playa de Shacks (Carr. 4466 in front of Villa Tropical) not only has good surfing and kitesurfing, it also has excellent snorkeling and diving. Blue Hole is touted as one of the north coast's best snorkeling spots. It's located in the surf just outside the office at Villa Tropical and about 500 meters east of Villa Montaña.

There are also underwater caverns accessible from the reef. Several dive shops offer excursions in the area, and horseback riding can be arranged at the resort. The only drawback to Shacks is the lack of parking, which is limited to the shoulders of the road or the occasional house where you're permitted to park for a small fee.

Punta Sardinera

Located on Punta Sardinera east of Playa de Jobos is Centro Empresarial Playero, a rustic recreation area containing patches of sandy beaches between coral outcroppings, a natural pool, basketball courts, and a cluster of kiosks selling fritters and booze tucked away in a thickly vegetated area overgrown with sea grape, devil's tongue, cedar trees, and palms. To get there, drive north on Carretera 112 through the central town of Isabela toward the beach. After you pass Carretera 446 on the left, continue straight past a condominium complex and turn right, following the road to a dead-end. If you turn left at the condominium complex, you will proceed along a short stretch of wilderness beach obscured by brush. There's no parking, but there are sandy pull-ins where you can park your car and walk down to the sea.

SIGHTS
Monumento al Indio

Monumento al Indio (intersection of Carr. 2

and Carr. 113 on the westbound side) is an astonishing artistic achievement made in memorial to the area's Taíno Indians and their cacique, Mabodamaca. A large bust of the chief has been carved into the side of a mountain, marking the road to Isabela and the west coast.

San Antonio de la Tuna Ruins

San Antonio de la Tuna ruins (from Carr. 2, turn south just west of Carr. 113) is the site of the area's first town, which was relocated and renamed Isabela in 1819. The original town was situated on Río Guajataca and was believed to have been established around 1725. The site is marked by the ruins of the town's church. Arrange a tour by trolley by contacting the tourism office (787/872-6400) in the *alcaldía* (city hall) on Plaza Recreo de Isabela.

◖ Bosque Estatal de Guajataca

Bosque Estatal de Guajataca (Carr. 446 south

© JASON ROSS/123RF.COM

WEST COAST

dense vegetation in Bosque Estatal de Guajataca

of Carr. 2, 787/724-3724) is a 2,357-acre forest reserve in a mountainous region south of Isabela. Be advised, though: The drive here is not for the fainthearted. The closer you get to the forest, the narrower the road becomes until it's just one car wide, despite the fact it's a two-way road. Adding to the thrill, the road climbs steadily upward and takes many sharp twists and turns around mountains with steep, unprotected drop-offs just inches from the road's pavement. You know you're close—and none too soon—when you encounter a sign warning drivers to roll down their windows, turn off their radios, and honk their horns as they travel around the blind curves.

The forest is well worth the hairy drive to get there, though. A subtropical moist forest that receives 75 inches of rain a year, it's distinguished by its unique karst topography featuring underground limestone caves and dramatic haystack hills called *mogotes*. Because its temperature wavers between 75°F and 79°F, it's a great place to escape the heat during the hot summer.

Bosque Estatal de Guajataca is rich in indigenous flora and fauna. It is home to 186 species of trees, including Honduras mahogany and teak hibiscus, and is home to 45 species of birds, including the Puerto Rican woodpecker, screech owl, and bullfinch. It's also where you can find the rare, endangered Puerto Rican boa constrictor.

There are 27 miles of trails in the forest that lead to such sites as a lookout tower and El Viento Cave, a natural limestone cave formation with stalactites, stalagmites, and columns. There is also a 1.5-mile interpretive trail. Primitive camping is allowed, but a permit is required.

SPORTS AND RECREATION
Water Sports

There are lots of hot **surfing** spots in Isabela. In addition to Playas Shacks and Jobos, you can find more great breaks by traveling eastward from Jobos on the dirt road that follows the coast to reach sites called Golondrinas, Secret Spot,

PASO FINO HORSES

Although not indigenous to Puerto Rico, the Paso Fino horse is closely associated with the island because it was here and in the Dominican Republic where the Spanish conquistadors first introduced the mixed-breed horse. Sharing a family tree with the Moorish Berber, Spanish jennet, and Andalusian breeds, the Paso Fino is a superb saddle horse thanks to its unusual gait. Unlike other horses, its feet fall in a natural lateral pattern instead of a diagonal pattern, which creates a smoother ride for its passenger.

Puerto Rico's Paso Fino horse is typically smaller than horses in the United States, coming in somewhere between 13 and 16 hands high. Their body shape varies from stocky to lithe, and they can be found in every equine color except the Appaloosa pattern. Besides their unusual gait, Paso Finos are characterized by a high level of endurance, great agility, and remarkable obedience.

Juan Ponce de Léon reportedly first introduced the horse to the island in 1521, bringing with him 50 specimens of the mixed breed from Spain. They were quickly put into service working farms, providing transportation, and participating in military maneuvers.

In 1610 the San Juan Races were established as part of the city's patron saint festivities. As a testament to their smooth gait and obedience, the horses were raced without the use of reins. In fact, riders reportedly crossed their arms over their chests and smoked tobacco while their steeds raced to the finish line.

Through the careful selection of mares and stallions that best embodied the horses' unique traits, a specific breed began to develop by the 1700s, although it wasn't until the mid-1800s that the Spanish government officially recognized the breed.

Today, there are about 8,000 registered pure-bred Puerto Rican Paso Fino horses. Although replaced by automation long ago, they're still used for transportation in rural parts of the island—most notably in Vieques and Culebra, where they also roam and graze freely throughout the islands.

Guided trail rides on Paso Finos are available along beaches and through tropical forests with **Tropical Trail Rides** (787/872-9256, www.tropicaltrailrides.com) in Isabela and **Pintos R Us** (787/516-7090, www.pintosrus.com) in Rincón on the west coast and **Hacienda Carabalí** (787/889-5820, www.haciendacarabalipuertorico.com) in Luquillo on the east coast.

and Middles, in that order. For expert advice on when and where the best spots are, visit **Hang Loose Surf Shop** (Carr. 4466, km 1.1, Playa Jobos, 787/872-2490, Tues.-Sat. 10 A.M.-5 P.M., Sun. 11 A.M.-3 P.M., $30 board rentals). This is the place to buy or rent boards, get your board replaced, or get private surfing lessons. Lessons must be scheduled and prepaid. No lessons are held on Sunday. The shop also sells beachwear and accessories, including towels, sunblock, sunglasses, sandals, bathing suits, beach chairs, snorkeling equipment, and souvenirs.

La Cueva Submarina (Carr. 466, km 6.3, 787/872-1390 or 787/872-1094 after 5:30 P.M., www.lacuevasubmarina.net, Mon.-Fri. 9 A.M.-5 P.M., Sat.-Sun. 8 A.M.-5 P.M., dive trips Thurs.-Mon. 9:30 A.M. and 1:30 P.M.

depending on weather, book at least 24 hours in advance) offers several tours, including snorkeling for $25; scuba for first-timers, $65; scuba for certified divers, $55; and a cavern dive, $55. It also offers diving certification instruction.

Horseback Riding

Isabela has great beaches for horseback riding, and **Tropical Trail Rides** (Carr. 4466, km 1.8, 787/872-9256, www.tropicaltrailrides.com, daily rides at 9 A.M. and 3:30 P.M., $45 per person for 2 hours) offers two-hour guided tours along tropical trails on Paso Fino horses through an almond forest, along secluded beaches, and to cliff-side caves. It includes a stop for a swim or exploring the caves. There's also a sunset tour available. Private rides can be arranged.

ENTERTAINMENT AND EVENTS
Festivals
Isabela celebrates **Festival del Tejido** (787/872-1045) in late April or early May, featuring needlecraft exhibits, live music, and vendors selling local food and drinks in Plaza de los Festivales.

Nightlife
Isabela's nightlife can be found along Carretera 466 at several very casual beachside bars that keep things hopping late into the night. One popular spot is **Happy Belly's Sports Bar and Grill** (Carr. 4466, Playa Jobos, 787/872-6566, daily noon-4 A.M.). Skip the tiny rustic bar inside and find a picnic table on the huge open-air deck on the beach. This is a hot party spot, especially on the weekends. It has the potential to be rowdy. It also serves a huge menu of American bar fare and Puerto Rican cuisine.

A similar ambience can be found at **Ocean Deck Park and Grill** (Ocean Front Hotel, Carr. 4466, km 0.1, 787/872-3339, www.oceanfrontpr.com, Wed.-Sun. 11:30 A.M.-11 P.M., bar and deck open until 3 A.M.). It's a traditional Puerto Rican beach bar: a wooden pavilion-style structure with deck flooring, no walls, and a pitched umbrella roof supported by a central post, around which the bar wraps. It's a terrific place to sip a rum punch and gaze at the water. It serves seafood for lunch and dinner, and there's live music starting at 8 P.M. Fridays and Saturdays.

High up on a bluff overlooking Isabela's coastline, **Karambola Sports Bar & Grill** (Carr. 446, km 6.4, Sun.-Thurs. 11 A.M.-midnight, Fri.-Sat. 11 A.M.-2 A.M., 787/969-9910, $10-25) is a no-frills, party-hardy haven with gorgeous views, a full bar and a big menu filled with pub fare and Puerto Rico specialties, including *chuleta Can Can* (fried pork chop) and *mofongo*.

SHOPPING
Located on the marginal road along Carretera 2, just east of José "Buga" Abreu coliseum, is **La Tiendita Tipica** (3560 Ave. Militar, Isabela, 787/609-6273 or 787/830-9527, daily 9 A.M.-6:30 P.M. including holidays). This little store stands out in more ways than one. It looks like a modest *jíbaro* house like the kind you would see in the mountains, but it is surrounded by fast food outlets and strip malls. Inside you will find every kind of traditional Puerto Rican sweet you can imagine, including candies, cakes, ice cream, puddings, fruit frappes, and local cheeses.

El Coral Market (Carr. 4446, km 5.7, 787/872-8388, Mon.-Tues. 9 A.M.-6 P.M., Wed.-Thurs. 8 A.M.-2 A.M., Fri.-Sun. 8 A.M.-2 A.M. or later) is conveniently located along the beachfront strip of Isabela, where it sells everything you need for a day of sun and surf, including ice, soft drinks, snacks, beer, liquor, and cigarettes. There is also a small bar serving cocktails and fritters.

ACCOMMODATIONS
$100-150
Ocean Front Hotel (Carr. 4466, km 0.1, 787/872-0444, www.oceanfrontpr.com, $85 d Sun.-Thurs., $100 d Fri.-Sat., $125 d holidays, plus tax) has undergone a dramatic transformation. The former crash pad for surfers and divers has been expanded and refurbished. The rooms have a new, light airy feel thanks to freshly painted walls, bleached wood furnishings, quality bedding, and new fixtures in the bathrooms. There's also a new sundeck. The small hotel is on the water and within walking distance to Playa de Jobos. Amenities include air-conditioning and cable TV. There is an upscale restaurant and bar downstairs and an open-air bar right on the water.

Villa Tropical (Shacks Beach, 326 Barrio Bajuras, 787/872-7172 or 787/354-7685, www.villatropical.com, $95-125 studio, $100-125 one-bedroom, $160-210 two-bedroom, $210-330 three-bedroom, plus tax) manages 27 oceanfront, fully equipped apartment units in several buildings along Shacks Beach. Each apartment is different, but they all come with full kitchens, satellite TV, air-conditioning, and free parking. Wireless Internet is available outside the main office and in some apartments. A coin-operated laundry is on-site. Weekly cleaning service is available. To get there from Carretera 4466, turn right just before you get to Carretera 110 at the Villa Montana and Villa Tropical signs.

Pelican Reef Apartments (Carr. 4466, km 0, Jobos Beach, 787/872-6518 or 866/444-9818, www.pelicanreefapartments.com, $110 studio, $125 one-bedroom) is a salmon-colored condo on the beach that rents studio and one-bedroom apartments by the day, week, or month. Accommodations are simple, clean, and modern. Rooms come with air-conditioning, cable TV, microwaves, refrigerators, and stovetops. All are oceanfront, although there's no beach, and have balconies. The building is purely self-serve, and part of it appears to be under renovation. There are laundry facilities on-site and wireless Internet.

$150-250

(**Parador Villas del Mar Hau** (Carr. 466, km 8.3, Playa Montones, 787/872-2021, fax 787/872-2045, www.hauhotevillas.com, $110 s, $150-160 d, $185 two-bedroom cottage, $260 three-bedroom, plus tax, reservations recommended by phone) is a quaint, casual paradise. Tucked away from civilization on a gorgeous stretch of beach and grassy plains, the property runs wild with bougainvillea, hibiscus, begonias, and sea grapes. A herd of horses grazes in a fenced field. At the center are two beaches, one a protected lagoon. Along the water's edge, shaded by palms, are individual cabanas, some with porches, and small clusters of studio apartments. Although authentically rustic, the interiors are plush, decorated in cool jewel tones that contrast smartly with the bright pastel exteriors. Rooms come with air-conditioning and cable TV. Other amenities include barbecue grills, a pool, a basketball court, laundry facilities, snorkel-equipment

rental, and horseback riding. The restaurant Olenas y Arenas offers lovely fine dining by the water.

Over $250

(**Villa Montaña Beach Resort** (Carr. 4466, km 1.9, 787/872-9554, 877/882-8082, or 888/780-9195, fax 787/872-9553, www.villa-montana.com, $225 standard room, $325 suite, $380 one-bedroom, $437 two-bedroom, $595 three-bedroom, plus tax) is a super-exclusive gated resort with meticulously landscaped grounds and posh accommodations decorated in an antique Caribbean style. The 26-acre property has 35 villas and 52 rooms with air-conditioning, phones, cable TV, kitchens or kitchenettes, and terraces. Some have whirlpool baths, roofless showers, and laundry facilities. There are two swimming pools, a fitness room, a rock-climbing wall, and spa services. Mountain-bike and sea-kayak rentals are available on-site. Eclipse Restaurant and Bar serves Caribbean-Asian fusion cuisine with an emphasis on seafood.

FOOD
Steak and Seafood

Ocean Front Restaurant (Ocean Front Hotel, Carr. 4466, km 0.1, 787/872-0444 or 787/872-3339, www.oceanfrontpr.com, Wed.-Sun. 11:30 A.M.-11 P.M., bar and deck open until 3 A.M., $16-22) serves creative Puerto Rican cuisine, including mahimahi ceviche with coconut milk, tamarind *churrasco,* guava-glazed shrimp, and lobster ravioli in pesto sauce. Dress up and eat in the upscale dining room or dress down and eat the same fare at the bar or at the open-air seaside bar next door.

Olas y Arenas (Villas del Mar Hau, Carr. 466, km 8.3, Isabela, 787/830-8315, daily 8 A.M.-10 P.M. in winter, Mon.-Fri. 5-10 P.M. and Sat.-Sun. 8 A.M.-10 P.M. in summer, $12-34) is a lovely, elegantly casual restaurant under a beachside pavilion. Specialties include *mofongo* paella, a creative combination of classic Puerto Rican and Spanish dishes, and a refreshing citrus dorado salad. Other menu items include the daily catch, steak, veal, and lamb chops. There's also a children's menu.

Situated across the street from the water, **Luna Marina** (Carr. 4466, km 5.2, 787/830-3455, Mon.-Thurs. 11 A.M.-10 P.M., Fri.-Sat. 11 A.M.-11 P.M., $12-29) is a bit more upscale than some of the other restaurants found in this beach community. The menu offers creative interpretations of *criolla* cuisine, featuring seafood, steak, *mofongo,* and rice dishes. The *mofongo de yuca* and *tres leches* cake are recommended. Service can be slow.

You couldn't ask for a better setting than **Eclipse** (Villa Montaña, Carr. 4466, km 1.9, 787/872-9554 or 877/882-8082 or 888/780-9195, www.villamontana.com, $12-24) for a romantic dining experience. Dinner is served on a covered terrace overlooking the ocean. The menu is not extensive, but it includes the very best in the way of steaks (strip, rib-eye, tenderloin, skirt) and seafood (shrimp brochette flamed with cognac, tuna tartare with black calamari ink, and catch of the day). In addition to the regular menu, a menu of creative specials is debuted each month featuring ambitious interpretations of appetizer and entrée classics.

American

Happy Belly's Sports Bar and Grill (Carr. 4466, Playa Jobos, 787/872-6566, daily 4:30 P.M.-late, $7-19) is a huge open-air beachside deck with an enormous menu. Happy Belly's specializes in typical pub fare—Buffalo wings, fried cheese sticks, and burgers—but it also serves pasta dishes, fajitas, steak, and seafood, as well as some traditional Puerto Rican fare. It has a full bar and modest wine list.

Breakfast

Catering to the surfing crowd that flocks to Isabela, **El Carey Café** (Carr. 4466, km 5.2, Isabela, 954/839-8356, Thurs.-Mon. 8 A.M.-4 P.M., $3-10) is a funky, bohemian spot specializing in *arepas,* a South American street food featuring a disc of fried corn meal stuffed with meat and cheese. Breakfast is available all day and it includes pancakes, French toast, omelets, and crepes. Lunch includes salads, burgers, wraps, quesadillas, and "tropical bowls," featuring your choice of sautéed meat, seafood, or chicken served on rice. Dessert crepes and smoothies round out the menu.

INFORMATION AND SERVICES

The **Isabela tourism office** (787/872-6400, Plaza Recreo) offers a free trolley tour of its major points of interest by appointment only. **Banco Popular** (73 Ave. Calero, 787/872-3100) has an ATM. For pharmacy needs, try **Isabela Farma Express** (1-350 G. Ave. Noel Estrada, 787/872-1930).

GETTING THERE AND AROUND

Isabela is 117 kilometers or 72 miles west of San Juan, and 20 kilometers or 12 miles northeast of Aguadilla. From San Juan, take Highway 2 west to Carretera 22 west to Carretera 113 west. From Aguadilla take Carretera 2 north to Carretera 459 northeast.

To call a **taxi** in Isabela, dial 787/918-5106.

Aguadilla

When the Rafael Hernández International Airport in Aguadilla expanded in 2005, it opened up more passenger service to Puerto Rico's west coast, and as a result the town of Aguadilla has undergone a transformation. What was once a bit of a rough-and-tumble town is fast becoming a destination for vacationing families, thanks to the addition of a new water park and the island's only ice skating rink. And the downtown area is being rapidly spruced up by multiple new-construction and renovation projects. There are still plenty of traditional wooden *criolla*-style houses remaining downtown, but sadly they are falling into disrepair.

Unlike in most coastal towns in Puerto Rico, much of the downtown area stretches along the waterfront. At its center is Plaza Degetau, a lovely old-fashioned square except for a striking modern steel fountain sculpture. It is flanked by the city hall and the San Carlos Borromeo Cathedral. Surrounding it is a bustling commercial district. A second, more modern plaza, Jardín del Atlántico, located right on the waterfront, is a popular gathering spot at night. Not only do its adobe-colored walls, balustrades, and wrought-ironwork provide an attractive setting for watching the sunset, a half dozen Spanish-tiled kiosks serve Puerto Rican cuisine and all manner of beverages without putting much of a dent in the wallet. Plans are underway to build a boardwalk along the beach.

Of course, Aguadilla has long been a popular destination for water sports enthusiasts—particularly surfers—thanks to a number of excellent beaches.

BEACHES
Playa Crash Boat (Carr. 458 to Carr. 107, Mon.-Sun. 7 A.M.-6 P.M., $3) is a beach with two parts to it. The first area you encounter is a small but wide public beach popular with families and groups who flock to the *balneario's*

bright blue and yellow picnic tables and huge pavilion tucked into a shady spot on the shore. There are bathroom facilities and tons of parking. Marring the view, though, are concrete pilings and a long concrete pier in the water.

A short distance farther down Carretera 458 is another beach area without facilities or entrance fees. You'll find more parking here and lots of food vendors selling drinks and fried treats. A mini underwater wall here makes it a popular dive spot, where you'll see lots of fish, sponges, and corals.

Wilderness Beach (from Carr. 107, turn west on a narrow unmarked road that passes through the Punta Borinquen Golf Club, Ramey) is also called El Natural. This remote beach is accessible by several small roads that branch off in different directions, but they all dead-end at the same place—a lovely patch of sand and sea. The beach is just past **Las Ruinas,** the ruins of the Punta Borinquen lighthouse, which was destroyed by a tsunami in 1918. There are no facilities at Wilderness Beach and minimal space for parking. Continue down the bumpy rutted road past Wilderness Beach to reach the big waves at **Surfer's Beach.** This is where you'll find the popular surfing spots Table Top and Survivor. Women traveling solo are ill-advised to hang around here. It's quite remote and attracts peeping Toms.

Parque Recreativo Cristóbal Colón (end of Carr. 440/442 dead-end, free) is a terrific little waterfront park featuring a boardwalk, playground, picnic pavilion, and basketball court. The highlight, though, is **Casa de Árbol,** a huge tree house built around a shady banyan tree. There are often vendors on the park grounds selling fritters, beverages, and produce. For more substantial sustenance, El Pabellon restaurant offers indoor and outdoor dining overlooking the ocean.

City Hall on Degetau Plaza in Aguadilla

SIGHTS

Aguadilla is a big enough town to have a couple of plazas, but **Degetau Plaza** is particularly attractive. In the center is a massive, modernist fountain with multiple levels, wind chimes, and angels that is something of a spectacle to behold. On one side of the plaza is **Iglesia San Carlos Borromeo,** a mission-style church built in 1783. On another side is the ubiquitous **Rex Cream,** selling ice cream cones. Also on the plaza is a curious clock made in 1912 by Mark Mayer Jr. It bears a plaque contains the following quote: "To know people is intelligence but to know yourself is true wisdom."

SPORTS AND RECREATION
Water Sports

Aguadilla has several fantastic **surfing** spots, especially along the former Ramey Air Force Base. As you travel north from Playa Crash Boat to Punta Agujereada, the island's farthest northwestern point, surf sites include (in order) Gas

Chamber, Wishing Well, Wilderness, Ponderosa Ruins, Surfer's Beach, and Table Tops. There are two surf shops in the area, which are great sources for surfing tips and advice on when and where to hit the best swells. Both can provide you with maps to all the great sites.

El Rincón Surf Shop (703 Belt Rd., Ramey Shopping Center, Ramey, Aguadilla, 787/890-3108, http://elrinconsurfshop.com, Mon.-Sat. 9 A.M.-6 P.M., Sun. 11 A.M.-5 P.M., $25-30 board rentals) rents and sells surfing, sailboarding, and snorkeling equipment. It has an excellent selection of quality bathing suits, sandals, sunglasses, and other beach accessories.

Aquatica (Carr. 110, km 10, Gate 5, Ramey, Aguadilla, 787/890-6071, Mon.-Sat. 10 A.M.-5:30 P.M., Sun. 9 A.M.-3 P.M., www.aquaticadive-surf.com, $25 board rentals) offers stand-up paddleboard lessons and tours ($65 pp), as well as dive and snorkeling trips and surf instruction. A two-tank dive is $85 per person. A two-hour guided snorkel tour is $45 per person.

Iglesia San Carlos Borromeo on Degetau Plaza in Aguadilla

Surfing instruction is $65 for 90 minutes. Rental equipment is available.

Golf
Punta Borinquen Golf and Country Club (Ramey Base, Aguadilla, 787/890-2987 or 787/890-1196, www.puntaborinquengolf. com, $20-22 green fees) is one of only a handful of courses in Puerto Rico that are not associated with a resort. Designed by Fred Garbin, it opened in 1940 to serve the military base. When the base closed, the course was opened to the public. It features 18 holes with straight and open fairways overlooking the ocean. Walking is permitted on certain days.

ENTERTAINMENT AND EVENTS
Las Cascadas de Aguadilla (Carr. 2, km 126.5, 787/819-1030, fax 787/819-0730, Mon.-Fri. 10 A.M.-5 P.M., Sat.-Sun. 10 A.M.-6 P.M. Mar.-Sept., $20 adults, $18 ages 4-12) is a new water park with tons of slides, tubes, and pools.

Aguadilla Ice Skating Arena (Calle Marina, Carr. 442, 787/819-5555, daily 10 A.M.-11 P.M., $10 day, $13 night) is a large new municipal facility that also features a sport shop, boxing rink, and two fast-food restaurants.

Crash Boat Summer Festival (787/891-1005) kicks off the high season in late May with a celebration of sun, surf, and water. Festivities include live music, beach games, and food vendors. It's held at Playa Crash Boat off Carretera 107.

ACCOMMODATIONS
Hotel Cielo Mar (84 Ave. Montemar, Carr. 111, km 1.3, 787/882-5959 or 787/882-5960, fax 787/882-5577, www.cielomar.com, $90-101 s, $106-117 d, plus tax) is a large corporate-style hotel that's a bit past its prime. High on a hill overlooking the ocean and the town of Aguadilla, the hotel has a flashy 1970s-style lobby with lots of elaborate chandeliers and a mirrored ceiling, and the rooms are pretty

WEST COAST

basic. Rooms have air-conditioning, DSL Internet, and satellite TV. The pool has recently been renovated and features a giant whale slide for the kids, a grotto, and a whirlpool. A large open-air restaurant and bar overlooks the Bay of Aguadilla. Unfortunately, that view is marred by an enormous abandoned sugarcane shipping operation below.

Parador El Faro (Carr. 107, km 2.1, Aguadilla, 787/882-8000, www.farohotels.net, $75 s, $85 d, $250 three-bedroom) is a modest budget hotel featuring 69 guest rooms with air-conditioning, satellite TV, free Internet, swimming pool, and room service. A bar and Mexican restaurant are on-site. All inclusive packages are available for couples and families.

Hotel El Pedregal (Carr. 111, km 1.1, 787/891-6068 or 888/568-6068, fax 787/882-2885, www.hotelelpedregal.com, $80-90 s/d/t, $263 two-bedroom villa, $316 three-bedroom, $329 four-bedroom, plus tax) is a popular spot for families with young children. The 27 modern, basic rooms come with air-conditioning, satellite TV, telephones, and wireless Internet. There's a small pool with a kiddie pool, a game room with pool tables and arcade games, and a small modest restaurant with a limited bar. Maintenance and upkeep is pretty slack, but the staff is friendly and there's a homespun charm about the place.

FOOD
Puerto Rican
El Pabellon (800 Ave. Cristóbal Colón, inside Parque Recreativo Cristóbal Colón, 787/997-2626, Mon. noon-6 P.M., Wed.-Thurs. and Sun. noon-9 P.M., Fri-Sat. noon-10 P.M., lunch specials Mon.-Fri. $9, dinner $9-20) serves Puerto Rican cuisine and a full bar in a fine-dining atmosphere downstairs and a casual open-air rooftop terrace overlooking the ocean upstairs.

Panadería Borinqueña (Carr. 107, Ramey, 787/882-4141, daily 5:30 A.M.-10 P.M.) and **El Ramey Bakery** (Belt Rd., Ramey

Shopping Center, Ramey, 787/890-2768, daily 6 A.M.-9 P.M.) serve pastries, sandwiches, and hot Puerto Rican fare from a steam table. You can also pick up essentials such as ice, toilet paper, and water.

Steak and Seafood
The upscale steakhouse **D'Grillade** (52 Calle José de Jesus Esteves/Calle Comercio, Aguadilla, 787/891-2010, lunch Wed.-Fri. 11 A.M.-4 P.M., dinner Wed.-Sat. 5-10 P.M. and Sun. 1-9 P.M., bar open until midnight Fri.-Sat., $15-29) serves Angus beef grilled to order, but the mahimahi ceviche and pumpkin cheesecake come highly recommended. The bar serves tapas 5-10 P.M. Friday and Saturday.

Oleana (57 Calle Stahl, Aguadilla, 787/882-7474, Wed.-Sat. 5-11 P.M., Sun. noon-10 P.M., $10-30) serves creative Caribbean cuisine, including lobster and steak, in a dramatic space with contemporary artwork on the walls.

International
Novecento Italian Bistro (61 Calle Stahl, Aguadilla, 787/882-7475, Mon.-Wed. 11 A.M.-11 P.M., Thurs.-Sat. 11 A.M.-2 A.M., Sun. noon-11 P.M., $5-20) serves tapas, thin crust pizza, and fondues, both sweet and savory, for lunch and dinner, but at night it turns into a lively dance club featuring live music on weekends. It has a full bar.

One Ten Thai (Carr. 110, km 9.2, Aguadilla, 787/890-0113, www.onetenthai.com, Wed.-Sun. 5-10 P.M., $10-14) serves Pan-Asian cuisine, including pad Thai, as well as red, green, and Massaman curry. A house favorite is steamed pork dumplings served with a chili soy dipping sauce. It also serves 90 local, craft, and international beers.

Breakfast
Café Aroma (Carr. 110, km 9.8, 787/819-5332, Tues.-Sat. 9 A.M.-5:30 P.M., $2-8) serves coffee drinks, tea, pastries, sandwiches, salads, and

breakfast dishes, including Belgian waffles, eggs Benedict, and huevos rancheros.

My Sweet Place (Carr. 110, km 1.2, San Jose Building, Aguadilla, 787/510-7692 or 787/604-6618, Mon.-Thurs. 11 A.M.-7:30 P.M., Fri.-Sat. 11 A.M.-9 P.M., Sun. 11 A.M.-8 P.M., $2-6 cash only) is a local chain of clean, modern coffeehouses serving a variety of coffee drinks, pancakes, and waffles made with Nutella, banana, mango, or strawberry.

INFORMATION AND SERVICES

The **tourism office** (787/890-3315, daily 8 A.M.-4:30 P.M.) is in Rafael Hernández International Airport. There are several banks, including **Banco Popular** (Carr. 2, km 129.2, 787/891-9500) and **Banco Santander** (Ave. Kennedy, 787/891-2190).

Walgreens (Carr. 2, km 129.7, 787/882-8005) operates a 24-hour pharmacy. Medical services are available at **Hospital Buen Samaritano** (Carr. 2, km 141.7, 787/658-0000).

GETTING THERE AND AROUND

Aguadilla is 133 kilometers or 82 miles west of San Juan. From San Juan, take Highway 22 west to Carretera 2 west.

Rafael Hernández International Airport (north of Carr. 2 on Carr. 110, between Isabela and Aguadilla, 787/891-2286) boasts the longest runway in the Caribbean. Several airlines have begun offering direct flights here from the United States.

Direct flights to Aguadilla are operated by JetBlue (from Orlando and from JFK airport in New York City), Spirit Airlines (from Fort Lauderdale); Delta (from Newark), and Continental (from Newark).

Several national **car-rental** agencies operate out of the airport, including Avis (787/890-3311), Budget (787/890-1110), Hertz (787/890-5650), and L&M (787/890-3010). Taxi service is available by calling **Mega Taxi** at 787/819-1235.

San Sebastián

Located inland in karst country, where limestone cave systems create dramatic sinkholes and exposed hilly outcroppings called *mogotes,* San Sebastián is a sleepy little agricultural town of dairy and coffee farms. But in July it explodes in a riot of color, music, and festivities for the annual Festival Nacional de la Hamaca, which celebrates the colorful hand-woven hammocks that are made here and can be bought from roadside vendors and shops throughout the island.

ENTERTAINMENT AND EVENTS

Festival Nacional de la Hamaca (Plaza Pública Román Baldorioty de Castro, 787/896-1550 or 787/896-2610) is a major annual festival that celebrates traditional Puerto Rican artisans and their crafts. Held for three days in early July, it specifically recognizes the handmade

hammocks that are crafted here. But it's oh-so-much more than hammocks: More than 200 artisans participate, selling everything from seed jewelry and cigars to wood carvings and masks. There's also plenty of food, music, and children's activities.

ACCOMMODATIONS

Hacienda El Jibarito (Carr. 445, km 6.5, Barrio Saltos, 787/280-4040 or 787/896-5010, www.haciendaeljibarito.com, $148-171 s, $194 d, $205 one-bedroom, $263-320 two-bedroom, tax included) is a newly developed property that combines tourism and agriculture to provide an educational stay in the lap of luxury. Originally a sugarcane farm that ceased operations in 1980, it has been transformed into a family-friendly resort where guests can commune with farm animals, witness farm technique demonstrations, and dine on the fruits and vegetables grown on-site. The lobby and fine-dining restaurant, Restaurante Laurnaga, are located in a striking Spanish-colonial plantation house with soaring ceilings and mission-style furniture. The 11 rooms and six villas are well furnished and come with all the amenities one would expect from an upscale resort, including air-conditioning, satellite TV, and wireless Internet. The grounds include a kidney-shaped pool with an octagonal bar that offers 360-degree views of the surrounding mountains, an indoor pool and whirlpool, a pond with a gazebo, greenhouses, and stables. A spa offers a menu of massages, body wraps, and nail services. In addition to the restaurant, Casa Café coffee shop and bakery serves delicious locally grown coffee in a variety of cold and hot beverages, plus fantastic pastries. Try the sticky, flaky *quesitos,* stuffed with cream cheese.

For a more economical option, **Hotel El Castillo** (Carr. 111, km 28.3, Barrio Eneas, 787/517-6233 or 787/896-2365, $65 s, $70 d) is a bright modern faux hacienda-style hotel with 18 rooms that have air-conditioning, satellite TV, and wireless Internet. Other amenities include a large pool with a waterfall, a kiddie pool, a barbecue pit, and a couple of arcade games in the large tiled lobby.

FOOD

Restaurante Laurnaga (at Hacienda El Jibarito, Carr. 445, km 6.5, Barrio Saltos, 787/280-4040 or 787/896-5010, www.haciendaeljibarito.com, Mon.-Thurs. 11 A.M.-8 P.M., Fri.-Sun. 11:30 A.M.-9:30 P.M., $13-20) is a lovely fine-dining restaurant in a cavernous two-level building made from dark roughhewn wood that imparts a rustic lodge vibe. A self-serve buffet of Puerto Rican cuisine is served during lunch for $13. The dinner menu specializes in seafood and pasta dishes. The fried shrimp are huge and crispy.

INFORMATION

The **Tourism Information Office** (787/896-2300, 787/896-1550, or 787/896-2610, www.sansebastianpr.com) is at 3 Padre Feliciano, on the main square at Ramon Baldorioty de Castro.

GETTING THERE AND AROUND

San Sebastián is 124 kilometers or miles west of San Juan, 26 kilometers or 16 miles southeast of Aguadilla. From San Juan, take Highway 22 to Carretera 129 south and follow a series of secondary roads to Carretera 111. From Aguadilla, take Carretera 2 south to Carretera 111 east. For transportation services, call **Acosta Taxi Service** (787/903-6723).

Rincón

Rincón is a fun-loving bohemian surf town, and the kind of place where people come to visit and never leave. Local lore says 80 percent of the beachfront property is owned by people from the States, and there are so many mainlanders here that it's often referred to as "Little America."

For many decades, tourism in Rincón catered primarily to surfers with cheap bare-bones accommodations, casual restaurants, and beachfront bars. But the world is quickly discovering this little burg's unparalleled charms. More upscale accommodations have set up shop, and restaurants that combine fine dining with a casual atmosphere are following suit. Rincón is also on the verge of a condo explosion that residents are trying to stem to mixed results.

Rincón has several distinct barrios (neighborhoods), each with its own characteristics. To the north is **Puntas,** a hilly point overlooking some of the area's best surf spots. It is home to

RINCÓN

★ RED DOOR BOUTIQUE
SANDY BEACH
CASA ISLEÑA/
TAPÁS BAR
CALLE MIRAMAR
LAS PALMAS
INN
CALYPSO CAFÉ ▼
CARR. 413 IBAMA
CALLE VISTA LINDA
EL FARO ★
EL FARO RD.
CAMINO CARRETAS
CARRETAS
413
115
LAZY
PARROT INN
MARIA'S ★
Cerro
Martinica
413
DOMES ★
413
LA ROSA INGLESA/
THE ENGLISH ROSE
STEPS ★
115
TAÍNO
DIVERS
BLUE BOY INN
BLACK EAGLE MARINA ★ ■
SHIPWRECK ▼
BLACK EAGLE ▼
CALLE CAUBIA
CALLE PARQUE
0   500 yds
0   500 m
BALNEARIO ★
Rincón
CALLE CAUBIA
Rincón
Plaza
DAS
▼ ALPEN
To Lemontree Oceanfront Cottages,
Horned Dorset Primavera,
and El Fogón de la Curva
© AVALON TRAVEL

restaurants, bars, and hotels that cater to the party-hardy crowd. Slightly south is **Ensenada,** where the **Black Eagle Marina** is located, as well as **Tres Palmas** and **Steps** surf spots. Further south is the town center, featuring a small plaza and a couple of good restaurants. Nearby is the public beach, **Balneario Rincón.** Farther south are the barrios of **Parcelas** and **Barrero,** and the town of **Añasco,** home to several quiet B&Bs and resorts.

Because surfing is best from December through April, winter through spring is high season in Rincón. Some businesses close in the summer or limit their hours of operation. February is peak season for whale-watching tours.

SIGHTS

A terrific new park has been built around **El Faro** (El Faro Rd., Carr. 4413 off Carr. 413, Barrio Puntas, 787/823-5024), a lighthouse built in 1922. You can't go inside, but the tower provides a lovely backdrop to the landscaped grounds complete with picnic tables, shelters, restrooms, and an observation deck offering gorgeous views of the coastline. There's plenty of parking on-site.

SPORTS AND RECREATION

Water-sports enthusiasts will think they've died and gone to heaven in Rincón. Not only is it world-renowned for its outstanding surfing, but the diving and fishing are stellar. The water

kayaking in Rincón

along the west coast can be choppy. If you plan to ride on a boat, take a motion-sickness pill the night before you go out, and then take another the next morning. Local pharmacies sell the pills for $0.10 apiece.

Surfing

The beaches in Rincón are legion for surfing thanks to the water's great breaks and long tubes, especially around the lighthouse during high season, December to April. Pick up a map of surf spots at any surf shop in town. The following is a list of hot surf spots in order of location if traveling north along Carretera 413 from Rincón:

- **Tres Palmas:** For pros only, this spot features long, powerful waves with occasional breaks over a rocky reef bottom. Waves can get up to 25 feet. It's rarely crowded.
- **Dogman:** A superior winter spot, Dogman is not for inexperienced surfers.

- **María's:** Beside the Calypso Café, on El Faro Road, off Carretera 413, this spot features long, fast waves running right and left over a rocky reef bottom. This regional classic is for experienced surfers only. It's very crowded on weekends.
- **Domes:** This spot is often referred to as BONUS, the acronym for the name of a retired nuclear power plant distinguished by two green domes that sit idle on the shore just north of the lighthouse. This is one of the most popular surfing sites in Rincón, and it can get quite crowded. The right point break is for experienced surfers.
- **Sandy Beach:** A great sandy-bottomed spot, this is ideal for beginners. It's in Barrio Puntas just west of Casa Isleña guesthouse.
- **Parking Lots:** Beside Sandy Beach just east of Casa Isleña guesthouse, this is a great spot for six-foot swells and a good alternative when adjacent Sandy Beach gets crowded.

SURF SHOPS AND INSTRUCTION
Rincón Surf School (787/823-0610, www.rinconsurfschool.com) conducts a surf school for

beginners and experienced surfers looking to up their game. You can get a 2.5-hour private lesson or 1-5 full days of class instruction. It also offers a Surf & Yoga Retreat for women. Individual instruction is $150 and for two people a 2.5-hour class costs $75 per person, which includes board rental. Day-long sessions for one to five days is $95-390 per person. A five-day women's surf and yoga retreat is $2,195 per person (price based on two people), including four nights of accommodations and three meals a day.

Mar Azul Surfboard Rental (Carr. 413, km 4.4, Barrio Puntas, 787/823-5632 or 787/214-7224, www.puertoricosurfinginfo.com, daily 8 A.M.-5 P.M.) rents long boards, short boards, and stand-up paddleboards by the day and week. Surfboards rent for $25 daily and $150 weekly. Guided paddleboard tours cost $40.

Surf Town Surf Shop (40 Muñoz Rivera, Pueblo, 787/823-2515, www.surftownpr.com, Mon.-Fri. 10 A.M.-6 P.M., Sun. 10 A.M.-4 P.M.) sells surfboards, skateboards, shoes, clothes, and sunglasses.

West Coast Surf Shop and School (2E Muñoz Rivera, Pueblo, 787/823-3935, www.westcoastsurf.com, daily 10 A.M.-5 P.M., $20-30 board rentals) sells surfboards, equipment, and clothes, and also offers surf instruction. Classes are one-to-three hours long and cost $20-60.

Surf 787 Summer Camp (Carr. 115, behind Angelo's Restaurant, 787/448-0968 or 949/547-6340, www.surf787.com) offers year-round surfing instruction. Kids Summer Day Camp is $85 per day, which includes lunch and snack. Adult instruction is $90 for a two-hour private lesson; group lessons are $70 per person.

Swimming

The size and ferocity of Rincón's waves make it better suited to surfing than swimming, but sandy beaches suitable for sunbathing and swimming can be had. **Balneario Rincón** (off Carr. 413, 0.5 mile south of downtown behind the junior high school and across from Costa Ensenada condominiums) offers a nice swimming beach with a small picnic shelter, restrooms, a playground, and a boardwalk. Wilderness beaches in Barrio Puntas include **Sandy Beach** (off Carr. 413 Int. just west of Casa Isleña guesthouse), which can get crowded and lively. If you want a quieter beach experience, walk a little ways east of Casa Isleña to reach the quieter **Antonio Beach.** There is also a small spit of sand at Black Eagle Marina. On the southern end of Rincón, you'll find a small sandy beach at the end of Calle 11 in Barrio Parcelas. Amenities include a playground, baseball field, basketball court, covered picnic shelters, restrooms, and a small pizzeria.

Diving and Snorkeling
◖ DIVING OFF DESECHEO ISLAND

Not only does the west coast have lots of great reef diving along its shore, but there is a small uninhabited island 12 miles offshore that offers exceptional diving spots in pristine waters.

From a distance, Desecheo looks like a gray mountain in the sea. Its tall peaks once served as a hideout for pirate ships that would lie in wait for unsuspecting cargo ships to pass by. Today the island is a protected wildlife refuge, and no one is allowed to enter it. But everyone's welcome to don a mask and explore its reefs. You can see all kinds of colorful marine life, including rays, parrot fish, grunts, porkpie fish, sharks, coral formations, and more.

There is no regularly scheduled transportation between Desecheo Island and Rincón, but all the tour operators in town offer snorkeling and scuba trips to its shores.

DIVE SHOP

Taíno Divers (Black Eagle Marina, Carr. 413, Barrio Ensenada, 787/823-6429, www.tainodivers.com, daily 9 A.M.-6 P.M.) offers daily snorkeling and dive trips to various dive sites, including Desecheo Island. Snorkeling trips are $50-95, scuba trips are $65-129, and Discovery scuba dives for first-timers are $119-170. Taíno

MONA ISLAND: RICH IN HISTORY AND WILDLIFE

Oh, the tales it could tell if Mona Island could speak. The 13,000-acre, virtually uninhabited island 47 miles southwest from Mayagüez and 37 miles east of the Dominican Republic has seen much drama through the years. At various times in its history, it was home to a thriving Taíno Indian village, a favorite stopover for marauding pirates, a secret hideaway for stolen treasure, the site of a lucrative mining operation, a vital breeding ground for migratory birds and sea turtles, and the final resting place for many a sailing ship sent careening into its unforgiving cliffs by rough waters and winds.

Today, Mona Island is a protected wildlife refuge, but unlike on Desecheo Island, up to 100 visitors per day are allowed to hike its trails, explore its ruins, camp on its beaches, dive or snorkel its crystal-clear shoreline, and hunt its feral pigs and goats, as long as permission is obtained from the **Department of Natural Resources** (787/722-1726). The island is a six-hour boat ride from Rincón or Mayagüez across the rough waters of Mona Passage, an important shipping lane that reaches 3,000 feet in depth. Several outfitters along the west coast offer overnight camping tours to the island, including **Mona Aquatics** (Calle José de Diego, next to Club Náutico, Boquerón, 787/851-2185, fax 787/254-0604, www.monaaquatics.com).

Commonly described as shaped like a lima bean, Mona is a semiarid subtropical island with 20 miles of coastline, most of it vertical cliffs rising from the sea to heights of more than 200 feet. The cliffs are penetrated by an intricate marine cave system that extends 150-800 feet under the island's surface in some places. There are also three sandy beaches on the south and southwest coast.

The surface of the island is mostly flat coastal plain with little vegetation, but it is home to a rich diversity of wildlife, most notably the world's only indigenous population of Mona iguanas. This prehistoric-looking reptile grows up to four feet long and wields its massive tail like a billy club. It has an aggressive appearance, thanks to a horned snout and jagged bony crest down its back, but it's a harmless vegetarian that can survive as long as 50 years. Mona is also an important habitat for the inch-long *geco oriundo* lizard, hawksbill and leatherback sea turtles, and the red-footed booby, among other sea birds.

The island was first visited by Christopher Columbus in 1493 or 1494. He was followed by Ponce de León, who arrived in 1508 and discovered a Taíno village of about 80 inhabitants, who fished the waters and cultivated yuca and sweet potatoes. During the early colonial years, Mona became an important source of agricultural products for the main island. Because of its location and lack of fortification, Mona became a pawn during Spain's defense of Puerto Rico and the Dominican Republic against the French, Dutch, and English. Enemy ships would often stop here to obtain freshwater, raid the Taíno of their food and goods, and sink their enemies' ships. In 1578 the 10-30 Taíno remaining on the island were transferred to Puerto Rico for protection from French raiders.

Mona remained virtually abandoned until the early 1800s, during which time its primary visitors were pirates, who stopped off to get water, repair their ships, or lie in wait to raid passing cargo ships. Infamous pirates, including Mateo Congo, Adrian Cornelis, William Kidd, and Roberto Cofresí all spent time on Mona. Around the mid-1800s, it was discovered that Mona was a rich source of guano, and several mining operations were established. Several significant shipwrecks along Mona's shore in the late 1800s contributed to the termination of operations. The last major operation on the island was the construction of a lighthouse by the United States in 1900.

Today Mona is home to a few rangers, employed by the Department of Natural Resources, who watch over conservation efforts and educate visitors on the unique environment. Three trails on the island connect its three beaches to the lighthouse on the eastern point. In addition to enjoying the island's great hiking, diving, and bird-watching, visitors can explore the faint remains of the Taíno civilization and mining operations. Petroglyphs, stone walls, cabins, and graves are enduring reminders of Mona's colorful past.

Many boating trips depart from Black Eagle Marina in Rincón.

also offers whale-watching cruises (late Jan.-mid-Mar.), as well as fishing charters and sunset cruises. Private excursions to Desecheo Island can be arranged. There is also equipment for rent or sale.

Boating

Katrina Sail Charters (Black Eagle Marina, Carr. 413, Rincón, Barrio Ensenada, 787/823-7245, www.sailrinconpuertorico.com) takes guests on snorkeling ($75 adults, $37.50 under age 12), sunset ($55, $27.50 under age 12), and full-moon sails ($55 adults only) aboard a 32-foot catamaran.

A bit of a misnomer, **Flying Fish Parasail** (Black Eagle Marina, Carr. 413, Rincón, Barrio Ensenada, 787/823-2FLY—787/823-2359, www.parasailpr.com, daily 9 A.M.-5 P.M.) does offer single and tandem parasail rides for $60 per person. But it offers a lot more, including glass-bottom boat rides ($30), sunset and whale-watch tours ($45), and reef snorkel tours ($55-85). Reservations are required, 12-passenger maximum.

Fishing

Taíno Divers (Black Eagle Marina, Carr. 413, Barrio Ensenada, 787/823-6429, www.tainodivers.com, daily 9 A.M.-6 P.M.) offers half-day offshore fishing charters including tackle, bait, lunch, and soft drinks for $1,200. It also offers snorkeling, dive, and whale-watching tours.

Makaira Fishing Charters (787/299-7374, www.makairafishingcharters.com, $575 half-day charter, $850 full-day charter) offers half-day and full-day charters aboard a 34-foot 2006 Contender. Rates include tackle and refreshments; there's a six-passenger maximum. Half-day charters are 7 A.M.-1 P.M. and 1-7 P.M. Full-day charters are 7 A.M.-4:30 P.M.

Whale-Watching

Migrating humpback whales can be spotted off the coast of Rincón during the winter, and several local operators offer boat tours to see them, including Taíno Divers.

WEST COAST

© JOHN THOMPSON

diving off the coast of Rincón

Horseback Riding

Pintos R Us (Carr. 413, across from Black Eagle Marina, Barrio Ensenada, 787/516-7090, www. pintosrus.com, no credit cards accepted) leads daily rides starting at 8:30 A.M. and 4 P.M. on Paso Fino horses for beginners and advanced riders. The trail takes you alongside lovely beaches, cliffs, and tropical trails. Pintos R Us also offers riding lessons, trail rides, and full moon rides. Two-hour guided tours, $55 per person.

ENTERTAINMENT AND EVENTS
Nightlife

Rincón may be famous for its fabulous water sports, but it is equally renowned for its hard-partying ways. Nothing complements a day spent surfing and diving like a pub crawl, and Rincón has no shortage of great bars and watering holes for partying into the wee hours.

A funky, casual open-air tiki bar and eatery, **Shipwreck Bar & Grill** (beside Taíno Divers at Black Eagle Marina off Carr. 413, Barrio

Ensenada, 787/823-6429, www.rinconship-wreck.com, daily 11 A.M.-late high season, Thurs.-Mon. noon-late off-season, $10-24) looks like something Gilligan might have built. Don't be put off by the gravel floor and the tin roof or the bathrooms that look like outhouses. It serves excellent, freshly prepared food ranging from hot wings to poached halibut. But it's the laid-back beach-bum vibe that invites visitors to tarry longer than you'd planned, sipping cocktails, noshing on fried shrimp with coconut curry dipping sauce, and chatting up the colorful characters who hang out here—especially during happy hour 3-6 P.M.

Located below Smilin' Joe's restaurant, nautical-themed open-air **Seaglass Bar** (Lazy Parrot Inn, Carr. 413, km 4.1, Barrio Puntas, 787/823-0101, www.lazyparrot.com, daily 5:30-10 P.M., $18-27) is heavy on atmosphere, especially at night when the lushly landscaped grounds are lit with torches. You can dine on the same great fare (jerked mahimahi, fried

Calypso Cafe

whole snapper, pad Thai) served upstairs but in a much more casual atmosphere. Check out the cocktail menu for fruity, frosty concoctions, such as the Bailey's banana daiquiri, featuring rum, Bailey's Irish Cream, fresh banana, and chocolate syrup.

At **Calypso Cafe** (on El Faro Rd., off Carr. 413, María's Beach, Barrio Puntas, 787/823-1626, daily 11:30 A.M.-10 P.M., bar open until 11 P.M. Sun.-Thurs., until 2 A.M. Fri.-Sat.), a funky laid-back spot on the water at María's Beach, happy hour (5-7 P.M.) happily coincides with sunset every day. Everyone in town seems to start the evening here, sipping rum punch and watching the glorious pink and orange light show courtesy of Mother Nature. The menu has expanded to include fish ceviche, grilled dorado burritos, and *churrasco*. And there's free wireless Internet.

Villa Cofresí Patio Bar (Villa Cofresí Hotel, Carr. 115, km 12, Barrio Parcelas, 787/823-2450, fax 787/823-1770, www.villacofresi.com) is named after Puerto Rico's claim to piracy fame—Roberto Cofresí, a seafaring Robin Hood who terrorized passing ships and stole their goods until he was captured and executed in 1825. This beachside bar is off the lobby of Villa Cofresí Hotel, and it's a popular spot for vacationing Puerto Ricans, who come to play pool, dance to live music or the jukebox, and break away for romantic walks on the beach. The patio bar is a great place to wrap up the night with the bar's drink special, called Pirata (pirate). The sweet, potent concoction features three kinds of rum, coconut juice, crème de cacao, and cinnamon, and it's served in a freshly cracked coconut.

Rock Bottom (at Casa Verde Guest House, Carr. 413, Sandy Beach, Barrio Puntas, 787/823-3756, www.enrincon.com/restaurant_bar.html, restaurant daily 9 A.M.-10 P.M., bar open until 2 A.M. during high season, $7-9) is a small, funky treetop bar and restaurant with a tin roof and palm-frond decor punctuated with surfing memorabilia. A sign proclaims: "Free beer for broken boards." True to its word, this nightspot is decorated with broken and (faux) shark-bitten surfboards that earned their owners a free beer each for the loss. A small menu offers pub food such as burgers, wings, and quesadillas. The inn has a few bare-bones rooms to rent, which are frequented by surfers. Rates are $60 for a studio, $120 for a two-bedroom apartment.

Festivals

Rincón honors Santa Rosa de Lima with its **Patron Saint Festival** (787/823-5024) on the beach in late August or early September with music, games, and food.

SHOPPING

Opened in 2011, **The Red Door Boutique & Gift Shop** (Carr. 413 Interior, km 4.4, 720/289-5079, www.reddoorboutique.net, Mon.-Sat. 11 A.M.-5 P.M.) stocks high quality goods by artisans both local and global, including Ethiopian pottery, seaglass jewelry, Tula straw hats, unusual candles, and more. Many items are made from recycled materials.

Part art gallery, part gift shop, **Playa Oeste Tropical Surf Art Gallery & Gift Shop** (Carr. 413, km 0.5, 787/823-4424, www.playaoeste-gallery.com, Tues.-Sun. 11 A.M.-5 P.M. in winter, Thurs.-Sun. 11 A.M.-5 P.M. in summer) specializes in collectible surf art by renowned artists, including John Severson, Ken Auster, and Wade Koniacowsky. It's also a great place to pick up imported batik sundresses, artisan-made jewelry, and local coffees.

Caribbean Casuals (El Faro Rd., off Carr. 413, Marías Beach, 787/823-3942, daily 10 A.M.-6 P.M. high season, call for hours off-season) sells casual beachwear, bathing suits, T-shirts, jewelry, and flip-flops.

ACCOMMODATIONS

Accommodations run the gamut in Rincón, from cheap basic crash pads for surfers and midrange B&Bs to upscale resorts and an exclusive enclave for the rich and famous.

$50-150

Casa Verde Guest House (Carr. 413, Barrio Puntas, Sandy Beach, 787/823-3756, www.enrincon.com, $70-129 studio, $169 two-bedroom) has been completely renovated and redecorated, making it a pleasant, convenient place to stay if you want to be close to popular bars, restaurants, and surfing spots. Rooms come with kitchenettes and air-conditioning. Rock Bottom bar and grill is right next door, and you can walk to Sandy Beach.

Owned and operated by the folks at Casa Isleña, **Las Palmas Inn** (Carr. 413, Rincón, 787/823-1530, www.palmasinn.com, $105-125 s/d, $165 suite) is a self-serve inn featuring 10 spacious, well-appointed guest rooms in a three-story structure on a hillside not far from the beach. Each room has a kitchenette with mini refrigerator and microwave, satellite TV, and super comfy beds. The suite on the third floor offers an ocean view. There is a small swimming pool but no restaurant, bar, or reception desk. Check-in is at Casa Isleña (Carr. 413 Int., km 4.8), just down the hill.

La Rosa Inglesa/The English Rose (Carr. Int. 413, km 2.0, Barrio Ensenada, 787/823-4032 or 787/207-4615, www.larosainglesa.com, $115-200, including full breakfast), newly constructed atop a high ridge overlooking the ocean, is an idyllic three-unit guesthouse offering everything you could want: peace and quiet; gorgeous views; a natural setting; proximity to restaurants, bars, and the ocean; comfortable contemporary accommodations; a small pool; and what's considered by many to be the best breakfast in Rincón. The place is operated by a friendly young couple who live on the top floor of the property: Ruth, who's British, and Jethro, who's Puerto Rican. Don't be intimidated by the steep drive up the hill to reach the inn. Once you do it

La Rosa Inglesa

a time or two, you won't even notice its dizzying heights. Even nonguests make the trek to dine on Ruth's amazing, freshly prepared dishes. Rooms come with air-conditioning, mini-kitchens, refrigerators, satellite TV, and free wireless Internet.

Lazy Parrot Inn (Carr. 413, km 4.1, Barrio Puntas, 787/823-5654 or 800/294-1752, fax 787/823-0224, www.lazyparrot.com, $125-165 s/d, plus tax and energy surcharge) is a 23-unit fun-loving hotel that has recently expanded. Stay in the original part of the hotel and you get a simple, modestly furnished no-frills room. Or stay in the recently built poolside suites, which are roomier and more nicely furnished. Either way, you get air-conditioning, a mini-refrigerator, a microwave, free continental breakfast buffet, and free wireless Internet by the pool. The pool and its recently renovated, grotto-style grounds are the best part. And you've got three restaurants on-site: Smilin' Joe's, Seaglass Bar, and the poolside Rum Shack.

Surf 787 Resort (Carr. 115, behind Angelo's Restaurant, 787/448-0968 or 949/547-6340, www.surf787.com, $150 private bath and ocean view, $100-120 shared bath) is a small, newly constructed year-round guest villa that also offers surf instruction for adults and children. Rooms come with air-conditioning, mini-refrigerators, TVs, and DVD players; there's a small pool on-site. No children are allowed from December through April, when it offers all-inclusive surf and board packages for adults only. From June through September, children ages 11-17 can attend the kids' day or overnight surf camp.

Pineapple Inn (2911 Calle 11, off Carr. 115, Barrio Parcelas, 787/823-1430 or 787/245-9067, fax 787/823-3963, www.thepineappleinn. net, $105-150 s/d) is run by the eco-conscious Nelson Santos and Mark Kelly, who have won multiple hospitality awards for their conservation efforts. Solar energy is used to heat water, the grounds' lush flora is fed recycled water, and guests' sheets and towels are laundered only every three days. The compact property is in a residential neighborhood just a half block away from a small public beach and offers small rooms with air-conditioning, mini-refrigerators, microwaves, coffeemakers, satellite TV, and wireless Internet. There's a small pool, and continental breakfast is delivered daily in a wicker basket. Beach chairs, boogie boards, noodles, and coolers are available for use. Honeymoon packages are available, as well as in-room massages. There is wheelchair accessibility.

$150-250

More shabby than chic, **Pools Beach Cabanas** (Carr. 413, Barrio Puntas, 787/823-8135 or 787/823-2583, www.poolsbeach.com, $150-225 per night, $950-1,500 week) offers four very basic, bohemian accommodations in a thickly wooded site across the street from the beach. The Love Shack is a small secluded house on a bluff overlooking the ocean, accessible by

WEST COAST

path. Two- and four-bedroom bungalows sleep 4-8 people and come with a kitchenette, air-conditioning, and cable TV. A two-bedroom A-frame apartment sleeps six and comes with a kitchen, air-conditioning, cable TV, laundry facilities, and porch. Amenities include pool, bar, and wireless Internet at the pool.

◖Lemontree Oceanfront Cottages (Carr. 429, km 4.1, Barrio Barrera, 787/823-6452 or 888/418-3733, www.lemontreepr.com, $165 studio, $195 one-bedroom, $295 three-bedroom; as low as $80 off-season) is operated by Bella Jane and Ted Davis. The six darling, recently renovated, connected units are named after fruits, and all are oceanfront with terraces, mini-kitchens, and small libraries. The rooms are tastefully furnished with contemporary dark wood and rattan furniture and whimsical art glass. Amenities include satellite TV, DVD players, wireless Internet, and flat-screen TVs. Some rooms come with big-screen TVs; the three-bedroom unit has a bar, and the Banana cottage has a two-person hot tub. The property is located on a swimmable beach, and beach chairs, a grill, floats, and tubes are available for use.

◖Casa Isleña Inn (Carr. 413 Int., km 4.8, Parking Lot Beach, Barrio Puntas, 787/823-1525 or 888/289-7750, fax 787/823-1530, www.casa-islena.com, $145-225 s/d) is a new, well-maintained luxury property designed to resemble a Spanish hacienda, complete with imported tile and mission-style furniture. There are only nine units, and each one comes with air-conditioning, cable TV, and a mini-refrigerator. Some have whirlpool baths and balconies. Other amenities include a pool and beachfront. There's an exceptional tapas restaurant on-site.

Beside the Pointe on the Beach (Carr. 413 Int., km 4.4, Punta Higüero Beach, 787/823-8550 or 888/823-8550, www.besidethepointe.com, $105-210 for rooms that sleep 2-6, plus tax) is a funky bare-bones beachside property with eight units with air-conditioning, cable

TV, refrigerators, and coffeepots. Some rooms have full kitchens and balconies. The decor appears to be secondhand and mismatched, and the walls feature palm-tree murals. The Tamboo Tavern and SeaSide Grill is open daily noon-10 P.M. high season, Thursday-Sunday low season. The bar is open daily noon-midnight year-round.

Villa Cofresí Hotel and Restaurant (Carr. 115, km 12, 787/823-2450, fax 787/823-1770, http://villacofresi.com, $145 d, $155 d with kitchenette, $170 two-bedroom apartment, plus tax) has 80 modern oceanside units with air-conditioning, mini-refrigerators, coffeepots, telephones, and cable TV. Some rooms have balconies, whirlpool baths, kitchens, and bathtubs. The large lobby is a tad shabby, but it contains an enormous and very popular bar. The rooms are recently renovated and very comfortable. Amenities include a pool, a game room, a gift shop, and a restaurant. Personal-watercraft and kayak rentals are available on-site.

◖Blue Boy Inn (556 Calle Black Eagle, off Carr. 413 by Black Eagle Marina, 787/823-2593, www.blueboyinn.com, $180 s/d, $215 studios, including breakfast) is an elegant, beachfront property featuring eight luxury rooms, each one appointed with a private entrance, a patio or terrace, flat-screen TV with digital cable, air-conditioning, fresh flowers, and custom tile work. Lushly landscaped grounds feature a pool with fountains, underwater bar stools, a hot tub, and a fire pit. This is a truly exceptional property.

Over $250

Rincón Beach Resort (Carr. 115, km 5.8, Añasco, 787/589-9000 or 866/589-0009, fax 787/589-9020 or 787/589-9040, www.rinconbeach.com, $240-285 s/d, $459 one-bedroom suite, $660 two-bedroom, plus resort fee and tax; inclusive packages available) is a 118-unit upscale oceanfront resort in Añasco, south of Rincón. The huge open-air lobby has high ceilings, a wrought-iron chandelier, and pink and adobe tile floors. On one end is a full bar; on the other is the reception desk. Outside the lobby is an open courtyard with patio umbrellas, tables, and chairs surrounded by *flamboyan* trees overlooking a long scalloped-edge pool with a swim-up bar and a hot tub. Other amenities include a boardwalk along a sandy beach, a playground, an exercise room, meeting rooms, and a gift shop, plus fine dining at Brasas Restaurant and casual dining at Pelican Grill.

◖ Horned Dorset Primavera (from Carr. 115, turn west on Carr. 429, bear right at the fork, discreet entrance on the right, 800/633-1857, www.horneddorset.com, $596-1,070 d, $1,695 two-bedroom, including all meals, plus tax and service fee) is where pop stars and Academy Award-winners stay for the most lavish and luxurious experience available in Puerto Rico. This Relais and Chateau property has 37 spacious, tastefully appointed suites and villas decked out with Italian lighting fixtures, custom-made mahogany furniture, Moroccan rugs, and Spanish tiles. Each unit has a private plunge pool, wet bar with mini-refrigerator, canopy beds, balconies, and oversized pedestal tubs. There are in-room massages, manicures and pedicures, and hair-care services. The white stucco main building, constructed in 1987 in a Spanish colonial style, contains a fabulous library with an ornate antique bar and a restaurant. The lushly landscaped grounds feature gardenias, hibiscuses, bougainvillea, and palm trees. It's the perfect backdrop for the property's long, gorgeous stretch of tranquil wilderness beach. Snorkeling equipment and kayaks are available at no charge. In-room massages are available.

FOOD

The dining options keep getting better and better in Rincón, but be prepared to pay top dollar even at the most casual places. And if you're traveling off-season, expect your options to be fewer. Many restaurants are open December-April only.

Puerto Rican

Restaurante El Coche (Carr. 115, km 6.6, Añasco, 787/826-5151, www.restauranteelcoche.com, daily 11 A.M.-11 P.M., $11-30) has been in business 45 years, serving *criolla* cuisine in your choice of an old-fashioned formal dining inside or a casual open-air terrace out back overlooking the ocean. Dishes include *asopao*, shrimp, lobster, and snapper served broiled, fried, stewed, and scampi-style.

One part American sports bar and one part Puerto Rican *lechonera*, **◖ El Fogón de la Curva** (Carr. 115, km 7.1, Añasco, 787/826-0096, Wed.-Mon. 10 A.M.-11 P.M., $9-20) is a popular restaurant and bar serving outstanding roast pig and fresh fish on a spot high up on a hill overlooking the ocean through big plate-glass windows. The billiard room is filled with sports memorabilia, and the dining room features a large, polished wood bar. Along a back wall is an enormous fish tank filled with the notorious lionfish, a colorful, spiny species not indigenous to Puerto Rico but introduced to the local waters, where they are destroying underwater reefs. Although they are poisonous to the touch, they are safe to eat and are served up fried for the adventurous diner. The **Sushi & Martini Den** next door opens 5-10 P.M. Thursday-Sunday.

Kaplash (Carr. 115, km 6.7, Curvas de Rincón, Añasco, 787/826-4582, Sun.-Thurs. 11 A.M.-10 P.M., Fri.-Sat. 11 A.M.-11 P.M., $1-3) serves a simple menu featuring nothing but beer and *empanadillas*—lobster, conch, crab, shark, grouper, shrimp, seafood combo, pizza, lasagna, and meat. The bright orange exterior welcomes visitors into a small bar inside decorated with Pedro Albizu Campos posters and kitschy beach tchotchkes. Upstairs are two levels of outside seating overlooking the ocean. The rooftop floor has its own bar.

Seafood

◖ Tapas Bar (Casa Isleña, Carr. 413 Int.,

Sushi & Martini Den

© SUZANNE VAN ATTEN

km 4.8, Parking Lot Beach, Barrio Puntas, 787/823-1525 or 888/289-7750, fax 787/823-1530, www.casa-islena.com, Wed.-Sun. 5-9 P.M. in winter, Thurs.-Sat. 5-9 P.M. in summer, Sun. brunch served year-round 10 A.M.-2 P.M., $4-20) is a lovely fine-dining restaurant situated in the breezeway between the patio bar and the pool of this small guesthouse. The expertly prepared, creatively conceived small plates change with the season. On a recent visit offerings included flash-fried cauliflower with lemon and fried capers and chargrilled octopus with black limas in a spicy Thai coconut sauce. Kick your meal off with a basil and lavender vodka *mojito*.

Black Eagle Restaurant (Black Eagle Marina, Carr. 413, 787/823-3510, www.rincononline.com/spot/home.htm, Wed.-Mon. 4:30 P.M.-late high season, closed late Apr.-Thanksgiving, $19-23) has undergone a renovation and is under new management. The menu includes filet mignon, shrimp, kabobs, and catch of the day, and it's best enjoyed on waterfront patio.

Shipwreck Bar & Grill (Black Eagle Marina, Carr. 413, beside Taíno Divers, Barrio Ensenada, daily noon-10 P.M. or later in high season, Thurs.-Mon. noon-10 P.M. or later in low season, 787/823-6429, $10-30) is a funky, casual open-air tiki bar and eatery that serves excellent freshly prepared food, including hot wings, mussels, burgers, veggie wraps, ravioli Florentine, and poached halibut.

Smilin' Joe's (Lazy Parrot Inn, Carr. 413, km 4.1, Barrio Puntas, 787/823-5654 or 800/294-1752, fax 787/823-0224, www.lazyparrot.com, daily 5:30-10 P.M., $18-27) is a pleasant, slightly formal restaurant serving jerked mahimahi, grilled shrimp, pad Thai, fried whole snapper, and coconut ceviche.

New American

Brasas Restaurant (Rincón Beach Resort, Carr. 115, km 5.8, Añasco, 787/589-9000 or 866/589-0009, www.rinconbeach.com, breakfast Mon.-Fri. 7-10:30 A.M., Sat.-Sun. 7-11 A.M., brunch

Sat.-Sun. 12:30-4:30 P.M., dinner daily 5-11 P.M., $18-27) offers fine dining in a dramatic setting featuring dark woods, adobe accents, a massive wrought iron chandelier, and an open kitchen. Outside dining is available on the terrace. Entrées include tuna tartare, rack of lamb, and duck breast glazed with honey and Grand Marnier.

International

Located atop a three-story structure on a mountaintop overlooking the ocean, **Ode to the Elephants** (Carr. 413, km 3.3, Barrio Puntas, 631/604-0948, Wed.-Fri. 5-10 P.M. and Sat.-Sun. noon-10 P.M. in summer, 5-10 P.M. daily in high season, bar open until 4 A.M. Wed.-Sun., www.odetotheelephants.com, $10-16) is a casual Thai restaurant with a short menu of appetizers, including spring rolls and chicken satay, and entrées including choice of protein (chicken, shrimp, beef, tofu) and sauce (Massaman, Thai sesame, ginger and pad Thai). But start things off with drink from the martini list featuring coconut, peach, guava, ginger, and Thai tea varieties. The setting is light and airy inside. A bar dominates the room and small black-and-white vintage photographs of surfing champions decorate the walls. At night, sit outside on the moonlit patio for a romantic setting. One floor below is the **Wine Cellar Café** (Carr. 413, km 4.3, 305/776-9859, Thurs.-Sun. 7 P.M.-midnight, $5-12), a tiny little hideaway serving wine, cheese, sandwiches, salads, and desserts.

Oddly enough, one of the best restaurants in Rincón serves German cuisine. **◖ Das Alpen Café** (Rincón Plaza, behind the church, 787/233 8009, www.dasalpencafe.com, Mon.-Sat. 5-10 P.M. and Sun. noon-9 P.M. in winter, Thurs.-Mon. 5-10 P.M. and Sun. noon-9 P.M. in summer, closed in September, $13-18) is a chef-owned restaurant and labor of love for Jake Elmstrom, a San Juan harbor pilot of German heritage. He uses his mother's recipes to create deliciously authentic wiener schnitzel, bratwurst, and apple strudel. Das Alpen is one of the first restaurants to serve draft beer, and it also has a long list of craft and international beers. Celebrate Oktoberfest with special events.

Pancho Villa Mexican Grill (115 Calle Progreso, Rincón plaza, 787/823-8226, www.panchovillarincon.com, Tues.-Sun. noon-10 P.M., $8-12) is a newly opened restaurant with a lovely Southwestern ambience, serving Mexican fare such as burritos and fish tacos.

Breakfast

Ask anyone in town where the best spot is for breakfast, and they will probably send you to **◖ La Rosa Inglesa/The English Rose** (Carr. 413 Int., km 2.0, Barrio Puntas, 787/823-4032 or 787/207-4615, www.larosainglesa.com, Thanksgiving-Easter daily 8-11 A.M., summer Thurs.-Mon. 8-11 A.M., $7-11). The steep drive up to the mountaintop hotel is a bit of a fright, but it's worth it to get the opportunity to dine here. Everything is fresh and local. Breads are baked on the premises and sausages are stuffed in-house. Dishes include the Dead Elvis, a dish of French toast and caramelized bananas, and The Full Monty, a nod to the chef-owner's British-born wife, featuring a traditional English breakfast with bacon, sausage, mushrooms, tomatoes and bubble and squeak (fried leftover vegetables). For heartier appetites, try the HRH Burger, a house-made chorizo patty topped with a fried egg, provolone cheese, tomato relish and chipotle mayonnaise.

Banana Dang (Carr. 314, km 4.1, Rincón, 787/823-0963, www.banana-dang.com, Wed.-Mon. 7 A.M.-3 P.M., $1-6) serves coffee drinks, teas, fruit frappes, and smoothies, with a small menu of food items, including vegetable panini and cinnamon toast.

INFORMATION AND SERVICES

Banking services can be found at **Banco Popular** (18 Calle Muñoz Rivera, 787/823-9378).

GETTING THERE AND AROUND

Rincón is 153 kilometers or 95 miles west of San Juan. It is a straight shot along Highway 22 to Carretera 2 to Aguadilla.

From Aguadilla it is 20 kilometers or 12 miles on Carretera 115.

Taxi service is provided by **AA Taxi Service** (Carr. 413, km 3.4, Barrio Punta, Rincón, 787/823-0906).

Mayagüez

Mayagüez is a lovely colonial city and a bustling mini-metropolis that has resisted the siren's call of tourism and mainland influence. It's as sophisticated as it is traditional. Not only is it home to a branch of the Universidad de Puerto Rico and other colleges, but the heart of the city—Plaza de Colón—features a pleasantly large and thriving central town square.

Mayagüez has endured more than its share

of hard times. Established in 1760, the city was destroyed in 1841 by a great fire. The town reportedly had 700 homes at the time, and only 10 percent survived the devastation. Much of the city was leveled again in 1918, this time by an earthquake estimated to have registered 7.5 on the Richter scale. That was followed by a tsunami that reached 19 feet in height.

The city has also struggled through

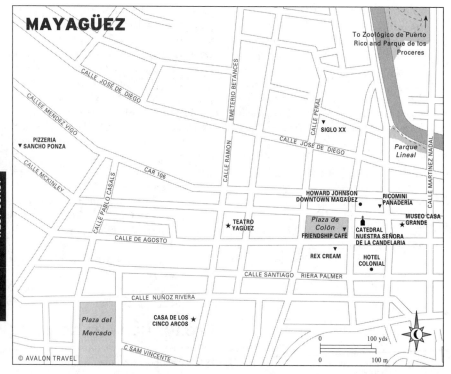

© SUZANNE VAN ATTEN

Plaza de Colón's Christopher Columbus sculpture, with Catedral Nuestra Señora de la Candelaria in the background

economic ups and downs. Under the Spanish crown, Mayagüez was a major shipping port for coffee production, but after the United States arrived, trade restrictions sent the island's coffee industry into decline. The void was filled by a massive tuna-canning industry, which reportedly produced more than half the canned tuna consumed by the United States, but that too has declined. Once the third-largest city in Puerto Rico, Mayagüez now ranks fifth, with 100,000 residents

In 2010, the city hosted the XXI Central American and Caribbean Games, which precipitated a significant effort to spruce up the town's cultural institutions and parks. The effect has given Mayagüez a shiny, new look that beckons visitors to linger awhile to explore its history and culture.

SIGHTS

Plaza de Colón (Calle McKinley) is a lovely, large, shady Spanish-style plaza with a huge statue of Christopher Columbus in the center surrounded by 16 lamp posts featuring intriguing bronze statues of figures representing other cultures, including Egypt, Africa, Spain, etc. There is also an outdoor café in the plaza where you can sip a *café con leche* and people-watch for a while.

Located on the plaza is **Catedral Nuestra Señora de la Candelaria** (Plaza Colón, 220 Apartado, 787/831-2444), a beautiful cathedral featuring marble floors, a wood-beamed ceiling, and stunning religious statuary. The first church on the site was a wooden structure built in 1763. Seventeen years later it was replaced with a masonry structure that was damaged in the 1918 earthquake and rebuilt in 1922.

WEST COAST

Teatro Yagüez

In 1976 the Diocese of Mayagüez was established and the church was rededicated as a cathedral. The church underwent a $3.5 million reconstruction in 2004. In the 18th century, the church's baptismal font, since replaced, was used to baptize slaves after they were bought by abolitionists who set them free. Listen for the church bells when they ring every day at 6 A.M. and 6 P.M.

Declared a National Historical Landmark in 1976, the recently renovated **Teatro Yagüez** (Calle McKinley, 787/834-0523) is a stunning example of Baroque architecture built in 1920 and still active as a cultural venue hosting operas, plays, and concerts. The original wooden structure was built in 1909 and was lavishly appointed with carpets from Spain and ceilings from Italy. It was destroyed in 1919 by a fire in which 150 perished.

Museo Casa Grande (104 Calle Méndez Vigo, 787/832-7435, Mon.-Fri. 8 A.M.-4:30 P.M., free) was once the private home of Don Guillermo Santos de la Mano, built in 1890, and it is an outstanding example of the city's turn-of-the-20th-century architecture, with its wide terrace, wrought-iron metalwork, and dramatic French doors. The recently renovated space is well-appointed with traditional furnishings and artwork from the era.

It's not open to the public, but **Casa de los Cinco Arcos** (Calle Betances between Calle San Vicente and Calle Munoz Rivera, downtown Mayagüez) is worth a drive-by. It's a striking example of *criolla* architecture and was built for Dr. Ramon Emeterio Betances (1827-1898), a surgeon, ophthalmologist, abolitionist, and nationalist who was very active in the island's independence movement. The home was built in 1865, and its name means House of the Five Arches.

Zoológico de Puerto Rico (Carr. 108, just north of Carr. 65, 787/832-6330, Wed.-Sun. 8:30 A.M.-4 P.M., Tues.-Sun. 8:30 A.M.-4 P.M. in summer, $13 adults, $8 ages 11-5, free for ages 4 and younger) is Puerto Rico's only zoo. It's a nicely landscaped, modern facility with 300 species divided into African Forest and African Savannah viewing compounds. Among its inhabitants are monkeys, zebras, lions, tigers, caimans, and hippos. Other features include a small lake and a children's playground.

Mayagüez is graced with several urban parks. Established in 1977, **Parque de los Proceres** (corner of Carr. 108 and Carr. 65, Mayagüez, dawn to dusk) is a picturesque park along Río Yagüez featuring formal gardens, a wrought-iron gazebo, walking paths, and plaques commemorating historic figures. It connects to **Parque Lineal** (Calle Martinez Nadal, Mayagüez, dawn to dusk), a nicely landscaped walking path that runs along the riverbank. The newest park is **Paseo del Litoral** (Carr. 102, south of Calle Mendez Vigo). Built in 2010, it contains walking paths that run along the shore of the bay and Plaza del las Banderas, commemorating the

the wrought iron gazebo in Parque de los Proceres

© SUZANNE VAN ATTEN

XXI Central American and Caribbean Games 2010, held in Mayagüez. Also located by the bay is **El Parque Infantil El Nuevo Milenio Rosa** (Tues.-Sun. 9 A.M.-10 P.M.), a fanciful children's playground with swings, jungle gyms, and picnic pavilions.

ENTERTAINMENT

Mayagüez is home to the west coast's only casinos, which are all open 24 hours daily. **Holiday Inn Tropical Casino Mayagüez** (Carr. 2, km 149.9, 787/265-4200 or 787/833-1100, fax 787/833-1300, www.hidpr.com/him_main.asp) has more than 400 slot machines and 13 gaming tables, including blackjack, Caribbean stud poker, craps, let it ride, mini-baccarat, poker, and roulette. **Mayagüez Resort and Casino** (Carr. 104, km 0.3, 787/832-3030, fax 787/265-3020, www.mayaguezresort.com) has slot machines, blackjack, craps, roulette, baccarat, and video poker.

SHOPPING

Plaza del Mercado (corner of Calle Pablo Casals and Calle Muñoz Rivera, 787/832-9240, daily 5 A.M.-6 P.M.) is a large structure containing booths filled with individual vendors selling everything from fresh fruits, vegetables, and meats to plants, birds, vitamins, and herbal remedies. There are also several food vendors serving fruit frappes, coffee, sandwiches, and more. This is a great place to get a real feel for daily life in Mayagüez.

Marine World (53 Calle Mendez Vigo, 787/833-2229, Mon.-Sat. 9 A.M.-6 P.M., Sun. noon-5 P.M.) sells beach, surf, and skate wear, including brands by Quiksilver, Billabong, and Crocs, as well as backpacks and skateboards.

ACCOMMODATIONS
$50-150

◖ **Howard Johnson Downtown Mayagüez** (70 Calle Méndez Vigo, 787/832-9191, fax 787/832-9122, www.hojo.com, $90 s, $100-130 d, $145 suite) is not your typical chain hotel. Once the home for priests serving at the city's cathedral, it was acquired by Howard Johnson, which renovated it and added lots of 21st-century amenities. Rooms have air-conditioning, cable TV, coffeemakers, and hair dryers. The suite has a kitchenette. There's a modest diner with a large wine list in the lobby, as well as a tiny pool oddly located inside a glassed-in courtyard.

The recently renovated **Hotel Colonial** (14 Iglesia Sur, 787/833-2150, www.hotelcolonial.com, $65 s, $75 d, $108 t, plus tax) is in a former convent built in 1920 that housed the nuns from Catedral Nuestra Señora de la Candelaria. If you can overlook the shabby neighborhood, this well-maintained, well-run property is the best deal in town. Continental breakfast and wireless Internet are free. If you don't mind the lack of windows, ask for room 23—it's in what was once the top of the chapel and features a fantastic dome ceiling.

WEST COAST

$150-250

Mayagüez Resort and Casino (Carr. 104, km 0.3, 787/832-3030, fax 787/265-3020, www. mayaguezresort.com, $185-245 s, $205-275 d, $335 suite, plus tax and resort fee) is an independently owned, modern hotel with a pool, casino, and restaurant on-site.

FOOD

⚫ **Ricomini Panadería** (131 Calle Méndez Vigo, 787/832-0565, daily 5 A.M.-midnight, $5-6) is much more than a bakery. This large modern restaurant serves eggs, ham, and *tortilla española* omelets for breakfast, as well as overstuffed hot sandwiches, barbecued chicken, stews, salads, and more. Plus there are five glass cases offering a huge selection of cakes and pastries. Buy a couple gift boxes of *brazo gitanos* for souvenirs. The jelly rolls, traditional to Mayagüez, are stuffed with a variety of fruits and cream cheese.

Siglo XX (9 Calle Peral at Calle de Diego, 787/833-1370 or 787/832-1370, Mon.-Sat. 6 A.M.-8:30 P.M., $7-15) is a small downtown diner serving cheap, homestyle Puerto Rican cuisine including fried pork, *carne guisado,* snapper fillet, and *churrasco.*

Office workers and students alike flock to **Pizzeria Sancho Panza** (87 Calle McKinley, 787/833-0215, daily noon-11 P.M., $4-17) to eat their weekday lunch. The very large, very casual open-kitchen eatery serves thin-crust pizza, a few basic Italian dishes, and a long list of Puerto Rican dishes, including *mofongo, churrasco,* and shrimp in garlic sauce. There are also a few dishes that blend cuisines, such as *churrasco Parmesan,* and unexpected pizza toppings like pastrami and chorizo. Every meal starts with a basket of garlic bread, and pizza is served by the slice on paper plates.

Brazo gitano, which literally means "gypsy arm," is a fruit-filled jelly roll cake brought to

Friends Café

© SUZANNE VAN ATTEN

Mayagüez in the 1850s by a Spanish company called E. Franco & Co. **Brazo Gitano Franco** (276 Calle Mendez Vigo, 787/832-0070, www.brazogitano.net, daily 6:30 A.M.-5 P.M., $5-9) still produces more than 20 varieties of the cakes, which come in flavors including guava and pineapple.

Before the beverage known as Sangria de Fido was professionally bottled and distributed throughout Puerto Rico and beyond, it was mixed up behind the bar of Fido's, a hole-in-the-wall bar and liquor store established 40 years ago by Wilfrido Aponte. The original establishment burned down, but **Fido's Sangria Garden** (78 Calle Fido—formerly Calle Dulievre, 787/833-4192, Wed.-Sat. 11 A.M.-midnight, Sun. and Mon. holidays 9 A.M.-6 P.M., $4-16) lives on in a modern new spot where Aponte's heirs still serve the powerful concoction of fruit juices, Bacardi 151 rum, and red wine. A mural wall depicts the original Fido's with Aponte still at the helm. A small menu of sandwiches and tapas, including chorizo in wine and calamari Francesca, is served.

Rex Cream (60 Calle Mendez Vigo, 787/832-8544, daily 9 A.M.-11 P.M.) is a popular ice cream chain based in Mayagüez that sells a soft ice cream in cones ($1.50-2.45), cups ($1.50-1.85), pints ($3), and quarts ($4). Flavors include chocolate, strawberry, pineapple, and coconut.

Friends Café (Plaza Colon, Mon.-Fri. 8 A.M.-11 P.M., Sat. 8 A.M.-midnight, Sun. noon-10 P.M., $1.25-3.50) is a pleasant sidewalk café serving coffee drinks, fruit frappes, croissants, bagels, pastries, and Argentine meat pies. Take it to go or enjoy it at one of the umbrella tables on the plaza.

INFORMATION AND SERVICES

There are several banks in town, including **Banco Popular** (locations at 1 Suau, Mayagüez, 787/831-6845, and 975 Ave. Hostos, Mayagüez, 787/834-4790). Medical services are available at **Hospital San Antonio** (Calle Post 18 N, 787/834-0050) and **Hostos Medical Services** (28 José de Diego, 787/833-0720 or 787/265-2929). **Walgreens** (Mayagüez Mall, Ave. Hostos, 787/831-9251) operates a 24-hour pharmacy.

The **Tourist Office** (51 Calle de la Candelaria, Plaza Colón, 787/832-5882, turismo@amayguezpr.gov, Mon.-Sat. 8 A.M.-4:30 P.M.) has a helpful staff and lots of brochures on local sights, but most of them are in Spanish.

GETTING THERE AND AROUND

Mayagüez is 191 kilometers or 118 miles west of San Juan along Highway 52 south to Carretera 2 west. It is 27 kilometers or 16 miles south of Aguadilla on Carretera 2.

Mayagüez is served by **Eugenio María de Hostos Airport** (north of town, Carr. 341, km 148.7, 787/265-7065). It is serviced primarily by **Cape Air** (800/352-0714, www.flycapeair.com), which provides several daily flights from San Juan. There are no direct flights from the United States to Mayagüez. Several car-rental agencies service Eugenio María de Hostos Airport, including **Avis** (787/833-7070), **Budget** (787/832-4570), **Hertz** (787/832-3314), and **Thrifty** (787/834-1590), among others.

There are several taxi services in Mayagüez. They include **City Taxi** (787/265-1992), **Taxi Western Bank** (787/832-0563), and **White Taxi** (787/832-1154).

Cabo Rojo

Because of its remote location and unusual topography, the municipality of Cabo Rojo is quite unlike anywhere else on the island. For one thing, it is hotter and more arid than the rest of the island, and the foliage gets scrubbier and browner the farther south you travel. Its geography is distinguished by two unique environments: more than 1,000 acres of natural salt flats along Bahía Salinas, and the red limestone cliffs along its southernmost tip that inspired the municipality's name, which means "red end."

Most visitors to the island don't make the trek this far southwest, but Puerto Ricans are very familiar with Cabo Rojo's charms thanks to three major points of interest: Joyuda, a fishing village with scores of terrific seafood restaurants; Boquerón, a popular summertime vacation town; and Cabo Rojo peninsula, site of the island's most picturesque lighthouse.

JOYUDA

Joyuda is home to a preponderance of fresh seafood restaurants. Many of them are open-air and located right on the water, with terraces perched on pilings in the sea. Locals often throw bits of their dinner over the railing to feed the enormous tarpon fish that come here to compete for snacks. The majority of the restaurants serve the same basic menu of seafood dishes prepared *criolla* style, and most of them are very casual—some perhaps more casual in cleanliness than one might like, so select your dining spot with care. The best rule of thumb is to look for the restaurants with the most cars, but be prepared to wait for your food. Even when restaurants aren't busy, service is exceedingly slow.

There are numerous hotels and guesthouses in Joyuda, but they are all fairly rustic with limited services. Joyuda caters to Puerto Rican vacationers, who tend to travel with extended family members, so a big selling point is how many people a unit can sleep. Kitchenettes are also popular. High season spans from Mother's Day to Labor Day, but it peaks in July.

Sights and Recreation

Isla Ratones is a tiny island (like a mouse, hence its name) half a mile off the coast of Joyuda managed by the Department of Natural and Environmental Resources. Its sandy beach and clear waters make it an excellent place to swim and snorkel. To get here, catch the ferry from the dock (Carr. 102, km 13.7) beside Island View Restaurant. It runs Tuesday-Sunday 9 A.M.-5 P.M. and costs $3 round-trip. For information call 787/851-7708.

Pelayo Marina (Carr. 102, km 12.3, Joyuda, 787/547-6084, daily 7 A.M.-6 P.M.) is a tiny rustic dock that can accommodate small boats and sells gasoline.

Capitán Red (Carr. 102, km 14.5, Joyuda, 787/451-1071 or 787/318-9216, Wed.-Mon. 9 A.M.-5 P.M.) is a source for fishing, boating, and scuba equipment.

Club Deportivo del Oeste (Carr. 102, km 15.4, Joyuda, 787/254-3748 or 787/851-8880, www.clubdeportivodeloeste.com) is a hilly nine-hole golf course with a practice putting green, a driving range, and club rentals. A PGA pro is available for lessons. It also has a golf shop and full-service restaurant.

Entertainment and Events

Along Carretera 102 around kilometer 10, there are numerous large bars with ample parking lots that jump late into the night on weekends, especially during the summer. They include **Sloe John's, Nocturno Oldies Night, Taino's Cave Bar & Beach, Casa del Mojito,** and **Punta Arenas Pool Room.**

Accommodations

Hotel Costa de Oro Inn (Carr. 102, km 14.7,

© SUZANNE VAN ATTEN

Joyuda

787/851-5010, $55 and up) is a small homespun guesthouse with a tiny pool and lobby and super-clean little rooms to match.

Parador Joyuda Beach (Carr. 102, km 11.7, 787/851-5650 or 800/981-5464, fax 787/255-3750, www.joyudabeach.com, $80 s/d Sun.-Thurs., $96 s/d Fri.-Sat., $159 waterfront room with refrigerator, tax included) has 41 no-frills units with air-conditioning, cable TV, telephones, Internet, and tubs or showers. Amenities include a small triangular pool, a waterside bar and restaurant, and a small beach area. The kitsch-crazy lobby with big gold statues of angels, fake flowers, and floral brocade upholstery on rattan furniture is quite a sight.

Parador Perichi's (Carr. 102, km 14.3, 787/851-3131 or 800/435-7197, fax 787/851-0560, www.hotelperichi.com, $64-115 s, $69-125 d, tax included) has a bright perky exterior, but the rooms in the main building are pretty drab. Some overlook the pool; others overlook the parking lot. All rooms have air-conditioning, cable TV, bathtubs or showers, and hair dryers. A better option is the higher-priced "hacienda" rooms, in a separate building on the back of the property. They have spiffier decor, refrigerators, and wireless Internet. Other amenities include a large pool with umbrella tables, wheelchair-accessible rooms, a restaurant, and a cocktail lounge.

Food

Parada Los Flamboyanes (Carr. 102, km 15.9, 787/255-3765, fax 787/255-6177, www.paradalosflamboyanes.com, Wed.-Thurs. 11 A.M.-11 P.M., Fri.-Sat. 11 A.M.-1 A.M., Sun. 11 A.M.-11 P.M., $1-15) is a casual, cheerful operation in an attractive salmon-colored structure with dining tables on a wraparound porch. Young families flock here to feast on affordable Puerto Rican seafood specialties, including *empanadillas, mofongo,* conch and octopus salad, and seafood soup.

Tino's Restaurant (Carr. 102, km 13.6,

WEST COAST

© SUZANNE VAN ATTEN

Isla Ratones off the coast of Joyuda

787/851-2976, Sun.-Mon. and Wed.-Thurs. 11 A.M.-10 P.M., Fri.-Sat. 11 A.M.-11 P.M., $13-32) is a slightly upscale eatery serving Puerto Rican seafood dishes and specializing in *mofongo*. The decor is simple, punctuated with stuffed fish hanging on the wall. It also offers monthly wine specials.

Vista Bahía Restaurant (Carr. 102, km 14.1, 787/851-4140, Wed.-Sun. and Mon. holidays 11 A.M.-10 P.M., $19-27) has a cool chrome-and-glass-block exterior with patio dining overlooking the water. It specializes in seafood *mofongo* and has a full bar.

A welcome departure from the *criolla*-style seafood restaurants that populate Joyuda, **Ceviche Restaurant** (Carr. 102, km 11, 787/255-0190, Wed.-Sat. 3-10 P.M., Sun. noon-9 P.M., $15-29) serves a variety of ceviches, paellas, and stuffed crepes.

Located by the hotel pool and overlooking the ocean, **Playa Joyuda Restaurant** (Parador Joyuda Beach, Carr. 102, km 11.8,

787/241-7140, daily 7:30 A.M.-8 P.M., bar open later, $14-28) is a pleasant patio restaurant serving *criolla* cuisine, including chicken breast stuffed with shrimp, rabbit in garlic sauce, octopus, conch, lobster and shrimp. Also serves breakfast and lunch.

El Gato Negro (Carr. 102, km 13.6, 787/851-2966, Wed.-Mon. 11 A.M.-10 P.M. or later, $13-22) is an enormous, rustic restaurant right on the water serving a huge menu of *criolla*-style seafood in a myriad of ways, including stewed, fried, grilled, or in salads, stews, and garlic sauce. It also serves a large selection of *empanadillas*. There is patio dining out back, overlooking the water. Karaoke is on Thursday nights.

Information and Services

In the municipality of Cabo Rojo, your best bet for tourist information, banking, or health-care needs is the town of Cabo Rojo, on Carretera 101, east of Carretera 100. Just outside of town is the **tourism office** (Carr. 100, km 13.7, Cabo Rojo, 787/851-7015, daily 8 A.M.-4:30 P.M.), which has tons of brochures and a helpful staff. In town you can find a hospital, **Hospital Metropolitano Cabo Rojo** (108 Muñoz Rivera, Cabo Rojo, 787/851-2816 or 787/851-0888), and a pharmacy, **Farmacia Encarnación** (45 Muñoz Rivera, 787/891-4723). For banking services, **Western Bank** with an ATM is on the corner of Carretera 100 and Carretera 102, on the way to Joyuda.

Getting There and Around

Joyuda is 39 kilometers or 24 miles south of Aguadilla, and 192 kilometers or 119 miles west of San Juan. From Aguadilla take Carretera 2 south and Carretera 100 west. From San Juan take Highway 52 south to Carretera 2 west and Carretera 100 west.

BOQUERÓN

Traveling south from Joyuda to Boquerón along Carretera 100 is a beautiful drive through

© SUZANNE VAN ATTEN

Boquerón

lush green hills and traffic medians filled with flowering plants. To the east is a lovely pastoral valley with mountains visible in the distance, and to the west is the sea. The scenery is a perfect prelude to a journey into Boquerón and one of the last sights of greenery you'll see as you continue south to El Combate, where the topography turns desert-like.

Boquerón, which means anchovy, is a sleepy little fishing village that explodes in the summer into a popular family beach destination. Puerto Rican families flock here to swim, fish, dine on seafood, browse souvenir shops, and bar-hop late into the night. Book early if you plan to come during a holiday. Boquerón gets really packed then, and the traffic getting into and out of town can be fierce.

Reminiscent of popular beach towns along the U.S. Eastern Seaboard, Boquerón's streets are lined with vendors selling T-shirts, hammocks, shell crafts, fresh oysters, and more. Carretera 101 Int. turns into Calle Jose de Diego as it passes through the heart of town, called Poblado de Boquerón. It's closed to automobile traffic Friday-Sunday, turning the road into a pedestrian promenade.

Because Boquerón primarily attracts Puerto Rican tourists, hotels and guesthouses cater to families who bunk together in single units. Many rooms sleep up to eight people and are priced accordingly.

Boquerón is 187 kilometers or 116 miles west of San Juan, and 50 kilometers or 31 miles south of Aguadilla. From San Juan take Highway 52 south to Carretera 2 west to Carretera 117 west to Carretera 101 west. From Aguadilla take Carretera 2 south to Carretera 100 south.

Sights

Refugio de Aves de Boquerón (Carr. 307, km 8.8, 787/851-7260, open 24-7) bird sanctuary is part of Bosque Estatal de Boquerón, a protected stretch of subtropical dry forest that spans from Mayagüez to Cabo Rojo to Lajas. The refuge has a short, well-maintained boardwalk through a mangrove swamp ideal for birdwatching. Keep an eye out for the endangered *mariquita,* a medium-sized bird with black plumage and a yellow spot on the shoulder. **The Caribbean Ecological Field Services Office** (787/851-7297, http://caribbean-ecoteam.fws. gov, daily 7 A.M.-noon and 1-3:30 P.M.), which oversees conservation efforts to protect the island's endangered species, is located here.

Refugio de Vida Silvestre (Camino Mediano Rodríguez, off Carr. 301 at km 5.1, south of Boquerón, 787/851-4795, Mon.-Fri. 8 A.M.-4 P.M., http://caribbean-ecoteam.fws. gov) is a wildlife refuge encompassing more than 400 acres of mangrove wetlands, an important breeding ground for birds, sea mammals, and fish. More than 60 species of birds have been identified here. The center has a few small nature exhibits featuring stuffed birds and a freshwater aquarium. Signage is in Spanish only, as are most of the printed educational materials. Several hiking trails start here.

WEST COAST

EL PIRATA COFRESÍ: PUERTO RICO'S PIRATE MARAUDER

The west coast of Puerto Rico abuts the 3,000-foot-deep Mona Passage, an important shipping lane since the early days of colonialism. The area was a popular hideout for pirates lying in wait for passing ships filled with goods traveling between Europe and the New World.

Among historical records are reports of pirate activity in Mona Passage that include the capture of a frigate in 1625 by the African pirate Mateo Congo. And in 1637, Dutch pirate Adrian Cornelis led 14 ships in the capture of an African ship carrying a load of cedar. It is believed that English pirate William Kidd hid out on Mona Island after capturing an Armenian vessel carrying goods worth 100,000 sterling pounds – some believe that treasure may still be found within Mona's intricate cave system.

Born more than 100 years later but likely inspired by tales of those notorious pirates, Roberto Cofresí took up the piracy game as a young man and gained hero status among many Puerto Ricans along the way.

Roberto Cofresí was born in Cabo Rojo in 1791, and as a young boy he had a small boat called *El Mosquito* that he used to putter around the shore of his hometown. For a brief time he was employed as a corsair, licensed to bring in foreign ships seeking authorization to dock. But he soon turned his attentions to raiding passing ships of their riches.

Acquiring a schooner he dubbed *Ana*, Cofresí and his men raided eight ships, including one from the United States, and crew members were killed in the process. Because he often shared his ill-gotten goods with fellow townspeople, he quickly gained a reputation as a Puerto Rican Robin Hood who robbed the exploiters and gave back to their victims. Although it had previously turned a blind eye toward pirates who attacked its enemy's ships, Spain's empire was beginning to crumble and it had begun to initiate trade with other countries to bolster its pocketbook. In collaboration with the United States, Spain set a trap for Cofresí and his men. Using as bait a U.S. Navy ship disguised as a commercial vessel, they captured Cofresí and his men, who were incarcerated at Castillo San Felipe del Morro in San Juan. Cofresí was tried by the Spanish Council of War and found guilty. He was executed at El Morro on March 29, 1825, and buried just outside the confines of the historic Old San Juan Cemetery.

Cofresí's legend has grown with time, and his memory is still celebrated in songs, books, and dance. A statue by artist José Cuscaglia Guillermety in Cabo Rojo's Boquerón Bay stands in monument to the notorious and beloved "El Pirata Cofresí."

(Balneario de Boquerón

Balneario de Boquerón (Carr. 101, km 18.1, 787/851-1900, daily 7:30 A.M.-7 P.M., $4) is one of Puerto Rico's most beautiful public beaches. The beach is a very long white crescent gently lapped by calm waters. Dozens of sailboats moored in the distance provide a picturesque sight. The property is very shady, thanks to all the palm trees and sea grapes that grow in the area, and the new facilities are very clean and modern. There's an enormous activities pavilion on the grounds, as well as picnic tables with umbrellas, a baseball field, and a cafeteria. The three huge parking lots are indicative of the crowds that descend here on weekends and during the summer.

Sports and Recreation

Boquerón is an excellent launching point for dive and snorkeling trips to Desecheo Island and Mona Island, two uninhabited wildlife refuges.

Mona Aquatics (Calle José de Diego, next to Club Náutico, 787/851-2185, fax 787/254-0604, www.monaaquatics.com) has been operating scuba-diving trips to Mona and Desecheo Islands for 20 years. The boat leaves Tuesday-Thursday at 8 A.M. Mona Aquatics also offers

© SUZANNE VAN ATTEN

Balneario de Boquerón

night dives Wednesday at 7 P.M., sunset cruises Saturday-Sunday at 6 P.M., night trips to the bioluminescent bay in La Parguera Friday-Sunday at 8 and 9:30 P.M., and transportation for overnight camping stays on Mona Island (permit required). Rental equipment is available.

Light Tackle Adventure (Boquerón pier, 787/849-1430 or 787/547-7380, www.lighttackleadventure.8k.com) specializes in light tackle and fly-fishing excursions. Excursions for two people are $340 for four hours, $425 for six hours, $550 for eight hours. A $100 reservation deposit is required. This company also provides kayak trips to the Cabo Rojo salt flats, Boquerón Bay, Joyuda, and La Parguera. Bird-watching tours in Cabo Rojo salt flats are also available.

Boquerón Kayak Rental (Calle Jose de Diego, Poblado de Boquerón, 787/255-1849, Sat.-Sun. and Mon. holidays 10 A.M.-5 P.M. in winter, daily 10 A.M.-5 P.M. in summer) offers banana boat rides for $10, or rent a kayak for $10 an hour.

Entertainment and Events

There is no shortage of bars in Boquerón. During the weekends, when the main street is closed to car traffic, partiers freely stroll from bar to bar, drink in hand.

Galloway's (Calle José de Diego, 787/254-3302, Sun.-Thurs. noon-midnight, Fri.-Sat. noon-1 A.M., kitchen until 10 P.M.) is a friendly, casual, open-air waterfront bar serving an excellent rum punch and good Puerto Rican cuisine.

Shamar (Calle José de Diego, beside Boquerón pier, 787/851-0542, Mon.-Thurs. 11 A.M.-midnight, Fri.-Sat. noon-1 A.M.) is a big popular beer hall with a full bar, pool tables, and a jukebox. This is the place to go for long happy hours and karaoke on Friday and Saturday nights. A small counter outside serves breakfast items, sandwiches, tacos, pizza, and fried treats ($5-10). Grab a cold Medalla beer from the bar, an *empanadilla* from the food counter, and walk out back to sit by the water.

WEST COAST

Accommodations

Parador Boquemar (Calle José de Diego, Poblado de Boquerón, 787/851-2158, www. boquemar.com, $108-128 s/d, $133 suite, plus tax) is a modern three-story hotel with 75 guest rooms with air-conditioning and cable TV. Each room can sleep up to four people, and some have small balconies. Amenities include a pool, wireless Internet in the lobby, and a restaurant and bar.

One of the better options for accommodations in Cabo Rojo is **Apartamentos Adamaris** (Calle Gil Boyet at Calle Jose de Diego, Poblado de Boquerón, 787/851-6860, www.adamarisapartments.com, $85 studio, $130 one-bedroom, $175 two-bedroom). The modest little complex of apartments offers neat, modern rooms with air-conditioning, wireless Internet, and cable TV. All but the studios have full kitchens. There's no pool or restaurant, but the beach is across the street, and restaurants and bars are within walking distance. Note that some rooms have balconies and some are windowless and dark.

Wildflowers Guest House (13 Calle Muñoz Rivera, 787/851-1793, www.wildflowersguesthouse.com, $115 s/d, $135 s/d with balcony, plus tax) is a small property with eight clean, compact rooms. Amenities include air-conditioning, cable TV, and mini-refrigerators.

Boquerón Beach Hotel (Carr. 101, by the entrance to Balneario de Boquerón, 787/851-7110, fax 787/851-7135, www.westernbayhotels.com, $109 s/d) is a modern bright blue-and-yellow high-rise hotel offering clean comfy accommodations. Rooms have air-conditioning, cable TV, and private balconies. Other amenities include a pool, uninvitingly located in the parking lot, and a restaurant.

Cofresí Beach House (57 Calle Muñoz Rivera, 787/254-3000, fax 787/254-1048, www.cofresibeach.com, $129 sleeps 4, $165 sleeps 6, $219 sleeps 8, plus tax) has a modernistic, art deco exterior with clean, simply furnished rooms. It offers 16 one-, two-, and three-bedroom apartments with air-conditioning, cable TV, VCRs, telephones, and fully equipped kitchens. Some rooms have balconies, and there's a pool on the fourth floor.

Food

Opened in 2011, **Mr. Mofongo Restaurant** (Poblado de Boquerón, by bridge to marina, 787/254-0799, Mon. and Wed. 10 A.M.-10 P.M., Thurs.-Sun. 10 P.M.-midnight, bar open later on weekends, $5-25) is a casual spot serving *criolla* cuisine, including *mofongo* stuffed with seafood, chicken, or *churrasco* and fish, pork, and chicken fried with onions. The daily lunch special is $7, and Medalla beer is $1 a can.

El Bulgao (35 Calle Jose de Diego, Poblado de Boquerón, 787/547-5020, Wed. 3 A.M.-midnight, Thurs. 8 P.M.-1 A.M., Fri.-Sat. 3 P.M.-3 A.M., Sun. 1 P.M.-midnight, $5-16) is a kitschy tiki bar touting itself as the home of natural Viagra, thanks to the local snails—*bulgao*—it serves. More bar than restaurant, its cocktails are made with fresh fruit juices, but there is a limited menu of burritos and salads made with lobster, octopus, shrimp, chicken, and, of course, snails.

Galloway's (Calle José de Diego, 787/254-3302, daily noon-10 P.M., $8-13) is a casual, open-air waterfront bar and restaurant serving a huge menu of seafood and Puerto Rican cuisine. Shrimp, lobster, snapper, and dorado are served in your choice of sauce, including garlic butter, creole, spicy creole, and *fra diabla*. Other items include *mofongo,* fried chicken, pork chops, and steak. The coconut shrimp with tamarind sauce is highly recommended. Daily lunch specials are served for $5. Diners can eat in the bar or cross a little bridge over the water into a separate dining room.

Roberto's Fish Net (Calle José de Diego, 787/851-6009, Wed.-Sun. 11 A.M.-9 P.M., $5-20) is so popular it operates two restaurants across the street from one another. They both reputedly serve the best, freshest seafood in town.

El Bulgao

Like a mirage, **La Frutera** fruit stand (Carr. 101, km 10.5, Llanos, daily 8 A.M.-6 P.M., $3) appears out of nowhere in the midst of flat farm land on the road between Boquerón and La Parguera in Lajas. With tin roof and wood shutters, it looks like a modest *jíbaro* house from years gone by, and it sells fruit frappes made to order with fresh pineapple, banana, mango, coconut, and papaya. People come from miles around to get one. It's only a two-person operation so be prepared to wait. It's worth it.

CABO ROJO PENINSULA

Cabo Rojo peninsula has such a dramatically different topography from the rest of Puerto Rico that you might think you've left the island altogether. It's incredibly flat, dry, and desolate, with little vegetation. Be sure to gas up before you leave Boquerón because there are few gas stations—or any other businesses, for that matter—in the area.

There are several interesting things to do and

see, though. El Combate is a quiet little fishing village with a nice beach for swimming. Farther south are more than 1,000 acres of salt flats, which have been mined for centuries and which are a great place for bird-watching. At the farthest tip of the island's southwest corner is the Cabo Rojo lighthouse, which sits atop dramatic red limestone cliffs that contain an intricate system of caves once frequented by the pirate Roberto Cofresí.

Cabo Rojo Peninsula is 197 kilometers or 122 miles southwest of San Juan, and 63 kilometers or 39 miles south of Aguadilla. From San Juan, take Highway 52 south to Carretera 2 west to Carretera 116 west to Carretera 305 west to Carretera 301 south. From Aguadilla take Carretera 2 south to Carretera 100 south to Carretera 301 south.

Sights

El Combate (end of Carr. 3301, off Carr. 301) is a small village that turns into something of a hot spot on weekends and holidays, thanks to a nice wilderness beach area and great fishing. It's also the peninsula's sole concentration—albeit a small one—of businesses such as gas stations, restaurants, and hotels that cater to visitors. The community has a small cluster of modest and luxury homes, with a couple of new condominium complexes cropping up.

There are two places to access the water in El Combate. Traveling toward Combate on Carretera 3301, turn left at the Combate Beach Hotel sign to reach a narrow sandy beach with calm, crystal-clear water. There's plenty of parking, little shade, and no facilities. To reach the fishing and small boat-launch area, continue along Carretera 3301 past the Combate Beach Hotel sign, past Annie's Place, to a small sandy parking lot on the left. Here you'll find small fishing boats moored in the water and a long wooden pier where fishers gather to drown worms. There are no facilities.

In 1999, the U.S. Fish and Wildlife Service bought 1,249 acres of the **Cabo Rojo salt flats** (Carr. 301, south of Combate), tripling the size of the Cabo Rojo National Wildlife Refuge. The salt flats have also been an important place for humans, who have mined the mineral since pre-Taíno times. The area encompasses coastline, mangroves, sea grass beds, and offshore reefs that are vital to migratory shorebirds and an important feeding ground for sea turtles and manatees. Local outfitters offer bird-watching tours of the area.

For a roadside view of the salt flats, there is an observation tower along Carretera 301 south of El Combate. Unfortunately, it's open sporadically, despite posted hours that claim it's open daily 8 A.M.-4 P.M.

El Faro de Cabo Rojo (end of Carr. 301, km 11.5), also called Los Morillos, built in 1882, is one of Puerto Rico's most picturesque lighthouses, although it's best viewed from the

El Faro de Cabo Rojo

water. That's the only way to appreciate its dramatic location 200 feet above the sea on top of enormous red limestone cliffs that line the coast in this remote corner of the island. To reach the lighthouse on foot, follow Carretera 301 to the end and continue along a bumpy dirt road through the dry scrubby wilderness area to a crude parking area. From here you can hike in along a rocky road closed to traffic. Another option is to turn left to another small parking area and the head of a narrow wilderness trail that will also take you there. Visitors are advised to go early in the day, apply lots of sunscreen, wear a hat, and bring water. It's scorching here, and there's no shade whatsoever.

Sports and Recreation

Light Tackle Adventure (Boquerón pier, 787/849-1430 or 787/547-7380, www. lighttackleadventure.8k.com) specializes in light tackle and fly-fishing excursions. Excursions for two people are $340 for four hours, $425 for six hours, $550 for eight hours. A $100 reservation deposit is required. This company also provides kayak trips to the Cabo Rojo salt flats, Boquerón Bay, Joyuda, and La Parguera. Bird-watching tours in Cabo Rojo salt flats are also available.

Paradise Puerto Rico Watersports (Combate Beach, 787/567-4386 or 888/787-4386, www.pprwatersports.com) offers Jet Ski rentals ($85 an hour, $45 half hour), tours ($30 an hour, $55 for two hours, three-person minimum), and banana boat rides.

Accommodations and Food

🄒 **Bahía Salinas Beach Hotel** (Carr. 301, km 11.5, 787/254-1212, fax 787/254-1215, www. bahiasalinas.com, $172 for 2 people, $194 for 3, $215 for 4, inclusive breakfast and lunch package available, limited dinner menu, plus tax and resort fees) is by far the best accommodation in all of Cabo Rojo if you don't mind the remote location. Across the street from the salt flats, this waterside paradise features lush, naturally landscaped grounds, a lovely open-air restaurant, covered terraces, verandas, porches, hammocks, an adult pool, a children's pool, a whirlpool bath, a mineral bath, and a small pier. The rooms are small, but they come with superior four-poster beds with thick, plush mattresses, air-conditioning, cable TV, and coffeepots. Suites have mini-refrigerators.

Combate Beach Hotel and Restaurant (Carr. 3301, km 2.7, 787/254-2358 or 787/254-7053, $99 for 2, $139-159 for 4, including tax) is a modern motel-style property on the beach. Rooms are simple and clean and come with air-conditioning and cable TV. A small pool and restaurant are on-site.

The restaurants in El Combate are all casual open-air affairs serving cheap Puerto Rican cuisine with an emphasis on seafood and *mofongo*. They also tend to do double duty as popular watering holes late into the night on weekends and holidays. Options include the recently renovated **Annie's Place** (Carr. 3301, km 2.9, 787/254-2553 or 787/254-0021, $5-15) and **Luichy's Seafood Restaurant and Guest House** (Carr. 3301, km 2.9, 787/254-7053 or 787/254-2358).

La Parguera

In the municipality of Lajas, La Parguera is a popular and picturesque vacation destination for Puerto Rican travelers. Much of what makes La Parguera special—its mangrove canals, coral reefs, and coastal forest—are part of the Parguera Natural Preserve, which is managed by the Department of Natural Resources. While there is plenty of swimming to be had in La Parguera, it's typically done from the bow of a boat because there isn't much in the way of sandy beaches. If you don't get on a boat while you're here, though, you won't experience the real La Parguera. Its main attraction is the Bahía Fosforescente, a bioluminescent bay, home to glowing microscopic organisms visible in the water on moonless nights. Unfortunately, the use of gas-powered boats, coupled with light pollution, has greatly diminished the bay's glow. But that doesn't stop visitors from flocking to the town's docks to catch boat rides to the bay after dark.

La Parguera is also the site of the famous La Pared, an underwater wall that is one of the most popular diving spots on the island. Deep-sea fishing and boat rides through mangrove channels, where enormous starfish, sea anemones, blowfish, and manatees live, are also popular activities.

The town of La Parguera is basically a small group of seafood restaurants, bars, and boating outfitters clustered around the waterfront docks. Radiating from that are lovely private homes—some situated on pilings over the water, where instead of cars there are boats floating in the garages. On the hills overlooking the town are expensive, architecturally daring homes.

SIGHTS
La Pared
La Pared is an underwater coral reef wall that runs parallel to the coast from Guánica to Cabo Rojo and is a world-class dive site. The wall drops from 55 feet to more than 1,500 feet in depth, and the water visibility ranges 60-150 feet. There are plenty of other outstanding dive sites in the area, where you can see rays, moray eels, parrot fish, grunts, sharks, rare black corals, and more.

Los Canales Manglares
Los Canales Manglares (787/899-1660 or 787/899-1335) is a cluster of more than 30 mangrove cays (islands) around the coast of La Parguera that form an intricate system of channels that are prime for wildlife exploration. On weekends and holidays, locals motor to their favorite cays and anchor for the day to swim and fish in shallow crystal-clear waters. Go to the boat docks in the heart of town to arrange a trip with one of several boating outfitters. The cost is $25 per person, or less for groups. Be sure to ask your captain to take you to see the enormous Mona iguanas that live on one of the cays. And watch the water for starfish, sea anemones, blowfish, manatees, and more.

Los Cayos
Los Cayos comprises 30 or more tiny islets, or cays, off the coast of La Parguera, accessible only by boat. They are ideal spots to swim, fish, and snorkel in shallow, clear waters. Each cay has its own personality. The most popular is **Caracoles,** which can get crowded with revelers. **Mata de la Gata** and **San Cristobal** are among the largest. **Enrique, Medialuna,** and **Majimo** are the best options for primitive camping. **Isla Cuevas** is full of rhesus monkeys, placed there by the now-closed La Parguera Primate Facility, so proceed with caution. They can be aggressive.

Bahía Fosforescente
Puerto Rico is blessed with several bioluminescent bays and lagoons. These are small warm

DRUG BLIMP

At first glance, the plump white dirigible floating above La Parguera looks like an albino version of the Goodyear blimp drifting overhead. That is, until you notice that it is tethered to a spot on the coast just west of town, surrounded by a high cyclone fence posted with No Trespassing signs. It is, in fact, a weapon in the U.S. war on drugs. Its proper name is aerostat unmanned radar system, and it is used to detect low-flying aircraft bringing in cocaine, heroin, and marijuana from Venezuela and the Dominican Republic.

One of 12 such radar systems operating in the southern United States and the Caribbean, the aerostat has a detection range of 200 miles. It's constructed of a lightweight polyurethane-coated fabric filled with helium, and it typically operates at 12,000 feet in the air. But keeping it in the air during high winds and rain is no small feat. The Las Lajas aerostat is grounded more often than it is airborne, and some believe it is a financial folly.

Some people think the blimp's true purpose is to detect intelligent life elsewhere in the universe, because many believe this part of the island has experienced extraterrestrial activity. Threatening to turn Lajas into the Roswell, New Mexico, of Puerto Rico, a local schoolteacher and farmer announced plans in 2005 to build a UFO landing strip near La Parguera, where some claim to have seen an alien craft crash in 1997.

bodies of water surrounded by mangrove forests that contain millions of dinoflagellates, unique microorganisms that emit a phosphorescent glow when they sense motion. The only way to see them is to enter the bay at night, preferably where the moon is not visible.

Puerto Rico's most spectacular bioluminescent bay is in Vieques, where there's little pollution or ambient light. But La Parguera's Bahía Fosforescente is probably the best-known and most popular one because of its easy access and long history as a tourist attraction.

Unlike in Vieques, gas-operated boats are permitted into La Parguera's Bahía Fosforescente, which has contributed to a diminishing number of dinoflagellates in the water.

Nevertheless, if you've never experienced the thrill of a nighttime boat ride into the sparkling waters of a bioluminescent bay, a trip into Bahía Fosforescente is in order. Several tour operators offer nightly rides into the bay on kayaks, fishing boats, and double-decker catamarans beginning at 7:30 P.M. from the docks in La Parguera.

SPORTS AND RECREATION
Diving and Snorkeling
Paradise Scuba Snorkeling and Kayaks (Carr.

304, km 3.2, 787/899-7611, paradisescubapr@ yahoo.com) offers scuba-dive tours ($70-80), night dives ($60), snorkeling tours ($50), sunset snorkeling tours ($50-65), phosphorescent bay tours ($25), gear rental, and dive instruction. Dive sites include El Pared, Enrique, El Mario, Chimney, and Old Buoy.

West Divers (Carr. 304, km 3.1, La Parguera, 787/899-3223 or 787/899-4171, www.westdiverspr.com) specializes in scuba trips to La Pared, an underwater wall and world-class dive site. It also offers snorkel trips, sunset cruises, kayak tours, and equipment rental. A one-day, two-tank dive is $100 per person. Kayak tours cost $20-30 per hour; kayak rentals are $10-15 per hour.

Paradise Scuba & Snorkeling Center (La Parguera, 787/899-7611, www.paradisescubas-norkelingpr.com) offers scuba and snorkel trips, night dives, sunset trips, bio bay tours, dive instruction, and equipment rental. A two-tank dive including equipment is $100 per person; snorkeling is $40 per person.

Fishing
Parguera Fishing Charters (Carr. 304,

La Parguera

WEST COAST

787/382-4698, www.puertoricofishingcharters.com) offers half-day ($500) and full-day ($850) charters to fish for dorado, tuna, blue marlin, and wahoo on a 31-foot, twin diesel Bertram Sportfisherman. Trips include bait, tackle, beverages, snacks, and lunch. It also offers light-tackle reef fishing, half-day snorkeling trips, and customized charters.

Boating

Along the docks in the heart of La Parguera are several boating operators, including **Cancel Boats** (787/899-5891 or 787/899-2972, call in advance for reservations) and **Johnny Boats** (787/299-2212, call in advance for reservations), which offer on-demand tours of the mangrove canals for $25 per person (less if you have a group) and nighttime tours of the phosphorescent bay for about $6.

Aleli Tours (Carr. 304, km 3.2, 787/899-6086 or 787/390-6086, http://alelitours.com) provides sailing, snorkeling, and mangrove channel tours around La Parguera and Guánica on a catamaran. It also has kayaks for rent.

Fondo de Cristal III (end of Carr. 304, La Parguera, 787/899-5891 or 787/344-0593) offers nighttime tours of Bahía Fosforescente on a 72-foot bilevel glass-bottomed catamaran that is wheelchair accessible. Not the best way to see the bay's glow, the boat packs in 150 people and blares loud dance music the whole time. Due to the size of the crowd, only a few can look through the glass bottom portals, and even then you can't see much. It's best suited for families and kids who just want to enjoy a nighttime boat ride.

Parguera Watersports (787/646-6777, www.prkbc.com) guides visitors on bio-bay or full moon kayaking adventures ($45 per person). Kiteboard instruction costs $95 for the first session, $75 additional sessions, including equipment. Rent kayaks by the hour for $20 double, $15 single, or paddleboards for $20 an hour. Day rates are available.

Excursiones EcoBoriken Inc. (La Parguera, 787/951-0683, www.excursionesecoboriken. com) provides guided kayak tours to the bioluminescent bay. A four-hour day tour or two-hour night tour is $40 per person for 2-15 people.

Surfing
Ventolera High-Wind Center & Surf Shop (Carr. 304, El Muelle Shopping Center, La Parguera, 787/808-0396 or 787/505-4541, Fri.-Sat. 9 A.M.-8 P.M., Sun. 9 A.M.-5 P.M. in winter; Mon.-Thurs. 10 A.M.-4 P.M., Fri.-Sat. 9 A.M.-8 P.M., Sun. 9 A.M.-5 P.M. in summer) is the source for buying surfboards, kayaks, paddleboards, wet suits, sunglasses, Crocs, and bathing suits.

ACCOMMODATIONS
$50-100
La Parguera Guest House (Carr. 304, km 3.3, 787/899-3993, www.pargueraguesthouse.com, $65 s, $76 d) is a modest little blue and yellow guesthouse with simple basic rooms that have air-conditioning, cable TV, and mini-refrigerators. There's no pool, restaurant, or bar, but there are barbecue grills on the grounds for guests' use.

Located in the heart of La Parguera, **Nautilus Hotel** (Carr. 304, 787/899-4565, www.nautiluspr.com, $80 s, $100 d, $120 t, plus tax) has 22 no-frills hotel rooms with air-conditioning and TVs. Amenities include pool with hot tub and laundry facilities.

Opened in 2011, **Turtle Bay Inn** (153 Calle 6, 787/508-9823 or 787/899-6633, www.turtlebayinn.com, $90 s, $125 d) is a small, two-story inn with 12 rooms appointed with satellite TV, plasma screens, wireless Internet, and air-conditioning. Amenities include pool, laundry facilities, and free continental breakfast.

$100-150
Parador Villa Parguera (Carr. 304, 787/899-7777, fax 787/899-6040, www.villaparguera.net, $97-106 s/d sea view, $96-144 s/d garden view, including breakfast; all-inclusive packages available) is one of the most romantically old-fashioned paradors in Puerto Rico. Time seems to have stopped still at this sprawling property. The low-profile, white clapboard hotel sits right on the bay in La Parguera. Although the lobby is fairly dated and underwhelming, the rooms are immaculate and comfortable, overlooking beautifully landscaped gardens and the water. Rooms come with air-conditioning, cable TV, telephones, showers and tubs, and balconies. Other amenities include a large pool, a good restaurant, and a small bar that serves a tasty piña colada made from scratch. There's also a cabaret show in Spanish on the weekends.

FOOD
Puerto Rican and Seafood
Villa Parguera Restaurant (Carr. 304, km 3.3, 787/899-7777, Sun.-Thurs. 7 A.M.-9:30 P.M., Fri.-Sat. 7 A.M.-11 P.M., $10-23) serves *criolla* cuisine with an emphasis on seafood served fried, in garlic sauce, in *criolla* sauce or stuffed in *mofongo*. For something a little more ambitious, try the mahimahi stuffed with lobster and shrimp in wine sauce. The kids' menu ranges $3-6, and there's a full bar.

El Karokal (in front of the boat dock, 787/899-5582, daily 11 A.M.-midnight or later) is a casual fast food-style establishment serving Puerto Rican cuisine and seafood. Thanks to the signs all over town hyping it, it's famous for its coconut sangria.

La Casita Seafood (Carr. 304, km 3.3, 787/899-1681, Tues.-Thurs. 4-10 P.M., Fri.-Sat. 11 A.M.-10 P.M., $8-25) is a large casual family-oriented restaurant serving Puerto Rican cuisine and seafood. Its specialties include whole fish and *asopao,* a seafood stew featuring octopus, lobster, or shrimp. There's no bar, but it does serve wine and beer.

Breakfast
Harbor Café (Carr. 304, 787/517-6666,

Mon.-Wed. 7 A.M.-3 P.M., Thurs.-Sun. 7 A.M.-midnight, $1-5) is a modest little coffeehouse selling sandwiches, breakfast pastries, coffee drinks, and fruit frappes. Try the chocolate stout latte and sugar-free cheesecake.

INFORMATION AND SERVICES

The **post office** is at 102 Avenue in Los Pescadores. An **ATM** is located at Parador Villa Parguera (Carr. 304).

GETTING THERE

La Parguera is 174 kilometers or 108 miles southwest of San Juan, and 58 kilometers or 36 miles from Aguadilla. From San Juan, take Highway 52 south to Carretera 2 west to Carretera 116 south to Carretera 324 west. From Aguadilla, take Carretera 2 west to Carretera 114 south to Carretera 116 south to Carretera 304 south.

San Germán

San Germán is the second-oldest colonial city in Puerto Rico. It was established in 1573 after the original village, built in 1511, was sacked by the French. It's a lovely town where many streets are lined with grand 18th- and 19th-century homes painted pastel shades of blue, pink, and green, and decked out with verandas,

© SUZANNE VAN ATTEN

one of the many lovely old homes in San Germán

columns, and intricate wrought-iron work. San Germán has two plazas. The oldest, Plazuela Santo Domingo, is the smaller of the two, and it is home to many historic houses and Porta Coéli, one of the oldest churches in the Americas. The largest plaza is Plaza Francisco Mariano Quiñones, and here you'll find the *alcaldía* (town hall) and Iglesia San Germán de Auxerre.

Accommodations are limited in San Germán, but in recent years the restaurant scene has expanded to include a couple of destination restaurants. The drive is a pleasant and shady venture through winding mountain roads, making it an ideal option for a leisurely day trip from Ponce or Mayagüez and a great opportunity to experience a colonial town mostly untouched by mainland influence.

SIGHTS

◖ Porta Coéli Chapel and Museum of Religious Art

Porta Coéli Chapel and Museum of Religious Art (at Calle Ramos and Calle Dr. Santiago Veve, on the south end of Plazuela Santo Domingo, 787/892-5845, Wed.-Sun. 8:30 A.M.-noon and 1-4:20 P.M., $1) is one of the few examples of Gothic architecture built in the New World, and it's the oldest chapel in Puerto Rico,

Porta Coéli Chapel and Museum of Religious Art

having been established in 1606. The original structure, now razed, was completed in 1607 as a chapel for the convent of Santo Domingo. It was rebuilt in 1692, and although many of its components have been rebuilt and restored over the years, it retains the original characteristics, featuring interior columns and a roof made from tile and wood, as was common in construction of the 17th and 18th centuries. Set high up on a hill overlooking Plazuela Santo Domingo, the structure appears to live up to its name, which translates to "gateway to heaven." Its primitive, dark sanctuary contains a fantastic collection of 18th- and 19th-century religious paintings and sculpture, including striking primitive-style wood carvings of the 12 stations of the cross. Beside the chapel are the brick ruins of a building that once housed the parish priests. Information is in Spanish only. Limited information in English is available at www.icp.gobierno.pr/icp/ingles/aboutus.htm.

San Germán de Auxerre Parish

Built in 1739, San Germán de Auxerre Parish (Plaza Francisco Mariano Quiñones, 787/892-1027) has been restored and rebuilt in part multiple times over the years, but it retains the classic beauty of its neoclassical origins. It contains three naves, 10 altars, two chapels, and a belfry tower, which was rebuilt after it was damaged in the 1918 earthquake. The ceiling and archways feature trompe-l'oeil painting made to resemble wood coffers, and in the choir loft is a painting by José Campeche, a renowned rococo artist from Puerto Rico, and 18th-century wood carvings.

ENTERTAINMENT AND EVENTS

La Fiesta del Acabe del Café celebrates the end of coffee harvest season in mid-February at a three-day celebration in Maricao, near San Germán. Festivities include musical performances, crafts, and food vendors.

WEST COAST

San Germán de Auxerre Parish

FOOD

Pierre P. Sauccy is the accomplished chef owner of ◖ **L'Auxerre** (16 Calle Estrella, 787/892-8844, www.lauxerre.com, Wed.-Thurs. 6-10 P.M., Fri.-Sat. 6 P.M.-midnight, Sun. brunch noon-4 P.M., $18-36, reservations recommended), a small, elegant restaurant tucked in the brick-floored basement of an 1871 house just off Plaza Francisco Mariano Quiñones. Having studied with world-renowned chef Jean-Georges Vongerichten, Sauccy brings that French influence to his seasonal menu at L'Auxerre. Selections may include foie gras and baked figs, cream of pumpkin soup, and turbot fillet in coconut ginger sauce. There's also an ambitious wine list with an emphasis on reds, including selections from Spain, France, Argentina, and California.

Sweet & Tasty Coffee (101 Ave. Universidad Interamericana, 787/340-4669, daily 10 A.M.-midnight, $2-12) is a large, welcoming hangout appointed with comfy couches and chairs tucked in cozy corners beneath large, colorful works of art. Although it purports to be a coffeehouse, it serves a full menu of breakfast, lunch, and dinner, including wraps, quesadillas, fajitas, burgers, *churrasco,* and salmon.

Opened in 2010, **La Tasca Restaurant and Bar** (12 Calle Dr. Santiago Veve, 787/892-3671, Mon.-Thurs. 11 A.M.-10 P.M., Fri. 11 A.M.-3 A.M., Sat. 5 P.M.-3 A.M., $8-26) serves *criolla* cuisine with an emphasis on seafood in a sophisticated space that was once a theater. Downstairs is a small, dark bar with a large patio. It's an excellent late-night spot to dine on weekends; the full menu is served until 1 A.M., and appetizers, including *empanadillas* and *tostones,* are served until 2 A.M.

A romantic little jewel of a spot, ◖ **Tapas Café** (50 Calle Dr. Santiago Veve, Santo Domingo Plaza, 787/264-0610 or 787/370-5227, Wed.-Thurs. 5-10 P.M., Fri. 5-11 P.M., Sat. 11 A.M.-11 P.M., Sun. 11 A.M.-9 P.M., $2-15) features a blue tiled bar and table tops, giving the place a Mediterranean vibe and providing the perfect setting for a menu of expertly prepared Spanish dishes. As its name implies, the menu primarily serves tapas, including *piquillo* peppers stuffed with tuna, sardine spread with mussels over toast, chorizo in red wine, and *tortilla española*. But a variety of paellas are available for two or more diners.

Chaparritas Bar and Restaurant (Calle Luna, 787/892-1078, Wed.-Thurs. 11:30 A.M.-3 P.M. and 6-9 P.M., Fri. 11:30 A.M.-3 P.M. and 5-10 P.M., Sat. 5-10 P.M., $11-15), a casual, brightly painted restaurant serving Mexican cuisine.

INFORMATION AND SERVICES

Hospital Metropolitano de San Germán (Javilla CDT, 787/892-5300) supplies medical services to San Germán, and **Walgreens** (10 Ave. Fenwal, 787/892-4482) has a pharmacy. Call the **Oficina de Turismo** (2nd floor, Casa Alcaldía Antigua, Plaza Francisco Mariano Quiñones, 787/892-3790 or 787/892-7195, Mon.-Fri. 8 A.M.-noon and 1-4 P.M.) to schedule a free walking or trolley tour.

GETTING THERE

San Germán is 173 kilometers or 107 miles southwest of San Juan, and 51 kilometers or 31 miles south of Aguadilla. From San Juan, take Highway 52 south to Carretera 2 to Carretera 362 north. From Aguadilla, take Carretera 2 south to Carretera 360 east to Carretera 396 west.

Guánica

Christopher Columbus is believed to have first disembarked on the island of Puerto Rico at **Bahía de Guánica** in 1493. At that time, Guánica was the indigenous capital of the island, led by the culture's most powerful Taíno Indian, Cacique Agüeybaná. Guánica also played a role in the Spanish-American War when it was fired on by the USS *Gloucester* and surrendered to U.S. troops in 1898.

Guánica is so completely different from the rest of Puerto Rico that you'd think you were on a whole other island. The flat, dry, desert-like landscape is so unusual, in fact, that a large part of the municipality has been designated a United Nations Biosphere Reserve in an effort to preserve and study its unique environment. Called Bosque Estatal de Guánica, the 10,000-acre reserve contains hiking trails, caves, beaches, and the ruins of a Spanish fort, among other sights. The coast offers great snorkeling and diving.

Guánica also has a burgeoning tourism infrastructure featuring several interesting accommodations varying from a quaint, funky B&B to an all-luxury resort.

◖ BOSQUE ESTATAL DE GUÁNICA

The primary draw for visitors to Guánica is the astounding landscape of Bosque Estatal de Guánica (Carr. 334, 787/821-5706, 787/724-3724, or 787/721-5495, Mon.-Fri. 7 A.M.-4 P.M., Sat.-Sun. 8:30 A.M.-4 P.M., free). This 10,000-acre subtropical dry forest sits atop petrified coral reefs millions of years old and features a variety of environments. On the southern side you'll find the dry scrub forest, featuring sun-bleached rocky soil, cacti, and stunted, twisted trees. There are also patches of evergreen forest along the upper eastern and western parts of the forest, where you can find Spanish moss, mistletoe, bromeliads, and orchids.

The rest of the forest has deciduous growth, where 40 percent of the trees lose their leaves between December and April. Agave and

WEST COAST

© SUZANNE VAN ATTEN

Bahía de Guánica

campeche trees, a source of red and black dye once exported to Europe for hundreds of years, are common to the area. Other flora among the forest's 700 species includes prickly pear cactus, sea grape, milkweed, mahogany, and yuca. Be sure to avoid the poisonous *chicharrón,* a shrub with reddish piney leaves that can irritate the skin on contact.

Guánica is of special interest to **bird-watchers.** More than 80 species have been identified here, including the pearly-eyed thrasher, a variety of hummingbirds, the Puerto Rican mango, and the Puerto Rican nightjar, a bird that nests on the ground and remains nearly motionless all day until dusk. Other species of wildlife include the crested toad, a variety of geckos and lizards, land crabs, and green and leatherback turtles. Mongooses are also present in the area, having been introduced to the island many years ago to kill rats on the sugar plantations. The vicious little varmints are to be avoided at all costs.

There are 36 miles of trails in the forest.

From the main entrance off Carretera 334, follow the long narrow road to the information center, where you'll find the trailheads and where you can obtain trail maps and tips from the helpful English-speaking rangers. The most popular hikes include: a 3-mile, 1.5-hour hike to the ruins of **Fuerte Capron,** once a look-out tower for the Spanish Armada and the site of an observation tower built by the Civilian Conservation Corps in the 1930s; a 40-minute loop trail ideal for bird-watching; a 35-minute hike to see the ancient *guayacán* tree (300 or 1,000 years old, depending on the source); and a 2-hour hike to underground caves, which requires special permission from the information center and accompaniment by a guide.

If you're planning to hike in the forest, be sure to wear sturdy shoes or hiking boots and bring a hat, insect repellent, sunscreen, and plenty of fresh drinking water.

Should you prefer a drive-by tour of Bosque Estatal de Guánica, take the breathtakingly

the coastline of Bosque Estatal de Guánica

beautiful **scenic route Carretera 333,** which starts in the town of Guánica and traverses eastward along the southern rim of the forest. The curvy road snakes up the side of a steep incline that grows thick with cactus and bougainvillea. When the road crests, prepare yourself for a stunning bird's-eye view of the ocean and Bahía de Guánica. Continue eastward and you pass the ruins of a Spanish lighthouse on the left, and on the right is **Area de Pesca Recreativa,** a shady remote patch of beach and a fishing spot with no facilities except for one picnic shelter. The road leading to the recreation area is bumpy and deeply rutted, but it is possible to travel without a four-wheel drive if you proceed with caution.

Continue eastward along Carretera 333 and you encounter **Balneario Caña Gorda** (Carr. 333, km 5.8), a large, modest, shady public beach with bathrooms, covered picnic shelters, a roped-off swimming area, and a wheelchair-accessible area. The facilities are fairly worn but

well maintained. Other features include a basketball court and lots of parking.

Next on the route is Punta San Jacinto, where you can catch a **ferry** (Carr. 333, 787/821-4941, Tues.-Sun. during high season and Fri.-Sun. during low season, 9 A.M.-5 P.M., every hour on the hour, $5) to **Gilligan's Island,** a small *cayo* just a few hundred yards offshore featuring a huge shallow lagoon of aquamarine water perfect for swimming and lots of great snorkeling and diving spots. It was tagged Gilligan's Island by the local tourist trade as a marketing gimmick, and the name caught on.

Carretera 333 ends at **Bahía de la Ballerna,** a lovely sandy beach area and a great snorkeling and diving spot known as Submarine Gardens.

SPORTS AND RECREATION

Sea Ventures Dive Copamarina (Copamarina Beach Resort, Carr. 333, km 6.5, 800/468-4553 or 877/348-3267, www.divecopamarina. com, daily 9 A.M.-6 P.M.) runs day and night

WEST COAST

dive excursions ($65-119) to sites including the 22-mile-long Guánica Wall, the Aquarium, and the Parthenon, a coral formation featuring a variety of sponges. Daily snorkeling excursions go to Gilligan's Island, Cayo Coral Reef, and Bahía de la Ballerna ($55 including equipment). Certification courses are offered. Also available are kayak, catamaran, and paddleboat rentals.

San Jacinto Boats and Seafood (Carr. 333, 787/821-4941) rents sea kayaks and equipment for diving and snorkeling. It also operates a ferry to Gilligan's Island every hour on the hour Tuesday-Sunday (high season) 9 A.M.-5 P.M. or Friday-Sunday (low season) for $5. Dine on fresh seafood dishes while you're there.

Island Scuba (392 Calle Marina Ensenada, Guánica, 787/309-6556 or 787/473-7997) provides daily dive and snorkeling trips, Discover scuba diving for first-timers, and diving certification.

ACCOMMODATIONS
$100-150

Mary Lee's by the Sea (off Carr. 333, first road on right just past the Copamarina Beach Resort tennis courts, 787/821-3600, fax 787/821-0744, www.maryleesbythesea.com, $110-300 plus $10 per additional person) is unlike any guesthouse in Puerto Rico—maybe the world! This bright, cheerful, sprawling guesthouse has a distinctive bohemian style reflective of its unique owner, Mary Lee, who came to Puerto Rico 50 years ago on a diving trip and never left. Each of the 11 rooms is different, but they all share two things: wall-to-wall thick straw mats and tons of hand-sewn curtains, bedspreads, and furniture upholstery made by the owner and her daughters, which gives the place a pleasant 1970s-era Southern California vibe. Rooms vary from small single units that sleep two ($100) to an enormous three-bedroom apartment with a living room, dining room, and furnished porch ($300). Each unit has some form of kitchen, whether it's a cleverly efficient "closet kitchen," a kitchenette, or a full kitchen. The grounds are basically a series of funky, small courtyards and seating areas with a lovely a view of Gilligan's Island. Amenities include a small dock, kayak rentals, and boat rides to Gilligan's Island, as well as swimming at the beach at Bahía de la Ballena. Rooms have air-conditioning but no phones; small TVs are available for rent. There is weekly maid service and laundry facilities are on-site. Be sure to book early: Mary Lee's by the Sea has a high return rate of regulars who come here every year.

Guánica Parador 1929 (Carr. 3116, km 2.5, Ave. Las Veteranos, 787/821-0099, www.Guanica1929.com, $114 s, $120 d, plus tax, includes breakfast; all inclusive packages available) is a two-story Spanish colonial-style structure built in 1929 as Hotel Americano. One of a small chain of hotels called Tropical Inns of Puerto Rico, this well-run, eco-friendly property located on Ensenada Bay has a lot to offer. Since reopening in 2008, the owners have extensively landscaped the grounds and added a delightful restaurant serving a creative Caribbean cuisine with indoor and outdoor dining. The environmentally conscious owners use only fluorescent lights, solar water heaters, and eco-friendly cleaning products. They also compost all organic materials from the restaurant and treat the pool with an ozone system and salt chlorination. In the small lobby there is a well-stocked collection of educational books for sale on Puerto Rico for adults and children. Amenities include fitness room, game room, pool, and laundry facilities.

Over $200

Copamarina Beach Resort (Carr. 333, km 6.5, 787/821-0505 or 800/468-4553, fax 787/821-0070, www.copamarina.com, $235-295 s/d, $400 suite, $1,000 villa, tax and resort fees) is a secluded full-service luxury resort featuring large comfortable rooms appointed with lovely, thick pine furniture, Dutch doors, and plantation windows that look out over the water. There is an excellent white-linen restaurant, Alexandra's, serving seafood and Puerto Rican cuisine, as well as a casual waterside eatery and bar, Las Palmas. The beautifully landscaped beachfront grounds feature two pools, two children's pools, two whirlpool baths, lighted tennis courts, and a lovely white-sand beach with a pier and a small boat dock. Other amenities include a spa and a fitness room. Sea Ventures Dive Copamarina is an on-site snorkeling and dive operator that also offers water taxi service taking guests to nearby Gilligan's Island. All-inclusive packages are available starting at $398 a night.

FOOD

Dine on traditional *criolla* cuisine on the wraparound porch at **Tropical Inn Restaurant** (Guánica Parador 1929, Carr. 3116, km 2.5, Ave. Las Veteranos, 787/821-0099, daily 8-10:30 A.M., noon-4 P.M., and 5-8 P.M., $10-20). Menu includes *mofongo,* halibut in caper sauce, linguine Alfredo with shrimp, and paella for two.

Restaurante Alexandra (Copamarina Beach Resort, Carr. 333, km 6.5, 787/821-0505, daily 6-10 P.M., $19-40) is that rare thing in Guánica: an upscale fine-dining establishment. The lovely enclosed oceanside restaurant features floor-to-ceiling windows hung with long sheer white curtains that set an elegant,

romantic mood for your meal. The menu serves classic continental and New American cuisine, including osso buco and pan-seared duck breast in port wine mango sauce.

San Jacinto Boats and Restaurant (Carr. 333, 787/821-4941, daily 9 A.M.-10 P.M., $5-25) is a rustic fish-camp kind of establishment in a rambling old two-story white clapboard building overlooking the water. The restaurant serves seafood Puerto Rican-style, including *mofongo* stuffed with lobster or shrimp, octopus salad, and fried whole fish, as well as steak and pork chops. Outside there is a small walk-up kiosk where water-sports enthusiasts can grab an *empanadilla* on their way to Gilligan's Island.

Festival del Juey, held in mid- to late June in the town of Guánica, celebrates the crab with a variety of local dishes made from the crustacean.

INFORMATION AND SERVICES

Banco Santander Puerto Rico has a branch in Guánica at Calle 25 de Julio. The **post office** is located at 39 Calle 13 de Marzo, Suite 101.

GETTING THERE

Guánica is 161 kilometers or 100 miles southwest from San Juan, and 76 kilometers or 47 miles south of Aguadilla. From San Juan take Highway 52 south to Carretera 2 west to Carretera 116 south to Carretera 3116. From Aguadilla, take Carretera 2 south to Carretera 116 south to Carretera 3116.

WEST COAST

NORTH COAST

The north coast of Puerto Rico is a wild expanse of rocky coastline and gorgeous ocean views, hilly karst country, and green farmland. It's also thick with industrial plants, shopping centers, fast-food restaurants, road construction, and traffic. Despite the urban sprawl, though, the north coast has a lot going for it.

Although craggy, rocky shores and rough waters can make finding the ideal swimming spot a challenge, there are several spectacular oceanside jewels worth seeking out—at the resorts in Dorado, Punta Cerro Gordo in Vega Alta, and Playa Mar Chiquita in Manatí. Meanwhile, the powerful waves along the north coast make for excellent surfing, especially around Manatí and Arecibo. The major sport on the north coast, though, is golf. Dorado is home to five classic courses.

There are three major attractions on the north coast. First there are the world-class golf courses in Dorado, just 30 minutes from San Juan. The other two are the Observatorio de Arecibo, which is the world's largest radio telescope, and Las Cavernas del Río Camuy, a major cave system with hiking trails and a nature park. Both are about a 30-minute drive south of Arecibo into the island's mountainous karst country. The unusual topography alone is worth the drive. An intricate system of underground limestone caves creates enormous sinkholes and haystack hills—called *mogotes*—on the earth's surface. It's a stunning

HIGHLIGHTS

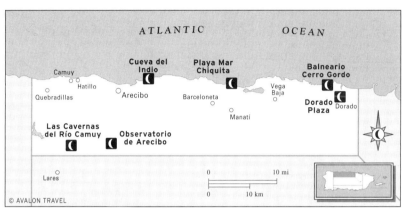

LOOK FOR ◖ TO FIND RECOMMENDED SIGHTS, ACTIVITIES, DINING, AND LODGING.

◖ **Dorado Plaza:** Museums, monuments, restaurants, and a charming mission-style church make this well-maintained town center a pleasant place to spend an afternoon (page 214).

◖ **Balneario Cerro Gordo:** Brand-new facilities and a superb campground just add to the idyllic setting of this publicly maintained beach on Punta Cerro Gordo in Vega Alta, making it a great spot to sun, swim, and surf (page 219).

◖ **Playa Mar Chiquita:** Tucked down at the bottom of a cliff, this small protected cove in Manatí offers calm waters for swimming and an intricate system of limestone caves where you can find Taíno petroglyphs (page 222).

◖ **Observatorio de Arecibo:** Check out the largest and most sensitive radio telescope in the world. The 18-acre dish is in a natural sinkhole created by the hilly karst landscape (page 223).

◖ **Cueva del Indio:** Explore the petrified sand dunes, natural arches, blow holes, and ancient Taíno petroglyphs found at this off-the-beaten-path site on the coast just east of Arecibo (page 225).

◖ **Las Cavernas del Río Camuy:** The third-largest river cave system in the world, the Camuy caves are located in a well-maintained park providing easy access to Puerto Rico's underground natural wonders (page 227).

sight completely unlike anywhere else on the island—and nearly the world.

PLANNING YOUR TIME

Puerto Rico's north coast is a great place for a day trip, an overnight stay, or a long weekend. Thanks to two major roadways it's easily accessible whether you're approaching it from San Juan or from the west coast.

Despite what you might think, Highway 22, a multilane divided toll road with six toll booths

between San Juan and Arecibo, is the best route along the north coast. Although construction projects and commuter rush hours can slow your progress, it is the most expeditious route. The alternative is Carretera 2, a congested multilane commercial route that bisects the island's longest, most unsightly stretch of urban sprawl. It should be avoided when possible.

Dorado is the farthest eastern municipality, about 17 miles and 30 minutes from San Juan. A popular vacation spot, it has lovely beaches, luxurious resorts,

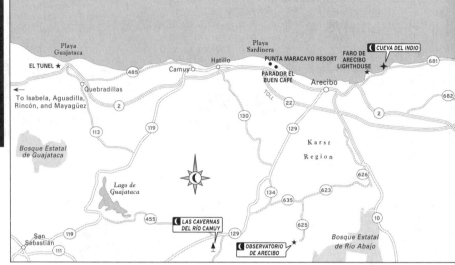

and world-class golf courses. Farther westward are the municipalities of Vega Alta and Manatí, which have some spectacular beaches—**Balneario Cerro Gordo** and **Playa Mar Chiquita,** respectively—that are ideal for swimming.

But the most popular sights along the north coast are **Las Cavernas del Río Camuy** and **Observatorio de Arecibo,** both in the southern tips of their respective municipalities and about 1.5 hours from San Juan. It's possible to visit both sights on a day trip if you get an early start. While in Arecibo, be sure to check out **Cueva del Indio,** an amazing geological and archaeological wonder featuring petrified sand dunes and Taíno petroglyphs.

The best selection of hotels and restaurants can be found at either end of the north coast. To the east is Dorado, where the accommodations are upscale resorts and pricier restaurants, and to the west is Hatillo, home to more budget-minded hotels and eateries.

Toa Baja and Toa Alta

Toa Baja and Toa Alta were once home to one of the largest Taíno Indian populations on the island, probably for the same reasons the Spanish colonists were drawn here—the excellent fishing and fertile soil. The land was taken and the Taíno enslaved in 1511 when Juan Ponce de León established the King's Farm on the rich shores of Río de la Plata, one of several rivers that converge in the area. The farm played an important role in the Spanish colony.

Not only did farmers use it to figure out how to cultivate European vegetables in the tropics, but it produced much of the produce consumed by the colonists.

Eventually settlers began to flock here to farm the fertile soil and fish the rich rivers. In 1776, just as the United States was gaining independence from England, the Spanish were establishing cattle ranches and sugarcane plantations throughout Toa Baja and Toa Alta.

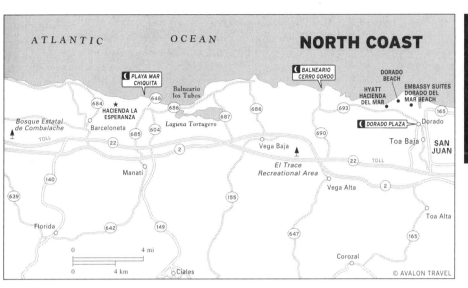

To many travelers, Toa Baja and Toa Alta are just municipalities you have to blow through to get to points farther west. But these communities have their charms. There are some good swimming and fishing spots to be found. And the town of Toa Alta boasts the Parroquia San Fernando Rey, a church built in 1752, and the beloved *bala de cañon* tree, which bears fruit that looks like cannonballs. The best reason to stop, though, is to dine at Millie's Place.

Toa Baja and Toa Alta are 31 kilometers or 19 miles west of San Juan. Take Highway 22 west and go north on Carretera 693 to Toa Baja and Carretera 165 south for Toa Alta.

SIGHTS AND RECREATION

The lovely drive along Carretera 165 east from Dorado toward **Balneario Punta Salinas** (daily 8:30 A.M.-6 P.M.) is reason alone to visit the publicly maintained beach. The highway runs between a picturesque stretch of roadway that divides an undeveloped palm grove from the rocky coastline. The beach lies on both sides of an isthmus that juts into the Atlantic and offers a great view of Old San Juan. The facilities include picnic shelters, bathrooms, and a snack bar. A space age-style geodesic dome sits on a hill overlooking the beach that houses the 140th Air Defense Squadron.

Area Recreativa de Lago La Plata (Carr. 824, km 4.9, Toa Alta, 787/723-6435, Tues.-Sun. 6 A.M.-6 P.M.) is a new recreation area popular with freshwater anglers. It features bathroom facilities, picnic shelters, and barbecue grills. The lake is stocked with fish, including largemouth bass, by the Maricao Fish Hatchery.

FOOD

It's well off the beaten path, but **◖ Millie's Place** (377 Calle Parque at Acueducto, Barrio Sabana Seca, Toa Baja, 787/784-3488, Wed.-Thurs. noon-4 P.M., Fri. noon-7 P.M., Sat.-Sun. noon-6 P.M., $16-45) is well worth the trip. People travel from far and wide to dine on Millie's magnificent land crabs. The big blue crustaceans are captured and corralled in pens behind the restaurant. The trick is how to find this modest blue concrete structure, across the street from a neighborhood ball park. From San Juan, travel west on Highway 22, and then go north on Carretera 866, which takes several turns. The road dead-ends at a T intersection in front of a pharmacy. To the left is Carretera 187, but you'll want to turn right. Go about a quarter mile and turn left onto Acueducto beside the El Semaforo auto parts store. Millie's Place is on the left across from the baseball field. The good thing is, if you get lost, just call. The English-speaking staff gives great directions.

At a sharp bend in the road between Dorado and Punta Salinas is **El Caracol** (Carr. 165, Toa Baja), a large, very casual open-air restaurant and pool hall right on the beach. In addition to selling bottles of beer for $1 during its "permanent happy hour," it has a great selection of fried fare, including empanadas, *pastelillos,* and *taquitos.*

Dorado

Dorado means "golden" in Spanish, but the only things that glitters here are the beautiful beaches and the resorts that began springing up in the '50s. Much of this land was grapefruit and pineapple plantations, and now it's home to some of the island's most celebrated golf courses. No longer just a vacation spot, Dorado has evolved into a bedroom community to San Juan. The town's central plaza was renovated in 2005, and it has charm to spare.

SIGHTS
◖ Dorado Plaza

Bounded by Calle Norte, Calle San Francisco, and Calle Jesus T. Pinero, the central plaza in Dorado is a lovely place for a stroll. In the center is *El Monumento a las Raíces Puertorriqueñas,* a statue composed of a Taíno Indian, an African, and a Spaniard, honoring the three races that came together to create Puerto Rican culture. Architectural sites around the plaza include **Parroquia San Antonio de Padua,** a charming mission-style church built in 1848, and **Anfiteatro Angel Hernández,** a concert hall.

Across the street from the plaza is **Casa Museo Alegría y Escuela de Artes** (Calle Norte, Dorado Plaza, 787/796-1433, Mon.-Fri. 8 A.M.-4 P.M., free). The bright yellow wooden house built in 1913 was home to Marcus Juan Alegría, an accomplished painter and art instructor from Dorado. Unlike the traditional *criolla* house, it sports twin gables and a side entrance. An addition on the back of the house is a art school, where classes are held on Saturdays.

Casa del Rey (292 Calle Méndez Vigo, Dorado Plaza, 787/796-5740, Mon.-Fri. 8 A.M.-4:30 P.M., free) is reportedly the first building in Dorado. The Spanish colonial structure was

© SUZANNE VAN ATTEN

El Monumento a las Raíces Puertorriqueñas

built in 1923, first as an inn before it housed Spanish government personnel. It became a residence in 1848 and was home at one time to the notable author Manuel Alonso y Pacheco.

Museo de Arte y Historia de Dorado (Méndez Vigo at Juan Francisco, Dorado, 787/796-5740, Mon.-Sat. 8 A.M.-3:30 P.M., free) has three exhibition halls featuring displays of art, archaeological artifacts, and illustrations depicting the city's history.

SPORTS AND RECREATION
Beaches and Recreation Areas

El Ojo del Buey (end of Carr. 698, Barrio Mameyal, Dorado, 787/796-5740 or 787/796-6001) is a primitive recreation area along the rocky coast with terrific views of the water. It's great for hiking, but be sure to wear sturdy shoes such as sneakers or hiking boots to help you navigate the hills and craters. And be sure to follow the path through the thick sea-grape bushes to the site's namesake—El Ojo del Buey (The Ox's Eye)—an impressive rock formation that resembles the head of an ox. Legend has it that the Puerto Rican pirate Roberto Cofresí buried his treasure here. Unfortunately, a recent visit revealed a disturbing amount of litter. From the Dorado plaza, travel north on Carretera 693 and turn right on Calle Pedro Albizu Campos. Pass Boston Scientific on the right, then fork left. Once you pass the school, turn right on Calle 13 and follow it to the end.

Much of the coastline along Dorado is rocky, except for that occupied by the resorts, but you can find a nice little patch of sandy beach at **Playa de Dorado** (end of Carr. 697, Dorado, daily 8:30 A.M.-5 P.M.) in town.

Opened in 2010, **El Dorado Gran Parque Agroturístico Ecológico Recreativo** (Carr. 165 at Carr. 693, south of Dorado, no phone, free) is an 850-acre park designed to educate and entertain the public with agricultural

© SUZANNE VAN ATTEN

entrance to El Ojo del Buey

NORTH COAST

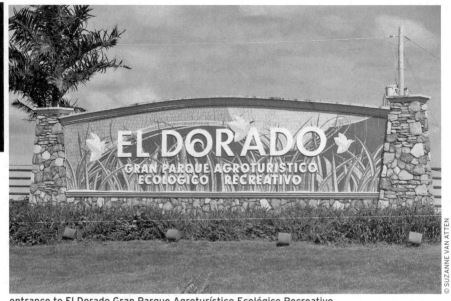

© SUZANNE VAN ATTEN

entrance to El Dorado Gran Parque Agroturístico Ecológico Recreativo

attractions and events. The majority of the acreage will be used to grow crops to sell, but visitors can stroll among experimental plantings of various strains of coffee, bananas, star fruit, tamarinds, and more. Features include a horse corral and ring for riding, a children's playground, picnic shelters, walking trails, and bathroom facilities.

Golf and Tennis

When it comes to sports in Dorado, golf reigns supreme. **Dorado Beach Club** (Carr. 693, Dorado, 787/796-1234 or 800/981-9066, ext. 3710, www.doradobeachclubs.com) has four 18-hole courses that have hosted the Senior PGA Tour Championship, the Chi Chi Rodriguez Pro Am Golf Classic, the Johnnie Walker International Pro Am, and the World Cup golf tournaments. The 72-par East Course (7 A.M.-5:30 P.M., $100-250 greens fees) was designed and built in 1958 by Robert Trent Jones Sr., modified by Raymond Floyd in 1999, and restored to Jones' original vision by his son, Robert Trent Jones Jr., in 2012. The 72-par West Course was closed for renovation in 2012. The challenge Sugarcane course and the ocean view Pineapple Course (7 A.M.-5:30 P.M., $47-137 greens fees) round out the club's courses.

Dorado del Mar Golf Club (Embassy Suites Dorado del Mar Beach and Golf Resort, 201 Dorado Del Mar Blvd., 787/796-3070, 6 A.M.-9 P.M., campgolf@coqui.com) is an 18-hole course designed by Chi Chi Rodriguez. Twelve holes are on the water.

ENTERTAINMENT AND EVENTS

In its effort to encourage tourism, Dorado hosts quite a few festivals, including **Carnaval de la Plata** in February, **Fiestas de la Cruz** in May, **Festival de la Cocolia** in August, **Discovery of Puerto Rico** in November, and a **Christmas Festival** in December. For details, call the tourism office at 787/796-5740.

ACCOMMODATIONS

Formerly the Hyatt Regency Cerromar Beach Resort, **Hyatt Hacienda del Mar** (301 Carr. 693, 787/796-3000, www.hyatthaciendadelmar.com, $149 studio, $299 one-bedroom, $428 two-bedroom, plus $20 resort fee and tax) now doubles as a time share property and a hotel. The good news is that the guest rooms are attractive and well appointed with full kitchens, spacious bathrooms with whirlpool garden tubs, big balconies, and large, comfy beds. The bad news is that one half of the building is abandoned and shut down, casting a mildly depressing pall on the place. The flowing river pool that once ran through the grounds has been disassembled, but there is still a large pool and a couple of hot tubs, as well as a modest fitness center, spa, game arcade, tennis courts, and a small private crescent of beach. The only available food and beverage service is provided by a poolside snack bar that closes at 8 P.M., but guests are permitted access to the amenities at Dorado Beach Resort & Club (www.doradobeachclub.com), including Zafra Restaurant and the golf courses. It's a great option for families traveling with young children.

Slated to open in the summer of 2013, **Dorado Beach, A Ritz-Carlton Reserve** (100 Dorado Beach Dr., 787/626-1001 or 787/253-1700, www.ritzcarlton.com) is the first Ritz Carlton Reserve to open in the Americas. In addition to private residences, it will contain 115 ultra-luxury guest rooms on 50 acres of a former pineapple plantation that includes one mile of pristine beach and the 11-mile Rockefeller Trail, a nod to Laurance Rockefeller, who built the first resort on the site in 1958. Amenities include the 8,000-square-foot Dorado Beach Fitness and Wellness Center, the Beach Club, a spa, four legendary golf courses designed by Robert Trent Jones Sr. and renovated by Robert Trent Jones Jr., and the Watermill, a $12 million water park.

Embassy Suites Dorado del Mar Beach & Golf Resort (201 Dorado Del Mar Blvd., 787/796-6125, www.embassysuites1.hilton.com, $169-209, plus tax and resort fee, including complimentary breakfast) features 175 suites featuring cable TV with HBO, microwave, refrigerator, and high-speed Internet. Amenities include the Dorado del Mar Gold Club, an 18-hole, 72-par golf course designed by Chi Chi Rodriguez, a lagoon pool overlooking the beach, a whirlpool bath, tennis courts, a fitness room, and two restaurants. Future plans include the construction of a $6.4 million casino.

FOOD

◖ **El Ladrillo** (334 Méndez Vigo, 787/796-2120, www.restauranteelladrillo.com, lunch Tues., Fri., and Sun. 11:30 A.M.-3 P.M., dinner Tues.-Sun. 6-10 P.M.) is a lovely Old World fine-dining restaurant that has been serving expertly prepared steaks, seafood, and Puerto Rican cuisine to locals and visitors alike for 30 years. Redbrick arches and colorful paintings by local artists contribute to the warm atmosphere. Specialties include plantain soup, rice dishes, and a variety of lobster dishes and steaks. It has a full bar and a well-stocked wine cellar.

With tongue planted firmly in cheek, ◖ **Made in Puerto Rico** (Carr. 693, km 8.5, Dorado, 787/626-6666, www.madeinpr.tv, Tues.-Sat. 11 A.M.-10 P.M., Sun. 11 A.M.-9 P.M., $12-18, $20 for Sun. buffet) is a chef-owned themed restaurant that is in on the good-natured joke as it re-creates a kitschy version of rural Puerto Rican life, circa 1950. Waitresses wear floral muumuus with curlers in their hair, and the waiters wear guayabera shirts and rustic straw hats. The waiting room is decked out in vintage furnishings to replicate a midcentury living room, complete with a TV showing old Puerto Rican shows, and the huge dining rooms look like thatched roof shacks. A separate bar and enormous outdoor patio with a kiosk selling traditional fritters round out the space. Chef Alexis Torres oversees preparation of the expertly prepared traditional *criolla* cuisine, including *mofongo, chuleta can can,* fricasseed goat, *arroz con pollo,* and more.

Striving for an upscale ambiance, **Villa Dorado D'Alberto** (99 Calle E. Costa de Oro, 787/278-1715, Sun.-Tues. 11 A.M.-9 P.M., Wed.-Thurs. 11 A.M.-10 P.M., Fri.-Sat. 11 A.M.-11 P.M., $13-29) misses the mark a bit with the plastic table cloths and garish sculptural mirror in the ladies' room, but the food is good if a bit pricey for what you get. The extensive menu includes all the usual suspects for seafood-oriented *criolla* cuisine, including whole fried snapper, *mofongo, chuleta can can,* and *asopao.*

The venerable Dorado restaurant **El Capitán** (511 Calle Extension Sur, 787/278-0011, Thurs.-Sat. 11 A.M.-9 P.M., Sun. noon-9 P.M., $9-24) serves an extensive menu of *mofongo,* seafood, *churrasco,* and rice dishes.

At the Dorado Beach Resort & Club, **Zafra Restaurant** (Plantation Clubhouse, 500 Plantation Dr., 787/626-1001, www.dorado-beachclubs.com, breakfast Fri.-Sun. 7-11 A.M., lunch daily 11 A.M.-5:30 P.M., dinner Wed.-Sun. 6-10 P.M., bar open later, $17-36) serves creative Caribbean cuisine, including fettuccine with shrimp in crab sauce and mahimahi casserole with spinach, chickpeas, and chorizo in an elegant setting overlooking the mountains.

Located on the Dorado plaza, **Café y Canela** (190 Calle Norte, Dorado Plaza, 787/626-3535, Mon.-Fri. 7 A.M.-3 P.M., Sat. 8 A.M.-midnight, $2-5) is an inviting little coffeehouse serving a variety of coffee drinks and fresh fruit juices, as well as breakfast and lunch items.

Punta Plena (279 Calle Mendez Vigo, Dorado Plaza, 787/796-7109, 787/796-3845, or 787/359-4893, Mon.-Thurs. and Sun. 9 A.M.-midnight, Fri.-Sat. 9 A.M.-2 A.M., $2-6) is a friendly, family-run bar serving a variety of *frituras.* The house specialty is stuffed *arepas,* fat little discs of fried corn bread stuffed with your choice of chicken, beef, or shrimp and topped with a house-made garlic sauce. Other menu items include wings, *alcapurrias, empanadillas,* and *tostones.*

La Terraza (Calle Marginal C-1, Costa de Oro, 787/796-1242, daily noon-midnight, $14-25) is a pricey tourist-friendly restaurant on an open-air terrace decked out in a cheery nautical theme. The menu features mostly traditional Puerto Rican cuisine, and its specialty is *mofongo* stuffed with everything from octopus to lobster to chicken. Other menu items include whole snapper, shrimp brochette, *picadillo,* and *chuleta can can.*

INFORMATION AND SERVICES

The **police department** (787/796-2020) is at Carretera 693, kilometer 7.2, Calle Méndez Vigo. For emergencies call 911. **The Dorado Medical Hospital** (Carr. 698 just off Calle Méndez Vigo, 787/796-6050) has a 24-hour emergency room. **Walgreens** (Carr. 693, 787/278-5800) is open 24 hours. **Banco Popular** (787/278-1171) has an ATM in the **Grande supermarket** (787/278-2400) on Calle Méndez Vigo.

GETTING THERE

Dorado is 34 kilometers or 21 miles west of San Juan. Take Highway 22 west to Carretera 165 north.

Vega Alta and Vega Baja

Vega Alta and Vega Baja are on fertile low-lying land divided by Río Cibuca, and it was here—not Dorado—where gold was found on the north coast. And naturally, where there was gold there were conquistadors. During colonization, the river's shores were populated by the Spanish, who used Taíno labor to mine the valuable mineral, which was washed into the river's channels by the strong ocean current. After the gold rush depleted the deposit, then came the sugar rush: The rich, level soil made the area perfect for growing sugarcane, and many slaves were brought in to work the land. In 1848 there was an attempted revolt among the slaves in Vega Baja, which was squelched when one of the main agitators was killed.

The highlight of the Vegas is definitely Punta Cerro Gordo, a gorgeous piece of coastline that boasts one of the island's best publicly maintained beaches and a great camping area.

SIGHTS
Museo de Arte Casa Alonso

Believed to have been built around the time Vega Baja was established, around 1776, Museo de Arte Casa Alonso (34 Calle Betances, Vega Baja, 787/855-1364, fax 787/855-1931, Tues.-Sat. 9 A.M.-noon and 1-4 P.M., free) is a two-story, 2,000-square-foot neoclassic creole-style home constructed of wood, bricks, and stone. The interior has been restored and now serves as an art and history museum, displaying, among other objects, many of the artifacts recovered from the home, including ceramics, tiles, stoneware, and coins. In the first-floor courtyard is a 40-foot well, which provided water to the home's residents, the first of whom was Vega Baja mayor Pablo Soliveras from Catalan. In addition to a collection of 19th-century furnishings, the house contains a room devoted to Puerto Rican popular music that includes photographs, phonographs, records, and radios.

Puerto Nuevo

Puerto Nuevo (Carr. 686, km 12, at Carr. 692, Vega Baja, 787/858-6447) has two parts to it. One part is a *balneario,* a free city-maintained recreation area with a lovely natural lagoon at its disposal. Facilities include lots of covered picnic shelters, outdoor showers, a playground, and a variety of food vendors selling fried snacks. Directly east of the *balneario* is a narrow road that takes you to a spot of wilderness coast where rocky outcroppings and soft patches of beach compete for space. Sandy pull-offs into the low-lying shrubs and trees that line the beach in some places suggest the area is something of a lovers' lane at night. But on weekend days and holidays, it's a popular party beach for teenagers and young adults. There are no facilities, and the property is not well-maintained, as evidenced by the amount of litter. Women should avoid going here alone, as it's very remote. And don't leave any valuables in the car.

El Trece Recreational Area

El Trece Recreational Area (Carr. 160, km 13, Vega Baja) is a 13-acre city-maintained sports and recreation park on the Indio River where visitors can swim in natural pools of fresh river water. There are also hiking trails, picnic shelters, bathroom facilities, a handball court, and a grass volleyball court.

◖ Balneario Cerro Gordo

Even if there weren't a shortage of beaches suitable for swimming on the north coast, Balneario Cerro Gordo (end of Carr. 6690, off Carr. 693, Vega Alta, 787/883-2730, daily 8:30 A.M.-6 P.M., parking $2 cars, $3 vans) would still be a wildly popular place to plunk down in the sun or frolic in the surf. It is a large, drop-dead gorgeous spot of forested coastline with dramatic cliffs, a rocky peninsula, and a palm-lined beach.

the view from the campgrounds at Balneario Cerro Gordo in Vega Alta

There's a large protected cove that's perfect for swimming, and on the other side of the point are rougher waters ideal for surfing.

Thanks to a multimillion-dollar investment by the government, this public beach received new facilities in 2006, including bathrooms, showers, food vendors, lifeguards, and picnic tables. On the eastern end, on a shady mountaintop, are some great campsites ($13 per person) with ocean views. Expect a crowd on weekends and holidays.

SPORTS AND RECREATION

Reserva Natural Laguna Tortuguero (Carr. 687, km 1.2, Vega Baja, 787/858-6617, reserve open Wed.-Sun. 6 A.M.-5 P.M., office open Mon.-Fri. 8 A.M.-4 P.M.) is a two-mile-long lagoon surrounded by swamps, marshlands, and karst mountains. A fishing dock provides a great place to angle for tilapia. In addition to fish, the lagoon is home to an estimated 1,000 caimans, a species of crocodile, believed to have originated from baby caimans that were imported from South America in the 1970s as pets and eventually released. They grow to six feet and can be vicious, but they're typically encountered only at night when the lagoon is closed.

The **Vega Baja Eco-Tourism Office** (Laguna Tortuguero, Carr. 687, km 1, 787/807-1822, Mon.-Fri. 8 A.M.-3 P.M., reservations required) offers guided nature tours through the lagoon. It also operates tours at El Trece recreation area and other areas.

ENTERTAINMENT AND EVENTS

It's all about the celebration of food in the Vegas. In mid-July, Vega Alta heralds the versatility of breadfruit with the **Festival de Panapén** (787/883-5900). In addition to performances by musicians and dancers, there are arts and crafts booths, food kiosks, and a breadfruit-cooking contest.

In Vega Baja, it's all about syrup at the **Festival del Melao Melao** (787/858-6617) held in early October. Artisans and food vendors line the Plaza de Recreo, where wood-carving competitions are held.

FOOD

Costa Norte Restaurante (Carr. 686, km 12 at Calle Joaquín Rosa Gomez, Vega Baja, 787/858-4247, daily 9 A.M.-9 P.M., $2-6) is easy to spot, thanks to the bright green metal fencing that encloses the patio at this glorified fry shack across from Balneario Puerto Nuevo, Vega Baja's public beach. It's an excellent place to pick up fried chunks of dorado, *mofongo,* and "tacos" filled with fish, meat, shrimp, or chicken.

INFORMATION AND SERVICES

Vega Baja Casa de Cultura y Turismo (Calle Betances at Tulio Otero, Vega Baja, 787/858-6447, Mon.-Fri. 8 A.M.-4:30 P.M.) offers information on the history and culture of the area and provides tours upon request.

GETTING THERE

Vega Alta is 39 kilometers or 21 miles west of San Juan. Take Highway 22 west to Carretera 690 south. Vega Baja is 49 kilometers or 30 miles west of San Juan. Take Highway 22 west to Carretera 2 west.

Manatí and Barceloneta

The town of Manatí proper, south of Highway 22, isn't much of a draw for visitors, but north of town along its coast is a lovely wonderland of rolling green hills and delightful beaches ideal for swimming and surfing. The thick vegetation and elevation make it a cool enclave for the fabulous new homes and condos that have cropped up here. Once known for their grand sugar plantations and haciendas, Manatí and Barceloneta's economies now revolve around pharmaceutical manufacturing and growing pineapples. Barceloneta is notable as the starting point for a spectacular scenic drive to Arecibo and as home to the Bosque Estatal de Combalache, a small forest popular for its wooded mountain-bike trails.

Manatí and Barceloneta are 55 kilometers or 34 miles west of San Juan on Highway 22.

SIGHTS

Balneario Playa Los Tubos

Balneario Playa Los Tubos (Carr. 686, Manatí, 787/884-3428, Wed.-Fri. 8 A.M.-4 P.M., Sat.-Sun. 9 A.M.-5 P.M.) has to hold the distinction of being the most fanciful public beach in all of Puerto Rico. Set high on a hill and ensconced

behind impressive steel gates are the standard facilities—bathrooms, showers, picnic shelters, food vendors, and so on—but they're tricked out like something from a Dr. Seuss book. Enormous animal statues in bright shades of yellow, green, and pink stand sentry over the elaborate columned picnic shelters with stacked pyramid rooftops and a magnificent view of the Atlantic. Beside the *balneario* is a stretch of wilderness beach that's renowned for its surfing.

Hacienda La Esperanza

Today, Hacienda La Esperanza (Carr. 616, Manatí, 787/854-2679, Fri., Sun., and holidays 8 A.M.-3 P.M., free) is a lovely, quiet natural preserve, but in the late 19th century it was one of the biggest, richest sugar plantations in Puerto Rico. In addition to the manor house, the sugar mill, and an ornate 1861 steam engine, the property encompasses more than 2,000 acres of karst formations. In addition, recent excavations have revealed that it was once occupied by indigenous people. A *batey* (a pre-Columbian ceremonial ball park), four plazas, a burial ground, and petroglyphs have been discovered. Although visitors are welcome

© SUZANNE VAN ATTEN

Playa Mar Chiquita

to enjoy the grounds, the structures and archae-ological sites are closed to the public while the Historic Conservation of Puerto Rico works to preserve the area.

Playa Mar Chiquita

If you're anywhere near Manatí, don't pass by without stopping at Playa Mar Chiquita (end of Carr. 648, off of Carr. 685, Manatí), an enchanting wonderland of natural beauty. Tucked down in the base of a wooded cliff is a perfectly formed natural pool almost completely enclosed by two long reaches of rocky coral that embrace a pristine crescent of sandy beach and crystal-clear water ideal for taking a dip.

The formation of Playa Mar Chiquita is so picture-perfect that a legend has grown up around it to explain its creation. As the story goes, a beautiful woman went to Mar Chiquita and fell into the ocean. She began to drown, but then the sea opened up and the waves washed her ashore. A few days later she returned to Mar

Chiquita and was surprised to discover that the lovely fan-shaped pool had formed.

There's more to Playa Mar Chiquita than its baby-safe beach, though. The mountain base contains an intricate system of caves, where the adventurous can discover stalagmites and stalactites, as well as petroglyphs left behind by indigenous people. Mangrove trees and sea grapes grow thick and low throughout the area, creating their own cave-like nooks where lovers park for rendezvous. Crumbling ruins of small buildings and walls add a bewitching quality. And set high into a cliff wall is a tiny shrine containing a likeness of the Virgin Mary, who looks down on all the mysterious beauty below.

Scenic Drive

A scenic drive from Barceloneta to Arecibo is one excellent reason to venture off Highway 22. This 10-mile stretch along Carretera 684 north and Carretera 681 is like Puerto Rico's own little version of California's Pacific Coast Highway, rich in gorgeous views of the ocean with lots of spots to pull over and go for a swim. There's also a great surfing point break at Machuca's Garden at La Boca off Carretera 684.

SPORTS AND RECREATION

Thanks to powerful waves and easy access, some of the best **surfing** in Puerto Rico can be found at **Los Tubos** (Carr. 686, Manatí), beside Balneario Playa Los Tubos. The best time to go is November-March, when the hollow swells can get up to 16 feet or more. It's rarely very crowded, and you can drive right down to the water. Just watch out for the sharp rocky bottom and sea urchins. Los Tubos is not for the inexperienced surfer.

Mountain-bike enthusiasts will want to check out **Bosque Estatal de Cambalache** (Carr. 682, km 6.3, beside the Job Corps facility, Barceloneta, 787/791-1004 or 787/878-7279, office Mon.-Fri. 8 A.M.-4:30 P.M.), a small wooded recreation area open Saturday-Sunday 9 A.M.-5 P.M., where trails meander through this 1,000-acre subtropical forest reserve distinguished by its dramatic hilly karst formations. There are also four miles of hiking trails, a wheelchair-accessible trail, and camping for up to 40 people. To obtain permits to camp ($4) or cycle ($1), call 787/724-3724. Unfortunately, there's no bike-rental outfitter, so bring your own gear.

SHOPPING

Puerto Rico Premium Outlets (1 Premium Outlets Blvd., Barceloneta, 787/846-5300, www.premiumoutlets. com/puertorico, Mon.-Sat. 9 A.M.-9 P.M., Sun. 9 A.M.-7 P.M.) boasts 90 stores offering discounts of 25 percent to 65 percent off designer labels, including Ann Taylor Factory Store, Calvin Klein, Izod, Kenneth Cole, Michael Kors, and Nautica. There are also restaurants and fast food outlets, including Panda Express, Subway, Taco Maker, and Wetzel Pretzel.

Arecibo

Before the Spanish arrived, Arecibo was home to a peaceful group of about 200 Taíno natives led by Cacique Arasibo, reputed to be a fair ruler over his village of fishermen. In 1515, Spain claimed the Arecibo area and enslaved the Taíno, most of whom died shortly thereafter. Today Arecibo is the most populated municipality on the north coast, with more than 100,000 residents who call it home. It is also a major industrial hub, producing textiles, chemicals, electronics, and medical instruments. As a result, Arecibo has been blighted by massive urban sprawl distinguished by traffic-clogged thoroughfares and unfettered commercial development.

Nevertheless, there are several good reasons to visit the municipality of Arecibo. In the mountainous karst country south of town is the world-famous Observatorio de Arecibo. On the coast is Cueva del Indio, a geographic wonder that illustrates what happens when crashing waves meet massive petrified sand dunes—it's also a natural repository for petroglyphs. And for children, there's the Faro de Arecibo Lighthouse and Historical Park with its themed playgrounds and welcoming patch of beach.

SIGHTS
◀ Observatorio de Arecibo

You know you're headed someplace unique as you travel south from the town of Arecibo toward the Observatorio de Arecibo (end of Carr. 625, 787/878-2612, www.naic.edu, daily 9 A.M.-4 P.M. June-July and Dec. 15-Jan. 15, Wed.-Sun. and Mon. holidays 9 A.M.-4 P.M. rest of the year, $4 adults, $2 children and seniors), the world's largest and most sensitive

COURTESY OF NATIONAL ASTRONOMY & IONOSPHERE CENTER

Observatorio de Arecibo

radio telescope. The bustle of commerce, industry, expressways, and road-construction projects eventually gives way to a bright green grassy landscape dotted with dramatic haystack-shaped hills called *mogotes.* Passing cars become few as the curvy road winds around the hills and ever upward, past sprawling cattle farms and errant chickens.

Be sure to bring sturdy walking shoes and an umbrella. Entry to the observatory requires a half-mile hike—mostly up stairs—from the parking lot to the entrance, and there's little shelter along the way. As you climb ever higher toward the observatory, the first glimpse between treetops of the telescope's suspension apparatus is a startling sight. Its cold, clinical, metal construction is in sharp contrast to the wilderness that surrounds it. The road ends at a guardhouse, where you park your car and begin the long uphill trek on a concrete surface to the top of the massive sinkhole that contains the telescope's dish. There are 500

steps, according to one source, and the hike can be so steep and arduous that there are little covered resting stations along the way for those who need to catch their breath. Visitors unable to make the journey by foot can get permission from the guard to drive up to the entrance.

Because there's not really much to do on a tour of the observatory, other than gawk at the sheer size of the telescope dish, a newly constructed educational center has been added. Inside are two levels of informative displays and interactive exhibits that educate visitors on the finer points of the study of space and the atmosphere. A short film on the telescope is screened throughout the day in both English and Spanish. But the highlight of the center is its observation deck, from which visitors can peer over the side of the massive dish. There's also a great gift shop that sells all kinds of great educational books, models, and toys. It's a good source for maps of the island too.

LOOK TO THE STARS

Built in 1963, the **Observatorio de Arecibo** is a curved dish telescope set into the earth on what was once a coffee plantation in the upper regions of Puerto Rico's karst country. The landscape is distinguished by an underground system of limestone caves that has transformed the topography into clusters of fertile green hills and sinkholes. It is because of the landscape's natural depressions, which were big enough to contain the telescope's dish, that the observatory was built here.

To convey a sense of its immensity, consider these statistics: The aluminum-lined dish is 1,000 feet wide from rim to rim and encompasses 18 acres. The receiver is on a 900-ton platform suspended 450 feet above the dish on a 304-foot moveable arm. Cornell University managed the observatory for four decades until 2011, when the National Science Foundation won a five-year bid to manage it. The observatory employs about 140 scientists and engineers from around the world.

Many significant astronomical discoveries have been made at the observatory in the last four decades. Joseph Taylor won the Nobel Prize in 1993 for discovering the first binary pulsar from Arecibo. Other discoveries made at Arecibo include the discovery of polar caps on Mercury and the existence of planets around a pulsar.

But Arecibo's most infamous contribution to science has been as the center of operations for the Search for Extraterrestrial Intelligence Institute's Phoenix Project, which monitored the telescope for signs of intelligent life in the universe. A respected organization of some of the world's foremost scientists, including three Nobel Prize winners, the SETI Institute and its Arecibo research project were funded through grants by NASA for many years before the organization became private in 1993. The project is not as "ET" as it sounds, though. The telescope doesn't so much "seek" intelligent life as listen for radio signals that might indicate its presence. Nevertheless, its otherworldly visage has made it a popular backdrop for filmmakers. In fact, much of the Jodie Foster movie *Contact* was filmed here.

There's one more thing about the Arecibo Observatory that is unique, and that is its longevity. Most major telescopes become obsolete after about 10 years as technological advancements are made, but not Arecibo. Multimillion-dollar upgrades have been made through the years that have extended its viability. Most recently a new "eye" was installed in 2004 that enables it to take photographs of space.

C Cueva del Indio

Because it's not technically an official tourist site—no government-sanctioned bathrooms, marked trails, information center, and so on— the Cueva del Indio (Carr. 681, km 7, $1) is Arecibo's lesser-known attraction, but it's well worth investigating. In fact, its down-home operation is part of its charm. A hand-painted sign marks the turn that takes visitors to the home of the caves' kindly overseer, Richard. Pay him $1, and he takes you for a personal tour of his amazing backyard.

The journey begins with a short trek through scrubby, prickly brush that soon gives way to what looks like a massive moonscape rising out

of the sea. The coral surface was formed from enormous petrified sand dunes whose guts have been scooped out through time from the pounding sea beating against its base. To the west is a large hole in the surface that leads down into a cave, which bottoms out on the sea floor. On its interior walls are faint petroglyphs—a sun, an owl, human faces—believed to have been made by the Taíno more than 500 years ago. To the east are huge natural arches where the sea has cut through the coral mass. During high tide, waves crash into it with such force that the water shoots 20-30 feet in the air.

Hiking shoes or sturdy sneakers are a must, as the coral surface is very rocky and covered

© SUZANNE VAN ATTEN

Cueva del Indio

with camouflaged tree roots in some places. Stay away from the precarious edges and keep your eyes peeled for holes in the surface. Perhaps the government chose not to make this an official tourist site because of the liability: Take one false step and it may be the last step you take.

Faro de Arecibo Lighthouse and Historical Park

Families will enjoy Faro de Arecibo Lighthouse and Historical Park (Rte. 655, Barrio Islote, Arecibo, 787/880-7540 or 787/880-7560, fax 787/880-7520, www.arecibolighthouse. com, Mon.-Fri. 9 A.M.-6 P.M., Sat.-Sun. 10 A.M.-7 P.M., $10 adults, $8 children 12-2, free for children under 2, parking $2). Built in 1898, the neoclassical-style lighthouse was the last one built by colonial Spain. It's on top of Punta Morrillo, a rocky mountain overlooking the north coast, and offers spectacular views of the Atlantic Ocean and surrounding area. The lighthouse is still operational, and inside

are historical displays and artifacts of curiosities found in the ocean, including a 1910 diving suit.

Road-tripping families will want to stop here to let their young children burn off some energy in the recently constructed historical park. Representing the island's historical eras are interactive, kid-friendly representations of an Arasibo Taíno Village; Columbus's ships the *Niña,* the *Pinta,* and the *Santa María;* African slave quarters; a replica of Blackbeard's pirate ship, the *Queen Anne's Revenge;* and a spooky Pirate's Cave containing tanks of sharks, turtles, and alligators. There's also a petting zoo and a standard playground with swings and so on.

The park also contains a small, well-maintained beach on the left as you approach the lighthouse. A smaller, scruffier patch of beach is outside the park just east of the lighthouse.

SPORTS AND RECREATION

Extreme-sports enthusiasts can enjoy caving, rappelling, and body-rafting expeditions along the Tanamá River with local outfit-ter **Expediciones Palenque** (787/407-2858, www.expedicionespalenque.com, $90). The daylong adventure starts in the parking lot of Observatorio de Arecibo and takes thrill-seekers over waterfalls, into natural swimming holes, and on an optional 15- to 20-foot cliff dive.

ACCOMMODATIONS AND FOOD

On a former coffee plantation, **TJ Ranch** (El Valle, Río Arriba, Arecibo, 787/880-1217, www.tjranch.com, $100, includes breakfast) is an oasis of quiet simplicity in a lovely spot of pristine nature between Arecibo and Utuado. The property has three little casitas, each with a bedroom, bathroom, and screened porch. There is also a pool, along with a restaurant specializing in seafood, local cuisine featuring goat and rabbit, and more continental dishes such as chicken marsala and lamb chops.

INFORMATION AND SERVICES

The **police department** (787/878-2020) is on Avenida Hostos. The 24-hour **hospital** (787/878-7272) is at Carretera 129 and Avenida Rotario. **Banco Popular** has an ATM (614 Ave. San Luis Arecibo, 787/878-4949).

GETTING THERE

Arecibo is 81 kilometers or 50 miles west of San Juan on Highway 22.

Camuy

Bypass the town of Camuy and go straight to Parque de las Cavernas del Río Camuy, a fantastic nature park in the island's karst country where visitors can explore caves and hike nature trails to their hearts' content.

Camuy is 103 kilometers or 64 miles west of San Juan. Take Highway 22 west to Carretera 2 west.

SIGHTS
◖ Las Cavernas del Río Camuy

Puerto Rico is home to one of the largest underground river-cave systems in the world, and the easiest way to explore the island's subterranean world is at Las Cavernas del Río Camuy (Carr. 129, km 18.9, 787/898-3100 or 787/898-3136, Wed.-Sun. 8:30 A.M.-3:30 P.M., $10 adults, $7 children under 12, free for senior citizens over 75, parking $2). The park is a well-maintained, tightly run ship, and it's a good thing. This place draws major crowds, including busloads of schoolchildren. Buy a ticket, browse the gift shop, and watch a 10-minute film (English and Spanish) while waiting for the trolley, which runs every 30 minutes.

Once aboard, you zip down, down, down toward the mouth of Cueva Clara. Along the way you pass a mind-boggling display of virgin tropical forest: African tulips, mamey apples, passion fruit, red ginger, bananas, begonias, ferns, and the tiniest, most delicate orchids you've ever seen are everywhere. Before you know it, you're standing at the entrance to Clara.

The cavern's natural opening has been preserved. Visitors enter to the right of it through a larger, artificially constructed opening. The path steeply descends, bottoming out just below the natural opening, through which the sun shines brilliantly, creating the sort of mystical scene that could inspire visions of hobbits and fairies. But farther down are even more magnificent sights as the cavern opens into a 170-foot room thick with stalactites and stalagmites, most notably the Giant Stalagmite, measuring 17 feet tall and 30 feet in diameter. There's also a subterranean waterfall created by the Río Camuy, which runs through parts of the cave. In addition to bats, crickets, and spiders, the cave is home to a creature that is

Las Cavernas del Río Camuy

so rare that this is the only place it lives. It's a microscopic crustacean called *Alloweckelia gurneii,* and it can't be seen by the naked eye.

Other natural sights in the park include Tres Pueblos sinkhole, seen from a viewing platform; Cathedral Cave; and Spiral Cave, accessible by a 200-step staircase to its mouth. There is also an interactive miniature gold mine where kids can pan for "nuggets," along with a snack bar, a gift shop, and trails. And although it's not publicized, there are a limited number of wooded campsites.

Of course, the part of the caves the general public sees is a tiny fraction of the wonders to be found. Luckily for experienced spelunkers, they can arrange tours to explore more remote parts of the caves. Sturdy, nonslip shoes are required; the cave paths get very slippery.

Expediciones Palenque (787/407-2858, www.expedicionespalenque.com, $90) offers a daylong adventure hiking, rappelling, caving, and body-rafting along the Río Camuy and into Resurgencia Cave.

Playa Peñón Brusi/Peñón Amador

Spend the day swimming, fishing, and hiking at Playa Peñón Brusi/Peñón Amador (Carr. 485, km 1.3, Camuy), a beautiful spot of natural beauty featuring a crescent of beach, a dingy dock, and mounds of petrified coral reef providing gorgeous panoramic views of the northern coast. Just be sure to bring a sturdy pair of lace-up shoes; the coral is sharp. Curiosities to explore include a six-foot wooden tiki totem on one reef and a cross planted in another. Lore has it that a grieving father made the cross from the wood of an old church and put it there to commemorate his daughter, who died at sea. Some people believe a 20-foot shark lives under the reef. There's also a terrific little food vendor called **El Pescadería Peñón** that serves up fresh seafood dishes.

Gran Parque del Norte

According to local lore, the people of Camuy and Hatillo fought like the Hatfields and the

© SUZANNE VAN ATTEN

totem at Playa Peñón

park located on the border between the two towns. Plans call for an observation deck, restaurants and food vendor booths, a playground, a driving range, and a bandstand.

FOOD

It looks like a community center snack bar, but **El Pescadería Peñón** (Playa Peñón Brusi/Peñón Amador, Carr. 485, km 1.3, Camuy, 787/356-4755, 787/356-3589, or 787/246-1404, Wed.-Thurs. 9 A.M.-3 P.M., Fri.-Sun. 9 A.M.-6 P.M., $1-20) serves excellent *pinchos, pastelillos,* and whole fried snapper.

Just a short distance south of the entrance to the Camuy caves, **Restaurant El Taíno** (Carr. 129, km 21.1, Camuy, 787/645-4591, Wed.-Sat. 10:30 A.M.-7 P.M., call for reservations) is the perfect place to grab a bite to eat after tromping through the nearby park's subterranean wonderland. The specialty of the house is rice with guinea hen, but the menu of traditional Puerto Rican fare also includes fried pork chops, rabbit in wine sauce, red snapper with scrambled eggplant, and *mofongo.* There's also a full bar and a recently constructed cocktail lounge made to resemble a Taíno hut. Business hours are not always observed, so call first.

McCoys. As a symbol of their newfound peace, or perhaps as a way to distract them from their rivalries, construction began in 2011 on Gran Parque del Norte (Carr. 119, between Hatillo and Camuy), a $2 million, 18-acre oceanfront

Hatillo

Hatillo is the land of dairy farms and the annual Festival de la Máscaras, a three-day celebration that culminates on December 28, when hundreds of elaborately costumed and masked men and women dance through the streets, gathering at the town plaza at 3 P.M. for a parade.

Milk production drives the local economy, which reportedly produces one-third of the milk consumed on the island. A bronze statue of a farmer holding a calf in the split between Carretera 2 and Carretera 485 is a testament to the community's reverence for the industry.

Hatillo's commercial district along Carretera 2 is mostly a thick tangle of urban sprawl, but it soon gives way to an amazing view of the sea as you approach Quebradillas. A long, curved descent out of the mountains seems to hurtle you downward toward an enormous expanse of blue as far as the eye can see.

SIGHTS

They're not necessarily worth going out of your way for, but if you're in the area and just need to get to a beach, there are a couple of options. **Paseo del Carmen** (Carr. 119) is a small patch of beach by a shady pull-over in town. A bright

© SUZANNE VAN ATTEN

Playa Sardinera in Hatillo

blue balustrade lines a short sea walk that ends at a matching pavilion. The other option is **Playa Sardinera** (at Carr. 2, km 84.6, turn beside entrance to Punta Maracayo Resort). This is the site of the **Luis Muñoz Marín Vacation Center** (787/820-0274, fax 787/820-9116, Mon.-Fri. 8 A.M.-4:30 P.M., Sat.-Sun. 8 A.M.-5 P.M., $3), which features a protected lagoon and a well-maintained beach lined by a wooden boardwalk. Facilities include bathrooms, a pool, a playground, a basketball court, a volleyball court, and a cafeteria, as well as a campground and villa rentals. The main drawback is that there's not a lick of shade in sight.

ENTERTAINMENT AND EVENTS

Hatillo hosts one of the island's most celebrated annual festivals. Originating in 1823 with the Spaniards who settled this part of the island, **Festival de la Máscaras** is a three-day costumed celebration held December 26-28.

Originally it was meant to retell the story of King Herod's attempt to kill the infant Jesus by ordering the death of all male babies. Men would don elaborate costumes and masks and travel house-to-house on horseback. After playfully harassing the residents and demanding money, which was donated to the church or a civic organization, they would receive homemade treats and beverages. Today festivities revolve around street parades, music, dance, food, and crafts on the main plaza. The last day is reserved for **Día de Inocentes,** a festival specifically for children.

ACCOMMODATIONS

Opened in 2004, **Punta Maracayo Resort** (Carr. 2, km 85, Hatillo, 787/544-2000 or 877/887-0100, www.hotelpuntamaracayopr.com, $100 d, $210 suite that sleeps 6, plus tax) is a bright yellow three-floor hotel in the middle of an enormous parking lot right on travel-clogged Carretera 2, but the property is quite plush, and the rooms are clean and modern with air-conditioning, mini-bars, and cable TV. Amenities include a pool and an upscale seafood restaurant and bar. Although the hotel isn't right on the ocean, it is within walking distance to Playa Sardinera, and rooms on the second and third floors have ocean views. You get a lot for your money here.

A welcome addition to the limited selection of hotels along the northern coast, **Hotel Rosa Del Mar** (Carr. 2, km 86.6, 1777 Calle Comercio, Hatillo, 787/262-1515, www.hotelrosadelmar.com, $119-139 s, 129-149 d, plus tax) is a modest, well-maintained hotel located in the commercial district of Hatillo. Catering primarily to business travelers, its rooms are large and comfortable with balconies overlooking the mountains or the ocean, which is located a few blocks away. Rooms are appointed with satellite TV and DVD player, microwave, hair dryer, and air-conditioning.

Amenities include a modest fitness center, business center, and penthouse pool. Mojitos Grill & Bar, a popular hot spot on weekend nights, serves a large menu of Puerto Rican and Cuban dishes.

Luis Muñoz Marín Vacation Center at Sardinera Beach (Carr. 2, km 84.6, Hatillo, 787/820-0274, fax 787/820-9116, $195-300, two-night minimum) is primarily a beach-side vacation site for Puerto Rican families. Accommodations include rustic wooden villas and cabanas with air-conditioning, but not much else in the way of amenities. There's also tent and trailer camping. Facilities include a swimming pool, a playground, a basketball and volleyball court, and a cafeteria with pool tables.

◖ **Parador El Buen Café** (Carr. 2, km 84, 381 Carrizales, Hatillo, 787/898-1000, fax 787/820-3013, www.elbuencafe.com, $90-105 s, $120 d, $195 suite, plus tax) is short on charm but long on clean, modern accommodations. The property has 33 rooms with air-conditioning, satellite TV, and mini-refrigerators. There's also a tiny pool. El Buen Café across the street serves breakfast, lunch, and dinner.

FOOD

Located on the top floor of Hotel Rosa Del Mar, **Mojitos Grill & Bar** (Carr. 2, km 86.6, 1777 Calle Comercio, Hatillo, 787/262-1515, www.hotelrosadelmar.com, Tues.-Thurs.

11 A.M.-10 P.M., Fri. 11 A.M.-10 P.M., Sat.-Sun. 4-10 P.M., bar open until 2 A.M. Fri.-Sat., $10-20) features a large U-shaped bar and three large TV screens playing music videos. The signature drink is the *mojito,* of course, and the bartender packs it with lots of fresh mint. The menu features Cuban and Puerto Rican dishes, along with a few Mexican offerings. Dishes include *ropa vieja, chuleta can can, mofongo,* and fajitas. Several samplers are offered if you can't choose just one. The bar is a popular hot spot on weekend nights.

For breakfast, **El Buen Café** (Carr. 2, km 84, 381 Calle Carrizales, Hatillo, 787/898-3495, fax 787/820-3013, www.elbuencafe.com, daily 5:30 A.M.-10 P.M., $4-20) is a good option. The cafeteria serves bacon and eggs, as well as sandwiches, soups, and heartier fare such as chicken and rice, *mofongo,* roast pork, and more. Other than breakfast and sandwiches, though, the food is only fair and it's a bit pricey for what it is, but the place really packs them in.

The prices are low and the atmosphere is pleasant at **El Truco de Güin** (Carr 2, km 86, Hatillo, 787/544-8260, Mon. 11 A.M.-8 P.M., Tues.-Thurs. 11 A.M.-11 P.M., Fri.-Sat. 11 A.M.-2 A.M., Sun. 11 A.M.-10 P.M., $10-18), an open-air restaurant specializing in pastrami, which comes stuffed in a sandwich or *mofongo.* Other offerings include quesadillas, wings, and *churrasco.* There is a $6 lunch special Monday through Friday.

Quebradillas

Notorious as a pirate's lair during the 17th century, Quebradillas was once part of Camuy before it established its independence in 1823. It is not an affluent town. It was once a leader in textile production, but manufacturers pulled out of the area in the 1990s, and tourist traffic typically bypasses the community.

But in a way, that is a part of the charm of its town center, which looks much the same as it did 150 years ago, and it's one of the few places you'll see wood buildings in town. Quebradillas has an edgy side, too, as seen in the presence of graffiti, tattoo parlors, and a motorcycle club.

NORTH COAST

SIGHTS

The drive westward on Carretera 2 at Quebradillas provides one of the most dramatic views in all of Puerto Rico as you crest a high mountain that gives way to steep decline, revealing a panoramic view of the Atlantic Ocean. **Guajataca Mirador** (Carr 2, km 103.7) is a newish observation tower that provides an ideal spot to pull over and take in the view. And there's a snack bar serving fritters and frozen drinks.

Merendero de Guajataca (Carr. 2, km 103.5, daily 9 A.M.-5 P.M.) is a fantastic little nature park that also offers dramatic views of Playa de Guajataca. Paved trails cut through the thick brush to stone picnic shelters and gorgeous views of the ocean. There are also clean, modern bathroom facilities and plenty of parking.

Playa de Guajataca (Carr. 2, km 103.8) is a primitive patch of sand with no facilities tucked down between two escarpments. The tide is too rough for swimming, but it's a popular surf spot that's great for beginners. The western escarpment bears a reminder of the sugarcane train that once connected one side of the island to the other: **El Tunel** is an abandoned train tunnel that can be seen disappearing into the mountain.

Located halfway between Camuy and Quebradillas, **Puerto Hermina** (Carr. 485 at Camino de la Cruz and el Pozo del Mago) is a tiny wedge of beach between cliffs that served as a hideout for 17th-century pirates. The waters are too rough for swimming, but it's a pretty patch of beach with a colorful history.

The simplicity of **Iglesia San Rafael** (110 Calle San Carlos, 787/895-2035), a mission-style church built in 1828, gives it a graceful beauty that sets it apart from the island's more opulent houses of worship. The interior features an unusual stamped ceiling. It's on Plaza de Luis Muñoz Rivera. Next door is **La Casa del Rey**

El Tunel, Playa de Guajataca

© SUZANNE VAN ATTEN

Iglesia San Rafael

FOOD AND NIGHTLIFE

Lucho's (105 Calle Ramon Savedra on Plaza de Luis Muñoz Rivera, 787/895-2717, Mon. 6 A.M.-4 P.M., Tues.-Sat. 6 A.M.-10 P.M., Sun. 6 A.M.-noon, $5-15) is a modest, homey place serving eggs, sandwiches, and *criolla* cuisine, including *carne guisada* and *arroz con pollo,* from a steam table. It has a full bar.

Restaurante La Llave del Mar (Calle Estación, off Carr. 2, directly across from Carr. 113 south, Mon.-Thurs. 11 A.M.-8 P.M., Fri.-Sat. 11 A.M.-11 P.M., Sun. 11 A.M.-10 P.M., 787/895-5843, $8-34) is an old-fashioned open-air restaurant dramatically perched on a cliff overlooking the pounding surf. As if the view weren't enough, it serves excellent Puerto Rican-style seafood dishes, including shrimp, enormous lobsters, dorado, snapper, and grouper with your choice of a selection of sauces, including garlic sauce, creole, thermidor, or *arrecife* (with shrimp, bacon, and cheese). It also serves a selection of Angus beef. The staff is very friendly.

Stone Riders Club House (152 Calle Socorro, Paseo Linares, Quebradillas, 787/955-3378, daily 9 A.M.-2 P.M.) is a cavernous, rustic bar and pool hall that is the headquarters for the Storm Riders motorcycle club, but it's also open to the public and more welcoming than one might expect.

(Plaza de Luis Muñoz Rivera), a yellow, three-story wood structure built in 1857 to accommodate the town hall, the Guard Corps, and a jail. It is not open to the public at this time. Nearby is **Teatro Liberty** (157 Calle Rafols), a small Spanish revival theater built in 1921 and on the National Registry of Historic Places.

CORDILLERA CENTRAL

It's hard for some visitors to wrap their heads around the idea of spending their time in Puerto Rico not in the water but in the mountains. That's what makes the Cordillera Central, Puerto Rico's central mountain region, one of the island's greatest hidden gems. Thousands of acres of undeveloped land thick with tropical jungle, high mountain peaks, waterfalls, rivers, caves, and canyons comprise the interior of the island, but the natural beauty isn't the only reason to visit. This is the place adventure junkies come to go hiking, rappelling, spelunking, and ziplining, and it's where history buffs go to explore the island's Taíno Indian roots.

Accommodations tend to be more rustic here than in San Juan, and the service may not be up to some travelers' standards. But there are some unusual and unique places to stay, like a coffee plantation dating back to 1858 in Jayuya and a 107-acre nature retreat among the peaks of Utuado. And the restaurants may not be on the cutting edge of the latest culinary trends, but you can dine on some of the best pit-cooked pork you'll ever taste at restaurants called *lechoneras,* which specialize in the delicacy.

PLANNING YOUR TIME

One of the great things about the Cordillera Central is that it's possible to get a taste of its charms on a day trip from just about anywhere on the island.

On the east side of the island, Highway 52 travels south from San Juan through Cayey to

© JOSÉ OQUENDO

HIGHLIGHTS

© AVALON TRAVEL

CORDILLERA CENTRAL

LOOK FOR ◖ TO FIND RECOMMENDED SIGHTS, ACTIVITIES, DINING, AND LODGING.

◖ **La Ruta Panorámica:** The well-marked scenic route runs through the Cordillera Central from east to west, offering stunning views of mountains and coast. In some spots, you can see the Atlantic and the Caribbean at the same time (page 236).

◖ **Jardín Botánico y Cultural de Caguas:** In addition to lushly landscaped grounds, tour ruins from Hacienda San José, a former sugar plantation and rum distillery, and recreated slave quarters (page 237).

◖ **Bosque Estatal de Toro Negro:** The forest preserve contains Puerto Rico's highest peak, Cerro Punta, which is 4,390 feet above sea level, and one of the island's highest waterfalls, Salto de Doña Juana (page 245).

◖ **Museo del Cemi:** Shaped like a Taíno amulet, this unique museum in Jayuya contains artifacts of Puerto Rico's indigenous culture (page 246).

◖ **La Piedra Escrita:** A boulder covered with Taíno petroglyphs is in a river by a large natural pool ideal for swimming (page 247).

◖ **Centro Ceremonial Indígena de Caguana:** The public can tour this significant Taíno Indian archaeological site, which dates to A.D. 1100. Many artifacts, petroglyphs, and ceremonial ball fields have been excavated here (page 250).

◖ **Cueva Ventana:** Take a 15-minute hike into a limestone cave and take in a stunning view of the northern karst country from the other side (page 251).

Salinas on the south coast. On the west side of the island, Highway 10 runs south from Arecibo to the mountain town of Utuado. Eventually the highway will continue farther south and connect with Adjuntas, but for now travelers must take Carretera 123 to Adjuntas, where Highway 10 starts again, ending in Ponce on the south coast.

Ambitious travelers who want to travel the whole length of the Cordillera Central can drive La Ruta Panorámica, a designated route following a series of well-marked secondary roads that travel along the highest peaks, offering stunning views of mountains and sea. Due to the sometimes narrow, twisty roads and scenic points along the way, it can take the better part of the day to drive the whole route one way.

The greatest number of dining options can be

CORDILLERA CENTRAL

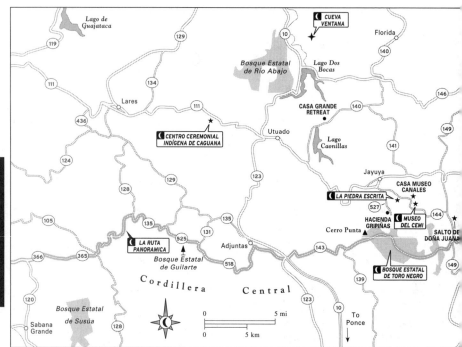

found on the eastern end of the mountain region near Cayey, where there is a high concentration of *lechoneras* roasting whole pigs over open fires. Near the center of the region is San Cristóbal Cañon, a verdant canyon between Aibonito and Barranquitas, where tour guides take thrill-seekers hiking and rappelling. But perhaps the most spectacular sights are on the western end. Jayuya is the site of **Bosque Estatal de Toro Negro,** home to the island's highest peaks; **La Piedra Escrita,** featuring a natural pool and large boulder covered in Taíno petroglyphs; and **Museo del Cemi,** a unique museum shaped like a Taíno amulet containing Indian artifacts found in the area. In Utuado is a 5,000-acre subtropical humid forest, **Bosque Estatal de Río Abajo,** as well as **Centro Ceremonial Indígena de Caguana,** a major Taíno archaeological site dating to A.D. 1100.

For accommodations, the municipalities

with the best options are Jayuya and Utuado. Note that it rains often in the mountains and it can be cool at night, so pack accordingly. And keep an eye on the weather. Heavy rains occasionally result in mudslides and flooding, which could close some roads. Also watch out for livestock. It's not unusual to see a cow or horse tied up to a house right smack beside the road, and chickens are forever crossing the asphalt.

🄲 La Ruta Panorámica

You couldn't ask for a better way to explore Cordillera Central than to drive this 167-mile route from Mayagüez on the west coast to Yabucoa on the southeast coast. The route takes visitors to breathtaking heights on the island's highest peaks, revealing panoramic views of both the Atlantic and the Caribbean, as well as the dramatic mountains and valleys that make up the island's spine. The well-maintained,

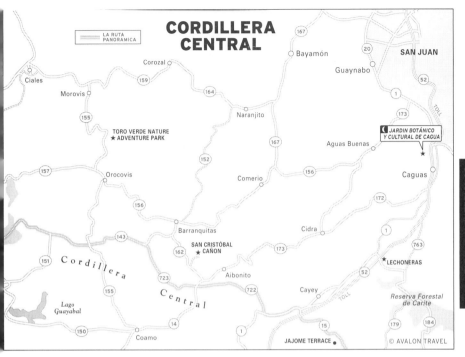

well-marked route traverses a network of secondary roads beginning on Carretera 105 in Mayagüez and ending on Carretera 182 in Yabucoa. It's clearly marked on most maps, including the ubiquitous tourist map (www. travelmaps.com) available at businesses throughout the island. If you only want to explore part of the route, drive the Carretera 143 leg between Adjuntas and Barranquitas, which traverses the island's highest mountains.

Caguas and Cayey

The eastern mountain towns of Caguas and Cayey don't boast the dramatic peaks and valleys of Jayuya and Utuado, but they have plenty to offer in the way of attractions. Caguas is home to the impressive botanical gardens at Jardín Botánico y Cultural de Caguas, and Cayey is graced with a dozen or so *lechoneras,* casual eateries that specialize in open-pit roasted pork. Many locals make a day of visiting the area to dine at all-you-can-eat buffets, dance to the live bands, and shop at roadside vendors, who sell everything from local crafts to homemade cheeses and sweets to gallons of *mavi,* a traditional Taíno beverage made from fermented tree bark of the *mavi* tree.

SIGHTS
◖ Jardín Botánico y Cultural de Caguas

Jardín Botánico y Cultural de Caguas (Hwy. 52 and Carr. 156, Caguas, 787/653-8990, www. visitacaguas.com, Thurs.-Sun. 10 A.M.-4 P.M.,

© JOSÉ OQUENDO

a bus navigates La Ruta Panorámica

$7 adults, $4 ages 7 and younger and 60 and older) is a gorgeous oasis of natural beauty that was once the site of Hacienda San Jose, a sugar plantation and rum distillery established in 1825. Ruins of the home still remain on the grounds, as do remnants of the rum distillery and sugar mill, including an iron sugarcane press and brick smokestacks. The well-maintained grounds provide a living laboratory of indigenous flora spanning 300 acres. In addition to an exhibition space, bookstore, and snack bar, there are trails, themed gardens, water features, and art sculptures, along with the ruins of Hacienda San Jose. There are also greenhouses where plants can be purchased (Mon.-Fri. 6:30-11:30 A.M. and 12:30-3 P.M.); for information call 787/633-0139.

Scenic Drive

Cayey is a 30-minute drive from San Juan or Ponce, and one of the best ways to experience its natural beauty and local culture is to take a short scenic drive that loops through the area. From San Juan, take Highway 52 south and exit at Carretera 184. At the end of the exit ramp, turn right and take an immediate left onto Carretera 184. At the intersection, turn left onto Carretera 763 (a right turn will take you to Reserva Forestal de Carite), then left onto Carretera 765 and right onto Carretera 1. Carretera 1 intersects with Highway 52 at the Caguas Sur Boriken exit. Not only does this drive give you some spectacular views of the mountains, but it will take you by many popular *lechoneras,* some of which have live music. On weekends street vendors sell crafts, homemade cheese, candied fruits, and *mavi* champagne along the way.

Moisty Skate & Family Park

You'll never hear a kid complain about being bored at Moisty Skate & Family Park (Ave. Jose Garrido at exit 18 off Hwy. 52, Caguas, 787/903-0504 or 787/903-6064, www.moisty.

© SUZANNE VAN ATTEN

a replica of slave quarters at Jardín Botánico y Cultural de Caguas

info, entrance $5, activities $8-30, American Express not accepted). In addition to a huge, challenging skate park and a water park, complete with super slides, wave pools, and boat rides, there are pony rides, a paintball field, petting zoo, zipline rides, inflatables, and more. Not surprisingly, it's a popular place for kids' birthday parties. Hours are seasonal: April-August the entire park opens daily 9 A.M.-6 P.M., while September-March the skate park opens Monday-Thursday noon-6 P.M., and the entire park opens Saturday-Sunday 9 A.M.-6 P.M.

Monumento al Jíbaro Puertorriqueño

Technically located in the municipality of Salinas, Monumento al Jíbaro Puertorriqueño (Hwy. 52, km 49.0, accessible only from the southbound lane) is located just south of Cayey, where it honors the Puerto Rican farmer. If you want a closer look, there is an exit just past the statue that ends at a parking lot. From there you can take the quarter-mile hike to the base

of the large, white statue depicting a hard-working man of the land, his solemn wife, and their infant child created by sculptor Tomás Batista of Luquillo.

Reserva Forestal de Carite

Reserva Forestal de Carite (Carr. 184, km 27.5, Cayey, 787/747-4510 or 787/747-4545, Mon.-Fri. 9 A.M.-4:30 P.M., Sat.-Sun. and holidays 8 A.M.-5 P.M., office Mon.-Fri. 7 A.M.-3:30 P.M.) is classified primarily as a subtropical humid forest rich in vegetation, including Honduran mahogany, hibiscuses, eucalyptus, giant ferns, and several varieties of palm. Unfortunately, this forest reserve was severely damaged by Hurricane Georges in 1998, and many of its hiking trails have never been restored. There is one 550-yard trail, though, that ends at Charco Azul, a lovely natural pool. If you don't mind camping in sight of the road, **Area Recreativa Guavate** (Carr. 184, km 27.2) offers nice, shady hillside camping with bathrooms, covered picnic tables, and an outdoor shower. Camping permits must be secured at least 15 days before arrival by calling the forest office or the Department of Natural Resources in San Juan at 787/723-1770.

Museo de Arte
Dr. Pío López Martínez

Museo de Arte Dr. Pío López Martínez (205 Ave. Antonio R. Barceló, Cayey, 787/738-2161, ext. 2209, museo@cayey.upr.edu, Mon.-Fri. 8 A.M.-4:30 P.M., Sat.-Sun. and holidays 11 A.M.-5 P.M.) is an art museum dedicated to local artists with an emphasis on the work of Ramon Frade (1875-1954), who celebrated the island's agricultural community with paintings that dignified the farmer and his contribution to society. Also featured are changing exhibitions of *cartels,* Puerto Rico's renowned poster art used to publicize festivals, plays, and social concerns.

FOOD

Cayey is famous for its many *lechoneras,* located in a sector called Guavate. From Highway 52, exit onto Carretera 184, where you'll find many restaurants serving pit-cooked pork as well as roast chicken stuffed with plantains, *pasteles* (mashed plantain or cassava stuffed with meat and steamed in banana leaves), and more. Drive around and check them out until you find one to your liking. Be sure to go hungry and bring a cooler to carry your leftovers home.

Lechonera El Mojito (Carr. 184, km 32.9, 787/263-4675, daily 9 A.M.-8 P.M., $2-20) is the first *lechonera* you encounter after exiting onto Carretera 184 from Highway 52, and you can't miss it thanks to its bright purple exterior. This casual, family-friendly concrete-block restaurant is a gastronomic emporium of fresh roast pork and all the fixings. Take a peek at the whole pigs cooking on a spit over an open fire before taking your place in line to peruse the long steam tables piled high with sliced pork, ribs, pork skins, whole roast chickens, rice and beans, sausages, *tostones, maduras,* yuca, and more. Point out the dishes you want to sample and take a seat at the common tables and wait for a server to deliver your feast. There's a full bar too. Expect a wait if you visit during the weekends or holidays.

Located at the busy intersection of Carretera 1 and Carretera 189 in Caguas, **Marcelo Restaurant** (3 Calle Muñoz Rivera, 787/743-8801, marcelorestaurant@gmail.com, daily 11 A.M.-10 P.M., $11-27) has been serving outstanding *criolla* fare and more since 1969. The low-slung building decorated in shades of beige looks like it hasn't been redecorated since the day it opened, but that's part of its charm. The reason to go is the house specialty—smoked chicken, an unusual offering that is delectably moist and packed with so much flavor, you'll want to lick your plate. Other dishes include baked chicken stuffed with shrimp, shrimp stuffed with cheese, lamb chops, fettuccine, *mofongo,* and paella. Daily lunch specials are $11-17. The service is especially professional in an old-school way, and there's a full bar, of course. Check out the dessert case at the entrance, filled with cakes and flans.

Restaurante Raíces (Urb. Villa Turabo, H-2, Hwy. 52, exit 21, across the street from Plaza del Carmen Mall, Caguas, 787/258-1570, fax 787/258-1560, www.restauranteraices.com, Mon.-Wed. 11 A.M.-8 P.M., Thurs.-Sat. 11 A.M.-10 P.M., Sun. noon-8 P.M., $12-39) serves excellent *criolla* cuisine, specializing in *mofongo, churrasco,* and *chuleta can can.*

INFORMATION AND SERVICES

For your banking needs, go to **Banco Popular** (Centro Comercial Sierra de Cayey, Ave. Antonio R. Barceló, Carr. 14, km 70.6, 787/738-2828). Cayey has two hospitals, **Hospital Menonita de Cayey** (4 Calle Mendoza, 787/263-1001) and **Family Health Center of Cayey** (5 Luis Barreras, 787/738-3011). For pharmacy needs, visit **Walgreens**

(Carr. 1, 1000 Ave., J.T. Pinero, Cayey Shopping Center, 787/738-2977).

GETTING THERE AND AROUND

Caguas is 32 kilometers or 20 miles south of San Juan on Highway 52. Cayey is 54 kilometers or 33 miles south of San Juan on Hwy 52. Cayey has two taxi services, **Cayey Metro Taxi** (787/738-8001) and **Cayey Taxi** (787/738-4344).

Aibonito and Barranquitas

Of these two mountain towns, Barranquitas offers the most charming plaza and city center. The recently renovated plaza features a beautiful wrought-iron gazebo in the middle, and the streets around it are lined with bustling shops and museums. But both municipalities have much to offer visitors in search of spectacular natural beauty, history, and annual festivals.

SIGHTS

San Cristóbal Cañon (Carr. 162/Carr. 725, between Aibonito and Barranquitas) is reportedly the biggest canyon in the Caribbean at 4.5 miles long and 500-800 feet deep. It's hard to believe this beautiful deep hole in the earth, now filled with verdant green vegetation, was once a garbage dump. Today it's a popular site for adventure-seeking outdoorsmen and -women who want to get away from it all and witness the canyon's natural beauty, including a spectacular river, waterfalls, and shoals. It is not advisable to enter the canyon without a trained guide.

Museo Luis Muñoz Rivera (10 Calle Muñoz Rivera, Barranquitas, 787/857-0230, Wed.-Sun. 8:30 A.M.-4:20 P.M., $1) is dedicated to one of Puerto Rico's most celebrated native sons, Luis Muñoz Rivera, a poet, journalist, politician, and defender of the island's independence both under Spanish and American rule. Inside this traditional Puerto Rican-style home built in 1857 are many artifacts of Rivera's life, including newspaper clippings, his impressive two-sided walnut desk from 1893, his death mask,

and the 1912 Pierce-Arrow that transported his body from his funeral services to his burial site in **Mausoleo Luis Muñoz Rivera** (Calle Padre Berrios, Tues.-Sat. 8 A.M.-4:30 P.M.).

Casa Museo Joaquín de Rojas (Calle Barceló, Barranquitas, 787/857-6293, Mon.-Fri. 8 A.M.-4:30 P.M., free) is a museum with a mishmash of interesting items that include vintage farm tools, *mundillo* lace, and newspaper clippings about the town's history. Most interesting is a large photograph of Barranquitas taken in 1950. Contemporary artists maintain studios here.

Mirador Piedra Degetau (Carr. 7718, km 0.8, Aibonito, Wed.-Sun. and Mon. holidays 9 A.M.-6 P.M.) is a new, pristinely landscaped park thick with blooming bougainvillea in a riot of colors. There are picnic shelters, bathrooms, a playground, and snack machines, but the focal point of the roadside attraction is the observation tower, which offers an amazing view of the mountains and even the sea when visibility is clear.

SPORTS AND RECREATION

San Cristóbal Hiking Tour (P.O. Box 678, Barranquitas, 787/857-2094 or 787/647-3402, http://barranquitaspr.org/viajes) offers a variety of weekend excursions in San Cristóbal Cañon, from moderate hiking and biking tours to extreme rappelling and mountaineering tours. It also offers tours to Bosque Estatal Toro Negro and other natural sights in the area. Prices range $50-140, depending on the excursion and the number of people in your party.

Acampa (1211 Ave. Piñero, San Juan, 787/706-0695, www.acampapr.com) offers rappelling and rock-climbing tours into San Cristóbal Cañon for experienced adventure travelers. Explore the canyon's waterfalls and river. Acampa also sells and rents camping, hiking, and mountaineering gear at its store in San Juan. The half-day zipline rainforest adventure is $115 per person, the full-day Toro Negro waterfall zipline tour is $159 per person, and the half-day coffee tasting tour is $109 per person. All prices include tax. All tours are for groups of 6-12 people.

ENTERTAINMENT AND EVENTS

Aibonito is known as the City of Flowers because every year it bursts into a riot of color and floral scents for the **Festival de las Flores** (Carr. 722, km 6.7, 787/735-4070, $3 adults, $2 children), held from the last weekend of June through the first weekend of July. On 25 acres of land, the festival grounds are filled with horticulture and landscaping exhibitions and more than 50 vendors selling flowers and plants, as well as pottery and garden accessories. There's also live music, and vendors sell food and crafts.

Feria Nacional de Artesanías (23 Calle Muñoz Rivera, Barranquitas, 787/857-6293), held in mid-July, features more than 200 artisans from all over the island who flock here to sell local arts and crafts, including wood carvings, musical instruments, ceramics, hammocks, and more.

FOOD

If gorging on pounds of meat is your idea of a fun night out, the wacky **Vaca Brava** (Carr. 771, km 9.3, Barranquitas, 787/857-2628, www.restaurantvacabrava.com, Thurs. and Sun. 11 A.M.-7 P.M., Fri. noon-9 P.M., Sat. 11 A.M.-9 P.M., $12-53) is for you. The restaurant serves enormous stacks of layered grilled

Feria Nacional de Artesanías in Barranquitas

© JOSE OQUENDO

chicken, beef ribs, *churrasco,* and sausage designed to share. To get an idea, a popular item on the menu is the $50 *la ubre de la vaca* (the cow's udder), featuring a large smoked ham stuffed to overflowing with rice and beef ribs. More modest options include grilled chicken or *churrasco.* A second location is in Old San Juan (253 Calle Recinto Sur).

La Piedra Restaurant (Carr. 7718, km 0.8, Aibonito, 787/735-1034, Mon.-Thurs. 11 A.M.-2 P.M., Fri.-Sun. 11 A.M.-11 P.M., $6-18) is a charming little home-style restaurant in a cozy Florida room that contains a full bar, a piano, and tons of potted plants. Puerto Rican cuisine is served, including a wide variety of seafood, steak, and chicken dishes. Be sure to try the desserts made on the premises, including an unusual and refreshing ginger flan.

INFORMATION AND SERVICES

Banking services are available at **Banco Popular** branches in Aibonito (Carr. 14, km 51, 787/735-3681) and Barranquitas (San Cristobal Shopping Center, Carr. 156, 787/857-4380). Health care is provided by **Mennonite General Hospital Aibonito** (Calle José at Calle Vazquez, Aibonito, 787/735-8001).

GETTING THERE AND AROUND

Aibonito is 73 kilometers or 45 miles south of San Juan. Take Highway 52 south to Carretera 14 west. Barranquitas is 53 kilometers or 33 miles south of San Juan. Take Carretera 2 south to Carretera 167 south to Carretera 147 south to Carretera 152 south. For getting around, taxi service is provided by **Aibonito Taxi** (787/735-7144).

CORDILLERA CENTRAL

Orocovis, Morovis, and Ciales

Orocovis and Morovis are small mountain towns with great views and a couple of popular cultural festivals that celebrate the music and foods of the area. Ciales is a charming mountain town where dramatic outcroppings of exposed limestone called *mogotes* tower overhead and the rivers Toro Negro, Yunes, Grande de Manatí, and Cialitos converge both above and below ground, creating an intricate cave system.

SIGHTS

Mirador Orocovis-Villalba (Carr. 143 between Orocovis and Villalba, Wed.-Sun. 9 A.M.-5 P.M.) is a newly constructed park and overlook 2,000 feet above sea level. From here you can see both the island's north and south coasts. Amenities include a children's playground and picnic tables.

The biggest draw to Ciales is its underground rivers and caves: **Yuyu Cave, La Virgen Cave, Las Archillas Cave,** and **Las Golondrina Cave,** where you can find sea fossils, stalactites, and

columns. For information call 787/871-3500, ext. 266, or contact one of several adventure-tour operators in the area who offer guided expeditions.

In addition to its spectacular caves, Ciales has several modest sights worth seeking out if you're in the area, including the **Museo del Café** (Calle Palmer at Paseo del Aroma, 787/857-6293, Mon.-Fri. 8 A.M.-4:30 P.M.), which celebrates Ciales as the only municipality on the island whose largest agricultural product is still coffee; **Museo Juan Antonio Corretjer** (7 Calle Betances, 787/871-3500, Sat. 8 A.M.-4 P.M.), dedicated to the renowned Puerto Rican poet; and **Puente Mata Plátano José Jiménez** (Carr. 149 at Carr. 132), a historic iron bridge.

SPORTS AND RECREATION

Claiming to be the largest aerial park in the western hemisphere with the longest zipline cable in the Americas, **Toro Verde Nature Adventure Park** (Carr. 155, km 32.9,

Orocovis, 787/944-1196, 787/944-1195, or 787/867-6606, fax 787/867-7022, www.toroverdetransportation.com, www.toroverdepr.com, Thurs.-Sun. 8 A.M.-5 P.M., $65-200, reservations required) has become one of the most popular new tourist sites in all of Puerto Rico, an adventure junkie's dream come true. It opened in 2010 and had more than 50,000 visitors its first year. The biggest attraction is The Beast, a 4,745-foot double cable, double harness zipline that has you flying through the air in a prone position like a bird. There are also zipline canopy tours, a hanging bridges tour, rappelling, and a mountain bike course. Activities can be enjoyed à la carte or combined in packages that include lunch, beverages, and snacks. Participants must be a minimum of four feet tall. Hotel pickup can be arranged.

Expediciones Palenque (787/407-2858, www.expedicionespalenque.com) offers daylong group tours throughout Cordillera Central. Tours include spelunking in Yuyu Cave in Ciales ($85); kayaking Guineo Lake in Jayuya ($85); hiking Guilarte Mountain in Adjuntas ($80); and tours combining hiking, rappelling, caving, and body rafting tours on the Tanamá River ($90).

Certified guides at **Aventuras Tierra Adentro** (268-A Ave. Jesus T. Piñero, San Juan, 787/766-0470, fax 787/754-7543, www.aventuraspr.com, Tues.-Fri. 10 A.M.-6 P.M., Sat. 10 A.M.-4 P.M.) lead cave and canyon tours that include rappelling, rock climbing, and ziplines for adventure seekers of all experience levels, including beginners. Reservations are required. Participants must be 15 or older. Cave tours are Fridays and Sundays ($170 per person). Canyon tours are Saturdays ($160 per person).

ArqueoTours Coabey (787/342-9317 or 787/470-1862, arqueotourscoabey@gmail.com, $65 adults, $20 ages 5-12, free for children 4 and younger) offers family-friendly hiking tours to Taíno archaeological sites including La Piedra Escrita. The tours are guided by a historian and archaeologist.

ENTERTAINMENT AND EVENTS

Festival de Cuatristas y Trovadores (Plaza de Recreo, Morovis, 787/862-2155) is a celebration of traditional Puerto Rican music and art held in mid-July. Local artisans who make *cuatros,* stringed guitarlike instruments, demonstrate their craft. *Cuatro* musicians and troubadours perform as well.

Festival de Pastel (Orocovis, 787/867-5000, ext. 2295) is a culinary festival held in late November for three days noon-midnight in honor of the *pastel,* a Taíno dish traditionally eaten during the Christmas holidays. Similar to a tamale, it's made of mashed, seasoned plantain filled with fried pork that's wrapped in a banana leaf and steamed. Festivities include live music and artisan vendors.

FOOD

◖**Casa Bavaria** (Carr. 15, km 38.3, Morovis, 787/862-7818, www.casabavaria.com, Thurs. noon-8 P.M., Fri.-Sat. noon-10 P.M., bar until 2 A.M., Sun. noon-8 P.M., bar until 10 P.M., $8-36) marks the unlikely intersection of Puerto Rican and German culture and is reason alone to take a day trip to Morovis. In a two-story open-air structure plastered with beer signs and banners, Casa Bavaria serves outstanding Puerto Rican and German cuisine. Alongside the usual *mofongo,* shrimp, lobster, and chicken, you can dine on heaping platters of bratwurst, wiener schnitzel, and sauerkraut. Cocktails are a mere $3.50, and there's an extensive wine list with offerings from Italy, Spain, Chile, and Germany. Dine in the crowded, pleasantly raucous bar, or go around back and take a seat in the quiet dining room overlooking a gorgeous mountain view. There's live music on Saturdays, and Oktoberfest is celebrated the first and second weekends of October with live bands all weekend long. Be forewarned: There's an infectious party atmosphere here that will have you drinking shots of Jägermeister before you know it!

Roka Dura Wine and Grill (Carr. 155, km

32.2, Orocovis, 787/867-4680, www.rokadurapr.com, Wed.-Sun. 11 A.M.-9 P.M., $8-17) is a casual, open-air restaurant offering fantastic mountain views, an extensive wine list, and a long list of traditional Puerto Rican and Cuban dishes, including fried whole snapper, *ropa vieja,* stuffed *mofongo,* chicken wings, and *churrasco.* For something out of the ordinary, try the longaniza hamburger, a patty made from garlicky sausage.

Morovis is known for its *pan de la patita echá,* a delicious braided bread. It's served at any number of the many *panaderías* (bakeries) found here, but the best-known place is **Panadería Patria y Repostería** (20 Calle Ruiz Belvis and 155 Carretera Desvio, Morovis, 787/862-2867). Believed to be one of the oldest bakeries in Puerto Rico, it was established in 1862. Other options include **Panadería**

y Repostería Barahona (Carr. 155, km 4.1, Morovis, 787/862-2538, daily 8 A.M.-10 P.M.).

INFORMATION AND SERVICES

Banking services are available at **Banco Popular** branches in Ciales (46A Calle Palmer, 787/871-1295) and Morovis (155 Carr. 6623 Int., 787/862-2160). For pharmacy needs, visit **Walgreens** (137 Carr. 200, 787/862-0104).

GETTING THERE

Morocovis is 60 kilometers or 37 miles southwest of San Juan. Take Highway 22 west to Carretera 137 south. Ciales is 74 kilometers or 46 miles southwest of San Juan. Take Highway 22 west of Carretera 149 south. Orocovis is 87 kilometers or 54 miles southwest of San Juan. Take Highway 22 west to Carretera 137 south.

Jayuya

If you visit only one place in Puerto Rico's Cordillera Central, go to Jayuya. The central town is a bit grim, offering little of interest to visitors. The reason to go is to experience the gorgeous mountain scenery and some of the highest peaks on the island, where it's possible to see both the Atlantic and the Caribbean, as well as vegetation thick with sierra palms, bamboo, banana trees, and brilliantly colorful impatiens. This is also the place to soak up the rich Taíno culture and explore other historic sights.

SIGHTS
Cacique Jayuya Monument
Unfortunately it's often closed, but the Cacique Jayuya Monument (Cultural Center, 24 Calle San Felipe, 787/828-1241) honors the great cacique who once ruled the Taíno who lived in the area now named in his memory. In addition to a sculpture of Cacique Jayuya by Tomás Batiste, here you'll see exhibits of archaeological finds from the area and the tomb of a Taíno Indian.

◖ Bosque Estatal de Toro Negro
If you want to see thick, virtually uninhabited tropical jungle as far as the eye can see and travel so high up in the mountains that you can see both coasts, Toro Negro Forest (along Ruta Panorámica on Carretera 143 south of Jayuya) is the place to go. From these heights you can see clouds drift between the peaks below you and you're surrounded by tangles of wild bamboo, banana trees, hibiscus, enormous ferns, impatiens, elephant ears, *flamboyan* trees, and miles of sierra palms, distinguished by their long straight trunks and pale green foliage towering 30-50 feet high. The roads are steep and twisty, putting a strain on small engines and inducing dizziness or—worse—motion sickness. But it's one of the most exotic sights you'll see on the island and well worth the effort.

The highest peaks in Puerto Rico can be found in Toro Negro, the tallest being Cerro Punta (4,390 feet). Driving through these mountains along La Ruta Panorámica, you can often catch a glimpse of the ocean off the southern coast. If visibility is clear, you can see the north coast, too.

Around kilometer 21 on Carretera 143 there is a small, rustic park on Cerro Maravillas where you can park and take in a stunning panoramic view of Ponce and the Caribbean Ocean. Unfortunately the picnic shelters and other structures are poorly maintained and marred with anti-American and anti-Semitic graffiti. It's hard to say if it's the work of rebellious teens or something more sinister. This was the site of a notorious incident in 1978 when police officers killed two *independistas* suspected of planning to sabotage a television transmission tower on the mountain's summit.

In Toro Negro you can also see one of the island's highest waterfalls, **Salto de Doña Juana** (Carr. 149, km 41.5). It can be viewed from the road (it's on the left if you're traveling south) if you look way up high. Although it's not particularly wide, the water propels off the mountaintop with great force, making it a spectacular sight.

The highest peaks of Toro Negro Forest contain dwarf or cloud forest, where the foliage has been stunted from the constant moisture in the atmosphere. The southern part of the forest features many rugged rock cliffs, jagged peaks, and waterfalls. Much of the forest has been subjected to clearing by the logging industry, but long-term reforestation efforts have helped repair some of the damage.

There are 10 trails in the forest, most of which originate from the **Doña Juana Recreation Center** (Carr. 143, km 32.4, 787/724-3724, daily 7:30 A.M.-4 P.M.). One trail is a 10-minute walk to a natural freshwater pool (open Sat.-Sun. and Mon. holidays 9 A.M.-5 P.M. Apr.-Sept., $1 adults, children under 10 free). Another hike is a 3-kilometer trek to **Torre Observación** lookout tower. A camping area with toilets and showers but no electricity is a 550-yard hike away.

◖ Museo del Cemi

Museo del Cemi (Carr. 144, km 9.3, 787/828-1241 or 787/828-4094, Wed.-Fri. 9:30 A.M.-4 P.M., Sat.-Sun. 10 A.M.-3 P.M. regularly, daily 9:30 A.M.-4 P.M. in summer, $1 adults, $0.50 children 15-5) makes quite a statement for itself as you drive along Carretera 144. Like a throwback to kitschy mid-century American architecture in which buildings were made to reflect their purpose (e.g., a hot-dog stand shaped like a hot dog), Museo del Cemi is shaped like a huge *cemi*—a triangular artifact with animal characteristics made by the Taíno Indians. Its significance is unknown, but it's believed to have represented a deity and to have contained many powers.

Downstairs is a small collection of Taíno artifacts: necklaces of stone and shells, ritual vomit spatulas, ceremonial maracas, a *dogolito* (a phallic symbol of power for caciques), and

Salto de Doña Juana, one of the island's highest waterfalls

© SUZANNE VAN ATTEN

Museo del Cemi

the mysterious stone collar/belt, the purpose of which is unknown. Upstairs are poster-size photographs of petroglyphs found in Jayuya, Comerio, Utuado, Naguabo, Luquillo, Corozal, and Río Piedras.

Next door is **Casa Museo Canales** (Carr. 144, km 9.3, daily 11 A.M.-4 P.M., 787/828-4618 or 787/828-1241, $1 adults, $0.50 ages 5-15, free for children under 5), a replica of the home of the celebrated author Nemesio R. Canales (1878-1923) and his revolutionary sister Blanca Canales (1906-1996). This traditional *criolla*-style wood frame structure contains many of the Canaleses' furnishings and a room devoted to the nationalist revolt Blanca led against the United States, the Jayuya Uprising, a.k.a. El Grito de Jayuya, in October 1950. One of several revolts orchestrated around the island that day, Blanca Canales's group attacked the police station, killing one policeman, and burned down the post office. The United States retaliated with infantry

troops, mortar fire, and grenades. Blanca was arrested and sentenced to a life sentence plus 60 years. She was pardoned in 1967. Objects on view include revolvers used in the revolt and a card identifying Blanca as a member of the Nationalist Party. Unfortunately the wall text is in Spanish only.

◖ La Piedra Escrita

La Piedra Escrita (Carr. 144, km 7.3, 787/828-1241, free) is one of Puerto Rico's most revered reminders of the island's Taíno culture. The enormous granite boulder measures 32 feet high and 13 feet wide and is located smack-dab in the middle of Río Saliente, creating a natural pool where visitors can go for a swim.

But it's what's on the boulder that is of interest to historians and archaeologists. On the rock's surface are 52 petroglyphs that were carved into the rock by members of indigenous groups sometime between A.D. 600 and 1200. Some of the symbols clearly depict faces of

CORDILLERA CENTRAL

humans and animals while others are geometric or abstract in shape. Because of the quantity of petroglyphs on the rock, some believe La Piedra Escrita was an important ceremonial site, but its significance is ultimately unknown.

Today La Piedra Escrita is a popular tourist sight. A long series of wheelchair-accessible switchback ramps has been built that descends from the stone escarpment overlooking the river down to the water where visitors can get a close-up look at the rock and go for a dip. It's a popular picnic spot on weekends.

Hacienda Pomarrosa

Hacienda Pomarrosa (Carr. 511 at Carr. 143, near Jayuya, 787/460-8934, www.cafepomarrosa.com, $15 per person, reservations required) is a working coffee plantation offering two-hour tours of its operation that end with a tasting of the product that is grown and processed on-site. Two modest B&B-style

© SUZANNE VAN ATTEN

La Piedra Escrita

accommodations are available for overnight stays for $125-150, including breakfast.

ENTERTAINMENT AND EVENTS

Festival Nacional Indígena de Jayuya (Plaza Nemesio R. Canales, Calles Nemesio R. Canales and Figuera, 787/828-1241) is an annual three-day celebration of the Taíno culture beginning November 19. Participants don Taíno-style clothing, prepare traditional foods, and perform traditional music and dances. More than 100 artisans sell handmade crafts as well, and many demonstrations and ceremonies are held.

Other festivals include **El Festival del Pueblo del Tomate,** held in mid-April to celebrate the municipality's production of tomatoes. Festivities include games, music, and food kiosks. The **Jayuya Patron Saint Festival** honors the Virgen de la Monserrate with religious processions, music, and food kiosks in early September. Christmas is celebrated with a **Magic Forest** featuring large holiday dioramas and storytelling December 1-January 15, and **Three Kings Day** on January 5 features traditional Christmas foods, music, and children's activities. All festivals are held in Complejo Deportivo Filiberto García on Carretera 144 at the entrance to Jayuya. For information call 787/828-1241.

ACCOMMODATIONS

◖ **Hacienda Gripiñas** (Carr. 527, km 2.5, 787/828-1717 or 787/828-1718, fax 787/828-1719, www.haciendagripinas.com, $104 s, $125 d, $153 t, $181 q, including full breakfast and dinner), built in 1858, was once one of the island's most prosperous coffee plantations. Today, its white wooden structures with green trim and red tin roofs are a unique hotel surrounded by the majestic mountains of the Cordillera Central. The accommodations are rustic but comfortable and include modern bathrooms, excellent beds, air-conditioning, local TV, and amazing mountain views. Some rooms have private balconies, but for those that

© SUZANNE VAN ATTEN

Hacienda Gripiñas

CORDILLERA CENTRAL

don't, there is a lovely large common porch with rocking chairs and hammocks overlooking the lush grounds thick with birds and coqui tree frogs. The Restaurante Don Pedro serves Puerto Rican cuisine but BYOB. Amenities include a swimming pool.

FOOD

Opened in 2011, **C El Lechón de la Piedra Escrita** (Carr. 144, km 7.3, Jayuya, 787/473-8559, Thurs.-Sun. 10 A.M.-11 P.M., Fri.-Sat. 10 A.M.-midnight, $8-13, $10 buffet Thurs.-Fri. 10 A.M.-4 P.M.) is a sprawling restaurant located beside the parking lot at La Piedra Escrita and specializing in whole, pit-cooked pig, sausages, chicken, and *churrasco.* Order individual platters or go family-style. Ten people can dine on three pounds of pork, stuffed *mofongo, pasteles,* and the house special rice for $85. There is a huge bar with big flat-screen TVs and live music and karaoke for entertainment.

Café Hacienda San Pedro Tienda y Museo

(Carr. 144, km 8.4, Jayuya, 787/828-2083, www.cafehsp.com, Fri.-Sun. 10 A.M.-5 P.M., free) is a coffee museum featuring exhibits of vintage coffee-processing equipment that dates back to the plantation's origins in 1931. There is also a shop serving coffee drinks and selling bags of whole beans and ground coffee to take home.

Restaurante Don Pedro (Hacienda Gripiñas, Carr. 527, km 2.5, 787/828-1717 or 787/828-1718, fax 787/828-1719, www.haciendagripinas.com, $8-35) serves breakfast and dinner, featuring seafood, steaks, and local cuisine. It's a good option if you stick to simple local dishes, such as the fried meaty ribs, which are tender and tasty. Stay away from more ambitious dishes, such as the onion soup, which comes with a gluey slice of American cheese on top. The attractive dining room in the middle of the hacienda is distinguished by a tree that grows from beneath the floor and spreads its limbs over the tables below.

Panadería Jayuya Cafeteria (Carr. 144, km

1.7, just west of Jayuya, 787/828-3186, daily 6 A.M.-10 P.M.) has a good selection of groceries, produce, baked goods, and a steam table with rice, beans, and other Puerto Rican dishes.

INFORMATION AND SERVICES

For travel information in Jayuya, visit the **tourism office** (Carr. 144, km 9.3,

787/828-1241, Mon.-Fri. 8 A.M.-4:30 P.M., Sat.-Sun. and holidays 10 A.M.-3 P.M.). Banking services are available at **Banco Popular** (84 Guillermo Estates, 787/828-4120).

GETTING THERE

Jayuya is 99 kilometers or 61 miles southwest of San Juan. Take Highway 22 west to Carretera 149 south.

Utuado

Utuado is one of the most accessible of Puerto Rico's mountain towns, via Highway 10 from Arecibo. The wide multilane thoroughfare is well-marked and well-maintained, and it offers a spectacular ascent into Puerto Rico's Cordillera Central, where you can see massive mountain peaks towering overhead. The road has been cut right through the mountains in some places, creating dramatic profiles that stand in testament to the engineering feat it took to build the passage. Note, though, that the narrow winding roads that lead off Highway 10 are not for the fainthearted. Proceed on them with caution, especially if it's raining, because mudslides and flooding are not uncommon. Otherwise, don't be deterred from venturing into this region. Its natural beauty is breathtaking, and Utuado is home to the island's most significant Taíno Indian archaeological site.

SIGHTS
C Centro Ceremonial Indígena de Caguana

Centro Ceremonial Indígena de Caguana (Carr. 111, km 12.5, between Utuado and Lares, 787/894-7325 or 787/894-7310, www.icp.gobierno.pr, daily 8:30 A.M.-4:20 P.M., $2 adults, $1 children 6-12, children under 6 and seniors free) is one of the island's most significant archaeological sites.

Taíno Indians did not live on the site in Caguana, but dating back to A.D. 1100 they congregated here for religious ceremonies and ball games, leaving behind 12 ceremonial ball fields called *bateyes,* two of which have yet to be excavated. All but one are rectangular fields rimmed with stones and small monoliths, some of which have animal faces and spiral symbols carved into their sides. One is an atypical horseshoe shape. *Bateyes* were central to Taíno culture. This is where men competed with neighboring Taíno groups in a game similar to soccer, played with a ball made from rubber plants and reeds.

A traditional Taíno hut made from tree trunks and palm fronds, called a *bohío,* has been recreated on the site, and there is a small museum of artifacts that unfortunately is closed indefinitely. Many of the artifacts excavated from the site, such as *cemíes* (amulets) and stone collars, have been relocated to the Institute of Puerto Rican Culture in San Juan.

Excavation first began on the park in 1915, and it has undergone various stages of excavation and restoration over the years, including a $500,000 overhaul in 2005 that made it more tourist-friendly by planting a promenade of palm trees at the entrance and creating picnic areas and attractive stone walkways through the park.

The best way to get there is to take Highway 10 south from Arecibo to Carretera 111, which is a tight, windy road featuring hairpin curve after hairpin curve. Beware of livestock on this

© JOSÉ OQUENDO

CORDILLERA CENTRAL

Centro Ceremonial Indígena de Caguana

road: Horses and cows can frequently be seen tied up to houses that hug the road, and chickens wander freely.

◉ Cueva Ventana

Located between Arecibo and Utuado, Cueva Ventana (Carr. 10, km 75, Arecibo/Utuado border) is a limestone cave that provides a stunning view of the north region's karst country. Park at the Texaco station ($2 fee) and follow the path on the right side of the building for about 15 minutes. The trail forks twice as it climbs in altitude; go left both times. The trail ends at the mouths of two caves. Both are accessible, but the one on the left with concrete steps is Cueva Ventana. Walk into the cave and through a dark passage that leads to another opening through which you can see a stunning view of the valley. Sturdy shoes with good tread and flashlights are essential to navigate the slick cave floor and dark passages.

Lago Dos Bocas

Lago Dos Bocas (Embarcadero Lago Dos Bocas, Carr. 123, Utuado) is a manmade lake lined with lakeside restaurants accessible by free boat ride from the *embarcadero* (pier). The restaurants ferry diners from the pier to the restaurants, but the government also operates a small ferry primarily for residents, but if there is availability, visitors can take the 45-minute ride around the lake. To reach the pier, travel south from Arecibo on Carretera 10 toward Utuado; turn left on Carretera 621; turn right on Carretera 123; the pier will be on the right. Boat rides are free.

Bosque Estatal de Río Abajo

Bosque Estatal de Río Abajo (Carr. 621, km 4.4, just west of Hwy. 10, 787/880-6557 or 787/724-3724) is a 5,000-acre mostly subtropical humid forest in the heart of Puerto Rico's karst country, spanning the municipalities of Utuado and Arecibo. Once heavily deforested by industry, the reserve was founded in 1943 and continues to undergo reforestation efforts.

The forest is home to 175 endangered plant species, 47 of which are in danger of extinction, and 34 species of birds. Although it is not open to the public, the forest contains an aviary where the indigenous Puerto Rican parrot is raised in captivity and released in hopes of restoring the endangered species to the island habitat. Recreational facilities include 24 hiking trails, campgrounds, and bare-bones cabins available for rent. Camping permits and guided tours can be arranged by calling 787/724-3724.

SPORTS AND RECREATION

Lago Dos Bocas (Carr. 123, north of Utuado, 787/894-3505) is a large artificial mountain lake perfect for kayaking and fishing for sunfish, largemouth bass, catfish, and tilapia. Boats are available from the municipal dock to take visitors to lakefront restaurants on weekends only.

Expediciones Palenque (787/407-2858, www.expedicionespalenque.com) is an adventure-tour operator that takes nature lovers hiking, rappelling, and body-rafting along the Tanamá River. Sights include Cueva del Arco (Arch Cave) and Tunnel Cave. A daylong tour is $90 per person.

ENTERTAINMENT AND EVENTS

The municipality of Utuado commemorates San Miguel Arcángel each year with a **Patron Saint Festival** (787/894-3505) in late September to early October. In addition to the usual religious processions, music, and food kiosks, there are amateur boxing matches, softball games, and domino competitions. It's held in Luis Muñoz Rivera Plaza.

ACCOMMODATIONS

◖**Casa Grande Mountain Retreat** (Carr. 612, km 0.3, at the intersection of Carr. 140, Barrio Caonillas, 787/894-3939 or 888/343-2272, www.hotelcasagrande.com, $125 s/d, plus tax)

is a truly unique hotel for visitors seeking a retreat from the 21st century deep in the tropical jungle. TVs and radios are prohibited, and the only entertainment at night is listening to the song of the coquí tree frog. The 107-acre property features 20 freestanding monastic cabins that contain a bed, a fan, a private bath, a hammock on the porch, and that's it. But what it lacks in luxuries, Casa Grande Mountain Retreat more than makes up for in setting. Deep in the Cordillera Central mountain region, the entire property—formerly a coffee plantation—is completely engulfed by lush, verdant forest. Amenities include a small pool, yoga classes (daily 8 A.M., $12, reservations required), hiking trails, a reading room, and board games. Casa Grande Café serves breakfast and dinner daily, lunch weekends only.

FOOD

Some of the tastiest and cheapest food in Puerto Rico can be purchased from street vendors, and the town of Utuado is a great place to experience that. All along Carretera 111 going into and out of town, there are vendors selling grilled *pinchos* (meat kabobs), *pollo al carbón* (barbecue chicken), *grandules* (pigeon peas), and fresh fruit.

Dinner at **El Fogón de Abuela** (Lago Dos Bocas, Utuado, 787/374-7793, http://elfogondeabuela.com, Fri.-Sun. 11 A.M.-7 P.M., $12-28) begins with a 10-minute boat ride to the lakeside restaurant (the last boat leaves the pier at 5 P.M.), where you can dine on a variety of traditional Puerto Rican dishes. Start with a fresh fruit frappe or the house cocktail, El Fiestón de Abuela, a refreshing mixture of vodka and tropical fruit juices. Then dine on whole fresh snapper, *churrasco,* stuffed *mofongo,* or shrimp in garlic sauce. The specialty of the house is choice of goat, veal, rabbit, or guinea hen served fricasseed. Service is extremely slow, so expect to spend a couple of hours at the restaurant. If you want to drive, continue south on Carretera

10 and turn left on Carretera 111. After the Lago Caonillas dam, turn left on Carretera 612 and drive to the end.

Rancho Marina (Lago Dos Bocas, Utuado, 787/894-8034, www.ranchomarina.com, Sat.-Sun. and Mon. holidays 10 A.M.-6 P.M., $11-22) is a charming open-air restaurant overlooking the lake serving traditional Puerto Rico dishes plus some unexpected creations, including rabbit in orange sauce and shrimp fried in *bacalaito* batter. For dessert have coffee flan or mango *tembleque*. Rancho Marina is accessible by boat from the pier.

Rasdan Panadería y Repostería (Carr. 111, km 4.0, Utuado, 787/814-0715, and 54 Calle Dr. Cueto, Ututado, 787/894-0621, 6 A.M.-10 P.M., $2-7) is a casual modern eatery that serves a wide selection of Puerto Rican cuisine, barbecue chicken, burgers, and sandwiches. But the real reason to go is fantastic selection of baked goods and pastries, including *mallorcas* (sweet buns), *budin* (bread pudding), and *pastelillo de guayaba* (guava turnover). There are also cakes, doughnuts, and cookies.

INFORMATION AND SERVICES

Banking services are available at **Banco Popular** (59 Calle Dr. Cueto, 787/894-2700). For pharmacy needs, visit **Walgreens** (Carr. 123, Edificio 940, 787/894-0574).

GETTING THERE

Utuado is 109 kilometers or 68 miles southwest of San Juan. Take Highway 22 west to Carretera 10 south.

Adjuntas

Situated along La Ruta Panorámico, Adjuntas is known as the "Switzerland of Puerto Rico" because of its cool temperatures. The municipality maintains an average 72 degrees year-round thanks to the high altitude. Adjuntas is also known as the "City of the Sleeping Giant," named after the shape of the mountain range's silhouette. The sleepy little agricultural town has a pleasant central plaza lined with a couple of pizza restaurants, a bakery, a souvenir shop, and a general store, selling everything from guitars to electric generators. In the early 1990s, Adjuntas gained notoriety for a rash of reports of UFO sightings in the area. An easy 20-mile drive up Highway 10 from Ponce, Adjuntas is a great centrally located place to explore the Cordillera Central for budget travelers looking for low-cost accommodations.

SIGHTS

Bosque Estatal de Guilarte (intersection of Carr. 518 and Carr. 131, 787/724-3647 or 787/829-5767, Mon.-Fri. 7 A.M.-3:30 P.M., Sat.-Sun. 9 A.M.-5:30 P.M.) is a 3,600-acre subtropical wet forest reserve featuring Monte Guilarte, the third-highest peak on the island at 3,953 feet above sea level. There is one marked trail, which offers a 30-minute hike to the mountain's summit. The forest has 26 bird species and 105 species of trees, including a eucalyptus grove. Unlike other forest reserves, Guilarte has five rustic cabins with bunk beds that rent for $20 a night. A permit is required, and visitors must provide their own bedding.

Take a 90-minute tour of a working coffee plantation at **Sandra Farms** (Carr. 548, km 4, Adjuntas, 787/409-8083, www.sandrafarms. com, daily 9 A.M.-3 P.M., $15, free for 12 and younger, 24-hour advance reservations required) and learn how coffee trees grow, learn about eco-processing, and discover why coffee grown in Adjuntas tastes so good.

Casa Pueblo (30 Calle Rodofo Gonzáles, 787/829-4842, www.casapueblo.org, daily

CORDILLERA CENTRAL

© JOSÉ OQUENDO

the pleasant Adjuntas town plaza

8 A.M.-4 P.M., $2 donation) is a 19th-century house that has been transformed by a local nonprofit environmental group into a cultural center with exhibition space, a small butterfly garden, a lending library, and a gift shop selling local coffee. The same group is restoring the nearby **Bosque del Pueblo,** a forest reserve that was once pit mined for copper. It now contains hiking trails and primitive campgrounds. Permits are required and can be obtained from Casa Pueblo.

SPORTS AND RECREATION

Lago Garzas (Carr. 518, south of Adjuntas), a 91-acre artificial lake, is primarily used to generate electricity. But it's also a great little fishing spot for largemouth bass, sunfish, catfish, and shad. A boat launch (787/829-3310) is open Monday-Friday 7 A.M.-7:30 P.M., Saturday-Sunday 9 A.M.-5:30 P.M.

Long-distance runners flock to Adjuntas for **El Gigante Marathon,** a 15-kilometer run held in mid-July. For details, call 787/829-3114.

ACCOMMODATIONS

Catering to Puerto Rican families, **Parador Villas Sotomayor** (Carr. 123, km 36.6, 787/829-1717 or 787/829-1774, www.paradorvillassotomayor.com, $121 s/d, $164 t/q, $203-250 two-bedroom for up to six people, $30 tent camping, $55 RV camping, plus tax) offers a modest place to stay for a modest price. The 14-acre grounds have 36 cabin-style accommodations including studios, suites, and two-bedroom apartments. Rooms come with air-conditioning, satellite TV, microwaves, coffeepots, and mini refrigerators. Larger rooms have full refrigerators and a stove top. Amenities include a swimming pool, tennis courts, game room, and playground. Horses, bikes, kayaks, and grills are available for rent. A restaurant and bar are on-site. All-inclusive packages are available.

FOOD

For an exclusive dining experience, a 19th-century coffee plantation provides the setting at

Casa Pueblo

Restaurante Vida Ventura (Hacienda Luz de Luna, Carr. 135, km 73.3, Adjuntas, 787/829-9096 or 787/210-6908, www.haciendaluzde-luna.com, $60 per person), where chef Ventura Vivoni serves an eight-course tasting menu to 36 lucky diners a couple times a month. Email the chef or check the Hacienda Luz de Luna website to find out when the next dining event is scheduled and make a reservation pronto. Vivoni's cuisine combines flavors from around the world and features mostly local ingredients.

Restaurant El Boricua (Carr. 5516, km 0.4, 787/829-1956, Mon.-Wed. 10 A.M.-9 P.M., Thurs. 10 A.M.-11 P.M., Fri. noon-1 P.M., Sat. 11 A.M.-4 A.M., Sun. 10 A.M.-11 P.M., $5-15) is a huge, rambling roadside restaurant featuring an enormous bar, pool tables, big-screen TVs, and a moderately priced menu serving everything from fried pork chops to crab stew to octopus salad. In typical fashion, there is a full bar and the restaurant is family friendly.

Traditional *criolla* cuisine is on the menu at **Restaurante Las Garzas** (Parador Villas Sotomayor, Carr. 123, km 36.6, 787/829-1717 or 787/829-1774, www.paradorvillassotomayor.com, Sun.-Thurs. 8 A.M.-8 P.M., Fri.-Sat. 8 A.M.-10 P.M., bar open until 10 P.M. Sun.-Thurs., until midnight Fri.-Sat., $5-23), and the selections are surprisingly diverse for such a small operation. There are several rabbit dishes as well as octopus salad, plantain soup, and *mofongo* stuffed with choice of octopus, *churrasco,* shrimp, chicken, or pork.

INFORMATION AND SERVICES

Medical services are provided by **Hospital Castañer** (Carr. 125, km 64.2, 787/829-1319). Banking services are available at **Banco Popular** (12-21 Calle San Joaquín, 787/829-2120).

GETTING THERE

Adjuntas is 125 kilometers or 77 miles southwest of San Juan. Take Highway 22 west to Carretera 10 south to Carretera 123 south. Adjuntas is 30 kilometers or 18 miles south of Ponce on Carretera 10.

CORDILLERA CENTRAL

Lares

CORDILLERA CENTRAL

Lares is considered the birthplace of Puerto Rican nationalism because it played a much-revered role in Puerto Rico's independence movement. On September 23, 1868, about 500 Puerto Ricans organized a revolt against Spanish rule in the town of Lares. Local stores and offices owned by Spanish merchants were looted, slaves were declared free, and city hall was stormed. For one day, Lares was free of foreign control for the first time since the arrival of Christopher Columbus.

The revolt was quickly squelched the next day, when rebel forces attempted to take over a neighboring town. The revolutionaries, including leaders Manuel Rojas and Juan Rius Rivera, were taken prisoner, found guilty of treason and sedition, and sentenced to death. But to ease the political tension that was brewing

on the island at that time, the revolutionaries were eventually released. Although the revolt, referred to as Grito de Lares, was ultimately unsuccessful, it did result in Spain giving the island more autonomy, and September 23 has become a national holiday.

Today Lares is best known for its production of Alto Grande coffee, a highly prized variety. And on its central plaza is a unique ice-cream shop that folks travel far and wide to visit.

SIGHTS

Centro 23 del Septiembre Plaza (Calle Dr. Pedro Albizu Campos, off Carr. 111) is the central plaza in Lares, and it is a testament to the town's brief independence from Spain's rule. In the plaza is a tamarind tree that was planted by beloved independence leader Dr. Pedro

the central plaza in Lares, Centro 23 del Septiembre Plaza

© JOSÉ OQUENDO

Albizu Campos in soil from several independent Spanish-speaking countries. Legend has it that when the tree bears an abundant amount of fruit, Puerto Rico will be free again.

FOOD

Heladería de Lares (Centro Calle 23 de Septiembre Plaza, Mon.-Thurs. 10 A.M.-5 P.M., Fri.-Sun. 9 A.M.-6 P.M., 787/897-3290 or 787/505-6299, $1.50 per scoop) has nothing like the 31 flavors at Baskin-Robbins. This unusual shop features a wide variety of uniquely flavored ice creams all made on the premises. The confection leans toward a light and fruity formula instead of a heavy butter base, but it's still very creamy and incredibly fresh. Try the sweet, nutty *maiz* (corn) flavor sprinkled with cinnamon. The outstanding pineapple flavor is studded with big chunks of fresh fruit. For something really unusual, try the rice and beans or plantain flavor.

INFORMATION AND SERVICES

Banking services are available at **Banco Popular** (12 Calle Vilella, 787/897-2670). For health services, go to **Lares Medical Center** (Carr. 111, km 2.9, 787/897-1444).

GETTING THERE

Lares is 114 kilometers or 71 miles southwest of San Juan. Take Highway 22 west to Carretera 129 south.

CORDILLERA CENTRAL

VIEQUES AND CULEBRA

Vieques and Culebra are two island municipalities a mere 8 and 17 miles, respectively, off the east coast of Puerto Rico, but the lifestyle there is light-years away from that of the main island. Referred to as the Spanish Virgin Islands, Vieques and Culebra are often described as "the way Puerto Rico used to be." The pace of life doesn't just slow down, it comes to a screeching halt. There are no fast-food restaurants or high-rise hotels, no golf courses or casinos, virtually no nightlife, and few tourist sights. And the only way to reach the islands is by plane or ferry. But what they do have are stunning beaches, world-class water sports, and lots of opportunity for R&R.

The small Spanish fort and museum El Fortín Conde de Mirasol on Vieques and the Museo Histórico de Culebra are the closest things to cultural attractions the islands have to offer. Instead, one of the main reasons to go is the islands' wide sandy beaches, the most popular being Balneario Sun Bay in Vieques and Playa Flamenco in Culebra. In addition to its beaches, Culebra and Vieques offer fantastic opportunities for diving and snorkeling. If you don't want to go on a group tour, excellent snorkeling from the beach at Playa Carlos Rosario in Culebra is easily accessible. And visitors to Vieques would be remiss not to visit the bioluminescent Mosquito Bay, which requires an overnight stay.

© SUZANNE VAN ATTEN

HIGHLIGHTS

© AVALON TRAVEL

LOOK FOR ◖ TO FIND RECOMMENDED SIGHTS, ACTIVITIES, DINING, AND LODGING.

◖ **El Fortín Conde de Mirasol:** Tour the last fort built by colonial Spain and see the 4,000-year-old remains of a man exhumed from an archaeological site in Vieques (page 262).

◖ **Mosquito Bay:** Take a guided kayak or electric pontoon boat to Vieques's biolumines-cent bay, where you can get up close and per-sonal with the water that glows an electric blue at night (page 263).

◖ **Balneario Sun Bay:** Vieques's mile-long, sandy, crescent-shaped beach on crystal-blue waters comes with bathroom, shower, and snack-bar facilities (page 265).

◖ **Playa Flamenco:** Puerto Rico's most cel-ebrated stretch of white sand and aquamarine water is in Culebra. It's considered one of the most beautiful beaches in the United States (page 281).

◖ **Diving in Culebra:** Culebra is surrounded by 50 dive sites, and excellent snorkeling can be found right off its beaches. One of the best sites is Playa Carlos Rosario, which features a long coral reef rich with sea life (page 283).

VIEQUES AND CULEBRA

PLANNING YOUR TIME

To get to Vieques and Culebra, you can fly from Ceiba or San Juan or take a ferry from Fajardo. If you're visiting for only a day or two, spring for the airfare to save time.

Although it's possible to get to your hotel and some of the islands' beaches using *públicos* (shared vans that carry multiple fares at a time), to fully explore the islands' remote beaches a rental car is recommended. Book early though, because they go fast.

Vieques and Culebra are such small islands that it's possible to spend a day and a night on

each one to get a cursory feel for them both. But the reason most people go is to experience the islands' unparalleled natural beauty and soak up plenty of R&R. To do those things properly, it takes a few days to reset your inter-nal clock to "island time" and achieve a blissful state of total relaxation.

HISTORY

Although details are sketchy, Vieques is be-lieved to have been inhabited by a series of in-digenous peoples possibly thousands of years before Christopher Columbus "discovered" Puerto Rico in 1493. Based on the discovery of remains found in Vieques, some historians date the earliest inhabitants to the Stone Age era more than 3,500 years ago.

Thanks to a few archaeological digs in Vieques, slightly more is known about the Saladoids, believed to have come from Venezuela around 250 B.C. They were followed by the Ostionoids around 400 B.C. and eventually the Taínos, a highly developed society of agriculturalists who lived on both Vieques and Culebra. The Taínos ruled Puerto Rico from about A.D. 1200 until the Spanish colonists wiped them out in the 1500s.

In the early 1500s, two Taíno brothers in Vieques journeyed to mainland Puerto Rico to help their fellow natives fight the Spanish conquerors. As a result, the governor of Puerto Rico sent troops to Vieques, where all the Taínos were killed or enslaved. For a long time after that, the islands became lawless havens for pirates who sought refuge in the protected harbors and ambushed passing ships.

In 1832 a Frenchman named Le Guillou, known as the founder of Vieques, arrived on the island. Under Spanish authority, he restored order to the island and helped launch a golden era of prosperity. He brought over other Frenchmen from Guadeloupe and Martinique who established sugarcane plantations and processing plants that exported the products to Spain. The operations were manned by hundreds of slaves from Africa and thousands of free workers from surrounding islands. In the early 1800s, the area around Esperanza was a thriving community with an opera house, a movie theater, and a cultural center. But as the town tried to expand to accommodate its growing population, difficulty in clearing the thick

vegetation led leaders to relocate the town center to Isabel Segunda in 1844. Vieques continued to enjoy its prosperity until around 1880, when the sugar industry began to decline because of the development of cheaper sources elsewhere.

It was around this time that Culebra was being settled in fits and starts. The first attempt was in 1875 by a black Englishman named Stevens, who was named governor and given the task of protecting the island's waters from pirates. Later that same year he was assassinated. He was followed in 1880 by a Spaniard, Cayetano Escudero Sanz, who established the first settlement, called San Ildefonso. The island's sole economy was agriculture.

Upon the ratification in 1898 of the Treaty of Paris, which ended the Spanish-American War, Vieques and Culebra came under the rule of the U.S. government. During World War II, the U.S. military became the major landholder on both islands and began to use them for bomb practice and defense-testing sites. Protests begun in Culebra in 1971 led the United States to abandon operations in 1975. But Vieques toughed through 24 more years until a civilian was accidentally killed by a bomb in 1999. Several years of persistent protesting followed, which captured international attention and led to the incarceration of many activists. In 2003, the Pentagon conceded and the Navy withdrew from Vieques. Its land— 15,000 acres on the east side, along with 3,100 acres on the west side that was ceded two years earlier—was handed over to the federal Fish and Wildlife Service, which has classified the property a National Wildlife Refuge.

Vieques

In a world where change is constant, it's nice to be reminded that some things stay the same. That is a big part of the charm of Vieques. Granted, a couple of new businesses have opened and a couple of them have closed. This hotel has changed names, and that one has a new coat of paint. But all in all, it's still just a sleepy little island where life moves at a snail's pace, cats and horses wander the island freely, and the only alarm clock you need is the crow of the roosters that run the place.

Just 21 miles long and 5 miles wide, Vieques is a natural wonderland. It is rimmed with primitive, fine-sand beaches, untouched by commercial development, and coral reefs that teem with undersea life. Among the island's mangrove forests is **Mosquito Bay,** one of the world's most spectacular bioluminescent bays. No visit to Vieques would be complete without a boat ride through luminescent blue waters. Inland Vieques is thickly forested hills and arid stretches of desert-like land. Bats are the only animal native to Vieques, but other wildlife commonly found includes geckos, iguanas, frogs, pelicans, seagulls, egrets, herons, doves, and horses, of course. Horses are a common mode of transportation in Vieques, and they can be seen following the same traffic laws as automobiles, stopping at four-way stops and so on. But they also graze and roam freely. The waters around the island are home to several endangered species, including the manatee and a variety of sea turtles, which nest on the beaches at night. The eastern side of the island is still off-limits to visitors, as the Navy continues to remove vestiges of its presence here. And 60 percent of the island is a protected wildlife sanctuary—**Refugio Nacional de Vida Silvestre de Vieques**—managed by the U.S. Fish and Wildlife Service. Some of the island's most beautiful primitive beaches are located here.

There are two primary communities on Vieques. On the north coast is **Isabel Segunda,** a.k.a. Isabel II, a traditional Puerto Rican town with a central plaza, an *alcaldía* (town hall), a post office, a grocery store, two banks—which contain the island's only ATMs—and the island's two gas stations. It is also where the ferry from Fajardo docks. There are a few shops, restaurants, and hotels here that cater to visitors, but Isabel Segunda is primarily a town where the island's residents conduct their daily business.

On the south coast is **Esperanza,** a funky, bohemian enclave where most tourists gravitate, thanks to the laid-back, "don't worry, be happy" atmosphere and the proximity of **Sun Bay,** one of the most gorgeous publicly maintained beaches in all of Puerto Rico. The main hub of Esperanza is along the oceanfront stretch of Calle Flamboyan, distinguished by the picturesque *malecón,* a boardwalk with balustrades, benches, and pavilions. From here you can also see Cayo Afuera, a small islet in spitting distance with excellent snorkeling on the western side. On the opposite side of the street is an inviting array of casual, open-air bars and restaurants that overlook the water and grow lively with tourists and locals—many of them "expats" from the mainland—as sundown approaches. There are also a handful of boutiques and a couple of guesthouses in the area, as well as the Vieques Conservation and Historical Trust, a modest institution but a great source of information on the island.

There are a few things travelers should know when visiting Vieques. The island has one of the highest unemployment rates in the United States, and petty theft from parked cars is a continuing problem. When in town, visitors are encouraged to keep their cars locked at all times and never to leave anything visible inside. The greatest threat to car break-ins is at

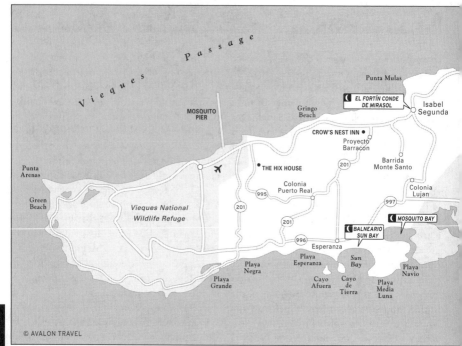

Punta Mulas

EL FORTÍN CONDE
DE MIRASOL

Isabel
Segunda

Gringo
Beach

CROW'S NEST INN

Proyecto
Barracón

Barrida
Monte Santo

201

MOSQUITO
PIER

THE HIX HOUSE

Colonia
Puerto Real

201

995

Colonia
Luján

997

201

MOSQUITO BAY

BALNEARIO
SUN BAY

Punta
Arenas

Green
Beach

Vieques National
Wildlife Refuge

996

Esperanza

Playa
Negra

Playa
Esperanza

Sun
Bay

Playa
Navio

Playa
Grande

Cayo
Afuera

Cayo
de
Tierra

Playa
Media
Luna

Vieques Passage

© AVALON TRAVEL

the beach. Drivers are encouraged to leave all the windows rolled down and the sunroof and glove box open to avoid having to pay the cost of replacing a broken window. And always park your car as close to you as possible—preferably away from any bushes and within sight range.

For well-heeled travelers, there are some outstanding and unique guesthouses that provide plenty of luxurious amenities. But outside those plush environs, there is a rustic quality to life here. Restaurants tend to be open-air, even nice ones, so don't expect a respite from the heat and humidity at dinner. When using public facilities, plumbing issues require toilet paper be disposed of in trash receptacles instead of being flushed, which can make for an odorous experience. And if you think restaurant service is slow on the main island of Puerto Rico, you haven't seen anything yet. Many businesses close or curtail hours during low season. Just when "low

season" is can be a topic of debate. To be safe, assume it's anything that isn't high season, which everyone seems to agree is mid-November through April. In fact, assume all hours of operation are more suggestions than fact. The secret to enjoying Vieques is to chill out and let things unfold in their own way and time.

SIGHTS
El Fortín Conde de Mirasol

Built between 1845 and 1855, El Fortín Conde de Mirasol (Fort Count Mirasol, Carr. 989, Isabel Segunda, 787/741-1717, www.enchanted-isle.com/elfortin/index.htm, Wed.-Sun. 10 A.M.-4 P.M., free) was the last fort built by the Spanish in the New World. Never attacked or used in battle, it originally housed Spanish troops and later became a jail and execution site. Among those incarcerated here were fugitive slaves from local sugar plantations and

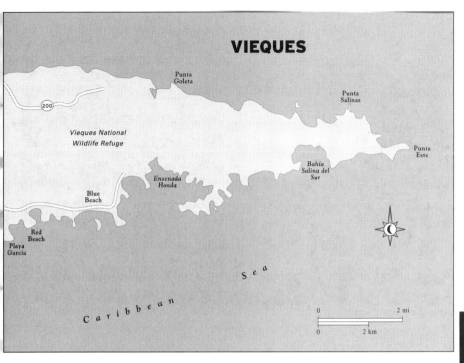

VIEQUES

Punta
Goleta

Punta
Salinas

200

*Vieques National
Wildlife Refuge*

Punta
Este

*Ensenada
Honda*

*Bahía
Salina del
Sur*

Blue
Beach

Red
Beach

Playa
Garcia

S e a

C a r i b b e a n

0   2 mi

0   2 km

VIEQUES AND CULEBRA

political prisoners who sought Puerto Rico's independence from Spain. Later it was used as a municipal jail until the 1940s, when it was closed and fell into disrepair. In 1989 the Institute of Puerto Rico began restoration of the fort, which still has its original brick floors, exterior walls, and hardwood beams. Today the fort is home to the **Vieques Museum of Art and History,** home of Hombre de Puerto Ferro, the 4,000-year-old remains of a man whose body was discovered in an archaeological site near Esperanza, as well as exhibits dedicated to the island's indigenous people, its historic sugarcane industry, and local artists. It also contains the Vieques Historic Archives.

Often referred to as Vieques Stonehenge, the archaeological site of Hombre de Puerto Ferro is on the south side of the island off Carretera 997. About 0.25 mile east of the entrance to Sun Bay, turn inland onto a dirt road that takes you to the fenced-off site. Giant boulders mark the spot where the remains were excavated in 1990. Some believe the boulders were placed around the grave; others say it's a natural phenomenon.

◖ Mosquito Bay

Mosquito Bay (off Carr. 997, near Esperanza, 787/741-0800) is the site of Vieques's celebrated bioluminescent bay, and no trip to the island is complete without a visit. Inside the Balneario Sun Bay complex, Mosquito Bay is a protected wildlife refuge not only because its fragile mangrove ecosystem is vital to the island's environmental health but also because it contains one of the most robust bioluminescent bays in the world. Harmless single-celled dinoflagellates that inhabit the warm water light up the bay with an electric blue glow when they sense motion.

Several outfitters in Vieques provide night excursions on kayaks or an electric pontoon

Isabel Segunda's *alcaldía*

© SUZANNE VAN ATTEN

boat for an up-close experience with the phenomenon. For best results, plan your trip during a new moon, when the bay glows brightest.

El Faro Punta Mulas

Built in the late 1800s, El Faro Punta Mulas (Calle Plinio Peterson, north of Isabel Segunda, 787/741-3141) looks less like a lighthouse and more like a modest, rectangular government building with a large light on top of it. It's still operational today but visitors can't enter the lighthouse.

Vieques Conservation and Historical Trust

Tucked between the bars and restaurants across from the *malecón* in Esperanza, Vieques Conservation and Historical Trust (138 Calle Flamboyan, Esperanza, 787/741-8850, www.vcht.org, daily 9 A.M.-5 P.M., free but donations accepted) is a small institution with a big mission to help protect and preserve the island's natural habitat. It was recently involved in a research project on the affect of light pollution on Mosquito Bay with the Scripps Institute of Oceanography in San Diego, California. It also runs a children's summer camp and leads tours to the Sugar Mill Ruins. Stop in to take a look at the aquariums containing local sea creatures or pick up some information on the island.

Refugio Nacional de Vida Silvestre de Vieques/National Wildlife Refuge

What was once the site of the U.S. Navy's Camp Garcia is now the largest wildlife refuge in the Caribbean (Carr. 997, halfway between Isabel Segunda and Esperanza, daily 6 A.M.-7:30 P.M. May-Aug., daily 6 A.M.-6:30 P.M. Sept.-Apr., free, 787/741-2138, www.fws.gov/caribbean/Refuges/Vieques). Encompassing 60 percent of the island, the 17,770-acre refuge contains a variety of natural habitats, including beaches, mangrove forests, and subtropical dry forest. It is home to four endangered plants and 10 endangered animals, including

the brown pelican and several species of sea turtles. Some of Vieques's finest primitive beaches are located in the refuge, including Playa Caracas/Red Beach, Playa Pata Prieta, Bahía de la Chiva/Blue Beach and Playa Plata/ Orchid Beach.

Sugar Mill Ruins

The Sugar Mill Ruins (off Carr. 201 near Playa Grande, west of Esperanza, call 787/741-8850 to schedule a tour, free) are what is left of Playa Grande Mill, one of four sugar mills that operated in Vieques beginning in the 1830s. It was closed in the early 1940s when the Navy arrived, and much of what was left has begun to

be reclaimed by Mother Nature, but there are still about a dozen buildings remaining.

BEACHES

Aside from Mosquito Bay, the main reason to come to Vieques is to enjoy the staggering beauty of its miles of remote, pristine beaches and clear, turquoise waters. Each beach has its own unique characteristics—some are calm and shallow, others have big crashing waves, and still others offer spectacular snorkeling. Several are accessible only from dirt trails, off road or by foot.

Although violent crime is uncommon in Vieques, the island has a petty theft problem, which can be avoided if you use caution. Be vigilant around beaches with bushes where culprits may hide. Never take anything of value to the beach, including digital cameras or personal ID. If someone can't watch your things while you swim, bring a "dry bag," available at dive shops, to contain a car key and a photocopy of your driver's license. Don't leave anything inside your car and be sure to roll all your windows down and open the glove box so it's apparent nothing is inside.

◖ Balneario Sun Bay

The island's best beaches are on the southern coast. The most spectacular is the long white crescent and calm waters of Balneario Sun Bay (Sombé) (Carr. 997, east of Esperanza, 787/741-8198, Wed.-Sun. 8:30 A.M.-5 P.M., $2-5). It's the only publicly maintained beach in Vieques. Surrounded by a tall cyclone fence, it has plenty of modern, fairly clean facilities, including bathrooms, showers, changing rooms, a snack bar, and guards. Camping is permitted for $10 a day, reservations required (787/741-8198). Adding to the charm of the place is the herd of horses that grazes here.

The Balneario Sun Bay complex also encompasses two smaller, more secluded beaches farther eastward along a sandy road. The first

THE ELECTRIC-BLUE WATERS OF MOSQUITO BAY

The evening starts at twilight with a bumpy ride through Esperanza in a rattly old school bus. The driver for Island Adventures motors along the seaside strip picking up adventurous patrons of all stripes along the way.

My fellow voyagers include an older couple and their adult daughter, a young family with two inquisitive little boys, a pregnant woman and her husband, and a half dozen rambunctious 20-somethings, whose high spirits suggest they've just left a nearby bar.

We arrive at the Island Adventures headquarters, a converted two-story house with a small office downstairs where we buy our tickets and peruse a small selection of T-shirts and postcards. We're instructed to go upstairs for a brief lecture. There we join others who had forgone the free pickup service and driven themselves.

The room resembles an elementary school science lab. Small tables and chairs fill the back of the room, bookshelves are lined with marine biology texts, and instructional posters fill the walls. Once everyone is assembled, we receive a child-friendly lecture, explaining just why the bioluminescent lagoon in Mosquito Bay glows.

The mangrove bay's rich nutrients and clean warm water create the perfect environment for sustaining the zillions of dinoflagellates that wash into the bay during high tide and remain trapped there when the tide recedes. The microscopic single-celled creature is unique in several ways. For one, it contains properties similar to both plants and animals. But more notably, when it senses motion, it experiences a chemical reaction that creates a burst of light not unlike that of a firefly.

Puerto Rico is said to have as many as seven bays rich in dinoflagellates, although only three are commonly known: Phosphorescent Bay in La Parguera on the southwest coast of Puerto Rico, Laguna Grande in Fajardo on the east coast, and Mosquito Bay in Vieques. Mosquito Bay is touted as one of the most spectacular bioluminescent bays in the world because of its high concentration of dinoflagellates and the absence of pollution and ambient light. Because darkness is required to see the glow, the best nights to tour the bay are when no moon is visible.

After our lecture we pile back into the bus and bounce our way over the rutted roads inside Balneario Sun Bay to reach Mosquito Bay Nature Reserve. Tonight is a new moon, and no matter how hard we peer out the windows, all we see is blackness. The bus pulls all the way up to the water's edge, where several guides and the boat captain await our arrival, and we unload, clutching our cameras and bug spray. A ramp appears from nowhere, and we walk across it to find our places on the bench seats that run along both sides of the electric pontoon boat.

Silently we motor across the calm waters into the dark lagoon. The sky is filled with constellations, which our guides point out and identify by name. We notice that the lip of the boat's wake looks an eerie pale blue. Then someone stomps loudly several times on the floor of the boat, and we see scores of blue zigzags radiating away from us—the underwater wakes of fish fleeing our path.

As we venture deeper into the lagoon, the night grows darker while the electric-blue glow of the water becomes more vivid.

Before April 2007, when the Department of Natural Resources banned swimming in the island's bioluminescent bays, the climax of the trip came when visitors were permitted to jump in and frolic in the bathtub-warm water, where they could swim, turn flips, and create water angels in the electric-blue drink. Now we must content ourselves with watching the boat's blue wake and spotting electric fish trails through the water. It's still a magical experience, but it's not quite the same.

After we motor back to shore and file onto the bus, we return to town in silence as everyone seems lost in thought. The bus makes intermittent stops in front of the crowded bars, restaurants, and guesthouses that line the strip in Esperanza. One at a time, we disembark and go our separate ways to eat dinner, have a few drinks, and marvel at the wonder of our nighttime journey through the electric-blue waters of Mosquito Bay.

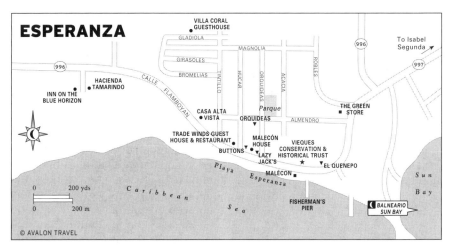

one you'll encounter is **Media Luna,** a protective cove where the water is shallow. Farther eastward is **Navio Beach,** which sometimes has large waves and is popular with gay beachgoers.

Other Beaches

Vieques has several remote and often deserted beaches that can be fun to explore. Some require a hike, so bring sturdy shoes. And don't forget the bug spray.

Playa Negra is a black-sand beach containing minute particles of lava, a reminder of the island's volcanic origins millions of years ago. To get there from the *malecón* in Esperanza, go west on Carretera 996 and turn left on Carretera 201. When you reach the sign for Gallery Galleon, pull off the road and park. Look for the bridge in the road and hike down into the dry creek bed beneath it. Follow the creek bed through a thickly wooded forest to the ocean.

Playa Grande is a long, thin strip of beach that curves around the southwestern tip of the island and is a great spot for walking and hunting for shells. Go when it's breezy because it can be buggy with sand fleas. It's located west of Esperanza off Carretera 201.

Green Beach is on Punta Arenas at the farthest most southwestern tip of the island, and

it features a shallow reef, making it ideal for snorkeling. Look for "flamingo tongues," a brightly colored sea snail that lives here. Nearby is Kiani Lagoon, a mangrove bay accessible by a wooden boardwalk that is rich with starfish. Green Beach is best visited early in the day or when it's breezy because it can be buggy with sand fleas. To access it take Carretera 200 as far west as possible, then follow the dirt road to the end. Look for the ancient ceiba tree with the massive trunk along the way.

Wilderness Refuge beaches are small, remote beaches tucked into the island's south central coastline, where the U.S. Navy's Camp Garcia was once located. From the entrance to the Refugio Nacional de Vida Silvestre de Vieques, located on Carretera 997 halfway between Isabel Segunda and Esperanza, there are four main wilderness beaches, and all of them are extraordinary.

Each one is a crescent of white, powdery sand, lapped by pale turquoise waters and rimmed with thick, lush vegetation. Measuring their distance from the entrance, they are **Playa Caracas/Red Beach** (2.4 miles), **Playa Pata Prieta** (2.7 miles), **Bahía de la Chiva/Blue Beach** (3 miles), and **Playa Plata/Orchid Beach** (4.4 miles). Note that the refuge closes at 6:30 P.M.,

© SUZANNE VAN ATTEN

horses grazing at Balneario Sun Bay

except May-August when it closes at 7:30 P.M. No camping, fires, or alcohol is permitted.

Esperanza Beach is a fairly unremarkable beach along Esperanza's strip of restaurants and guesthouses. But it's within walking distance if you're staying in town and offers excellent snorkeling, especially around Cayo Afuera, a tiny islet just offshore.

SPORTS AND RECREATION
Mosquito Bay Tours

Any trip to Vieques would be incomplete without a trip to the bioluminescent Mosquito Bay—unless, of course, you visit during a full moon, when the ambient light diminishes the visibility of the bioluminescent organisms that light up the water.

Island Adventures (787/741-0720, www.bio-bay.com, $25) operates a well-run tour of the bay that lasts about 2.5 hours and starts with a short bilingual lecture. Then guests are bused to Mosquito Bay, where they board an electric pontoon boat

that tools around the electric-blue water. Guides are exceedingly friendly and informative. You'll also get a lesson on the constellations.

If you want a more up-close and personal tour of the bay, **Blue Caribe Kayaks** (149 Calle Flamboyan, Esperanza, 787/741-2522) provides kayak tours of Mosquito Bay for $30 per person. Kayak rentals are also available for $10-15 per hour, $25-35 for four hours, and $45-55 all day. Snorkel-equipment rentals are also available.

Travesías Isleñas Yaureibo/Vieques Outdoors (Calle Flamboyan, Esperanza, 787/447-4104 or 939/630-1267, www.vieques-outdoors.com) offers snorkeling, kayaking, hiking, and biking tours. Bioluminescent bay kayak tours are offered nightly ($25 adults, $15 children). Meet at the *malecón* in front of Trade Winds Guest House. Snorkel tours cost $30, and hiking/biking tours are $30.

Abe's Snorkeling & Bio-Bay Tours (787/741-2134 or 787/436-2686, www.abes-norkeling.com, reservations required) offers a variety of kayak tours, ideal for exploring beaches, mangrove bays, the bio-bay, or undersea life. The two-hour bioluminescent tour in a double kayak is $40 adults, $20 children.

Snorkeling and Diving

The best diving in Vieques can be found along the fringe reefs on the southern side of the island. **Nan-Sea Charters** (787/741-2390, www.nanseacharters.com) offers half-day, two-dive trips starting at $100 from a 28-foot dive boat. One-tank shore dives are $60. Custom coral tours and diving certification courses are also available.

Combine a day of sailing and snorkeling with **Sail Vieques** in Isabel Segunda (787/508-7245, billwillo@yahoo.com). A half-day trip with snorkeling is $50, and a daylong trip to the southern tip of the Bermuda Triangle with snorkeling is $110. Captain Bill also offers a two-hour sunset cruise for $30.

Vieques Adventure Company (69 Calle Orquideas, Esperanza, 787/692-9162, www.bikevieques.com) offers kayak rentals ($45) and tours, as well as individual kayak fishing tours ($150).

Abe's Snorkeling & Bio-Bay Tours (787/741-2134 or 787/436-2686, www.abessnorkeling.com, reservations required) offers a variety of kayak tours, ideal for exploring beaches, mangrove bays, the bio-bay, or undersea life. The Cayo Afuera kayak and snorkel tour is $35 adults, $17.50 children. A Mosquito Pier snorkeling excursion designed for beginners costs $30 adults, $15 children. Custom tours are available.

Fun Brothers Hut (grass hut on the *malecón* across from El Quenepo, 787/435-9372, www.funbrothers-vieques.com) rents scooters, Jet Skis, and snorkel equipment. Take a guided kayak and snorkeling tour, with or without water scooters, or charter a 21-foot boat and captain for a custom outing to fish, ski, snorkel, wakeboard, or sightsee. Two-passenger scooters rent for $50 a day. Jet Skis and Waverunners are $60 for a half hour, $100 an hour. Snorkel gear

rents for $10 a day. A guided kayak and snorkel tour costs $35, or $50 with water scooter. Boat charters are $400 half day, $750 full day.

Blackbeard Sports (101 Calle Muñoz Rivera, Isabel Segunda, 787/741-1892, www.blackbeardsports.com, Mon.-Tues. 8 A.M.-5 P.M., Wed. 8 A.M.-5:30 P.M., Thurs.-Fri. 8 A.M.-5 P.M., Sat. 8 A.M.-4:30 P.M., Sun. 9 A.M.-3 P.M.) is the place to go to buy or rent mountain bikes or gear for snorkeling, diving, camping, and kayaking. You can also pick up all your needs for the beach. Kayak tours cost $75.

Fishing

Go inshore fishing for kingfish, amberjack, barracuda, pompano, and tarpon on a 21-foot Ranger bay boat with Captain Franco Gonzalez of **Caribbean Fly Fishing** (61 Calle Orquideas, Esperanza, 787/741-1337 or 787/450-3744, www.caribbeanflyfishingco.com, $375 half day, $650 full day, including gear and tackle, two-person maximum).

Fun Brothers Hut (grass hut on the *malecón* across from El Quenepo, 787/435-9372, www.funbrothers-vieques.com) charters a 21-foot boat and captain for custom outings to fish, ski, snorkel, wakeboard or sightsee ($400 half day, $750 full day).

Paddleboarding

The stand-up paddleboard is a great way to explore the island. At **Vieques Paddleboarding** (787/366-5202, www.viequespaddleboarding.com) the four-hour downwind tour travels 2-4 miles, depending on wind conditions, along the north and south shores ($85). Or take a three-hour tour across the bay, through a mangrove forest, ending at a beach with a snorkel ($65). Kids 11 and younger can ride with adults for $20.

Horseback Riding

Explore the island atop a locally bred Paso Fino horse with **Esperanza Riding Company** (787/435-0073, www.esperanzaridingcompany.

com, cash only, reservations required). Two-hour guided tours through hills, meadows, riverbeds, and beaches cost $70. A private guided tour is $100. Children 7 and younger can take a 20-minute, hand-led pony trail ride for $15. Due to the small stature of the breed, there is a weight limit of 225 pounds for riders. Long pants and closed-toe shoes are recommended.

Mountain Biking

Landlubbers looking to explore inland Vieques can get a guided, off-the-beaten-path mountain-bike tour with **Vieques Adventure Company** (69 Calle Orquideas, Esperanza, 787/692-9162, www.bikevieques.com). Bikes rent for $25 a day, two-day minimum, and include a helmet, a lock, and a trail repair kit. Half-day tours are $95. Combination bike-kayak-snorkel tours are also available.

ENTERTAINMENT AND EVENTS
Cockfights

If there is such a thing as politically correct cockfighting, it exists in Vieques, where the birds do not fight until death. Winners are proclaimed by judges before the birds are seriously harmed. Fights are held at **Gallera Puerto Real** (Carr. 200, about three miles west of Isabel Segunda, no telephone), typically on Friday nights and Sunday afternoons, although the schedule changes. Admission is $10; women are admitted free. Food and alcohol are served.

Bars

If partying into the wee hours is your idea of the perfect vacation, Vieques may not be the place for you. There are no nightclubs, discos, or casinos on the island, and many of the restaurants close by 10 P.M. There are a couple of watering holes that stay open late, though. Salty sea dogs gravitate to the no-frills **Bananas Guesthouse, Beach Bar & Grill** (Calle Flamboyan, Esperanza, 787/741-8700, www.bananasguesthouse.com, daily 11 A.M.-10 P.M.,

bar stays open later). A sign behind the bar proudly proclaims: "This Is A Gin-u-wine Sleazy Waterfront Bar." Ask the bartender what the drink special is, and she's likely to respond: "A beer and a shot." But it also serves a potent rum punch made with three kinds of rum. There are eight small guest rooms on-site if you drink too much and can't drive home.

Apologies to Bananas, but the real "gin-u-wine sleazy waterfront bar" in Vieques is **Al's Mar Azul** (577 Calle Plinio Peterson, Isabel Segunda, 787/741-3400, Sun.-Thurs. 11 A.M.-1 A.M., Fri.-Sat. 11 A.M.-2:30 A.M.). Hanging right over the water, this pleasant dive bar is cluttered with a random collection of junk that looks as if it has been sitting around the place for decades: old lifesaving rings, an inflated blowfish, paper lanterns, the grill off a jeep, a huge plastic turtle, a carved coconut head. It doesn't serve food, but someone will call your order in and pick it up for you at Mamasonga across the street. It's also home of the annual Spam Cookoff every May. There are some worn pool tables and video poker games if you're compelled to do something besides drink and chat up the locals who hang here. And if you really get bored, there's a dusty bookshelf filled with tattered paperbacks. It's the perfect place to nurse a hangover with a spicy Bloody Mary on Sundays.

Lazy Jack's Pub (61A Calle Orquideas, corner of Calle Flamboyan, Esperanza, 787/741-1447, www.lazyjacksvieques.com, daily noon-late, $8-14) serves food, but the reason to come is the well-stocked bar, the entertainment, and the convivial patrons. Beginning at 9 P.M., there's entertainment every night, ranging from live bands to DJs to karaoke to Wii competitions. The menu features pub fare like jalapeño poppers and chicken fingers, as well as a selection of hand-rolled thin-crust pizzas.

Duffy's Esperanza (on the *malecón*, 787/741-7600, www.duffysesperanza.com, 11 A.M.-11 P.M., bar closes 2:30 A.M. Fri.-Sat.,

$6-13) is primarily a great bar where you can down a few cold ones, rub elbows with the locals, and watch the ocean waves roll in. The bar serves artisan beers from Abita, Anchor, Goose Island, North Coast, and Old Harbour in San Juan, as well as a menu of creative cocktails, including the Viequense, a combination of vodka, passion fruit liqueur, orange juice, and cranberry juice. The menu features pub fare such as nachos, burritos, burgers, and an Italian hoagie. For something more substantial, try the Caribbean crab cakes or curry chicken *pastelillos*. Brunch is served 10 A.M.-2 P.M. Sundays and features a Bloody Mary bar.

If you're looking for something less rustic and more chic, **Living Room Bar** (W Retreat & Spa, Carr. 200, km 3.2, 787/741-4100, www.wvieques.com) is a cool, sleek oceanfront lounge serving creative cocktails and tapas.

Festivals

There are two major festivals in Vieques. The biggest one is **Fiestas Patronales de Nuestra Señora del Carmen** (787/741-5000), which is held on the plaza of Isabel Segunda Wednesday-Sunday during the third weekend of July. Attractions include parades, religious processions, a small carnival, and lots of live Latin music and dancing. Entertainment usually starts around 9 P.M. and lasts until the wee hours of the morning. Festivities are fueled by *bili*, a traditional beverage made from a local fruit called *quenepa* mixed with white rum, cinnamon, and sugar.

The other big event is the **Cultural Festival** (787/741-1717), sponsored by the Institute of Puerto Rican Culture at El Fortín Conde de Mirasol in Isabel Segunda after Easter. Festivities include folk music and dance performances, a craft fair, and a book fair.

SHOPPING
Clothing
Vieques Yacht Club Shopping Court (Calle Orquideas, Esperanza, 787/741-1447, daily noon-5 P.M.) boasts a quartet of pocket shops situated around a gravel courtyard. Vendors include Modamar, selling jewelry and handbags; Tropical Treasures, a resort wear boutique; Tropical Footprints, a shoe store and Crocs dealer; and VQS Emporium, a variety store selling housewares, cigars, and books, among other items.

Diva's Closet (134 Calle Flamboyan, Esperanza, 787/741-7595, daily 10 A.M.-5 P.M.) is the place to go for funky, chunky jewelry, floral print bathing suits, and a variety of resort wear.

Kim's Cabin Clothing Boutique and Gifts (136 Calle Flamboyan, Esperanza, 787/741-3145, daily 9:30 A.M.-5 P.M.) sells Haitian metal art, sea-glass earrings, and cotton beach wear.

Sol Creation (370 Calle Antonio G. Mellado, Isabel Segunda, 787/741-1694 or 808/280-6223, www.solcreationclothing.com, Mon.-Sat. 10:30 A.M.-4:30 P.M.) is a clothing boutique specializing in floaty, bohemian styles in silk and cotton, plus jewelry, bags, and more.

Jewelry
The Crystal Dolphin (134 Calle Flamboyan, Esperanza, 787/741-2424, castilloenvieques@ gmail.com, daily 10 A.M.-5 P.M.) sells beautiful hand-crafted silver jewelry by husband-and-wife proprietors, as well as other artisans.

Arts and Crafts
At first glance you might think **Vieques Flower and Gifts** (134 Calle Flamboyan, Esperanza, 787/741-4197, www.viequesgifts-andflowers.com, daily 9 A.M.-6 P.M. Nov.-May, daily 10 A.M.-5 P.M. summer) is another souvenir shop selling T-shirts and tchotchkes, but you'll also find artisan-made *vejigante* masks and pottery made by local artists.

Billing itself as Vieques's first craft gallery, **Caribbean Walk** (353 Calle Antonio G. Mellado, Isabel Segunda, 787/741-7770, www.caribbeanwalk.com, Mon.-Sat. 9 A.M.-5 P.M.) sells hand-crafted items by 55 artisans, including jewelry, dolls, paintings, carvings, and more.

Vibrant original paintings and prints on canvas of tropical flowers, fish, palm trees, and jungle scenes by local artist Siddhia Hutchinson can be found at **Siddhia Hutchinson Fine Art Design Studio and Gallery** (Carmen Hotel, Calle Muñoz Rivera, 787/741-1343, http://siddhiahutchinson.com, Mon.-Sat. 10 A.M.-4 P.M.). The artwork has also been tastefully reproduced on ceramics, dinnerware, rugs, and pillows.

Food Markets

Buen Provecho (353 Calle Antonio G. Mellado, Isabel Segunda, 787/529-7316, Tues.-Sat. 10 A.M.-6 P.M.) is a gourmet market selling organic goods, fresh produce, and specialty foods, including artisan cheeses and live lobsters.

The Green Store/La Tienda Verde (corner of Calle Flamboyan/Carr. 996 and Calle Robles, 787/741-8711, daily 9 A.M.-9 P.M.) is a small market selling everything you need to set up house for a week—coffee, toilet paper, bug spray, beer, etc.

ACCOMMODATIONS
$50-100

If you don't mind not staying on the beach, there are several options for the budget-minded traveler. **Villa Coral Guesthouse** (485 Calle Gladiolas, Esperanza, 787/741-1967, www.villacoralguesthouse.com, $80-85 s/d, $160-185 two-bedroom apartment) is a clean, comfortable six-room guesthouse in a residential neighborhood several blocks from the *malecón*. Rooms come with a queen bed, window air-conditioning unit, ceiling fan, a mini-refrigerator, and a coffeepot—but alas, no coffee. Towels are refreshed every four days, and laundry facilities are reserved for weekly guests. There's a covered porch with wireless Internet, board games, magazines, and a microwave, plus a rooftop terrace with a view of the ocean. The

owners also have a one-bedroom cottage with a full kitchen and satellite TV a couple blocks away that rents for $795-895 a week.

Casa Alta Vista (297 Calle Flamboyan, Esperanza, 787/741-3296, fax 787/741-3296, www.casaaltavista.net, $80 s, $90-95 d, $115-175 for 4 people, plus tax) is a small, tidy 10-room guesthouse featuring modern bathrooms and extra-comfy mattresses. There's no TV, telephone, or pool, but the air-conditioning and mini-refrigerator keep things cool. A rooftop sundeck offers a 360-degree view of the island, three-quarters of it ocean. If it's available, ask for room 12—it has got the best view of the ocean and hillsides. Registration is in the small market on the first floor. Scooter, bicycle, snorkeling gear, beach chair, umbrella, and cooler rentals are available on-site. There is also a one-bedroom apartment, and some rooms are wheelchair-accessible.

Trade Winds Guest House and Restaurant (Calle Flamboyan, Esperanza, 787/741-8666, fax 787/741-2964, www.tradewindsvieques. com, $80-90 s/d, plus tax) is a better restaurant than it is a guesthouse, but it's conveniently situated in the middle of Esperanza and across the street from the *malecón* (sea walk). The 10 rooms are small, windowless, and spartan, but they're clean and have firm mattresses. There's no TV or telephone, but some rooms have air-conditioning. The rooms open onto a scrappy courtyard with plastic patio furniture, and there's a decent restaurant and bar upstairs.

Just want a cheap place to crash? If you don't plan to spend much time in your room, **Bananas Guesthouse, Beach Bar & Grill** (Calle Flamboyan, Esperanza, 787/741-8700, www.bananasguesthouse.com, $70-90 s/d, $100 d with private terrace, plus tax) may meet your needs. In the back of the popular Bananas bar and restaurant, this bare-bones guesthouse has eight small, rustic, dimly lit rooms with deck flooring. There's no TV or telephone, but some rooms have air-conditioning, screened porches, and mini-refrigerators.

$100-150

Perched on an inland hillside overlooking the main island is the lovely, lushly landscaped ◖ **Crow's Nest Inn** (Carr. 201, km 1.1, Isabel Segunda, 787/741-0033 or 877/276-9763, www.crowsnestvieques.com, $115-139 s/d, $139 one-bedroom suite, $250 two-bedroom suite, plus tax, includes continental breakfast). The Spanish hacienda-style inn has 16 well-appointed modern rooms, all with air-conditioning, TV, and a kitchen or kitchenette. Amenities include a small pool and an excellent restaurant, Island Steakhouse. Snorkel-gear rental is available.

There's something positively Mediterranean about the exterior appearance of **Casa La Lanchita** (374 N. Shore Rd., Isabel Segunda, 787/741-8449 or 800/774-4717, www.viequeslalanchita.com, $120-190, four-night minimum stay). The bright white four-story structure with archways and balustrades is built right on the sandy beach of a brilliant blue sea and is surrounded by flowering bougainvillea. Despite the posh exterior, the rooms are modestly appointed with budget rattan and metal furnishings, but each room has a private terrace and full-size kitchen.

$150-250

Luxury has many different definitions, and Vieques seems to have a unique hotel to match each one. The ultramodern boutique hotel **Bravo Beach Hotel** (1 N. Shore Rd., Isabel Segunda, 787/741-1128, www.bravobeach-hotel.com, $125-225 s/d, $425 villa, plus tax; no children under 18 permitted) is a study in glamorous minimalism. Nine rooms and a two-bedroom villa are located in a cluster of small bungalows painted pastel shades of green, blue, and yellow. Each room is different, but the spacious interiors all feature stark white walls that create a dramatic contrast to the dark mahogany platform beds and modular furnishings made of wood and glass. Some rooms have ocean-view balconies and floor-to-ceiling windows. One room has 180-degree windows and a king-size canopy bed. Each room has satellite TV, air-conditioning, a mini-refrigerator, wireless Internet, a DVD player, and a PlayStation. The bathroom is stocked with Aveda bath products, and the beds are made with Italian Frette linens. Although it's on the ocean, the hotel doesn't have a swimmable beach. Instead there are two swimming pools, one oceanside. A poolside bar and lounge serves a limited menu, and the newly opened BBH restaurant serves tapas ranging $8-14 and boasts a large wine selection.

◖ **Malecón House** (105 Calle Flamboyan, Esperanza, 787/741-0663, www.malecon-house.com, $175-265 s/d, $235-305 t/q, plus tax; two-night minimum required) is a modern two-story guesthouse overlooking the *malecón*. It was built in 2010 and has brought a new level of sophistication to the area. Rooms come with air-conditioning and ceiling fans; some rooms have mini refrigerators and balconies. Amenities include a small pool, rooftop deck, wireless Internet in common areas, and continental breakfast.

Victorian elegance is the theme at ◖ **Hacienda Tamarindo** (Calle Flamboyan, just west of Esperanza, 787/741-8525, fax 787/741-3215, www.haciendatamarindo.com, $125-245 s, $135-285 d, $175-245 suites, $240-300 two-bedroom suites, $350 penthouse or two-bedroom villa, plus tax and service charge). Built around a 200-year-old tamarind tree that's rooted in the lobby and shades the second-floor breakfast room, this beautifully appointed hotel is furnished in a tasteful combination of antique Caribbean and Victorian styles. Folk art, wall murals, and vintage circus posters provide playful touches. There are 13 rooms and three suites. Each one is different, but they all contain basket-weave furnishings, brightly colored bedspreads, and air-conditioning. Rooms have neither TVs nor telephones, but each one comes with folding chairs,

© SUZANNE VAN ATTEN

view from the *malecón* in Esperanza

oversize towels, and coolers for the beach or pool. The hotel doesn't have a restaurant per se, but it does serve a free breakfast, and a box lunch can be prepared if requested the night before. There's also a 24-hour honor bar. No one under age 15 is permitted.

A romantic getaway doesn't get any more lovely or secluded than **Inn on the Blue Horizon** (Calle Flamboyan, west of Esperanza, 787/741-3318 or 787/741-0527, fax 787/741-0522, www.innonthebluehorizon.com, $160-375 s/d, plus tax and energy charge). The small 10-room inn perched on a cliff overlooking the ocean hosts many weddings and is geared primarily toward couples. Rooms are exquisitely furnished with poster beds, antiques, and original artwork. Amenities include a small gym, pool, lighted tennis courts, and an inviting pavilion bar. Rooms have air-conditioning but no TV or telephone. **Carambola** restaurant serves upscale Caribbean fusion cuisine, and the **Blue Moon Bar and Grill** serves breakfast and lunch

in a lovely open-air pavilion-style restaurant overlooking the ocean.

Avant-garde architecture in a thickly wooded setting distinguishes the most unusual hotel in Puerto Rico, **◖The Hix House** (Carr. 995, km 1.6, 787/741-2302, www.hixislandhouse.com, $135-450 s/d, plus tax and service charge). Four unpainted concrete buildings house 13 "lofts," many with open sides, outdoor showers, and ocean views. Designed by architect John Hix to have as little impact on its 13 acres as possible, the property uses solar energy and recycles used water to replenish the vegetation. There's no TV or telephone, but the linens are Frette, the pool is spectacular, and each morning the kitchen is stocked with juices, cereal, breads, and coffee. Yoga classes are conducted in the pavilion, and in-room or garden massages are available.

Over $250

An anomaly in every way, **W Retreat & Spa** (Carr 200, km 3.2, 787/741-4100, www.

© SUZANNE VAN ATTEN

For a tasty, budget-friendly breakfast or lunch, try Belly Buttons.

wvieques.com, $419-1,339 s/d, plus resort fee and taxes) is a megaresort that brings chic style and plush luxury to the rustic environs of Vieques. Located on a low cliff right on the beach, the resort has 156 accommodations ranging from standard rooms with garden views to high design "retreats" with direct access to the ocean. Amenities include chef Alain Ducasse's MiX on the Beach plus two other restaurants, a lounge, a spa, tennis courts, a fitness room, a business center and infinity pool. Rooms come with air-conditioning, flat-screen TVs, coffeemakers, hair dryers, and balconies.

FOOD
Breakfast
There are several terrific breakfast spots in Vieques. In addition to your typical eggs, **Mamasonga** (Calle Plinio Peterson, Isabel Segunda, 787/741-0103, Wed.-Mon. 9 A.M.-2 P.M., $4-9) serves great German apple pancakes and French toast, plus muesli for the health-conscious. Lunch items include black-bean soup, burgers, nachos, Cuban sandwiches, quesadillas, and salads. There's also a full bar.

You can't miss **Belly Buttons** (62 Calle Flamboyan, Esperanza, 787/741-3336, daily 7:30 A.M.-2 P.M., Thurs. and Sun. 5-9 P.M., breakfast $4-8, lunch $6-9), just look for two tin-roofed shacks trimmed in neon green with brightly colored picnic tables and umbrellas out front. That's the place to go for a cheap lunch or breakfast. In addition to typical breakfast fare, check out the specials. If you're lucky the thick, tasty banana pancakes will be on the menu. Lunch includes burgers, hot wings, fish and chips and tuna salad. Thursday night is Mexican night and Sunday night is rib night.

Puerto Rican and Caribbean
◖ **El Quenepo** (148 Calle Flamboyan, Esperanza, 787/741-1215, reservations@ elquenepovieques.com, Wed.-Sun. 5:30-9:30 P.M. June-Aug., Tues.-Sun. 5:30-10 P.M.

Thanksgiving-May, closed Sept. to mid-Nov., $20-32) is hands-down the finest restaurant in Vieques. Owner-chef Scott Cole is creating sublime new interpretations of *criolla* cuisine, and his wife Kate, who runs the front of the house, knows how to provide the kind of service diners expect from a top-dollar establishment. Together they have created a casually elegant oasis of fine dining. Open to the sea on one side, the interior is hung with long white sheers, and wall sconces provide just enough lighting to make everyone look more attractive than they really are. Soft jazz noodles in the background. The effect is instantly calming. And then there is the food. The menu includes calabaza gnocchi pan-seared in brown butter and served with toasted pumpkin seeds, goat cheese, and pomegranate molasses; jasmine rice-crusted calamari, Peking duck pad Thai; breadfruit *mofongo* stuffed with lobster. And that's just the regular menu. There are usually several daily specials to choose from as well.

French chef Alain Ducasse brings his impressive pedigree to **MiX on the Beach** (W Retreat & Spa, Carr. 200, km 3.2, 787/741-4100, www.wvieques.com/mix, daily 7:30-11 A.M. and 6-10 P.M., $22-39), an elegant, ocean-side restaurant specializing in Caribbean cuisine. Breakfast includes short-rib hash served with poached egg and hollandaise sauce and MiX Benedict, served with choice of crab or lobster and a spicy hollandaise. Dinner options include almond-coconut gazpacho, roasted lobster with curry, and pineapple tart.

Restaurante Bili (144 Calle Flamboyan, 787/741-1382 or 787/402-0357, www.viequescatering.com, daily 11 A.M.-11 P.M., lunch $8-16, dinner $10-29) is a veteran restaurant that must be doing something right because it has been in business for many years, but every time I visit, I become so frustrated with the service I never make it past my first cocktail. It's not that the service is slow; it's nonexistent and borders on rude. I can heartily recommend

the watermelon *mojito,* though. It's made with fresh pulp and really hits the spot. The extensive menu features wraps, sandwiches, and salads for lunch. Dinner includes *chuletas can can,* whole fried snapper, paella, and various lobster dishes. Seating is provided inside the open-air restaurant or alfresco on a patio overlooking Calle Flamboyan and the ocean.

Because many restaurants on Vieques close early, it's good to know where to find a decent restaurant open later in the evening every day. That place is **Richard's Café Restaurant** (Carr. 200, just west of downtown Isabel Segunda, 787/741-5242, daily 11 A.M.-3 P.M. and 5-11 P.M., $7-19). The dim lighting, fast-food decor, and fake flowers don't create much of an atmosphere inside the pink concrete structure. But it serves good traditional Puerto Rican cuisine, including *pastelillos, mofongo,* steak, seafood, and lobster. The full bar serves a terrific passion fruit punch, made with Grand Marnier, rum, and pineapple juice.

Coconuts (59 Calle Benitez Guzman, Isabel Segunda, 787/741-9325, Fri.-Tues. 5:30-10 P.M., $10-20) is a casual eatery serving Caribbean fare, including fish and chips, shrimp *pincho* (kabobs) with coconut noodle salad, and beer-steamed pork ribs in a Malta barbecue sauce.

American

Tucked behind Lazy Jack's on the *malecón,* **Orquideas** (61 Calle Orquideas, Esperanza, 787/741-1864, www.orquideasvqs.com, lunch daily 10 A.M.-7 P.M., dinner Wed.-Mon. 6-10 P.M., lunch $10-16, dinner $19-30) is a quaint little spot containing two independent restaurants. During the day it serves basic deli fare, such as club sandwiches and tuna salad, which can be served to guests on the covered wooden porch or prepared to go for pickup. At night, the fare is more ambitious, including pan-seared duck in plum wine reduction and seafood-stuffed lobster.

Bananas Guesthouse, Beach Bar & Grill

(Calle Flamboyan, Esperanza, 787/741-8700, www.bananasguesthouse.com, daily 11 A.M.-about 10 P.M., bar stays open later, $5-17) is a casual drinking hole serving mostly American pub fare, including burgers, wings, and hotdogs, as well as jerk chicken, ribs, and grilled fish. There are eight small guest rooms in the back.

Veritas Restaurant (Crows Nest Inn, Carr. 201, km 1.1, Isabel Segunda, 787/741-0011, http://veritasvqs.com, Tues.-Sat. 5-10:30 P.M., Sun. brunch 10 A.M.-2:30 P.M., $10-25) boasts a romantic setting surrounded by thick foliage and twinkle lights, providing a charming backdrop to the ambitious menu that includes wild mushroom ravioli in sage and port wine reduction sauce and Caribbean lobster macaroni and cheese. Place your order by 8:30 P.M. the night before, and Veritas will deliver a picnic lunch basket to your hotel room or guesthouse the next morning, ideal for taking to the beach. The menu includes salads, wraps, a cheese plate, and more for $7-10.

Seafood and Steak

Chez Shack (Carr. 995, km 1.8, 787/741-2175, Mon. and Wed.-Sat. 5:30-10 P.M., $16-26) really is a shack. It's constructed of tacked-up sheets of corrugated metal strung with twinkle lights and surrounded by thick forest, but folks flock here for the homestyle food, the steel-drum band, and the convivial spirit. The menu is always changing, so check the chalkboard. Options often include grilled mahimahi and barbecue ribs. Mondays are Reggae Grill Night.

Carambola (Inn at the Blue Horizon, Calle Flamboyan, west of Esperanza, 787/741-3318, www.innonthebluehorizon.com, daily 8 A.M.-3 P.M., 5-10 P.M., $18-29, reservations recommended for dinner) serves Caribbean cuisine in an elegant setting overlooking the sea. Menu includes conch ceviche, grilled mahimahi with *amarillos* and chorizo salad, and whole fried snapper.

Trade Winds Restaurant (Calle Flamboyan,

Esperanza, 787/741-8666, fax 787/741-2964, www.tradewindsvieques.com, Thurs.-Mon. 7:30 A.M.-2 P.M. and 6-9:30 P.M., dinner daily 5-9:30 P.M., $14-34) is a casual open-air restaurant that overlooks the water and serves grilled fish, steak, lobster, pork loin, pasta, *mofongo,* and coconut curry. For dessert, try the piña colada bread pudding with warm rum sauce. There are 10 small guest rooms behind the restaurant.

Mexican

Decorated with vintage pictures of banditos and revolutionaries, **Cantina La Reina** (351 Calle Antonio G. Mellado, Isabel Segunda, 787/741-2700, www.cantina-lareina.com, Tues.-Sat. 5-10 P.M., Sun. brunch 11 A.M.-2 P.M., $13-20) serves typical Mexican fare with flair, including fish tacos, fajitas, burritos, and the catch of the day served with mango salsa. And the bar serves a long list of tequilas, as well as a variety of margaritas, specialty cocktails, sangria, and a short list of beers and wines. Reservations are accepted.

INFORMATION AND SERVICES

All of the services on Vieques are in Isabel Segunda. The **tourism office** (787/741-0800, Mon.-Fri. 9 A.M.-4 P.M.) is on the plaza in Casa Alcaldía (town hall). But for the most comprehensive, up-to-date information, visit www.enchanted-isle.com, www.vieques-island.com, www.viequestravelguide.com, and www.travelandsports.com/vie.htm.

To stay abreast of local goings-on, pick up a copy of *Vieques Events* (www.viequesevents.net), both printed in English and Spanish.

The island's only bank, with an ATM, is **Banco Popular** (115 Calle Muñoz Rivera, 787/741-2071). Nearby, on the same street, is the **post office** (787/741-3891). You'll find the **police station** (Carr. 200, km 0.2, 787/741-2020 or 787/741-2121) at the corner of Carretera 200 and Carretera 997, and the **fire department** can be reached by calling 787/741-2111.

For health services, **Centro de Salud de Familia** (Carr. 997) is open Monday-Friday 7 A.M.-3:30 P.M., and the emergency room is open 24 hours. Serving visitors' pharmacy needs is **Farmacia San Antonio** (Calle Benitez Guzman across from Casa Alcaldía, 787/741-8397).

Self-serve laundry **Familia Ríos** (Calle Benítez Castaño, 787/438-1846) is open Sunday-Monday and Wednesday-Friday 6 A.M.-7 P.M., and Saturday 6 A.M.-5 P.M.

GETTING THERE
By Ferry

The **Puerto Rico Port Authority** (in Vieques 787/741-4761 or 787/863-0705, or 800/981-2005, daily 8-11 A.M. and 1-3 P.M.) operates a daily ferry service between Vieques and Fajardo.

The **passenger ferry** is primarily a commuter operation, and it can often be crowded—especially on the weekends and holidays when vacationers swell the number of passengers. Reservations are not accepted, but you can buy tickets in advance. Arrive no later than one hour before departure. Sometimes the ferry cannot accommodate everyone, in which case passengers with a Puerto Rico ID get priority over visitors. The trip typically takes about an hour to travel between Fajardo and Vieques, and the fare is $4 round-trip per person. Note that ferry schedules can change, but the schedule was as follows:

- **Fajardo to Vieques:** daily 9:30 A.M., 1 P.M., 4:30 P.M., and 8 P.M.
- **Vieques to Fajardo:** daily 6:30 A.M., 11 A.M., 3 P.M., and 6 P.M.

There is also a weekday **cargo/car ferry,** for which reservations are required. But be aware that most car-rental agencies in Puerto Rico do not permit their automobiles to leave the main island. The best option is to leave your car in Fajardo and rent another car on Vieques. The trip usually takes about two hours, and the cost

is $15 for small vehicles and $19 for large vehicles. The schedule is as follows:

- **Fajardo to Vieques:** Monday-Friday 4 A.M., 9:30 A.M., and 4:30 P.M.
- **Vieques to Fajardo:** Monday-Friday 6 A.M., 1:30 P.M., 6 P.M.

By Air

As almost anyone who's taken the commuter ferry from Fajardo to Vieques will tell you, the best way to get to the island is by air. Several small airlines fly to Vieques from the main island, and the flights are fairly inexpensive and speedy.

In San Juan, flights can be arranged from Luis Muñoz Marín International Airport near Isla Verde or from the smaller Isla Grande Airport near Old San Juan. But the shortest, cheapest flight is from the newly opened José Aponte de la Torre Airport on the former Roosevelt Roads Naval Base in Ceiba on the east coast. Round-trip flights are about $125 from San Juan and $60 from Ceiba. Flights between Vieques and Culebra are about $70.

Vieques Air Link (787/534-4221, 787/534-4222, or 787/741-8331) offers flights to Vieques from San Juan International, Isla Grande, St. Croix, and Ceiba.

Seaborne Airlines (340/773-6442 or 866/359-8784, www.seaborneairlines.com) flies to Vieques from San Juan International, Isla Grande, St. Thomas, St. Croix, and Beef Island, Tortola.

Air Flamenco (787/724-1818, 787/721-7332, 877/535-2636, www.airflamenco.net) offers flights from Ceiba and Isla Grande. Charter flights are available.

Air Sunshine (787/741-7900 or 800/327-8900, www.airsunshine.com) has flights to Vieques from San Juan International, St. Croix, and St. Thomas.

Cape Air (787/741-7734 or 800/352-0714, www.capeair.net) offers flights to Vieques from San Juan International and St. Croix.

GETTING AROUND

Unless you plan to park yourself at one of the island's full-service hotels and never leave it, you're going to need a rental car to get around. *Públicos* are a great way to get from the ferry or airport to your hotel, but beyond that, they're not as reliable as the taxi service mainland Americans may be accustomed to.

If you do rent a car, book it well in advance of your arrival. They get snapped up quickly. Rental fees start around $80 per day, and penalties can be accrued if you return it with excessive sand inside, damp seats, or less gas in the tank than when you got it. Most vehicles are four-wheel drives because many of the beaches require off-roading to reach. Blowouts are not unusual, so make sure your car has a full-size replacement tire and the tools necessary to change it. If you need assistance changing the tire, the rental-car agency may send someone to help, but again, it will cost you. The seatbelt law is enforced, as are speed limits, which are mostly 35 miles per hour, except in town and on beach roads, where it's 10-15 miles per hour.

There are only two gas stations on the island, and they're both on Carretera 200 in Isabel Segunda, just west of the plaza. Because gas is shipped from San Juan on weekdays only, gas shortages are not unusual, and sometimes gas stations close early on Sundays, since that's the day everyone goes to the beach, including the gas-station operators.

Remember that semiwild horses roam freely on Vieques. Because many roads in Vieques are unlit, it's nearly impossible to see the horses in the dark, so take extra care when driving at night.

Público

Públicos can typically can be found waiting for fares at the airport or ferry. They can also be called randomly throughout the day for pickup service, although some travelers report that they are not always reliable or timely. Fares are typically $5 in town and $8 to various sites and beaches on the island.

You can usually pick up a list of *público* operators at the airport. Here is a partial list: **Jorge Belardo** (787/206-3130 or 787/741-2116), **Diego Quiñones** (787/364-7895), **Miguel Diaz** (787/485-3470), and **Fernando Roldán** (407/446-4299).

Taxi service is provided by **Ana** (787/313-0599) and **Rafael** (787/385-2318).

For travelers seeking transportation from San Juan to Fajardo to catch the ferry to Vieques, **Travel with Padin** (787/355-6746 after 6 P.M. for English, 787/644-3091 8 A.M.-6 P.M. for Spanish, http://enchanted-isle.com/padin/) operates 24-hour *público* service between Fajardo and the Luis Muñoz Marín International Airport in San Juan.

Car Rentals

Car rentals start at about $80 per day in Vieques, and most vehicles are jeeps or other four-wheel-drive automobiles. Some agencies will deliver a rental to the airport or your hotel; others require a *público* ride to the office. Agencies include **Martineau Car Rental** (787/741-0087 or 787/741-3948, www.martineaucarrental.com), **Vieques Car and Jeep Rental** (787/741-1037, www.viequescarrental.com), and **Steve's Car Rental** (787/741-8135, www.enchanted-isle.com/steves).

Culebra

As laid-back as Vieques is, it's practically Las Vegas compared to Culebra. Halfway between mainland Puerto Rico and St. Thomas, the tiny amoeba-shaped archipelago with 23 surrounding cays is just four miles by seven miles. The island is home to 3,000 residents and has one small community—**Dewey** (commonly called "Pueblo" or "Town")—on **Ensenada Honda harbor,** where the ferry docks.

Culebra has yet to be discovered by the tourism industry, but experienced divers know it as one of the best diving spots in the Caribbean. The clear clean waters are practically untouched by people and their polluting by-products, thanks in part to the arid island's absence of rivers or streams. The result is superb underwater visibility and healthy, intact coral systems that support a wide variety of sea life.

Recognizing the island's vital role as a natural wildlife habitat, President Theodore Roosevelt proclaimed much of the island a National Wildlife Refuge in 1909, which today encompasses 1,568 acres. Nonetheless, in 1939 the U.S. Navy made Culebra its primary gunnery and bomb practice site and continued its operations here until 1975, when it turned its focus to Vieques.

The island is a combination of hilly terrain with dry subtropical forest and a highly irregular coastline punctuated by cliffs, mangrove forests, and spectacular sandy coral beaches. Because it is so sparsely inhabited, Culebra is home to many endangered species and is an important nesting site for birds and sea turtles. Playa Flamenco is celebrated as one of the best beaches in the United States. But there are many other smaller beaches to discover, some completely deserted much of the time.

Accommodations in Culebra are mostly small mom-and-pop guesthouses, some little more than spare bedrooms. The operations here are mostly self-serve. In fact, it's not unusual for visitors to have the run of the place when owners decide to head to the beach or bar to while away the day. But a handful of small luxury hotels and condo rental units service travelers who want more modern-day amenities. At the dozen or so restaurants service typically moves at a snail's pace, and there are a couple of bars, but little real nightlife.

Because water is shipped from San Juan, shortages are not unusual, and pressure is often low. Some smaller properties have limited hot water or none at all. Plumbing in general can be problematic—the standard practice is to discard toilet paper in the trash instead of flushing it. And alarm clocks are never necessary, because you're sure to be woken by one of the roosters that roam the island. An anomaly in the world, Culebra is virtually crime-free. Instead of petty theft, visitors need only brace themselves against the voracious mosquitoes and sand gnats that tend to invade around dusk.

Culebra is one of the last vestiges of pre-tourism Puerto Rico. Nobody's in a hurry, modern conveniences are few, and all anybody really wants to do is go to the beach. That's the way people in Culebra like it, and most of them want to keep it that way. Visitors are advised to embrace the island's quirky inconveniences and sleepy pace of life to fully appreciate its many rare charms.

SIGHTS

If you spend any time in Culebra, you're bound to enter the **Culebra National Wildlife Refuge** (787/742-0115, Mon.-Fri. 7:30 A.M.-4 P.M., free). It encompasses 1,568 acres, including much of Flamenco Peninsula, where 60,000 sooty terns nest, as well as mangrove forests, wetlands, coastline, surrounding cays (except Cayo Norte), and **Monte Resaca,** the island's

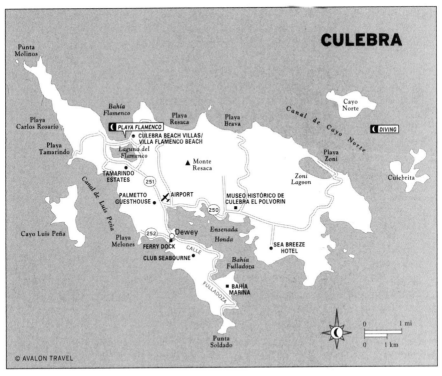

highest point at 650 feet, which contains forested canyons, ravines, and a unique habitat known as the boulder forest. The refuge contains excellent beaches, diving, bird-watching, and hiking. Culebrita, Cayo Luis Peña, and Monte Resaca are open daily sunrise-sunset. Other areas are off-limits to visitors. For maps and information, visit the refuge office, east on Carretera 250, just past the cemetery.

Museo Histórico de Culebra El Polvorin (off Carr. 250 toward Playa Brava, 787/405-3768 or 787/742-3832, Thurs. Sun. 10 A.M.-3 P.M.) is a newly created museum of history on the island that features old maps and photographs of Culebra, Taíno artifacts, traditional canoes made from the zinc plant, and Navy artifacts. It's located at the site of the first settlement in Culebra, in a 1905-era stone building that once stored ammunition for the Navy.

BEACHES

Once you see Culebra's craggy coastline of hidden coves, private beaches, coral outcroppings, and cays, it's easy to imagine why pirates liked to hide out here. Playa Flamenco is the island's most celebrated beach, and rightly so. But there are many less populated and more remote beaches to be found for those willing to hike in.

◖ Playa Flamenco

Named one of "America's Best Beaches" by the Travel Channel, Playa Flamenco (north on Carr. 251 at dead-end) is one of the main reasons people come to Culebra. It's a wide, mile-long, horseshoe-shaped beach with calm, shallow waters and fine white sand. The island's only publicly maintained beach, it has bathroom facilities, picnic tables, lounge-chair

© SUZANNE VAN ATTEN

Ensenada Honda harbor, Dewey

and umbrella rentals, and a camping area. You can buy sandwiches and alcoholic beverages at Coconuts Beach Grill in front of Culebra Beach Villa, as well as from vendors who set up grills and blenders in the ample parking lot. An abandoned, graffiti-covered tank remains as a reminder of the Navy's presence. It can get crowded on summer weekends and holidays—especially Easter and Christmas.

Other Beaches

If Playa Flamenco is too crowded, take a 20-minute hike over the ridge and bypass the first small beach you encounter to reach the more private **Playa Carlos Rosario,** a pleasant, narrow beach flanked by coral reef and boulders. It offers excellent snorkeling around the long, vibrant stretch of coral reef not too far offshore. Other great snorkeling and diving beaches are **Punta Soldado** (south of Dewey, at the end of Calle Fulladoza), which also has beautiful coral reefs; **Playa Melones,** a rocky beach

and subtropical forest within walking distance of Dewey; and **Playa Tamarindo,** where you'll find a diversity of soft corals and sea anemones.

Excellent deserted beaches can also be found on two of Culebra's cays—**Cayo Luis Peña** and **Culebrita,** which is distinguished by a lovely but crumbling abandoned lighthouse and several tidal pools. To gain access, it is necessary to either rent a boat or arrange a water taxi. And be sure to bring water, sunscreen, and other provisions; there are no facilities or services on the islands.

At the far eastern side of the island at the end of Carretera 250 is **Playa Zoni,** which features a frequently deserted sandy beach and great views of Culebrita, Cayo Norte, and St. Thomas.

Playa Brava has the biggest surf on the island, but it requires a bit of a hike to get there. To reach the trailhead, travel east on Carretera 250 and turn left after the cemetery, and then hike downhill and fork to the left. Note that Playa Brava is a turtle-nesting site, so it may be off-limits during nesting season from April to June.

© SUZANNE VAN ATTEN

Playa Flamenco

Like Playa Brava, **Playa Resaca** is an important nesting site for sea turtles, but it is ill-suited for swimming because of the coral reef along the beach. The hike to Playa Resaca is fairly arduous, but it traverses a fascinating topography through a mangrove and boulder forest. To get there, turn on the road just east of the airport off Carretera 250, drive to the end, and hike the rest of the way in.

Turtle-Watching

Culebra is one of three nesting grounds for hawksbill and leatherback turtles, the latter of which is the largest species of turtle in the world, weighing between 500 and 1,600 pounds. From April to early June, the sea turtles spend the evenings trudging up the beach at Playa Resaca and Playa Brava to dig holes and lay eggs before returning to the sea in grand displays of sand-tossing to cover their tracks. Visitors are not permitted on the beaches at night during nesting season.

SPORTS AND RECREATION
◖ Diving

Culebra more than makes up for its dearth of entertainment options with its wealth of diving opportunities. There are reportedly 50 dive sites surrounding the island. They're mostly along the island's fringe reefs and around the cays. In addition to huge diverse coral formations, divers commonly spot sea turtles, stingrays, puffer fish, angel fish, nurse sharks, and more.

Among the most popular dive sites are **Carlos Rosario (Impact),** which features a long, healthy coral reef teeming with sea life, including huge sea fans, and **Shipwreck,** the site of *The Wit Power,* a tugboat sunk in 1984. Here you can play out your *Titanic* fantasies and witness how the sea has claimed the boat for its habitat.

Many of the best dive sites are around Culebra's many cays. **Cayo Agua Rock** is a single 45-foot-tall rock surrounded by sand and has been known to attract barracudas, nurse

SEA TURTLES

© JOHN THOMPSON

One of the most magnificent sights you can witness in the waters around Vieques and Culebra is a sea turtle. A chance encounter is reason enough to go diving or snorkeling in the area. Three species of sea turtles can be found in the area, all of them are endangered and protected.

The **leatherback sea turtle** is the largest species of sea turtle, weighing between 500 and 2,000 pounds and reaching lengths from four to eight feet. It is distinguished by seven pronounced ridges that run down the length of the shell, which has a rubbery texture and is primarily black with white spots. Leatherback sea turtles feed mostly on jellyfish, but they also like to eat sea urchins, squids, crustaceans, fish, seaweed, and algae. They dive as deep as 4,200 feet and can stay submerged for up to 85 minutes.

The **green sea turtle** has a hard, smooth shell mottled in shades of black, gray, green, brown, and yellow. Its head is small and its lower jaw is hooked. It tops out at 350 pounds, is around three feet long, and is the only sea turtle that just eats plants.

The **hawksbill sea turtle** is the smallest species at 180 pounds and three feet long. It is distinguished by the serrated edges of its shell, its beak-shaped mouth, and the brown and white pattern of its shell and skin. The hawksbill lives in coral reefs and primarily eats sea sponges, but also sea anemones, jellyfish, and Portuguese Man o' War.

Sea turtles mate every couple of years, and the females return to the beaches of their birth to lay their eggs in pits they dig in the sand. When they hatch, the tiny turtles crawl to the water where they swim to offshore feeding sites. This is a vulnerable time in their life cycle because birds and lizards feed on the eggs and hatchlings. Nesting may occur anytime between March and October, depending on the species, during which time beaches may be closed to the public unless they are part of a turtle watch program, approved by the Puerto Rico Department of Natural and Environmental Resources.

For more information about the turtles and conservation efforts, visit the **Wider Caribbean Coastal Sea Turtle Conservation Network**'s website at www.widecast.org.

sharks, and sea turtles. **Cayo Ballena** provides a 120-foot wall dive with spectacular coral. **Cayo Raton** is said to attract an inordinate number and variety of fish. And **Cayo Yerba** features an underwater arch covered in yellow cup coral, best seen at night when they "bloom," and a good chance to see stingrays.

The island's sole diving and snorkeling source, **Culebra Divers** (across from the ferry terminal in Dewey, 787/742-0803, www.culebradivers.com), offers daily snorkeling trips for $45. One-tank dives are $60, and two-tank dives are $85, including tanks and weights. Snorkeling and dive gear is available for rent. It's also a good place to go for advice on snorkeling from the beach.

Other Water Sports

Aquafari Culebra (787/245-4545, http://kayakingpuertorico.com) offers a kayaking and snorkeling tour of Culebra, including ferry tickets from Fajardo ($70 per person).

Mamacita's

Las Palmas Paddle (508/237-9652) offers paddleboard tours starting at $40 per person. Introductory tours for beginners as well as adventure packages for experienced paddlers are available.

Day & Night Boat Tours (787/435-4498) offers day-long snorkeling trips to Culebrita, including drinks, snacks, and gear ($75 per person). Custom fishing, snorkeling, and sightseeing tours can be arranged.

Bicycling

Culebra Bike Shop (Calle Fulladoza, 787/742-0589, daily 9 A.M.-6 P.M.) rents bikes, tents, umbrellas, chairs, ice chests, kayaks, and snorkel gear.

Dick & Cathie's Bike Rental (787/742-0062) rents mountain bikes and delivers to your hotel ($17 a day).

Yoga

Culebra Yoga (787/435-3629, www.culebrayoga.com) offers yoga classes at various outdoor locations around the island, including a sunset yoga class at Flamenco Beach. Drop-in classes are $12. Private classes are available.

ENTERTAINMENT

Nightlife is limited on Culebra, but sometimes even nature lovers and beachcombers need to cut loose. **El Batey** (Carr. 250, km 1.1, 787/742-3828, Fri.-Sat. 10 P.M.-2 A.M., also serves lunch) provides that opportunity. Dancing is the primary attraction at this large no-frills establishment, where DJs spin salsa, merengue, and disco on Friday and Saturday nights. It also serves deli sandwiches and burgers ($3-5) during the day.

Everybody who goes to Culebra ends up at **Mamacita's** (64 Calle Castelar, 787/742-0090, www.mamacitaspr.com, Sun.-Thurs. 4-10 P.M., Fri.-Sat. 4-11 P.M.) at some point. The popular open-air watering hole right on the canal in Dewey attracts both locals and visitors. Two side-by-side tin-roofed pavilions provide shade for the cozy oasis appointed with brightly painted tables and chairs surrounded by potted palms. The blue tiled bar is tricked out with colorful folk art touches painted in shades of turquoise, lime green, and lavender. Behind the bar you can buy cigarettes and condoms, and you can get a spritz of bug spray free of charge when the sand gnats attack. Happy hour is 3-6 P.M. daily. Try the house special cocktail, the Bushwhacker, a frozen concoction of Kahlúa, Bailey's Irish Cream, coconut cream, rum, and amaretto. Check the chalkboard for excellent daily dinner specials.

The Sandbar (ferry dock, 787/742-1060, Mon.-Thurs. 3 P.M.-midnight, Fri.-Sat. 3 P.M.-2 A.M., Sun. 3 P.M.-midnight, $3-7) is a pleasant dive bar serving a variety of beers and cocktails in a small, cool spot with colorful paintings of sea creatures on the walls and ceiling.

SHOPPING

Shopping is limited to mostly shops selling tourist trinkets, but **Butiki** (74 Calle Romero, Dewey, daily 9 A.M.-2 P.M. and 4-8 P.M., 708/935-2542, www.butikiculebra.com) stands out for offering a great selection of batik fabrics, purses, jewelry by local artisans, and seascape oil paintings by owner Evan Schwarze.

Located across the street from airport entrance, **Colmado Costa del Sol** (Calle 1, 787/742-0599, Mon.-Sat. 7 A.M.-9 P.M., Sun. 7 A.M.-noon) is a bright yellow building selling a good selection of dry goods, meats, produce, and frozen foods.

Island Boutique (ferry dock, 787/742-0343, daily 10 A.M.-1 P.M. ad 3-5 P.M.) is a small boutique selling silver jewelry, sun dresses, floppy hats, and postcards.

ACCOMMODATIONS

Some properties require a minimum stay, although exceptions may be made for a surcharge. It's worth asking if you don't mind the extra cost.

Under $50

Playa Flamenco Campground (Playa Flamenco, 787/742-7000, $20, cash only) is not necessarily the place to go if you want a quiet spot to commune with nature. It's more like party central on weekends, holidays, and in summer, when the grounds can get crowded. Facilities include toilets, outdoor showers, and picnic tables. Reservations are required. If you can't get through by phone, write to Autoridad de Conservación y Desarrollo de Culebra (Attn.: Playa Flamenco, Apartado 217, Culebra, PR 00775).

$50-100

The Spanish-style guesthouse 🎧 **Posada La Hamaca** (68 Calle Castelar, Dewey, 787/742-3516, www.posada.com, $83-97 s/d, $115 studio, $145 one-bedroom that sleeps 8, plus tax) is under new management and has updated itself with new furnishings and fresh paint inside and out. The 10 rooms are light, airy, and tidy, and they come with satellite TV, air-conditioning, mini-refrigerators, free Internet, and hot water. There's a large shady deck overlooking the canal out back with two gas grills. Beach towels, coolers, and free ice are provided for trips to the beach. It's within walking distance of the ferry dock.

In town on Ensenada Honda is **Casa Ensenada** (142 Calle Escudero, 787/241-4441 or 866/210-00709, www.casaensenada.com, $85-100 s/d, $100-150 studio, $115-175 one-bedroom, plus tax). Despite its small size and modest aesthetics, this three-room guesthouse has everything you could need. Rooms are outfitted with air-conditioning, satellite TV, VCRs, hot showers, and kitchenettes, and a telephone, high-speed Internet, fax, and copier are on-site. For trips to the beach, towels, chairs, coolers, umbrellas, and ice are available.

$100-150

Mamacita's Guesthouse (64 Calle Castelar, 787/742-0090, $102 s, $115 d, including tax)

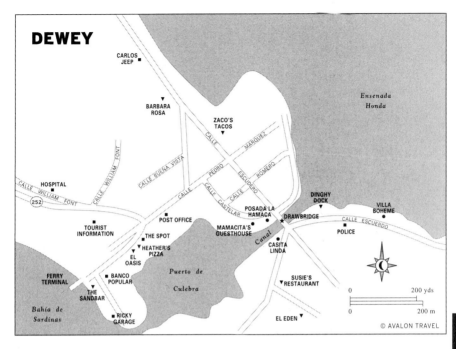

DEWEY

CARLOS JEEP

BARBARA ROSA

ZACO'S TACOS

CALLE MARQUEZ

CALLE BUENA VISTA

CALLE PEDRO

CALLE ESCUDERO

CALLE ROMERO

CALLE WILLIAM FONT

HOSPITAL

CALLE WILLIAM FONT

252

CALLE CASTELAR

POST OFFICE

TOURIST INFORMATION

THE SPOT

HEATHER'S PIZZA

EL OASIS

MAMACITA'S GUESTHOUSE

POSADA LA HAMACA

DRAWBRIDGE

CASITA LINDA

Canal

DINGHY DOCK

VILLA BOHEME

CALLE ESCUERDO

POLICE

FERRY TERMINAL

BANCO POPULAR

THE SANDBAR

RICKY GARAGE

Puerto de Culebra

Bahía de Sardinas

SUSIE'S RESTAURANT

EL EDEN

Ensenada Honda

0   200 yds

0   200 m

© AVALON TRAVEL

is a pastel-colored hodgepodge of balconies and archways squeezed between Calle Castelar and the canal. The hostel-like accommodations are strictly functional and feature air-conditioning and satellite TV in the bedrooms. It's best suited for those just looking for a place to crash and a hopping bar and excellent restaurant on-site. Laundry facilities and boat dockage are available for guests. Internet access is available for a fee.

Palmetto Guesthouse (128 Manuel Vasquez, two blocks behind Carlos Jeep, 787/742-0257 or 787/235-6736, www.palmettoculebra.com, $95 s, $130 d) is a modest six-unit property in the residential part of Dewey, within walking distance of the airport. One of the few properties that don't boast a view of the water, it makes up for its location with the "we aim to please" attitude of its owners, former Peace Corps volunteers Mark and Terrie Hayward. The small, tidy rooms are appointed with modern furnishings, air-conditioning, and

mini-refrigerators. Common areas include two kitchens, a computer with Internet access, and a TV with a DVD/VCR player (but no cable or satellite access). Beach chairs, umbrellas, boogie boards, and coolers are provided free of charge for a small deposit. The shady backyard has a deck and gas grill. Co-owner Mark Hayward also operates an informational website on Culebra at http://culebrablog.com.

Vista Bella Apartments (on Ensenada Honda, 787/644-6300 or 787/742-0549, www.islaculebra.com/puerto-rico/vista-bella-apartments.htm, $120 studio, $163 one-bedroom that sleeps four, $218 two-bedroom that sleeps six) has four new, modern, and spacious apartments that come with kitchens, air-conditioning, large covered balconies, and a spectacular view of Ensenada Honda.

An option right on Playa Flamenco is **Villa Flamenco Beach** (Playa Flamenco, 787/742-0023, Jan.-Apr., $125-135 studio, $150

© SUZANNE VAN ATTEN

camping on Playa Flamenco

one-bedroom, plus tax). The two-story pink-and-green concrete structure contains six tidy, basic units. There are four studio apartments with kitchenettes, air-conditioning, and hot water, which sleep two, and two efficiency apartments with full kitchens, hot water in the shower only, and no air-conditioning, which sleep four. A couple of rooms have beachfront balconies. The place is low-key and self-serve. Bring insect repellent.

$150-250

€ **Villa Boheme** (368 Calle Fulladoza, 787/742-3508, www.villaboheme.com, $115-150 s, $165-215 d, plus tax) has a lovely Spanish hacienda-style exterior and landscaped grounds right on Fulladoza Bay. Inside are 11 cheerfully appointed rooms with air-conditioning and hot water. Some rooms have private balconies and small kitchens; others share a communal kitchen in the patio area, which also contains satellite TV. A large terrace spans the length

of the rambling property and overlooks the bay. Guests may use the dock, equipped with water and electricity, for $2 per foot per night. Moorings are also available for rent.

Right on Playa Flamenco, **Culebra Beach Villas** (Playa Flamenco, 787/767-7575 or 787/754-6236, or 877/767-7575, www.culebra-beachrental.com, www.culebrabeach.com, $125 studio, $175-195 one-bedroom, $215-225 two-bedroom, $300 three-bedroom, plus tax) offers 33 individually owned cottages and rooms with air-conditioning and kitchens, some with TVs but no Internet or telephones. The rooms are fairly spartan, but the cottages have decks and covered porches. The service is minimal, although linens and towels are provided. Request a newer unit in the back of the complex if available. Basic pub fare can be had at the open-air waterside Coconuts Beach Grill. Just be sure to bring your insect repellent—it gets buggy.

€ **Club Seabourne** (Carr. 252, Calle Fulladoza on Ensenada Honda, 787/742-3169

the canal in Dewey

or 800/981-4435, fax 787/742-0210, www. clubseabourne.com, $189 pool cabana room, $219 one-bedroom villa, $329 two-bedroom, including tax), is a charming property with 14 units overlooking Fulladoza Bay. There is a New England vibe to the gray clapboard villas with pitched tin roofs dotted around the wooded property. The rooms are quite luxe, with super plush canopy beds and balconies. Rooms have air-conditioning but no TV or telephone. A lovely landscaped pool surrounded by umbrella tables overlooks the bay, as does the poolside bar. Fine dining can be had at Club Seabourne Restaurant, serving Caribbean cuisine on a screened porch on Fridays and Saturdays. Rates include breakfast, courtesy cocktails, one hour of free kayak rental, and transportation to and from the airport and ferry. Kayaks, snorkeling equipment, bikes, beach chairs, and umbrellas are available for rental, and picnic lunches are available by request.

Even more modern amenities can also be found at **Bahía Marina** (Punta Soldado Rd., km 2.4, 787/742-0535 or 866/285-3272, fax 787/742-0536, www.bahiamarina.net, $151-179 one-bedroom apartment, $295 two-bedroom, plus tax). This hilltop row of 16 corporate-looking apartments with sleeper sofas in the sitting rooms comes with kitchenettes, air-conditioning, cable TV, and ocean-view balconies. There's also a large pool and an open-air bar and restaurant.

For total seclusion, you can't do much better than **Tamarindo Estates** (off Carr. 251 just south of Playa Flamenco, 787/742-3343, www.tamarindoestates.com, $160-175 one-bedroom, $240 two-bedroom, two-bath, plus tax). The property is on the wildlife refuge and features 12 simply furnished, hillside cottages on 60 acres overlooking the water and Cayo Luis Peña. Units are three or six to a building, and they look like they were furnished by a flea market, which gives them a quaint homespun vibe. Each one contains a TV, a

VCR, air-conditioning in the bedroom, a fully equipped kitchen, a screened porch, and a roof-top veranda. Internet access is available in the common computer room. The rocky beach directly in front of the property offers great snorkeling, and a short hike north is a sandy beach for swimming. There's also a small pool on-site, but no restaurant or bar.

Over $250

Sea Breeze Hotel (Carr. 250, km 1.8, 855/285-3272, www.seabreezeculebra.com, $250-295) is a large complex overlooking the bay featuring 160 units, more than half of which are privately owned condominium units. The rest are hotel suites with microwaves, mini refrigerators, air-conditioning, and balconies. There are no TVs or daily housekeeping services. Amenities include a swimming pool, a pool-side bar and grill, and Juanita Bananas, a popular local restaurant that relocated to the hotel's lobby in 2011.

FOOD

The concept of service is very different here from what stateside dwellers may be accustomed to. Things move at a slow, casual pace, so it's best to be patient and prepared to linger for awhile. Also, note that operating hours can change unexpectedly, and some restaurants close up shop completely for weeks at a time.

Puerto Rican

Barbara Rosa (Carr. 250, 787/742-0073, Thurs.-Mon. 5-9 P.M., $8-14) is located between the airport and the school in a modest house with a large front porch. When the Christmas lights are on and the bed sheet has been removed from the sign, Barbara Rosa is in business. Diners place their orders at the kitchen, pick up their plates when their names are called, and clear their own dishes when they're done. Dining is alfresco on the front porch and the food is homey and filling. The menu includes grilled kingfish, plantain-crusted mahi, fried shrimp, and *churrasco*. The pumpkin soup and red beans are especially good. Note that Barbara Rosa is probably the only restaurant in all of Puerto Rico that doesn't have a bar, but you're welcome to bring your own bottle. And be prepared to wait. The restaurant gets crowded and it is a one-woman operation.

The name says it all. At **Dinghy Dock** (Calle Fulladoza, south of the drawbridge, on Ensenada Honda, 787/742-0233, or 787/742-0518, daily 8 A.M.-2:30 P.M. and 6-9:30 P.M., dinner $9-30) boats literally dock beside your table at this casual waterfront spot. Plastic patio chairs line a narrow dock under a hanging roof. The cuisine is standard Puerto Rican featuring Angus steaks, tuna, and lobster. Breakfast includes waffles and French toast. Check out the huge tarpon swimming below waiting for a handout. There is a full bar, which is a good thing because service takes forever.

Seafood and Steak

One of Culebra's finest restaurants, **Juanita Bananas** (Carr. 250, km 1.8, 787/742-3171, 787/742-3855, or 787/402-5852, www.juanitabananas.com, daily noon-10 P.M., $12-32) is owned by chef Jennifer Daubon, born to a family of restaurateurs in Culebra who received her culinary training at Johnson and Wales University before opening Juanita Bananas in 2004. In 2011 she moved the restaurant to the open-air lobby of the Sea Breeze Hotel, where she continues to serve fresh, seasonal cuisine featuring locally caught seafood and produce and herbs from her own garden. The menu includes such dishes as chili-stuffed plantain baskets, grouper tempura, and salmon in honey mustard sauce.

Mamacita's (64 Calle Castelar, by the canal south of the drawbridge, 787/742-0322, restaurant daily 8 A.M.-3 P.M. and 6-9 P.M., bar Sun.-Thurs. 10 A.M.-10 P.M., Fri. 10 A.M.-11 P.M., $14-20, plus 15 percent gratuity) is a colorful open-air restaurant and bar serving excellent Caribbean-American-style dishes featuring dorado, *churrasco*, pork, and pasta, as well as a few pub-style appetizers. The dinner menu changes nightly and recently included a terrific dish of grilled dorado in cilantro lime aioli. Mamacita's doubles as a popular watering hole at night and rents rooms too.

Susie's Restaurant (on the canal, Dewey, 787/742-0574 or 787/340-7058, www.susiesculebra.com, Fri.-Wed. 6-9:30 P.M., reservations recommended, $18-25) serves creative Caribbean cuisine inside this modest concrete restaurant located at the end of nameless road on the canal in Dewey. The seasonal menu may include such delicacies as coriander-crusted tuna loin, shrimp glazed in a tamarind coconut sauce, and whole fried snapper.

Shipwreck Bar and Grill (at Bahía Marina, Calle Punta Soldado, km 2.4, 787/742-0535, www.bahiamarina.net, daily 4-10 P.M., $10-24) is a casual open-air eatery at Bahía Marina hotel, high up on a hill overlooking the water. The menu serves everything from burgers and conch fritters to whole snapper, *mofongo,* and New York strips.

International
Located in a brightly colored house on a dead-end street in town, **◖ Zaco's Tacos** (21 Calle Pedro Marquez, 787/742-0243, www.zacostacos.com, Sat.-Wed. noon-8 P.M., $3-9) is a happy new addition to the dining scene serving fresh fruit cocktails and creative tacos and burritos stuffed with goodies like pork belly or blackened tofu. Order and pick up at the bar and take a seat on the covered deck out back. It also serves milk shakes and smoothies.

The Spot (16 Calle Pedro Marquez, Culebra, 787/742-0203, Mon., Tues., Thurs., and Sun. 6:30 P.M.-midnight, Fri.-Sat. 6:30 P.M.-2 A.M., $6-18) serves Middle Eastern-inspired dishes, including couscous with curry chicken, gyros, and a burger made from hummus, olives, and feta cheese.

Lunch and Light Fare
Pandeli Bakery (17 Calle Pedro Marquez

at the corner of Calle Escudero, Carr. 250, 787/402-3510, Mon.-Sat. 5:30 A.M.-5 P.M., Sun. 6:30 A.M.-5 P.M., $2-6) is a cool, modern, cozy bakery serving breakfast, sandwiches, burgers, empanadas, and pastries. There's also a small selection of dry goods and wines.

Heather's Pizza & Sports Bar (14 Calle Pedro Marquez, 787/742-3175, Mon.-Tues and Thurs.-Sun. 5-10 P.M., bar open until 11 P.M., $2-15) is a friendly spot where locals gather to watch the game, have a drink, and chow down on pizza, served by the slice or pie. Options include unusual combinations such as the Boricua Pizza, featuring ground beef, garlic, sweet plantains, and cilantro. Panini and pasta round out the menu.

INFORMATION AND SERVICES
The **Culebra Tourism Department** (787/742-3521 or 787/742-3116, ext. 441 or 442, Mon.-Fri. 8 A.M.-4:30 P.M.) is in the yellow concrete building on Calle William Font in Dewey. For the most up-to-date information on the island, visit www.culebra-island.com, www.islaculebra.com, and www.culebra.org.

Because many businesses accept only cash, it's important to know where the island's ATM is. **Banco Popular** (787/742-3572, Mon.-Fri. 8:30 A.M.-3:30 P.M.) is across from the ferry terminal on Calle Pedro Marquez. You'll find the **post office** (787/742-3862, Mon.-Fri. 8 A.M.-4:30 P.M.) at 26 Calle Pedro Marquez, and **laundry facilities** can be found at Mamacita's Guesthouse (64 Calle Castelar, 787/742-0090).

The **police department** (787/742-3501) is on Calle Fulladoza just past Dinghy Dock. For medical services, **Hospital de Culebra** (Calle William Font, 787/742-3511 or 787/742-0001, ambulance 787/742-0208) operates a clinic Monday-Friday 7 A.M.-4:30 P.M., as well as 24 hour emergency service and the island's only pharmacy.

GETTING THERE
By Ferry
The **Puerto Rico Port Authority** (in Culebra 787/742-3161, 787/741-4761, 787/863-0705,

FERRY RIDING TIPS

In January 2012, business owners in Culebra bemoaned the erratic service of the passenger ferry from Fajardo, which they said was hurting business. While the schedule set by the Puerto Rico Port Authority clearly stated that the passenger ferry arrived and departed three times a day, every day, on some days it only arrived once or not at all. Because more travelers go to Vieques than Culebra, the latter island is more likely to be cut from service when a problem arises. A new 600-passenger ferry, the fleet's largest, has since been added, but the system is still plagued with inconsistencies. Nevertheless, the ferry is a cheap way to get to Vieques and Culebra from the main island, and for some travelers it is worth putting up with the inconvenience. If you plan to take a ferry to Vieques or Culebra, here are a few things worth noting.

- Tickets may be bought in advance, but they do not guarantee space on the ferry.

- Ferries often sellout, especially on weekends and holidays. Therefore, passengers typically line up hours in advance.

- If a ferry is oversold, ticket holders with a Puerto Rico Permanent Resident Card get priority over visitors.

- If you are prone to motion sickness, take preventive medication. The ride is sometimes choppy.

- Ferries do not always arrive or depart on time.

- There is an additional $2 charge for camping or beach equipment

- Rental cars may not be transported on the car ferry.

---

or 800/981-2005) operates a daily ferry service between Culebra and Fajardo.

The **passenger ferry** is primarily a commuter operation, and it can often be crowded—especially on the weekends and holidays. Reservations are not accepted, but you can buy tickets in advance. Be aware that on weekends and holidays, the ferry can sell out, leaving disappointed travelers behind. Passengers with a Puerto Rico ID are given priority access. The trip typically takes about 1.5 hours to travel between Fajardo and Culebra. The fare is $4.50 round-trip per person, with an additional charge of $2 for beach or camping equipment. The Culebra ferry does not always adhere to its schedule, which is subject to change, but at press time it was as follows:

- **Fajardo to Culebra:** Daily 9 A.M., 3 P.M., and 7 P.M.
- **Culebra to Fajardo:** Daily 6:30 A.M., 1 P.M., and 5 P.M.

There is also a weekday **cargo/car ferry** between Culebra and Fajardo, for which reservations are required. But be aware that most car-rental agencies in Puerto Rico do not permit their automobiles to leave the main island. The best option is to leave your car in Fajardo and rent another car on Culebra. The trip usually takes about 2.5 hours, and the cost is $15 for small vehicles and $19 for large vehicles. The schedule is as follows:

- **Fajardo to Culebra:** Monday, Tuesday, and Thursday 4 A.M. and 4:30 P.M.; Wednesday and Friday 4 A.M., 9:30 A.M., and 4:30 P.M.
- **Culebra to Fajardo:** Monday, Tuesday, and Thursday 7 A.M. and 6 P.M.; Wednesday and Friday 7 A.M., 1 P.M., and 6 P.M.

By Air

Several small airlines fly to Culebra from the main island, and the flights are fairly inexpensive and speedy. The only catch is that it's not for the faint of heart. Landing on the tiny island requires a steep descent over a mountaintop that takes your breath away.

In San Juan, flights can be arranged from Isla Grande Airport for about $190 round-trip, or from the new José Aponte de la Torre

Airport in Ceiba, on the east coast of the big island, for about $66 round-trip.

Vieques Air Link (787/534-4221, 787/534-4222, or 787/741-8331; for service to Culebra, call 888/901-9247) flies to and from Ceiba.

Air Flamenco (787/724-1818, 787/721-7332, 877/535-2636, www.airflamenco.net) offers flights from Ceiba and Isla Grande. Charter flights are available.

GETTING AROUND

It is possible to get around Culebra without renting a vehicle, but it is not advisable. If you want to explore the island, jeeps, scooters, and golf carts are available for rent. Just be sure to book early—two to three months in advance is recommended.

There are few roads on Culebra, but they can be narrow, steep, and riddled with potholes. Parking and seatbelt laws are strictly enforced, and for some odd reason, driving bare-chested can get you a ticket.

Note that many places don't have traditional addresses with street names and numbers. If you ask people for an address, they're more likely to describe its physical location in relation to something else, as in "beside El Batey," or "across from the ferry." Also, nobody who lives in Culebra calls Dewey by its name. It's usually just referred to as "Pueblo" or "Town."

Público

If you arrive at the airport and there aren't any *públicos* waiting, strike out walking a short distance to Willys. From the airport turn left and go one block past the stop sign; he's on the right. Otherwise, you can give one a call. Operators include **Willys** (787/742-3537 or

787/396-0076), **Kiko** (787/514-0453, 787/361-7453, or 787/363-2183), **Adrianos** (787/590-1375), **Isla Bonita** (787/223-3428), **Natas** (787/510-0736), and **Pichi** (787/455-5569). It costs about $4 to go from the airport to "downtown" Dewey or from Dewey to Flamenco Bay.

For travelers seeking transportation from San Juan to Fajardo to catch the ferry to Culebra, **Travel with Padin** (787/355-6746 after 6 P.M. for English, 787/644-3091 8 A.M.-6 P.M. for Spanish, http://enchanted-isle.com/padin) operates 24-hour *público* service between Fajardo and the Luis Muñoz Marín International Airport in San Juan.

Car Rentals

Several agencies provide jeep rentals for about $65 per day, although some travelers report success at negotiating a better rate. Bring a copy of your insurance policy to avoid steep insurance charges.

Carlos Jeep Rental (office 787/742-3514, airport 787/742-1111, cell 787/613-7049, www.carlosjeeprental.com) is conveniently located at the airport and has a well-maintained fleet of 2011 jeeps for $65 a day. Golf carts are $40 a day. Other options include **Jerry's Jeeps** (787/742-0587 or 787/742-0526) and **Dick and Cathie's Jeep Rental** (787/742-0062, cash only).

Culebra Scooter Rental (at the Culebra airport, 787/742-0195, www.culebrascooterrental.com, 8 A.M.-6:30 P.M.) rents two-wheelers for $45 a day.

For gassing up your vehicle, **Garage Ricky** (ferry dock, 787/742-3174, daily 8 A.M.-6 P.M.) has the only gas pump in Culebra, so allow plenty of time to wait in line to use it. The small store sells soft drinks, cigarettes, bug spray, and liquor.

VIEQUES AND CULEBRA

BACKGROUND

The Land

GEOGRAPHY

Puerto Rico is a rectangular island, situated roughly in the middle of the **Antilles,** a chain of islands that stretches from Florida to Venezuela and forms the dividing line between the Atlantic Ocean and the Caribbean Sea. The Antilles are divided into two regions—Greater Antilles and Lesser Antilles. Puerto Rico is the smallest and easternmost island of the Greater Antilles, which include Cuba, Hispañola (Dominican Republic and Haiti), and Jamaica.

In addition to the main island, which is 111 miles east to west and 36 miles north to south, Puerto Rico comprises several tiny islands or *cayos,* including Mona and Desecheo off the west coast and Vieques, Culebra, Palomino, Icacos, and others off the east coast. The northern and eastern shores of Puerto Rico are on the Atlantic Ocean, and the southern shores are on the Caribbean Sea. To the west is Mona Passage, an important shipping lane that is 75 miles wide and 3,300 feet deep.

The island was believed to have been formed between 135 million and 185 million years ago when a massive shift of tectonic plates crumpled the earth's surface, pushing parts of it

© SUZANNE VAN ATTEN

down into deep recesses below the ocean floor and pushing parts of it up to create the island. This tectonic activity resulted in volcanic eruptions, both underwater and above it.

Two significant things happened as a result of all this geologic activity. The **Puerto Rico Trench** was formed off the island's north coast. At its greatest depth, it is 28,000 feet below sea level, making it the deepest point known in the Atlantic Ocean. Secondly, it formed the mountainous core of Puerto Rico that spans nearly the entire island from east to west and reaches heights of 4,390 feet above sea level. Volcanic activity is believed to have been dormant in Puerto Rico for 45 million years, but the earth is always changing. The Caribbean plate is shifting eastward against the westward-shifting North American plate, which has resulted in occasional earth tremors through the years. Although this activity is suspected to have led to the volcanic activity in Montserrat in recent years, its danger to Puerto Rico is its potential to cause earthquakes, not volcanic activity.

Puerto Rico has three main geographic regions: mountains, coastal lowlands, and karst country. More than 60 percent of the island is mountainous. The island's mountains, which dominate the island's interior, comprise four ranges: **Cordillera Central, Sierra de Cayey, Sierra de Luquillo,** and **Sierra de Bermeja.** The largest and highest range is Cordillera Central, which spans from Caguas in the east to Lares in the west. Its highest point is Cerro Punta (4,390 feet above sea level), in the Bosque Estatal de Toro Negro near Jayuya. Sierra de Luquillo is in the northeast and contains the Caribbean National Forest, home to El Yunque rainforest. These two mountain ranges feature dramatic pointed peaks and lush tropical vegetation. Sierra de Cayey, in the southeast between Cayey and Humacao, and Sierra de Bermeja, in the southwest between Guánica and the island's southwestern tip, are smaller in area and height, drier, and less forested.

The **coastal lowlands** span more than 300 miles around the rim of the island, 8-12 miles inland in the north and 2-8 miles inland in the south. Formed through time by erosion of the mountains, the coastal lowlands are important agricultural areas that benefit from the rich soil and water that wash down from the mountains. Much of the area is defined by sandy or rocky beaches and mangrove swamps, although the mangrove forests are being whittled away by development.

The island's third region is unique. The **karst region** spans the island's northern interior, from San Juan in the east to Aguadilla in the west, and the southern interior, from Ponce in the east to San Germán in the west. It can also be found in isolated pockets throughout the island, as well as on Mona Island off the west coast. The karst region is distinguished by a fascinating landscape of sinkholes, cliffs, caves, and conical, haystack-shaped hills called *mogotes*. More than 27 percent of Puerto Rico's surface is made up of limestone, and its erosion from rain helped create the beguiling patchwork of hills and holes. One of limestone's unique properties is that it reprecipitates and forms case rock that is impervious to chemical and climatic change, which has basically frozen the odd formations in time. In addition, water produced by reprecipitation bubbles up to hydrate the earth's surface, and drips down, creating subterranean rivers and caves.

As a result of its karst region, Puerto Rico has some of the most significant cave systems in the western hemisphere and the third-largest underground river, Río Camuy. The public can tour part of the massive cave system at **Las Cavernas del Río Camuy** in the municipality of Camuy.

In addition to Río Camuy, Puerto Rico's other major rivers include the north-running **Grande de Arecibo,** the island's longest; **La Plata, Cibuco, Loíza,** and **Bayamón,** which run north; and **Grande de Añasco,** which runs west. There are no natural lakes in Puerto Rico, although 15 reservoirs have been created by damming rivers. But there are several natural lagoons, including **Condado** and **San José** in San Juan, **Piñones** and **Torrecilla** in Loíza, **Joyuda** in Cabo Rojo, **Tortuguero** in Vega Baja, and **Grande** in Fajardo.

CLIMATE

Puerto Rico's climate is classified as **tropical marine,** which means it's typically sunny, hot, and humid year-round. The temperature fluctuates between 76°F and 88°F in the coastal plains and 73-78°F in the mountains. Humidity is a steady 80 percent, but a northeasterly wind keeps things pretty breezy, particularly on the northeast side of the island.

Nobody wants rain during a tropical vacation, but precipitation is very much a part of life in Puerto Rico. Although there are periods when the deluge is so heavy that you might think it's time to build an ark, rains are generally brief and occur in the afternoons. The average annual rainfall is 62 inches. Although it rains throughout the year, the heaviest precipitation is from May to October, which is also hurricane season. The driest period is January to April, which coincides with the tourism industry's high season. Keep in mind that the north coast receives twice as much rain as the south coast, so if the outlook is rainy in San Juan, head south.

Hurricanes are a very real threat to Puerto Rico. It is estimated that the island will be hit by a major hurricane every 30 years. The most devastating storm in recent history was Hurricane Georges, a category 3 storm that struck in September 1998 and rendered $2 billion of damage.

For the latest information on weather conditions in Puerto Rico, visit the National Weather Service at www.srh.noaa.gov/sju.

ENVIRONMENTAL ISSUES

Because Puerto Rico is part of the United States, local industry is subject to the same federal environmental regulations and restrictions as in the United States.

Puerto Rico's greatest environmental threats concern its vanishing natural habitat and the resulting impact on soil erosion and wildlife. Reforestation efforts are under way in many of the island's national parks and forest reserves, and organized efforts are under way to protect and rebuild endangered wildlife populations, especially the Puerto Rican parrot, the manatee, and the leatherback sea turtle.

Many of the island's environmental protection efforts are overseen by the Conservation Trust of Puerto Rico, whose headquarters is based in **Casa de Ramón Power y Giraut** (155 Calle Tetuán, San Juan, 787/722-5834, www. fideicomiso.org, Tues.-Sat. 10 A.M.-4 P.M.), where visitors can peruse exhibits and pick up printed information on its projects.

In Vieques, the biggest environmental concern surrounds the ongoing cleanup of the grounds once occupied by the U.S. Navy, which stored munitions and performed bombing practice on the island. After years of protest by local residents, the Navy withdrew in 2003, but much of its land (18,000 acres) is still off-limits to the public while efforts to clear it of contaminants and the live artillery that still litters the ocean floor are under way. The cancer rate in Vieques is 27 percent higher than that of the main island, and many blame it on the presence of unexploded artillery leaking chemicals into the water and the release of chemicals into the air when the artillery is detonated, which is the Navy's way of disposing of it.

Flora

For such a small island, Puerto Rico has a wide diversity of biological environments.

For instance, Bosque Estatal de Guánica in the southwestern corner of the island is classified as a subtropical dry forest, where cacti, grasses, and evergreen trees hosting Spanish moss and mistletoe compete for water and nutrients from sun-bleached rocky soil. On the opposite end of the island is the Caribbean National Forest, which contains subtropical moist forest, also called rainforest. Palm trees, a multitude of ferns, *tabonuco* trees, orchids, and bromeliads grow here. And along the coast are mangrove forests, where the mighty land-building trees flourish in the salty water and provide vital habitat to marine life.

The first extensive study of Puerto Rico's diverse flora was undertaken in the early 1900s, thanks to American botanists Nathaniel and Elizabeth Britton, founders of the New York Botanical Gardens. Their annual trips to the Caribbean, beginning in 1906, led to the publication in 1933 of *The Scientific Survey of Puerto Rico and the Virgin Islands,* the first systematic natural history survey in the Caribbean region.

TREES

The official tree of Puerto Rico is the **ceiba,** also called silk-cotton tree or kapok tree. Often the tallest tree in the forest, the ceiba attains heights of 150 feet and has a ridged columnar trunk and a massive umbrella-shaped canopy. Its far-reaching limbs often host aerial plants, such as moss and bromeliads.

The ceiba was important to the island's indigenous Taínos because its thick trunks were perfect for carving into canoes. Its flowers are small and inconspicuous, but it produces a large ellipsoid fruit that, when split open, reveals an abundance of fluffy fibers, called kapok.

Arguably Puerto Rico's most beautiful tree, though, is the *flamboyan,* also known as royal poinciana. If you visit the island between June and August, you're sure to notice the abundance of reddish-orange blooms that cover the umbrella-shaped canopy of the *flamboyan.* It is a gorgeous sight to behold. The tree is also distinguished by fernlike leaves and the long brown seedpods it produces.

Probably the most plentiful and easily identifiable tree in Puerto Rico is the mighty palm, which grows throughout the island. There are actually many varieties of palm in Puerto Rico. Among them are the **coconut palm,** which has a smooth gray bark marked by ring scars from fallen fronds and which bears the beloved coconut in abundance; the **royal palm,** distinguished by its tall, thin straight trunk, which grows to 25 feet and sports a crown of leaves that are silver on the underside; the **Puerto Rican hat palm,** featuring a fat tubular trunk and fan-shaped frond; and the **sierra palm,** which has a thin straight trunk and thick thatch.

Puerto Rico's **mangrove** forests are found in swampy coastal areas throughout the island. Much of the island's coast was once covered in mangrove, but a lot of it has been destroyed to make way for commercial development. Fortunately efforts are under way to preserve many of the island's last remaining mangrove forests in parks in Piñones, Boquerón, Fajardo, Vieques, and elsewhere.

The mangrove tree is a unique plant. For one thing, it is able to grow along the ocean's shallow edges, absorbing, processing, and secreting salt from the water. But what's truly amazing about the mangrove, and what makes it so vital to marine life, is its adaptive root system. Because the trees grow in thick, oxygen-deprived mud, they sprout aerial roots to absorb oxygen from the air and nutrients from the surface of the water. The aerial roots take many

© SUZANNE VAN ATTEN

a coconut palm

The **mamey** is prized not only for the delicious fruit it bears but also for its fragrant flowers and lovely appearance. Resembling a Southern magnolia, the mamey grows to 60 feet high and features a short stout trunk and dense foliage with long, glossy, leathery dark-green leaves. The flowers feature 4-6 white petals and have a lovely fragrance. The fruit is brown and leathery on the outside, and inside can be sweet and tender or crisp and sour, depending on the variety. Another popular tree that bears edible fruit is the **mango.** The ubiquitous leafy tree grows in forests, backyards, and alongside roadways, and in the summer each tree bears what appear to be hundreds of mangoes. When ripe, the fruit is covered with a thick yellow and brown skin, but inside is a soft succulent fruit similar to a peach. You'll often see locals on the side of the road selling bags of them out of their trucks.

The curious **calabash tree** served an entirely different purpose in Taíno culture. Its greatest value was in the large, round, gourd-like fruit that sprouts directly from the tree's trunk. After the fruit was cleansed of its pulp, the remaining shell was dried and used as a bowl for food preparation and storage. Sometimes the bowls were decorated with elaborate carvings etched into the sides before the shell dried. Carved calabash bowls are popular souvenir items today.

FLOWERING PLANTS

Like any good tropical island, Puerto Rico has a bounty of flowering plants. Probably the one most commonly encountered, particularly in gardens but also in the wild, is the beautiful sun-loving **bougainvillea.** The plant produces great clusters of blossoms with thin papery petals, which come in an assortment of colors, including pink, magenta, purple, red, orange, white, and yellow. The plant is actually a vine, but in Puerto Rico bougainvillea often grows freestanding, with its long thin branches hanging heavy with blooms.

different forms, including thousands of tiny pencil-shaped roots sticking up from shallow waters; big knee-shaped roots that emerge from the ground and loop back down; and roots that sprout from branches.

Between its complex tangle of roots and its low-lying compact canopy, the mangrove forest plays several important roles in the environment, primarily by providing habitat to local wildlife. Its branches are a haven to nesting birds, and its underwater root systems protect crabs, snails, crustaceans, and small fish from predators. Mangrove forests also help protect the coastal plains from violent storms, reduce erosion, and filter the ocean waters. And finally, mangrove forests actually build land by providing nooks and crannies within their root systems that capture soil, aerate it, and create conditions where other plants can grow.

Puerto Rico is rich in plants that have edible, medicinal, or other practical uses. For the Taíno Indians, the island's forests served as their pharmacy and grocery store.

© SUZANNE VAN ATTEN

An orchid grows on a mango tree.

The mountains are home to many varieties of flowering plants, including one that home gardeners in the States may recognize—the shade-loving **impatiens,** a lovely ground-covering plant with white blooms. They can be seen blooming in great drifts along mountain banks. Other mountain flowering plants include more than 50 varieties of **orchids,** but don't look for corsage-sized blossoms—Puerto Rico's orchids tend to be small, some the size of a fingernail. Where you find orchids, you can usually find **bromeliads,** which, like orchids, grow on other plants that serve as hosts. Bromeliads are typically distinguished by overlapping spirals of leaves with a tubular punch of color in the center, but the family includes some atypical variations, including **Spanish moss** and the **pineapple,** both of which grow on the island.

Other plants found commonly in Puerto Rico are a large variety of ferns, large and small, in the mountains. Along the beaches, the sea grape, a low-lying compact shrub that grows in clusters, creates a cave-like reprieve from the sun. Several varieties of cactus grow in the subtropical dry forest along the southwestern coast and on the islands of Vieques and Culebra.

Fauna

MAMMALS

The only mammal native to Puerto Rico is the bat. Eleven species live on the island, including the **red fig-eating bat,** which roosts in the forest canopy in the Caribbean National Forest, and the **Greater Antillean long-tongued bat,** which lives in caves and feeds on fruits and nectar from flowers.

Thanks to colonial trade ships, **rats** were introduced to the island in the late 1400s. They thrived here in great abundance, causing havoc on sugar plantations. Then someone had the brilliant idea of introducing **mongooses** from India to keep the rat population down. Unfortunately, mongooses are active during the day, and rats are active at night, so the effort failed, and now there's a mongoose problem. They have no natural predators on the island, and they live up to 40 years. Mongooses are to be avoided at all costs as they are major carriers of rabies.

Paso Fino horses are a common form of transportation in rural areas of Puerto Rico, especially in Vieques and Culebra, where they roam the island freely.

Some parts of Puerto Rico also have a **feral dog** problem. It's not uncommon to see roving packs of mangy, skeletal canines rummaging for scraps in small towns and rural areas.

BIRDS AND INSECTS

Puerto Rico is a bird-watcher's paradise, but the one endemic bird you probably won't see is the **Puerto Rican parrot.** Although once prolific throughout the island, the endangered bird's population is a mere 35 or so that live in the wild today because of the loss of habitat to development. They are found in the Caribbean National Forest.

In 1987 the U.S. Fish and Wildlife Service initiated a program to raise Puerto Rican parrots in captivity and release them into the Caribbean National Forest in hopes of building up the population. Unfortunately, success has been stymied by hurricanes and predators, primarily the red-tailed hawk. But the efforts continue, and today there are about 150 living in captivity in aviaries in Luquillo and Bosque Estatal Río Abajo.

It's highly unlikely a visitor to El Yunque will see a Puerto Rican parrot, but just in case, keep your eyes peeled for a foot-long, bright green Amazon parrot with blue wingtips, white eye rings, and a red band above its beak. When in flight, it emits a repetitive call that sounds like a bugle.

Other species of birds found in more plentiful numbers in Puerto Rico include **sharp-skinned hawks, broad-wing hawks, bananaquits, Puerto Rican todies, red-legged thrushes, stripe-headed tanagers, brown pelicans, lizard cuckoos, elfin woods warblers, hummingbirds,** and **nightjars,** which nest silently on the ground by day and fly in search of prey at night.

At dusk, many of Puerto Rico's wilderness beaches come under attack by **sand fleas,** also called no-see-ums: vicious, minuscule buggers that have a fierce bite. If they attack, your best defense is to pack up as quickly as possible and call it a day.

REPTILES AND AMPHIBIANS

Of all the creatures that call Puerto Rico home, none are as beloved as the tiny **coqui tree frog,** the island's national symbol. A mere 1-1.5 inches long fully grown, the coqui is difficult to spot, but you can definitely hear the male's distinctive "co-QUI" call at dusk or after a rain. Despite the ubiquity of their cheerful chirp, of the 16 varieties that live in Puerto Rico, only two make the eponymous sound, which serves to attract a mate and repel reproductive competitors.

Unlike many frogs, the coqui does not

brown pelican

have webbed appendages and does not require water to live or reproduce. In fact, coquis are never tadpoles. The female coqui lays its eggs on leaves, and tiny little froglets emerge fully formed from the eggs. Although they're born with tails, they lose them posthaste.

It is considered good luck to spot a coqui, and there are many other legends surrounding them. One is that a little boy was transformed into a frog because he misbehaved, and now he comes out and sings at sunset. Another involves a bird that was stripped of its wings but was later turned into a frog so it could climb back into the trees where it once lived.

The one creature visitors to Puerto Rico are sure to spot is a **lizard.** The island is literally crawling with them, varying in species from the ubiquitous four-inch **emerald anoli,** which is sure to slip inside the house if a window is left open, to the **Puerto Rican giant green lizard,** an imposing reptile that can grow up to 16 inches long and lives mostly in the limestone hills.

But Puerto Rico's mack-daddy lizard is the prehistoric-looking **Mona iguana,** which grows up to four feet long. Mona Island off the west coast of Puerto Rico is the only natural habitat for the Mona iguana, but there is a tiny mangrove *cayo* in the bay at La Parguera where a small population is kept for research purposes and which can be seen by boat. Although an herbivore, the Mona iguana has an intimidating appearance because of its horned snout and the jagged bony crest down its back. The Mona iguana lives up to 50 years.

Snakes are few in Puerto Rico, but they do exist. Fortunately, they are all nonpoisonous. The **Puerto Rican boa** is an endangered species. The longest snake on the island, it grows up to six feet and is quite elusive.

MARINE LIFE

Unlike on many islands in the Caribbean, Puerto Rico's underwater coral reef systems are still mostly healthy and intact. And where

THE SWEET SOUNDS OF THE COQUI TREE FROG

© KIM CHEN, CAT'S CRADLE PHOTOGRAPHY (WWW.CATSCRADLEPHOTO.COM)

a tiny coqui tree frog

There is one sweet sound unlike any other that you can hear throughout the island of Puerto Rico at night, and that is the song of the coqui tree frog. Rarely seen but often heard, these tiny translucent amphibians are the beloved mascot of the island. The scientific name is *Eleutherodactylus,* and they differ from other frogs in two key ways: First, instead of webbed feet, they have tiny pads on their feet that facilitate climbing to the tops of trees, where they like to gather at night to mate and feed on insects, including mosquitoes, termites, and centipedes. Second, they do not begin life as tadpoles but hatch fully formed from eggs. There are 17 varieties of coquis in Puerto Rico, but only two of them sing the famous songs: the *coqui comun* and the *coqui de la montaña,* also

known as the *coqui puertorriqueño.* And only the male sings the "co-QUI!" call after dusk. Coquis can be found throughout the Caribbean and Latin America, but only those in Puerto Rico sing the song. In recent years the coqui inadvertently has been introduced to Hawaii, hidden in plants shipped there from Puerto Rico. But while Puerto Ricans love the sound of their coquis, many people in Hawaii do not. In fact, they consider the frogs to be a scourge to the island and the state government is trying to have them eradicated. Meanwhile, in Puerto Rico, some species of coquis have been put on the endangered list, including the tiniest one, the *coqui llanero,* which was only discovered in 2005 and whose song is so high-pitched it is barely perceivable by humans.

© SUZANNE VAN ATTEN

Mona iguanas can live up to 50 years of age.

there's a healthy reef system, there is an abundance of marine life.

Among Puerto Rico's endangered marine creatures is the **manatee,** a 1,000-pound submarine-shaped mammal with a tail, two small flippers, and a wrinkled, whiskered face. The slow-moving herbivore lives in shallow, still waters, such as lagoons and bays. Their only natural predator is man, and because they often float near the water's surface, they are particularly susceptible to collision with watercraft. The U.S. Fish and Wildlife Service operates a recovery program for the manatee, and if you spot one, you're likely to see its tracking device, which looks like a walkie-talkie attached to its back.

Also endangered are the **hawksbill** and **leatherback sea turtles,** the latter of which is the world's largest species of sea turtle, weighing between 500 and 1,600 pounds. There are several important turtle nesting sites in Puerto Rico, along the north shore and on the islands of Mona and Culebra. The turtles nest between April and June by climbing up on the beach at night and burying their eggs in the sand before returning to the sea. Unfortunately, turtle nests are vulnerable to animals and poachers, who prize the eggs. Several government agencies are involved in protected the nesting sites. If visitors want to help out, they should contact the Puerto Rico Department of Natural and Environmental Resources (787/556-6234 or 877/772-6725, fax 530/618-4605, www.coralations.org/turtles), which accepts volunteers to catalog the turtles during nesting season.

Besides its endangered species, Puerto Rico has numerous other varieties of thriving marine life, from **rays** and **nurse sharks** to **puffer fish** and **parrot fish.** The reefs themselves are sights to behold, with their **brain coral, sea fans,** and **yellow cup coral,** which blooms at night.

And although typically associated with colder waters, migrating **humpback whales** can be spotted along the island's west coast between January and March.

History

INDIGENOUS CULTURES

The earliest known inhabitants of Puerto Rico were the **Archaic** or **Pre-Ceramic** cultures, which are believed to have lived on the island from 3000 B.C. until A.D. 150. They were loosely organized in small nomadic groups of about 30 who occupied encampments for brief periods. What little is known about this culture has been deduced from a couple of burial sites and a few excavated stone and shell artifacts, such as flint chips, scrapers, and pestles. They are believed to have been primarily hunters and gatherers who did not cultivate crops or make pottery. There are two main theories about the origins of the Archaic culture. It is believed they either originated in South America and migrated to Puerto Rico by way of the Lesser Antilles or they originated in the Yucatán Peninsula and crossed from Cuba and Hispañola.

The Archaic were followed by the **Arawak,** who migrated from Venezuela. The earliest Arawak were classified as **Igneri** or **Saladoid,** and they lived in Puerto Rico from 300 B.C. to A.D. 600. The Igneri were superb potters, whose ceramics were distinguished by white paint on a red background. They also produced small *cemies,* three-sided amulets believed to have religious significance. Their society was organized in villages of extended-family houses situated around a central plaza, under which the dead were buried. In addition to hunting and gathering, the Igneri cultivated crops.

Around A.D. 600, the Igneri culture evolved into two separate cultures that are grouped together under the name **Pre-Taíno.** The **Elenoid** lived on the eastern two-thirds of the island while the **Ostionoid** lived on the western third of the island. The Elenoid culture is distinguished by a coarse, thick style of unpainted ceramics. The Ostionoid produced pottery similar to the Igneri's, except that it was painted in shades of pink and lilac. Little is known about Pre-Taíno culture. Both cultures continued to hunt, fish, gather, and farm. Although they had centralized villages, there is evidence that many Pre-Taíno split into nuclear families and lived in houses separate from one another scattered throughout the island. It is during this time that many Taíno customs began to appear. The Pre-Taíno were the first to construct *bateyes* (rectangular ball courts) and central plazas, which were square or round. They produced larger *cemi* amulets than found in Igneri culture, and they began carving petroglyphs—typically human or animal faces—into stones.

The most significant Igneri and Pre-Taíno archaeological site in Puerto Rico is **Centro Ceremonial Indígena de Tibes** near Ponce. In addition to seven *bateyes* and two plazas, a cemetery containing the remains of 187 people was discovered here.

Around A.D. 1200, the Pre-Taíno evolved into the **Taíno** culture. Of all the indigenous groups that lived in Puerto Rico, the most is known about the Taíno, perhaps because they were the ones to greet Christopher Columbus when he arrived in 1493, and several Spanish settlers wrote historical accounts about their culture.

The Taíno society was highly organized and hierarchal. They lived in self-governing villages called *yucayeques.* Commoners lived in conical wood-and-thatch huts called *bohíos* while the chief, or cacique, lived in a rectangular hut called a *caney.* They were a highly spiritual culture and would gather on sacred grounds, distinguished by plazas and *bateyes* (ball courts), to perform their religious ceremonies and compete in ball games.

The Taínos produced highly complex ceramics, as well as wood and stone implements, such as axes, daggers, *dujos* (ceremonial stools), and stone collars, the purpose of which is unknown.

In addition to hunting, fishing, and gathering, they were highly developed farmers. The Taínos were also highly spiritual, and they created many *cemi* amulets, which were much more complex than those of past cultures, and stone carvings.

The Taínos were a peaceful culture, a fact that was severely challenged by the arrival of the Spanish conquistadors as well as the marauding Caribs, a highly aggressive, warrior culture that originated in Venezuela and roamed the Antilles plundering goods and capturing women. A hotly debated topic in scholarly discussions about the Caribs is whether or not they practiced cannibalism. The Taíno culture vanished around 1500 after the arrival of the Spanish conquistadors. Those not killed and enslaved by the Spanish died from a smallpox epidemic.

When Taíno Indians Ruled Boriken

The Taínos were an indigenous group of people who ruled the island of Puerto Rico (which they called Boriken) when Christopher Columbus and his expedition arrived in 1493. A little more than two decades later, they were virtually wiped out.

But surprising developments have recently revealed that the Taínos may live on in Puerto Rico, and not just in the vestiges of their customs, cuisine, and language that are still prevalent today. Preliminary results from DNA studies recently conducted at the Universidad de Puerto Rico in Mayagüez indicate that nearly half the island's Puerto Rican residents may contain indigenous DNA.

The study of Taíno history and culture is a fairly recent academic undertaking. Previously, what little was known of the peaceful, agrarian society was derived from written accounts by Spanish settlers. But the ongoing study of archaeological sites has uncovered new details about the highly politicized and spiritual society.

The Taínos are thought to have originated

© SUZANNE VAN ATTEN

Taíno petroglyphs, La Piedra Escrita in Jayuya

in South America before migrating to the Caribbean, where they settled in Puerto Rico, Haiti, the Dominican Republic, and Cuba. Taíno society in Puerto Rico is believed to have developed between A.D. 1100 and 1500. By the time of Columbus's arrival, the island comprised about 20 political chiefdoms, each one ruled by a cacique (chief). Unlike the laboring class, who mostly wore nothing, the cacique wore a resplendent headdress made of parrot feathers, a gold amulet, and a *mao,* a white cotton shawl-like garment that protected the shoulders and chest from the sun.

Second in power to the caciques were the *bohiques* (shamans). Ornamenting their faces with paint and charcoal, they led spiritual rituals and ceremonies, using herbs, chants, maracas, and tobacco to heal the sick. To communicate with the gods and see visions of the future, *bohiques* and caciques inhaled a hallucinogenic powder made from the bright red seeds of the *cohoba* tree. It was ingested in a ceremony that began with a ritual cleansing that involved inducing vomiting with ornately carved spatulas. The powder was then inhaled through tubes created from tubers or bones.

Of special spiritual importance to the Taínos was the enigmatic *cemi,* a three-pointed object carved from stone or wood. Its significance is a mystery, but some believe it was thought to contain the spirit of the god Yocahu. *Cemies* were plentiful, powerful objects, believed to control everything from weather and crops to health and childbirth. Most *cemies,* which were kept in shrine rooms, were representations of animals and men with froglike legs. Some were ornamented with semiprecious stones and gold and are believed to represent the *cohoba*-fueled visions of the caciques and *bohiques.*

The Taínos saw spirituality in every natural thing, even death. Laborers were buried under their houses, called *bohios*—conical huts made from cane, straw, and palm leaves. But chiefs and shamans had special funerary rites. Their bodies

were left to decompose in the open, and then their bones and skulls were cleaned and preserved in wooden urns or gourds, which were hung from the rafters. Pity the poor wives of the caciques, who were polygamists. Their favorite wives were buried alive when their husbands died.

Religious ceremonies, called *areytos,* were held in ceremonial plazas or rectangular ball courts, called *bateyes.* Lining its perimeter were monoliths adorned with petroglyphs—carvings of faces, animals, and the sun. This is where feasts, celebrations, sporting events, and ritual dances were held. Music was performed on conch trumpets, bone flutes, wooden drums, maracas, and *güiros,* a washboard-type percussion instrument made from gourds. Sometimes neighboring villagers would join in the festivities, participating in mock fights, footraces, or ball games similar to soccer, played with a heavy bouncing ball made from rubber plants and reeds. As in our modern-day ball games, the consumption of alcoholic beverages—corn beer in Taíno times— was also a highlight of the activities.

When they weren't whooping it up at the *batey,* the Taínos were hard at work growing, gathering, and hunting food. Luckily for them, the island was rich in resources. Peanuts, guavas, pineapples, sea grapes, black-eyed peas, and lima beans grew wild. Fields were cleared for the cultivation of corn, sweet potatoes, yams, squashes, papayas, and yucas, a staple that was processed into a type of flour used to make cassava bread. Cotton was also grown for the making of hammocks. Iguanas, snakes, birds, and manatees were hunted. The sea provided fish, conchs, oysters, and crabs. Canoes, carved from tree trunks, were used to fish and conduct trade with nearby islands. Some canoes were so huge that they could hold 100 men.

The Taínos were a matrilineal society. Women held a special place in the culture because nobility was passed down through their families. The only commoners to don clothing, married women wore cotton aprons; the longer the *nagua,* the higher the social rank of the wearer. Women spent their time making pottery, weaving hammocks, and processing yuca, a time-consuming and complicated procedure. Babies were carried on their mothers' backs on boards that were tied to the babies' foreheads, a practice that produced the flat heads that Taínos found attractive.

Columbus's arrival marked the beginning of the end for Taíno society. They were already weakened from attacks by the Caribs, an aggressive, possibly cannibalistic indigenous group from South America who captured Taíno women and forced them into slavery. The Spanish followed suit by enslaving many of the remaining Taínos.

It didn't take long for unrest to grow among the Taínos. In 1510, Cacique Urayoan ordered his warriors to capture and drown a Spanish settler to determine if the colonists were mortal. Upon Diego Salcedo's death, the Taínos revolted against the Spanish, but they were quickly overpowered by the Spaniards' firearms. Thousands of Taínos were shot to death, many are believed to have committed mass suicide, and others fled to the mountains.

Several devastating hurricanes hit the island during the next several years, which killed many more Taínos. It has been reported that by 1514, there were fewer than 4,000 Taínos left, and in 1519 a smallpox epidemic is said to have virtually wiped out the rest of the remaining population.

In the last decade, interest in learning more about the Taínos has increased. As pride in the legacy of Taíno society grows, so do efforts to preserve its heritage.

In 2007, what experts are calling the largest and most significant pre-Columbian site in the Caribbean was discovered during the construction of a dam in Jacana near Ponce. The five-acre site contains plazas, *bateyes,* burial grounds, residences, and a midden mound—a pile of ritual refuse. After a preliminary four-month investigation that included the removal of 75 boxes of skeletons, ceramics, and petroglyphs, the site has been covered back up to preserve it until a full-scale excavation can begin. It is expected to take 15 to 20 years to unearth all the secrets the site contains.

There are two archaeological sites open to the public: **Centro Ceremonial Indígena de Caguana** (Carr. 111, km 12.5, 787/894-7325 or 787/894-7310, www.icp.gobierno.pr) in Utuado and **Centro Ceremonial Indígena de Tibes** (Carr. 503, km 2.5, 787/840-2255, www.nps.gov/nr/travel/prvi/pr15.htm) in Ponce.

And for a taste of Taíno culture, visit Jayuya in November for the Festival Nacional Indígena, featuring traditional music, dance, food, and crafts.

To learn more about Taíno history and culture, visit the websites of the United Federation of Taíno People (www.uctp.org) and the Jatibonicu Taíno Tribal Nation of Boriken (www.taino-tribe.org).

COLONIZATION

Christopher Columbus was on his second voyage in his quest to "discover" the New World when he arrived in Puerto Rico in 1493. There is debate as to where exactly Columbus, called Cristóbal Colón by the Spanish, first disembarked on the island. That momentous occasion is claimed by Aguada, on the northwest coast of the Atlantic, and Guánica, on the southwest coast of the Caribbean. Either way, he didn't stick around long enough to do much more than christen the island San Juan Bautista, after John the Baptist.

It wasn't until 1508 that Juan Ponce de León, who had been on the voyage with Columbus, returned to the island to establish a settlement. The Taíno provided no resistance to his arrival. In fact, Taíno cacique Agueybana allowed Ponce de León to pick any spot he wanted for a settlement so long as the Spanish would help defend the Taíno against the Caribs. His choice of Caparra, a marshy mosquito-ridden spot just west of what is now San Juan, was a poor one.

Around 1521 the settlement was relocated to what is now Old San Juan, and in 1523 Casa Blanca was built to house Ponce de León and his family, although by that time the explorer had left for Florida, where he met his demise. Originally the new settlement was called Puerto Rico for its "rich port." It's not clear why—possibly a cartographer's mistake—but soon after it was founded, the name of the settlement was switched with the name of the island.

San Juan quickly became a vital port to the Spanish empire. An important stopover for ships transporting goods from the New World to Europe, it soon became a target for foreign powers. To protect its interests, Spain began a centuries-long effort to construct a formidable series of fortresses to defend the harbor and the city.

Construction of the island's first Spanish fort, La Fortaleza, began in 1533. The small structure, which to this day serves as home to the island's governor, was built to store gold and protect it from Carib attacks. The port quickly grew in importance, and Spain's enemies—England, Holland, and France—began to threaten it with attacks. More elaborate defense systems were needed. To protect the city's all-important harbor, construction of Castillo San Felipe del Morro began in 1539, forming the nucleus of the city's fortifications. Through the years it was expanded to four levels and five acres before completion in 1787.

To protect the city from attack by land, San Cristóbal castle was begun in 1634. By the time it was completed in 1783, it was the city's largest fort, spanning 27 acres. That same year began the 200-year construction of La Muralla, the massive stone wall that once encircled the city and much of which still stands. It contained five gates, which were closed at night and guarded at all times.

The English were the first to significantly damage the city. In 1595, Sir Francis Drake led 26 vessels in an attack that partially burned the city but was successfully repelled. The next

English attack proved more fruitful. Led by George Clifford, the earl of Cumberland, troops landed in Santurce in 1598 and occupied the city for several months before illness and exhaustion forced them to abandon their stronghold.

The most devastating attack to date came when 17 Dutch ships led by Boudoin Hendricks attacked in 1625. And in 1797 the British, led by Sir Ralph Abercrombie, attacked again.

Meanwhile, other settlements were being established throughout the island. The area now known as Aguada was established as Villa de Sotomayor in 1508, but it was destroyed by Indians in 1511. In 1516, Franciscan friars built a monastery nearby, which was destroyed by Indians 12 years later. A new monastery was built in 1590, followed by a chapel in 1639. Also an important stopover for ships on their way to Spain from South America, it suffered attacks by the English, French, and Dutch. San Germán was founded in 1573 and was attacked by pirates, the English, and the Dutch. Arecibo followed in 1606.

Attack by foreign powers waned in the 1800s, and the island's sugarcane and coffee plantations flourished because of the slave labor that was brought in from Africa. But by the 1860s, a new challenge to Spanish rule arose in the form of an independence rebellion that was brewing among the island's rural class.

On September 23, 1868, about 500 Puerto Ricans organized a revolt, proclaiming the mountain town of Lares free of Spanish rule. Local stores and offices owned by Spanish merchants were looted, slaves were declared free, and city hall was stormed. The revolt was quickly squelched the next day, when rebel forces attempted to take over a neighboring town. The revolutionaries, including leaders Manuel Rojas and Juan Rius Rivera, were taken prisoner, found guilty of treason and sedition, and sentenced to death. But to ease the political tension that was brewing on the island at that time, the revolutionaries were eventually released. Although the revolt, referred to as **Grito de Lares,** was unsuccessful, it did result in Spain's giving the island more autonomy.

Colonial reforms were made, national political parties were established, and slavery was abolished. But at the same time, restrictions were imposed on human rights, such as freedom of the press and the right to gather. Meanwhile, the Spanish empire was beginning to crumble. It eventually lost all its Caribbean colonies except Cuba and Puerto Rico, and increased tariffs and taxes were imposed on imports and exports to help fund Spain's efforts to regain control of the nearby Dominican Republic. Living conditions in Puerto Rico deteriorated as the economy declined. Illiteracy was high; malnutrition and poverty were rampant. Violent clashes broke out between desperate residents and Spanish merchants, who monopolized trade on the island.

SPANISH-AMERICAN WAR

As the 19th century drew to a close, tensions had grown between Spain's declining empire and the rising world power of the United States, which had set its sights on the Caribbean islands to protect its growing sea trade. Under pressure from the United States, Spain granted Puerto Rico constitutional autonomy, and the island was preparing to hold its first self-governing elections when the Spanish-American War was declared in April 1898.

The war was fought mostly in the waters around Cuba and the Philippines, but in May San Juan was pounded with artillery for three hours from U.S. warships led by Admiral William T. Sampson. The attack was a misguided effort to flush out a Spanish squadron commander who was not in San Juan at the time. Both of San Juan's major forts sustained damage. The top of Castillo San Felipe del Morro's lighthouse was destroyed, and several residences and government buildings were damaged.

In July, 18,000 U.S. troops were sent to secure Puerto Rico. Landing in Guánica, ground troops began working their way northwest to San Juan, but before they could arrive, Spain agreed to relinquish sovereignty over the West Indies. With the signing of the Treaty of Paris in December 1898, Puerto Rico was ceded to the United States.

U.S. RULE AND THE FIGHT FOR INDEPENDENCE

For two years after the Spanish-American War, the United States operated a military government in Puerto Rico until 1900, when the first civilian government was established. The governor, his cabinet, and the senate-like Higher House of Delegates were appointed by the U.S. president. A 35-member Local House of Delegates and a resident commissioner, who represented Puerto Rico in the U.S. House of Representatives but had no vote, were elected by popular vote. In 1917, Puerto Ricans were granted U.S. citizenship by President Woodrow Wilson.

Living conditions in Puerto Rico advanced very little in the first 30 years under U.S. rule. A couple of hurricanes between 1928 and 1932 left the economy—dependent solely on agriculture—in ruins. Homelessness and poverty were rife. The unhappy state of affairs fueled the organization of another independence movement led by the Harvard-educated nationalist leader Pedro Albizu Campos. The doctor chafed against U.S. rule and asserted it had no claims to the island because it had been given its independence from Spain before the Spanish-American War broke out.

A gifted orator, Campos traveled throughout Latin America garnering support for Puerto Rico's independence and was named president of the island's Nationalist Party, which had formed in 1922. In 1935, four nationalists were killed by local police under the command of a Colonel E. Francis Riggs in an event referred to today as the Río Piedras Massacre. The next year, Riggs was killed in retaliation by two

NATIONALIST HERO: DON PEDRO ALBIZU CAMPOS

Dr. Pedro Albizu Campos has been dead since 1965, but the beloved nationalist leader lives on in the memory of Puerto Ricans everywhere. Nearly every town in Puerto Rico has a street or school named after him, and on the side of a building on Calle San Sebastián in Old San Juan, local artist Dennis Mario Rivera has memorialized him with a stunning graffiti portrait, helping make Campos a pop-culture icon among Puerto Ricans akin to Che Guevara in other Latin American countries.

Born in Ponce in 1891, Campos was a brilliant man who was fluent in eight languages and earned five degrees at Harvard University—in law, literature, philosophy, chemical engineering, and military sciences. So how did a man with such a promising future end up spending the last 25 years of his life in and out of prison? By leading the charge for Puerto Rico's independence from the United States.

Campos was reportedly not anti-American, nor was he communist. But he passionately believed that the 1898 Treaty of Paris, which ended the Spanish-American War, wrongfully gave the United States sovereignty over Puerto Rico. After all, Spain had granted autonomy to Puerto Rico in 1897. The island had established its own currency, postal service, and customs department. It's hard to deny Campos's belief that Spain had no authority to bequeath the island to the United States.

Nevertheless, the island did become a property of the United States, and Campos even went on to serve as a first lieutenant in the U.S. Infantry during World War I. After he was discharged, he completed his studies at Harvard and returned to Puerto Rico, where he joined the Nationalist Party in 1924.

A gifted orator, Campos traveled throughout the island, as well as the Caribbean and Latin America, seeking support for the independence movement with such eloquent speeches that he was nicknamed El Maestro. And he was eventually elected president of the Nationalist Party. Although the Nationalist Party fared poorly in local elections, during the next six years Campos kept the movement in the forefront of political discourse by staging a protest at the San Juan capitol, implicating the U.S.-based Rockefeller Institute in the deaths of patients who were the subject of medical testing without their consent, and by serving as legal representation for striking sugarcane workers.

The beginning of Campos's downfall came in 1935, when four nationalists were killed by police under the command of Colonel E. Francis Riggs in an event referred to as the Río Piedras Massacre. The next year, two nationalists killed Riggs, a crime that resulted in their being arrested and executed without trial. That same year, the federal court in San Juan ordered the arrest of Campos and several other nationalists on the grounds of seditious conspiracy to overthrow the U.S. government in Puerto Rico. A jury trial found him innocent, but a new jury was ordered and Campos was found guilty. The verdict was upheld on appeal, and Campos was sent to the federal penitentiary in Atlanta.

Campos returned to Puerto Rico in 1947 and is believed to have become involved in a plot to incite armed struggle against the United States. Three years later, two nationalist attacks—one on La Fortaleza, the governor's residence in San Juan, and one on Blair House, the temporary home of President Harry Truman—led to Campos's rearrest, conviction, and imprisonment for sedition. His imprisonment at La Princesa in Old San Juan was marked by a serious decline in his health, which he attributed to radiation experiments performed on him without his consent.

Governor Luis Muñoz Marín pardoned Campos in 1953, but the pardon was overthrown when there was another attempted attack made on the U.S. House of Representatives. In 1964, Marín successfully pardoned Campos, who was by then a sick and broken man. A year later he died of a stroke in Hato Rey. More than 75,000 Puerto Ricans reportedly joined the procession that carried Campos's body to his burial in Cementerio de Santa María Magdalena de Pazzis, Old San Juan's historic cemetery.

Although the independence movement still has little political clout in Puerto Rico today, Campos is revered as a man who gave his life for liberty—an ideal the island has never fully achieved.

graffiti portrait of Don Pedro Albizu Campos by local artist Dennis Mario Rivera on Calle de San Sebastián

was getting under way, police fired on the crowd, killing 19 people and injuring 200 in what went down in history as the Ponce Massacre. It was a huge blow to the independence movement, and with Campos imprisoned, it seemed as though the fight for freedom had been quelled. Instead, the incident merely drove the movement underground and possibly fueled its embrace of violent tactics.

To quell the brewing unrest, protect its interests, and benefit from the island's resources, the United States took several momentous steps beginning in the 1940s that had far-reaching effects on Puerto Rico's culture. During World War II, several large military bases were established on the island—Fort Buchanan Army Base in Guaynabo, Ramey Air Force Base in Aguadilla, Roosevelt Roads Naval Station in Ceiba, and Vieques Navy Base—which significantly boosted the economy. In 1940 a major hydroelectric-power expansion program was undertaken, providing electrical power throughout the island and attracting U.S. industry. In 1947, President Harry S. Truman agreed to give Puerto Rico more control of its local government, and the next year the island chose its first self-elected governor, Luis Muñoz Marín, a member of the Popular Democratic Party.

But by this time, Campos had finished serving his time and returned to Puerto Rico, where he reinvigorated efforts to achieve independence—this time, at any cost.

On November 1, 1950, two Puerto Rican nationalists—Oscar Collazo and Griselio Torresola—attempted to assassinate President Truman at the Blair House, where the president and his family were living while the White House was being renovated. Approaching the house from opposite sides, they attempted but failed to shoot their way in. After the gunfire ended, Torresola and one police officer were dead, and two police officers were wounded. Collazo was sentenced to death, but Truman commuted the sentence to life. Campos was

nationalists, who were arrested and executed without a trial. Campos was arrested for his suspected role in the death. The first jury trial found him innocent, but a second trial found him guilty and he was sentenced to prison.

On Palm Sunday in 1937, a Nationalist Party demonstration was organized in Ponce, Campos's hometown, to protest the independence leader's incarceration. Just as the march again arrested and found guilty of his role in planning the assassination attempt. He spent the remainder of his life in and out of prison until his death in 1965.

In 1952, Puerto Rico adopted a new constitution, and commonwealth status was established. The island had more self-governing powers than ever before. This was the beginning of the long debate that still rages today over Puerto Rico's political status. While roughly half the population is content with commonwealth status, an equal number of residents have worked steadily toward trying to achieve statehood.

Puerto Rico's first self-elected governor, Luis Muñoz Marín, was a New Deal-style reformist with progressive ideas who served four terms as governor of Puerto Rico. In partnership with the United States, he initiated many programs that advanced economic and cultural development throughout the island and significantly improved the infrastructure. Under his leadership, an economic development program called Operation Bootstrap was successfully launched to entice global industry to the island with federal and local tax exemptions. *The Economist* described it as "one century of economic development...achieved in a decade." The standard of living leapt to new heights, and the tourist trade soon exploded. The next three decades, from the 1950s through the 1970s, was a huge period of growth and development for the island. But some believed Operation Bootstrap was a throwback to colonial ideals in which the island's resources were exploited without fair compensation, rendering the island increasingly more dependent on the United States.

The island suffered several setbacks in the 1980s. The energy crisis and U.S. recession sent the tourist trade into decline, and many of San Juan's glamorous high-rise hotels fell into disrepair, some shuttering altogether. Hurricane Hugo in 1989 dealt a devastating blow, and Operation Bootstrap was discontinued, which sent many manufacturers packing.

Meanwhile, the independence movement was quietly gaining momentum, and peaceful protest was not part of the agenda. Two pro-independence organizations formed in the 1970s. The Popular Boricua Army, commonly known as Los Macheteros, primarily operated in Puerto Rico. The Armed Forces of Puerto Rican National Liberation (FALN) operated in the United States. The two organizations communicated their desire for independence with terrorist attacks.

One of FALN's most notorious attacks was setting off a briefcase bomb in 1975 in New York City's Fraunces Tavern, a historic landmark where George Washington delivered his farewell speech to colonial troops during the Revolutionary War. Four patrons were killed. Other bombs were detonated in a Harlem tenement, Penn Station, and JFK Airport. All told, FALN set off 72 bombs in New York City and Chicago, killing five people and injuring 83.

In 1981, Los Macheteros infiltrated the Puerto Rican Air National Guard base and blew up 11 military planes, causing $45 million in damage. In 1983 members of Los Macheteros raided a Wells Fargo depot in Hartford, Connecticut, wounding a policeman and making off with $7.2 million, ostensibly to fund the organization's efforts.

Sixteen instigators from both organizations were eventually captured and sentenced to federal prison, bringing the terrorist acts to a halt. In 1999, President Clinton granted them clemency.

TODAY

The dawn of a new century found Puerto Rico in a heated contest with the U.S. military over its naval base in Vieques. For years the military had been using the island for bombing practice and ammunitions storage. But in 1999, civilian David Sanes was accidentally killed by a bomb in Vieques, which set off an organized protest effort that raged for several years and grew stronger in numbers through time. The military finally relented, pulling out of Vieques in 2003. Without the base in Vieques, the U.S. Navy decided it didn't need the Roosevelt Roads Naval Station in Ceiba, and it was closed in 2004, taking with it its estimated $250 million-a-year infusion into the local economy. With Ramey Air Force Base having closed in the mid-1970s, Fort Buchanan is the last remaining U.S. military base on the island.

The independence movement in Puerto Rico has long since abandoned its violent ways, and in truth, only 5 percent of the population wants independence. But every once in a while, something occurs that reminds islanders of the movement's presence and its bloody history. As recently as 2005, the FBI killed—some say ambushed—Los Macheteros organizer Filiberto Ojeda Ríos in a shoot-out at his home in Hormigueros. The 72-year-old man was the ringleader in the 1983 Wells Fargo attack and had evaded authorities ever since. To some, the fact that Ojeda was killed on September 23—a holiday honoring the independence movement's 1868 uprising against Spain—seemed to send a clear reminder to *independistas* that their past activities had not been forgotten.

The single most defining characteristic of Puerto Rico's political climate today is the decades-old debate over whether it should remain a territory of the United States or become a state. Which way the tides would turn if residents were given the opportunity to decide is anyone's guess because popular opinion is fairly equally divided between those who are pro-commonwealth and those who are pro-statehood.

Economy and Government

ECONOMY

Puerto Rico has one of the best economies in the Caribbean, but it's still well below U.S. standards. Approximately 41 percent of the population lives below the poverty level. In 2012 the unemployment rate was 12 percent, and the median household income was $18,862. The island is heavily dependent on U.S. aid, and the government is the largest employer.

From colonial times until the 1940s, the island's largest industry was sugar production. But that industry went into decline when sugar prices plummeted as other sources became available.

In 1948 the federal and local governments came together to introduce an economic development program called Operation Bootstrap. In addition to bringing land reforms, roads, and schools to neglected parts of the island, it stimulated industrial growth by giving federal and local tax exemptions to U.S. corporations that established operations in Puerto Rico. Many major manufacturing firms set up shop, and before long the production of pharmaceuticals and electronics far eclipsed agriculture on the island. The period from the 1950s through the 1970s was a huge period of growth and development. The standard of living achieved new heights very quickly, and the tourism industry began to blossom.

But in the latter part of the 20th century, Puerto Rico's economy suffered a series of setbacks. First the energy crisis and U.S. recession put a damper on the tourist trade in the 1980s. Then in the 1990s, Operation Bootstrap's tax incentives were discontinued and the North American Free Trade Agreement (NAFTA) was enacted, which sent industries packing to Mexico, where labor was cheaper. Adding insult to injury, in 2004 the United States closed the Roosevelt Roads Naval Station, which had contributed $250 million a year to the local economy.

But there is a new vigor fueling the economy

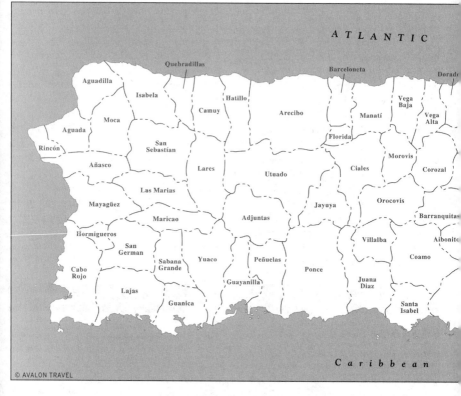

ATLANTIC

Quebradillas

Aguadilla

Isabela

Barceloneta

Dorado

Moca

Camuy

Hatillo

Vega Baja

Aguada

Arecibo

Manatí

Vega Alta

Rincón

San Sebastián

Florida

Añasco

Lares

Morovis

Ciales

Corozal

Utuado

Mayagüez

Las Marias

Jayuya

Orocovis

Barranquitas

Maricao

Adjuntas

Villalba

Aibonito

Hormigueros

San German

Coamo

Cabo Rojo

Sabana Grande

Yuaco

Peñuelas

Ponce

Juana Diaz

Lajas

Guayanilla

Santa Isabel

Guanica

Caribbean

© AVALON TRAVEL

of Puerto Rico today, and it's apparent in the many cranes and construction projects under way throughout the island. Economic development has turned its attention aggressively toward tourism during a time, especially after 9/11, when U.S. travelers are seeking destinations closer to home. Port Authority improvements to San Juan's 12 ship docks and seven piers have made it the largest port in the Caribbean. The brand-new 113-acre Puerto Rico Convention Center beside the Isla Grande Airport near Old San Juan was completed in late 2005, making it the largest convention center in the Caribbean. New road construction projects are under way, and seemingly every town is renovating its central plaza. An estimated five million tourists visit the island each year.

GOVERNMENT ORGANIZATION

Puerto Rico is a self-governing commonwealth of the United States. Its residents are U.S. citizens, but they can't vote for members of Congress or the president. A resident commissioner represents the island's interests in Washington but cannot vote on legislative matters. Businesses pay federal taxes, but individuals do not, although they do contribute to federal programs such as Social Security and Medicare. Individuals also pay about 32 percent of their income in local taxes.

Ever since Puerto Rico became a commonwealth in the early 1950s, its residents have debated the best course for the island's political future. A small but fervent number want independence, but the rest of the island is evenly

PUERTO RICO MUNICIPALITIES

divided between pro-statehood and pro-commonwealth factions. Statehood would mean more federal funding and a voice in national decisions. Those opposed to statehood fear losing their Spanish language and heritage in the rush toward Americanization.

In some ways, Puerto Rico is already like a state. The United States oversees all federal affairs, including interstate trade, foreign relations, customs, immigration, currency, military service, judicial procedures, transportation, communications, agriculture, mining, and the postal service. The local Puerto Rican government oversees internal affairs. The head of government is an elected governor, and there are two legislative chambers—the House and the Senate. The island's capital is based in San Juan. The island is divided into 78 municipalities, and each one is governed by a popularly elected mayor and municipal assembly.

For the first time since the United States claimed the island as a territory in 1898, Puerto Rico may be in the position to help decide its own fate. In 2011, the island's governor put into action a two-step referendum. The first vote that takes place in August 2012, allows Puerto Rican residents to vote on whether they wanted to maintain their current commonwealth status or pursue non-territorial status. If they vote for non-territorial status, the second vote that takes place in November 2012, would allow voters to decide whether they prefer statehood or independence. The outcomes of both votes occurred after this book went to press. But no matter how the vote turned out, the ultimate decision will be up to the U.S. Congress.

POLITICAL PARTIES

Puerto Ricans are passionate about politics. Political rallies are frequent, and during election years, political alliances are proclaimed by flag-waving caravans that drive through towns honking their horns and broadcasting speeches from loudspeakers. Puerto Rico has one of the highest percentages of voter turnout in the United States, with 81.7 percent in 2004.

There are three political parties in Puerto Rico. The **Popular Democratic Party** is pro-commonwealth, the **New Progressive Party** is pro-statehood, and the **Puerto Rican Independence Party** is pro-independence. Those who embrace independence represent only 5 percent of the population. The rest of the island is fairly evenly divided between pro-statehood and pro-commonwealth factions.

How Puerto Ricans might vote should they be given the option of remaining a commonwealth or becoming a state is hard to say. It will be interesting to see what path Puerto Rico chooses should the United States give it the power to decide.

JUDICIAL SYSTEM

The judicial system in Puerto Rico is structured the same as in the United States. The highest local court is the Supreme Court, consisting of a chief justice and six associate justices appointed by the governor. There is a Court of Appeals, Superior Court, a civil and criminal District Court, and Municipal Court. The U.S. Federal Court, based in San Juan, has final authority.

People and Culture

POPULATION

Today more Puerto Ricans live on the U.S. mainland than in Puerto Rico, and the island's population is continuing to shrink as the high unemployment rate sends residents—mostly educated professionals—stateside in pursuit of work. Between April 2010 and July 2011, the population dropped 19,100 to 3.7 million. About 45 percent of the island's residents live below the poverty level and at least 10 municipalities (primarily those in the Cordillera Central) have poverty rates greater than 60 percent. The economy is also blamed for the slide in the birth rate down from 60,000 in 2000 to 42,000 in 2012.

NATIONAL IDENTITY

There is a saying on the island that Puerto Ricans are like porpoises: They can barely keep their heads above water, but they're always smiling. It's an apt description. In 2005, Puerto Ricans were proclaimed the happiest people on earth, according to a highly reported study by the Stockholm-based organization World Values Survey. Despite high poverty and unemployment rates, it seems nothing can put a damper on the lively, fun-loving Puerto Rican spirit. Most Puerto Ricans like to celebrate big and often. In fact, there are reportedly more than 500 festivals a year on the island, and everything is a family affair involving multiple generations of relatives. Music is usually at the heart of most gatherings, and Puerto Ricans are passionate about their opinions and love few things more than to debate politics or sports for hours.

The culture of Puerto Rican life has been significantly shaped by its history. It was originally inhabited by a society of peaceful, agriculturally based indigenous people who migrated to the island from South America. But beginning in 1508, the island became a Spanish colony, and for the next four centuries European influence

graffiti reflecting Puerto Ricans' sense of pride

reigned. Towns were developed according to Spanish custom around central plazas and churches. The church spread Catholicism, and Spanish became the official language.

Because the majority of colonists were men, the Spanish Crown officially supported marriage between Spanish men and Taíno women, leading to a population of mixed offspring. The Spanish also brought in slaves from Africa to work the island's many coffee and sugar plantations, and they too produced offspring with the Taíno and Spanish colonists, producing what for years was called a population of mulattoes.

Perhaps because of this historic mixing of races, racial tensions are relatively minimal in Puerto Rico. There are some levels of society that proudly claim to be of pure European blood, and darker-skinned populations are sometimes discriminated against. But in general, Puerto Rico is a true melting pot of races in which skin comes in all shades of white and brown, and the general population is fairly accepting of everyone else.

When the United States took control of Puerto Rico in 1898, the island underwent another enormous cultural transformation. Suddenly U.S. customs and practices were imposed. English became a common second language, and has at times been proclaimed the official language. The U.S. dollar became the legal tender. American corporations set up shop, bringing with them an influx of American expatriates whose ways of dress, cuisine, and art were integrated into the existing culture. Much of this influence came in the form of the military, due to the many military bases that were established on the island. Some people credit that influence on the relative stability and orderliness of public life, particularly as compared to other Caribbean islands. The island's governmental and judicial systems are organized similarly to the United States, and many U.S. social services are offered on the island.

Inroads of contemporary American culture have been made into much of island life, but Puerto Ricans are fiercely proud of their

JÍBARO CULTURE: FROM RIDICULE TO REVERENCE

After the Taíno Indians succumbed to the Spanish conquistadors, an agrarian culture developed in the mountains of Puerto Rico. By the 19th century, wealthy Europeans arrived by ship to establish grand haciendas. Along with slaves, locals were employed to work the land, growing coffee and sugar. Isolated from developing port cities by unnavigable forest, dependent upon their own two hands to feed and shelter their families, and governed by a strict moral code informed by both Catholicism and Taíno spiritual beliefs, the early Puerto Rican men and women were poor, hard-working people who made up for their lack of formal education with common sense. When they did venture into the cities, townspeople jeered at them for their straw hats, their neckerchiefs, and their country ways, calling them *jíbaros*, a word similar in meaning to hillbilly.

The word *jíbaro* first appeared in a song and poem in 1820, but it gained widespread acceptance in 1849 when Dr. Manuel Alonzo published his book *El Gíbaro*, a collection of folktales about rustic life. Because they had to create their own entertainment, a big part of *jíbaro* culture was music. Steeped in Spanish roots, *jíbaro* music emphasizes stringed instruments, particularly the four-string *cuatro*. It is similar in sound to the *guajiro* sound from Cuba, and is often likened to the folk music of the Appalachian region of the United States. *Jíbaro* music is still quite popular in Puerto Rico and is performed at weddings and Christmas celebrations.

Once a source of embarrassment, the *jíbaro* identity has evolved over time to become a source of Puerto Rican pride. The symbol for the Popular Democratic Party formed in 1938 is the *jíbaro's* straw hat. A monument in Salinas, depicting a man, woman, and child, pays tribute to the *jíbaro* culture. And popular restaurants, such as Restaurante Raíces in Old San Juan, dress their servers as *jíbaros* in straw hats and neckerchiefs. To be called a *jíbaro* today is to be called a true Puerto Rican, and that's a good reason to feel proud.

Spanish heritage. Since becoming a U.S. territory a little more than 100 years ago, Puerto Rico has undergone a seismic shift in its national identity that has divided the island politically. Puerto Ricans are U.S. citizens, and they enjoy many—but not all—the privileges that entails. The issue of Puerto Rico's future political status has been an ongoing debate for more than 50 years, and it is as much a part of the island's national identity as its Spanish language and customs. Roughly half the island's population wants to remain a U.S. commonwealth, in large part because they believe that status ensures the preservation of their Spanish culture. The other half wants to become a U.S. state so they can have full privileges of citizenship, including the ability to vote for the U.S. president and have full representation in Congress.

In 2012, Congress took actions that could put the future of Puerto Rico's political status to a popular vote on the island. Until a vote is held, the future of Puerto Rico's 3.7 million citizens hangs in the balance between two cultures. Regardless of the outcome of Puerto Rico's 2012 referendums on whether to maintain commonwealth status or seek non-territorial status, Puerto Rico's political standing will probably remain in flux for the time being.

GENDER ROLES

When it comes to gender roles, Puerto Ricans are fairly traditional. However, as in the rest of the industrial world, women have made inroads into the formerly male world of business and sports, particularly in urban areas. At one time it was common practice among the island's most traditional families for young women to be accompanied by chaperones in the form of an aunt or older sister when they began dating, but that practice is quickly vanishing.

Vestiges of machismo still exist. Attractive young women may attract unwanted catcalls, usually expressed with a "s-s-s" sound, or calls of *"Mira, mami!"* ("Look, mama!"). But in general, Puerto Rican men can be quite chivalrous in ways American women may be unaccustomed to. Having a bus seat relinquished for their comfort and the holding of doors are courtesies commonly encountered.

RELIGION

Before the arrival of Christopher Columbus in 1493, Puerto Rico's indigenous population was composed of highly spiritual individuals who worshipped multiple gods believed to reside in nature. It was a common belief that these gods controlled everything from the success or failure of crops to one's choice of a spouse.

All that began to change when Ponce de León arrived in 1508, bringing with him several Roman Catholic priests who ministered to the new colony and set about converting the Taíno Indians to the faith, beginning with baptisms. In 1511, Pope Julius II created a diocese in Caparra, the island's first settlement.

Today, depending on the source, Puerto Rico's population is between 75 and 85 percent Roman Catholic. Although weekly church attendance is far below that figure, the Catholic Church has great influence on Puerto Rican

AN ISLAND CHRISTMAS

The Twelve Days of Christmas have nothing on Puerto Rico. Here, Las Navidades (the Christmas holidays) start the day after Thanksgiving and end in mid-January with the San Sebastián Street Festival. On any given day during the Christmas holiday period (usually after 10 P.M.), a roving band of *parranderos* – like carolers but dressed in straw hats and playing guitars and maracas – will wake an unsuspecting friend with Christmas songs and raucous demands for food and drink. After the visitors have emptied the pantry and the refrigerator, the owners of the home close up the house and join the *parranderos* at the next house, and the next house, and so on, until dawn, when the last house serves everyone the traditional *asopao de pollo* (chicken and rice stew).

Nochebuena (Christmas Eve) is an official half-day holiday when friends and family come together over a large meal, followed by midnight Mass. Many Puerto Ricans have adopted the tradition of Santa Claus on Christmas Day, called **Navidad.** In addition to presents from St. Nick, the highlight is a day-long party that usually involves roasting a whole pig over wood charcoal.

On December 28, the north coast town of Hatillo commemorates Herod's slaughter of innocents in Bethlehem with **Día de los Inocentes,** a celebration featuring costumed parades throughout the countryside where tricks are played on friends and family.

At the stroke of midnight on New Year's Eve or **Año Viejo** (Old Year), tradition dictates that locals eat 12 grapes, sprinkle sugar outside the house for good luck, and throw a bucket of water out the window to get rid of the old and make room for the new. Fireworks light up the sky at the Puerto Rico Convention Center in San Juan at midnight.

Puerto Rico's traditional Christian holiday is **Día de los Reyes** (Three Kings Day) on January 6. Festivities begin the night before with **Víspera de los Reyes** (Eve of the Epiphany of the Kings), when children fill drinking glasses with water for thirsty Wise Men and fill shoeboxes with grass for their camels. The next morning children discover that the water and grass have been consumed and find gifts that have been left beneath their beds.

The **San Sebastián Street Festival** in Old San Juan originated as a day to honor Saint Sebastian. It takes place mid-January, which makes it a natural bookend to the island's holiday season. The four-day festival is likened to Mardi Gras without the beads when hundreds of thousands of people descend on Old San Juan for parades, concerts, artisan booths, and lots of eating and drinking.

FIESTAS PATRONALES

The most elaborate and renowned *fiestas patronales* take place in San Juan and Loíza, but all of the municipalities' celebrations honoring their patron saints offer visitors a unique opportunity to get a concentrated dose of local culture. Here is a list of some of the island's *fiestas patronales*.

FEBRUARY

- **Manatí:** La Virgen de la Candelaria, February 2

- **Mayagüez:** La Virgen de la Candelaria, February 2

- **Coamo:** La Virgen de la Candelaria and San Blas, February 3

MARCH

- **Loíza:** San Patricio, March 17

- **Lares:** San José, March 19

- **Luquillo:** San José, March 19

MAY

- **Arecibo:** Apóstol San Felipe, May 1

- **Maunabo:** San Isidro, May 15

- **Toa Alta:** San Fernando, May 30

JUNE

- **Barranquitas:** San Antonio de Padua, June 13

- **Dorado:** San Antonio de Padua, June 13

- **Isabela:** San Antonio de Padua, June 13

- **San Juan:** San Juan Bautista, June 23

- **Orocovis:** San Juan Bautista, June 24

- **Toa Baja:** San Pedro Apóstol, June 30

JULY

- **Culebra:** Virgen del Carmen, July 16

- **Hatillo:** Virgen del Carmen, July 16

- **Morovis:** Virgen del Carmen, July 16

- **Aibonito:** Santiago Apóstol, July 25

- **Fajardo:** Santiago Apóstol, July 25

- **Guánica:** Santiago Apóstol, July 25

- **Loíza:** Santiago Apóstol, July 25

- **San Germán:** San Germán, July 31

AUGUST

- **Cayey:** Nuestra Señora de la Asunción, August 15

- **Adjuntas:** San Joaquín and Santa Ana, August 21

- **Rincón:** Santa Rosa de Lima, August 30

SEPTEMBER

- **Jayuya:** Nuestra Señora de la Monserrate, September 8

- **Moca:** Nuestra Señora de la Monserrate, September 8

- **Salinas:** Nuestra Señora de la Monserrate, September 8

- **Cabo Rojo:** San Miguel Arcangel, September 29

- **Utuado:** San Miguel Arcangel, September 29

OCTOBER

- **Yabucoa:** Los Angeles Custodios, October 2

- **Naguabo:** Nuestra Señora del Rosario, October 7

- **Vega Baja:** Nuestra Señora del Rosario, October 7

- **Quebradillas:** San Rafael Arcangel, October 24

NOVEMBER

- **Aguadilla:** San Carlos Borromeo, November 4

DECEMBER

- **Vega Alta:** La Inmaculada Concepción de María, December 8

- **Vieques:** La Inmaculada Concepción de María, December 8

- **Ponce:** Nuestra Señora de la Guadalupe, December 12

© LAGUSTIN/123RF.COM

Carnaval in Ponce

life. Each town has a Catholic church at its center and celebrates its patron saint with an annual festival. Although many patron-saint festivals have become much more secular over time, they typically include a religious procession and special Mass to mark the day. Images of saints are common items in traditional households, and you can't enter a church without seeing clusters of women lighting candles, praying, or kissing the hem of the dress worn by a statue of Mary.

Some Puerto Ricans practice a hybrid form of religion called *espiritismo,* which combines elements of the Catholic religion and Indian beliefs in nature-dwelling spirits that can be called on to effect change in one's life. Similarly, some Puerto Ricans of African descent practice Santería, introduced to the island by Yoruba slaves from West Africa. It also observes multiple gods and combines elements of Catholicism. Practitioners of both religions patronize the island's *botanicas,* stores that sell roots, herbs, candles, soaps, and amulets that are employed to sway the spirits to help individuals achieve success, whether it be in business, love, or starting a family.

Once the United States arrived in Puerto Rico in 1898, Protestantism began to grow on the island, and all major sects are represented. Pentecostal fundamentalism has developed in recent decades, and there is a small Jewish community on the island as well.

HOLIDAYS AND FESTIVALS

No matter when you visit Puerto Rico, there's a good chance there's a holiday or festival going on somewhere on the island. Among the biggest festivals are Ponce's **Carnaval** in February;

Hatillo's **Festival de Máscaras** and **Día de los Inocentes** in December; and **Festival Nacional Indígena** in Jayuya in November.

Being a U.S. commonwealth, Puerto Rico has adopted an American-style celebration of Christmas, but it also celebrates the more traditional **Los Reyes Magos,** also known as **Three Kings Day,** on January 6. On January 5, children fill shoeboxes with grass to feed the Wise Men's camels and place them under their beds. In the morning, the grass is gone and in its place is a present.

But most notably, all 78 municipalities in Puerto Rico honor their patron saints with annual festivals called *fiestas patronales.* Although special Masses and religious processions may be a part of the celebrations, secular festivities such as musical performances, dancing, traditional foods, artisan booths, and games often take precedence. The festivals typically take place in the main plaza.

LANGUAGE

Puerto Rico has two official languages: Spanish and English. Many Puerto Ricans living in metropolitan areas are bilingual, but by far the majority of the population uses primarily Spanish. Spanish is spoken in the public school system, and English is taught as a foreign language.

In recent years, the designation of Puerto Rico's official language has been caught in a political volley between the pro-statehood and pro-commonwealth factions. In 1991, Governor Rafael Hernández Colón, a proponent of commonwealth status, declared Spanish as the sole official language. He was preceded by Governor Pedro Rosselló, a proponent of statehood, who changed the official language to English. But for now, both languages enjoy official status.

EDUCATION

Puerto Rico has a 94 percent literacy rate, and its educational system is structured the same as in the United States—kindergarten through 12th grade. In addition to the public school system, the Catholic Church operates a private school system. Both systems teach in Spanish. There are also several English-language private schools on the island.

There are several institutions of higher learning in Puerto Rico, the largest one being the Universidad de Puerto Rico, with campuses in Mayagüez, San Juan, Río Piedras, and Humacao. Other schools include Universidad Polytechnica de Puerto Rico, Universidad Intermericana de Puerto Rico, Universidad Carlos Albizu, and Universidad del Sagrado Corazón. There are also two arts schools— Escuela de Artes Plásticas de Puerto Rico and Conservatorio de Música de Puerto Rico.

The Arts

Puerto Rico is a melting pot of indigenous, Spanish, and African influences, and nowhere is that more apparent than in the island's rich cultural life. Food, music, art, dance—they all reflect different aspects of the cultures that came together over time to create *la vida criolla* (the Creole life).

MUSIC

Music is a huge part of Puerto Rican life. Sometimes it seems as though the whole island reverberates to a syncopated beat, thanks to the strains of music that waft from outdoor concerts, open windows, barrooms, passing cars, and boom boxes. Nearly every weekend there is a holiday or festival in Puerto Rico, and at the core of its celebration is always music. During a recent stay in Old San Juan, each morning began with the sound of a lone elderly man walking up the deserted street singing a heartbreaking lament that echoed off the 18th-century buildings.

The island has made many significant contributions to the world of music at large, starting with the birth of a couple of uniquely Puerto Rican instruments. The national instrument of Puerto Rico is the *cuatro,* an adaptation of the Spanish guitar that features 10 strings arranged in five pairs and is typically carved from solid blocks of laurel. Several classic Puerto Rican instruments date to the indigenous people, including the popular *güiro.* Similar in principle to the washboard, the *güiro* is a hollowed gourd with ridges cut into its surface, which is scraped rhythmically with a comblike object. Other prevalent local instruments that reflect African influence are the *barrtl,* a large drum originally made by stretching animal skin over the top of a barrel; the *tambour,* a handheld drum similar to a tambourine but without the cymbals; and the maraca, made from gourds and seeds.

Some of Puerto Rico's earliest known musical styles are *bomba* and *plena,* which have roots in the African slave culture. They're both heavy on percussion and lightning-fast rhythms. *Bomba* features call-and-response vocals and is accompanied by frenzied dancing in which the dancers match their steps to every beat of the drum. In *plena,* the emphasis is on the vocals, which are more European in origin and retell current events or local scandals. Local *bomba* masters include Los Hermanos Ayala (traditionalists from Loíza) and the more contemporary Cepedas (based in Santurce, San Juan). Reviving interest in *plena* is the band Plena Libre.

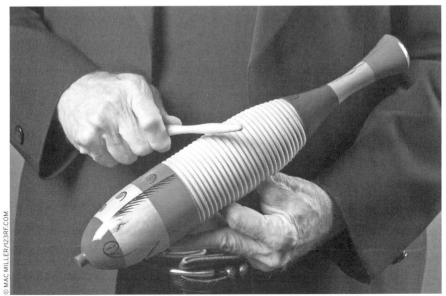

a *güiro* being played

Akin in philosophy to the origins of American country music, *música jíbara* is the folk sound of Puerto Rico's rural mountain dwellers, called *jíbaros*. Performed by small ensembles on *cuatro, güiro,* bongos, and occasionally clarinets and trumpets, *música jíbara* is more Spanish in origin than *bomba* or *plena,* although the Caribbean influence is unmistakable. Vocals, which play an important part in *música jíbara,* are usually about the virtues of a simpler way of life. There are two types of *música jíbara*—seis and *aguinalda. Seis* is typically named after a particular town, and the lyrics are often improvised and sung in 10-syllable couplets. *Aguinaldos* are performed around Christmas by roaming carolers. Ramito (1915-1990) is considered Puerto Rico's quintessential *jíbaro* artist.

While Puerto Rican slaves grooved to *bomba* and the farmers played their folk tunes, Puerto Rico's moneyed Europeans turned their attentions to classical music, eventually giving birth around 1900 to *danza,* a romantic classical style of music often described as Afro-Caribbean waltz. Originating in Ponce, *danza* was performed on piano, cello, violin, and *bombardino* (similar to a trombone) for dancers who performed structured, ballroom-style steps. The form is celebrated in Ponce with the annual Semana de la Danza in May. The most famous composers of *danza* were Manuel Gregorio Tavarez (1843-1883) and his pupil, Juan Morel Campos (1857-1896).

In 1956, renowned Catalan cellist and composer Pablo Casals moved to Puerto Rico, and a year later Festival Casals was born. The international celebration of classical music continues today in concert halls in San Juan, Ponce, and Mayagüez every June and July. In Old San Juan there is a museum dedicated to Casals, featuring his music manuscripts, instruments, and recordings.

Of course, salsa is the music most associated with Puerto Rico today. A lively, highly danceable fusion of jazz, African polyrhythms, and Caribbean flair, salsa is performed by large ensembles on drums, keyboards, and horns. When people refer to Latin music, they usually mean salsa. It is the predominant form of music heard on the island, so just stop in almost any bar or restaurant advertising live music and you're likely to hear it. Watching expert salsa dancers move to the music is as entertaining as listening to the music. Born in New York City but Puerto Rican by heritage, percussionist and composer Tito Puente (1923-2000) was a major influence on salsa music. Other masters include Celia Cruz (1924-2003) and Willie Colón, but there are scores of popular Puerto Rican salsa artists who perform today.

The biggest thing happening in Puerto Rican music now, though, is reggaetón. An exciting blend of American hip-hop, *bomba, plena,* and Jamaican dancehall, the musical form is Puerto Rican-born and bred, and it's starting to gain notice worldwide. A big part of its explosive growth is due to the popularity of Daddy Yankee, who grew up in the public housing projects of San Juan and who's managed to cross over into the American market. Reggaetón festivals have become a popular pastime in Puerto Rico, but you can also hear it in nightclubs and blasting from car windows. And once again, Puerto Rico's culture comes back to its Afro-Caribbean roots. Other popular reggaetón artists include Don Omar, Tego Calderón, Ivy Queen, and Calle 13.

VISUAL ARTS

The visual arts have been a thriving art form in Puerto Rico for centuries, and its artists' output runs the gamut from baroque European-influenced paintings to contemporary conceptual pieces that challenge the definition of art.

Puerto Rico's best-known early artists were José Campeche (1751-1809) and Francisco Oller (1833-1917). Campeche was of mixed race, born in San Juan to a freed slave, Tomás Campeche, and a native of the Canary Islands, María

Jordán Marqué. He was primarily a self-taught artist, first learning the skill from his father, but he studied for a time with Luis Paret, an exiled Spanish painter who lived in Puerto Rico for awhile. As was common at the time, Campeche primarily painted portraits of wealthy landowners and religious scenes in heavily ornamented detail, which was in keeping with the rococo style of the day. He painted more than 400 paintings during his lifetime, the majority of them commissions. Campeche's *Virgen de la Soledad de la Victoria* was the first acquisition of the Museo de Arte de Puerto Rico, where you can see many other examples of his work.

Oller was born in Bayamón and studied art at the Academia de Bellas Artes in Madrid from 1851 to 1853. He also studied in Paris from 1858 to 1863, where he was a contemporary of Pissarro, Cézanne, and Guillaumins and exhibited at several Paris salons. Influenced by realist and impressionist styles, his work encompassed portraits, landscapes, and still lifes. But once he returned for good to Puerto Rico in 1884, his work became primarily realist in nature, typically rendered in somber colors. His subjects tended to focus on traditional Puerto Rican ways of life. One of his most famous paintings is *El Velorio (The Wake),* which depicts a rural family gathered in a home for an infant's wake and which can be seen in a gallery at the Universidad de Puerto Rico in Río Piedras. Oller's work has been acquired by many important museums, including the Musée d'Orsay in Paris.

Two other important early artists were Miguel Pou (1880-1968) and Ramón Frade (1875-1954), whose paintings celebrated the dignity of *jíbaro* (peasant) life.

Another internationally recognized artist was island transplant Jack Delano (1914-1997), a significant photographer who chronicled the Puerto Rican people and way of life from 1941 until his death. Born in Kiev, Ukraine, he first came to Puerto Rico in 1941 on assignment for the U.S. Farm Security Administration in conjunction with President Franklin D. Roosevelt's New Deal programs. The program sent many famous photographers throughout the United States to document rural life. In addition to Delano, they included Walker Evans, Dorothea Lange, Marjory Collins, and Gordon Parks, among others. After the war, Delano returned to Puerto Rico in 1946, settled there permanently, and continued to photograph the island's changing culture. His work is journalistic in nature but is deeply imbued with a respect for the human condition. In addition to his photography, Delano was a musical composer of sonatas.

Beginning in the 1940s, a radical new art form exploded in Puerto Rico that reflected growing concern among artists and writers that the island's native culture was being subsumed by American influence. That sentiment was expressed in visually striking representations of graphic poster art, called *cartels*. Originally funded by the local government, artists produced colorful illustrations of important books, plays, songs, and poems, as well as political slogans and quotations. Eventually the art form evolved away from its boosterish origins. Some artists used the form to criticize the government and social issues, while others celebrated the island's natural and architectural beauty. Today it's most commonly seen advertising festivals. Among its most celebrated artists is Lorenzo Homar (1913-2004), who was a recipient of the National Medal of Honor and cofounder of the Centro de Arte de Puertorriqueño, which played an important role in advancing the graphic art form. The Museo de Arte de Puerto Rico has a gallery devoted to an excellent collection of *cartels*.

Another significant artist was Rafael Tufiño (1922-2008), whose somber paintings captured the island's people and customs, as well as its pockets of squalor. Tufiño was also a cofounder of the Centro de Arte de Puertorriqueña and a faculty member for the Puerto Rico Institute of Culture's art school, Escuela de Artes Plásticas.

Puerto Rico's arts scene continues to evolve. Recognizing the positive impact art can have on the economy, in 2001 Governor Sila M. Calderón initiated a $25 million program to fund the **Puerto Rico Public Art Project,** which has put in place scores of contemporary site-specific public art installations throughout the island. Many works are meant to be functional, in the form of bus stops, park benches, and vendor kiosks, or to enliven the roadways of major thoroughfares and stops along the new commuter rail service (Tren Urbano). Pieces vary from murals to conceptual multimedia installations to earthworks, and 20 percent of the works were created by Puerto Rican artists. Among the local and international artists involved were Ana Rosa Rivera, Víctor Vázquez, Ramón Berríos, Lourdes Correa Carlo, Charles Juhasz, and Liliana Porter.

For details on the project, including maps and descriptions of the pieces, visit www.arte-publicopr.com, in English and Spanish.

CRAFTS

Puerto Rican artisans produce a variety of crafts unique to the island's culture. The most distinctive craft is the **vejigante mask,** a brilliantly colored object made from coconut shells or papier-mâché featuring large protruding horns. The masks represent the Moors in annual festivals revolving around street pageants that re-enact Spain's defeat of the Moors in the 13th century. Although there are several artists who create the masks, the Ayala family artists in Loíza are considered the masters of the form. Prices range about $30-250. *Vejigante* figurines made from a variety of materials, including ceramic, glass, and metal, are also popular collectible items made by local artisans and come in all price ranges.

Puerto Rico's oldest and most traditional craft form is the **santo,** primitive-looking woodcarvings of Catholic saints. Santos originated with low-income families who wanted representations of their favorite saints to display in their homes, but who couldn't afford the expensive plaster ones available for purchase. Today, santos are highly collectible, and many museums, including Museo de las Americas in Old San Juan, exhibit priceless collections of vintage santos. New santos can be found in the island's finer crafts and gift shops and cost $80-500.

Mundillo is a delicate, handmade lace created by tying fine threads using bobbins, which facilitate weaving the threads into an intricate pattern. The lace is used to embellish tablecloths, handkerchiefs, and christening gowns, among other things. The art form has roots in Spain, but the *mundillo* pattern is specific to Puerto Rico. It's primarily produced in and around the tiny town of Moca near Aguadilla on the west coast, where several artisans live. *Mundillo* can be purchased at finer gift shops around the island and at some festivals. Because it is so labor-intensive, *mundillo* is somewhat pricey. A handkerchief rimmed with a small amount of *mundillo* starts around $30, but a handkerchief made entirely of *mundillo* can cost more than $100.

The crafting of woven cotton **hammocks** is an art form that continues a tradition started by the Taíno Indians, who used them not only to sleep on but also for food storage and other utilitarian purposes. The town of San Sebastián in the western fringe of the Cordillera Central is the best known source of the hammock, but they're available at most crafts and gift shops throughout the island starting at about $30.

Other popular low-priced craft items include **seed jewelry,** colorful earrings, bracelets, and necklaces made from the seeds of trees and plants on the island; **güiros,** percussion instruments made from gourds; and landscape paintings on pieces of rough-hewn wood.

LITERATURE

Literature in Puerto Rico has historically revolved around national identity and the tension of being U.S. citizens in a Latino culture. Its literary heritage began to emerge in the mid-1800s, and among its earliest notable works was *El Gibaro* (1849) by Manuel Alonso y Pacheco. Part prose, part poetry, *El Gibaro* celebrated the simple life of Puerto Rico's farmers, called *jíbaros.*

But the first writer to receive literary prominence was Alejandro Tapia y Rivera (1826-1882) of San Juan, a playwright and abolitionist who wrote many works, including biographical pieces on important Puerto Ricans such as Spanish admiral Ramón Power y Giralt, artist José Campeche, and the pirate Roberto Cofresí.

One of Puerto Rico's early writers who was revered throughout the Caribbean and South America was Eugenio María de Hostos (1839-1903), a writer and educator who led civic-reform movements throughout Latin America. His seminal work is *Peregrinación de Bayoán* (1863), a work of fiction that illustrated injustices under the Spanish regime and called for independence from Spain.

After Puerto Rico came under control of the United States, a new crop of writers, called the Generation of 1998, began to flourish. Fueled primarily by politics, several writers of this era combined the art of poetry with the craft of journalism. José de Diego (1867-1918) of Aguadilla and Luís Muñoz Rivera (1859-1916) of Barranquitas were significant poets and journalists who fueled the island's independence movement with their words. Diego, considered a precursor of the modernist movement in Puerto Rico, produced several books of poetry, including *Pomarrosas, Jovillos, Cantos de Rebeldia,* and *Cantos del Pitirre.* Rivera's most significant work was a book of poems called *Tropicales.*

One of the most important writers of this era was Antonio S. Pedriera (1899-1939), whose work *Insularismo* examined how U.S. political

control had affected Puerto Rican culture in the first 35 years.

In the 1940s, there was a mass migration of Puerto Ricans to the United States—primarily New York City—and the island's literature took a significant shift reflecting that phenomenon. Suddenly there was an output of work by Puerto Rican immigrants who found themselves grappling with issues of dual identity. In 1951, playwright René Marqués (1919-1974) of Arecibo wrote his most critically acclaimed play, *The Oxcart,* which chronicled the mass exodus of Puerto Ricans to New York City. Also noteworthy is *A Puerto Rican in New York* (1961), by Jesús Colón (1918-1974), who was born in Cayey but grew up in the United States.

The 1960s and 1970s saw the birth of a literary movement called Nuyorican literature. Nuyorican is the name given to New Yorkers of Puerto Rican heritage. Some of the most notable writers of this movement were Piri Thomas, author of *Down These Mean Streets* (1967), and Nicholasa Mohr, who wrote *Nilda* (1973), both of which dealt with life in the urban barrios of New York City. By the 1980s, the Nuyorican movement exploded on the spoken-word scene with work that had a strong political message. New York's Nuyorican Poets Café was and still is the epicenter of this movement, providing a forum for such celebrated poets as Ponce-born Pedro Pietri (1944-2004), for whom a street in New York City was recently named, and New York-born Felipe Luciano, founder of the Young Lords activist group. Also once a regular at Nuyorican Poets Café was Gurabo-born Miguel Piñero (1946-1988), who was a playwright and actor. His play *Short Eyes,* about life in prison, won the New York Drama Critics Award for Best American Play in 1974. His life was depicted in a film starring Benjamin Bratt called *Piñero.*

Puerto Rican literature continues to flourish today thanks to many contemporary writers living on the island and in the United States, including poet Victor Hernández Cruz and authors Esmeralda Santiago and Ernesto

Quiñonez. Santiago wrote *Conquistador* (2011), a historical novel about a sugar plantation owner in 19th-century Puerto Rico, and *When I Was Puerto Rican* (1993), a memoir about growing up on the island. Quiñonez wrote *Bodega Dreams* (2000) and *Chango's Fire* (2004).

For an excellent survey of Puerto Rican literature, read *Boricuas: The Influential Puerto Rican Writings, an Anthology* (Ballantine, 1995), featuring excerpts of works by some of the writers mentioned here, as well as many others.

DANCE

Dance plays an important role in Puerto Rican culture because it goes hand in hand with the island's rich musical heritage. But for the most part, dance is about moving to the groove of live music or DJs, whether it's at a nightclub, an outdoor concert in the town plaza, or at one of the island's countless festivals. Dance is integral to *bomba, plena,* salsa, and reggaetón music, and the thing all those forms of movement have in common is this: It's all in the hips! The exception is the ballroom style of *danza.*

When it comes to dance performance, the island leader is Guateque, the folkloric ballet of Puerto Rico. For more than 20 years this 40-member dance company and school based on Corozal has been preserving and performing the island's traditional dances, as well as adapting them into new productions. Past productions include *Los Taínos de Borkén* and *Los Dioses (The Gods),* which depict daily life and spirituality of the island's indigenous Indians.

ESSENTIALS

Getting There

BY AIR

Puerto Rico has two international airports, **Luis Muñoz Marín International Airport** (Aeropuerto Internacional Luis Muñoz Marín, SJU) in Isla Verde, San Juan, and **Rafael Hernández International Airport** (Aeropuerto Internacional Rafael Hernández, BQN) in Aguadilla on the west coast. The only other airport to service flights from the United States is **Mercedita International Airport** (Aeropuerto Internacional Mercedita, PSE) in Ponce on the south coast.

Regional airports serving commercial travel are Isla Grande Airport (SIG) near Old San Juan; José Aponte de la Torre Airport (RVR) in Ceiba; Eugenio María de Hostos Airport (MAZ) in Mayagüez; Vieques Airport (VQS) in Isabel Segunda; and Culebra Airport (CPX) in Culebra. Airports in Fajardo and Humacao have been closed to commercial service.

Airfares to Puerto Rico fluctuate in price throughout the year, but the cheapest rates can typically be secured during the off-season, May-October, which is also hurricane season.

From North America

Direct flights to San Juan are available

from Atlanta, Boston, Chicago, Dallas/Fort Worth, Fort Lauderdale, Miami, New York City, Newark, Orlando, Philadelphia, and Washington, D.C.

These airlines offer flights to San Juan from the United States:

- **AirTran** (800/247-8726, www.airtran.com)
- **American Airlines** (800/433-7300, www.aa.com)
- **Continental Airlines** (800/231-0856 or 800/523-3273, www.continental.com)
- **Delta Air Lines** (800/221-1212 or 800/325-1999, www.delta.com)
- **JetBlue Airways** (800/538-2583, www.jetblue.com)
- **Spirit Airlines** (800/772-7117, www.spiritairlines.com)
- **United Airlines** (800/864-8331, www.ual.com)
- **U.S. Airways** (800/428-4322, www.usairways.com)

Direct flights to Aguadilla are operated by JetBlue (from Orlando and from JFK in New York City); Spirit Airlines (from Fort Lauderdale); Delta (from Newark); and Continental (from Newark). Direct flights to Ponce are operated by JetBlue (from JFK in New York City and from Orlando).

In Canada, direct flights to San Juan are operated by Air Canada (888/247-2262, www.aircanada.com) from Montréal and Toronto.

From Europe

British Airways (www.britishairways.com) offers connecting flights from the United Kingdom to San Juan via New York City or Miami. **Iberia** (www.iberia.com) offers direct flights to San Juan from Madrid.

From Australia

Connecting flights from Australia are operated by **United** (through Los Angeles and Chicago) and **American Airlines** (through New York City).

From the Caribbean

Several small airlines offer flights to San Juan from throughout the Caribbean. They include **Air Sunshine** (888/879-8900, www.airsunshine.com) from St. Croix, St. Thomas, Tortola, Virgin Gorda, and Vieques; **Cape Air** (800/352-0714, www.flycapeair.com) from St. Croix, St. Thomas, and Tortola; and **Liat Airline** (888/844-5428, www.liatairline.com) from 22 destinations in the eastern Caribbean.

BY CRUISE SHIP

San Juan is the largest port in the Caribbean, and it is a port of call or point of origin for nearly two dozen cruise lines. The cruise ship docks lie along Calle La Marina in Old San Juan.

A few of the most popular cruise lines serving San Juan include:

- **Carnival Cruise Lines** (866/299-5698, www.carnival.com)
- **Celebrity Cruises** (800/647-2251, www.celebritycruises.com)
- **Holland America Line** (877/724-5425, www.hollandamerica.com)
- **Norwegian Cruise Line** (800/327-7030, www.ncl.com)
- **Princess Cruises** (800/PRINCESS-800/774-6237, www.princess.com)
- **Radisson Seven Seas Cruises** (877/505-5370, www.rssc.com)

Getting Around

Puerto Rico's easy accessibility from the States and the compact lay of the land make it a great place to go for a long weekend. Many visitors simply fly into San Juan and stay there. There are plenty of great restaurants, nightclubs, shops, beaches, and historical sights within walking or taxi distance. A reliable bus transit system and a new rail line called Tren Urbano provide inexpensive transportation throughout the city. It's understandable why some visitors are hesitant to leave behind the capital city's charms.

But escaping the bustle of the city and experiencing the island's unique natural beauty is highly recommended and easily achieved. Car-rental agencies are plentiful, and the roads are well marked and maintained. Because the island is so small, it's possible to make a day trip to any sight on the island. Just keep in mind that Puerto Rico has a high volume of traffic, which can slow your progress. Travel through the central mountain region especially can take longer than might be expected because of the narrow winding roads. Always figure in extra travel time when planning a road trip.

CAR

Visitors who plan to venture outside of San Juan should plan to rent a car. This is by far the best way to explore the island. Most of the major American car-rental agencies have locations throughout the island, and there are several local agencies as well. For the most part, roads are well maintained and well marked. Gasoline is sold by the liter, speed limits are measured in miles per hour, and distance is measured in kilometers. And all road signs are in Spanish. International driving licenses are required for drivers from countries other than the United States.

Driving around San Juan can be bit nerve-racking for those not accustomed to inner-city driving. The sheer number of cars on the island guarantees congested roadways, so be sure to schedule extra time for road trips. Drivers tend to speed and don't leave much space between cars. They also can be creative when it comes to navigating traffic—rolling through stops and driving on the shoulder of the highway is not uncommon. Ponce has, hands-down, the worst drivers. It's practically a free-for-all, and they blow their car horns constantly.

Take extra precautions when driving in the mountains. Fortunately the traffic is light, but the roads are narrow and winding. Drivers who travel these roads every day tend to proceed at a perilously fast clip. If the driver behind you appears impatient or tailgates, pull over and let him or her pass. On roads with a lot of blind curves, it is common practice to blow the car horn to alert oncoming traffic you're approaching. If it's raining, beware of small mudslides and overflowing riverbanks, which sometimes close roads. And whatever you do, don't look down! But really, it's not as bad as it sounds. Driving through Puerto Rico's majestic mountains is well worth a few shattered nerves.

There is an excellent, major, limited-access highway system called *autopista* that dissects and nearly encircles the island, parts of which are toll roads ($0.25-1.25 per toll). The speed limits range 50-65 miles per hour.

The rest of the island's numbered roads are called *carreteras,* typically written as the abbreviation *carr.,* followed by a number, such as Carr. 193. Major *carreteras* often have spur routes that go either into a town's center or along its beachfront. A road number followed by the letter R or the word *ramal* indicates a spur route that goes through a town's commercial district. Beachfront routes are often indicated by the abbreviation *int.* or an addition of the numeral 3 after a road number.

PUERTO RICO'S HIGHWAYS AND DRIVING DISTANCES

MAJOR HIGHWAYS

- **PR 26:** East-west, San Juan airport to Condado; also known as Baldorioty de Castro Avenue
- **PR 18:** North-south, connecting PR 22 and PR 52, San Juan
- **PR 66:** Northwest-southeast, Canovanas to San Juan
- **PR 22:** East-west, San Juan to Arecibo (toll); also known as Jose de Diego Expressway
- **PR 52:** North-southwest, San Juan to Ponce (partially toll); also known as Luis A. Ferré Expressway
- **PR 30:** Northwest-southeast, Caguas to Humacao
- **PR 53:** North-south, Fajardo to Yabucoa

DRIVING DISTANCES FROM SAN JUAN

- **Aguadilla:** 81 miles (130 kilometers)
- **Arecibo:** 48 miles (77 kilometers)
- **Barranquitas:** 34 miles (55 kilometers)
- **Cabo Rojo:** 111 miles (179 kilometers)
- **Cayey:** 30 miles (48 kilometers)
- **Dorado:** 17 miles (27 kilometers)
- **Fajardo:** 32 miles (52 kilometers)
- **Guánica:** 94 miles (151 kilometers)
- **Humacao:** 34 miles (55 kilometers)
- **Jayuya:** 58 miles (93 kilometers)
- **La Parguera:** 107 miles (172 kilometers)
- **Luquillo:** 28 miles (45 kilometers)
- **Mayagüez:** 98 miles (158 kilometers)
- **Ponce:** 70 miles (113 kilometers)
- **Rincón:** 93 miles (150 kilometers)
- **Salinas:** 46 miles (74 kilometers)
- **Utuado:** 65 miles (105 kilometers)

Addresses are typically identified by road and kilometer numbers, for instance: Carr. 193, km 2. Look for the white numbered kilometer posts alongside the road to identify your location. In towns, streets are called **avenidas** (abbreviated as Ave.) and **calles.**

TAXI

Most towns in Puerto Rico are served by at least one taxi service. San Juan has several reliable tourist-taxi services that serve the areas where visitors congregate. It's possible to flag one down day or night in Isla Verde and Condado, and in Old San Juan, there are two taxi stands—on Plaza de Colón and Plaza de Armas. You can also call one.

Operators include **Metro Taxi** (787/725-2870), **Major Taxi** (787/723-2460), **Rochdale Radio Taxi** (787/721-1900), and **Capetillo Taxi** (787/758-7000).

Fares between the airport and the piers in Old San Juan are fixed rates. From the airport, the rates are $10 to Isla Verde, $15 to Condado, $19 to Old San Juan, and $15 to Isla Grande Airport and the Puerto Rico Convention Center. From the piers, the rates are $12 to Condado and $19 to Isla Verde. There is a $1.50 gas surcharge, and each piece of luggage is $1. Metered fares are $3 minimum, $1.75 initial charge, and $0.10 every 19th of a mile. Customers pay all road tolls.

PÚBLICO

Públicos, also known as *guaguas* or *carros públicos,* are privately owned transport services that operate communal van routes throughout specific regions of the island. In addition, most towns are served by local *públicos.* *Público* stops are usually found on a town's

DRIVING VOCABULARY

USEFUL WORDS
al centro: downtown
autopista: limited access toll road
calle: street
carr. or *carretera:* highway
cruce: crossroads
cruzar: to cross
cuadras: blocks
esquina: corner
estacionamiento: parking
derecha: right
derecho: straight ahead
doble: turn
izquierda: left
lejos: far
luces: traffic lights

luz: traffic light
vaya: go

ROAD SIGNS
alto: stop
calle sin salida: dead-end street
cuidado: be careful
despacio: slow
desvio: detour
este: east
hacia: to
int. : approaching intersection, or interior route
norte: north
oeste: west
ramal: business route
salida: exit
sur: south

main plaza. This is a very inexpensive but slow way to travel because as riders get off at their appointed stops, the van will wait indefinitely until it fills up with new riders before heading to the next stop.

Público transportation from San Juan to outlying areas is provided by **Blue Line** (787/765-7733) to Río Piedras, Aguadilla, Aguada, Moca, Isabela, and other areas; **Choferes Unidos de Ponce** (787/764-0540) to Ponce and other areas; **Lina Boricua** (787/765-1908) to Lares, Ponce, Jayuya, Utuado, San Sebastián, and other areas; **Linea Caborrojeña** (787/723-9155) to Cabo Rojo, San Germán, and other areas; **Linea Sultana** (787/765-9377) to Mayagüez and other areas; and **Terminal de Transportación Publica** (787/250-0717) to Fajardo and other areas.

BUS
Autoridad Metropolitana de Autobuses (787/250-6064 or 787/294-0500, ext. 514, www.dtop.gov.pr/ama/mapaindex.htm) is an excellent public bus system that serves the entire metropolitan San Juan area until about 9 P.M. It's serviced by large, air-conditioned vehicles with wheelchair access, and the cost is typically a low $0.75 per fare (exact change required). Bus stops are clearly marked along the routes with green signs that say "Parada," except in Old San Juan, where you have to catch the bus at **Covadonga Bus and Trolley Terminal,** the large terminal near the cruise-ship piers at the corner of Calle la Marina and Calle J. A. Corretjer. When waiting for a bus at a *parada,* it is necessary to wave to get the driver to stop.

RAIL
In 2005, San Juan launched **Tren Urbano,** its first long-awaited commuter train service. The system runs mostly aboveground and has 15 stations, many of which house a terrific collection of specially commissioned public art. The train connects the communities of Bayamón, the Universidad de Puerto Rico in Río Piedras, Hato Rey, and Santurce at Universidad del Sagrado Corazón. The train runs daily 5:30 A.M.-11:30 P.M. Fares are $1.50. For information call 866/900-1284 or visit www.ati.gobierno.pr.

AIR

Local air service within Puerto Rico, including Vieques and Culebra, is provided by several airlines, including **Vieques Air Link** (787/741-8331 or 888/901-9247, www.viequesairlink.com); **M&N Aviation** (787/791-7008, www.mnaviation.com); and **Air Flamenco** (787/724-1818, www.airflamenco.net).

FERRY

The **Puerto Rico Port Authority** (in Vieques 787/741-4761, 787/863-0705, or 800/981-2005; in Culebra 787/742-3161, 787/741-4761, 787/863-0705, or 800/981-2005; in Fajardo 787/863-0705 or 787/863-4560) operates daily passenger ferry service and weekday cargo and car ferry service between Fajardo on the east coast to the islands of Vieques and Culebra. Reservations are not accepted, but you can buy tickets in advance. Arrive no later than one hour before departure. Sometimes the ferry cannot accommodate everyone who wants to ride. The passenger ferry takes about one hour to get from Fajardo to Vieques and 1.5 hours from Fajardo to Culebra. The fare is $4.50 round-trip per person. The cargo/car ferry trip takes about two hours to get from Fajardo to Vieques and about 2.5 hours from Fajardo to Culebra. The cost is $15 for small vehicles and $19 for large vehicles. Note that car-rental agencies in Puerto Rico prohibit taking rental cars off the main island.

Sports and Recreation

Puerto Ricans are rabid sports enthusiasts, and their three biggest passions can be described as the three B's: boxing, baseball, and basketball.

BOXING

Puerto Rico has produced many world-class boxers, starting with the island's first National Boxing Association world champion in the bantamweight class, Barceloneta native Sixto Escobar, who first won the title in 1934. In 1948, bantamweight boxer Juan Evangelista Venegas became the first Puerto Rican to win an Olympic medal. To date, Puerto Rico has won six Olympic medals in boxing. Isabela native Juan Ruíz made history by becoming the first Latino World Boxing Association heavyweight champion by beating Evander Holyfield in 2001.

Félix "Tito" Trinidad is considered by many to be Puerto Rico's best all-time boxer. A champion in both welterweight and middleweight divisions, Trinidad announced his retirement in 2002 with a record of 42 wins (35 by knockout) and only two losses. Since then he has come out of retirement twice to compete three more times, losing his last match in 2008 to Roy Jones. Trinidad's most celebrated win was the defeat of welterweight champion Oscar de la Hoya in an event called The Fight of the Millennium held at Mandalay Bay in Las Vegas in 1999. His victorious return to the island was marked by a jubilant turnout of thousands of fans who greeted him at the Luis Muñoz Marín International Airport in San Juan.

BASEBALL

With origins dating back to the late 19th century, baseball was the first team sport to emerge in Puerto Rico's modern times. Currently the island is home to a winter league featuring four regional teams. Each year the winning team competes in the Caribbean Series in February, playing against winning teams from Dominican Republic, Mexico, and Venezuela.

For the first time in history, opening day for Major League baseball was held in San Juan in 2001 with a game between the Toronto Blue Jays and the Texas Rangers. The game was appropriately held in San Juan's Hiram Bithorn

Stadium, named after the Chicago Cubs pitcher and the first Puerto Rican to play in the Major Leagues.

Today more than 100 Major League players are from Puerto Rico, but the island's most famous player is undoubtedly Hall of Famer Roberto Clemente, who played 18 seasons with the Pittsburgh Pirates. Clemente died in an airplane crash off the coast of San Juan on New Year's Eve in 1972 on his way to deliver aid to earthquake victims in Nicaragua.

BASKETBALL

Although once extremely popular, basketball has seen a decline in interest in recent years, which has put the future of the National Superior Basketball League in jeopardy. Established in 1932, it currently consists of 12 regional teams. The island is also home to the Puerto Rican National Basketball Team, which competes in international events. The team made history in the 2004 when it defeated the U.S. Dream Team in the Olympics in Greece.

Puerto Rican athletes who have gone on to play for the NBA include Carlos Arroyo (Orlando Magic) and Jose Barea (Dallas Mavericks).

GOLF

Because of its verdant natural beauty, Puerto Rico has become something of a golf mecca for travelers. There are more than 20 courses on the island, most of them resort courses that tend to be upgraded and improved on a regular basis. The majority of courses are located on the eastern side of the island, from Dorado in the north to Humacao on the southeast coast.

Puerto Rico hosted its first PGA tour event, the Puerto Rico Open, in 2008 at the Trump International Golf Club in Rio Grande. The island's best known professional golfer is Juan "Chi Chi" Rodriguez. The story has it that the PGA Hall of Famer was first introduced to the game when he was a child working as a water carrier on a sugar plantation and discovered golf caddies were better paid.

HORSE RACING AND RIDING

The development of the Paso Fino breed of horse is closely intertwined with the history of Puerto Rico, starting with the arrival of Juan Ponce de León in 1508. Among the explorer's cargo were 50 horses from which the birth of the breed can be traced.

Horse races were once held in the streets of Old San Juan as far back as 1610. Today gamblers can bet on winners at the big modern Hipódromo Camarero in Canóvanas, about 10 miles east of San Juan. Races are held Wednesday through Sunday.

Horses are still used as a mode of transportation in rural parts of the main island and throughout Vieques and Culebra. There are several stables that offer trail rides, including **Pintos R Us** (787/361-3639, www.pintosrus. com) in Rincón, **Hacienda Carabalí** (787/889-5820 or 787/889-4954, www.haciendacarabalipuertorico.com) in Luquillo, and **Tropical Trail Rides** (787/872-9256, www.tropicaltrailrides.com) in Isabela.

COCKFIGHTING

Pitting spur-wearing gamecocks against each other in a battle for the finish is a legal and a popular sport with gamblers—so much so that it's televised. Although birds do sometimes fight to the death, efforts have been made to make the sport more humane. Spurs have been shortened from 2.5 inches to 1.5 inches in length, and injured cocks may be removed from a fight.

There are more than 100 licensed cockfighting arenas in Puerto Rico. Arenas are typically found in barnlike structures in rural areas of the island, but San Juan has a modern facility in Isla Verde, Club Gallistico de Puerto Rico, which caters to a more urban crowd with food and beverage service.

WATER SPORTS

As noted throughout this book, water sports are a huge draw in Puerto Rico. Visitors come from all over the world to surf its western shores, where regional and national competitions are held. Diving and snorkeling are popular on the southwest coast and around the smaller islands off the east coast. Sailing, big game fishing, and kite-boarding are other popular sports.

TOUR OPERATORS

Puerto Rico has a slew of tour operators offering a variety of adventures that span the spectrum from guided city walks to deep-sea dives to mountain-climbing hikes. All tour companies require reservations.

Historical Walking Tours

ArqueoTours Coabey (787/342-9317 or 787/470-1862, arqueotourscoabey@gmail.com) offers family-friendly hiking tours to Taíno archaeological sites around Jayuya, including La Piedra Escrita. Rates are $65 adults, $20 ages 5-12, free for children 4 and younger. The tours are guided by a historian and archaeologist.

Legends of Puerto Rico (Old San Juan, 787/605-9060, fax 787/764-2354, www.legendsofpr.com) offers daytime and nighttime walking tours of Old San Juan that revolve around topics from history, pirate legends, and crafts. It also offers a Modern San Juan tour and hiking tours of the karst region, El Yunque, and mangrove forests. Tours range $35-85 per person.

Adventure Nature Tours

Acampa (1211 Ave. Piñero, San Juan, 787/706-0695, www.acampapr.com) offers a large selection of hiking, rappelling, ziplining, and rock-climbing adventure tours throughout the island. Sights include San Cristóbal Cañon, Río Tanamá, El Yunque, Bosque Estatal de Toro Negro, Mona Island, and Caja de Muerto Island. Acampa also sells and rents camping, hiking, and mountaineering gear at its store in San Juan. Rates are $80-170.

Aventuras Tierra Adentro (268-A Ave. Jesus T. Piñero, San Juan, 787/766-0470, fax 787/754-7543, www.aventuraspr.com, Tues.-Fri. 10 A.M.-6 P.M., Sat. 10 A.M.-4 P.M.) leads cave and canyon tours that include rappelling, rock climbing, and ziplining for adventure seekers of all experience levels, including beginners. Reservations are required. Participants must be 15 or older. Cave tours take place Friday and Sunday for $170 per person. Canyon tours are on Saturday and cost $160 per person.

Expediciones Palenque (787/407-2858, www.expedicionespalenque.com) offers day-long group tours throughout Cordillera Central. Tours include spelunking in Yuyu Cave in Ciales, $85; kayaking Guineo Lake in Jayuya, $85; hiking Guilarte Mountain in Adjuntas, $80; and tours combining hiking, rappelling, caving, and body rafting tours on the Río Tanamá, $90.

Toro Verde Nature Adventure Park (Carr. 155, km 32.9, Orocovis, 787/944-1196, 787/944-1195, or 787/867-6606, fax 787/867-7022, www.toroverdetransportation.com, www.toroverdepr.com, Thurs.-Sun. 8 A.M.-5 P.M.) offers zipline canopy tours, hanging bridge tours, mountain bike tours, and rappelling. Packages are $65-200. Reservations are required. Participants must be at least four feet tall. Hotel pickup can be arranged.

Diving, Snorkeling, and Boating Tours

Abe's Snorkeling & Bio-bay Tours (787/741-2134 or 787/436-2686, www.abessnorkeling.com, reservations required) offers a variety of kayak tours, ideal for exploring beaches, mangrove bays, the bioluminescent bay (bio-bay), or undersea life in Vieques. A two-hour bio-bay tour in a double kayak is $40 adults, $20 children.

Blue Caribe Kayaks (149 Calle Flamboyan, Esperanza, Vieques, 787/741-2522) provides kayak tours of Mosquito Bay for $30 per person. Kayak rentals are also available for $10-15 per hour, $25-35 for four hours, and $45-55 all day.

Cancel Boats (Carr. 3304, on the waterfront in La Parguera, 787/899-5891 or

787/899-2972) and **Johnny Boats** (Carr. 3304, on the waterfront in La Parguera, 787/299-2212) offer on-demand tours of the La Parguera mangrove canals for $25 per person (less if you have a group) and nighttime tours of the phosphorescent bay for about $6.

Capt. Suarez Electric Boat (Carr. 987, Las Croabas dock, Fajardo, 787/655-2739 or 787/472-3128, captainsuarezbiobaypr@gmail.com) offers electric boat rides into the Laguna Grande bio-bay in Fajardo ($45 adults, $35 children).

Caribbean School of Aquatics (1 Calle Taft, Santurce, San Juan, 787/728-6606 or 787/383-5700, www.saildiveparty.com) offers full- and half-day sail, scuba, snorkel, and fishing trips from San Juan and Fajardo on a luxury catamaran with Captain Greg Korwek. Snorkel trips start at $69 per person; scuba trips start at $119 per person.

Day & Night Boat Tours (Dewey boatyard, 787/435-4498) offers a day-long snorkeling trip from Culebra to Culebrita. Cost (including drinks, snacks, and gear) is $75 per person. Custom fishing, snorkeling, and sightseeing tours can be arranged.

East Island Excursions (Puerto Del Rey Marina, Fajardo, 787/860-3434 or 877/937-4386, fax 787/860-1656, www.eastwindcats.com) offers sailing and snorkeling trips to Culebrita ($69 adults, $49 children ages 2-9).

Eco Adventures (787/206-0290, www.ecoadventurespr.com) offers bio-bay tours of Laguna Grande in Fajardo ($45 per person) and sailing snorkel tours ($65 per person). Transportation from San Juan to Las Croabas costs $20.

Flying Fish Parasail (Black Eagle Marina, Carr. 413, Rincón, Barrio Ensenada, 787/823-2FLY-787/823-2359, www.parasallpr.com, daily 9 A.M.-5 P.M.) offers single and tandem parasail rides ($60), glass-bottom boat rides ($30), sunset and whale-watching tours ($45), and reef snorkel tours ($55-85). Reservations are required, and there's a 12-passenger maximum.

Island Adventures (Carr. 996, km 4.5,

Esperanza, 787/741-0720, www.biobay.com) operates a tour of Mosquito Bay in Vieques on an electric pontoon boat that tools around the electric-blue water ($25 per person). Guides are friendly and informative.

Island Kayaking Adventures (787/444-0059 or 787/225-1808, www.ikapr.com) offers bio-bay kayak tours to Laguna Grande ($45 per person, six-person minimum). Rainforest and bio-bay combo tours cost $100 per person.

Katrina Sail Charters (Black Eagle Marina, Carr. 413, Rincón, Barrio Ensenada, 787/823-7245, www.sailrinconpuertorico.com) takes guests on snorkeling ($75 adults, $37.50 under age 12), sunset ($55, $27.50 under age 12), and full-moon sails ($55 adults only) aboard a 32-foot catamaran.

Kayaking Puerto Rico (787/435-1665 or 787/564-5629, www.kayakingpuertorico.com) offers bio-bay tours in Laguna Grande ($45 per person). Combination kayak and snorkel expeditions are also available.

La Cueva Submarina (Carr. 466, km 6.3, Isabela, 787/872-1390 or 787/872-1094 after 5:30 P.M., www.lacuevasubmarina.net, Mon.-Fri. 9 A.M.-5 P.M., Sat.-Sun. 8 A.M.-5 P.M., dive trips Thurs.-Mon. 9:30 A.M. and 1:30 P.M. depending on weather, book at least 24 hours in advance) offers several tours, including snorkeling ($25); scuba for first-timers ($65); scuba for certified divers ($55); and a cavern dive ($55). It also offers diving certification instruction.

The **Vieques Dive Company** (787/672-6565, www.viequesdivers.com) offers one-tank ($55-65) and two-tank dive tours ($75-100) and Discover tours for first-time divers ($135).

Paradise Puerto Rico Watersports (Combate Beach, Cabo Rojo, 787/567-4386 or 888/787-4386, www.pprwatersports.com) offers Jet Ski rentals ($85 per hour, $45 per half hour) and tours ($30 an hour, $55 for two hours, three person minimum).

Paradise Scuba Snorkeling and Kayaks (Carr. 304, km 3.2, La Parguera, 787/899-7611, paradisescubapr@yahoo.com) offers dive tours

($70-80), night dives ($60), snorkeling tours ($50), sunset snorkeling tours ($50-65), phosphorescent bay tours ($25), gear rental, and dive instruction. Dive sites include El Pared, Enrique, El Mario, Chimney, and Old Buoy.

Parguera Watersports (Carr. 3304, on the waterfront in La Parguera, 787/646-6777, www.prkbc.com) guides visitors in La Parguera on bio-bay or full moon kayaking adventures ($45 per person). Kiteboard instruction is $95 for the first session, $75 for additional sessions, including equipment. Rent kayaks by the hour for $20 double, $15 single, or paddleboards for $20 an hour. Day rates are available.

Sail Vieques (Carr. 200, on the waterfront in Isabel Segunda, Vieques, 787/508-7245, billwillo@yahoo.com) offers a half-day snorkeling tour ($50) and a daylong snorkel trip to the southern tip of the Bermuda Triangle ($110). Captain Bill also offers a two-hour sunset cruise for $30.

Salty Dog (1 Calle 1, El Batey, Fajardo, 787/717-6378 or 787/717-7259, www.saltydreams.com) offers catamaran snorkeling tours including all-you-can-eat lunch buffet and unlimited rum drinks ($60 per person). A sunset cruise includes cocktails and light snacks ($50 per person).

Scuba Dogs (Balneario El Escambrón, Avenida Muñoz Rivera, 787/783-6377 or 787/977-0000, www.scubadogs.net, Mon.-Thurs. 8 A.M.-4 P.M., Fri.-Sun. 8 A.M.-5 P.M.) offers snorkel tours ($55 adults, $45 kids), scuba tours ($75 for certified divers, $95 for instructional tours for first-timers), and kayak tours ($65 adults, $55 children).

Sea Ventures Dive Center (Marina Puerto del Rey, Carr. 3, km 51.2, Fajardo, 787/863-3483 or 800/739-3483, www.divepuertorico.com) offers dive and snorkel trips to local reefs. A two-tank dive for certified divers is $120. A two-tank dive for beginners is $150. Snorkel tours cost $60. Prices include gear.

Sea Ventures Dive Copamarina (Copamarina Beach Resort, Carr. 333, km 6.5, 800/468-4553 or 877/348-3267, www.divecopamarina.com, daily 9 A.M.-6 P.M.) runs day and night dive excursions ($65-119) to sites including the 22-mile-long Guánica Wall, the Aquarium, and the Parthenon, a coral formation featuring a variety of sponges. Daily snorkeling excursions go to Gilligan's Island, Cayo Coral Reef, and Bahía de la Ballerna ($55 including equipment). Certification courses are offered. Also available are kayak, catamaran, and paddleboat rentals.

Taíno Divers (Black Eagle Marina, Carr. 413, Barrio Ensenada, 787/823-6429, www.tainodivers.com, daily 9 A.M.-6 P.M.) offers daily snorkeling and dive trips to various dive sites, including Desecheo Island. Snorkeling trips are $50-95, scuba trips are $65-129, and Discovery scuba dives for first-timers are $119-170. Taíno also offers whale-watching cruises (late Jan.-mid-Mar.), as well as fishing charters and sunset cruises. Private excursions to Desecheo Island can be arranged. There is also equipment for rent or sale.

Travesías Isleñas Yaureibo/Vieques Outdoors (Calle Flamboyan, Esperanza, Vieques, 787/447-4104 or 939/630-1267, www.viequesoutdoors.com) offers snorkeling, kayaking, hiking, and biking tours. Bioluminescent bay kayak tours are offered nightly ($25 adults, $15 children). Meet at the *malecón* in front of Trade Winds Guest House. Snorkel, hiking, and biking tours are $30.

West Divers (Carr. 304, km 3.1, La Parguera, 787/899-3223 or 787/899-4171, www.westdiverspr.com) specializes in scuba trips to La Pared, an underwater wall and world-class dive site. Snorkel trips, sunset cruises, kayak tours, and equipment rental are also offered. A one-day, two-tank dive is $100 per person. Kayak tours cost $20-30 per hour; kayak rentals are $10-15 per hour.

Yokahu Kayaks (Carr. 987, km 6.2, Las Croabas, Fajardo, 787/604-7375, yokahukayaks@hotmail.com) offers kayak tours to

Laguna Grande in Las Cabezas de San Juan with licensed guides and equipment included ($45 per person).

Fishing Tours

Bill Wraps Fishing Charters PR (Marina Puerta Real, Fajardo, 787/364-4216, 787/347-9668 or 787/278-2729, www.billwrapsfishingpr.com) offers half-day charters for $650 and full-day charters for $950, including tackle, bait and snacks. Lunch is included with a full-day charter.

Caribbean Fly Fishing (61 Calle Orquideas, Esperanza, Vieques, 787/741-1337 or 787/450-3744, www.caribbeanflyfishingco.com) charters cost $375 for a half day, $650 for a full day, including gear and tackle. There is a two-person maximum.

Light Tackle Adventure (Boquerón pier, 787/849-1430 or 787/547-7380, www.lighttackleadventure.8k.com) specializes in light tackle and fly-fishing excursions. Excursions for two people are $340 for four hours, $425 for six hours, $550 for eight hours. A $100 reservation deposit is required. This company also provides kayak trips to the Cabo Rojo salt flats, Boquerón Bay, Joyuda, and La Parguera. Bird-watching tours in Cabo Rojo salt flats are also available.

Light Tackle Paradise (Marina Puerto Chico, Carr. Road 987, km 2.4, Fajardo, 787/347-4464, $350-450 half day for 4 or 6 people) offers fishing excursions on 22-foot and 26-foot catamarans or 17-foot skiffs.

Magic Tarpon (Cangrejos Yacht Club, 787/644-1444, www.puertoricomagictarpon.com) offers half-day fishing charters for $330-460 for 1-4 people.

Makaira Fishing Charters (Black Eagle Marina, Rincón, 787/299-7374) offers half-day ($575) and full-day ($850) fishing charters aboard a 34-foot 2006 Contender. Rates include tackle and refreshments; there's a six-passenger maximum.

Parguera Fishing Charters (Carr. 304, La Parguera, 787/382-4698, www.puertoricofishingcharters.com) offers half-day ($500) and full-day ($850) charters to fish for dorado, tuna, blue marlin, and wahoo on a 31-foot, twin diesel Bertram Sportfisherman. Trips include bait, tackle, beverages, snacks, and lunch. It also offers light-tackle reef fishing, half-day snorkeling trips, and customized charters.

Taíno Divers (Black Eagle Marina, Carr. 413, Barrio Ensenada, 787/823-6429, www.tainodivers.com, daily 9 A.M.-6 P.M.) offers half-day offshore fishing charters including tackle, bait, lunch, and soft drinks for $1,200.

Surfing

Surf 787 Summer Camp (Carr. 115, behind Angelo's Restaurant, 787/448-0968 or 949/547-6340, www.surf787.com) offers year-round surfing instruction.

Located on the beach at The Ritz Carlton San Juan and El San Juan Resort & Casino in Isla Verde, **Wow Surfing School & Water Sports** (787/955-6059, www.wowsurfingschool.com, daily 9 A.M.-5 P.M.) gives two-hour surf lessons for $85, including board. Group rates are available. Equipment rentals include surfboards ($25 an hour), paddleboards ($30), kayaks ($25), and snorkel equipment ($15 and up). Jet Ski rentals and tours are available from La Concha Resort in Condado and San Juan Bay Marina. Call for prices.

Paddleboarding

Las Palmas Paddle (508/237-9652) offers paddleboard tours around Culebra starting at $40 per person. Introductory tours for beginners as well as adventure packages for experienced paddlers are available.

Velauno Paddleboarding (2430 Calle Loíza, Isla Verde, 787/982-0543, www.velaunopaddleboarding.com, Mon.-Fri. 10 A.M.-7 P.M., Sat. 11 A.M.-7 P.M.) offers paddleboarding lessons ($100 first hour, $50 each subsequent hour) and tours ($75 for two hours, $25 subsequent hours).

Vieques Paddleboarding (787/366-5202, www.viequespaddleboarding.com) offers tours on stand-up paddleboards, a great way to explore the island. The four-hour downwind tour travels 2-4 miles, depending on wind conditions, along the north and south shores ($85). Or take a three-hour tour across the bay, through a mangrove forest, ending at a beach with a snorkel ($65). Kids 11 and younger can ride with adults for $20.

Accommodations and Food

Accommodations in Puerto Rico run the gamut from world-class luxury resorts to rustic self-serve guesthouses, which offer little more than a bed to crash on and a help-yourself attitude when it comes to getting clean linens, ice, and other items you might need. In between are a variety of American hotel chains in all price ranges and a number of small, independent hotels and inns. There are also some unique hotels of historic significance, such as **Hotel El Convento** in San Juan, a former Carmelite convent built in 1651, and **Hacienda Gripiñas,** a former coffee plantation in Jayuya located high up in the Cordillera Central.

Outside San Juan there are accommodations designated by the Puerto Rico Tourism Co. as *paradores* (www.gotoparadores.com), independently owned and operated country inns. There are 18 properties in all, with the largest concentration located on the western half of the island. Note, though, that the designation of *parador* is not a recommendation, and the quality of the properties is wildly divergent between the superior and the inferior. For details, visit the website.

ACCOMMODATION RATES

Overnight stays in Puerto Rico can range from $39 at Hotel Colonial in Mayagüez to $1,070 for a Cliffside suite at the **Horned Dorset Primavera** in Rincón. Generally, however, room rates fall between $100 and $250. There are no traditional all-inclusive resorts in Puerto Rico, where meals are included with the price of the room, although Copamarina Resort in Guánica and the Horned Dorset Primavera in Rincón offer all-inclusive packages.

A tax is applied to all accommodations, but many properties include the tax in the rate, so ask to be sure. Typically the tax is 9 percent of the rate, but hotels with casinos charge 11 percent tax. Resorts usually add on a resort service fee, which is typically an additional 9 percent.

Many accommodations offer two rates—the most expensive is during high season (typically January-April), the least expensive is during low season (May-December). If you're traveling during high season, be sure to book your room early or you may find your options limited. Note that the high season for destinations and accommodations catering to Puerto Rican travelers may be during the summer months. Some accommodations have a third rate charged during the Christmas holiday season, which may be even more pricey than the high-season rates. Most accommodations may be booked online.

PUERTO RICAN CUISINE

Puerto Rican cuisine is a hearty fare called *cocina criolla,* which means creole cooking. A typical *criolla* dish contains fried or stewed meat, chicken, or seafood, combined with or accompanied by rice and beans. Stewed dishes usually begin with a seasoning mix called *sofrito,* which includes salt pork, ham, lard, onions, green peppers, chili peppers, cilantro, and garlic. *Adobo,* a seasoning mix comprising peppercorn, oregano, garlic, salt, olive oil, and vinegar or fresh lime juice, is rubbed into meats and poultry before frying or grilling. Tomato sauce, capers, pimento-stuffed olives, and raisins are also common ingredients in Puerto

mini *mofongo* cups stuffed with land crab and *ropa vieja* spring rolls

Rican cuisine. Two items are integral to the preparation of *cocina criolla:* a *caldero* (a cast-iron or cast-aluminum cauldron with a round base, straight sides, and a lid) and a mortar and pestle (used to grind herbs and seeds).

The **plantain** is a major staple of the Puerto Rican diet. Similar to a banana but larger, firmer, and less sweet, it is prepared in a variety of ways. *Tostones* are a popular plantain dish. The fruit is sliced into rounds, fried until soft, mashed flat, and fried again until crisp. They're typically eaten like bread, as a starchy accompaniment to a meal. They're sometimes served with a tomato-garlic dipping sauce or something akin to Thousand Island dressing.

But probably the most popular way plantain is served is in *mofongo,* a mashed mound of fried, unripe plantain, garlic, olive oil, and *chicharrón* (pork crackling). *Mofongo relleno* is *mofongo* stuffed with meat, poultry, or seafood, and *piononos* are appetizer-size stuffed *mofongo.* *Amarillos,* which translates as "yellows," is the same thing as the Cuban *maduras* and is made from overripe plantains that have been sliced lengthwise and fried in oil until soft and sweetly caramelized. Bananas are also popular in *cocina criolla,* especially *guineitos en escabeche,* a green-banana salad marinated with pimento-stuffed olives in vinegar and lime juice.

Rice also figures prominently in Puerto Rican food. Most restaurants serving *comida criolla* will list several *arroz* (rice) dishes, such as *arroz con habichuelas* (beans), *arroz con pollo* (chicken), *arroz con juyeyes* (crab), *arroz con camarones* (shrimp), and *arroz con gandules* (pigeon peas). Typically in this dish the ingredients have been stewed until damp and sticky in a mixture of tomatoes and *sofrito.* A similar dish is paella, a Spanish import featuring an assortment of seafood. *Asopao,* a thick stew, is another popular rice dish, and *arroz con leche* (milk) is a favorite dessert similar to rice pudding.

Pork is very popular in Puerto Rico, and it has a variety of names: *lechón, pernil, cerdo.* But

POPULAR *CRIOLLA COCINA* DISHES

Traditional Puerto Rican cuisine is called *criolla cocina*. Like the people of Puerto Rico, the cuisine's roots can be found at the intersection of the Taíno, Spanish, and African cultures. Most dishes are either slowly stewed throughout the day or quickly fried just before eating.

Many Puerto Rican dishes start with *sofrito*. Similar to a roux in Cajun cooking, it is a reduction of tomatoes, green bell pepper, onion, garlic, and cilantro. And plantains, both ripe and green, are eaten at just about every meal.

Here are some dishes commonly served in the homes and restaurants throughout Puerto Rico.

- *a la criolla:* a cut of meat or fish served in a sauce made from tomatoes, green bell pepper, onion, garlic, and cilantro
- *amarillos:* a side dish of ripe plantains sliced lengthwise and slowly fried in oil until caramelized
- *arañitas:* fried balls of shredded plantain; often served as a snack or appetizer
- *arroz con gandules:* a thick pigeon peas and rice dish seasoned with *sofrito*
- *arroz con jueyes:* a thick land crab and rice dish seasoned with *sofrito*
- *arroz con pollo:* a thick chicken and rice dish seasoned with *sofrito*
- *asopao:* a thick rice stew made with chicken, pork, beef or seafood
- *carne guisado:* beef stew
- *chicharrones de pollo:* fried chunks of chicken
- *chillo entero frito:* whole fried snapper with the head on
- *chuleta can can:* a thick, deep-fried pork chop specially cut to retain a thick rind of fat and a strip of ribs
- *churrasco* with *chimichurri* sauce: an Argentine-style grilled skirt steak served with a piquant green sauce made from olive oil, garlic, and parsley
- *empanado bifstec:* a slice of steak pounded thin, breaded, and fried
- *encebollado bifstec:* a slice of steak pounded thin and served with caramelized onions
- *flan:* caramel custard
- *frituras:* fritters, such as *alcapurrias, empanadillas,* and *bacalaito,* typically sold from street-side kiosks, trucks, tents, and vans
- *guineitos en escabeche:* pickled green banana salad with onions and green olives
- *lechón:* whole roasted pig
- *mallorca:* a slightly sweet knot of bread dough, baked and dusted with powdered sugar—served split, buttered, and toasted or stuffed with hot ham and cheese for breakfast
- *mofongo:* a cone-shaped dish of mashed fried plantain seasoned with olive oil and garlic and fried bits of pork skin, bacon, or ham
- *mofongo rellenas: mofongo* stuffed with chicken, meat, or seafood
- *paella:* Spanish dish similar to *arroz con pollo* but with saffron and filled with a variety of seafood instead of chicken
- *pasteles:* like tamales; mashed plantain or cassava stuffed with pork or chicken and steamed in banana leaves, typically served around around the Christmas holidays—don't eat the leaf!
- *pescado in escabeche:* pickled fish served cold; raw fillets are marinated in seasoned vinegar, similar to ceviche
- *pique:* hot sauce made from vinegar, lime juice, and hot peppers
- *quesito:* a sweet, sticky twist of puff pastry with a dab of cream cheese inside
- *salmorejo de jueyes:* stewed land crabmeat served over rice
- *tembleque:* coconut custard; often served around Christmas
- *tostones:* slices of green plantain fried twice and smashed; served like bread as an accompaniment to other dishes

chicken and beef are common, and occasionally you'll come across *cabro* (goat) and guinea hen. Popular meat dishes include *carne guisada* (beef stew), *chuletas fritas* (fried pork chops), *carne empanado* (breaded and fried steak), *carne encebollado* (fried steak smothered in cooked onions), and *churrasco,* an Argentine-style grilled skirt steak. Restaurants along the coast usually specialize in a wide range of seafood, including *camarones* (shrimp), *langosta* (lobster), *pulpo* (octopus), and *carrucho* (conch). Fish—typically fried whole—can be found on nearly every menu, the choices usually being *chillo* (red snapper), dorado (mahimahi), or occasionally *bacalao* (dried salted cod).

Interestingly, you'll usually find the exact same dessert options at most restaurants. They will include flan (a baked caramel custard), *helados* (ice cream), and *dulce de guayaba* (guava in syrup) or *dulce de lechosa* (papaya in syrup) served with *queso del país,* a soft white cheese. Occasionally restaurants will offer *tembleque,* a coconut custard, particularly around the Christmas holidays.

An American-style breakfast is fairly commonly found, although Puerto Ricans often eat their eggs and ham in toasted sandwiches called *bocadillos.* American coffee can sometimes be found, but the traditional *café con leche,* a strong brew with steamed milk, is highly recommended. *Bocadillos* are often eaten for lunch, particularly the *cubano,* a toasted sandwich with ham, roasted pork, and cheese. The *media noche* is similar to the *cubano,* but it's served on a softer, sweeter bread.

Although American fast-food restaurant chains can be found in Puerto Rico, the island has its own traditional style of fast-food fare often sold from roadside kiosks. Offerings usually include fried savory pies and fritters made from various combinations of plantain, meat, chicken, cheese, crab, potato, and fish.

Puerto Rican Cocktails

The legal drinking age in Puerto Rico is 18. Although all types of alcoholic beverages are available, rum is the number one seller. There are three types of rum: white or silver, which is dry, pale, and light-bodied; gold, which is amber-colored and aged in charred oak casks; and black, a strong, 151-proof variety often used in flambés. Favorite rum drinks are the Cuba libre, a simple mix of rum and Coke with a wedge of lime; the piña colada, a frozen blended combination of rum, cream of coco, and pineapple juice; and the *mojito,* a Cuban import made from rum, simple syrup, club soda, fresh lime juice, and tons of fresh muddled mint.

When it comes to beer, Puerto Ricans prefer a light pilsner, and you can't go wrong with Medalla. It's brewed in Mayagüez and won the bronze in its class at the World Beer Cup 1999. Presidente beer, made in the Dominican Republic, is also popular.

Conduct and Customs

ETIQUETTE

A certain formality permeates life in Puerto Rico. It's customary to acknowledge one another, including shop owners, with a greeting: *buenas dias* for good day, *buenas tardes* for good afternoon, and *buenas noches* for good evening. If you approach someone to ask the time or for directions, preface your question with *perdóneme* (excuse me). When a waiter delivers your meal, he or she will say *buen provecho,* and it's customary to say the same to diners already eating when you enter a restaurant.

Traditionally Puerto Ricans are exceedingly cordial. Even in San Juan, rudeness is rarely encountered. If you're lost or need help, they will cheerfully point you in the right direction. But Puerto Ricans don't typically display much interest in fraternizing with tourists. Americans who venture into bars catering primarily to the local dating scene may get a chilly reception if they're perceived as romantic rivals. The exception is bars that depend on the tourist dollar or that are in towns with a large U.S. expatriate population, such as Rincón or Vieques, where you're likely to know everybody's name by the time you leave.

Dress appropriately for the occasion. Although most upscale restaurants don't necessarily require a coat and tie, some do, so inquire. Otherwise, a well-groomed, nicely attired appearance is expected. And never wear beach attire, skimpy halter tops, or short shorts anywhere but the beach or pool. Although young fashionable Puerto Rican women may sometimes dress provocatively, visiting American women are advised to use some modesty or risk attracting unwanted male attention.

To the relief of nonsmokers, smoking has been banned in all restaurants, lounges, clubs, and bars in Puerto Rico, with the exception of establishments with outdoor seating. Public drinking has also been banned.

MACHISMO

Machismo appears to be becoming somewhat a thing of the past, particularly in San Juan, where mainland American influence is heaviest. The days of men verbally harassing or flashing young women is no longer a common occurrence, although vestiges of it remain around some wilderness beaches where perpetrators are far from the eyes of the *policía.* Nevertheless, it is interesting that *cabron* is a favored, mock-aggressive greeting among many men in Puerto Rico. Technically it means "goat," but its idiomatic translation is a man who's cuckolded by a cheating wife. There was a time when calling a man a *cabron* was a sure way to get a black eye, and used in the heat of an argument, it still is. But today it's more commonly used as a term of affection between male friends.

Meanwhile, the flip side of machismo—Old World chivalry—is still very much alive and well in Puerto Rico, especially among older men who appear to take pride in their gestures of kindness toward women.

CONCEPTS OF TIME

San Juan operates much like any big American city. The pace of life is fast, service is expedient, and everybody's in a hurry. But the farther you get away from San Juan, and most markedly in Culebra and Vieques, things tend to operate on "island time"—that is, at an extremely leisurely pace. You may be the only person in the restaurant, but it may still take 30 minutes or longer to receive your meal. Posted hours of operation are more suggestion than reality. Visitors are best advised to chill out and accept that this is just the way things are in Puerto Rico. If fawning service is required to have a good time, then stick with the resorts.

Tips for Travelers

VISAS AND OFFICIALDOM

No passports or visas are required for U.S. citizens entering Puerto Rico. Those visiting the island from other countries must have the same documentation required to enter the United States. Visitors from the United Kingdom are required to have a British passport but do not need a visa unless their passports are endorsed with British Subject, British Dependent Territories Citizen, British Protected Person, British Overseas Citizen, or British National (Overseas) Citizen. A return ticket or proof of onward travel is necessary. Australian visitors must have a passport and can stay up to 90 days without a visa.

CUSTOMS

Travelers must pass through customs at the airport in Puerto Rico before leaving the island to make sure no prohibited plants or fruits are taken off the island. Permitted items include avocados, coconuts, papayas, and plantains. Mangoes, passion fruits, and plants potted in soil are not permitted. Pre-Columbian items or items from Afghanistan, Cuba, Iran, Iraq, Libya, Serbia, Montenegro, and Sudan may not be brought into the United States. There are no customs duties on items brought into the United States from Puerto Rico.

EMBASSIES

Because Puerto Rico is a commonwealth, there are no U.S. embassies or consulates here. Several countries are represented locally by consulates, though, including the United Kingdom (Torre Chardon, Ste. 1236, 350 Ave. Chardon, San Juan, PR 00918, 787/758- 9828, fax 787/758-9809, btopr1@coqui.net) and Canada (33 Calle Bolivia, 7th Floor, Hato Rey, San Juan, PR 00917-2010, 787/759-6629, fax 787/294-1205).

GAY AND LESBIAN TRAVELERS

Homosexuality is illegal in Puerto Rico; however, the law is rarely, if ever, enforced. Despite Puerto Rico's strong patriarchal society in which a traditional sense of manhood is highly prized, homosexuality is generally accepted, especially in San Juan, which is something of a mecca for the LGBT traveler. There are a number of nightclubs that cater specifically to a gay and lesbian clientele, and certain beaches are known to attract a gay crowd. San Juan is also a popular port of call for gay cruises.

WOMEN TRAVELING ALONE

Puerto Rico is safe for women traveling alone or in groups. But precautions should be taken. Dressing provocatively can attract catcalls and other forms of unwanted attention, and bathing suits should never be worn anywhere but at the beach or pool. Women traveling solo should avoid remote wilderness beaches and late-night bars that cater primarily to locals. Safety in numbers is a good rule to follow when going out at night.

TRAVELING WITH CHILDREN

San Juan offers lots to do for families with children of all ages. The historic forts and museums hold plenty of interest for youngsters, and many water sports are suitable as well, including fishing, boating, and swimming. And with a few exceptions, most restaurants welcome young diners. As in any urban center, parents should keep a close watch on their children at the pool and beach, especially if there is no lifeguard on duty, and along busy sidewalks where there is car traffic. It is advisable to keep sunscreen, bug spray, and bottled water on hand at all times.

TRAVELERS WITH DISABILITIES

As a territory of the United States, Puerto Rico must adhere to the Americans with Disabilities Act, which ensures access to public buildings for all. While some historic buildings may be exempt, most have been adapted for access with ramps, elevators, and wheelchair-accessible restrooms. The majority of hotels have at least one accessible hotel room. Most sidewalks have curb cuts at crosswalks to accommodate wheelchairs, scooters, and walkers, and traffic lights have audible signals to assist visitors with sight impairments with street crossings.

STUDY AND VOLUNTEER OPPORTUNITIES

Spanish Abroad (5112 N. 40th St., Ste. 203, Phoenix, AZ 85018, 888/722-7623 or 602/778-6791, www.spanishabroad.com) offers Spanish-language immersion classes with homestays in Hato Rey, San Juan. The **Vieques Humane Society** (787/741-0209, www.viequeshs.org) offers a private room, shared bath and kitchen (and limited transportation) in exchange for volunteering to work with animals and/or a clinic for 20 hours a week.

WHAT TO TAKE

The activities you plan to pursue in Puerto Rico will dictate what you will need to pack. If you plan to sunbathe by day and hit the discos by night, pack your swimsuit and trendiest club wear. If a shopping marathon is on the agenda, pack comfortable walking shoes and an empty duffel bag for carrying back your loot. If you want to go hiking in the mountains, long lightweight pants and hiking boots are in order. If you stay in the mountains overnight, bring a light jacket.

No matter what you do, bring sunscreen, bug spray, a wide-brimmed hat, an umbrella, and some bottled water. You'll need protection from the sun and the occasional sand-flea attack while you're on the beach. And if you're traveling during the rainy season, expect a brief shower every day. You'll be grateful for some light raingear, such as a poncho and waterproof shoes or sandals.

Light cotton fabrics are always recommended. Puerto Rico's temperatures fluctuate between 76-88°F on the coastal plains and 73-78°F in the mountain region. The humidity hovers around a steady 80 percent. Note that wearing bathing suits or short shorts is inappropriate anyplace other than the pool or beach, and a few restaurants require a jacket and tie.

If you plan to navigate the island by car, bring a Spanish-English dictionary and a current, detailed road map. Just about every business on the island accepts credit cards and debit cards, and virtually every town has at least one ATM. The only time you'll need cash is if you plan to shop or buy food from roadside vendors, which you definitely should do.

HEALTH AND SAFETY

The quality of health care in Puerto Rico is comparable to that in the United States, and all major towns have at least one hospital and pharmacy, including Walgreens. Unlike in Mexico, the water is as safe to drink as it is in the United States, and fruits and vegetables are fine to eat.

There are no major health issues facing the island, save the occasional outbreak of dengue fever, a viral infection spread by mosquitoes. Symptoms include fever, headache, body aches, and a rash, and it lasts about seven days. In rare cases it can be fatal—usually when the victim has been previously infected with the disease. Visitors are at low risk for contracting dengue fever unless there's an active outbreak, but using mosquito repellent is a good preventative measure.

A visitor's biggest physical threat is most likely sunstroke. Summer can be brutally hot, especially in urban areas. It's important to drink lots of water, especially if you're doing a lot of walking or other physical activity. A hat and sunscreen are recommended. Or you could do as some of the local women do and use umbrellas to keep the beating rays at bay.

Crime

Most of the crime in Puerto Rico revolves around the drug trade. The island is on a drug-transportation route that begins in Venezuela and passes through the Dominican Republic and into Puerto Rico on the way to the U.S. mainland. Add to that a poverty level of 44 percent, and you have a certain level of desperation. Ponce and Loíza have experienced high rates of murder, but most crimes are of the petty street variety—especially theft from automobiles or snatched purses. The street drug trade in San Juan operates out of La Perla, a former squatter's village outside the city wall beside Old San Juan.

Prostitution is illegal in Puerto Rico, although there's at least one strip club in San Juan that's reputed to be a bordello. Prostitutes do sometimes work the streets—even in quiet towns such as Mayagüez—and they're often more likely to be transgendered men than women.

The most common threat to visitors is having their possessions stolen from a rental car. Never leave anything of value visible in your car and always keep it locked. There are also occasional reports of carjackings and stolen vehicles. The police patrol San Juan regularly, and they keep their blue lights flashing all night long to announce their presence. For any emergency—crime, fire, wreck, injury—dial 911 for help.

Information and Services

MAPS AND TOURIST INFORMATION

Before you go, contact the **Puerto Rico Tourism Company** (800/866-7827) to request that it send you free of charge its extensive tourist-information packet, which includes brochures, maps, pictures, and details on hotels, tours, and attractions. It's a great planning tool. You can also visit its website at www.gotopuertorico.com for more information. Another great site is www.travelandsports.com.

Once you've arrived on the island, visit the Puerto Rico Tourism Company's information center, in Old San Juan near the cruise-ship piers in a small yellow colonial structure called **La Casita** (Plaza de Dársenes, Old San Juan, 787/722-5208 or 787/724-6829, fax 787/722-5208, www.gotopuertorico.com, Sat.-Wed. 9 A.M.-8 P.M., Thurs.-Fri. 9 A.M.-6:30 P.M.). It's not only a great source for maps and promotional brochures on various tourist sites, hotels, and tours, but you can also sip on a free rum cocktail. Call 800/866-7827 to order travel information.

For information specifically on the capital city, visit the **Tourism Office of San Juan** (250 Calle Teután at Calle San Justo, Old San Juan, 787/721-6363, Mon.-Sat. 8 A.M.-4 P.M.). It offers self-guided audio tours of Old San Juan in English and Spanish for $10 per person. There's also a small selection of promotional materials for local tourist sites, hotels, and tours.

Many of the island's towns have their own tourist offices, usually on or near the plaza and often in the *alcaldía* (city hall) building. Unfortunately, many of them tend to be open sporadically, despite posted hours of operation.

There are also free maps and travel publications, such as *Places to Go, Bienvenidos,* and *Qué Pasa!* magazines, available at many stores, restaurants, and hotels.

For a detailed road map of the island, International Travel Maps of Canada (www.itmb.com) is your best option, but you'll have to order online before you go. The same goes for National Geographic's excellent illustrated map of the Caribbean National Forest, available from its website, www.nationalgeographic.com/maps.

MONEY

Puerto Rico's form of currency is the U.S. dollar, which is sometimes referred to as *peso.* Full-service banks with ATMs are plentiful, the most common one being Banco Popular. Banking hours are Monday-Friday 9 A.M.-3:30 P.M. Credit cards and debit cards are accepted virtually everywhere. The only time cash is required is when buying items from roadside vendors and occasionally even they will accept plastic.

A sales tax, between 5.5 percent and 6.7 percent depending on the municipality, has recently been instituted in Puerto Rico, and hotel taxes can vary depending on the type of property. Hotels with casinos charge 11 percent tax, and hotels without casinos charge 9 percent tax. There may also be resort fees, energy surcharge fees, and other charges. When determining the price of a hotel room, ask whether or not the tax is included in the stated price.

Tipping practices are the same as in the United States—15-20 percent of the bill, unless a gratuity has already been added.

COMMUNICATIONS AND MEDIA
Postal Service
Mail service is provided by the U.S. Postal Service. Although mailing letters and postcards to and from the island costs the same as in the United States, international rates apply when shipping items to the island. United Parcel Service and overnight shipping companies such as Federal Express also operate on the island.

Telephone
Puerto Rico has one area code—787—and it must always be dialed when placing a call. Nevertheless, all calls are not local, so long-distance rates may apply. U.S. cell phones with nationwide service should function fine in Puerto Rico.

Newspapers and Magazines
Daily newspapers include *El Nuevo Día* and

Primera Hora, both in Spanish. Ponce has a newsweekly, *La Perla del Sur. The New York Times* and *The Miami Herald* can be commonly found in hotels and newsstands in San Juan.

Television
Broadcasting is regulated by the U.S. Federal Communications Commission. There are three commercial channels: **Telemundo** (channel 2), **Televicentro** (channel 4), and **Univision** (channel 11), and one public channel—**TUTV** (channel 6). Local programming features sitcoms, talk shows, news, and soap operas, all in Spanish. Multichannel cable and satellite TV is also available.

Radio
- **WRTU:** 89.7 FM (Universidad de Puerto Rico); music, news, culture
- **Cadena Salsoul:** 98.5 FM (San Juan), 101.1 FM (south), 100.3 FM (west); salsa
- **WOSO:** 1030 AM; news, information, entertainment, and sports in English
- **Alfa Rock:** 105.7 FM (northeast), 106.1 FM (southwest); rock music
- **La Mega Station:** 106.9 FM (San Juan); pop music

WEIGHTS AND MEASURES
Puerto Rico uses the metric system. Gasoline is bought in liters (1 gallon = 3.7 liters), and distance is measured in kilometers (1 mile = 1.61 kilometers). The exception is speed, which is measured in miles per hour.

Time Zone
Puerto Rico observes Atlantic standard time and does not practice daylight saving time. Therefore, time in Puerto Rico is one hour later than eastern standard time November-March and the same as eastern daylight time from the second Sunday in March until the first Sunday in November.

RESOURCES

Glossary

ajillo: garlic

a la criolla: a cut of meat or fish served in a sauce made from tomatoes, green bell pepper, onion, garlic, and cilantro

alcapurria: fritter of mashed yautia, yuca, and green banana stuffed with meat or crab and deep fried

al centro: downtown

alto: stop

amarillos: fried ripe plantains

appertivos: appetizers

arañitas: fried balls of shredded plantain; often served as a snack or appetizer

arepa: a small, round patty of corn meal batter fried, split open on one side, and stuffed with meat or seafood

arroz: rice

arroz con gandules: a thick pigeon peas and rice dish seasoned with *sofrito*

arroz con jueyes: a thick land crab and rice dish seasoned with *sofrito*

arroz con pollo: a thick chicken and rice dish seasoned with *sofrito*

asado: roasted

asopao: rice stew

autopista: divided limited-access highway

avenida: avenue

azúcar: sugar

bacalaito: codfish fritter

bahía: bay

balneario: publicly maintained beach

barbacoa: meat grilled over a fire or charcoal; also the name of the grill

barcazas: whole plantains sliced lengthwise, stuffed with ground beef, and topped with cheese

barrio: neighborhood

batata: white yam

batey: ceremonial ball field used by Taíno people

bebida: beverage

bio-bay: shorthand for bioluminescent bay, one of three mangrove lagoons in Puerto Rico that contain micro-organisms called dinoflagellates that glow in the dark

bocadillo: sandwich, typically toasted

bohique: Taíno spiritual leader

Borinquen: Taíno name for Puerto Rico

bosque estatal: public forest

botánica: shop that sells herbs, scents, and candles used by practitioners of *espiritismo* or Santería

brazo gitano: translates as "gypsy arm," but it refers to a jellyroll cake filled with fruit traditional to Mayagüez

cabro: goat

cacique: Taíno chief

café: coffee

calle: street

camarones: shrimp

capilla: chapel

carbón: grilled

carne: beef

carne guisado: beef stew

carretera: road

carrucho: conch

cayos: cays, islets

cebollado: onion

cemi: Taíno amulet

cerdo: pork

chicharrones de pollo: fried chunks of chicken

chillo: red snapper

chillo entero frito: whole fried snapper with the head on

chorizo: spicy pork sausage

chuleta can can: a thick, deep-fried pork chop specially cut to retain a thick rind of fat and a strip of ribs

chuletas: chops, typically pork

churrasco: grilled, marinated skirt steak

criolla cocina: Puerto Rican cuisine

coco: coconut

coco dulce: an immensely sweet confection of fresh, coarsely grated coconut and caramelized sugar

coco frio: chilled coconuts still in their green husks served with a hole cut in the top and a straw stuck through it; inside is refreshing thin coconut milk

conejo: rabbit

coqui: tiny tree frog that emits an eponymous chirp

cordero: lamb

criolla: creole; means "Puerto Rican-style"

cruce: crossroads

cruzar: to cross

cuadras: blocks

cubano: toasted sandwich with pork, ham, cheese, and pickles

derecha: right

derecho: straight

doble: turn

dorado: mahimahi

empanadilla: savory turnover stuffed with meat, chicken, seafood, or cheese

empanado: breaded and fried meat

encebollado bifstec: a slice of steak pounded thin and served with caramelized onions

ensalada: salad

espiritismo: Taíno-based religion that believes deities reside in nature

esquina: corner

estacionamiento: parking

este: east

faro: lighthouse

fiestas patronales: festivals that celebrate the patron saints of towns

flan: caramel custard

frito: fried

frituras: fritters

gandules: pigeon peas

guayaba: guava

guineitos en escabeche: pickled green banana salad with onions and green olives

habichuelas: beans

helado: ice cream

hielo: ice

horno: baked

izquierda: left

jámon: ham

jíbaro: rural resident, hillbilly

juevos: eggs

juyeyes: land crab

laguna: lagoon

langosta: rock lobster

leche: milk

lechón: pork

lechonera: restaurant serving pit-roasted pork and other local delicacies

lechosa: papaya

lejos: far

luces: traffic lights

luz: traffic light

malécon: seawall promenade

mallorca: a slightly sweet knot of bread dough, baked and dusted with powdered sugar—served split, buttered, and toasted or stuffed with hot ham and cheese for breakfast

mantequilla: butter

mariscos: seafood

máscaras: masks

mavi: a fermented Taíno beverage made from the bark of the *mavi* tree

media noche: sandwich similar to a *cubano,* but on a softer, sweeter bread

mercardo: market

mofongo: cooked unripe plantain mashed with garlic and olive oil

mofongo rellenas: *mofongo* stuffed with chicken, meat, or seafood *mogote:* conical, haystack-shaped hill

mondongo: beef tripe stew

mundillo: handmade lace that's created with bobbins

muralla: wall

ñame: yam

norte: north

Nuyorican: a Puerto Rican person who migrated to New York

oeste: west

paella: Spanish dish similar to *arroz con pollo* but with saffron and filled with a variety of seafood instead of chicken

pan: bread

panadería: bakery

panapén: breadfruit

papas: potatoes

papas rellenas: a big lump of mashed potatoes stuffed with meat and deep-fried

parador: privately owned inn in a rural area

parque: park

pasteles: like tamales; mashed plantain or cassava stuffed with pork or chicken and steamed in banana leaves, typically served around around the Christmas holidays—don't eat the leaf!

pastelillos: savory turnover stuffed with meat, chicken, seafood, or cheese

pechuga de pollo: chicken breast

pernil: pork

pescado: fish

pescado in escabeche: pickled fish served cold; raw fillets are marinated in seasoned vinegar, similar to ceviche

picadillo: seasoned ground beef used to stuff *empanadillas*

pimento: pepper

piña: pineapple

pinchos: chunks of chicken, pork, or fish threaded on a skewer and grilled shish-kebab style

pionono: seasoned ground beef wrapped mummy style in slices of plantain and deep-fried

pique: hot sauce made from vinegar, lime juice, and hot peppers

platano: plantain

playa: beach

postre: dessert

públicos: public transportation in vans that pick up multiple riders along an established route

pueblo: town center

pulpo: octopus

quesito: a sweet, sticky twist of puff pastry with a dab of cream cheese inside

queso: cheese

queso del país: soft white cow cheese

relleno: stuffed food item, as in *mofongo relleno*

reserva forestal: forest reserve

sal: salt

salida: exit

salmorejo de jueyes: stewed land crabmeat served over rice

Santería: Afro-Caribbean-based religion that observes multiple gods

santos: small wood carvings of Catholic saints

setas: mushrooms

sopa: soup

sorullos or sorullitos: fried cheese and cornmeal sticks

sur: south

Taíno: people who were indigenous to Puerto Rico when it became a Spanish colony

taquitos: chicken, ground beef, crab, or fish rolled up in a tortilla and deep-fried

tembleque: coconut custard; often served around Christmas

tocino: bacon

tortilla española: a baked egg and potato dish

tostones: twice-fried, flattened pieces of plantain

vaya: go

vejigante: horned mask worn in festivals

yautia: taro root, similar to a potato

yuca: cassava, a root vegetable

ABBREVIATIONS

Ave.: Avenida

Bo.: Barrio

Carr.: Carretera

Int.: approaching intersection, or interior route

km: kilometer

Spanish Phrasebook

Your Puerto Rico adventure will be more fun if you use a little Spanish. Puerto Ricans, although they may smile at your funny accent, will appreciate your halting efforts to break the ice and transform yourself from a foreigner to a potential friend.

Spanish commonly uses 30 letters—the familiar English 26, plus four straightforward additions: ch, ll, ñ, and rr, which are explained in "Consonants," below.

PRONUNCIATION

Once you learn them, Spanish pronunciation rules—in contrast to English—don't change. Spanish vowels generally sound softer than in English. (*Note:* The capitalized syllables below receive stronger accents.)

Vowels

a   like ah, as in "hah": *agua* AH-gooah (water), *pan* PAHN (bread), and *casa* CAH-sah (house)

e   like ay, as in "may:" *mesa* MAY-sah (table), *tela* TAY-lah (cloth), and *de* DAY (of, from)

i   like ee, as in "need": *diez* dee-AYZ (ten), *comida* ko-MEE-dah (meal), and *fin* FEEN (end)

o   like oh, as in "go": *peso* PAY-soh (weight), *ocho* OH-choh (eight), and *poco* POH-koh (a bit)

u   like oo, as in "cool": *uno* OO-noh (one), *cuarto* KOOAHR-toh (room), and *usted* oos-TAYD (you); when it follows a "q" the **u** is silent; when it follows an "h" or has an umlaut, it's pronounced like "w"

Consonants

b, d, f, k, l, m, n, p, q, s, t, v, w, x, y, z, and ch   pronounced almost as in English; **h** occurs, but is silent—not pronounced at all

c   like k as in "keep": *cuarto* KOOAR-toh (room), Tepic tay-PEEK (capital of Nayarit state); when it precedes "e" or "i," pro-

nounce **c** like s, as in "sit": *cerveza* sayr-VAY-sah (beer), *encima* ayn-SEE-mah (atop)

g   like g as in "gift" when it precedes "a," "o," "u," or a consonant: *gato* GAH-toh (cat), *hago* AH-goh (I do, make); otherwise, pronounce **g** like h as in "hat": *giro* HEE-roh (money order), *gente* HAYN-tay (people)

j   like h, as in "has": *Jueves* HOOAY-vays (Thursday), *mejor* may-HOR (better)

ll   like y, as in "yes": *toalla* toh-AH-yah (towel), *ellos* AY-yohs (they, them)

ñ   like ny, as in "canyon": *año* AH-nyo (year), *señor* SAY-nyor (Mr., sir)

r   is lightly trilled, with tongue at the roof of your mouth like a very light English d, as in "ready": *pero* PAY-doh (but), *tres* TDAYS (three), *cuatro* KOOAH-tdoh (four)

rr   like a Spanish r, but with much more emphasis and trill. Let your tongue flap. Practice with *burro* (donkey), *carretera* (highway), and Carrillo (proper name), then really let go with *ferrocarril* (railroad)

Note: The single small but common exception to all of the above is the pronunciation of Spanish **y** when it's being used as the Spanish word for "and," as in "Ron y Kathy." In such case, pronounce it like the English ee, as in "keep": Ron "ee" Kathy (Ron and Kathy).

Accent

The rule for accent, the relative stress given to syllables within a given word, is straightforward. If a word ends in a vowel, an n, or an s, accent the next-to-last syllable; if not, accent the last syllable.

Pronounce *gracias* GRAH-seeahs (thank you), *orden* OHR-dayn (order), and *carretera* kah-ray-TAY-rah (highway) with stress on the next-to-last syllable.

Otherwise, accent the last syllable: *venir* vay-

NEER (to come), *terrocarril* tay-roh-cah-REEL (railroad), and *edad* ay-DAHD (age).

   Exceptions to the accent rule are always marked with an accent sign: (á, é, í, ó, or ú), such as *teléfono* tay-LAY-foh-noh (telephone), *jabón* hah-BON (soap), and *rápido* RAH-pee-doh (rapid).

BASIC AND COURTEOUS EXPRESSIONS

Most Spanish-speaking people consider formalities important. Whenever approaching anyone for information or some other reason, do not forget the appropriate salutation–good morning, good evening, etc. Standing alone, the greeting *hola* (hello) can sound brusque.

Hello. *Hola.*

Good morning. *Buenos días.*

Good afternoon. *Buenas tardes.*

Good evening. *Buenas noches.*

How are you? *¿Cómo está usted?*

Very well, thank you. *Muy bien, gracias.*

Okay; good. *Bien.*

Not okay; bad. *Mal or feo.*

So-so. *Más o menos.*

And you? *¿Y usted?*

Thank you. *Gracias.*

Thank you very much. *Muchas gracias.*

You're very kind. *Muy amable.*

You're welcome. *De nada.*

Goodbye. *Adios.*

See you later. *Hasta luego.*

please *por favor*

yes *sí*

no *no*

I don't know. *No sé.*

Just a moment, please. *Momentito, por favor.*

Excuse me, please (when you're trying to get attention). *Disculpe or Con permiso.*

Excuse me (when you've made a boo-boo). *Lo siento.*

Pleased to meet you. *Mucho gusto.*

How do you say... in Spanish? *¿Cómo se dice... en español?*

What is your name? *¿Cómo se llama usted?*

Do you speak English? *¿Habla usted inglés?*

Is English spoken here? (Does anyone here speak English?) *¿Se habla inglés?*

I don't speak Spanish well. *No hablo bien el español.*

I don't understand. *No entiendo.*

How do you say... in Spanish? *¿Cómo se dice... en español?*

My name is... *Me llamo...*

Would you like... *¿Quisiera usted...*

Let's go to... *Vamos a...*

TERMS OF ADDRESS

When in doubt, use the formal *usted* (you) as a form of address.

I *yo*

you (formal) *usted*

you (familiar) *tu*

he/him *él*

she/her *ella*

we/us *nosotros*

you (plural) *ustedes*

they/them *ellos* (all males or mixed gender); *ellas* (all females)

Mr., sir *señor*

Mrs., madam *señora*

miss, young lady *señorita*

wife *esposa*

husband *esposo*

friend *amigo* (male); *amiga* (female)

sweetheart *novio* (male); *novia* (female)

son; daughter *hijo; hija*

brother; sister *hermano; hermana*

father; mother *padre; madre*

grandfather; grandmother *abuelo; abuela*

TRANSPORTATION

Where is...? *¿Dónde está...?*

How far is it to...? *¿A cuánto está...?*

from... to... *de... a...*

How many blocks? *¿Cuántas cuadras?*

Where (Which) is the way to...? *¿Dónde está el camino a...?*

the bus station *la terminal de autobuses*

the bus stop *la parada de autobuses*
Where is this bus going? *¿Adónde va este autobús?*
the taxi stand *la parada de taxis*
the train station *la estación de ferrocarril*
the boat *el barco*
the launch *lancha; tiburonera*
the dock *el muelle*
the airport *el aeropuerto*
I'd like a ticket to... *Quisiera un boleto a...*
first (second) class *primera (segunda) clase*
roundtrip *ida y vuelta*
reservation *reservación*
baggage *equipaje*
Stop here, please. *Pare aquí, por favor.*
the entrance *la entrada*
the exit *la salida*
the ticket office *la oficina de boletos*
(very) near; far *(muy) cerca; lejos*
to; toward *a*
by; through *por*
from *de*
the right *la derecha*
the left *la izquierda*
straight ahead *derecho; directo*
in front *en frente*
beside *al lado*
behind *atrás*
the corner *la esquina*
the stoplight *la semáforo*
a turn *una vuelta*
right here *aquí*
somewhere around here *por acá*
right there *allí*
somewhere around there *por allá*
road *el camino*
street; boulevard *calle; bulevar*
block *la cuadra*
highway *carretera*
kilometer *kilómetro*
bridge; toll *puente; cuota*
address *dirección*
north; south *norte; sur*
east; west *oriente (este); poniente (oeste)*

ACCOMMODATIONS

hotel *hotel*
Is there a room? *¿Hay cuarto?*
May I (may we) see it? *¿Puedo (podemos) verlo?*
What is the rate? *¿Cuál es el precio?*
Is that your best rate? *¿Es su mejor precio?*
Is there something cheaper? *¿Hay algo más económico?*
a single room *un cuarto sencillo*
a double room *un cuarto doble*
double bed *cama matrimonial*
twin beds *camas gemelas*
with private bath *con baño*
hot water *agua caliente*
shower *ducha*
towels *toallas*
soap *jabón*
toilet paper *papel higiénico*
blanket *frazada; manta*
sheets *sábanas*
air-conditioned *aire acondicionado*
fan *abanico; ventilador*
key *llave*
manager *gerente*

FOOD

I'm hungry *Tengo hambre.*
I'm thirsty. *Tengo sed.*
menu *carta; menú*
order *orden*
glass *vaso*
fork *tenedor*
knife *cuchillo*
spoon *cuchara*
napkin *servilleta*
soft drink *refresco*
coffee *café*
tea *té*
drinking water *agua pura; agua potable*
bottled carbonated water *agua mineral*
bottled uncarbonated water *agua sin gas*
beer *cerveza*
wine *vino*

milk *leche*
juice *jugo*
cream *crema*
sugar *azúcar*
cheese *queso*
snack *antojo; botana*
breakfast *desayuno*
lunch *almuerzo*
daily lunch special *comida corrida* (or *el menú del día* depending on region)
dinner *comida* (often eaten in late afternoon); *cena* (a late-night snack)
the check *la cuenta*
eggs *huevos*
bread *pan*
salad *ensalada*
fruit *fruta*
mango *mango*
watermelon *sandía*
papaya *papaya*
banana *plátano*
apple *manzana*
orange *naranja*
lime *limón*
fish *pescado*
shellfish *mariscos*
shrimp *camarones*
meat (without) *(sin) carne*
chicken *pollo*
pork *puerco*
beef; steak *res; bistec*
bacon; ham *tocino; jamón*
fried *frito*
roasted *asada*
barbecue; barbecued *barbacoa; al carbón*

SHOPPING

money *dinero*
money-exchange bureau *casa de cambio*
I would like to exchange traveler's checks. *Quisiera cambiar cheques de viajero.*
What is the exchange rate? *¿Cuál es el tipo de cambio?*

How much is the commission? *¿Cuánto cuesta la comisión?*
Do you accept credit cards? *¿Aceptan tarjetas de crédito?*
money order *giro*
How much does it cost? *¿Cuánto cuesta?*
What is your final price? *¿Cuál es su último precio?*
expensive *caro*
cheap *barato; económico*
more *más*
less *menos*
a little *un poco*
too much *demasiado*

HEALTH

Help me please. *Ayúdeme por favor.*
I am ill. *Estoy enfermo.*
Call a doctor. *Llame un doctor.*
Take me to… *Lléveme a…*
hospital *hospital; sanatorio*
drugstore *farmacia*
pain *dolor*
fever *fiebre*
headache *dolor de cabeza*
stomach ache *dolor de estómago*
burn *quemadura*
cramp *calambre*
nausea *náusea*
vomiting *vomitar*
medicine *medicina*
antibiotic *antibiótico*
pill; tablet *pastilla*
aspirin *aspirina*
ointment; cream *pomada; crema*
bandage *venda*
cotton *algodón*
sanitary napkins use brand name, e.g., Kotex
birth control pills *pastillas anticonceptivas*
contraceptive foam *espuma anticonceptiva*
condoms *preservativos; condones*
toothbrush *cepilla dental*
dental floss *hilo dental*
toothpaste *crema dental*

dentist *dentista*
toothache *dolor de muelas*

POST OFFICE AND COMMUNICATIONS

long-distance telephone *teléfono larga distancia*
I would like to call... *Quisiera llamar a...*
collect *por cobrar*
station to station *a quien contesta*
person to person *persona a persona*
credit card *tarjeta de crédito*
post office *correo*
general delivery *lista de correo*
letter *carta*
stamp *estampilla, timbre*
postcard *tarjeta*
aerogram *aerograma*
air mail *correo aereo*
registered *registrado*
money order *giro*
package; box *paquete; caja*
string; tape *cuerda; cinta*

CUSTOMS

border *frontera*
customs *aduana*
immigration *migración*
tourist card *tarjeta de turista*
inspection *inspección; revisión*
passport *pasaporte*
profession *profesión*
marital status *estado civil*
single *soltero*
married; divorced *casado; divorciado*
widowed *viudado*
insurance *seguros*
title *título*
driver's license *licencia de manejar*

AT THE GAS STATION

gas station *gasolinera*
gasoline *gasolina*
unleaded *sin plomo*

full, please *lleno, por favor*
tire *llanta*
tire repair shop *vulcanizadora*
air *aire*
water *agua*
oil (change) *aceite (cambio)*
grease *grasa*
My... doesn't work. *Mi... no sirve.*
battery *batería*
radiator *radiador*
alternator *alternador*
generator *generador*
tow truck *grúa*
repair shop *taller mecánico*
tune-up *afinación*
auto parts store *refaccionería*

VERBS

Verbs are the key to getting along in Spanish. They employ mostly predictable forms and come in three classes, which end in *ar*, *er*, and *ir*, respectively:

to buy *comprar*
I buy, you (he, she, it) buys *compro, compra*
we buy, you (they) buy *compramos, compran*

to eat *comer*
I eat, you (he, she, it) eats *como, come*
we eat, you (they) eat *comemos, comen*

to climb *subir*
I climb, you (he, she, it) climbs *subo, sube*
we climb, you (they) climb *subimos, suben*

Here are more (with irregularities indicated):

to do or make *hacer* (regular except for *hago*, I do or make)
to go *ir* (very irregular: *voy, va, vamos, van*)
to go (walk) *andar*
to love *amar*
to work *trabajar*
to want *desear, querer*

to need *necesitar*
to read *leer*
to write *escribir*
to repair *reparar*
to stop *parar*
to get off (the bus) *bajar*
to arrive *llegar*
to stay (remain) *quedar*
to stay (lodge) *hospedar*
to leave *salir* (regular except for *salgo*, I leave)
to look at *mirar*
to look for *buscar*
to give *dar* (regular except for *doy*, I give)
to carry *llevar*
to have *tener* (irregular but important: *tengo, tiene, tenemos, tienen*)
to come *venir* (similarly irregular: *vengo, viene, venimos, vienen*)

Spanish has two forms of "to be":

to be *estar* (regular except for *estoy*, I am)
to be *ser* (very irregular: *soy, es, somos, son*)

Use *estar* when speaking of location or a temporary state of being: "I am at home." "*Estoy en casa.*" "I'm sick." "*Estoy enfermo.*" Use *ser* for a permanent state of being: "I am a doctor." "*Soy doctora.*"

NUMBERS

zero *cero*
one *uno*
two *dos*
three *tres*
four *cuatro*
five *cinco*
six *seis*
seven *siete*
eight *ocho*
nine *nueve*
10 *diez*
11 *once*
12 *doce*

13 *trece*
14 *catorce*
15 *quince*
16 *dieciseis*
17 *diecisiete*
18 *dieciocho*
19 *diecinueve*
20 *veinte*
21 *veinte y uno* or *veintiuno*
30 *treinta*
40 *cuarenta*
50 *cincuenta*
60 *sesenta*
70 *setenta*
80 *ochenta*
90 *noventa*
100 *ciento*
101 *ciento y uno* or *cientiuno*
200 *doscientos*
500 *quinientos*
1,000 *mil*
10,000 *diez mil*
100,000 *cien mil*
1,000,000 *millón*
one half *medio*
one third *un tercio*
one fourth *un cuarto*

TIME
What time is it? *¿Qué hora es?*
It's one o'clock. *Es la una.*
It's three in the afternoon. *Son las tres de la tarde.*
It's 4 a.m. *Son las cuatro de la mañana.*
six-thirty *seis y media*
a quarter till eleven *un cuarto para las once*
a quarter past five *las cinco y cuarto*
an hour *una hora*

DAYS AND MONTHS
Monday *lunes*
Tuesday *martes*
Wednesday *miércoles*
Thursday *jueves*

Friday *viernes*	**August** *agosto*
Saturday *sábado*	**September** *septiembre*
Sunday *domingo*	**October** *octubre*
today *hoy*	**November** *noviembre*
tomorrow *mañana*	**December** *diciembre*
yesterday *ayer*	**a week** *una semana*
January *enero*	**a month** *un mes*
February *febrero*	**after** *después*
March *marzo*	**before** *antes*
April *abril*	
May *mayo*	(Courtesy of Bruce Whipperman, author of *Moon*
June *junio*	*Pacific Mexico.*)
July *julio*	

Suggested Reading

ARTS AND CULTURE

Delano, Jack. *Puerto Rico Mio: Four Decades of Change.* Washington: Smithsonian Books, 1990. Includes 175 duotones of former Farm Security Administration photographer Jack Delano's visual chronicle of the island and its people. Includes essays in Spanish and English by educator Arturo Morales Carrión, historian Alan Fern, and anthropologist Sidney W. Mintz.

Muckley, Robert L., and Adela Martinez-Santiago. *Stories from Puerto Rico.* New York: McGraw-Hill, 1999. A collection of legends, ghost stories, and beloved true accounts that reflect the island's folklore. In English and Spanish.

Santiago, Roberto, ed. *Boricuas: Influential Puerto Rican Writings—An Anthology.* New York: One World/Ballantine, 1995. A fantastic collection of poems, speeches, stories, and excerpts by Puerto Rico's greatest writers, past and present, including Jesús Colón, Pablo Guzman, Julia de Burgos, and many more.

CHILDREN'S BOOKS

Bernier-Grand, Carmen T. (author), and Ernesto Ramos Nieves (illustrator). *Juan Bobo:*

Four Folktales from Puerto Rico. New York: HarperTrophy, 1995. Four humorous folktales about the trials and tribulations of the lovable, misguided little boy Juan Bobo.

Ramirez, Michael Rose (author), and Margaret Sanfilippo (illustrator). *The Legend of the Hummingbird: A Tale from Puerto Rico.* New York: Mondo, 1998. Learn about Puerto Rico's history, climate, and traditions in this beguiling tale of transformation.

HISTORY AND POLITICS

Carrión, Arturo Morales. *Puerto Rico: A Political and Cultural History.* New York: W.W. Norton & Co., 1984. An examination of Puerto Rico's commonwealth status and how it got there.

Monge, José Trias. *Puerto Rico: The Trials of the Oldest Colony in the World.* New Haven: Yale University Press, 1999 (paperback). An examination of Puerto Rico's political status through history and an outlook on its future.

Odishelidze, Alexander, and Arthur Laffer. *Pay to the Order of Puerto Rico: The Cost of Dependence.* Dover: Allegiance Press, 2004. A look at Puerto

Rico's political status from an outsider—a Russian native. Although Puerto Rico's options for future political status are well documented, the author openly favors statehood.

Rouse, Irving. *The Taínos: Rise and Decline of the People Who Greeted Columbus.* New Haven: Yale University Press, reissue 1993. A history of the Taíno culture based on intensive study of archaeological sites.

LITERATURE

Santiago, Esmeralda. *Conquistadora.* New York: Knopf, 2012. Historical fiction about a strong-willed Spanish woman who sails to Puerto Rico with her husband and brother-in-law in 1844 to run a sugar plantation.

Santiago, Esmeralda. *When I Was Puerto Rican.* Cambridge: Da Capo Press, 2006. A memoir about growing up in Puerto Rico and immigrating to the United States.

Santiago, Roberto. *Boricua: The Influential Puerto Rican Writings, an Anthology.* New York: Ballantine, 1995. Fifty selections of 19th and 20th century works by Puerto Rican writers.

NATURE AND WILDLIFE

Lee, Alfonso Silva. *Natural Puerto Rico/Puerto Rico Natural.* Saint Paul: Pangaea, 1998. An examination of the fauna of Puerto Rico by Cuban biologist Alfonso Silva Lee. In Spanish and English.

Oberle, Mark W. *Puerto Rico's Birds in Photographs.* Bucharest: Humanitas, 2000. More than 300 color photographs document 181 species of birds found in Puerto Rico. Comes with a CD-ROM including audio clips and more photographs.

Raffaele, Herbert. *A Guide to the Birds of Puerto Rico and the Virgin Islands.* Princeton: Princeton University Press, 1989. Contains information on 284 documented species as well as 273 illustrations.

Simonsen, Steve. *Diving and Snorkeling Guide to Puerto Rico.* Deland: Pisces Books, 1996. A guide to the best diving and snorkeling sites around the island.

Internet Resources

TRAVEL INFORMATION

En Culebra Magazine
www.enculebra.com
Well-researched and well-written articles cover various aspects of life in Culebra, with lots of great travel information.

Isla Culebra
www.islaculebra.com
A terrific source for vacation rentals on Culebra. The best feature is its very active, informative travel forum. Post a question and someone will know the answer.

Puerto Rico Day Trips
www.puertoricodaytrips.com
This individually owned and operated site is well researched and updated on a regular basis. Lots of good practical information.

Puerto Rico Tourism Co.
www.seepuertorico.com
Produced by the Puerto Rico Tourism Co., this is an excellent source of well-researched information on history, culture, events, and sights with a promotional slant.

Tourism Association of Rincón
www.rincon.org

In addition to a plethora of general tourist information on Rincón, this site provides info services of interest to residents, including locations for churches, hair salons, and cleaners. Plus, there's some great photography.

Travel and Sports Inc.
http://travelandsports.com

An enormous database of travel information, including hotels, restaurants, sights, transportation, water sports, and more. It has a great interactive map. Many of the phone numbers are incorrect.

Vieques Travel Guide
www.viequestravelguide.com

A reliable source of vacation rentals, tourist sights, shops, transportation, and more on Vieques

.

Welcome to Puerto Rico
www.topuertorico.org

Individually owned and operated site offering extensive information on the history, government, and geography of all 78 municipalities.

HISTORY, POLITICS, AND CULTURE

Historic Places in Puerto Rico
www.nps.gov/history/nr/travel/prvi

The National Park Service site provides details on all the historic sites that fall under its purview.

Music of Puerto Rico
www.musicofpuertorico.com

Excellent source for information on Puerto Rican music, from folk and *danza* to *bomba* and salsa to reggaetón. Also contains audio clips, biographies of native musicians, lyrics, and musical history.

Public Art
www.artepublicopr.com/english

Official source for Puerto Rico's $25 million public art project, including project proposals, artists' biographies, and maps to the sites.

Puerto Rican Painter
www.puertoricanpainter.com

An all-inclusive look at local artists currently working in Puerto Rico, the site includes a list of galleries, artist biographies, and galleries of artwork.

Puerto Rico and the Dream
www.prdream.com

An intelligent and discriminating site about the history, culture, and politics of Puerto Rico that includes audio files of oral histories, galleries of select art exhibitions, historical timelines, archival photos, and discussion forums. The site really has its finger on the pulse of all matters important to Puerto Ricans.

Taíno Cyber Culture Center
www.indio.net/taino

A clearinghouse for links to articles on Taíno history, news, research, and culture.

NATURE AND WILDLIFE

The Conservation Trust of Puerto Rico
www.fideicomiso.org

In addition to working to preserve the island's natural beauty, the Conservation Trust of Puerto Rico offers a variety of educational nature and culture tours.

U.S. Fish and Wildlife Service
www.fws.gov/caribbean

The U.S. Fish and Wildlife Service operates this site featuring information on the island's wildlife refuges, geographic regions, and efforts to restore the population of Puerto Rican parrots.

Index

List of Maps

Acknowledgments

I want to thank my parents, Ted and Jo Teagle, who instilled in me a passion for travel. Had they not been adventurous enough to move our family to Puerto Rico in the early 1970s, this book would never have happened. I also want to thank my sons, Derrick and Drew, who bring so much joy to my life and inspire me to be my best every day.

Very special thanks go to Holly Aguirre, Jennifer Bhagia-Lewis, Lea Holland, Evelyn Amaya Ortega and Emilio Williams for their expert fact-checking skills and to photographers Anne Murray Mozingo and John Thompson for allowing me to use their images.

I owe much gratitude to my dear friends and traveling companions, Shelly Williams, Scottie Williams, and Amy Tinaglia. Thanks for coming along for the ride. I will always treasure our friendship.

And special thanks go to my lifelong friend Caryl Altman Howard for introducing me to this beguiling island and for playing a major role in some of my fondest memories of life in Puerto Rico.

www.moon.com

DESTINATIONS | ACTIVITIES | BLOGS | MAPS | BOOKS

MOON.COM is ready to help plan your next trip! Filled with fresh trip ideas and strategies, author interviews, informative travel blogs, a detailed map library, and descriptions of all the Moon guidebooks, Moon.com is all you need to get out and explore the world—or even places in your own backyard. While at Moon.com, sign up for our monthly e-newsletter for updates on new releases, travel tips, and expert advice from our on-the-go Moon authors. As always, when you travel with Moon, expect an experience that is uncommon and truly unique.

KEEP UP WITH MOON ON FACEBOOK AND TWITTER
JOIN THE MOON PHOTO GROUP ON FLICKR

MAP SYMBOLS

▭ Expressway	◖ Highlight	✗ Airfield	⚲ Golf Course
▭ Primary Road	○ City/Town	✈ Airport	℗ Parking Area
▭ Secondary Road	◉ State Capital	▲ Mountain	▲ Archaeological Site
▭ Unpaved Road	⊛ National Capital	✦ Unique Natural Feature	▮ Church
- - - - - Trail	★ Point of Interest		▯ Gas Station
.... Ferry	• Accommodation	⚲ Waterfall	◯ Glacier
▭ Railroad	▾ Restaurant/Bar	▲ Park	▱ Mangrove
▭ Pedestrian Walkway	▪ Other Location	◨ Trailhead	▱ Reef
▭ Stairs	⋀ Campground	✗ Skiing Area	▱ Swamp

CONVERSION TABLES

°C = (°F - 32) / 1.8
°F = (°C x 1.8) + 32
1 inch = 2.54 centimeters (cm)
1 foot = 0.304 meters (m)
1 yard = 0.914 meters
1 mile = 1.6093 kilometers (km)
1 km = 0.6214 miles
1 fathom = 1.8288 m
1 chain = 20.1168 m
1 furlong = 201.168 m
1 acre = 0.4047 hectares
1 sq km = 100 hectares
1 sq mile = 2.59 square km
1 ounce = 28.35 grams
1 pound = 0.4536 kilograms
1 short ton = 0.90718 metric ton
1 short ton = 2,000 pounds
1 long ton = 1.016 metric tons
1 long ton = 2,240 pounds
1 metric ton = 1,000 kilograms
1 quart = 0.94635 liters
1 US gallon = 3.7854 liters
1 Imperial gallon = 4.5459 liters
1 nautical mile = 1.852 km

°FAHRENHEIT   °CELSIUS

°FAHRENHEIT	°CELSIUS	
230	110	
220	100	WATER BOILS
210		
200	90	
190		
180	80	
170		
160	70	
150		
140	60	
130		
120	50	
110		
100	40	
90		
80	30	
70		
60	20	
50		
40	10	
30		
20	0	WATER FREEZES
10		
0	-10	
-10		
-20	-20	
-30	-30	
-40	-40	

INCH
0   1   2   3   4

CM
0 1 2 3 4 5 6 7 8 9 10

MOON PUERTO RICO

Avalon Travel
a member of the Perseus Books Group
1700 Fourth Street
Berkeley, CA 94710, USA
www.moon.com

Editor: Erin Raber
Series Manager: Kathryn Ettinger
Copy Editor: Deana Shields
Graphics Coordinator and Production Coordinator:
  Elizabeth Jang
Cover Designer: Elizabeth Jang
Map Editor: Kat Bennett
Cartographers: Andy Butkovic, Claire Sarraille,
  Chris Henrick, Kat Bennett
Indexer: Deana Shields

ISBN-13: 978-1-61238-338-5
ISSN: 1932-0957

Printing History
1st Edition – 2006
3rd Edition – December 2012
5 4 3 2 1

Front cover photo: Seven Seas Beach, near Fajardo.
© Colin Young/123rf.com

Title page photo: Turret at Castillo de San Cristóbal
in San Juan © Sean Pavone/123rf.com

Interior color photos: p. 4 © John Thompson; p. 5
© José Oquendo; p. 6 (inset) © Suzanne Van Atten;
(bottom) Old San Juan © Angela Williams Duea/123rf
.com; p. 7 (top left) male anole in Bosque Estatal de
Guilarte, Adjuntas © José Oquendo; (top right) *La
Rogativa* by sculptor Lindsay Daen, Plazuela de la
Rogativa © José Oquendo; (bottom left) *malecón*
in Vieques © Robert Lerich/123rf.com; (bottom
right) at El Morro © Steven Gaertner/123rf.com;
p. 8 © Suzanne Van Atten; p. 9 © Anne Murray
Mozingo; p. 10 © José Oquendo; p. 11 © Amy Jo
Richards-Ellis/123rf.com; p. 12 © capricornis/
123rf.com; p. 13 © Carlos A. Aviles/www.flickr.com;
pp. 14-23 © Suzanne Van Atten; p. 24 © JEDphoto/
123rf.com

Printed in Canada by Friesens

KEEPING CURRENT

If you have a favorite gem you'd like to see included in the next edition, or see anything
that needs updating, clarification, or correction, please drop us a line. Send your comments via email to feedback@moon.com, or use the address above.